THE OXFORD

Essential Spelling Dictionary

AMERICAN EDITION

Also available

THE OXFORD DESK DICTIONARY AND THESAURUS

THE OXFORD ESSENTIAL DICTIONARY

THE OXFORD ESSENTIAL QUOTATIONS DICTIONARY

THE OXFORD ESSENTIAL THESAURUS

THE OXFORD FRENCH DICTIONARY

THE OXFORD GERMAN DICTIONARY

THE OXFORD ITALIAN DICTIONARY

THE OXFORD PORTUGUESE DICTIONARY

THE OXFORD RUSSIAN DICTIONARY

THE OXFORD SPANISH DICTIONARY

THE OXFORD

Essential
Spelling
Dictionary

AMERICAN EDITION

BERKLEY BOOKS, NEW YORK

THE OXFORD ESSENTIAL SPELLING DICTIONARY

A Berkley Book / published in mass market paperback
by arrangement with Oxford University Press, Inc.

PRINTING HISTORY
Berkley edition / August 1998

The Penguin Putnam Inc. World Wide Web site address is
http://www.penguinputnam.com

ISBN: 0-425-16388-1

BERKLEY®
Berkley Books are published by The Berkley Publishing Group,
a member of Penguin Putnam Inc.,
200 Madison Avenue, New York, New York 10016.
BERKLEY and the "B" design
are trademarks belonging to Berkley Publishing Corporation.

PRINTED IN THE UNITED STATES OF AMERICA

10 9 8 7 6 5

Contents

Project Staff

Editor-in-Chief: Frank R. Abate
Managing Editor: Elizabeth J. Jewell
Editors: Deborah Argosy, Ruth Handlin
Manley, Christine A. Lindberg,
Andrea R. Nagy, Laurie H. Ongley
Proofreader: Linda M. Costa

Introduction and How to Use This Book

The *Oxford Essential Spelling Dictionary* is a handy and reliable guide to American spelling and word division for more than 50,000 entries. Unlike other spelling dictionaries, the *Oxford Essential Spelling Dictionary* includes thousands of proper names (of people, places, and cultural entities) as well as the most frequently occurring words in American English. Other unique features—including coverage of "sound-alike" words (homophones) and a convenient **Good Speller's Toolkit**—make the *Oxford Essential Spelling Dictionary* a superior choice for home, school, and office.

For greater ease of use, inflected forms (plurals of nouns, past and past participles of verbs, comparative and superlative forms of adjectives), phrases, and common derivative forms are given at the entry for the main form, unless the derivative is alphabetically quite different from the main form. This allows the dictionary to be used for studying patterns of English word formation and suffixes.

"Sound-alikes" or Homophones

A unique feature of the *Oxford Essential Spelling Dictionary* is the indication of words that sound alike (homophones), with cross references to the other word or words in each set of homophones. Additionally, each homophone is given a brief definition to distinguish its use from that of the other word or words in the set. For example:

soar (*fly*; see SORE)
sore (*painful; see* SOAR)

Word Division

In the *Oxford Essential Spelling Dictionary*, each entry that consists of more than one syllable is marked for division at the syllable breaks. The word division points are indicated by centered dots (*ab•a•cus*). For hyphenated terms, the hyphen is also a word-division point (*tid•dly-winks*).

Proper word division is important to writers and editors, who may need to break a word at the end of a line of text. The foremost rule governing end-of-line word division is to separate the word at word-division breaks whenever possible. There are, however, several other rules that, by convention, also apply:

1. The breaking of short words, particularly those of five or fewer letters (*icy, cola, nasal*), should be avoided.
2. Contractions (*couldn't, wasn't*) should not be divided.
3. If a word has adjoining vowels that are pronounced separately, the preferable division is between the two vowels (*re-ality*, not "real-ity").
4. It is best to break a compound word between its root elements (*motor-cycle*, not "motorcy-cle").

5. The division of a hyphenated term should occur only at the hyphen (*heavy-handed*, not "heav-y-handed" or "heavy-hand-ed").

6. If a syllable at the beginning or end of a word consists of only one letter, the single-letter syllable should not be separated from the rest of the word (*Amer-ica*, not "A-merica" or "Americ-a").

7. If a syllable within a word consists of only one letter, the division should not separate the single-letter syllable from the preceding syllable (*paci-fist*, not "*pac-ifist*"), EXCEPT *in the instances described in the following rule:*

8. *It is better to separate a single-letter syllable from the preceding syllable if the single-letter syllable is the first syllable of a root word (un-available*, not "una-vailable") *or if the single-letter syllable is part of the suffix* -able *or* -ible (*laugh-able*, not "laugha-ble"; *aud-ible*, not "audi-ble").

Using the word divisions given in this dictionary along with the rules above, the vast majority of word-division problems can be easily resolved.

Good Speller's Toolkit

Another unique feature of the *Oxford Essential Spelling Dictionary* is the concise set of spelling tips and rules that follow the A–Z entries, the **Good Speller's Toolkit**. For those who need a better grounding in some of the key principles of good spelling, or a quick review, the **Toolkit** offers reliable guidelines that will help you avoid the most common pitfalls of spelling.

THE OXFORD

Essential
Spelling
Dictionary

AMERICAN EDITION

A

Aa·chen

aard·vark

Aar·on

a·back

ab·a·cus
  pl. ab·a·cus·es *or* ab·a·ci

a·baft

ab·a·lo·ne

a·ban·don
  a·ban·do·ner
  a·ban·don·ment

a·ban·doned

a·base
  a·base·ment

a·bash
  a·bash·ment

a·bate
  a·bate·ment

ab·at·toir

ab·bé

ab·bess

ab·bey
  pl. ab·beys

ab·bot

ab·bre·vi·ate
  ab·bre·vi·a·tion

ab·di·cate
  ab·di·ca·tion
  ab·di·ca·tor

ab·do·men
  ab·dom·i·nal
  ab·dom·i·nal·ly

ab·duct
  ab·duc·tion
  ab·duc·tor

a·beam

a·bed

Ab·e·lard

Ab·e·na·ki
  pl. same *or* Ab·e·na·kis

Ab·er·deen

ab·er·ra·tion
  ab·er·rant
  ab·er·ra·tion·al

a·bet
  a·bet·ted, a·bet·ting
  a·bet·ment
  a·bet·tor *or* a·bet·ter

a·bey·ance
  a·bey·ant

ab·hor
  ab·horred, ab·hor·ring
  ab·hor·rence
  ab·hor·rer

ab·hor·rent

a·bide
  past a·bode *or* a·bid·ed
  a·bid·ance

a·bid·ing
  a·bid·ing·ly

Ab·i·djan

Ab·i·lene

a·bil·i·ty
  pl. a·bil·i·ties

ab·ject
  ab·jec·tion
  ab·ject·ly
  ab·ject·ness

ab·jure
  ab·ju·ra·tion

ab·la·tive

a·blaze

a·ble
  a·bler, a·blest
  a·ble-bod·ied

ab·lu·tion
  ab·lu·tion·ar·y

a·bly

ab·ne·gate
  ab·ne·ga·tion
  ab·ne·ga·tor

ab·nor·mal
  ab·nor·mal·i·ty
  ab·nor·mal·ly

a·board

a·bode

a·bol·ish
  a·bol·ish·a·ble
  a·bol·ish·er
  a·bol·ish·ment

ab·o·li·tion
  ab·o·li·tion·ist

a·bom·i·na·ble
  a·bom·i·na·bly

a·bom·i·nate
  a·bom·i·na·tion
  a·bom·i·na·tor

ab·o·rig·i·nal

ab·o·rig·i·ne
  usu. Ab·o·rig·ine

a·bort

a·bor·tion
  a·bor·tion·ist

a·bor·tive
  a·bor·tive·ly

a·bound

a·bout

a·bout-face

a•bove

a•bove•board

ab•ra•ca•da•bra

a•brade
a•brad•er

A•bra•ham

ab•ra•sion

ab•ra•sive

a•breast

a•bridge
a•bridg•a•ble or
a•bridge•a•ble
a•bridg•er
a•bridg•ment or
a•bridge•ment

a•broad

ab•ro•gate
ab•ro•ga•tion
ab•ro•ga•tor

ab•rupt
ab•rupt•ly
ab•rupt•ness

ab•scess
ab•scessed

ab•scis•sa
pl. ab•scis•sae or
ab•scis•sas

ab•scond
ab•scond•er

ab•sence

ab•sent
ab•sent•ly

ab•sen•tee

ab•sen•tee•ism

ab•sent•mind•ed
ab•sent•mind•ed•ly
ab•sent•mind•ed•ness

ab•sinthe
also ab•sinth

ab•so•lute
ab•so•lute•ness

ab•so•lute•ly

ab•so•lu•tion

ab•so•lut•ism
ab•so•lut•ist

ab•solve
ab•solv•er

ab•sorb
ab•sorb•a•ble
ab•sorb•a•bil•i•ty
ab•sorb•er

ab•sorbed
ab•sorb•ed•ly

ab•sor•bent
ab•sor•ben•cy

ab•sorb•ing
ab•sorb•ing•ly

ab•sorp•tion
a•bsorp•tive

ab•stain
ab•stain•er
ab•sten•tion

ab•ste•mi•ous
ab•ste•mi•ous•ly
ab•ste•mi•ous•ness

ab•sti•nence
ab•sti•nent

ab•stract
ab•stract•ly
ab•stract•or

ab•strac•tion

ab•struse
ab•struse•ly
ab•struse•ness

ab•surd
ab•surd•i•ty
ab•surd•ly

A•bu Dha•bi

A•bu•ja

a•bun•dance
a•bun•dant
a•bun•dant•ly

a•buse
a•bused
a•bus•er
a•bu•sive
a•bu•sive•ly
a•bu•sive•ness

a•but
a•but•ted, a•but•ting

a•but•ment

a•bys•mal
a•bys•mal•ly

a•byss

a•ca•cia

ac•a•de•mi•a
also ac•a•deme
ac•a•de•mi•cian

ac•a•dem•ic
ac•a•dem•i•cal•ly

a•cad•e•my
pl. a•cad•e•mies

A•ca•di•a

a•can•thus

a cap•pel•la

A•ca•pul•co

ac•cede

ac•cel•er•ate
ac•cel•er•a•tion

ac•cel•er•a•tor

ac•cent
ac•cen•tu•al

ac•cen•tu•ate
ac•cen•tu•a•tion

ac•cept

ac•cept•a•ble
ac•cept•a•bil•i•ty
ac•cept•a•ble•ness
ac•cept•a•bly

ac•cept•ance

ac•cess

ac•ces•si•ble
ac•ces•si•bil•i•ty
ac•ces•si•bly

ac•ces•sion

ac•ces•so•ry
pl. ac•ces•so•ries
ac•ces•so•ri•al

ac•ci•dent
ac•ci•dent-prone

ac•ci•den•tal
ac•ci•den•tal•ly

ac•claim
ac•claim•er

ac•cla•ma•tion

ac•cli•mate

ac•cli•ma•tize
ac•cli•ma•tiz•a•tion

ac•co•lade

ac•com•mo•date

ac•com•mo•dat•ing
ac•com•mo•dat•ing•ly

ac•com•mo•da•tion

ac•com•pa•ni•ment
ac•com•pa•nist

ac•com•pa•ny
ac•com•pa•nies,
   ac•com•pa•nied

ac•com•plice

ac•com•plish
ac•com•plish•a•ble

ac•comp•lished

ac•com•plish•ment

ac•cord

ac•cord•ance

ac•cord•ing

ac•cord•ing•ly

ac•cor•di•on
ac•cor•di•on•ist

ac•cost

ac•count

ac•count•a•ble
ac•count•a•bil•i•ty
ac•count•a•ble•ness
ac•count•a•bly

ac•count•ant
ac•count•an•cy

ac•count•ing

ac•cou•ter•ment
also ac•cou•tre•ment

Ac•cra

ac•cred•it
ac•cred•i•ta•tion
ac•cred•it•ed

ac•cre•tion
ac•cre•tive

ac•crue
ac•crued, ac•cru•ing
ac•cru•al
ac•crue•ment

ac•cu•mu•late
ac•cu•mu•la•tion
ac•cu•mu•la•tive
ac•cu•mu•la•tor

ac•cu•ra•cy

ac•cu•rate
ac•cu•rate•ly
ac•cu•rate•ness

ac•curs•ed

ac•cu•sa•tion
ac•cu•sa•to•ry

ac•cu•sa•tive
ac•cu•sa•ti•val
ac•cu•sa•tive•ly

ac•cuse
ac•cus•er
ac•cus•ing•ly

ac•cus•tom

ac•cus•tomed

ace

a•cer•bic
a•cer•bi•cal•ly
a•cer•bi•ty
pl. a•cer•bi•ties

a•ce•ta•min•o•phen

ac•e•tate

a•ce•tic

ac•e•tone

a•cet•y•lene

ache
ach•ing•ly
ach•y
ach•i•er, ach•i•est

A•che•be

Ach•e•son

a•chieve
a•chiev•a•ble
a•chiev•er

a•chieve•ment

A•chil•les

ach•ro•mat•ic
ach•ro•ma•tic•al•ly
ach•ro•ma•tic•i•ty
a•chro•ma•tism

ac•id
a•cid•ic
a•cid•i•fy
a•cid•i•ty
ac•id•ly
ac•id•ness

a•cid•u•lous

ac•knowl•edge
ac•knowl•edge•a•ble
ac•knowl•edge•ment *or*
ac•knowl•edg•ment

ac•me

ac•ne
ac•ned

ac•o•lyte

A•con•ca•gua

ac•o•nite
  ac•o•nit•ic

a•corn

a•cous•tic
  a•cous•ti•cal
  a•cous•ti•cal•ly
  ac•ous•ti•cian

ac•quaint

ac•quaint•ance
  ac•quaint•ance•ship

ac•qui•esce
  ac•qui•es•cence
  ac•qui•es•cent

ac•quire
  ac•quir•a•ble
  ac•quire•ment

ac•qui•si•tion

ac•quis•i•tive
  ac•quis•i•tive•ly
  ac•quis•i•tive•ness

ac•quit
  ac•quit•ted,
    ac•quit•ting
  ac•quit•tal

a•cre
  a•cred

a•cre•age

ac•rid
  ac•rid•er, ac•rid•est
  a•crid•i•ty
  ac•rid•ly

ac•ri•mo•ni•ous
  ac•ri•mo•ni•ous•ly
  ac•ri•mo•ny

ac•ro•bat
  ac•ro•bat•ic
  ac•ro•bat•i•cal•ly

ac•ro•bat•ics

ac•ro•nym

ac•ro•pho•bi•a
  ac•ro•pho•bic

a•crop•o•lis
  also A•crop•o•lis

a•cross

a•cros•tic

a•cryl•ic

act

act•ing

ac•tin•i•um

ac•tion

ac•tion•a•ble
  ac•tion•a•bly

ac•ti•vate
  ac•ti•va•tion
  ac•ti•va•tor

ac•tive
  ac•tive•ly
  ac•tive•ness

ac•tiv•ism
  ac•tiv•ist

ac•tiv•i•ty
  pl. ac•tiv•i•ties

ac•tor

ac•tress

ac•tu•al
  ac•tu•al•i•za•tion
  ac•tu•al•ize

ac•tu•al•i•ty
  pl. ac•tu•al•i•ties

ac•tu•al•ly

ac•tu•ar•y
  pl. ac•tu•ar•ies
  ac•tu•ar•i•al
  ac•tu•ar•i•al•ly

ac•tu•ate
  ac•tu•a•tion
  ac•tu•a•tor

a•cu•i•ty

a•cu•men

ac•u•pres•sure

ac•u•punc•ture
  ac•u•punc•tur•ist

a•cute
  a•cut•er, a•cut•est
  a•cute•ly
  a•cute•ness

ad

ad•age

a•da•gio
  pl. a•da•gios

Ad•am

ad•a•mant
  ad•a•mant•ly

Ad•ams

a•dapt
  a•dapt•a•ble
  ad•ap•ta•tion
  a•dapt•er *or*
  a•dap•tor
  a•dap•tive
  a•dap•tive•ly

add
  add•ed

Ad•dams

ad•den•dum
  pl. ad•den•da

ad•der

ad•dict
  ad•dic•tion
  ad•dic•tive

Ad•dis A•ba•ba

Ad•di•son

ad•di•tion

ad•di•tion•al
  ad•di•tion•al•ly

ad•di•tive

ad•dle

ad·dress
  ad·dress·er

ad·dress·ee

ad·duce
  ad·duc·i·ble

ad·duc·tor

Ad·e·laide

A·den

A·de·nau·er

ad·e·noids
  ad·e·noi·dal

a·dept
  a·dept·ly
  a·dept·ness

ad·e·quate
  ad·e·qua·cy
  ad·e·quate·ly

ad·here

ad·her·ent
  ad·her·ence

ad·he·sion

ad·he·sive
  ad·he·sive·ly
  ad·he·sive·ness

ad hoc

a·dieu
  pl. a·dieus or a·dieux

ad in·fi·ni·tum

ad·i·os

ad·i·pose
  ad·i·pos·i·ty

Ad·i·ron·dack

ad·ja·cent
  ad·ja·cen·cy

ad·jec·tive
  ad·jec·ti·val
  ad·jec·ti·val·ly

ad·join

ad·journ
  ad·journ·ment

ad·judge

ad·ju·di·cate
  ad·ju·di·ca·tion
  ad·ju·di·ca·tive
  ad·ju·di·ca·tor

ad·junct
  ad·junc·tive
  ad·junc·tive·ly

ad·jure
  ad·ju·ra·tion
  ad·jur·a·to·ry

ad·just
  ad·just·a·ble
  ad·just·a·bil·i·ty
  ad·just·er
  ad·just·ment

ad·ju·tant
  ad·ju·tan·cy

Ad·ler

ad lib
  ad libbed, ad lib·bing

ad·man
  pl. ad·men

ad·min·is·ter
  ad·min·is·tra·ble

ad·min·is·trate
  ad·min·is·tra·tive
  ad·min·is·tra·tive·ly

ad·min·is·tra·tion

ad·min·is·tra·tor

ad·mi·ra·ble
  ad·mi·ra·bly

ad·mi·ral
  ad·mi·ral·ship

Ad·mi·ral·ty
  pl. Ad·mi·ral·ties

ad·mi·ra·tion

ad·mire
  ad·mir·er

ad·mir·ing
  ad·mir·ing·ly

ad·mis·si·ble
  ad·mis·si·bil·i·ty

ad·mis·sion

ad·mit
  ad·mit·ted, ad·mit·ting
  ad·mit·ta·ble
  ad·mit·tance

ad·mit·ted·ly

ad·mix·ture

ad·mon·ish
  ad·mon·ish·ment
  ad·mo·ni·tion
  ad·mon·i·to·ry

ad nau·se·am

a·do
  pl. a·dos

a·do·be

ad·o·les·cent
  ad·o·les·cence

A·don·is

a·dopt
  a·dop·tion
  a·dop·tive

a·dor·a·ble
  a·dor·a·bly

a·dore
  ad·o·ra·tion
  a·dor·er
  a·dor·ing
  a·dor·ing·ly

a·dorn
  a·dorn·ment

a·dre·nal

a·dren·a·line

A·dri·at·ic Sea

a·drift

a·droit
  a·droit·ly
  a·droit·ness

ad·sorb
  ad·sorb·a·ble
  ad·sorb·ent
  ad·sorp·tion
  also ad·sorb·tion

ad·u·late
  ad·u·la·tion
  ad·u·la·tor
  ad·u·la·to·ry

a·dult
  a·dult·hood
  a·dult·ly

a·dul·ter·ate
  a·dul·ter·ant
  a·dul·ter·a·tion
  a·dul·ter·a·tor

a·dul·tery
  a·dul·ter·er
  a·dul·ter·ous
  a·dul·ter·ous·ly

ad·um·brate
  ad·um·bra·tion
  ad·um·bra·tive

ad·vance
  ad·vance·ment
  ad·vanc·er

ad·van·tage
  ad·van·ta·geous
  ad·van·ta·geous·ly

Ad·vent
  also ad·vent

adven·ti·tious
  ad·ven·ti·tious·ly

ad·ven·ture
  ad·ven·ture·some
  ad·ven·tur·ous

ad·ven·tur·er
  fem. ad·ven·tur·ess

ad·verb
  ad·ver·bi·al

ad·ver·sar·y
  pl. ad·ver·sar·ies
  ad·ver·sar·i·al

ad·verse
  ad·verse·ly

ad·ver·si·ty
  pl. ad·ver·si·ties

ad·vert

ad·ver·tise
  ad·ver·tis·er

ad·ver·tise·ment

ad·vice

ad·vis·a·ble
  ad·vis·a·bil·i·ty
  ad·vis·a·bly

ad·vise
  ad·vis·er *or*
  ad·vi·sor

ad·vi·so·ry
  pl. ad·vi·so·ries

ad·vo·cate
  ad·vo·ca·cy
  ad·vo·cate·ship
  ad·voc·a·to·ry

adze
  also adz

Ae·ge·an Sea

ae·gis

Ael·fric

ae·on
  var. of e·on

aer·ate
  aer·a·tion
  aer·a·tor

ae·ri·al
  aer·i·al·ly

aer·i·al·ist

aer·ie
  also ey·rie

aer·o·bat·ics

aer·o·bic

aer·o·bics

aer·o·dy·nam·ics
  aer·o·dy·nam·ic
  aer·o·dy·nam·i·cal·ly
  aer·o·dy·nam·i·cist

aer·o·nau·tics
  aer·o·nau·tic
  aer·o·nau·ti·cal

aer·o·sol

aer·o·space

Aes·chy·lus

Ae·sop

aes·thete
  also es·thete

aes·thet·ic
  also es·thet·ic
  aes·thet·i·cal·ly
  aes·thet·i·cism

Aet·na, Mount
  var. of Et·na

a·far

af·fa·ble
  af·fa·bil·i·ty
  af·fa·bly

af·fair

af·fect (*have influence on;*
  see EFFECT)
  af·fect·ing
  af·fect·ing·ly

af·fec·ta·tion

af·fect·ed

af·fec·tion·ate
  af·fec·tion·ate·ly

af·fi·da·vit

af·fil·i·ate

af·fin·i·ty
  pl. af·fin·i·ties

af·firm

af·firm·a·tive

af·flic·tion

af·flu·ent

af·ford

af·fray

af·front

Af·ghan·i·stan
  Af·ghan

a·flame

a·float

a·foot

a·fore·men·tioned

a·fore·thought

a·foul

a·fraid

a·fresh

Af·ri·ca
  Af·ri·can

Af·ri·kaans

Af·ri·ka·ner

Af·ro
  pl. Af·ros

Af·ro-A·mer·i·can

Af·ro-Car·ib·be·an

aft

af·ter

af·ter·birth

af·ter·burn·er

af·ter·care

af·ter·ef·fect

af·ter·life

af·ter·math

af·ter·noon

af·ter·thought

af·ter·ward
  also af·ter·wards

a·gain

a·gainst

a·gape

a·gar
  also a·gar-a·gar

Ag·as·siz

ag·ate

a·ga·ve

age
  ag·ing, age·ing

a·ged

age·ism
  also ag·ism
  age·ist

age·less

a·gen·cy
  pl. a·gen·cies

a·gen·da
  pl. agen·das

a·gent
  a·gen·tial

a·gent pro·voc·a·teur
  pl. a·gents
  pro·voc·a·teurs

ag·glom·er·ate

ag·glu·ti·nate
  ag·glu·ti·na·tion
  ag·glu·ti·na·tive

ag·gran·dize
  ag·gran·dize·ment
  ag·gran·diz·er

ag·gra·vate
  ag·gra·va·tion

ag·gre·gate
  ag·gre·ga·tion
  ag·gre·ga·tive

ag·gres·sion
  ag·gres·sor

ag·gres·sive
  ag·gres·sive·ly
  ag·gres·sive·ness

ag·grieved
  ag·griev·ed·ly

a·ghast

ag·ile
  ag·ile·ly
  a·gil·i·ty

ag·i·tate
  ag·i·tat·ed·ly
  ag·i·ta·tion
  ag·i·ta·tive
  ag·i·ta·tor

a·glow

Ag·new

ag·nos·tic
  ag·nos·ti·cism

a·go

a·gog

ag·o·nize
  ag·o·niz·ing·ly

ag·o·ny
  pl. ag·o·nies

ag·o·ra·pho·bi·a
  ag·o·ra·pho·bic

A·gra

a·grar·i·an

a·gree
  a·grees, a·greed,
  a·gree·ing

a·gree·a·ble
  a·gree·a·bil·i·ty
  a·gree·a·ble·ness
  a·gree·a·bly

a·gree·ment

ag·ri·busi·ness

ag·ri·cul·ture
  ag·ri·cul·tur·al
  ag·ri·cul·tur·al·ist
  ag·ri·cul·tur·al·ly
  ag·ri·cul·tur·ist

a·gron·o·my
  ag·ro·nom·ic
  a·gron·o·mist

a·ground

A·guas·ca·lien·tes

a·gue
  a·gued
  a·gu·ish

ah

a·ha

a·head

a·hem

Ah·mad·a·bad

a·hoy

aid

aide

aide-de-camp
  pl. aides-de-camp

Ai·ken

ail

ai·le·ron

ail·ment

aim

aim·less
  aim·less·ly
  aim·less·ness

ain't

air (*atmosphere;* see ERE, HEIR)
  air-con·di·tioned
  air-con·di·tion·ing
  air·less
  air·less·ness

air·borne

air·craft
  pl. same

Aire·dale

air·field

air·head

air·lift

air·line

air·lin·er

air·lock

air·mail

air·man
  pl. air·men

air·plane

air·port

air·ship

air·sick
  air·sick·ness

air·space

air·speed

air·strip

air·tight

air·waves

air·way

air·wom·an
  pl. air·wom·en

air·wor·thy

air·y
  air·i·er, air·i·est
  air·i·ly
  air·i·ness

aisle (*passage;* see ISLE, I'LL)
  aisled

aitch

Aix-en-Pro·vence

a·jar

Ak·bar

Akh·na·ton

A·ki·hi·to

a·kim·bo

a·kin

Ak·ron

Al·a·bam·a
  Al·a·bam·i·an *or*
  Al·a·bam·an

al·a·bas·ter
  al·a·bas·trine

à la carte

a·lac·ri·ty

à la mode

Al·a·ric

a·larm
  a·larm·ing
  a·larm·ing·ly

a·larm·ist
  a·larm·ism

a·las

A·las·ka
  A·las·kan

alb

al·ba·core

Al·ba·ni·a
  Al·ba·ni·an

Al·ba·ny

al·ba·tross

Al·bee

al·be·it

Al·ber·ta

al·bi·no
  pl. al·bi·nos
  al·bi·nism
  al·bi·not·ic

Al·bright

al·bum

al·bu·men

al·bu·min
  al·bu·min·ous

Al·bu·quer·que

Al·ca·traz

al·che·my
  pl. al·che·mies
  al·chem·ic
  al·chem·i·cal
  al·che·mist
  al·che·mize

Al·ci·bi·a·des

al·co·hol

al·co·hol·ic

al·co·hol·ism

Al·cott

al·cove

Al·cuin

al den·te

al·der

al·der·man
  pl. al·der·men; *fem.*
  al·der·wom·an, *pl.*
  al·der·wom·en
  al·der·man·ic
  al·der·man·ship

ale

a·le·a·to·ry

a·lem·bic

A·lep·po

a·lert
  a·lert·ly
  a·lert·ness

Al·eut
  A·leu·tian

A·leu·tian Is·lands
  also A·leu·tians

Al·ex·an·der

Al·ex·an·dri·a

al·fal·fa

Al·fred

al·fres·co

al·ga
  pl. al·gae *also* al·gas
  al·gal
  al·goid

al·ge·bra
  al·ge·bra·ic
  al·ge·bra·i·cal
  al·ge·bra·i·cal·ly

Al·ge·ri·a
  Al·ge·ri·an

Al·giers

Al·gon·qui·an (*language family*)

Al·gon·quin (*a Native American people or their language*)
  also Al·gon·ki·an

al·go·rithm
  al·go·rith·mic

A·li

a·li·as

al·i·bi
  pl. al·i·bis
  al·i·bis, al·i·bied,
  al·i·bi·ing

al·ien
  al·ien·ness

al·ien·ate
  al·ien·a·tion
  al·ien·a·tor

A·li·ghie·ri

a·light

a·lign
  also a·line
  a·lign·ment

a·like

al·i·men·ta·ry
  al·i·men·ta·tion

al·i·mo·ny

a·live
  a·live·ness

al·ka·li
  pl. al·ka·lis
  al·ka·line
  al·ka·lin·i·ty

al·ka·loid

al·kyd

all (*everything*; see AWL
  all-A·mer·i·ca(n)
  all-a·round

Al·lah

Al·lah·a·bad

al·lay

al·le·ga·tion

al·lege
  al·leged
  al·leg·ed·ly

Al·le·ghe·ny

al·le·giance

al·le·go·ry
  pl. al·le·go·ries
  al·le·go·rist

al·le·gret·to
  pl. al·le·gret·tos

al·le·gro
  pl. al·le·gros

al·le·lu·ia
  also al·le·lu·ya,
  hal·le·lu·jah

Al·len

All·en·de Gos·sens

Al·len·town

al·ler·gen
  al·ler·gen·ic

al·ler·gic

al·ler·gy
pl. al·ler·gies
al·ler·gist

al·le·vi·ate
al·le·vi·a·tion
al·le·vi·a·tive
al·le·vi·a·tor
al·le·vi·a·to·ry

al·ley
pl. al·leys
also al·ley·way

al·li·ance

al·lied
also Al·lied

al·li·ga·tor

al·lit·er·a·tion
al·lit·er·ate
al·lit·er·a·tive

al·lo·cate
al·lo·ca·ble
al·lo·ca·tion
al·lo·ca·tor

al·lot
al·lot·ted, al·lot·ting
al·lot·ment

al·low
al·low·a·ble
al·low·a·bly

al·low·ance

al·loy

all·spice

al·lude

al·lure
al·lure·ment
al·lur·ing
al·lur·ing·ly

al·lu·sion (*reference;* see
  ILLUSION)
al·lu·sive

al·lu·vi·um
pl. al·lu·vi·ums *or*
  al·lu·vi·a
al·lu·vi·al

al·ly
pl. al·lies
al·lies, al·lied

al·ma ma·ter
also Al·ma Ma·ter

al·ma·nac

al·Ma·nam·ah

Al·ma·ty
formerly Al·ma-A·ta

al·might·y

al·mond

al·most

alms

alms·house

al·oe

a·loft

a·lo·ha

a·lone
a·lone·ness

a·long

a·long·side

a·loof
a·loof·ness

a·loud

alp

al·pac·a

al·pha

al·pha·bet
al·pha·bet·i·cal
al·pha·bet·i·cal·ly

al·pha·bet·ize
al·pha·bet·i·za·tion

al·pha·nu·mer·ic
also
  al·pha·nu·mer·i·cal

al·pine
also Al·pine

Alps

al·read·y

al·so
al·so-ran

al·tar (*table;* see ALTER)

al·tar·piece

al·ter (*change;* see ALTAR)
al·ter·a·ble
al·ter·a·tion

al·ter·cate
al·ter·ca·tion

al·ter·nate
al·ter·nate·ly
al·ter·na·tion

al·ter·na·tive
al·ter·na·tive·ly

al·ter·na·tor

al·though

al·tim·e·ter

al·ti·tude

al·to
pl. al·tos

al·to·geth·er

al·tru·ism
al·tru·ist
al·tru·is·tic
al·tru·is·ti·cal·ly

al·um

a·lu·mi·na

a·lu·mi·num

a·lum·nus
pl. a·lum·ni; *fem.*
  a·lum·na, *pl.*
  a·lum·nae

al·ways

Alz·hei·mer's dis·ease

a·mal·gam

a·mal·ga·mate
a·mal·ga·ma·tion

a·man·u·en·sis
pl. a·man·u·en·ses

am·a·ranth
am·a·ran·thine

Am·a·ril·lo

am·a·ryl·lis

a·mass
a·mass·er
a·mass·ment

am·a·teur
am·a·teur·ish
am·a·teur·ish·ly

A·ma·ti

am·a·to·ry

a·maze
a·maze·ment
a·maz·ing
a·maz·ing·ly

Am·a·zon
also am·a·zon
Am·a·zo·ni·an

am·bas·sa·dor
am·bas·sa·do·ri·al
am·bas·sa·dor·ship

am·ber

am·ber·gris

am·bi·dex·trous
am·bi·dex·ter·i·ty
am·bi·dex·trous·ly
am·bi·dex·trous·ness

am·bi·ence
also am·bi·ance

am·bi·ent

am·big·u·ous
am·big·u·i·ty
am·big·u·ous·ly

am·bi·tion

am·bi·tious
am·bi·tious·ly

am·biv·a·lence
also am·biv·a·lency
am·biv·a·lent
am·biv·a·lent·ly

am·ble

am·bro·sia
am·bro·sial
am·bro·sian

am·bu·lance

am·bu·la·to·ry

am·bus·cade

am·bush

a·me·ba
var. of a·moe·ba

a·me·lio·rate
a·mel·io·ra·tion
am·el·io·ra·tive
a·mel·io·ra·tor

a·men

a·me·na·ble
a·me·na·bil·i·ty
a·me·na·bly

a·mend
a·mend·a·ble
a·mend·er

a·mend·ment

a·mends

A·men·ho·tep
also Am·e·no·phis

a·men·i·ty
pl. a·men·i·ties

Am·er·a·sian

a·merce
a·merce·ment

A·mer·i·ca
A·mer·i·can

A·mer·i·can·i·za·tion
A·mer·i·can·ize

A·mer·i·ca·na

A·mer·i·can·ism

am·er·i·ci·um

Am·er·in·di·an
also Am·er·ind
Am·er·in·dic

am·e·thyst
am·e·thys·tine

a·mi·a·ble
a·mi·a·bil·i·ty
a·mi·a·ble·ness
a·mi·a·bly

am·i·ca·ble
am·i·ca·bil·i·ty
am·i·ca·bly

a·mid
also a·midst

am·ide

a·mid·ships
also a·mid·ship

Am·i·ens

a·mi·go
pl. a·mi·gos

A·min

a·mine

a·mi·no ac·id

a·miss

am·i·ty

Am·man

am·me·ter

am·mo

am·mo·nia

am·mu·ni·tion

am·ne·sia
am·ne·si·ac
am·ne·sic

am·nes·ty
  pl. am·nes·ties
  am·nes·ties,
  am·nes·tied

am·ni·o·cen·te·sis
  pl. am·ni·o·cen·te·ses

am·ni·on
  pl. am·ni·a
  am·ni·ot·ic

a·moe·ba
  also a·me·ba
  pl. a·moe·bas *or*
  a·moe·bae
  a·moe·bic
  a·moe·boid

a·mok
  also a·muck

a·mong
  also a·mongst

a·mor·al
  a·mor·al·ism
  a·mor·al·i·ty

am·o·rous
  am·o·rous·ly
  am·o·rous·ness

a·mor·phous
  a·mor·phous·ly
  a·mor·phous·ness

am·or·ti·za·tion

am·or·tize

a·mount

a·mour

a·mour pro·pre

amp·er·age

am·pere

am·per·sand

am·phet·a·mine

am·phib·i·an
  am·phib·i·ous
  am·phib·i·ous·ly

am·phi·the·a·ter

am·pho·ra
  pl. am·pho·rae *or*
  am·pho·ras

am·ple
  am·pler, am·plest
  am·ple·ness
  am·ply

am·pli·fi·er

am·pli·fy
  am·pli·fies, am·pli·fied
  am·pli·fi·ca·tion

am·pli·tude

am·poule
  also am·pule *or* am·pul

am·pu·tate
  am·pu·ta·tion
  am·pu·ta·tor

am·pu·tee

Am·rit·sar

Am·ster·dam

Am·trak

a·muck
  var. of a·mok

am·u·let

a·muse
  a·mus·ing
  a·mus·ing·ly

a·muse·ment

a·my·o·troph·ic
  lat·er·al scle·ro·sis

an·a·bol·ic

a·nab·o·lism

a·nach·ro·nism
  a·nach·ro·nis·tic
  a·nach·ro·nis·ti·cal·ly

an·a·con·da

an·aer·obe
  an·aer·o·bic

an·a·gram
  an·a·gram·ma·tic
  an·a·gram·mat·i·cal
  an·a·gram·ma·tize

An·a·heim

a·nal
  a·nal·ly

an·al·ge·si·a

an·al·ge·sic

an·a·log

a·nal·o·gize

a·nal·o·gous
  a·nal·o·gous·ly

a·nal·o·gy
  pl. a·nal·o·gies
  an·a·log·i·cal
  an·a·log·i·cal·ly

a·nal·y·sis
  pl. a·nal·y·ses
  an·a·lyt·ic
  an·a·lyt·i·cal
  an·a·lyt·i·cal·ly

an·a·lyst

an·a·lyze
  an·a·lyz·a·ble
  an·a·lyz·er

an·a·pest
  an·a·pes·tic

an·a·phy·lax·is
  pl. an·a·phy·lax·es
  an·a·phy·lac·tic

an·ar·chism
  an·ar·chist
  an·ar·chis·tic

an·ar·chy
  an·ar·chic
  an·ar·chi·cal
  an·ar·chi·cal·ly

A·na·sa·zi

a·nath·e·ma
  pl. a·nath·e·mas

a·nath·e·ma·tize

a·nat·o·mize

a·nat·o·my
pl. a·nat·o·mies
an·a·tom·i·cal
a·nat·o·mist

An·ax·ag·o·ras

an·ces·tor
fem. an·ces·tress
an·ces·tral

an·ces·try
pl. an·ces·tries

an·chor

An·chor·age (*city*)

an·chor·age (*harbor*)

an·cho·rite

an·cho·vy
pl. an·cho·vies

an·cient
an·cient·ness

an·cil·lar·y
pl. an·cil·lar·ies

An·da·man Is·lands

an·dan·te

An·der·sen

An·der·son

An·des
An·de·an

and·i·ron

An·dor·ra

an·dro·gen
an·dro·gen·ic

an·drog·y·nous
an·drog·y·ny

an·droid

An·dro·pov

an·ec·dote
an·ec·do·tal
an·ec·do·tal·ist

an·ec·dot·ic
an·ec·dot·ist

a·ne·mi·a

a·ne·mic

an·e·mom·e·ter

a·nem·o·ne

an·er·oid

an·es·the·sia
an·es·the·si·ol·o·gy

an·es·thet·ic
an·es·the·tize

an·es·the·tist

an·eu·rysm
also an·eu·rism
an·eu·rys·mal
also an·eu·ris·mal

a·new

an·gel
an·gel·ic
an·gel·i·cal
an·gel·i·cal·ly

An·ge·lou

an·ger

an·gi·na
in full an·gi·na
pec·tor·is

an·gi·o·sperm
an·gi·o·sper·mous

an·gle
an·gled

An·gli·can
An·gli·can·ism

An·gli·cism
An·gli·cize

An·glo
pl. An·glos

An·glo-French

An·glo·phile

An·glo-Sa·xon

An·go·la
An·go·lan

an·go·ra

an·gry
an·gri·er, an·gri·est
an·gri·ly

angst

ang·strom
also ång·ström

An·guil·la

an·guish

an·gu·lar
an·gu·lar·i·ty
an·gu·lar·ly

an·i·line

an·i·mad·vert
an·i·mad·ver·sion

an·i·mal

an·i·mal·ism

an·i·mate

an·i·mat·ed
an·i·mat·ed·ly
an·i·ma·tor

an·i·ma·tion

an·i·mism
an·i·mist
an·i·mis·tic

an·i·mos·i·ty
pl. an·i·mos·i·ties

an·i·mus

an·i·on
an·i·on·ic

an·ise

An·ka·ra

ankh

an·kle

ank·let

an·ky·lo·sis
an·ky·lot·ic

an·nals
  an·nal·ist
  an·nal·is·tic
  an·nal·is·ti·cal·ly

An·nan

An·nap·o·lis

Ann Ar·bor

an·neal
  an·neal·er

Anne Bol·eyn

an·ne·lid

An·nen·berg

Anne of Cleves

an·nex
  an·nex·a·tion

an·ni·hi·late
  an·ni·hi·la·tion
  an·ni·hi·la·tor

an·ni·ver·sa·ry
  pl. an·ni·ver·sa·ries

an·no·tate
  an·no·ta·tion
  an·no·ta·tive
  an·no·ta·tor

an·nounce
  an·nounce·ment

an·nounc·er

an·noy
  an·noy·ance
  an·noy·er
  an·noy·ing

an·nu·al
  an·nu·al·ly

an·nu·i·ty
  pl. an·nu·i·ties

an·nul
  an·nulled, an·nul·ling
  an·nul·ment

an·nu·lar
  an·nu·lar·ly

an·nun·ci·a·tion
  also An·nun·ci·a·tion

an·ode
  an·od·ic

an·o·dize
  an·o·diz·er

an·o·dyne

a·noint
  a·noint·er

a·nom·a·lous
  a·nom·a·lous·ly
  a·nom·a·lous·ness

a·nom·a·ly
  pl. a·nom·a·lies

a·non

a·non·y·mous
  an·o·nym·i·ty
  a·non·y·mous·ly

a·noph·e·les

an·o·rak

an·o·rex·i·a
  in full an·o·rex·ia
  ner·vo·sa
  an·o·rex·ic

an·oth·er

A·nou·ilh

An·selm, St.

an·swer
  an·swer·a·ble

ant *(insect; see* AUNT)

ant·ac·id

an·tag·o·nism

an·tag·o·nist
  an·tag·o·nis·tic
  an·tag·o·nis·ti·cal·ly

an·tag·o·nize
  an·tag·o·ni·za·tion

An·ta·na·na·ri·vo

Ant·arc·ti·ca
  Ant·arc·tic

an·te
  an·tes, an·ted

ant·eat·er

an·te·bel·lum

an·te·ced·ent
  an·te·ce·dence
  an·te·ced·ent·ly

an·te·cham·ber

an·te·date

an·te·di·lu·vi·an

an·te·lope
  pl. same *or* an·te·lopes

an·ten·na
  pl. an·ten·nae *or*
  an·ten·nas

an·te·ri·or
  an·te·ri·or·i·ty
  an·te·ri·or·ly

an·te·room

an·them

an·ther
  an·the·ral

ant·hill

an·thol·o·gy
  pl. an·thol·o·gies
  an·thol·o·gist
  an·thol·o·gize

An·tho·ny

an·thra·cite
  an·thra·cit·ic

an·thrax

an·thro·po·cen·tric
  an·thro·po·cen·tri·
  cal·ly
  an·thro·po·cen·trism

an·thro·poid

an·thro·pol·o·gy
  an·thro·po·log·i·cal
  an·thro·pol·o·gist

an·thro·po·mor·phism
  an·thro·po·mor·phic
  an·thro·po·mor·phi·
    cal·ly
  an·thro·po·mor·phize

an·thro·po·mor·phous

an·ti
  pl. an·tis

an·ti·air·craft

an·ti·bi·ot·ic

an·ti·bod·y
  pl. an·ti·bod·ies

an·tic

An·ti·christ

an·tic·i·pate
  an·tic·i·pa·tion
  an·tic·i·pat·or
  an·tic·i·pa·tor·y

an·ti·cli·max
  an·ti·cli·mac·tic
  an·ti·cli·mac·ti·cal·ly

an·ti·de·pres·sant

an·ti·dote
  an·ti·dot·al

an·ti·freeze

an·ti·gen
  an·ti·gen·ic

An·ti·gua and
  Bar·bu·da

an·ti·he·ro
  pl. an·ti·he·roes

an·ti·his·ta·mine

An·til·les

an·ti·lock

an·ti·log·a·rithm

an·ti·mat·ter

an·ti·mo·ny

an·ti·par·ti·cle

an·ti·pas·to
  pl. an·ti·pas·tos or
    an·ti·pas·ti

an·ti·pa·thy
  pl. an·tip·a·thies

an·ti·per·spi·rant

an·ti·phon
  an·tiph·o·nal
  an·tiph·o·nal·ly

An·tip·o·des (New
  Zealand islands)

an·tip·o·des (opposite
  places)
  an·tip·o·dal
  an·tip·o·de·an

an·ti·quar·i·an
  an·ti·quar·i·an·ism

an·ti·quar·y
  pl. an·ti·quar·ies

an·ti·quat·ed

an·tique
  an·tiques, an·tiqued,
    an·ti·quing

an·tiq·ui·ty
  pl. an·tiq·ui·ties

an·ti-Sem·ite
  an·ti-Se·mit·ic
  an·ti-Sem·i·tism

an·ti·sep·tic
  an·ti·sep·ti·cal·ly

an·ti·se·rum
  pl. an·ti·se·ra

an·ti·so·cial

an·tith·e·sis
  pl. an·tith·e·ses
  an·ti·thet·i·cal
  an·ti·thet·i·cal·ly

an·ti·tox·in
  an·ti·tox·ic

an·ti·trust

an·ti·vi·ral

ant·ler
  ant·lered

An·to·ni·nus Pi·us

An·to·ny

an·to·nym
  an·ton·y·mous

Ant·werp

a·nus

an·vil

anx·i·e·ty
  pl. anx·i·e·ties

anx·ious
  anx·ious·ly
  anx·ious·ness

an·y

an·y·bod·y

an·y·how

an·y·one

an·y·thing

an·y·way
  also an·y·ways

an·y·where

a·or·ta
  pl. a·or·tas
  a·or·tic

a·pace

A·pach·e

Ap·a·lach·ee
  also Ap·a·lach·i

a·part

a·part·heid

a·part·ment

ap·a·thy
  ap·a·thet·ic
  ap·a·thet·i·cal·ly

ap·a·to·sau·rus

ape

Ap•en•nines

a•pe•ri•tif

ap•er•ture

a•pex
 pl. a•pex•es *or* a•pi•ces

a•pha•si•a
 a•pha•sic

aph•e•li•on
 pl. a•phe•li•a

a•phid

aph•o•rism
 aph•o•rist
 aph•o•ris•tic
 aph•o•ris•ti•cal•ly
 aph•o•rize

aph•ro•di•si•ac

A•pi•a

a•pi•ar•y
 pl. a•pi•ar•ies
 a•pi•a•rist

ap•i•cal
 a•pi•cal•ly

a•piece

a•plomb

a•poc•a•lypse
 a•poc•a•lyp•tic
 a•poc•a•lyp•ti•cal•ly

A•poc•ry•pha
 also a•poc•ry•pha

a•poc•ry•phal

ap•o•gee
 ap•o•ge•an

a•po•lit•i•cal

Ap•ol•lo•ni•us

a•pol•o•get•ic
 a•pol•o•get•i•cal•ly

a•pol•o•gist

a•pol•o•gize

a•pol•o•gy
 pl. a•pol•o•gies

ap•o•plec•tic

ap•o•plex•y

a•pos•ta•sy
 pl. a•pos•ta•sies

a•pos•tate
 ap•o•stat•i•cal
 a•pos•ta•tize

a pos•te•ri•o•ri

a•pos•tle
 also A•pos•tle
 a•pos•tle•ship

ap•os•tol•ic

a•pos•tro•phe

a•poth•e•car•y
 pl. a•poth•e•car•ies

ap•o•thegm
 ap•o•theg•mat•ic

a•po•the•o•sis
 pl. a•poth•e•o•ses

Ap•pa•la•chi•an

ap•pall
 also ap•pal
 ap•palled, ap•pal•ling
 ap•pal•ling•ly

ap•pa•rat•us

ap•par•el
 ap•par•eled,
 ap•par•el•ing;
 ap•par•elled,
 ap•par•el•ling

ap•par•ent
 ap•par•ent•ly

ap•pa•ri•tion

ap•peal
 ap•peal•er

ap•peal•ing
 ap•peal•ing•ly

ap•pear

ap•pear•ance

ap•pease
 ap•pease•ment
 ap•peas•er

ap•pel•lant

ap•pel•late

ap•pel•la•tion

ap•pend

ap•pend•age

ap•pen•dec•to•my
 pl. ap•pen•dec•to•mies

ap•pen•di•ci•tis

ap•pen•dix
 pl. ap•pen•di•ces;
 ap•pen•dix•es

ap•per•tain

ap•pe•tite
 ap•pe•ti•tive

ap•pe•tiz•er

ap•pe•tiz•ing
 ap•pe•tiz•ing•ly

ap•plaud

ap•plause

ap•ple

ap•ple•jack

ap•pli•ance

ap•pli•ca•ble
 ap•pli•ca•bil•i•ty
 ap•pli•ca•bly

ap•pli•cant

ap•pli•ca•tion

ap•pli•ca•tor

ap•plied

ap·pli·qué
ap·pli·qués,
ap·pli·quéd,
ap·pli·qué·ing

ap·ply
ap·plies, ap·plied
ap·pli·er

ap·point
ap·point·ee
ap·point·er
ap·poin·tive

ap·point·ment

Ap·po·mat·tox

ap·por·tion
ap·por·tion·a·ble
ap·por·tion·ment

ap·po·site
ap·po·site·ly
ap·po·site·ness

ap·po·si·tion
ap·po·si·tion·al

ap·praise
ap·prais·a·ble
ap·prais·al
ap·prais·er

ap·pre·cia·ble
ap·pre·cia·bly

ap·pre·ci·ate
ap·pre·cia·tive
ap·pre·cia·tive·ly
ap·pre·cia·tive·ness
ap·pre·ci·a·tor
ap·pre·ci·a·to·ry

ap·pre·ci·a·tion

ap·pre·hend

ap·pre·hen·sion

ap·pre·hen·sive
ap·pre·hen·sive·ly
ap·pre·hen·sive·ness

ap·pren·tice
ap·pren·tice·ship

ap·prise

ap·proach

ap·proach·a·ble
ap·proach·a·bil·i·ty

ap·pro·ba·tion
ap·pro·ba·tive
ap·pro·ba·to·ry

ap·pro·pri·ate
ap·pro·pri·ate·ly
ap·pro·pri·ate·ness
ap·pro·pri·a·tion
ap·pro·pri·a·tor

ap·prov·al

ap·prove
ap·prov·er
ap·prov·ing·ly

ap·prox·i·mate
ap·prox·i·mate·ly
ap·prox·i·ma·tion

ap·pur·te·nance

ap·ri·cot

A·pril

a pri·o·ri
a·pri·o·rism

a·pron
a·proned
a·pron·ful
pl. a·pron·fuls

ap·ro·pos

apse

apt
apt·ly
apt·ness

ap·ti·tude

A·pu·lci·us

aq·ua

aq·ua·ma·rine

aq·ua·naut

aq·ua·plane

a·quar·ium
pl. a·quar·i·ums *or*
a·quar·i·a

A·quar·ius
A·quar·i·an

a·quat·ic

aq·ua vi·tae

aq·ue·duct

a·que·ous

aq·ui·fer

aq·ui·line

A·qui·nas

Ar·ab

ar·a·besque

A·ra·bi·a
A·ra·bi·an

Ar·a·bic

ar·a·ble

a·rach·nid
a·rach·ni·dan

Ar·a·fat

Ar·al Sea

Ar·a·ma·ic

A·rap·a·ho

Ar·a·rat, Mt.

ar·bi·ter

ar·bi·trar·y
ar·bi·trar·i·ly
ar·bi·trar·i·ness

ar·bi·trate
ar·bi·tra·tion

ar·bi·trat·or

ar·bor
ar·bored

ar·bo·re·al

ar·bo·re·tum
pl. ar·bo·re·tums *or*
ar·bo·re·ta**

ar•bor vi•tae

ar•bu•tus

arc (*curved line*; see ARK)
arced, arc•ing

ar•cade
ar•cad•ed

ar•cane
ar•cane•ly

arch
arch•ly
arch•ness

ar•chae•ol•o•gy
also ar•che•ol•o•gy
ar•chae•o•log•ic
ar•chae•o•log•i•cal
ar•chae•ol•o•gist

ar•cha•ic
ar•cha•i•cal•ly

ar•cha•ism
ar•cha•ist
ar•cha•is•tic

Arch•an•gel (*city*)

arch•an•gel (*angel*)

arch•bish•op
arch•bish•op•ric

arch•dea•con
arch•dea•con•ry
pl. arch•dea•con•ries
arch•dea•con•ship

arch•di•o•cese
arch•di•oc•e•san

arch•duke
fem. arch•duch•ess
arch•du•cal
arch•duch•y
pl. arch•duch•ies

arch•en•e•my
pl. arch•en•e•mies

ar•che•ol•o•gy
var. of ar•chae•ol•o•gy

arch•er

ar•cher•y

ar•che•type
ar•che•typ•al
ar•che•typ•i•cal

ar•chi•pel•a•go
pl. ar•chi•pel•a•gos *or*
ar•chi•pel•a•goes

ar•chi•tect

ar•chi•tec•ton•ic

ar•chi•tec•ture
ar•chi•tec•tur•al
ar•chi•tec•tur•al•ly

ar•chi•trave

ar•chive
ar•chi•val
ar•chi•vist

arch•way

Arc•tic
also arctic

ar•dent
ar•den•cy
ar•dent•ly

ar•dor

ar•du•ous
ar•du•ous•ly
ar•du•ous•ness

are

a•re•a
a•re•al

a•re•na

aren't

Ar•gen•ti•na
Ar•gen•tine
Ar•gen•tin•e•an

ar•gon

ar•go•sy
pl. ar•go•sies

ar•got

ar•gue
ar•gues, ar•gued,
ar•gu•ing

ar•gu•a•ble
ar•gu•a•bly
ar•gu•er

ar•gu•ment

ar•gu•men•ta•tion

ar•gu•men•ta•tive
ar•gu•men•ta•tive•ly
ar•gu•men•ta•tive•ness

a•ri•a

ar•id
a•rid•i•ty
ar•id•ly
ar•id•ness

A•ries
Ar•i•an

a•right

A•ri•os•to

a•rise
past a•rose; *past part.*
a•risen

Ar•is•ti•des

ar•is•to•cra•cy
pl. ar•is•to•cra•cies

a•ris•to•crat
a•ris•to•crat•ic
a•ris•to•crat•i•cal•ly

Ar•is•toph•a•nes

Ar•is•tot•le

ar•ith•me•tic
also ar•ith•met•i•cal
a•rith•me•ti•cian

Ar•i•zo•na
Ar•i•zo•nan,
Ar•i•zo•ni•an

ark (*Noah's ship*; see ARC)

Ar•kan•sas
Ar•kan•san

Ar•khan•gelsk

Ar•ling•ton

arm
arm•ful
pl. arm•fuls
arm•less

ar•ma•da

ar•ma•dil•lo
pl. ar•ma•dil•los

Ar•ma•ged•don

ar•ma•ment

ar•ma•ture

arm•chair

Ar•me•ni•a
Ar•me•ni•an

arm•hole

arm•i•stice

arm•let

ar•moire

ar•mor

ar•mor•y
pl. ar•mor•ies

arm•pit

arm•rest

Arm•strong

ar•my
pl. ar•mies

Ar•nold

a•ro•ma

ar•o•ma•tic
ar•o•mat•ic•al•ly

a•rose

Ar•ouet

a•round

a•rouse
a•rous•a•ble
a•rous•al
a•rous•er

ar•peg•gio
pl. ar•peg•gios

ar•raign
ar•raign•ment

ar•range
ar•range•a•ble
ar•rang•er

ar•range•ment

ar•rant
ar•rant•ly

ar•ras

ar•ray

ar•rears
ar•rear•age

ar•rest
ar•rest•ing
ar•rest•ing•ly

ar•riv•al

ar•rive

ar•ri•viste

ar•ro•gant
ar•ro•gance
ar•ro•gant•ly

ar•ro•gate
ar•ro•ga•tion

ar•row

ar•row•head

ar•row•root

ar•se•nal

ar•se•nic
ar•sen•i•cal

ar•son
ar•son•ist

art

Ar•ta•xerx•es

ar•te•ri•al

ar•te•rio•scle•ro•sis
ar•te•ri•o•scle•rot•ic

ar•te•ry
pl. ar•te•ries

ar•te•sian

art•ful
art•ful•ly
art•ful•ness

ar•thri•tis
ar•thrit•ic

ar•thro•pod

Ar•thur
Ar•thu•ri•an

ar•ti•choke

ar•ti•cle

ar•tic•u•lar

ar•tic•u•late
ar•tic•u•late•ly
ar•tic•u•late•ness
ar•tic•u•la•tion

ar•ti•fact

ar•ti•fice

ar•ti•fi•cer

ar•ti•fi•cial
ar•ti•fi•ci•al•i•ty
ar•ti•fi•cial•ly

ar•til•ler•y
pl. ar•til•ler•ies
ar•til•ler•y•man

ar•ti•san

art•ist
art•ist•ry

ar•tis•tic
ar•tis•ti•cal•ly

art•less
art•less•ly
art•less•ness

art•work

art•y
art•i•er, art•i•est
art•i•ness

A·ru·ba

a·rum

Ar·y·an

as·bes·tos

as·cend

as·cen·dan·cy
also as·cen·den·cy

as·cen·dant

as·cen·sion
also As·cen·sion
as·cen·sion·al

as·cent (*upward
movement*; see
ASSENT)

as·cer·tain
as·cer·tain·a·ble
as·cer·tain·ment

as·cet·ic
as·cet·i·cal·ly
as·cet·i·cism

a·scor·bic ac·id

as·cot

as·cribe
a·scrib·a·ble
as·crip·tion

a·sep·sis
a·sep·tic

a·sex·u·al
a·sex·u·al·i·ty
a·sex·u·al·ly

ash

a·shamed
a·sham·ed·ly

Ashe

ash·en

Ash·ga·bat
also Ash·kha·bad

ash·lar

a·shore

ash·ram

ash·tray

ash·y
ash·i·er, ash·i·est

A·sia
A·sian

A·sia Mi·nor

A·si·at·ic

a·side

As·i·mov

as·i·nine
as·i·nin·i·ty

ask
ask·er

a·skance
also a·skant

a·skew

a·slant

a·sleep

As·ma·ra
also As·me·ra

asp

as·par·a·gus

as·pect

as·pen

as·per·i·ty
pl. as·per·i·ties

as·per·sion

as·phalt
as·phalt·er
as·phal·tic

as·pho·del

as·phyx·i·ate
as·phyx·i·a·tion
as·phyx·i·a·tor

as·pic

as·pi·rant

as·pi·rate

as·pi·ra·tion

as·pi·ra·tor

as·pire

as·pi·rin
pl. same *or* as·pir·ins

ass

As·sad

as·sail
as·sail·a·ble
as·sail·ant

as·sas·sin

as·sas·si·nate
as·sas·si·na·tion
as·sas·si·na·tor

as·sault
as·sault·er

as·say
as·say·er

as·sem·blage

as·sem·ble
as·sem·bler

as·sem·bly
pl. as·sem·blies

as·sent (*consent*; see
ASCENT)
as·sen·tor
also as·sent·er

as·sert
as·ser·tor

as·ser·tion

as·ser·tive
as·ser·tive·ly
as·ser·tive·ness

as·sess
as·sess·a·ble
as·sess·ment
as·ses·sor

as·set

as·sev·er·ate
  as·sev·er·a·tion
  as·sev·er·a·tive

as·sid·u·ous
  as·sid·u·ous·ly
  as·sid·u·ous·ness

as·sign
  as·sign·a·ble
  as·sign·er

as·sig·na·tion

as·sign·ee

as·sign·ment

as·sim·i·late
  as·sim·i·la·tion
  as·sim·i·la·tive
  as·sim·i·la·tor

As·sin·i·boin

as·sist
  as·sis·tance
  as·sist·er

as·sis·tant

as·so·ci·ate
  as·so·ci·ate·ship
  as·so·ci·a·tive

as·so·ci·a·tion

as·so·nance
  as·so·nant
  as·so·nate

as·sort

as·sort·ed

as·sort·ment

as·suage
  as·suage·ment
  as·suag·er

as·sume
  as·sum·a·ble
  as·sum·ed·ly

as·sumed

as·sum·ing

as·sump·tion
  also As·sump·tion

as·sur·ance

as·sure
  as·sur·a·ble
  as·sur·er

A·staire

as·ta·tine

as·ter

as·ter·isk

a·stern

as·ter·oid
  as·ter·oi·dal

asth·ma
  asth·mat·ic

a·stig·ma·tism
  as·tig·mat·ic

a·stir

as·ton·ish
  as·ton·ish·ing
  ast·on·ish·ing·ly
  as·ton·ish·ment

As·tor

as·tound
  as·tound·ing
  as·tound·ing·ly

a·strad·dle

as·tra·khan

as·tral

a·stray

a·stride

as·trin·gent
  as·trin·gen·cy
  as·trin·gent·ly

as·tro·labe

as·trol·o·gy
  as·trol·o·ger
  as·tro·log·i·cal
  as·trol·o·gist

as·tro·naut
  as·tro·nau·ti·cal
  as·tro·nau·tics

as·tro·nom·i·cal
  also as·tro·nom·ic
  as·tro·nom·i·cal·ly

as·tron·o·my
  as·tron·o·mer

as·tro·phys·ics
  as·tro·phys·i·cal
  as·tro·phys·i·cist

As·tu·ri·as

as·tute
  as·tute·ly
  as·tute·ness

A·sun·ción

a·sun·der

As·wan

a·sy·lum

a·sym·me·try
  a·sym·met·ric
  a·sym·met·ri·cal
  a·sym·met·ri·cal·ly

A·syut

at

A·ta·ca·ma Des·ert

A·ta·türk

at·a·vism
  at·a·vis·tic
  at·a·vis·ti·cal·ly

at·ax·i·a
  also a·tax·y
  a·tax·ic

ate (*consumed food*; see EIGHT)

a·te·lier

Ath·a·bas·ka, Lake

a·the·ism
  a·the·ist
  a·the·is·tic
  a·the·is·ti·cal

Ath·ens
  A·the·ni·an

ath·er·o·scle·ro·sis
  ath·er·o·scle·rot·ic

ath·lete

ath·let·ic
  ath·let·i·cal·ly
  ath·let·i·cism

ath·let·ics

At·lan·ta

At·lan·tic

At·las (*mountains, mythological figure*)

at·las (*book of maps*)

at·mo·sphere
  at·mos·pher·ic
  at·mos·pher·i·cal
  at·mos·pher·i·cal·ly

a·tom·ic
  a·tom·i·cal·ly

at·om·ize
  at·om·i·za·tion

at·om·iz·er

a·ton·al
  a·to·nal·i·ty

a·tone

a·tone·ment

a·tri·um
  pl. a·tri·ums *or* a·tri·a
  a·tri·al

a·tro·cious
  a·tro·cious·ly

a·troc·i·ty
  pl. a·troc·i·ties

at·ro·phy
  at·ro·phies, at·ro·phied

at·ro·pine

at·tach
  at·tach·a·ble
  at·tach·er

at·ta·ché

at·tach·ment

at·tack
  at·tack·er

at·tain
  at·tain·a·ble
  at·tain·a·bil·i·ty
  at·tain·ment

at·tar
  also ot·to

at·tempt
  at·tempt·a·ble

at·tend
  at·tend·er

at·tend·ance

at·tend·ant

at·tend·ee

at·ten·tion

at·ten·tive
  at·ten·tive·ly
  at·ten·tive·ness

at·ten·u·ate
  at·ten·u·at·ed
  at·ten·u·a·tion
  at·ten·u·a·tor

at·test
  at·test·a·ble
  at·tes·ta·tion
  at·tes·tor

At·tic (*of ancient Athens*)

at·tic (*uppermost story in a house*)

At·ti·la

at·tire

at·ti·tude
  at·ti·tu·di·nal

at·ti·tu·di·nize

Att·lee

at·tor·ney
  pl. at·tor·neys

at·tract
  at·tract·a·ble
  at·trac·tor

at·trac·tion

at·trac·tive
  at·trac·tive·ly
  at·trac·tive·ness

at·tri·bute
  at·trib·ut·a·ble
  at·tri·bu·tion

at·trib·u·tive
  at·trib·u·tive·ly

at·tri·tion
  at·tri·tion·al

At·tucks

at·tune

At·wood

a·typ·i·cal
  a·typ·i·cal·ly

au·burn

Auck·land

auc·tion

auc·tion·eer
  auc·tion·eer·ing

au·da·cious
  au·da·cious·ly
  au·da·cious·ness
  au·dac·i·ty

Au·den

au·di·ble
  au·di·bil·i·ty
  au·di·ble·ness
  au·di·bly

au·di·ence

au·di·o

au·di·o·phile

au·di·o·vi·su·al

au·dit

au·di·tion

au·di·tor

au·di·to·ri·um
   pl. au·di·to·ri·ums *or*
   au·di·to·ri·a

au·di·to·ry

Au·du·bon

au fait

au·ger (*tool;* see AUGUR)

aught (*any, zero;* see
   OUGHT)

aug·ment
   aug·men·ta·tion
   aug·men·ta·tive
   aug·ment·er

au gra·tin

Augs·burg

au·gur (*portend;* see
   AUGUR)

au·gu·ry
   pl. au·gu·ries
   au·gu·ral

Au·gust (*month*)

au·gust (*impressive*)
   au·gust·ly
   au·gust·ness

Au·gus·ta

Au·gus·tan

Au·gus·tine
   Au·gus·tin·i·an

Au·gus·tus

auk

auld lang syne

Aung San Suu Kyi

aunt (*relative;* see ANT)

au pair

au·ra
   pl. au·rae *or* au·ras

au·ral (*of the ear;* see
   ORAL)
   au·ral·ly

Au·re·li·us

au·re·ole
   also au·re·o·la

au re·voir

au·ri·cle

Au·ro·ra (*goddess, city*)

au·ro·ra (*streamers of
   light*)
   pl. au·ro·ras *or*
   au·ro·rae

aus·cul·ta·tion

aus·pice

aus·pi·cious
   aus·pi·cious·ly
   aus·pi·cious·ness

Aus·sie
   also Os·sie, Oz·zie

Aus·ten (*proper name;*
   see AUSTIN)

aus·tere
   aus·ter·er, aus·ter·est
   aus·tere·ly

aus·ter·i·ty
   pl. aus·ter·i·ties

Aus·tin (*city;* see
   AUSTEN)

Aus·tral·a·sia

Aus·tral·ia
   Aus·tral·i·an
   Aus·tral·ian·ism

Aus·tri·a
   Aus·tri·an

au·then·tic
   au·then·ti·cal·ly
   au·then·tic·i·ty

au·then·ti·cate
   au·then·ti·ca·tion
   au·then·ti·ca·tor

au·thor
   fem. au·thor·ess
   au·tho·ri·al
   au·thor·ship

au·thor·i·tar·i·an
   au·thor·i·tar·i·an·ism

au·thor·i·ta·tive
   au·thor·i·ta·tive·ly
   au·thor·i·ta·tive·ness

au·thor·i·ty
   pl. au·thor·i·ties

au·thor·ize
   au·thor·i·za·tion

au·tism
   au·tis·tic

au·to
   pl. au·tos

au·to·bi·og·ra·phy
   pl. au·to·bi·og·ra·phies
   au·to·bi·og·ra·pher
   au·to·bi·o·graph·ic
   au·to·bi·o·graph·i·cal

au·to·clave

au·toc·ra·cy
   pl. au·toc·ra·cies
   au·to·crat
   au·to·crat·ic
   au·to·crat·i·cal·ly

au·to-da-fé
   pl. au·tos-da-fé

au·to·di·dact
   au·to·di·dac·tic

au·to·graph

au·to·im·mune
   au·to·im·mu·ni·ty

au·to·mate

au·to·mat·ic
  au·to·mat·i·cal·ly
  au·to·mat·ic·i·ty

au·to·ma·tion

au·tom·a·tism

au·tom·a·ton
  pl. au·tom·a·ta *or*
  au·tom·a·tons

au·to·mo·bile

au·to·mo·tive

au·to·nom·ic

au·ton·o·mous
  au·ton·o·mous·ly

au·ton·o·my
  pl. au·ton·o·mies
  au·ton·o·mist

au·to·pi·lot

au·top·sy
  pl. au·top·sies

au·to sug·ges·tion

au·tumn
  au·tum·nal

aux·il·ia·ry
  pl. aux·il·ia·ries

a·vail

a·vail·a·ble
  a·vail·a·bil·i·ty
  a·vail·a·bly

av·a·lanche

a·vant-garde
  a·vant-gard·ism
  a·vant-gard·ist

av·a·rice
  av·a·ri·cious
  av·a·ri·cious·ly
  av·a·ri·cious·ness

a·vast

av·a·tar

a·venge
  a·veng·er

av·e·nue

a·ver
  a·verred, a·ver·ring

av·er·age

A·ver·ro·ës

a·verse

a·ver·sion

a·vert

a·vi·an

a·vi·ar·y
  pl. a·vi·ar·ies

a·vi·a·tion

a·vi·a·tor
  fem. a·vi·a·trix

A·vi·cen·na

av·id
  a·vid·i·ty
  a·vid·ly

a·vi·on·ics

av·o·ca·do
  pl. av·o·ca·dos

av·o·ca·tion

a·void
  a·void·a·ble
  a·void·a·bly
  a·void·ance
  a·void·er

av·oir·du·pois

a·vow
  a·vow·al
  a·vow·ed·ly

a·vun·cu·lar

a·wait

a·wake
  past a·woke; *past part.*
  a·wok·en

a·wak·en

a·ward
  a·ward·er

a·ware
  a·ware·ness

a·wash

a·way (*at a distance;* see
  AWEIGH)

awe
  awe-in·spir·ing

a·weigh ([*of an anchor*]
  clear of the sea bed; see
  AWAY)

awe·some
  awe·some·ly
  awe·some·ness

aw·ful (*horrible;* see
  OFFAL)
  aw·ful·ness

aw·ful·ly

a·while

awk·ward
  awk·ward·ly
  awk·ward·ness

awl (*tool;* see ALL)

awn

awn·ing

a·woke

a·wok·en

a·wry

ax
  also axe
  ax·ing

ax·i·al
  ax·i·al·ly

ax·i·om
  ax·i·o·mat·ic
  ax·i·o·mat·i·cal·ly

ax·is
  pl. ax·es

ax·le

ax·o·lotl

ax·on

a·ya·tol·loh

aye (*yes*; see EYE)
  also ay

Ayer

a·za·lea

Az·er·bai·jan
  Az·er·bai·ja·ni

az·i·muth
  az·i·muth·al

A·zores

A·zov, Sea of

Az·tec

az·ure

B

baa
baas, baaed *or* baa'd
pl. baas

bab·ble
bab·bler

babe

ba·bel

Ba·ber
also Ba·bar, Ba·bur

ba·boon

ba·by
pl. ba·bies
ba·bies, ba·bied
ba·by-sit
ba·by-sit·ter
ba·by·hood
ba·by·ish

bac·ca·lau·re·ate

bac·cha·nal
also bac·cha·na·li·a

Bach

bach·e·lor
bach·e·lor·hood

ba·cil·lus
pl. ba·cil·li

back
back·er
back·less

back·ache

back·bite
back·bit·er

back·bone

back·break·ing

back·date

back·door

back·drop

back·fire

back·gam·mon

back·ground

back·hand

back·hand·ed

back·ing

back·lash

back·log

back·pack
back·pack·er

back·ped·al
back·ped·aled,
back·ped·al·ing

back·rest

back·seat

back·side

back·slash

back·slide
past back·slid; *past part.*
back·slid *or*
back·slid·den
back·slid·er

back·space

back·spin

back·stage

back·stairs
also back·stair

back·stop

back·stroke

back·track

back·up

back·ward
also back·wards
back·ward·ness

back·wash

back·wa·ter

back·woods
back·woods·man
pl. back·woods·men

back·yard

Ba·con (*proper name*)

ba·con (*meat*)

bac·te·ri·cide
bac·te·ri·ci·dal

bac·te·ri·ol·o·gy
bac·te·ri·o·log·i·cal
bac·te·ri·o·log·i·cal·ly
bac·te·ri·ol·o·gist

bac·te·ri·um
pl. bac·te·ri·a
bac·te·ri·al

bad (*not good; see* BADE)
worse, worst
bad·der, bad·dest
bad·ness

bade (*past of bid; see* BAD)

Ba·den-Pow·ell

badge

bad·ger

bad·i·nage

Bad·lands (*national
park*)

bad·lands (*barren area*)

bad·ly
worse, worst

bad·min·ton

bad-tem·pered

Baf·fin Bay

baf·fle
baf·fle·ment
baf·fling
baf·fling·ly

bag
bagged, bag·ging
bag·ful
pl. bag·fuls

bag·a·telle

ba·gel

bag·gage

bag·gy
bag·gi·er, bag·gi·est
bag·gi·ly
bag·gi·ness

Bagh·dad

bag·pipe
bag·pip·er

ba·guette

bah

Ba·ha·mas
Ba·ha·mi·an

Bah·rain

Bai·kal, Lake

bail (*security for release of a prisoner*; see BALE)
bail·a·ble

bail (*scoop water from*; see BALE)
bail·er

bai·liff

bai·li·wick

bail·out

bait (*enticement*; see BATE)

baize

Ba·ja Ca·li·for·nia

bake
bak·er
bak·ing

Ba·kers·field

bak·er·y
pl. bak·er·ies

bak·la·va

bak·sheesh

Ba·ku

bal·a·cla·va

bal·a·lai·ka

bal·ance
bal·anc·er

Bal·an·chine

Bal·boa

bal·co·ny
pl. bal·co·nies
bal·co·nied

bald
bald·ing
bald·ish
bald·ly
bald·ness

bal·der·dash

Bald·win

bale (*large bundle*; see BAIL)

Bâle

Bal·e·ar·ic Is·lands

ba·leen

bale·ful
bale·ful·ly
bale·ful·ness

Bal·four

Ba·li

balk
balk·er

Bal·kan

ball (*round object*; see BAWL)
ball-and-sock·et joint

bal·lad
bal·lad·eer
bal·lad·ry

bal·last

ball·boy
fem. ball·girl

bal·le·ri·na

bal·let
bal·let·ic

bal·lis·tic
bal·lis·ti·cal·ly

bal·lis·tics

bal·loon
bal·loon·ist

bal·lot
bal·lot·ed, bal·lot·ing

ball·park

ball·point

ball·room

bal·ly·hoo

balm (*ointment*; see BOMB)

balm·y
balm·i·er, balm·i·est
balm·i·ly
balm·i·ness

ba·lo·ney (*nonsense*; see BOLOGNA)
pl. ba·lo·neys

bal·sa

bal·sam
bal·sam·ic

Bal·tic

Bal·ti·more

bal·us·ter

bal·us·trade

Bal·zac

Ba·ma·ko

bam·boo

bam·boo cur·tain

bam·boo·zle
bam·boo·zle·ment
bam·boo·zler

ban
banned (*prohibited*; see
BAND), ban·ning

ba·nal
ba·nal·i·ty
pl. ba·nal·i·ties
ba·nal·ly

ba·nan·a

band (*group*; see *banned*
[BAN])

band·age

Band-Aid (*trademark*)

ban·dan·na
also ban·dan·a

band·box

ban·deau
pl. ban·deaux

ban·dit
ban·dit·ry

ban·do·lier
also ban·do·leer·

bands·man
pl. bands·men

band·stand

Ban·dung

band·wag·on

ban·dy
ban·di·er, ban·di·est
also ban·dy-leg·ged
ban·dies, ban·died

bane
bane·ful
bane·ful·ly

bang

Ban·ga·lore

Bang·kok

Ban·gla·desh
Ban·gla·desh·i

ban·gle

Ban·gui

ban·ish
ban·ish·ment

ban·is·ter
also ban·nis·ter

ban·jo
pl. ban·jos *or* ban·joes
ban·jo·ist

Ban·jul

bank
bank·a·ble

bank·book

bank·card

bank·er

bank·ing

bank·note

bank·rupt
bank·rupt·cy
pl. bank·rupt·cies

ban·ner
ban·nered

ban·nis·ter
var. of ban·is·ter

banns

ban·quet
ban·quet·er

ban·quette

ban·shee

ban·tam

ban·tam·weight

ban·ter
ban·ter·er

Ban·tu
pl. same *or* Ban·tus

ban·yan

ba·o·bab

bap·tism
bap·tis·mal

Bap·tist

bap·tis·ter·y
also bap·tis·try
pl. bap·tis·tries

bap·tize

bar (*long rod*; see BARRE)
barred (*having bars*;
see BARD), bar·ring

barb

Bar·ba·dos
Bar·ba·di·an

bar·bar·i·an

bar·bar·ic
bar·bar·i·cal·ly

bar·ba·rism

bar·bar·i·ty
pl. bar·bar·i·ties

Bar·ba·ros·sa

bar·ba·rous
bar·ba·rous·ly
bar·ba·rous·ness

Bar·ba·ry

bar·be·cue
bar·be·cues,
bar·be·cued,
bar·be·cuing

bar·bel

bar·bell

bar·ber
bar·ber·shop

bar·ber·ry
pl. bar·ber·ries

bar·bi·tu·rate

bar•ca•role
  also bar•ca•rolle

Bar•ce•lo•na

bard (*poet*; see *barred*
  [BARD])
  bard•ic

bare (*uncovered*; see
  BEAR)
  bare•ness

bare•back

bare•faced

bare•foot
  also bare•foot•ed

bare•head•ed

bare•ly

bar•gain
  bar•gain•er

barge

Ba•ri
  also Ba•ri del•le Pu•glie

bar•i•tone

bar•i•um

bark

bar•keep•er
  also bar•keep

bark•er

bar•ley

bar•maid

bar•man
  pl. bar•men

bar mitz•vah

barn

bar•na•cle
  bar•na•cled

Bar•nard

barn•storm
  barn•storm•er

Bar•num

barn•yard

Ba•ro•da

ba•rom•e•ter
  bar•o•met•ric
  bar•o•met•ri•cal
  ba•rom•e•try

bar•on (*nobleman*; see
  BARREN)

bar•on•ess

bar•on•et

bar•o•ny
  pl. bar•o•nies

ba•roque

bar•rack

bar•ra•cu•da
  pl. same *or*
  bar•ra•cu•das

bar•rage

Bar•ran•qui•lla

barre (*bar used for dance*;
  see BAR)

bar•rel
  bar•reled, bar•rel•ing;
  bar•relled, bar•rel•ling

bar•ren (*unproductive*;
  see BARON)
  bar•ren•ly
  bar•ren•ness

Bar•rett

bar•rette

bar•ri•cade

Bar•rie

bar•ri•er

bar•ring

bar•ri•o
  pl. bar•ri•os

bar•room

bar•row

Bar•ry•more

bar•tend•er

bar•ter
  bar•ter•er

Barth

Barthes

Bar•tók

Bar•ton

bar•y•on
  bar•y•on•ic

Ba•rysh•ni•kov

ba•sal

ba•salt
  ba•sal•tic

base (*foundation,
  despicable*; see BASS)
  base•ly
  base•ness

base•ball

base•board

Ba•sel

base•less
  base•less•ly
  base•less•ness

base•line

base•ment

bash
  bash•er

bash•ful
  bash•ful•ly
  bash•ful•ness

bas•ic
  ba•si•cal•ly

Ba•sie

ba•sil

ba•sil•i•ca

ba·sin
ba·sin·ful
pl. ba·sin·fuls

ba·sis
pl. ba·ses

bask (*relax in warmth*;
see BASQUE)

bas·ket
bas·ket·ful
pl. bas·ket·fuls

bas·ket·ball

bas·ket·ry

bas·ket·work

bas mitz·vah
also bat mitz·vah

Basque (*European people*;
see BASK)

Bas·ra

bas-re·lief

bass (*fish*)
pl. same or bass·es

bass (*singer*; see BASE)
bass·ist

bas·set

Basse·terre
also Basse-Terre

bas·si·net

bas·so
pl. bas·sos or bas·si

bas·soon

bast

bas·tard
bas·tard·y

bas·tard·ize
bas·tard·i·za·tion

baste

bas·tion

Ba·su·to·land

bat
bat·ted, bat·ting

batch

bate (*moderate*; see BAIT)

bat·ed

bath
pl. baths

bathe

bath·house

ba·thos
ba·thet·ic

bath·robe

bath·room

bath·tub

bath·y·scaphe

bath·y·sphere

ba·tik

Ba·tis·ta

bat mitz·vah
var. of bas mitz·vah

ba·ton

Bat·on Rouge

bat·tal·ion

bat·ten

bat·ter
bat·ter·er
bat·ter·ing

bat·ter·y
pl. bat·ter·ies

bat·tle
bat·tle-ax
bat·tler

Bat·tle Creek

bat·tle·field
also bat·tle·ground

bat·tle·ment

bat·tle·ship

bat·ty
bat·ti·er, bat·ti·est

bau·ble

baud (*electronic code speed*;
see BAWD)
pl. same or bauds

Bau·de·laire

baux·ite

bawd (*woman who runs
a brothel*; see BAUD)

bawd·y
bawd·i·er, bawd·i·est
bawd·i·ly
bawd·i·ness

bawl (*cry*; see BALL)
bawl·er

bay

Ba·ya·món

bay·ber·ry
pl. bay·ber·ries

bay·o·net

bay·ou

ba·zaar (*market*; see
BIZARRE)

ba·zoo·ka

be (*exist*; see BEE)

beach (*shore*; see BEECH)

beach·comb·er

beach·head

bea·con

bead
bead·ed

bead·ing

bead·y
bead·i·er, bead·i·est
bead·y-eyed
bead·i·ly
bead·i·ness

bea·gle

beak
  beaked
  beak·y

beak·er

beam

bean

bean·bag

bean·pole

bear (*animal*; see BARE)
  bear·ish

bear (*carry*; see BARE)
  past bore; *past part.*
    borne, born
  bear·a·ble
  bear·a·bly
  bear·er

beard
  beard·ed
  beard·less

Beards·ley

bear·ing

Bé·ar·naise sauce

bear·skin

beast

beast·ly
  beast·li·er, beast·li·est
  beast·li·ness

beat (*hit*; see BEET)
  past beat; *past part.*
    beat·en
  beat-up
  beat·a·ble

beat·en

beat·er

be·a·tif·ic
  be·a·tif·i·ca·lly

be·at·i·fy
  be·at·i·fies, be·at·i·fied
  be·at·i·fi·ca·tion

beat·ing

be·at·i·tude

beat·nik

Be·a·trix

beau (*suitor*; see BOW)
  pl. beaux *or* beaus

Beau·fort

Beau·mar·chais

Beau·mont

beau·te·ous

beau·ti·cian

beau·ti·ful
  beau·ti·ful·ly

beau·ti·fy
  beau·ti·fies,
    beau·ti·fied
  beau·ti·fi·ca·tion
  beau·ti·fi·er

beau·ty
  pl. beau·ties

Beau·voir

bea·ver
  pl. same *or* bea·vers

Bea·ver·ton

be·bop
  be·bop·per

be·calm

be·came

be·cause

bé·cha·mel

beck

Beck·et

Beck·ett

beck·on

be·come
  past be·came; *past part.*
    be·come
  be·com·ing·ly

bed
  bed·ded, bed·ding

be·daz·zle
  be·daz·zle·ment

bed·bug

bed·clothes

bed·ding

Bede

be·deck

be·dev·il
  be·dev·iled,
    be·dev·il·ing
  be·dev·il·ment

bed·fel·low

bed·lam

Bed·ou·in
  also Bed·u·in

bed·pan

be·drag·gle

bed·rid·den

bed·rock

bed·room

bed·side

bed·sore

bed·spread

bed·stead

bed·wet·ting

bee (*insect*; see BE)

beech (*tree*; see BEACH)

Bee·cher

beef
  pl. beeves *or* beefs

beef•cake

beef•steak

beef•y
beef•i•er, beef•i•est
beef•i•ly
beef•i•ness

bee•hive

bee•keep•er
bee•keep•ing

bee•line

Be•el•ze•bub

been (*past part. of be*;
see BIN)

beep

beep•er

beer (*beverage*; see BIER)

Beer•bohm

Beer•she•ba

beet (*vegetable*; see BEAT)

Bee•tho•ven

bee•tle (*insect*; see BETEL)
bee•tle-browed

beeves

be•fall
past be•fell; *past part.*
be•fall•en

be•fit
be•fit•ted, be•fit•ting
be•fit•ting
be•fit•ting•ly

be•fog
be•fogged, be•fog•ging

be•fore

be•fore•hand

be•fud•dle
be•fud•dle•ment

beg
begged, beg•ging

be•get
be•get•ting; *past* be•got;
be•gat; *past part.*
be•got•ten
be•get•ter

beg•gar
beg•gar•ly
beg•gar•y

Be•gin (*proper name*)

be•gin (*start*)
be•gin•ning; *past*
be•gan; *past part.*
be•gun

be•gin•ner

be•gin•ning

be•gone

be•go•nia

be•got

be•got•ten

be•grudge
be•grudg•ing•ly

be•guile
be•guile•ment
be•guil•er
be•guil•ing
be•guil•ing•ly

be•guine

be•gun

be•half

Be•han

be•have

be•hav•ior
be•hav•ior•al

be•head

be•held

be•he•moth

be•hest

be•hind

be•hold
past & past part. be•held
be•hold•er

be•hold•en

be•hoove

beige

Bei•jing

be•ing

Bei•rut

bel can•to

be•la•bor

Bel•a•rus

be•lat•ed
be•lat•ed•ly
be•lat•ed•ness

be•lay

belch

be•lea•guer

Bel•fast

bel•fry
pl. bel•fries

Bel•gium
Bel•gian

Bel•go•rod

Bel•grade

be•lie
be•lied, be•ly•ing

be•lief

be•lieve
be•liev•a•ble
be•liev•a•bil•i•ty
be•liev•er

be•lit•tle
be•lit•tle•ment
be•lit•tler
be•lit•tling•ly

Be•lize

Bell (*proper name*)

bell (*chime*; see BELLE)
bell-bot•tom

bel•la•don•na

bell•boy

belle (*beauty*; see BELL)

bel•les let•tres
bel•le•trism
bel•let•rist
bel•let•ris•tic

Belle•vue

bell•hop

bel•li•cose
bel•li•cos•i•ty

bel•lig•er•ent
bel•lig•er•ence
bel•lig•er•ent•ly

Bel•li•ni

Bel•low (*proper name*)

bel•low (*yell*)

bel•lows

bel•ly
pl. bel•lies
bel•lies, bel•lied

bel•ly•ache
bel•ly•ach•er

bel•ly•flop

bel•ly•ful
pl. bel•ly•fuls

Bel•mo•pan

belt
belt•er

belt•way

be•muse
be•mus•ed•ly
be•muse•ment

Be•na•res

bench

bench•mark

bend
past bent; *past part.* bent
bend•a•ble

bend•er

he•neath

Ben•e•dict

ben•e•dic•tion

ben•e•fac•tion

ben•e•fac•tor
fem. ben•e•fac•tress

ben•e•fice

be•nef•i•cent
be•nef•i•cence
be•nef•i•cent•ly

ben•e•fi•cial
ben•e•fi•cial•ly

ben•e•fi•ci•ar•y
pl. ben•e•fi•ci•ar•ies

ben•efit
ben•e•fit•ed,
ben•e•fit•ing;
ben•e•fit•ted,
ben•e•fit•ting

Ben•e•lux

Be•nét

be•nev•o•lent
be•nev•o•lence
be•nev•o•lent•ly

Ben•gal, Bay of

Ben•gha•zi

Ben-Gu•ri•on

be•night•ed
be•night•ed•ness

be•nign
be•nign•ly

be•nig•nant
be•nig•nan•cy
be•nig•nant•ly

be•nig•ni•ty
pl. be•nig•ni•ties

Be•nin

bent

Ben•tham

Ben•ton

Bent•sen

bent•wood

be•numb

Benz

ben•zene

be•queath
be•queath•al
be•queath•er

be•quest

be•rate

Ber•ber

be•reave
be•reave•ment

be•reft

be•ret

berg

Ber•gen

Berg•son

ber•i•ber•i

Ber•ing Sea

Berke•ley

ber•ke•li•um

Ber•lin
Ber•li•ner

Ber•li•oz

Ber•mu•da
also Bermu•das
Ber•mu•dan,
Ber•mu•di•an

Bern
also Berne
Ber•nese

Ber•na•dette

Ber•nard

Bern•hardt

Ber•ni•ni

Bern•stein

Ber•ry (*proper name*)

ber•ry (*fruit*; see BURY)
pl. ber•ries
ber•ried

ber•serk

berth (*bunk*; see BIRTH)

ber•yl

be•ryl•li•um

be•seech
past and *past part.*
be•sought *or*
be•seeched
be•seech•ing

be•set
be•set•ting; *past* and
past part. be•set
be•set•ment

be•side

be•sides

be•siege
be•sieg•er

be•smirch

be•sot•ted

be•sought

be•spat•ter

be•speak
past be•spoke; *past part.*
be•spo•ken *or*
be•spoke

Bes•se•mer

best

bes•tial
bes•tial•ize
bes•tial•ly

bes•ti•al•i•ty
pl. bes•ti•al•i•ties

bes•ti•ar•y
pl. bes•ti•ar•ies

be•stir
be•stirred, be•stir•ring

be•stow
be•stow•al

be•strew
past part. be•strewed
or be•strewn

bet
bet•ting; *past* and *past
part.* bet *or* bet•ted
bet•tor *or* bet•ter

be•ta
be•ta-block•er

be•ta•tron

be•tel (*plant*; see BEETLE)

bête noire
pl. bêtes noires

Be•thes•da

be•think
past and *past part.*
be•thought

Be•thune

Bet•je•man

be•tray
be•tray•al
be•tray•er

be•troth
be•troth•al

bet•ter

bet•ter•ment

be•tween

be•twixt

bev•el
bev•eled, bev•el•ing;
bev•elled, bev•el•ling

bev•er•age

bev•y
pl. bev•ies

be•wail
be•wail•er

be•ware

be•wil•der
be•wil•dered•ly
be•wil•der•ing
be•wil•der•ing•ly
be•wil•der•ment

be•witch
be•witch•ing
be•witch•ing•ly

Beyle

be•yond

bez•el

Bho•pal

Bhu•tan

Bhut•to

Bia•ly•stok

bi•an•nu•al
bi•an•nu•al•ly

bi•as
bi•ased, bi•as•ing

bi•ath•lon
bi•ath•lete

bib

Bi•ble
also bi•ble
bib•li•cal
bib•li•cal•ly

bib•li•og•ra•phy
pl. bib•li•og•ra•phies
bib•li•og•ra•pher
bib•li•o•graph•ic
bib•li•o•graph•i•cal
bib•li•o•graph•i•cal•ly

bib·li·o·phile
  bib·li·o·phil·ic
  bib·li·oph·i·ly

bib·u·lous
  bib·u·lous·ly
  bib·u·lous·ness

bi·cam·er·al
  bi·cam·er·al·ism

bi·carb

bi·car·bon·ate

bi·cen·ten·ni·al

bi·ceps

bick·er

bi·con·cave

bi·con·vex

bi·cus·pid
  bi·cus·pi·date

bi·cy·cle

bid
  bid·ding; *past* bid,
  bade; *past part.* bid
  bid·da·bil·i·ty
  bid·da·ble
  bid·der

bid·ding

bid·dy
  pl. bid·dies

bide

bi·det

Bie·le·feld

bi·en·ni·al
  bi·en·ni·al·ly

bier (*coffin frame*; see
  BEER)

Bierce

bi·fo·cal

bi·fur·cate
  bi·fur·ca·tion

big
  big·ger, big·gest
  big·gish
  big·ness

big·a·my
  pl. big·a·mies
  big·a·mist
  big·a·mous

big·heart·ed

big·horn

bight (*curve*; see BITE,
  BYTE)

big·mouth

big·ot
  big·ot·ed
  big·ot·ry

Big Sur

big·wig

bike
  bik·er

bi·ki·ni

Bi·ko

bi·lat·er·al
  bi·lat·er·al·ly

Bil·ba·o

bile

bilge

bi·lin·e·ar

bi·lin·gual
  bi·lin·gual·ism

bil·ious
  bil·ious·ly
  bil·ious·ness

bilk
  bilk·er

bill
  bill·a·ble
  billed (*past of bill*; see
  BUILD)

bill·board

bil·let
  bil·let·er

bil·let-doux
  pl. bil·lets-doux

bill·fold

bil·liards

Bil·lings

bil·lion
  pl. same *or* bil·lions
  bil·lionth

bil·lion·aire

bil·low
  bil·low·y

bil·ly
  pl. bil·lies
  in full bil·ly club

bil·ly goat

bim·bo
  pl. bim·bos *or* bim·boes

bi·me·tal·lic

bi·month·ly
  pl. bi·month·lies

bin (*receptacle*; see BEEN)

bi·na·ry
  pl. bi·na·ries

bin·au·ral

bind

bind·er

bind·er·y
  pl. bind·er·ies

bind·ing

binge

bin·go

bin·oc·u·lar

bin·oc·u·lars

bi·no·mi·al
  bi·no·mi·al·ly

bi·o

bi·o·chem·is·try
  bi·o·chem·i·cal
  bi·o·chem·ist

bi·o·de·grad·a·ble
  bi·o·de·grad·a·bil·i·ty
  bi·o·deg·ra·da·tion

bi·o·feed·back

bi·o·gen·e·sis
  bi·o·ge·net·ic

bi·og·ra·phy
  pl. bi·og·ra·phies
  bi·og·ra·pher
  bi·o·graph·ic
  bi·o·graph·i·cal

bi·o·log·i·cal
  bi·o·log·i·cal·ly

bi·ol·o·gy
  bi·ol·o·gist

bi·o·mass

bi·on·ic
  bi·on·i·cal·ly

bi·on·ics

bi·o·phys·ics
  bi·o·phys·i·cal
  bi·o·phys·i·cist

bi·op·sy
  pl. bi·op·sies

bi·o·rhythm
  bi·o·rhyth·mic
  bi·o·rhyth·mi·cal·ly

bi·o·sphere

bi·o·syn·the·sis
  bi·o·syn·thet·ic

bi·o·tech·nol·o·gy

bi·o·tin

bi·par·ti·san
  bi·par·ti·san·ship

bi·par·tite

bi·ped
  bi·ped·al

bi·plane

bi·ra·cial

birch

bird
  bird's-eye view

bird·bath

bird·brain
  bird·brained

bird·ie
  bird·ies, bird·ied,
  bird·ie·ing

bi·ret·ta

Bir·ming·ham

birth (*coming into
    existence*; see BERTH)

birth·day

birth·mark

birth·place

birth·right

birth·stone

Bis·cay, Bay of

bis·cuit

bi·sect
  bi·sec·tion
  bi·sec·tor

bi·sex·u·al
  bi·sex·u·al·i·ty

Bish·kek

bish·op

bish·op·ric

Bis·marck

bis·muth

bi·son
  pl. same

bisque

Bis·sau

bis·tro
  pl. bis·tros

bit

bitch

bitch·y
  bitch·i·er, bitch·i·est
  bitch·i·ly
  bitch·i·ness

bite (*cut with teeth*; see
    BIGHT, BYTE)
    past bit; *past part.*
    bit·ten
    bit·er

bit·ing
  bit·ing·ly

bit·ter
  bit·ter·ly
  bit·ter·ness

bit·tern

bit·ter·sweet

bi·tu·men

bi·tu·mi·nous

bi·valve

biv·ou·ac
  biv·ou·acked,
  biv·ou·ack·ing

biz

bi·zarre (*strange*; see
    BAZAAR)
    bi·zarre·ly
    bi·zarre·ness

Bi·zet

blab
  blabbed, blab·bing

black
  black-eyed Su·san

black·ish
black·ly
black·ness

black·ball

black·ber·ry
pl. black·ber·ries

black·bird

black·board

black·en

Black·foot

black·guard
black·guard·ly

black·head

black·jack

black·list

black·mail
black·mail·er

black·out

Black·pool

black·smith

black·thorn

black·top

blad·der

blade
blad·ed

Blair

Blake

blame
blam·a·ble *or*
blame·a·ble
blame·ful

blame·less
blame·less·ly
blame·less·ness

Blanc, Mont

blanch

bland
bland·ly
bland·ness

blan·dish
blan·dish·ment

blank
blank·ly
blank·ness

blan·ket

blare

blar·ney
blar·neys, blar·neyed

bla·sé

blas·pheme
blas·phem·er

blas·phe·my
pl. blas·phe·mies
blas·phe·mous
blas·phe·mous·ly

blast

bla·tant
bla·tan·cy
bla·tant·ly

blaze
blaz·ing
blaz·ing·ly

blaz·er

bla·zon

bleach

bleach·er

bleak
bleak·ly
bleak·ness

blear·y
blear·i·er, blear·i·est
blear·y-eyed
blear·i·ly
blear·i·ness

bleat
bleat·er
bleat·ing·ly

bleed
past and *past part.* bled

bleed·er

bleep

blem·ish

blench

blend

blend·er

bless
past and *past part.*
bless·ed, blest

bless·ed
also blest
bless·ed·ly
bless·ed·ness

bless·ing

blew (*past of blow*; see
BLUE)

blight

blimp

blind
blind·ly
blind·ness

blind·er

blind·fold

blind·side

blink

blink·er

blip
blipped, blip·ping

bliss
bliss·ful
bliss·ful·ly
bliss·ful·ness

blis·ter
blis·ter·y

blithe
blithe·ly
blithe·ness
blithe·some

blitz

blitz·krieg

bliz·zard

bloat

blob

bloc (*coalition*; see BLOCK)

block (*chunk, obstruct*; see BLOC)
block·er

block·ade

block·bust·er

block·head
block·head·ed

block·house

Bloem·fon·tein

blond
also fem. blonde
blond·ish
blond·ness

blood

blood·cur·dling

blood·hound

blood·less
blood·less·ly
blood·less·ness

blood·mo·bile

blood·shed

blood·shot

blood·stain
blood·stained

blood·stream

blood·suck·er
blood·suck·ing

blood·thirst·y
blood·thirst·i·er,
blood·thirst·i·est

blood·thirst·i·ly
blood·thirst·i·ness

blood·y
blood·i·er, blood·i·est
blood·ies, blood·ied
blood·i·ly
blood·i·ness

bloom

bloom·ers

bloom·ing

Bloo·ming·ton

blos·som
blos·som·y

blot
blot·ted, blot·ting

blotch
blotch·y
blotch·i·er, blotch·i·est

blot·ter

blouse

blow
past blew; *past part.*
blown
blow-dry
blow-up

blow·fly
pl. blow·flies

blow·gun

blow·hole

blown

blow·out

blow·pipe

blow·torch

blow·zy
blow·zi·er, blow·zi·est
blow·zi·ly
blow·zi·ness

blub·ber
blub·ber·er
blub·ber·ing·ly
blub·ber·y

blud·geon

blue (*color*; see BLEW)
blue-chip
blue-col·lar
blue·pen·ciled,
blue·pen·cil·ing

blue·bell

blue·ber·ry
pl. blue·ber·ries

blue·bird

blue·bot·tle

blue·grass

Blue·grass Re·gion

blue·print

Blue Ridge Moun·tains

blues
blues·y

bluff
bluff·er
bluff·ly
bluff·ness

blun·der
blun·der·er
blun·der·ing·ly

blun·der·buss

blunt
blunt·ly
blunt·ness

blur
blurred, blur·ring
blur·ry
blur·ri·er, blur·ri·est

blurb

blurt

blush

blush·er

blus·ter
blus·ter·er
blus·ter·y

bo·a

Bo·ad·i·cea
also Bou·dic·ca

boar (*animal*; see BORE, BOER)

board
board·er

board·ing·house

board·walk

boast
boast·er
boast·ful
boast·ful·ly
boast·ful·ness
boast·ing·ly

boat
boat·ful
pl. boat·fuls

boat·er

boat·house

boat·ing

boat·swain
also bo'·sun, bo·sun, bo's'n

bob
bobbed, bob·bing

bob·bin

bob·ble

bob·by pin

bob·by socks
also bob·by sox

bob·cat

bob·sled

bob·white

Boc·cac·ci·o

bode
bod·ing

bod·ice

bod·i·ly

bod·kin

bod·y
pl. bod·ies

bod·y·build·ing

bod·y·guard

bod·y·suit

Boer (*Dutch African*; see BOAR, BORE)

Bo·e·thi·us

bog
bogged, bog·ging
bog·gi·er, bog·gi·est
bog·gi·ness
bog·gy

Bo·gart

bo·gey
pl. bo·geys
bo·geys, bo·geyed

bo·gey·man
also bo·gy·man, boog·ey·man, boog·ie·man
pl. bo·gey·men

bog·gle

Bo·go·tá

bo·gus
bo·gus·ly
bo·gus·ness

Bo·he·mi·an
also bo·he·mi·an
bo·he·mi·an·ism

Bohr

bohr·i·um

boil

boil·er

boil·ing point

Boi·se

bois·ter·ous
bois·ter·ous·ly
bois·ter·ous·ness

bold
bold·ly
bold·ness

bole (*tree trunk, clay*; see BOLL, BOWL)

bo·le·ro
pl. bo·le·ros

Bol·eyn

Bol·i·var

Bo·liv·i·a
Bo·liv·i·an

boll (*seed*; see BOLE, BOWL)

Bo·lo·gna (*city*)
Bo·lo·gnese

bo·lo·gna (*sausage*; see BALONEY)

Bol·she·vik
Bol·she·vism
Bol·she·vist

bol·ster
bol·ster·er

bolt
bolt·er

bomb (*explosive device*; see BALM)

bom·bard
bom·bard·ment

bom·bar·dier

bom·bast
bom·bas·tic
bom·bas·ti·cal·ly

Bom·bay

bomb·er

bomb·shell

bo·na fi·de

bo·nan·za

Bo·na·parte

bon·bon

bond

bond·age

bonds·man
pl. bonds·men

bone
bone-dry
bone·less

bone·meal

bon·fire

bon·go
pl. bon·gos or bon·goes

bo·ni·to
pl. same or bo·ni·tos

bonk
bonk·er

bon·kers

bon mot
pl. bons mots

Bonn

bon·net

Bon·ne·ville

bon·sai
pl. same

bo·nus

bon vo·yage

bon·y
bon·i·er, bon·i·est
bon·i·ness

boo
boos, booed

boob

boo·boo

boo·by
pl. boo·bies
boo·by-trap

boo·dle

boog·ey·man
var. of bog·ey·man

boo·gie
boo·gies, boo·gied,
boo·gy·ing

boog·ie·man
var. of bog·ey·man

boog·ie-woog·ie

book

book·bind·er
book·bind·ing

book·case

book·end

book·ie

book·ing

book·ish
book·ish·ly
book·ish·ness

book·keep·er
book·keep·ing

book·let

book·mak·er
book·mak·ing

book·mark

book·mo·bile

book·plate

book·sell·er

book·store

boom

boo·mer·ang

boon

boon·docks
also boon·ies

boon·dog·gle

Boone

boor
boor·ish
boor·ish·ly
boor·ish·ness

Boor·stin

boost

boost·er
also boost·er shot

boot
boot·ed

booth
pl. booths

boot·leg
boot·legged,
boot·leg·ging
boot·leg·ger

boot·less

boot·strap

boo·ty

booze
booz·er

bop
bopped, bop·ping
bop·per

bo·rax

Bor·deaux

bor·der

bor·der·land

bor·der·line

bore (drill, tiresome person;
see BOAR, BOER)
bor·ing

bore·dom

Bor·ges

Bor·gi·a

bor·ic

Born (proper name)

born (*existing as a result of birth*; see BORNE)
born·a·gain

borne (*past part. of bear*; see BORN)

Bor·ne·o

bo·ron

bor·ough (*municipality*; see BURRO, BURROW)

bor·row
bor·row·er
bor·row·ing

borscht
also borsch

bor·zoi

Bosch (*proper name*; see BOSH)

bosh (*nonsense, part of a blast furnace*; see BOSCH)

bo's'n
var. of boat·swain

Bos·ni·a and Her·ze·go·vi·na
also Bos·nia-Her·ze·go·vi·na

bo·som
bos·om·y

Bos·po·rus

boss

bos·sa no·va

boss·y
boss·i·er, boss·i·est
boss·i·ly
boss·i·ness

Bos·ton
Bos·ton·i·an

bo·sun
also bo'·sun
var. of boat·swain

Bos·well

bot·a·ny
bo·tan·ic
bo·tan·i·cal
bo·tan·i·cal·ly
bot·a·nist

botch
botch·er

both

both·er
both·er·some

Both·ni·a, Gulf of

Bot·swa·na

Bot·ti·cel·li

bot·tle
bot·tle·ful
pl. bot·tle·fuls
bot·tler

bot·tle·neck

bot·tom
bot·tom·most

bot·tom·less

bot·u·lism

bou·doir

bouf·fant

bou·gain·vil·le·a

bough (*tree branch*; see BOW)

bought

bouil·la·baisse

bouil·lon

Boul·der (*city*)

boul·der

bou·le·vard

Bou·lez

bounce
bounc·i·ness
bounc·y
bounc·i·er, bounc·i·est

bounc·er

bounc·ing

bound

bound·a·ry
pl. bound·a·ries

bound·en

bound·less
bound·less·ly
bound·less·ness

boun·te·ous
boun·te·ous·ly
boun·te·ous·ness

boun·ti·ful
boun·ti·ful·ly

boun·ty
pl. boun·ties

bou·quet

bour·bon

bour·geois

bour·geoi·sie

Bourke-White

Bourne·mouth

bout

bou·tique

bou·ton·niere
also bou·ton·nière

Bou·tros-Gha·li

bo·vine
bo·vine·ly

bow (*decoration*, see BEAU; *bend*, see BOUGH)

bowd·ler·ize
bowd·ler·ism
bowd·ler·i·za·tion

bow·el

bow·er
bow·er·y

bowl (*dish, game*; see
   BOLE, BOLL)
   bowl•ful
   pl. bowl•fuls

bow•legs
   bow•leg•ged

bowl•er

bowl•ing

bow•man
   pl. bow•men

bow•sprit

bow•string

box
   box•ful
   pl. box•fuls
   box•like

box•car

box•er
   also box•ers

box•ing

boy
   boy•hood
   boy•ish
   boy•ish•ly
   boy•ish•ness

boy•cott

boy•friend

bra

brace
   pl. same
   brac•ing•ly
   brac•ing•ness

brace•let

brack•en

brack•et

brack•ish
   brack•ish•ness

bract
   brac•te•al
   brac•te•ate

brad

Brad•bur•y

Brad•ford

Brad•ley

Bra•dy

brag
   bragged, brag•ging
   brag•ger
   brag•ging•ly

brag•gart

Brahe

Brah•ma

Brah•man
   also brah•man
   pl. Brah•mans
   Brah•man•ic
   Brah•man•i•cal
   Brah•man•ism

Brah•min

Brahms

braid
   braid•er
   braid•ing

Braille

brain

brain•child
   pl. brain•chil•dren

brain•less

brain•storm
   brain•storm•ing

brain•wash
   brain•wash•ing

brain•y
   brain•i•er, brain•i•est
   brain•i•ly
   brain•i•ness

braise (*cook*; see BRAZE)

brake (*curb*; see BREAK)
   brake•less

brake•man
   pl. brake•men

bram•ble
   bram•bly

Bramp•ton

bran

branch
   branched
   branch•let
   branch•like

brand
   brand-new
   brand•er

Bran•deis

bran•dish
   bran•dish•er

Bran•do

Brandt

bran•dy
   pl. bran•dies

brash
   brash•ly
   brash•ness

Bra•sil•ia

brass

bras•siere

brass•y
   brass•i•er, brass•i•est
   brass•i•ly
   brass•i•ness

brat
   brat•ty

Bra•ti•sla•va

Braun

bra•va•do

brave
   brave•ly
   brave•ness
   brav•er•y

bra·vo
   pl. bra·vos

bra·vu·ra

brawl
   brawl·er

brawn
   brawn·i·er, brawn·i·est
   brawn·i·ness
   brawn·y

bray

braze (*solder*; see BRAISE)

bra·zen
   also bra·zen-faced
   bra·zen·ly
   bra·zen·ness

bra·zier

Bra·zil
   Bra·zil·ian

Braz·za·ville

breach (*failure*; see
   BREECH)

bread (*food*; see BRED)
   also dai·ly bread

breadth
   breadth·ways
   breadth·wise

bread·win·ner

break (*shatter*; see
   BRAKE)
   past broke; *past part.*
   bro·ken
   break·a·ble
   break-in

break·age

break·down

break·er

break·fast
   break·fas·ter

break·neck

break·through

break·up

break·wa·ter

breast
   breast·ed
   breast·less

breast·bone

breast·stroke

breath

breathe

breath·er

breath·ing

breath·less
   breath·less·ly
   breath·less·ness

breath·tak·ing
   breath·tak·ing·ly

breath·y
   breath·i·er, breath·i·est
   breath·i·ly
   breath·i·ness

Brecht

bred (*past of breed*; see
   BREAD)

breech (*childbirth*; see
   BREACH)

breech·es

breed
   breed·er

breed·ing

breeze

breez·y
   breez·i·er, breez·i·est
   breez·i·ly
   breez·i·ness

Brem·en

Brem·er·ha·ven

Bre·scia

Brest

breth·ren

Breu·ghel

breve

bre·vi·ar·y
   pl. bre·vi·ar·ies

brev·i·ty

brew
   brew·er

brew·er·y
   pl. brew·er·ies

Brey·er

Brezh·nev

bri·ar
   var. of bri·er

bribe
   brib·a·ble
   brib·er
   brib·er·y

bric-à-brac
   also bric-a-brac,
   bric·a·brac

brick

brick·bat

brick·lay·er
   brick·lay·ing

brid·al (*wedding*; see
   BRIDLE)

Brid·al·veil

bride

bride·groom

brides·maid

bridge
   bridge·a·ble

bridge·head

Bridge·port

Bridg·es

Bridge·town

bridge·work

bri·dle (*horse gear;* see BRIDAL)

brief
  brief·ly
  brief·ness

brief·case

bri·er
  also bri·ar
  bri·er·y

brig

bri·gade

brig·a·dier

brig·and
  brig·and·age

brig·an·tine

bright
  bright·ish
  bright·ly
  bright·ness

bright·en

Brigh·ton

bril·liant
  bril·liance
  bril·liant·ly

bril·lian·tine

brim
  brimmed, brim·ming
  brim·less
  brimmed

brim·stone

brin·dled
  also brin·dle

brine
  brin·y
  brin·i·er, brin·i·est
  brin·i·ness

bring
  past and *past part.*
  brought
  bring·er

brink

brink·man·ship

bri·quette
  also bri·quet

Bris·bane

brisk
  brisk·ly
  brisk·ness

bris·ket

bris·tle

Bris·tol

Brit

Brit·ain (*country;* see BRITON, BRITTEN)

Bri·tan·nia

Brit·i·cism
  also Brit·ish·ism

Brit·ish
  Brit·ish·ness

Brit·ish Co·lum·bi·a

Brit·on (*British person;* see BRITAIN)

Brit·ten

brit·tle
  brit·tle·ly
  brit·tle·ness

Br·no

broach (*mention;* see BROOCH)

broad
  broad-mind·ed
  broad·ly
  broad--mind·ed·ly
  broad--mind·ed·ness
  broad·ness

broad·ways
broad·wise

broad·cast
  past broad·cast *or*
  broad·cast·ed; *past
  part.* broad·cast
  broad·cast·er
  broad·cast·ing

broad·cloth

broad·en

broad·loom

broad·side

broad·sword

Broad·way

bro·cade

broc·co·li

bro·chure

Brock·ton

Brod·sky

brogue

broil

broil·er

broke

bro·ken
  bro·ken-down
  bro·ken·ly
  bro·ken·ness

bro·ken·heart·ed
  bro·ken·heart·ed·ness

brok·er
  bro·ker·age
  bro·ker·ing

bro·mide

bro·mine

bron·chi·al

bron·chi·tis
  bron·chit·ic

bron·chus
  pl. bron·chi

bron·co
  pl. bron·cos

Bron·të

bron·to·sau·rus
  also bron·to·saur

Bronx

bronze
  bronz·y

brooch (*pin;* see
  BROACH)

brood
  brood·ing·ly

brook
  brook·let

Brook·lyn

broom

broom·stick

broth

broth·el

broth·er
  pl. also breth·ren
  broth·er-in-law
  pl. broth·ers-in-law
  broth·er·less
  broth·er·ly
  broth·er·li·ness

broth·er·hood

brought

brou·ha·ha

brow
  browed

brow·beat
  past brow·beat; *past*
  part. brow·beat·en
  brow·beat·er

Brown (*proper name*)

brown (*color*)
  brown-bag
  brown·ish

brown·ness

brown·y

brown·ie
  also Brownie

Brown·ing

brown·out

brown·stone

Browns·ville

browse
  brows·er

Brue·gel
  also Breu·ghel,
  Brue·ghel

Bruges
  also Brug·ge

bruise

bruis·er

bruit (*spread widely;*
  see BRUTE)

brunch

Bru·nei

Bru·nel·les·chi
  also Bru·nel·les·co

bru·nette
  also masc. bru·net

brunt

brush
  brush-off
  brush·like
  brush·y

brush·wood

brush·work

brusque
  brusque·ly
  brusque·ness

Brus·sels

Brus·sels sprout

bru·tal
  bru·tal·i·ty
  pl. bru·tal·i·ties
  bru·tal·ly

bru·tal·ize
  bru·tal·i·za·tion

brute (*beast;* see BRUIT)
  brut·ish
  brut·ish·ly
  brut·ish·ness

Bru·tus

Bry·an

Bry·ansk

Bry·ant

Bryce

Bryn·ner

bub·ble

bub·bly
  bub·bli·er, bub·bli·est

Bu·ber

bu·bo
  pl. bu·boes

bu·bon·ic plague

buc·ca·neer
  buc·ca·neer·ing
  buc·ca·neer·ish

Bu·chan·an

Bu·cha·rest

Buck (*proper name*)

buck (*deer, dollar, jump*)
  buck·er

buck·board

buck·et
  buck·et·ful
  pl. buck·et·fuls

buck·le

Buck·ley

buck·ram

buck·saw

buck·shot

buck·skin

buck·tooth

buck·wheat

bu·col·ic
bu·col·i·cal·ly

bud
bud·ded, bud·ding

Bu·da·pest

Bud·dha

Bud·dhism
Bud·dhist

bud·dy
pl. bud·dies
bud·dies, bud·died

budge

bud·ger·i·gar

bud·get
budg·et·ar·y

Bue·nos Ai·res

buff

Buf·fa·lo (*city*)

buf·fa·lo (*animal*)
pl. same *or* buf·fa·loes
buf·fa·loes, buf·fa·loed

buf·fer

buf·fet

buf·foon
buf·foon·er·y
buf·foon·ish

bug
bugged, bug·ging
bug-eyed

bug·a·boo

bug·bear

bug·gy
pl. bug·gies

bu·gle
bu·gler
bu·glet

build (*construct;* see *billed*
[BILL])
past and *past. part.* built
built-in
built-up
build·er

build·ing

build·up

built

Bu·jum·bu·ra

bulb

bul·bous

Bul·gar·i·a
Bul·gar·i·an

bulge
bulg·ing·ly
bulg·y

bu·li·ma·rex·i·a
bu·lim·a·rex·ic

bu·lim·i·a
bu·lim·ic

bulk

bulk·head

bulk·y
bulk·i·er, bulk·i·est
bulk·i·ly
bulk·i·ness

bull
bull's-eye
bull·ish

bull·dog

bull·doze

bull·doz·er

bul·let

bul·le·tin

bul·let·proof

bull·fight
bull·fight·er
bull·fight·ing

bull·frog

bull·head·ed
bull·head·ed·ly
bull·head·ed·ness

bull·horn

bul·lion

bull·ish

bul·lock

bull·ring

bul·ly
pl. bul·lies
bul·lies, bul·lied

bul·rush

Bult·mann

bul·wark

bum
bummed, bum·ming

bum·ble
bum·bler

bum·ble·bee

bump
bump·i·ly
bump·i·ness
bump·y
bump·i·er, bump·i·est

bump·er

bump·kin

bump·tious
bump·tious·ly
bump·tious·ness

bun

bunch
bunch·y

Bunche

bun·co
  also bun·ko
  pl. bun·cos

bun·dle

bung

bun·ga·low

bun·gee

bun·gle
  bun·gler

Bu·nin

bun·ion

bunk

bunk·er

bun·kum

bun·ny
  pl. bun·nies

Bun·sen burn·er

bunt

bun·ting

Bun·yan

bu·oy

buoy·ant
  buoy·an·cy
  buoy·ant·ly

bur
  var. of burr

Bur·bank

bur·den
  bur·den·some
  bur·den·some·ness

bur·dock

bu·reau
  pl. bu·reaus *or* bu·reaux

bu·reau·cra·cy
  pl. bu·reau·cra·cies
  bu·reau·crat
  bu·reau·crat·ic
  bu·reau·crat·i·cal·ly

bur·geon

Bur·ger (*proper name*)

burg·er (*hamburger*; see
  BURGHER)

bur·gher (*citizen*; see
  BURGER)

bur·glar

bur·glar·ize

bur·gla·ry
  pl. bur·gla·ries

bur·gle

Bur·gos

bur·gun·dy
  pl. bur·gun·dies

bur·i·al

Burke

Bur·ki·na Fa·so

bur·lesque
  bur·lesques,
    bur·lesqued, bur·
    lesqu·ing
  bur·lesqu·er

bur·ly
  bur·li·er, bur·li·est
  bur·li·ness

Bur·ma
  Bur·mese

burn
  past and *past part.*
    burned *or* burnt

burn·er

Bur·nett

burn·ing
  burn·ing·ly

bur·nish
  bur·nish·er

bur·noose

burn·out

Burns

Burn·side

burnt

burp

Burr (*proper name*)

burr (*thistle*)

bur·ri·to
  pl. bur·ri·tos

bur·ro (*donkey*; see
  BOROUGH, BURROW)
  pl. bur·ros

Bur·roughs

bur·row (*tunnel*; see
  BOROUGH, BURRO)
  bur·row·er

Bur·sa (*city*)

bur·sa (*anatomical sac*)
  pl. bur·sae *or* bur·sas
  bur·sal

bur·sar

bur·si·tis

burst
  past and *past part.* burst

Bur·ton

Bu·run·di

bur·y (*put underground*;
  see BERRY)
  bur·ies, bur·ied

bus (*vehicle*; see BUSS)
  pl. bus·es *or* bus·ses
  bus·es, bused, bus·ing;
    bus·ses, bussed,
    bus·sing

bus·boy

bus·by
  pl. bus·bies

Bush (*proper name*)

bush (*shrub*)
  bush•i•ly
  bush•i•ness
  bush•y
  bush•i•er, bush•i•est

bushed

bush•el
  bush•el•ful
  pl. bush•el•fuls

bush•ing

bush•man
  pl. bush•men
  also Bushman

bush•mas•ter

bush•whack

busi•ness

busi•ness•like

busi•ness•man
  pl. busi•ness•men; *fem.*
  busi•ness•wom•an, *pl.*
  busi•ness•wom•en

bus•man
  pl. bus•men

buss (*kiss;* see BUS)

bust
  past and *past part.*
  bust•ed *or* bust
  also bust•ed

bust•er

bus•tle
  bus•tler

bus•y
  bus•i•er, bus•i•est
  bus•ies, bus•ied
  bus•i•ly
  bus•y•ness

bus•y•bod•y
  pl. bus•y•bod•ies

but (*however;* see BUTT)

bu•tane

butch

butch•er

butch•er•y
  pl. butch•er•ies

But•ler (*proper name*)

but•ler (*domestic servant*)

butt (*buttocks, hit, object
  of joke;* see BUT)

Butte•sels

but•ter

but•ter•fat

but•ter•fin•gers

but•ter•fly
  pl. but•ter•flies

but•ter•milk

but•ter•scotch

but•ter•y
  pl. but•ter•ies
  but•ter•i•ness

but•tock

but•ton
  but•toned
  but•ton•less

but•ton•hole

but•tress

bu•xom
  bux•om•ly
  bux•om•ness

buy (*purchase;* see BY,
  BYE)
  buys, buy•ing; *past* and
  past part. bought

buy•er

buy•out

buzz

buz•zard

buzz•er

buzz•word

by (*near;* see BUY, BYE)

bye (*goodbye;* see BUY,
  BYE)

Bye•lo•rus•sia

by•gone

by•law
  also bye•law

by•line

by•pass

by•play

by•prod•uct

Byrd

by•road

By•ron

by•stand•er

byte (*computer unit;* see
  BITE, BIGHT)

by•way

by•word

Byz•an•tine
  By•zan•tin•ism
  Byz•an•tin•ist

By•zan•ti•um

C

cab

cabal

ca·ban·a

cab·a·ret

cab·bage

cab·by
  also cab·bie
  pl. cab·bies

cab·in

cab·i·net

cab·i·net·mak·er

cab·i·net·ry

ca·ble
  ca·ble-read·y

ca·ble·gram

ca·boo·dle

ca·boose

Cab·ot

Ca·bri·ni

ca·ca·o
  pl. ca·ca·os

cache (hidden items; see CASH)

ca·chet

cack·le

cac·o·de·mon
  also cac·o·dae·mon

ca·coph·o·ny
  pl. ca·coph·o·nies
  ca·coph·o·nous

cac·tus
  pl. cac·ti or cac·tus·es

cad
  cad·dish
  cad·dish·ly
  cad·dish·ness

ca·dav·er

ca·dav·er·ous

cad·die (golfer's assistant; see CADDY)
  also cad·dy
  pl. cad·dies
  cad·dies, cad·died, cad·dy·ing

cad·dy (small container; see CADDIE)
  pl. cad·dies

ca·dence
  ca·denced

ca·den·za

ca·det

cadge
  cadg·er

Cad·il·lac

Cá·diz

cad·mi·um

cad·re

ca·du·ce·us
  pl. ca·du·ce·i

Caen

Cae·sar

Cae·sar·e·an
  also Cae·sar·i·an
  var. of Ce·sar·e·an

cae·su·ra
  pl. cae·su·ras or cae·su·rae
  cae·su·ral

ca·fé
  also ca·fe

caf·e·te·ri·a

caf·fe·ine

caf·tan
  also kaf·tan

cage

ca·gey
  also cag·y
  cag·i·er, cag·i·est
  cag·i·ly
  cag·i·ness

Cag·ney

Ca·guas

ca·hoots

Cain (Biblical first murderer; see CANE)

cairn

Cai·ro

cais·son

ca·jole
  ca·jole·ment
  ca·jol·er
  ca·jol·ery

cake

cal·a·bash

cal·a·boose

cal·a·mine

ca·lam·i·ty
  pl. ca·lam·i·ties
  ca·lam·i·tous
  ca·lam·i·tous·ly

cal·cif·er·ous

cal·ci·fy
  cal·ci·fies, cal·ci·fied
  cal·cif·ic
  cal·ci·fi·ca·tion

cal·cine
  cal·ci·na·tion

cal·cite

cal·ci·um

cal·cu·late
cal·cu·la·ble
cal·cu·la·tive

cal·cu·lat·ed
cal·cu·lat·ed·ly

cal·cu·lat·ing

cal·cu·la·tion

cal·cu·la·tor

cal·cu·lus
pl. cal·cu·li *or*
cal·cu·lus·es

Cal·cut·ta

Cal·der

cal·dron
var. of caul·dron

cal·en·dar (*system for dividing the year;* see CALENDER)

cal·en·der (*roller;* see CALENDAR)

calf
pl. calves
calf·hood
calf·ish
calf·like

calf·skin

Cal·ga·ry

Cal·houn

Ca·li

cal·i·ber
cal·i·bered

cal·i·brate
cal·i·bra·tion
cal·i·bra·tor

cal·i·co
pl. cal·i·coes *or* cal·i·cos

Cal·i·for·nia
Cal·i·for·ni·an

cal·i·for·ni·um

Ca·lig·u·la

cal·i·per

ca·liph
ca·liph·ate

cal·is·then·ics
cal·is·then·ic

calk
var. of caulk

call

Cal·las

call·er

cal·lig·ra·phy
cal·lig·ra·pher
cal·li·graph·ic
cal·lig·ra·phist

call·ing

cal·li·o·pe

cal·los·i·ty
pl. cal·los·i·ties

cal·lous (*unfeeling;* see CALLUS)
cal·lous·ly
cal·lous·ness

cal·low

cal·lus (*hardened skin;* see CALLOUS)

calm
calm·ly
calm·ness

ca·lo·ric

cal·o·rie

cal·o·rif·ic

cal·u·met

ca·lum·ni·ate
ca·lum·ni·a·tion
ca·lum·ni·a·tor

cal·um·ny
pl. cal·um·nies
ca·lum·ni·ous

cal·va·dos
also Cal·va·dos

calve

Cal·vert

calves

Cal·vin

Cal·vin·ism
Cal·vin·ist
Cal·vin·is·tic

ca·lyp·so
pl. ca·lyp·sos

ca·lyx
pl. ca·lyx·es *or* ca·ly·ces

cam

Ca·ma·güey

ca·ma·ra·de·rie

cam·ber

Cam·bo·di·a
Cam·bo·di·an

Cam·bri·an

cam·bric

Cam·bridge

cam·cor·der

Cam·den

came

cam·el

ca·mel·li·a

Cam·em·bert

cam·e·o
pl. cam·e·os

cam·er·a

Cam·er·oon

cam·i·sole

cam·o·mile
var. of cham·o·mile

cam·ou·flage

camp (*affected,*
outrageous)
camp·y
camp·i·er, camp·i·est
camp·i·ly
camp·i·ness

camp (*temporary*
accommodations)
camp·ing

cam·paign
cam·paign·er

cam·pa·ni·le

Camp Da·vid

Cam·pe·che

camp·er

cam·phor

Cam·pi·nas

camp·site

cam·pus
pl. cam·pus·es

cam·shaft

Ca·mus

can (*able*)
past could

can (*container*)
canned, can·ning
can·ner

Can·a·da
Ca·na·di·an

ca·nal

Ca·na·let·to

ca·na·pé (*food, sofa;* see
CANOPY)

ca·nard

ca·nar·y
pl. ca·nar·ies

Ca·nar·y Is·lands

ca·nas·ta

Ca·nav·er·al, Cape

Can·ber·ra

can·can

can·cel
can·celed, can·cel·ing
can·celled,
can·cel·ling
can·cel·la·tion

can·cer
can·cer·ous

can·de·la·brum
also can·de·la·bra
pl. can·de·la·bra,
can·de·la·brums,
can·de·la·bras

can·des·cence

can·did
can·did·ly
can·did·ness

can·di·date
can·di·da·cy

can·dle
can·dler

can·dle·light
can·dle·lit

can·dle·pow·er

can·dle·stick

can·dor

can·dy
pl. can·dies
can·dies, can·died

cane (*stick;* see CAIN)
can·er
can·ing

ca·nine

can·is·ter

can·ker
can·ker·ous

can·na·bis

canned

can·nel·lo·ni

can·ner·y
pl. can·ner·ies

can·ni·bal
can·ni·bal·ism
can·ni·bal·is·tic

can·ni·bal·ize
can·ni·bal·i·za·tion

can·non (*gun;* see
CANON)
pl. same

can·non·ade

can·non·ball

can·not

can·ny
can·ni·er, can·ni·est
can·ni·ly
can·ni·ness

ca·noe
ca·noes, ca·noed,
ca·noe·ing
ca·noe·ist

can·o·la oil

can·on (*laws, round;* see
CANNON)
fem. can·on·ess

ca·non·i·cal
also ca·non·ic
ca·non·i·cal·ly

can·on·ize
can·on·i·za·tion

can·o·py (*covering;* see
CANAPÉ)
pl. can·o·pies

Ca·no·va

cant (*humbug, slanting*
surface; see CAN'T)

can't (*cannot*; see CANT)

can·ta·loupe

can·tan·ker·ous
can·tan·ker·ous·ly
can·tan·ker·ous·ness

can·ta·ta

can·teen

cant·er (*gallop*; see
CANTOR)

Can·ter·bur·y

can·ti·cle

can·ti·le·ver

can·to
pl. can·tos

Can·ton (*city*)

can·ton (*district, division*)
can·ton·al

can·tor (*vocalist*; see
CANTER)

Ca·nute
also Cnut, Knut

can·vas (*cloth*; see
CANVASS)
can·vased, can·vas·ing;
can·vassed,
can·vass·ing

can·vass (*electioneer*; see
CANVAS)
can·vass·er

can·yon

cap
capped, cap·ping
cap·ful
pl. cap·fuls
cap·ping

ca·pa·bil·i·ty
pl. ca·pa·bil·i·ties

ca·pa·ble
ca·pa·bly

ca·pa·cious
ca·pa·cious·ly
ca·pa·cious·ness

ca·pac·i·tance

ca·pac·i·tor

ca·pac·i·ty
pl. ca·pac·i·ties
ca·pac·i·ta·tive

ca·par·i·son

cape

Cape Hat·ter·as

Cape Horn

Cape of Good Hope

ca·per
ca·per·er

Ca·pet

Cape Town

Cape Verde

cap·il·lar·y
pl. cap·il·lar·ies

cap·i·tal (*city, money*;
see CAPITOL)
cap·i·tal·ly

cap·i·tal·ism

cap·i·tal·ist
cap·i·tal·is·tic
cap·i·tal·is·ti·cal·ly

cap·i·tal·ize
cap·i·tal·i·za·tion

cap·i·tol (*building*; see
CAPITAL)

ca·pit·u·late
ca·pit·u·la·tor
ca·pit·u·la·to·ry

ca·po
in full ca·po·tas·to
pl. ca·pos *or*
ca·po·tas·tos

ca·pon

Ca·pone

Ca·po·te

cap·puc·ci·no
pl. cap·puc·ci·nos

ca·price

ca·pri·cious
ca·pri·cious·ly
ca·pri·cious·ness

Cap·ri·corn

cap·size
cap·siz·al

cap·stan

cap·sule
cap·su·lar
cap·su·late

cap·sul·ize

cap·tain
cap·tain·cy
pl. cap·tain·cies
cap·tain·ship

cap·tion

cap·tious
cap·tious·ly
cap·tious·ness

cap·ti·vate
cap·ti·vat·ing
cap·ti·vat·ing·ly
cap·ti·va·tion

cap·tive
cap·tiv·i·ty

cap·tor

cap·ture
cap·tur·er

cap·y·ba·ra

car
car·ful
pl. car·fuls

Ca·ra·cas

ca·rafe

car·a·mel
  car·a·mel·i·za·tion
  car·a·mel·ize

car·a·pace

car·at (*unit of weight;*
  see CARET, CARROT,
  KARAT)

Ca·ra·vag·gio

car·a·van
  car·a·van·ner

car·a·van·sa·ry
  also car·a·van·se·rai

car·a·vel
  also car·vel

car·a·way

car·bide

car·bine

car·bo·hy·drate

car·bol·ic

car·bon

car·bon·ate
  car·bon·a·tion

car·bon·ic

car·bon·if·er·ous

car·bo·run·dum

car·boy

car·bun·cle
  car·bun·cu·lar

car·bu·ret·or
  also car·bu·rat·or

car·cass

car·cin·o·gen
  car·cin·o·gen·ic

car·ci·no·ma
  pl. car·ci·no·mas *or*
  car·ci·no·ma·ta
  car·ci·no·ma·tous

card
  card-car·ry·ing

card·board

car·di·ac

Car·diff

car·di·gan

car·di·nal
  as a title Car·di·nal
  car·di·nal·ate
  car·di·nal·ly
  car·din·al·ship

car·di·o·gram

car·di·o·graph
  car·di·og·raph·er
  car·di·og·ra·phy

car·di·ol·o·gy
  car·di·ol·o·gist

car·di·o·pul·mo·nar·y

car·di·o·vas·cu·lar

card·sharp
  also card·sharp·er

care

ca·reen
  ca·reen·age

ca·reer

care·free

care·ful
  care·ful·ly
  care·ful·ness

care·giv·er

care·less
  care·less·ly
  care·less·ness

ca·ress

car·et (*editorial mark;*
  see CARAT, CARROT,
  KARAT)

care·tak·er

care·worn

car·go
  pl. car·goes *or* car·gos

Car·ib

Car·ib·be·an

car·i·bou
  pl. same

car·i·ca·ture
  car·i·ca·tur·al
  car·i·ca·tur·ist

car·ies
  pl. same
  car·i·ous

car·il·lon

car·ing

car·jack·ing
  car·jack·er

Carls·bad Cav·erns

Car·lyle

Car·mi·chael

car·mine

car·nage

car·nal
  car·nal·i·ty
  car·nal·ize
  car·nal·ly

car·na·tion

Car·ne·gie

car·ne·lian
  also cor·ne·lian

car·ni·val

car·ni·vore

car·niv·o·rous
  car·niv·o·rous·ly
  car·niv·o·rous·ness

car·ob

car·ol (*song;* see CARREL)
  car·ol·er

Car·o·li·na

Car·o·line Is·lands

Car·o·lus Mag·nus

car·o·tene

ca·rot·id

ca·rouse
ca·rous·al
ca·rous·er

car·ou·sel

carp
pl. same
carp·er

car·pal

Car·pa·thi·an
Moun·tains

car·pel
car·pel·lar·y

car·pen·ter
car·pen·try

car·pet

car·pet·bag·ger

car·pet·ing

car·pool
also car pool; car-pool

car·port

car·pus
pl. car·pi

Car·rac·ci

car·rel (*desk*; see CAROL)

Car·re·ras

car·riage

car·ri·er

car·ri·on

Car·roll

car·rot (*vegetable*; see
CARAT, CARET,
KARAT)
car·rot·y

car·ry
car·ries, car·ried
pl. car·ries

car·sick
car·sick·ness

Car·son

Car·son Cit·y

cart
cart·er
cart·ful
pl. cart·fuls

Car·ta·ge·na

carte blanche

car·tel
car·tel·ize

Car·ter

Car·thage
Car·tha·gin·i·an

Car·tier

car·ti·lage
car·ti·lag·i·noid
car·ti·lag·i·nous

car·tog·ra·phy
car·tog·ra·pher
car·to·graph·ic

car·ton

car·toon
car·toon·ist

car·touche

car·tridge

cart·wheel

Ca·ru·so

carve
carv·er

Car·ver

carv·ing

Cas·a·blan·ca

Ca·sals

Cas·a·no·va

cas·cade

Cas·cade Range

case

case·ment

case·work
case·work·er

Cash (*proper name*)

cash (*money;* see CACHE)
cash·a·ble
cash·less

ca·shew

cash·ier

cash·mere

cas·ing

ca·si·no
pl. ca·si·nos

cask

cas·ket

Cas·pi·an Sea

Cas·satt

cas·sa·va

cas·se·role

cas·sette

cas·si·a

Cas·sius

cas·sock
cas·socked

cas·so·war·y
pl. cas·so·war·ies

cast (throw, direct; see
CASTE)
cast-i·ron
cast-off

cas·ta·net
usu. cas·ta·nets

cast•a•way

caste (*social class*; see
   CAST)

cas•tel•lat•ed
   cas•tel•la•tion

cast•er (*bottle, wheel*; see
   castor [CASTOR OIL])

cas•ti•gate
   cas•ti•ga•tion
   cas•ti•ga•tor
   cas•ti•ga•to•ry

cast•ing

cas•tle
   cas•tled

cast•off

cas•tor oil

cas•trate
   cas•tra•tion
   cas•tra•tor

Cas•tries

Cas•tro

cas•u•al
   cas•u•al•ly
   cas•u•al•ness

ca•su•al•ty
   pl. ca•su•al•ties

ca•su•ist
   cas•u•is•tic
   cas•u•is•ti•cal
   cas•u•is•ti•cal•ly
   cas•u•ist•ry

cat
   cat-o'-nine-tails
   cat's-paw

cat•a•clysm
   cat•a•clys•mal
   cat•a•clys•mic
   cat•a•clys•mi•cal•ly

cat•a•comb

cat•a•falque

Cat•a•lan

cat•a•lep•sy
   cat•a•lep•tic

Cat•a•li•na Is•land

cat•a•log
   also cat•a•logue
   cat•a•logs, cat•a•loged,
      cat•a•log•ing;
      cat•a•logues,
      cat•a•logued,
      cat•a•log•uing
   cat•a•log•er
   also cat•a•logu•er

ca•tal•y•sis
   pl. ca•tal•y•ses

cat•a•lyst

cat•a•ly•tic

cat•a•ma•ran

Ca•ta•nia

cat•a•pult

cat•a•ract

ca•tarrh

ca•tas•tro•phe
   cat•a•stroph•ic
   cat•a•stroph•i•cal•ly

cat•a•to•nia
   cat•a•ton•ic

cat•call

catch
   past and *past part.*
      caught
   catch•a•ble

catch–22

catch•all

catch•ing

catch•phrase

catch•word

catch•y
   catch•i•er, catch•i•est
   catch•i•ly
   catch•i•ness

cat•e•chism
   cat•e•chis•mal

cat•e•chize
   cat•e•chiz•er

cat•e•gor•i•cal
   also cat•e•gor•ic
   cat•e•gor•i•cal•ly

cat•e•go•rize
   cat•e•go•ri•za•tion

cat•e•go•ry
   pl. cat•e•go•ries
   cat•e•go•ri•al

ca•ter

ca•ter•cor•nered
   also cat•er•cor•ner,
      cat•ty-cor•nered,
      kit•ty-cor•ner

ca•ter•er

cat•er•pil•lar

cat•er•waul

cat•fish

cat•gut

ca•thar•sis
   pl. ca•thar•ses

ca•thar•tic
   ca•thar•ti•cal•ly

ca•the•dral

Cath•er

**Cath•er•ine de
   Méd•i•cis**
   also Ca•te•ri•na de'
   Med•i•ci

Cath•er•ine of Ar•a•gon

cath•e•ter
   cath•e•ter•ize

cath•ode
   cath•o•dal
   ca•thod•ic

cath·o·lic
  also Cath·o·lic
  ca·thol·i·cal·ly
  Ca·thol·i·cism
  cath·o·lic·i·ty

cat·i·on
  cat·i·on·ic

cat·kin

cat·nap
  cat·napped,
  cat·nap·ping

cat·nip

Ca·to

CAT scan
  CAT scan·ner

Cats·kill Moun·tains

cat·sup
  var. of ketch·up

Catt

cat·tle

cat·ty
  cat·ti·er, cat·ti·est
  cat·ti·ly
  cat·ti·ness

Ca·tul·lus

cat·walk

Cau·ca·sian
  Cau·ca·soid

Cau·ca·sus, the

cau·cus

cau·dal
  cau·dal·ly

caught

caul·dron
  also cal·dron

cau·li·flow·er

caulk
  also calk
  caulk·er

caus·al
  caus·al·ly

cau·sal·i·ty

cau·sa·tion

caus·a·tive
  caus·a·tive·ly

cause
  caus·a·ble
  cause·less
  caus·er

cause cé·lè·bre
  pl. causes cé·lè·bres

cau·se·rie
  pl. cau·se·ries

cause·way

caus·tic
  caus·ti·cal·ly
  caus·tic·i·ty

cau·ter·ize
  cau·ter·i·za·tion

cau·tion

cau·tion·ar·y

cau·tious
  cau·tious·ly
  cau·tious·ness

cav·al·cade

cav·a·lier
  cav·a·lier·ly

cav·al·ry
  pl. cav·al·ries

cave
  cave·like
  cav·er

ca·ve·at

cave·man
  pl. cave·men

cav·ern
  cav·ern·ous
  cav·ern·ous·ly

cav·i·ar
  also cav·i·are

cav·il
  cav·il·er

cav·ing

cav·i·ty
  pl. cav·i·ties

ca·vort

Ca·vour

caw

Cay·enne (*city*)

cay·enne (*pepper*)

Cay·man Is·lands

ca·yu·ga

cease
  cease-fire

cease·less
  cease·less·ly

Ceau·ses·cu

ce·cum
  pl. ce·ca
  ce·cal

ce·dar
  ce·darn

Ce·dar Rap·ids

cede (*yield;* see SEED)

ce·dil·la

ceil·ing

Cel·e·bes

cel·e·brant

cel·e·brate
  cel·e·bra·tion
  cel·e·bra·tor
  cel·e·bra·to·ry

ce·leb·ri·ty
  pl. ce·leb·ri·ties

ce·ler·i·ty

cel·er·y

ce·les·tial
  ce·les·tial·ly

cel·i·bate
  cel·i·ba·cy

cell (small room; see SELL)
  celled

cel·lar (basement; see
  seller [SELL])

Cel·li·ni

cel·lo
  pl. cel·los
  cel·list

cel·lo·phane

cell·phone

cel·lu·lar
  cel·lu·lar·i·ty
  cel·lu·late
  cel·lu·la·tion

cel·lu·lite

cel·lu·loid

cel·lu·lose

Cel·si·us

Celt
  also Kelt

Celt·ic
  also Kelt·ic

ce·ment
  ce·ment·er

cem·e·ter·y
  pl. cem·e·ter·ies

cen·o·taph

Ce·no·zo·ic
  also Cai·no·zo·ic,
  Cae·no·zo·ic

cen·ser (vessel; see
  CENSOR, SENSOR)

cen·sor (suppress; see
  CENSER, SENSOR)
  cen·so·ri·al

cen·so·ri·ous
cen·sor·ship

cen·sure
  cen·sur·a·ble

cen·sus
  pl. cen·sus·es

cent (monetary unit; see
  SCENT, SENT)

cen·taur

cen·te·nar·i·an

cen·te·na·ry
  pl. cen·te·na·ries

cen·ten·ni·al

cen·ter
  cen·tered
  cen·ter·most
  cen·tric

cen·ter·board

cen·ter·fold

cen·ter·piece

cen·ti·grade

cen·ti·me·ter

cen·ti·pede

cen·tral
  cen·tral·i·ty
  cen·tral·ly

**Cen·tral Af·ri·can
Re·pub·lic**

cen·tral·ize
  cen·tral·i·za·tion

cen·trif·u·gal
  cen·trif·u·gal·ly

cen·tri·fuge

cen·trip·e·tal
  cen·trip·e·tal·ly

cen·trist
  cen·trism

cen·tu·ri·on

cen·tu·ry
  pl. cen·tu·ries

ce·phal·ic

ceph·a·lo·pod

ce·ram·ic

ce·ram·ics

ce·re·al (grain; see
  SERIAL)

cer·e·bel·lum
  pl. cer·e·bel·lums or
  cer·e·bel·la

ce·re·bral
  ce·re·bral·ly

ce·re·brum
  pl. cer·e·brums or
  cer·e·bra

cer·e·mo·ni·al
  cer·e·mo·ni·al·ism
  cer·e·mo·ni·al·ist
  cer·e·mo·ni·al·ly

cer·e·mo·ni·ous
  cer·e·mo·ni·ous·ly

cer·e·mo·ny
  pl. cer·e·mo·nies

ce·rise

ce·ri·um

cer·tain

cer·tain·ly

cer·tain·ty
  pl. cer·tain·ties

cer·ti·fi·a·ble

cer·tif·i·cate
  cer·ti·fi·ca·tion

cer·ti·fy
  cer·ti·fies, cer·ti·fied

cer·ti·tude

ce·ru·le·an

Cer·van·tes

cer·vi·cal

cer·vix
  pl. cer·vic·es or
  cer·vix·es

Ce·sar·e·an
  also Ce·sar·i·an,
  Cae·sar·e·an,
  Cae·sar·i·an

ce·si·um

ces·sa·tion

ces·sion (giving up; see
  SESSION)

cess·pool

ce·ta·cean
  ce·ta·ceous

Cey·lon

Cé·zanne

Cha·blis
  pl. same

cha-cha
  also cha-cha-cha

Chad
  Chad·i·an

chafe

chaff
  chaff·y

chaf·ing dish

Cha·gall

cha·grin

chain

chair

chair·lift

chair·man
  pl. chair·men; fem.
  chair·wom·an, pl.
  chair·wom·en
  chair·man·ship

chair·per·son

chaise longue

cha·let

chal·ice (cup; see
  CHALLIS)

chalk
  chalk·y
  chalk·i·er, chalk·i·est
  chalk·i·ness

Chal·lans

chal·lenge
  chal·lenge·a·ble
  chal·leng·er

chal·lis (fabric; see
  CHALICE)

cham·ber

Cham·ber·lain (proper
  name)

cham·ber·lain (steward)

cham·ber·maid

cham·bray

cha·me·le·on
  cha·me·le·on·ic

cham·ois
  pl. same

cham·o·mile
  also cam·o·mile

champ

cham·pagne (drink; see
  CHAMPAIGN)

Cham·paign (city; see
  CHAMPAGNE)

cham·pi·on

cham·pi·on·ship

Cham·plain

chance

chan·cel

chan·cel·ler·y
  pl. chan·cel·ler·ies

chan·cel·lor
  chan·cel·lor·ship

chan·cer·y
  pl. chan·cer·ies

chanc·y
  chanc·i·er, chanc·i·est
  chanc·i·ly
  chanc·i·ness

chan·de·lier

Chan·dler

Cha·nel

Chang
  also Chang Jiang

change
  change·ful
  chang·er

change·a·ble
  change·a·bil·i·ty
  change·a·ble·ness
  change·a·bly

change·less

change·ling

change·o·ver

chan·nel

Chan·nel Is·lands

chant

chan·teuse

chan·tey (sailors' song;
  see SHANTY)

chan·ti·cleer

Cha·nu·kah
  var. of Ha·nuk·kah

cha·os
  cha·ot·ic
  cha·ot·i·cal·ly

chap
  chapped, chap·ping

chap·ar·ral

chap·el

chap·er·on
  also chap·er·one
  chap·er·on·age

chap·lain (*member of the clergy;* see CHAPLIN)
  chap·lain·cy
  pl. chap·lain·cies

chap·let
  chap·let·ed

Chap·lin (*proper name;* see CHAPLAIN)

chap·ter

char
  charred, char·ring

char·ac·ter
  char·ac·ter·less

char·ac·ter·is·tic
  char·ac·ter·is·ti·cal·ly

char·ac·ter·ize
  char·ac·ter·i·za·tion

cha·rade

char·coal

charge
  charge·a·ble

char·gé d'af·faires

char·ger

char·i·ot
  char·i·o·teer

cha·ris·ma
  pl. cha·ris·ma·ta
  char·is·mat·ic
  char·is·mat·ic·al·ly

char·i·ta·ble
  char·i·ta·ble·ness
  char·i·ta·bly

char·i·ty
  pl. char·i·ties

char·la·tan
  char·la·tan·ism
  char·la·tan·ry

Char·le·magne

Charles Mar·tel

Charles·ton

char·ley horse

Char·lotte

Char·lotte·town

charm
  charm·er

charm·ing
  charm·ing·ly

chart

charter
  char·ter·er

char·treuse

char·y
  char·i·er, char·i·est
  char·i·ly
  char·i·ness

Chase (*proper name*)

chase (*follow*)

chas·er

chasm
  chas·mic

chas·sis
  pl. same

chaste
  chaste·ly
  chaste·ness

chast·en
  chas·ten·er

chas·tise
  chas·tise·ment
  chas·tis·er

chas·ti·ty

cha·su·ble

chat
  chat·ted, chat·ting
  chat·ty
  chat·ti·er, chat·ti·est

chat·ti·ly
chat·ti·ness

châ·teau
  pl. châ·teaus *or*
  châ·teaux

Cha·teau·bri·and

chat·e·laine

Chat·ta·hoo·chee Riv·er

Chat·ta·noo·ga

chat·tel

chat·ter
  chat·ter·er
  chat·ter·y

chat·ter·box

Chau·cer

chauf·feur

chau·vin·ism

chau·vin·ist
  chau·vin·is·tic
  chau·vin·is·ti·cal·ly

cheap (*inexpensive, shoddy;* see CHEEP)
  cheap·ish
  cheap·ly
  cheap·ness

cheap·en

cheap·skate

cheat
  cheat·er
  cheat·ing·ly

check (*examine, bank order;* see CZECH)
  check·a·ble

check·er

check·er·board

check·ing ac·count

check·mate

check·out

check•point

check•up

ched•dar

cheek

cheek•bone

cheek•y
cheek•i•er, cheek•i•est
cheek•i•ly
cheek•i•ness

cheep (*peep*; see CHEAP)

cheer

cheer•ful
cheer•ful•ly
cheer•ful•ness

cheer•lead•er

cheer•less
cheer•less•ly
cheer•less•ness

cheer•y
cheer•i•er, cheer•i•est
cheer•i•ly
cheer•i•ness

cheese

cheese•burg•er

cheese•cake

cheese•cloth

chees•y
chees•i•er, chees•i•est
chees•i•ness

chee•tah

Chee•ver

chef

Che•khov

Chel•ya•binsk

chem•i•cal
chem•i•cal•ly

che•mise

chem•ist

chem•is•try
pl. chem•is•tries

Chem•nitz

che•mo•ther•a•py
che•mo•ther•a•pist

che•nille

Che•ops
also Khu•fu

cher•ish

Cher•o•kee

che•root

cher•ry
pl. cher•ries

cher•ub
pl. cher•u•bim
che•ru•bic
che•ru•bi•cal•ly

cher•vil

Ches•a•peake

chess

chess•board

chess•man
pl. chess•men

chest

Ches•ter•ton

chest•nut

chest•y
chest•i•er, chest•i•est
chest•i•ly
chest•i•ness

Che•tu•mal

che•va•lier

chev•ron

chew
chew•a•ble
chew•er

chew•y
chew•i•er, chew•i•est
chew•i•ness

Chey•enne

chi

Chiang Kai-shek

Chi•an•ti
pl. Chi•an•tis

Chi•a•pas

chi•ar•o•scu•ro

Chi•ba

chic
chic•er, chic•est
chic•ly

Chi•ca•go
Chi•ca•go•an

chi•ca•ner•y
pl. chi•ca•ner•ies

Chi•ca•no
pl. Chi•ca•nos; *fem.*
chi•ca•na, *pl.*
Chi•ca•nas

chick

chick•a•dee

Chick•a•saw

chick•en
pl. same *or* chick•ens

chick•pea

chick•weed

chic•le

chic•o•ry
pl. chic•o•ries

chide
past chid•ed *or* chid;
past part. chid•ed *or*
chid *or* chid•den
chid•er
chid•ing•ly

chief

chief•ly

chief·tain
  fem. chief·tain·ess
  chief·tain·cy
  pl. chief·tain·cies
  chief·tain·ship

chif·fon

chig·ger

chi·gnon

Chi·hua·hua

chil·blain
  chil·blained

child
  pl. chil·dren
  child·less
  child·less·ness

child·bear·ing

child·birth

child·hood

child·ish
  child·ish·ly
  child·ish·ness

child·like

Chil·e (*country*; see
  CHILI, CHILLY)
  Chil·e·an

chil·i (*seasoning*; see
  CHILE, CHILLY)
  pl. chil·ies

chill
  chill·er
  chill·ing·ly

chill·y (*cool*; see CHILE,
  CHILI)
  chill·i·er, chill·i·est
  chill·i·ness

Chil·pan·cin·go

Chi·lung

chime
  chim·er

chi·me·ra
  also chi·mae·ra
  chi·mer·ic
  chi·mer·i·cal
  chi·mer·i·cal·ly

chim·ney
  pl. chim·neys

chim·pan·zee

chin
  chin-up

Chi·na (*country*)
  Chi·nese

chi·na (*ceramic*)

Chi·nan

chin·chil·la

chine

chink

chi·no
  pl. chi·nos

Chi·nook

chintz

chintz·y
  chintz·i·er, chintz·i·est
  chintz·i·ly
  chintz·i·ness

chip
  chipped, chip·ping

chip·munk

chip·per

Chip·pe·wa

Chi·rac

Chi·ri·co

chi·rog·ra·phy

chi·ro·man·cy

chi·rop·o·dy
  chi·rop·o·dist

chi·ro·prac·tic
  chi·ro·prac·tor

chirp

chirp·er

chir·rup
  chir·ruped,
   chir·rup·ing
  chir·rup·y

chis·el
  chis·el·er

Chis·holm Trail

Chi·și·nă·u

chit

chit·chat
  chit·chat·ted,
   chit·chat·ting

chi·tin
  chi·tin·ous

Chit·ta·gong

chit·ter·lings
  also chit·lings, chit·lins

chiv·al·rous
  chiv·al·rous·ly

chiv·al·ry
  chi·val·ric

chive

chla·myd·i·a

chlo·ride

chlo·ri·nate
  chlo·ri·na·tion
  chlo·ri·na·tor

chlo·rine

chlo·ro·fluor·o·car·bon

chlo·ro·form

chlo·ro·phyll
  chlo·ro·phyl·lous

chock
  chock-full

chock·a·block

choc·o·late
  choc·o·lat·y
  also choc·o·late·y

Choc·taw
  pl. same *or* Choc·taws

choice
  choice·ly

choir (*singers*; see QUIRE)

choke

chok·er

cho·ler (*anger*; see COLLAR)

chol·er·a
  chol·e·ra·ic

chol·er·ic
  chol·er·i·cal·ly

cho·les·ter·ol

chomp

Chom·sky

Chong·qing

Chon·ju

choose
  past chose; *past part.*
    chos·en
  choos·er

choos·y
  choos·i·er, choos·i·est
  choos·i·ly
  choos·i·ness

chop
  chopped, chop·ping

Cho·pin

chop·per

chop·py
  chop·pi·er, chop·pi·est
  chop·pi·ly
  chop·pi·ness

chop·stick

chop su·ey
  pl. chop su·eys

cho·ral (*music*; see
    CORAL)
  cho·ral·ly

cho·rale
  also cho·ral

chord (*music*; see CORD)
  chord·al

chor·date

chore

cho·re·o·graph
  cho·re·og·ra·pher

cho·re·og·ra·phy
  cho·re·o·graph·ic
  cho·re·o·graph·i·cal·ly

cho·ris·ter

chor·tle

cho·rus
  pl. cho·rus·es

chose

cho·sen

Chou En-lai
  also Zhou En·lai

chow

chow·der

chow mein

Chré·tien de Troyes

Christ

Christ·church

chris·ten
  chris·ten·er
  chris·ten·ing

Chris·ten·dom

Chris·tian
  Chris·tian·ize
  Chris·tian·i·za·tion

Chris·ti·an·i·ty

Chris·tie

Christ·mas
  pl. Christ·mas·es
  Christ·mas·sy

chro·mat·ic
  chro·mat·i·cal·ly
  chro·mat·i·cism

chro·ma·tin

chrome

chro·mi·um

chro·mo·some
  chro·mo·so·mal

chron·ic
  chron·i·cal·ly
  chro·nic·i·ty

chron·i·cle
  chron·i·cler

chro·nol·o·gy
  pl. chro·nol·o·gies
  chron·o·log·i·cal
  chro·nol·o·gist
  chron·o·log·i·cal·ly
  chro·nol·o·gize

chro·nom·e·ter
  chro·nom·e·try
  chron·o·met·ric
  chron·o·met·ri·cal
  chron·o·met·ri·cal·ly

chrys·a·lis
  also chrys·a·lid
  pl. chrys·a·lis·es *or*
    chry·sal·i·des

chry·san·the·mum

chub·by
  chub·bi·er, chub·bi·est
  chub·bi·ly
  chub·bi·ness

chuck

chuck·le
  chuck·ler

chug
  chugged, chug·ging

Chuk·chi Sea

Chu·la Vis·ta

chum
  chum·my
  chum·mi·er,
    chum·mi·est
  chum·mi·ly
  chum·mi·ness

chump

Chung·king
  var. of Chong·qing

chunk

chunk·y
  chunk·i·er, chunk·i·est
  chunk·i·ness

church

church·go·er
  church·go·ing

Church·ill

church·yard

churl

churl·ish
  churl·ish·ly
  churl·ish·ness

churn

chute (tunnel; see
  SHOOT)
  chut·ist

chut·ney
  pl. chut·neys

chutz·pah
  also chutz·pa

chyme
  chy·mous

ciao

ci·ca·da
  pl. ci·ca·das or ci·ca·dae

cic·a·trix
  also cic·a·trice
  pl. cic·a·tri·ces
  cic·a·tri·cial

Cic·e·ro

Cid

ci·der

ci·de·vant

ci·gar

cig·a·rette
  also cig·a·ret

cil·i·um
  pl. cil·ia
  cil·i·ar·y
  cil·i·ate
  cil·i·at·ed
  cil·i·a·tion

cinch

cin·cho·na
  cin·chon·ic
  cin·cho·nine

Cin·cin·nat·i

cinc·ture

cin·der
  cin·der·y

Cin·der·el·la

cin·e·ma
  cin·e·mat·ic
  cin·e·mat·i·cal·ly

cin·e·ma·tog·ra·phy
  cin·e·ma·tog·ra·pher
  cin·e·mat·o·graph·ic
  cin·e·mat·o·graph·
    i·cal·ly

cin·na·bar

cin·na·mon

ci·pher

cir·ca

cir·ca·di·an

cir·cle
  cir·cler

cir·clet

cir·cuit

cir·cu·i·tous
  cir·cu·i·tous·ly
  cir·cu·i·tous·ness

cir·cuit·ry
  pl. cir·cuit·ries

cir·cu·lar
  cir·cu·lar·i·ty
  cir·cu·lar·ly

cir·cu·lar·ize
  cir·cu·lar·i·za·tion

cir·cu·late
  cir·cu·la·tive
  cir·cu·la·tor

cir·cu·la·tion

cir·cu·la·to·ry

cir·cum·cise
  cir·cum·ci·sion

cir·cum·fer·ence
  cir·cum·fer·en·tial
  cir·cum·fer·en·tial·ly

cir·cum·flex

cir·cum·ja·cent

cir·cum·lo·cu·tion
  cir·cum·lo·cu·tion·al
  cir·cum·lo·cu·tion·a·ry
  cir·cum·lo·cu·tion·ist
  cir·cum·loc·u·to·ry

cir·cum·nav·i·gate
  cir·cum·nav·i·ga·tion
  cir·cum·nav·i·ga·tor

cir·cum·scribe
  cir·cum·scrib·a·ble
  cir·cum·scrib·er
  cir·cum·scrip·tion

cir·cum·spect
  cir·cum·spec·tion
  cir·cum·spect·ly

cir·cum·stance
  cir·cum·stanced

cir·cum·stan·tial
  cir·cum·stan·ti·al·i·ty
  cir·cum·stan·tial·ly

cir·cum·vent
  cir·cum·ven·tion

cir·cus
  pl. cir·cus·es

cir·rho·sis
  cir·rhot·ic

cir·rus
  pl. cir·ri
  cir·rose
  cir·rous

cis·tern

cit·a·del

ci·ta·tion

cite (*quote*; see SIGHT,
  SITE)
  cit·a·ble

cit·i·zen
  cit·i·zen·ry
  cit·i·zen·ship

cit·ric
  cit·rate

cit·ron

cit·ro·nel·la

cit·rus
  cit·rous

cit·y
  pl. cit·ies
  cit·y·ward
  cit·y·wards

cit·y·scape

Ciu·dad Gua·ya·na

Ciu·dad Juá·rez

Ciu·dad Vic·to·ria

civ·et

civ·ic
  civ·i·cal·ly

civ·ics

civ·il
  civ·il·ly

ci·vil·ian

ci·vil·i·ty
  pl. ci·vil·i·ties

civ·i·li·za·tion

civ·i·lize
  civ·i·liz·a·ble
  civ·i·liz·er

civ·vies

clack (*noise*; see CLAQUE)
  clack·er

clad

clad·ding

claim
  claim·a·ble
  claim·ant
  claim·er

clair·voy·ance
  clair·voy·ant
  clair·voy·ant·ly

clam
  clammed, clam·ming

clam·bake

clam·ber

clam·my
  clam·mi·er,
    clam·mi·est
  clam·mi·ly
  clam·mi·ness

clam·or
  clam·or·ous
  clam·or·ous·ly
  clam·or·ous·ness

clamp

clan
  clan·nish
  clan·nish·ly
  clan·nish·ness

clan·des·tine
  clan·des·tine·ly

clang

clan·gor
  clan·gor·ous
  clan·gor·ous·ly

clank
  clank·ing·ly

clap
  clapped, clap·ping

clap·per

Clap·ton

clap·trap

claque (*followers*; see
  CLACK)

clar·et

clar·i·fy
  clar·i·fies, clar·i·fied
  clar·i·fi·ca·tion
  clar·i·fi·er

clar·i·net
  clar·i·net·ist
  also clar·i·net·tist

clar·i·on

clar·i·ty

Clark

Clarke

clash
  clash·er

clasp
  clasp·er

class
  class-con·scious
  class-con·scious·ness

clas·sic

clas·si·cal
  clas·si·cal·ism
  clas·si·cal·ist
  clas·si·cal·ly

clas·si·cism
  clas·si·cist

clas·si·fy
  clas·si·fies, clas·si·fied
  clas·si·fi·able

clas•si•fi•ca•tion
clas•si•fi•ca•to•ry
clas•si•fied
clas•si•fi•er

class•less
class•less•ness

class•mate

class•room

class•y
class•i•er, class•i•est
class•i•ly
class•i•ness

clat•ter

Claude Lor•raine

Clau•di•us

clause
claus•al

Clau•se•witz

claus•tro•pho•bi•a
claus•tro•phobe
claus•tro•pho•bic

Cla•vell

clav•i•chord

clav•i•cle
cla•vic•u•lar

claw
clawed
claw•er
claw•less

Clay (*proper name*)

clay (*molding material*)
clay•ey
clay•ish
clay•like

clean
clean-cut
clean•a•ble
clean•ish
clean•ness

clean•er

clean•ly
clean•li•er, clean•li•est
clean•li•ness

cleanse
cleans•er

clear
clear-cut
clear•a•ble
clear•er
clear•ly
clear•ness

clear•ance

clear•ing

clear•ing•house

Clear•wa•ter

cleat

cleav•age

cleave
past cleaved *or* cleft
or clove; *past part.*
cleaved *or* cleft *or*
clo•ven
cleav•a•ble

cleav•er

clef

cleft

cle•ma•tis

Cle•men•ceau

Clem•ens

clem•ent
clem•en•cy

clem•en•tine

clench

Cle•o•pat•ra

clere•sto•ry
also clear•sto•ry
pl. clere•sto•ries

cler•gy
pl. cler•gies

cler•gy•man
pl. cler•gy•men; *fem.*
cler•gy•wom•an, *pl.*
cler•gy•wom•en

cler•ic

cler•i•cal
cler•i•cal•ism
cler•i•cal•ist
cler•i•cal•ly

clerk
clerk•ish
clerk•ly
clerk•ship

Cleve•land

clev•er
clev•er•er, clev•er•est
clev•er•ly
clev•er•ness

cli•ché
also cli•che
cli•chéd

click (*noise*; see CLIQUE)
click•er

cli•ent

cli•en•tele

cliff
cliff-hang•er
cliff•like

cli•mac•ter•ic

cli•mate
cli•mat•ic
cli•mat•i•cal
cli•mat•i•cal•ly

cli•max
cli•mac•tic

climb (*mount*; see
CLIME)
climb•a•ble
climb•er

clime (*region, climate*;
see CLIMB)

clinch

clinch•er

cling
past and *past part.* clung
cling•er
cling•y
cling•i•er, cling•i•est
cling•ing•ly
cling•i•ness

clin•ic
cli•ni•cian

clin•i•cal
clin•i•cal•ly

clink

clink•er

Clin•ton

clip
clipped, clip•ping
clip•pa•ble

clip•board

clip•per

clip•ping

clique (*group*; see CLICK)
cli•quey
cliqu•i•er, cliqu•i•est
cli•quish
cli•quish•ness
cli•quism

cli•to•ris
cli•to•ral

cloak

clob•ber

cloche

clock

clock•wise

clock•work

clod

clod•hop•per

clog
clogged, clog•ging

clois•ter
clois•tered
clois•tral

clomp

clone
clon•al

clonk

close (*shut*; see CLOTHES)
close-knit
close-up
close•ly
close•ness
clos•a•ble
clos•er

closed
closed-cir•cuit

clos•et
clos•et•ed, clos•et•ing

clo•sure

clot
clot•ted, clot•ting

cloth
pl. cloths

clothe
past and *past part.*
clothed *or* clad

clothes (*garments*; see
CLOSE)

cloth•ier

cloth•ing

clo•ture

cloud
cloud•less
cloud•less•ly
cloud•let

cloud•burst

cloud•y
cloud•i•er, cloud•i•est
cloud•i•ly
cloud•i•ness

clout

clove

clo•ven
clo•ven-foot•ed
clo•ven-hoofed

clo•ver

Clo•vis

clown
clown•er•y
clown•ish
clown•ish•ly
clown•ish•ness

cloy
cloy•ing
cloy•ing•ly

club
clubbed, club•bing
club•ber

club•foot
club•foot•ed

club•house

cluck

clue
clues, clued, clue•ing
or clu•ing

clue•less
clue•less•ly
clue•less•ness

clump
also clomp
clump•y
clump•i•er, clump•i•est

clum•sy
clum•si•er, clum•si•est
clum•si•ly
clum•si•ness

clung

clunk

clus•ter

clutch

clut•ter

Cnut

coach

co·ag·u·late
co·ag·u·la·ble
co·ag·u·lant
co·ag·u·la·tion
co·ag·u·la·tive
co·ag·u·la·tor

Co·a·hui·la

coal (*black rock*; see
COLE)

co·a·lesce
co·a·les·cence
co·a·les·cent

co·a·li·tion
co·a·li·tion·ist

coarse (*rough*; see
COURSE)
coarse·ly
coarse·ness

coars·en

coast
coast·al

coast·er

coast·line

coat (*garment, cover*; see
COTE)
coat·ed

coat·ing

coat·tail

coax
coax·er
coax·ing·ly

co·ax·i·al
co·ax·i·al·ly

cob

co·balt

cob·ble

cob·bler

Co·blenz
also Ko·blenz

co·bra

cob·web
cob·webbed

co·ca

co·caine

coc·cyx
pl. coc·cy·ges
coc·cyg·e·al

Co·chise

cock
cock-and-bull sto·ry

cock·ade
cock·ad·ed

cock·a·too

cock·er
in full cock·er span·iel

cock·er·el

cock·eyed

cock·fight
cock·fight·ing

cock·le

cock·le·shell

cock·ney
pl. cock·neys
cock·ney·ism

cock·pit

cock·roach

cock·sure
cock·sure·ly
cock·sure·ness

cock·tail

cock·y
cock·i·er, cock·i·est
cock·i·ly
cock·i·ness

co·co (*palm tree*; see
COCOA)
pl. co·cos

co·coa (*drink*; see COCO)

co·co·nut
also co·coa·nut

co·coon

Coc·teau

cod
pl. same
cod-liv·er oil

Cod, Cape

co·da

cod·dle
cod·dler

code

co·de·fen·dant

co·deine

co·dex
pl. co·di·ces

cod·fish

cod·ger

cod·i·cil
cod·i·cil·la·ry

cod·i·fy
cod·i·fies, cod·i·fied
cod·i·fi·ca·tion
cod·i·fi·er

cod·piece

Co·dy

co·ed

co·ed·u·ca·tion
co·ed·u·ca·tion·al

co·ef·fi·cient

coe·len·ter·ate

co·e·qual
co·e·qual·i·ty
co·e·qual·ly

co·erce
  co·er·ci·ble
  co·er·cion
  co·er·cive

Coeur d'A·lene

co·e·val
  co·e·val·i·ty
  co·e·val·ly

co·ex·ist
  co·ex·ist·ence
  co·ex·is·tent

co·ex·ten·sive

cof·fee

cof·fee·house

cof·fer
  cof·fered

cof·fer·dam

cof·fin

cog
  cogged

co·gent
  co·gen·cy
  co·gent·ly

cog·i·tate
  cog·i·ta·tion
  cog·i·ta·tive
  cog·i·ta·tor

cog·nac

cog·nate
  cog·nate·ly

cog·ni·tion
  cog·ni·tion·al
  cog·ni·tive

cog·ni·zance

cog·ni·zant

cog·no·men

cog·wheel

co·hab·it
  co·hab·it·ed,
    co·hab·it·ing

co·hab·it·ant
co·hab·i·ta·tion

Co·han

co·here

co·her·ent
  co·her·ence
  co·her·ency
  co·her·ent·ly

co·he·sion
  co·he·sive
  co·he·sive·ly
  co·he·sive·ness

co·hort

coif·fure

coil

coin (money; see QUOIN)
  coin·age

co·in·cide

co·in·ci·dence

co·in·ci·den·tal
  co·in·ci·den·tal·ly

co·i·tus
  co·i·tal

coke

co·la
  also ko·la

col·an·der

cold
  cold·ish
  cold·ly
  cold·ness

cold-blood·ed
  cold·-blood·ed·ly
  cold·-blood·ed·ness

cold-heart·ed
  cold·-heart·ed·ly
  cold·-heart·ed·ness

Cole (proper name; see
    COAL)

Cole·ridge

cole·slaw

Co·lette

co·le·us

col·ic
  col·ick·y

Co·li·ma

col·i·se·um (stadium;
    see COLOSSEUM)

co·li·tis

col·lab·o·rate
  col·lab·o·ra·tion
  col·lab·o·ra·tion·ist
  col·lab·o·ra·tive
  col·lab·o·ra·tor

col·lage
  col·lag·ist

col·lapse
  col·lap·si·ble
  col·lap·si·bil·i·ty

col·lar (part of shirt; see
    CHOLER)
  col·lared
  col·lar·less

col·lar·bone

col·late
  col·la·tor

col·lat·er·al
  col·lat·er·al·ly

col·la·tion

col·league

col·lect
  col·lect·a·ble
  col·lect·ed·ly

col·lect·i·ble

col·lec·tion

col·lec·tive
  col·lec·tive·ly
  col·lec·tive·ness

col·lec·tiv·ism
  col·lec·tiv·ist
  col·lec·tiv·is·tic

col·lec·tor

col·lege
  col·le·gi·al

col·le·giate
  col·le·giate·ly

col·lide

col·lie

col·lier·y
  pl. col·lier·ies

col·li·sion

col·loid
  col·loi·dal

col·lo·qui·al
  col·lo·qui·al·ism
  col·lo·qui·al·ly

col·lo·qui·um
  pl. col·lo·qui·ums or
  col·lo·qui·a

col·lo·quy
  pl. col·lo·quies

col·lude
  col·lud·er
  col·lu·sion
  col·lu·sive
  col·lu·sive·ly

Co·logne (city)

co·logne (fragrance)

Co·lom·bi·a (country;
  see COLUMBIA)
  Co·lom·bi·an

Co·lom·bo

co·lon
  co·lon·ic

col·o·nel (officer; see
  KERNEL)
  col·o·nel·cy
  pl. col·o·nel·cies

co·lo·ni·al
  co·lo·ni·al·ly

co·lo·ni·al·ism
  co·lo·ni·al·ist

col·o·nize
  col·o·ni·za·tion
  col·o·niz·er

col·on·nade
  col·on·nad·ed

col·o·ny
  pl. col·o·nies
  col·o·nist

col·o·phon

col·or
  col·or-blind
  col·or-blind·ness
  col·or·a·tion

Col·o·ra·do
  Col·o·ra·dan or
  Col·o·ra·do·an

col·or·a·tu·ra

col·ored

col·or·fast
  col·or·fast·ness

col·or·ful
  col·or·ful·ly
  col·or·ful·ness

col·or·ing

col·or·ize

col·or·less
  col·or·less·ly

co·los·sal

Col·os·se·um (Roman
  amphitheater; see
  COLISEUM)

co·los·sus
  pl. co·los·si or
  co·los·sus·es

co·los·to·my
  pl. co·los·to·mies

Colt (proper name,
  revolver)

colt (young horse)

Co·lum·ba

Co·lum·bi·a (river, city,
  space shuttle; see
  COLOMBIA)

col·um·bine

Co·lum·bus

col·umn
  co·lum·nar
  col·umned

col·um·nist

co·ma

Co·man·che

co·ma·tose

comb

com·bat

com·bat·ant

com·bat·ive

com·bi·na·tion

com·bine

com·bo
  pl. com·bos

com·bus·ti·ble
  com·bus·ti·bil·i·ty

com·bus·tion
  com·bus·tive

come
  past came; past part.
  come
  come-on

come·back

co·me·di·an

co·me·di·enne

come·down

com·e·dy
  pl. com·e·dies
  co·me·dic

come·ly
  come·li·er, come·li·est
  come·li·ness

co·mes·ti·ble

com·et

come·up·pance

com·fort

com·fort·a·ble

com·fort·er

com·fy
  com·fi·er, com·fi·est
  com·fi·ly
  com·fi·ness

com·ic
  com·i·cal
  com·i·cal·ly

com·ing

com·i·ty
  pl. com·i·ties

com·ma

com·mand

com·man·dant

com·man·deer

com·mand·er

com·mand·ing

com·mand·ment

com·man·do
  pl. com·man·dos

com·mem·o·rate
  com·mem·o·ra·tive
  com·mem·o·ra·tion

com·mence

com·mence·ment

com·mend

com·mend·a·ble

com·men·da·tion

com·men·su·ra·ble

com·men·su·rate

com·ment

com·men·tar·y
  pl. com·men·tar·ies

com·men·ta·tor
  com·men·tate

com·merce

com·mer·cial
  com·mer·cial·ism
  com·mer·cial·i·za·tion
  com·mer·cial·ize

com·min·gle

com·mis·er·ate
  com·mis·er·a·tion
  com·mis·er·a·tive
  com·mis·er·a·tor

com·mis·sar

com·mis·sar·y
  pl. com·mis·sar·ies

com·mis·sion

com·mis·sion·er

com·mit
  com·mit·ted,
    com·mit·ting

com·mit·ment

com·mit·tal

com·mit·tee

com·mode

com·mo·di·ous

com·mod·i·ty
  pl. com·mod·i·ties

com·mo·dore

com·mon

com·mon·al·i·ty
  pl. com·mon·al·i·ties

com·mon·er

com·mon·place

com·mons

com·mon·wealth

com·mo·tion

com·mu·nal
  com·mu·nal·ize
  com·mu·nal·ly

com·mune

com·mu·ni·ca·ble
  com·mu·ni·ca·bil·i·ty
  com·mu·ni·ca·bly

com·mu·ni·cant

com·mu·ni·cate
  com·mu·ni·ca·tor

com·mu·ni·ca·tion

com·mu·ni·ca·tive
  com·mu·ni·ca·tive·ly

com·mu·nion

com·mu·ni·qué

com·mu·nism

com·mu·nist
  com·mu·nis·tic

com·mu·ni·ty
  pl. com·mu·ni·ties

com·mu·ta·tive

com·mute

com·mut·er

Com·o·ros
  Com·o·ran or
  Co·mo·ri·an

com·pact
  com·pact·ly
  com·pact·ness

com·pan·ion

com·pan·ion·a·ble
  com·pan·ion·a·bly

com·pan·ion·ship

com·pan·ion·way

com·pa·ny
pl. com·pa·nies

com·pa·ra·ble
com·pa·ra·bil·i·ty
com·pa·ra·bly

com·par·a·tive
com·par·a·tive·ly

com·pare

com·par·i·son

com·part·ment

com·part·men·tal
com·part·men·tal·ly

com·part·men·tal·ize
com·part·men·tal·
i·za·tion

com·pass

com·pas·sion

com·pas·sion·ate
com·pas·sion·ate·ly

com·pat·i·ble
com·pat·i·bil·i·ty
com·pat·i·bly

com·pa·tri·ot

com·pel
com·pel·led,
com·pel·ling
com·pel·ling·ly

com·pen·di·ous

com·pen·di·um
pl. com·pen·di·ums *or*
com·pen·di·a

com·pen·sate
com·pen·sa·to·ry

com·pen·sa·tion
com·pen·sa·tion·al

com·pete

com·pe·tence
also com·pe·ten·cy

com·pe·tent
com·pe·tent·ly

com·pe·ti·tion

com·pet·i·tive
com·pet·i·tive·ly
com·pet·i·tive·ness

com·pet·i·tor

com·pile
com·pi·la·tion
com·pil·er

com·pla·cent (*smug*; see
COMPLAISANT)
com·pla·cence
com·pla·cen·cy
com·pla·cent·ly

com·plain
com·plain·er
com·plain·ing·ly

com·plain·ant

com·plaint

com·plai·sant
(*deferential*; see
COMPLACENT)
com·plai·sance

com·ple·ment
(*completion*; see
COMPLIMENT)
com·ple·men·tal

com·ple·men·ta·ry
(*completing*; see
COMPLIMENTARY)

com·plete
com·plete·ly
com·plete·ness
com·ple·tion

com·plex
com·plex·i·ty
pl. com·plex·i·ties

com·plex·ion

com·pli·ance

com·pli·ant
com·pli·ant·ly

com·pli·cate

com·pli·ca·tion

com·plic·i·ty

com·pli·ment (*praise*;
see COMPLEMENT)

com·pli·men·ta·ry
(*praising*; see
COMPLEMENTARY)

com·ply
com·plies, com·plied

com·po·nent
com·po·nen·tial

com·port
com·port·ment

com·pose
com·pos·er

com·pos·ite

com·po·si·tion
com·po·si·tion·al
com·po·si·tion·al·ly

com·pos·i·tor

com·post

com·po·sure

com·pote

com·pound

com·pre·hend
com·pre·hen·si·bil·i·ty
com·pre·hen·si·ble
com·pre·hen·si·bly
com·pre·hen·sion

com·pre·hen·sive
com·pre·hen·sive·ly
com·pre·hen·sive·ness

com·press
com·press·i·ble
com·press·i·bil·i·ty

com·pres·sion

com·pres·sor

com·prise

com•pro•mise
  com•pro•mis•er
  com•pro•mis•ing•ly

comp•trol•ler (*used in titles*; see CONTROLLER)

com•pul•sion

com•pul•sive
  com•pul•sive•ly
  com•pul•sive•ness

com•pul•so•ry
  com•pul•so•ri•ly

com•punc•tion
  com•punc•tious

com•pute
  com•put•a•bil•i•ty
  com•put•a•ble
  com•pu•ta•tion
  com•pu•ta•tion•al

com•put•er

com•put•er•ize
  com•put•er•i•za•tion

com•rade
  com•rade•ly
  com•rade•ship

Comte

con (*deceive, against*; see KHAN)
  conned, con•ning

Co•na•kry

con•cat•e•nate
  con•cat•e•na•tion

con•cave
  con•cav•i•ty

con•ceal
  con•ceal•er
  con•ceal•ment

con•cede

con•ceit

con•ceit•ed
  con•ceit•ed•ly

con•ceiv•a•ble
  con•ceiv•a•bly

con•ceive

con•cen•trate
  con•cen•tra•tor

con•cen•tra•tion

con•cen•tric
  con•cen•tri•cal•ly
  con•cen•tric•i•ty

Con•cep•ción

con•cept

con•cep•tion
  con•cep•tion•al

con•cep•tu•al
  con•cep•tu•al•ly

con•cep•tu•al•ize
  con•cep•tu•al•i•za•tion

con•cern

con•cerned
  con•cern•ed•ly

con•cern•ing

con•cert

con•cert•ed

con•cer•ti•na

con•cer•to
  pl. con•cer•ti *or*
  con•cer•tos

con•ces•sion
  con•ces•sion•ar•y
  also con•ces•sion•al.

conch
  pl. conchs *or* conches

con•ci•erge

con•cil•i•ate
  con•cil•i•a•tive
  con•cil•i•a•tor
  con•cil•i•a•tory

con•cise
  con•cise•ly
  con•cise•ness

con•clave

con•clude

con•clu•sion

con•clu•sive
  con•clu•sive•ly
  con•clu•sive•ness

con•coct
  con•coc•tion

con•com•i•tant
  con•com•i•tance
  con•com•i•tant•ly

Con•cord (*city, grape*; see CONCORDE)

con•cord (*agreement*; see CONCORDE)

con•cor•dance

Con•corde (*aircraft*; see CONCORD)

con•course

con•crete
  con•crete•ly
  con•crete•ness

con•cre•tion

con•cu•bine

con•cu•pis•cence
  con•cu•pis•cent

con•cur
  con•curred,
  con•cur•ring

con•cur•rent
  con•cur•rent•ly

con•cus•sion

con•demn
  con•dem•na•ble
  con•dem•na•tion
  con•dem•na•to•ry

con•den•sa•tion

con•dense

con•dens•er

con·de·scend
  con·de·scend·ing·ly
  con·de·scen·sion

con·dign
  con·dign·ly

con·di·ment

con·di·tion

con·di·tion·al
  con·di·tion·al·ly

con·di·tion·er

con·do
  pl. con·dos

con·do·lence

con·dom

con·do·min·i·um

con·done

con·dor

con·du·cive

con·duct
  con·duct·i·ble
  con·duct·i·bil·i·ty

con·duc·tance

con·duc·tion
  con·duc·tive
  con·duc·tiv·i·ty

con·duc·tor

con·duit

cone

Con·es·to·ga

con·fec·tion

con·fec·tion·er

con·fed·er·a·cy
  pl. con·fed·er·a·cies
  also Con·fed·er·a·cy

con·fed·er·ate
  also Con·fed·er·ate

con·fed·er·a·tion

con·fer
  con·ferred,
  con·fer·ring
  con·fer·ment
  con·fer·ra·ble

con·fer·ence

con·fer·ral

con·fess

con·fes·sion
  con·fes·sion·ar·y

con·fes·sion·al

con·fes·sor

con·fet·ti

con·fi·dant
  fem. con·fi·dante

con·fide

con·fi·dence

con·fi·dent
  con·fi·dent·ly

con·fi·den·tial
  con·fi·den·ti·al·i·ty
  con·fi·den·tial·ly

con·fig·u·ra·tion

con·fine

con·fine·ment

con·firm
  con·firm·a·tive
  con·firm·a·to·ry

con·fir·ma·tion
  (*assurance*; see
  CONFORMATION)

con·firmed

con·fis·cate
  con·fis·ca·tion
  con·fis·ca·tor

con·fla·gra·tion

con·flate
  con·fla·tion

con·flict

con·flu·ence

con·form

con·form·a·ble
  con·form·a·bil·i·ty
  con·form·a·bly

con·for·ma·tion
  (*compliance*; see
  CONFIRMATION)

con·form·ist
  con·form·ism

con·form·i·ty

con·found

con·frere

con·front
  con·fron·ta·tion
  con·fron·ta·tion·al

Con·fu·cian
  Con·fu·cian·ism
  Con·fu·cian·ist

Con·fu·cius
  Con·fu·cian

con·fuse
  con·fus·ed·ly
  con·fus·ing
  con·fus·ing·ly

con·fu·sion

con·fute
  con·fu·ta·tion

con·ga

con·geal

con·ge·nial
  con·ge·ni·al·i·ty
  con·gen·ial·ly

con·gen·i·tal
  con·gen·i·tal·ly

con·ger

con·ge·ries
  pl. same

con·gest
  con·ges·tive

con·ges·tion

con·glom·er·ate
  con·glom·er·a·tion

Con·go
  Con·go·lese

con·grat·u·late
  con·grat·u·la·to·ry

con·grat·u·la·tion

con·gre·gate

con·gre·ga·tion

con·gre·ga·tion·al
  also Con·gre·ga·tion·al
  Con·gre·ga·tion·al·ist

con·gress
  con·gres·sion·al

con·gress·man
  pl. con·gress·men; *fem.*
  con·gress·wom·an,
  pl. con·gress·wom·en

Con·greve

con·gru·ent
  con·gru·ence

con·gru·ous
  con·gru·i·ty
  con·gru·ous·ly

con·ic
  con·i·cal
  con·i·cal·ly

co·ni·fer
  co·nif·er·ous

con·jec·ture
  con·jec·tur·al

con·join

con·joint
  con·joint·ly

con·ju·gal
  con·ju·gal·i·ty
  con·ju·gal·ly

con·ju·gate

con·ju·ga·tion
  con·ju·ga·tion·al

con·junct

con·junc·tion

con·junc·ti·va
  pl. con·junc·ti·vas *or*
  con·junc·ti·vae
  con·junc·ti·val

con·junc·tive

con·junc·ti·vi·tis

con·jure

conk

con·nect
  con·nec·tor

Con·nect·i·cut

con·nec·tion

con·nec·tive

Con·ner·y

conn·ing tow·er

con·nive

con·nois·seur

con·note
  con·no·ta·tion
  con·no·ta·tive

con·nu·bi·al
  con·nu·bi·al·ly

con·quer
  con·quer·a·ble
  con·quer·or

con·quest

con·quis·ta·dor
  pl. con·quis·ta·dor·es
  or con·quis·ta·dors

Con·rad

con·san·guin·e·ous
  con·san·guin·i·ty

con·science

con·sci·en·tious
  con·sci·en·tious·ly
  con·sci·en·tious·ness

con·scious
  con·scious·ly
  con·scious·ness

con·script
  con·scrip·tion

con·se·crate
  con·se·cra·tion
  con·se·cra·tor

con·sec·u·tive
  con·sec·u·tive·ly
  con·sec·u·tive·ness

con·sen·sus

con·sent

con·se·quence

con·se·quent

con·se·quen·tial
  con·se·quen·tial·ly

con·se·quent·ly

con·ser·van·cy
  pl. con·ser·van·cies

con·ser·va·tion
  con·ser·va·tion·al
  con·ser·va·tion·ist

con·ser·va·tive
  con·ser·va·tism
  con·ser·va·tive·ly
  con·ser·va·tive·ness

con·ser·va·to·ry
  pl. con·ser·va·to·ries

con·serve

con·sid·er

con·sid·er·a·ble
  con·sid·er·a·bly

con·sid·er·ate
  con·sid·er·ate·ly

con·sid·er·a·tion

con·sid·er·ing

con·sign
  con·sign·ee
  con·sign·or

con·sign·ment

con·sist

con·sis·ten·cy
  pl. con·sis·ten·cies

con·sis·tent
  con·sist·ent·ly

con·so·la·tion

con·sole
  con·sol·a·ble
  con·sol·er
  con·sol·ing·ly

con·sol·i·date
  con·sol·i·da·tion
  con·sol·i·da·tor

con·som·mé

con·so·nance

con·so·nant

con·sort

con·sor·tium
  pl. con·sor·ti·a *or*
  con·sor·ti·ums

con·spic·u·ous
  con·spic·u·ous·ly
  con·spic·u·ous·ness

con·spir·a·cy
  pl. con·spir·a·cies

con·spir·a·tor
  con·spir·a·to·ri·al

con·spire

Con·sta·ble (*proper name*)

con·sta·ble (*peace officer*)

con·stab·u·lar·y
  pl. con·stab·u·lar·ies

con·stan·cy

con·stant
  con·stant·ly

Con·stan·tine

Con·stan·ti·no·ple

con·stel·la·tion

con·ster·na·tion

con·sti·pate

con·sti·pa·tion

con·stit·u·en·cy
  pl. con·stit·u·en·cies

con·stit·u·ent

con·sti·tute
  con·sti·tu·tor

con·sti·tu·tion

con·sti·tu·tion·al
  con·sti·tu·tion·al·i·ty
  con·sti·tu·tion·al·ly

con·strain

con·straint

con·strict
  con·stric·tion
  con·stric·tive

con·stric·tor

con·struct
  con·struc·tor

con·struc·tion
  con·struc·tion·al

con·struc·tive
  con·struc·tive·ly

con·strue

con·sul
  con·sul·ar
  con·sul·ship

con·sul·ate

con·sult
  con·sul·ta·tive

con·sult·ant

con·sul·ta·tion

con·sume
  con·sum·a·ble

con·sum·er

con·sum·er·ism
  con·sum·er·ist

con·sum·mate
  con·sum·mate·ly
  con·sum·ma·tion
  con·sum·ma·tive
  con·sum·ma·tor

con·sump·tion

con·tact

con·ta·gion

con·ta·gious

con·tain

con·tain·er

con·tain·er·ize
  con·tain·er·i·za·tion

con·tain·ment

con·tam·i·nate
  con·tam·i·nant
  con·tam·i·na·tion
  con·tam·i·na·tor

con·tem·plate
  con·tem·pla·tion
  con·tem·pla·tive

con·tem·po·ra·ne·ous
  con·tem·po·ra·ne·
  ous·ly

con·tem·po·rar·y
  pl. con·tem·po·rar·ies

con·tempt

con·tempt·i·ble
  con·tempt·i·bly

con·temp·tu·ous
  con·temp·tu·ous·ly

con·tend
  con·tend·er

con·tent

con·tent·ed
  con·tent·ed·ly
  con·tent·ed·ness

con·ten·tion

con·ten·tious
  con·ten·tious·ly
  con·ten·tious·ness

con·tent·ment

con·test
  con·test·a·ble

con·test·ant

con·text
  con·tex·tu·al
  con·tex·tu·al·ize
  con·tex·tu·al·i·za·tion
  con·tex·tu·al·ly

con·tig·u·ous
  con·tig·u·ous·ly

con·ti·nent
  con·ti·nence

con·ti·nen·tal

con·tin·gen·cy
  pl. con·tin·gen·cies

con·tin·gent

con·tin·u·al
  con·tin·u·al·ly

con·tin·u·ance

con·tin·u·a·tion

con·tin·ue

con·ti·nu·i·ty
  pl. con·ti·nu·i·ties

con·tin·u·ous
  con·tin·u·ous·ly

con·tin·u·um
  pl. con·tin·ua *or*
  con·tin·u·ums

con·tort
  con·tor·tion

con·tor·tion·ist

con·tour

con·tra·band

con·tra·cep·tion
  con·tra·cep·tive

con·tract

con·trac·tile
  con·trac·til·i·ty

con·trac·tion

con·trac·tor

con·trac·tu·al
  con·trac·tu·al·ly

con·tra·dict
  con·tra·dic·tion
  con·tra·dic·to·ry

con·tra·dis·tinc·tion

con·trail

con·tral·to
  pl. con·tral·tos

con·trap·tion

con·tra·pun·tal
  con·tra·pun·tal·ly
  con·tra·pun·tist

con·trar·i·wise

con·trar·y
  pl. con·trar·ies
  con·trar·i·ly
  con·trar·i·ness

con·trast

con·tra·vene
  con·tra·ven·tion

con·tre·temps

con·trib·ute
  con·trib·u·tor

con·tri·bu·tion

con·trite
  con·trite·ly
  con·trite·ness
  con·tri·tion

con·triv·ance

con·trive

con·trived

con·trol
  con·trolled,
  con·trol·ling
  con·trol·la·ble
  con·trol·la·bil·i·ty
  con·trol·la·bly

con·trol·ler (*person who controls;* see COMPTROLLER)

con·tro·ver·sial
  con·tro·ver·sial·ly

con·tro·ver·sy
  pl. con·tro·ver·sies

con·tro·vert
  con·tro·vert·i·ble

con·tu·ma·cious

con·tu·me·li·ous

con·tu·me·ly

con·tuse
  con·tu·sion

co·nun·drum

con·ur·ba·tion

con·va·lesce
  con·va·les·cence
  con·va·les·cent

con·vec·tion

con·vene

con·ven·ience

con·ven·ient
  con·ven·ient·ly

con·vent

con·ven·tion

con·ven·tion·al
  con·ven·tion·al·ism
  con·ven·tion·al·ist
  con·ven·tion·al·i·ty
  con·ven·tion·al·ly

con•verge
  con•ver•gence
  con•ver•gent

con•ver•sant

con•ver•sa•tion
  con•ver•sa•tion•al
  con•ver•sa•tion•al•ist

con•verse
  con•verse•ly

con•ver•sion

con•vert
  con•ver•ter

con•vert•i•ble
  con•vert•i•bil•i•ty
  con•vert•i•bly

con•vex
  con•vex•i•ty
  con•vex•ly

con•vey
  con•vey•a•ble
  con•vey•or

con•vey•ance

con•vict

con•vic•tion

con•vince
  con•vinc•ing
  con•vinc•ing•ly

con•viv•i•al
  con•viv•i•al•i•ty
  con•viv•i•al•ly

con•vo•ca•tion
  con•vo•ca•tion•al

con•voke

con•vo•lut•ed
  con•vo•lut•ed•ly

con•vo•lu•tion

con•voy

con•vulse

con•vul•sion
  con•vul•sive
  con•vul•sive•ly

coo (*soft sound*; see COUP)

Cook (*proper name*)

cook (*prepare food*)
  cook•ing

cook•book

cook•er•y

cook•ie
  also cook•y
  pl. cook•ies

cook•out

cook•ware

cool
  cool•ly (see COOLIE)
  cool•ness

cool•ant

cool•er

Cool•idge

coo•lie (*laborer*; see *coolly*
  [COOL])

coon

coop (*cage*; see COUPE)

co-op

Coop•er

co•op•er•ate
  co•op•er•a•tion

co•op•er•a•tive
  co•op•er•a•tive•ly

co-opt
  co-op•tion
  co-op•tive

co•or•di•nate
  co•or•di•na•tion
  co•or•di•na•tor

coot

cop
  copped, cop•ping

co•pa•cet•ic

cope

Co•pen•ha•gen

Co•per•ni•cus

cop•i•er

co•pi•lot

cop•ing

co•pi•ous
  co•pi•ous•ly
  co•pi•ous•ness

Cop•land

Cop•ley

cop•per

cop•per•head

co•pra

copse

cop•ter

cop•u•la
  pl. cop•u•las *or*
  cop•u•lae
  cop•u•lar

cop•u•late
  cop•u•la•tion

cop•u•la•tive
  cop•u•la•tive•ly

cop•y
  pl. cop•ies
  cop•ies, cop•ied

cop•y•cat

cop•y•right

cop•y•writ•er
  cop•y•writ•ing

co•quette
  co•quet•tish
  co•quet•tish•ly
  co•quet•tish•ness

cor•al (*ocean stone*; see
  CHORAL)

cor·bel

cord (*rope; see* CHORD)

Cor·day d'Ar·mont

cor·dial
  cor·di·al·i·ty
  cor·dial·ly

cord·ite

cord·less

Cór·do·ba
  also Cor·do·va

cor·don

cor·do·van

cor·du·roy

core (*center; see* CORPS)

co·re·spon·dent (*person cited in divorce case; see* CORRESPONDENT)

Cor·fu

cor·gi
  pl. cor·gis

co·ri·an·der

Co·rin·thi·an

Cor·i·o·la·nus

cork

cork·screw

corm

cor·mo·rant

corn

corn·ball

corn·cob

cor·ne·a
  cor·ne·al

Cor·neille

cor·ner

cor·ner·stone

cor·net
  cor·net·ist or
  cor·net·tist

corn·flow·er

cor·nice

corn·meal

corn·row

corn·starch

cor·nu·co·pi·a
  cor·nu·co·pi·an

Corn·wall

Corn·wal·lis

corn·y
  corn·i·er, corn·i·est
  corn·i·ly
  corn·i·ness

co·rol·la

cor·ol·lar·y
  pl. cor·ol·lar·ies

co·ro·na
  pl. co·ro·nas or
  co·ro·nae

Co·ro·na·do

cor·o·nar·y
  pl. cor·o·nar·ies

cor·o·na·tion

cor·o·ner

cor·o·net
  cor·o·net·ed

Co·rot

cor·po·ra

cor·po·ral
  cor·po·ral·ly

cor·po·rate

cor·po·ra·tion

cor·po·re·al
  cor·po·re·al·i·ty
  cor·po·re·al·ly

corps (*army division; see* CORE)
  pl. corps

corpse

cor·pu·lent
  cor·pu·lence

cor·pus
  pl. cor·po·ra or
  corpuses

Cor·pus Chris·ti

cor·pus·cle
  cor·pus·cu·lar

cor·pus de·lic·ti

cor·ral
  cor·ralled, cor·ral·ling

cor·rect
  cor·rect·ly
  cor·rect·ness

cor·rec·tion
  cor·rec·tion·al

cor·rec·tive
  cor·rec·tive·ly

Cor·reg·gio

cor·re·late
  cor·re·la·tion
  cor·re·la·tion·al

cor·rel·a·tive
  cor·rel·a·tive·ly
  cor·rel·a·tiv·i·ty

cor·re·spond
  cor·re·spond·ing·ly

cor·re·spon·dence

cor·re·spond·ent
  (*person who writes; see* CORESPONDENT)
  cor·re·spond·ent·ly

cor·ri·dor

cor·rob·o·rate
  cor·rob·o·ra·tion
  cor·rob·o·ra·tive
  cor·rob·o·ra·tor

cor•rode
cor•rod•i•ble

cor•ro•sion
cor•ro•sive
cor•ro•sive•ly
cor•ro•sive•ness

cor•ru•gate
cor•ru•ga•tion

cor•rupt
cor•rup•ter
cor•rupt•i•ble
cor•rupt•i•bil•i•ty
cor•rup•tive
cor•rupt•ly
cor•rupt•ness

cor•rup•tion

cor•sage

cor•sair

cor•set
cor•set•ed

Cor•si•ca
Cor•si•can

cor•tege
also cor•tège

Cor•tés
also Cor•tez

cor•tex
pl. cor•ti•ces *or*
cor•tex•es
cor•ti•cal

cor•ti•sone

co•run•dum

cor•us•cate
cor•us•ca•tion

cor•vette

cos

co•se•cant

co•sign (*sign jointly*; see
COSINE)
co•sign•er

co•sig•na•to•ry
pl. co•sig•na•to•ries

co•sine (*mathematical*
term; see COSIGN)

cos•met•ic
cos•met•i•cal•ly

cos•me•tol•o•gy
cos•me•tol•o•gist

cos•mic
cos•mi•cal
cos•mi•cal•ly

cos•mog•o•ny
pl. cos•mog•o•nies
cos•mo•gon•ic
cos•mo•gon•i•cal
cos•mog•o•nist

cos•mol•o•gy
cos•mo•log•i•cal
cos•mol•o•gist

cos•mo•naut

cos•mo•pol•i•tan
cos•mo•pol•i•tan•ism

cos•mos

Cos•sack

cost
past and *past part.* cost
cost-ben•e•fit
cost-ef•fec•tive

Cos•ta Bra•va

Cos•ta del Sol

Cos•ta Me•sa

Cos•ta Ri•ca
Cos•ta Ric•an

cost•ly
cost•li•er, cost•li•est
cost•li•ness

cos•tume

cot

co•tan•gent

cote (*shelter*; see COAT)

Côte d'A•zur

Côte d'I•voire

co•te•rie

co•ter•mi•nous

co•til•lion

Co•to•nou

cot•tage

cot•ter

cot•ton
cot•ton-pick•ing
cot•ton•y

cot•ton•mouth

cot•ton•tail

cot•ton•wood

cot•y•le•don

couch

cou•gar

cough

could

could•n't

cou•lomb

coun•cil (*body of persons*;
see COUNSEL)

coun•cil•man
pl. coun•cil•men; *fem.*
coun•cil•wom•an, *pl.*
coun•cil•wom•en

coun•sel (*advice, advise*;
see COUNCIL)
pl. same
couseled, coun•sel•ing;
counselled, counselling

coun•sel•or *also*
counsellor

count

count•a•ble

count•down

coun·te·nance

count·er

coun·ter·act
  coun·ter·ac·tion
  coun·ter·ac·tive

coun·ter·at·tack

coun·ter·bal·ance

coun·ter·clock·wise

coun·ter·cul·ture

coun·ter·es·pi·o·nage

coun·ter·feit
  coun·ter·feit·er

coun·ter·in·tel·li·gence

coun·ter·mand

coun·ter·meas·ure

coun·ter·pane

coun·ter·part

coun·ter·point

coun·ter·poise

coun·ter·pro·duc·tive

coun·ter·rev·o·lu·tion
  coun·ter·rev·o·lu·
    tion·ar·y
  pl. coun·ter·rev·o·lu·
    tion·ar·ies

coun·ter·sign
  coun·ter·sig·na·ture

coun·ter·sink
  past and *past part.*
    coun·ter·sunk

coun·ter·ten·or

coun·ter·top

coun·ter·vail

coun·ter·weight

count·ess

count·less

coun·tri·fied

coun·try
  pl. coun·tries

coun·try·man
  pl. coun·try·men; *fem.*
    coun·try·wom·an, *pl.*
    coun·try·wom·en

coun·try·side

coun·try·wide

coun·ty
  pl. coun·ties

coup (*triumph*; see COO)
  pl. coups

coup de grâce

coup d'é·tat

coupe (*shallow dish, car*;
  see COOP)

Cou·pe·rin

cou·ple

cou·plet

cou·pling

cou·pon

cour·age

cou·ra·geous
  cou·ra·geous·ly

cou·ri·er

course (*direction, class*;
  see COARSE)

cours·er

court

cour·te·ous
  cour·te·ous·ly
  cour·te·ous·ness

cour·te·san

cour·te·sy
  pl. cour·te·sies

court·house

cour·ti·er

court·ly
  court·li·er, court·li·est
  court·li·ness

court-mar·tial
  pl. courts-mar·tial

court·room

court·ship

court·yard

cous·cous

cous·in (*relative*; see
  COZEN)

cou·ture

cou·tu·ri·er
  fem. cou·tu·ri·ère

co·va·len·cy
  co·va·lent

cove

co·ven

cov·e·nant
  also Cov·e·nant
  cov·e·nan·tal
  cov·e·nan·tor

Cov·en·try

cov·er
  cov·er-up

cov·er·age

cov·er·all

cov·er·let

co·vert
  co·vert·ly
  co·vert·ness

cov·et
  cov·et·a·ble

cov·et·ous
  cov·et·ous·ly
  cov·et·ous·ness

cov·ey
  pl. cov·eys

cow

Cow•ard (*proper name*)

cow•ard (*fearful person*)

cow•ard•ice

cow•ard•ly
cow•ard•li•ness

cow•boy
fem. cow•girl

cow•catch•er

cow•er

cow•hand

cow•hide

cowl
cowled

cow•lick

cowl•ing

co•work•er

Cow•per

cow•poke

cow•pox

cox•comb

cox•swain

coy
coy•er, coy•est
coy•ly
coy•ness

coy•o•te
pl. same *or* coy•o•tes

coz•en (*deceive; see* COUSIN)
coz•en•age

co•zy
co•zi•er, co•zi•est
pl. co•zies
co•zi•ly
co•zi•ness

crab
crab•bed, crab•bing
crab•like

crab•bed
crab•bed•ly
crab•bed•ness

crab•by
crab•bi•er, crab•bi•est
crab•bi•ly
crab•bi•ness

crab•grass

crack

crack•down

crack•er

crack•er•jack

crack•ers

crack•le
crack•ly

crack•pot

Crac•ow
also Krak•ów

cra•dle
cra•dle-rob•ber *or* -snatch•er

craft
pl. craft

crafts•man
pl. crafts•men; *fem.*
crafts•wom•an, *pl.*
crafts•wom•en
crafts•man•ship

craft•y
craft•i•er, craft•i•est
craft•i•ly
craft•i•ness

crag

crag•gy
crag•gi•er, crag•gi•est
crag•gi•ly
crag•gi•ness

cram
crammed, cram•ming

cramp

cram•pon

cran•ber•ry
pl. cran•ber•ries

Crane (*proper name*)

crane (*machine, bird*)

cra•ni•um
pl. cra•ni•ums *or*
cra•ni•a
cra•ni•al

crank

crank•case

crank•shaft

crank•y
crank•i•er, crank•i•est
crank•i•ly
crank•i•ness

Cran•mer

cran•ny
pl. cran•nies
cran•nied

crap
crapped, crap•ping
crap•py

crape (*black fabric; see* CREPE)

craps

crap•shoot

crap•u•lent
crap•u•lence
crap•u•lous

crash
crash-dive
crash-land

crass
crass•ly
crass•ness

Cras•sus

crate
crate•ful
pl. crate•fuls

cra•ter
cra•ter•ous

Cra•ter Lake

cra•vat
cra•vat•ted

crave

cra•ven
cra•ven•ly
cra•ven•ness

crav•ing

craw

craw•fish
var. of cray•fish

crawl
crawl•ing•ly
crawl•y

cray•fish
pl. same

cray•on

craze

cra•zy
cra•zi•er, cra•zi•est
cra•zi•ly
cra•zi•ness

Cra•zy Horse

creak (*noise*; see CREEK)
creak•ing•ly
creak•y

cream

cream•er

cream•er•y
pl. cream•er•ies

cream•y
cream•i•er, cream•i•est
cream•i•ness

crease

cre•ate

cre•a•tion
also Cre•a•tion

cre•a•tion•ism
cre•a•tion•ist

cre•a•tive
cre•a•tive•ly
cre•a•tive•ness
cre•a•tiv•i•ty

cre•a•tor

crea•ture

crèche

cre•dence

cre•den•tial

cre•den•za

cred•i•bil•i•ty

cred•i•ble
cred•i•bly

cred•it

cred•it•a•ble
cred•it•a•bil•i•ty
cred•it•a•bly

cred•i•tor

cre•do
pl. cre•dos

cred•u•lous
cre•du•li•ty
cred•u•lous•ly
cred•u•lous•ness

Cree
pl. same *or* Crees

creed
also Creed
creed•al *or*
cred•al

Creek (*Native Americans*)

creek (*stream*; see
CREAK)

creel

creep
past and past part. crept

creep•y
creep•i•er, creep•i•est
creep•i•ly
creep•i•ness

cre•mate
cre•ma•tion
cre•ma•tor
cre•ma•to•ry

cre•ma•to•ri•um
pl. cre•ma•to•ri•ums *or*
cre•ma•to•ri•a

crème de la crème

cren•el•late
cren•el•la•tion

Cre•ole
also cre•ole

cre•o•sote

crepe (*wrinkled fabric,
pancake*; see CRAPE)
also crêpe
crep•ey
also crep•y.

crept

cre•scen•do
pl. cre•scen•dos
cre•scen•does,
cre•scen•doed

cres•cent

cress

crest
crest•ed

crest•fall•en

cre•ta•ceous
also Cre•ta•ceous

Crete

cre•tin
cre•tin•ism
cre•tin•ize
cre•tin•ous

cre•vasse

crev·ice

crew

crew·el (*needlework*; see
CRUEL)

crew·el·work

crib
cribbed, crib·bing

crib·bage

Crick (*proper name*)

crick (*painful spasm*)

crick·et

cried

cri·er
also cry·er

crime

Cri·me·a
Cri·me·an

crim·i·nal
crim·i·nal·i·ty
crim·i·nal·ly

crim·i·nol·o·gy
crim·i·no·log·i·cal
crim·i·nol·o·gist

crimp
crimp·er
crimp·y
crimp·i·ness

crim·son

cringe
cring·er

crin·kle
crin·kle-cut
crin·kly

crin·o·line

crip·ple

cri·sis
pl. cri·ses

crisp
crisp·ly
crisp·ness

crisp·er

crisp·y
crisp·i·er, crisp·i·est
crisp·i·ness

criss·cross

cri·te·ri·on
pl. cri·te·ri·a *or*
cri·te·ri·ons

crit·ic

crit·i·cal
crit·i·cal·ly
crit·i·cal·ness

crit·i·cism

crit·i·cize
crit·i·ciz·able
crit·i·ciz·er

cri·tique
cri·tiques, cri·tiqued,
cri·ti·quing

crit·ter

croak

Cro·a·tia
Cro·at *or* Cro·a·tian

cro·chet
cro·chet·er

crock

crock·er·y

Crock·ett

croc·o·dile
croc·o·dil·i·an

cro·cus
pl. cro·cus·es

Croe·sus

crois·sant

Cro-Mag·non

Crom·well

crone

Cro·nin

Cron·kite

cro·ny
pl. cro·nies

crook

crook·ed
crook·ed·ly
crook·ed·ness

croon
croon·er

crop
cropped, crop·ping

crop·per

cro·quet

cro·quette

cro·sier
also cro·zier

cross
cross-dress
cross·ly
cross·ness

cross·bar

cross·bow
cross·bow·man
pl. cross·bow·men

cross·breed
past and *past part.*
cross·bred

cross-check

cross-coun·try

cross·cut

cross-ex·am·ine
cross-ex·am·in·a·tion
cross-ex·am·in·er

cross-eyed

cross-fer·til·ize
cross-fer·ti·li·za·tion

cross·fire
also cross fire

cross•ing

cross•o•ver

cross•piece

cross-ref•er•ence

cross•road

cross sec•tion
cross-sec•tion•al

cross•walk

cross•wind

cross•wise

cross•word

crotch

crotch•et•y
crotch•et•i•ness

crouch

croup
croup•y

crou•pi•er

crou•ton

Crow (*Native Americans*)

crow (*bird*)
crow's-foot
pl. crow's-feet

crow•bar

crowd
crowd•ed•ness

crown

cro•zier

cru•ces

cru•cial
cru•ci•al•i•ty
pl. cru•ci•al•i•ties
cru•cial•ly

cru•ci•ble

cru•cif•er•ous

cru•ci•fix

cru•ci•fix•ion
also Cru•ci•fix•ion

cru•ci•form

cru•ci•fy
cru•ci•fies, cru•ci•fied
cru•ci•fi•er

crud
crud•dy
crud•di•er, crud•di•est

crude
crude•ly
crude•ness
cru•di•ty

cru•di•tés

cru•el (*harsh*; see
CREWEL)
cru•el•ly
cru•el•ness
cru•el•ty
pl. cru•el•ties

cru•et

cruise

cruis•er

cruis•er•weight

crul•ler

crumb

crum•ble
crum•bli•ness
crum•bly
crum•bli•er,
crum•bli•est

crumb•y (*lots of crumbs*;
see CRUMMY)
crumb•i•er,
crumb•i•est

crum•my (*unpleasant*;
see CRUMBY)
crum•mi•er,
crum•mi•est
crum•mi•ly
crum•mi•ness

crum•ple
crum•ply

crunch
crunch•i•ly
crunch•i•ness
crunch•y
crunch•i•er,
crunch•i•est

cru•sade
cru•sad•er

crush

crust
crus•tal

crus•ta•cean

crust•y
crust•i•er, crust•i•est
crust•i•ly
crust•i•ness

crutch

crux
pl. crux•es *or* cru•ces

cry
cries, cried
pl. cries

cry•ba•by

cry•er
var. of cri•er

cry•ing

cry•o•gen•ics
cry•o•gen•ic

crypt

cryp•tic
cryp•ti•cal•ly

cryp•to•gram

cryp•tog•ra•phy
cryp•to•gra•pher
cryp•to•graph•ic
cryp•to•graph•i•cal•ly

crys•tal

crys·tal·line
  crys·tal·lin·i·ty

crys·tal·lize
  crys·tal·li·za·tion

cub

Cu·ba
  Cu·ban

cub·by
  pl. cub·bies
  in full cub·by·hole

cube

cu·bic

cu·bi·cal (*cube-shaped*;
    see CUBICLE)
  cu·bi·cal·ly

cu·bi·cle (*compartment*;
    see CUBICAL)

cub·ism
  cub·ist

cu·bit

cuck·old
  cuck·old·ry

cuck·oo

cu·cum·ber

cud

cud·dle
  cud·dle·some
  cud·dly
  cud·dli·er, cud·dli·est

cud·gel

cue (*signal*; see QUEUE)
  cues, cued, cu·ing *or*
    cue·ing
  cue·ist

Cuer·na·va·ca

cuff
  cuffed

cui·sine

cul-de-sac
  pl. culs-de-sac

Cu·lia·cán

cu·li·nar·y

cull

cul·mi·nate
  cul·mi·na·tion

cu·lottes

cul·pa·ble
  cul·pa·bil·i·ty

cul·prit

cult
  cult·ism
  cult·ist

cul·ti·vate
  cul·ti·va·tion

cul·tur·al
  cul·tur·al·ly

cul·ture
  cul·tured

cul·vert

cum

Cum·ber·land

cum·ber·some

cum·in

cum·mer·bund

Cum·mings

cu·mu·la·tive
  cu·mu·la·tive·ly
  cu·mu·la·tive·ness

cu·mu·lus
  pl. cu·mu·li
  cu·mu·lous

cu·ne·i·form

cun·ning
  cun·ning·ly

cup
  cupped, cup·ping

cup·board

cup·cake

cup·ful
  pl. cup·fuls

Cu·pid
  also cu·pid

cu·pid·i·ty

cu·po·la

cu·pric

cu·prous

cur

cur·a·ble
  cur·a·bil·i·ty

Cu·ra·çao

cu·ra·çao

cu·ra·re

cu·rate

cu·ra·tive

cu·ra·tor
  cu·ra·to·ri·al
  cu·ra·tor·ship

curb

curd

cur·dle
  cur·dler

cure
  cure-all

cu·rette

cur·few

cu·ri·a
  also Cu·ri·a
  pl. cu·ri·ae
  Cu·ri·al

Cu·rie (*proper name*)

cu·rie (*unit of
    radioactivity*)

cu·ri·o
  pl. cu·ri·os

cu·ri·os·i·ty
  pl. cu·ri·os·i·ties

cu•ri•ous
  cu•ri•ous•ly
  cu•ri•ous•ness

cu•ri•um

curl

curl•er

cur•lew

cur•li•cue

curl•ing

curl•y
  curl•i•er, curl•i•est
  curl•i•ness

cur•mud•geon
  cur•mud•geon•ly

cur•rant (*fruit*; see
  CURRENT)

cur•ren•cy
  pl. cur•ren•cies

cur•rent (*ongoing,
  stream*; see CURRANT)

cur•rent•ly

cur•ric•u•lum
  pl. cur•ric•u•la *or*
    cur•ric•u•lums
  cur•ric•u•lar

cur•ric•u•lum vi•tae
  pl. cur•ric•u•la vi•tae

cur•ry
  pl. cur•ries
  cur•ries, cur•ried

cur•ry•comb

curse

cursed
  curs•ed•ly
  curs•ed•ness

cur•sive
  cur•sive•ly

cur•sor

cur•so•ry
  cur•so•ri•ly
  cur•so•ri•ness

curt
  curt•ly
  curt•ness

cur•tail
  cur•tail•ment

cur•tain

Cur•tiss

curt•sy
  also curt•sey
  pl. curt•sies *or* curt•seys
  curt•sies, curt•sied *or*
    curt•seys, curt•seyed

cur•va•ceous

cur•va•ture

curve
  curved
  cur•vi•ness
  curv•y
  curv•i•er, curv•i•est.

cush•ion
  cush•ion•y

cush•y
  cush•i•er, cush•i•est
  cush•i•ness

cusp

cus•tard

Cus•ter

cus•to•di•an
  cus•to•di•an•ship

cus•to•dy
  cus•to•di•al

cus•tom

cus•tom•ar•y
  cus•tom•ar•i•ly

cus•tom•er

cus•tom•ize

cut
  cut•ting; *past and past
  part.* cut

cu•ta•ne•ous

cut•a•way

cut•back

cute
  cute•ly
  cute•ness

cu•ti•cle

cut•lass

cut•ler•y

cut•let

cut•off

cut•throat

cut•ting
  cut•ting•ly

cut•tle•fish

cut•worm

cy•an

cy•a•nide

cy•a•no•sis
  cy•a•not•ic

cy•ber•net•ics
  cy•ber•net•ic
  cy•ber•net•i•cist

cy•borg

cy•cla•men

cy•cle

cy•clic
  also cy•cli•cal
  cy•cli•cal•ly

cy•clist

cy•clone
  cy•clon•ic
  cy•clon•i•cal•ly

cy•clo•tron

cyg•net (*swan*; see SIGNET)

cyl•in•der
  cy•lin•dri•cal
  cy•lin•dri•cal•ly

cym•bal (*musical instrument*; see SYMBOL)
  cym•bal•ist

Cym•be•line

cyn•ic
  cyn•i•cal
  cyn•i•cism

cy•no•sure

cy•press (*tree*; see CYPRUS)

Cy•prus (*country*; see CYPRESS)

Cyr•a•no de Ber•ge•rac

Cyr•il

Cy•ril•lic

Cy•rus the Great

cyst

cys•tic

cy•tol•o•gy
  cy•to•log•i•cal
  cy•to•log•i•cal•ly
  cy•tol•o•gist

cy•to•plasm

cy•to•plas•mic

czar
  also tsar; *fem.* cza•ri•na, tsa•ri•na
  czar dom
  czar•ism
  czar•ist

Czech (*nationality*; see CHECK)

Czech•o•slo•vak
  also Czech•o•slo•va•ki•an

Czech•o•slo•va•ki•a

Cze•sto•cho•wa

D

dab
dabbed, dab•bing
dab•ber

dab•ble
dab•bler

da•cha

dachs•hund

Da•cron

dac•tyl
dac•tyl•ic

dad

dad•dy
pl. dad•dies

da•do
pl. da•dos

daf•fo•dil

daf•fy
daf•fi•er, daf•fi•est
daf•fi•ness

daft
daft•ly
daft•ness

dag•ger

da•go
pl. da•gos or da•goes

da•guerre•o•type

Dahl

dahl•ia

dai•ly
pl. dai•lies

dain•ty
dain•ti•er, dain•ti•est
pl. dain•ties
dain•ti•ly
dain•ti•ness

dai•qui•ri

dair•y
pl. dair•ies

da•is

dai•sy
pl. dai•sies

Da•kar

Da•ko•ta
Da•ko•tan

Da•lai La•ma

dale

Da•li

Da•lian

Dal•las
Dal•las•ite

dal•li•ance

dal•ly
dal•lies, dal•lied

Dal•ma•tian

dam (barrier holding back
water; see DAMN)
dammed, dam•ming

dam•age
dam•ag•ing•ly

Da•mas•cus

dam•ask

dame

dam•mit

damn (curse; see DAM)
damn•ing•ly

dam•na•ble
dam•na•bly

dam•na•tion

damned

damp
damp•ly
damp•ness

damp•en
damp•en•er

damp•er

dam•sel

dam•sel•fly
pl. dam•sel•flies

Da•na

Da•nang

dance
dance•a•ble
danc•er

dan•de•lion

dan•der

dan•dle

dan•druff

dan•dy
pl. dan•dies
dan•di•er, dan•di•est
dan•dy•ish
dan•dy•ism

Dane (person from
Denmark; see DEIGN)

dan•ger

dan•ger•ous
dan•ger•ous•ly
dan•ger•ous•ness

dan•gle
dan•gler

Dan•ish

dank
dank•ly
dank•ness

d'An•nun•zio

Dan•te

Dan•ton

Dan•ube

dap•per
dap•per•ly
dap•per•ness

dap•ple

Dar•da•nelles

dare

dare•dev•il
dare•dev•il•ry

Dar es Sa•laam

dar•ing
dar•ing•ly

Da•ri•us I

dark
dark•ly
dark•ness

dark•en

dark•room

dar•ling

darn

Dar•row

dart

dart•board

Dar•win

dash

dash•board

dash•ing
dash•ing•ly

das•tard•ly
das•tard•li•ness

da•ta

da•ta•base

date

dat•ed

date•line

da•tive

da•tum
pl. da•ta

daub

Dau•det

daugh•ter
daugh•ter-in-law
pl. daugh•ters-in-law
daugh•ter•ly

Dau•mier

daunt
daunt•ing
daunt•ing•ly

daunt•less
daunt•less•ly
daunt•less•ness

dau•phin

Dav•en•port (*proper name, city*)

dav•en•port (*sofa*)

Da•vid

da Vin•ci

Da•vis

daw•dle

dawn

dawn•ing

day
day-to-day

Da•yan

day•break

day•dream
day•dream•er

day•light

day•time

Day•ton

daze
daz•ed•ly

daz•zle
daz•zling
daz•zling•ly

dea•con

de•ac•ti•vate
de•ac•ti•va•tion
de•ac•ti•va•tor

dead

dead•beat

dead•en
dead•en•er

dead•line

dead•lock

dead•ly
dead•li•er, dead•li•est

dead•pan

dead•wood

deaf
deaf•ness

deal
past and *past part.* dealt

deal•er
deal•er•ship

deal•ings

dealt

dean

dear (*beloved*; see DEER)
dear•ly

Dear•born

dearth

death
death•less
death•like

death•bed

death•blow

death•ly
dcath•li•er, death•li•est

deb

de·ba·cle
also dé·bâ·cle

de·bar
de·barred, de·bar·ring
de·bar·ment

de·bark
de·bar·ka·tion

de·base
de·base·ment
de·bas·er

de·bat·a·ble
de·bat·a·bly

de·bate
de·bat·er

de·bauch

deb·au·chee

de·bauch·er·y

de Beau·voir

de·ben·ture

de·bil·i·tate
de·bil·i·ta·tion

de·bil·i·ty

deb·it

deb·o·nair

de·brief
de·brief·ing

de·bris

Debs

debt

debt·or

de·bug
de·bugged, de·bug·
ging

de·bunk
de·bunk·er

De·bus·sy

de·but
also dé·but

deb·u·tante

dec·ade

dec·a·dence

dec·a·dent
dec·a·dent·ly

de·caf·fein·at·ed

dec·a·gon
de·cag·o·nal

de·cal

de·cal·co·ma·ni·a

Dec·a·logue

de·camp

de·cant

de·cant·er

de·cap·i·tate
de·cap·i·ta·tion

de·cath·lon
de·cath·lete

De·ca·tur

de·cay

de·ceased

de·ceit

de·ceit·ful
de·ceit·ful·ly
de·ceit·ful·ness

de·ceive
de·ceiv·er

de·cel·er·ate
de·cel·er·a·tion

De·cem·ber

de·cen·cy
pl. de·cen·cies

de·cen·ni·al
de·cen·ni·al·ly

de·cent
de·cent·ly

de·cen·tral·ize
de·cen·tral·i·za·tion

de·cep·tion

de·cep·tive
de·cep·tive·ly
de·cep·tive·ness

dec·i·bel

de·cide
de·cid·a·ble

de·cid·ed

de·cid·ed·ly

de·cid·u·ous

dec·i·mal

dec·i·mate
dec·i·ma·tion

de·ci·pher
de·ci·pher·a·ble

de·ci·sion

de·ci·sive
de·ci·sive·ly
de·ci·sive·ness

deck

de·claim
de·claim·er
dec·la·ma·tion
de·clam·a·to·ry

dec·la·ra·tion

de·clare
de·clar·a·ble
de·clar·a·tive
de·clar·a·tive·ly
de·clar·a·to·ry
de·clar·er

dé·clas·sé
fem. dé·clas·sée

de·clas·si·fy
de·clas·si·fies, de·clas·
si·fied
de·clas·si·fi·ca·tion

de·clen·sion

dec·li·na·tion
  dec·li·na·tion·al

de·cline

de·cliv·i·ty
  pl. de·cliv·i·ties
  de·cliv·i·tous

de·coc·tion

de·code
  de·cod·er

dé·colle·tage

dé·colle·té

de·com·mis·sion

de·com·pose
  de·com·po·si·tion

de·com·pres·sion
  de·com·press·

de·con·ges·tant

de·con·struc·tion
  de·con·struc·tion·ism
  de·con·struc·tion·ist

de·con·tam·i·nate
  de·con·tam·i·na·tion

de·cor
  also dé·cor

dec·o·rate
  dec·o·ra·tive
  dec·o·ra·tive·ly
  dec·o·ra·tive·ness

dec·o·ra·tion

dec·o·ra·tor

dec·o·rous
  dec·o·rous·ly
  dec·o·rous·ness

de·co·rum

de·cou·page
  also dé·cou·page

de·coy

de·crease
  de·creas·ing·ly

de·cree

de·crep·it
  de·crep·i·tude

de·crim·i·nal·ize
  de·crim·i·nal·i·za·tion

de·cry
  de·cries, de·cried

ded·i·cate
  ded·i·ca·tor
  ded·i·ca·to·ry

ded·i·ca·tion

de·duce
  de·duc·i·ble

de·duct

de·duct·i·ble

de·duc·tion

de·duc·tive
  de·duc·tive·ly

deed

deem

deep
  deep-freeze
  deep-fry
  deep-fries, deep-fried
  deep·ly

deep·en

deer (*animal*; see DEAR)
  pl. same

deer·skin

de-es·ca·late
  de-es·ca·la·tion

de·face
  de·face·ment

de fac·to

de·fal·ca·tion

de Fal·la

de·fame
  def·a·ma·tion
  de·fam·a·to·ry

de·fault

de·feat

de·feat·ism
  de·feat·ist

def·e·cate
  def·e·ca·tion

de·fect
  de·fec·tion
  de·fec·tor

de·fec·tive
  de·fec·tive·ly
  de·fec·tive·ness

de·fend
  de·fend·er

de·fend·ant

de·fense
  de·fense·less
  de·fense·less·ly
  de·fense·less·ness

de·fen·si·ble
  de·fen·si·bil·i·ty
  de·fen·si·bly

de·fen·sive
  de·fen·sive·ly
  de·fen·sive·ness

de·fer
  de·ferred, de·fer·ring
  de·fer·ment
  de·fer·ral
  de·fer·rer

def·er·ence

def·er·en·tial
  def·er·en·tial·ly

de·fi·ance

de·fi·ant
  de·fi·ant·ly

de·fi·cien·cy
  pl. de·fi·cien·cies

de·fi·cient

def·i·cit

de·file
  de·file·ment

de·fine
  de·fin·a·ble

def·i·nite
  def·i·nite·ly

def·i·ni·tion

de·fin·i·tive
  de·fin·i·tive·ly

de·flate
  de·fla·tor

de·fla·tion
  de·fla·tion·ar·y

de·flect
  de·flec·tion
  de·flec·tor

de·flow·er

De·foe

de·fo·li·ate
  de·fo·li·ant
  de·fo·li·a·tion

de·form
  de·form·a·ble
  de·for·ma·tion
  de·formed·
  de·for·mi·ty
  pl. de·for·mi·ties

de·fraud

de·fray
  de·fray·al

de·frost
  de·frost·er

deft
  deft·ly
  deft·ness

de·funct

de·fuse

de·fy
  de·fies, de·fied

De·gas

de Gaulle

de·gen·er·ate
  de·gen·er·a·cy
  de·gen·er·ate·ly

de·gen·er·a·tion
  de·gen·er·a·tive

de·grade
  de·grad·a·ble
  deg·ra·da·tion
  de·grad·er

de·grad·ing
  de·grad·ing·ly

de·gree

de·hu·man·ize
  de·hu·man·i·za·tion

de·hu·mid·i·fy
  de·hu·mid·i·fies, de·
    hu·mid·i·fied
  de·hu·mid·i·fi·ca·tion
  de·hu·mid·i·fi·er

de·hy·drate
  de·hy·dra·tion
  de·hy·dra·tor

de·ice
  de·ic·er

de·i·fy
  de·i·fies, de·i·fied
  de·i·fi·ca·tion

deign (*condescend*; see
  DANE)

de·ism
  de·ist
  de·is·tic
  de·is·ti·cal

de·i·ty
  pl. de·i·ties

dé·jà vu

de·ject
  de·ject·ed·ly
  de·jec·tion

de ju·re

de Klerk

de Koo·ning

De·la·croix

de la Mare

Del·a·ware
  Del·a·war·e·an

de·lay
  de·layed-ac·tion
  de·lay·er

de·lec·ta·ble
  de·lec·ta·bil·i·ty
  de·lec·ta·bly

de·lec·ta·tion

del·e·gate

del·e·ga·tion

de·lete
  de·le·tion

del·e·te·ri·ous

delft
  also delft·ware

Del·hi

del·i
  pl. del·is

de·lib·er·ate
  de·lib·er·ate·ly
  de·lib·er·ate·ness
  de·lib·er·a·tive
  de·lib·er·a·tive·ly
  de·lib·er·a·tive·ness
  de·lib·er·a·tor

de·lib·er·a·tion

del·i·ca·cy
  pl. del·i·ca·cies

del·i·cate
  del·i·cate·ly

del·i·ca·tes·sen

de·li·cious
  de·li·cious·ly

de·light
  de·light·ed
  de·light·ed·ly

de·light·ful
    de·light·ful·ly

de·lim·it
    de·lim·i·ta·tion

de·lin·e·ate
    de·lin·e·a·tion

de·lin·quent
    de·lin·quen·cy
    de·lin·quent·ly

del·i·quesce
    del·i·ques·cence
    del·i·ques·cent

de·lir·i·ous
    de·lir·i·ous·ly

de·lir·i·um

De·li·us

de·liv·er

de·liv·er·ance

de·liv·er·y
    pl. de·liv·er·ies

dell

Del·mar·va
    Pen·in·su·la

del·phin·i·um

del·ta

del·toid

de·lude

del·uge

de·lu·sion
    de·lu·sion·al

de·luxe

delve

de·mag·ne·tize
    de·mag·ne·ti·zation
    de·mag·ne·tiz·er

dem·a·gogue
    also dem·a·gog
    dem·a·gog·ic

dem·a·gogu·er·y
dem·a·go·gy

de·mand
    de·mand·ing·ly

de·mar·ca·tion
    de·mar·cate
    de·mar·ca·tor

de·mean

de·mean·or

de·ment·ed
    de·ment·ed·ly
    de·ment·ed·ness

de·men·tia

de·mer·it

de·mesne

dem·i·god
    fem. dem·i·god·dess

dem·i·john

de·mil·i·ta·rize
    de·mil·i·ta·ri·za·tion

dem·i·monde

de·mise

dem·i·tasse

dem·o
    pl. dem·os

de·mo·bi·lize
    de·mo·bi·li·za·tion

de·moc·ra·cy
    pl. de·moc·ra·cies

dem·o·crat
    also Dem·o·crat

dem·o·crat·ic
    dem·o·crat·i·cal·ly

de·moc·ra·tize
    de·moc·ra·ti·za·tion

De·moc·ri·tus

de·mod·u·late
    de·mod·u·la·tion
    de·mod·u·la·tor

de·mog·ra·phy
    de·mog·ra·pher
    dem·o·graph·ic
    dem·o·graph·i·cal
    dem·o·graph·i·cal·ly

de·mol·ish
    de·mol·ish·er
    dem·o·li·tion
    dem·o·li·tion·ist

de·mon
    de·mon·ic
    de·mon·ize

de·mo·ni·ac
    de·mo·ni·a·cal
    de·mo·ni·a·cal·ly

de·mon·stra·ble
    de·mon·stra·bly

dem·on·strate
    dem·on·stra·tor

dem·on·stra·tion
    dem·on·stra·tion·al

de·mon·stra·tive
    de·mon·stra·tive·ly
    de·mon·stra·tive·ness

de·mor·al·ize
    de·mor·al·i·za·tion
    de·mor·al·iz·ing
    de·mor·al·iz·ing·ly

De·mos·the·nes

de·mote
    de·mo·tion

Demp·sey

de·mur (object; see
    DEMURE)
    de·murred, de·mur·
    ring
    also de·mur·ral

de·mure (modest; see
    DEMUR)
    de·mur·er, de·mur·est
    de·mure·ly
    de·mure·ness

de·mur·rer

de·mys·ti·fy
  de·mys·ti·fies, de·mys·ti·fied
  de·mys·ti·fi·ca·tion

de·my·thol·o·gize

den

De·na·li

de·na·ture
  de·na·tur·ant
  de·na·tur·a·tion

den·drite
  den·drit·ic

den·drol·o·gy
  den·dro·log·i·cal
  den·drol·o·gist

den·gue

Deng Xiao·ping
  also Teng Hsiao-p'ing

de·ni·al

de·nier

den·i·grate
  den·i·gra·tion

den·im

den·i·zen

Den·mark

de·nom·i·nate

de·nom·i·na·tion
  de·nom·i·na·tion·al

de·nom·i·na·tor

de·note
  de·no·ta·tion
  de·no·ta·tive

de·noue·ment
  also dé·noue·ment

de·nounce
  de·nounce·ment
  de·nounc·er

dense
  dense·ly
  dense·ness

den·si·ty
  pl. den·si·ties

dent

den·tal

den·ti·frice

den·tin
  also den·tine

den·tist
  den·tist·ry

den·ti·tion

den·ture

de·nude
  den·u·da·tion

de·nun·ci·a·tion
  de·nun·ci·ate
  de·nun·ci·a·tor

Den·ver

de·ny
  de·nies, de·nied

de·o·dor·ant

de·o·dor·ize
  de·o·dor·i·za·tion
  de·o·dor·iz·er

de·ox·y·ri·bo·nu·cle·ic ac·id

de·part

de·part·ed

de·part·ment
  de·part·men·tal
  de·part·men·tal·ize
  de·part·men·tal·ly

de·par·ture

de·pend

de·pend·a·ble
  de·pend·a·bil·i·ty
  de·pend·a·ble·ness
  de·pend·a·bly

de·pend·ence

de·pen·den·cy
  pl. de·pen·den·cies

de·pen·dent

de·pict
  de·pict·er
  de·pic·tion
  de·pic·tive
  de·pic·tor

de·pil·a·to·ry
  pl. de·pil·a·to·ries

de·plane

de·plete
  de·ple·tion

de·plor·a·ble
  de·plor·a·bly

de·plore
  de·plor·ing·ly

de·ploy
  de·ploy·ment

de·po·lit·i·cize
  de·po·lit·i·ci·za·tion

de·pop·u·late
  de·pop·u·la·tion

de·port
  de·por·ta·tion

de·por·tee

de·port·ment

de·pose

de·pos·it

dep·o·si·tion

de·pos·i·to·ry
  pl. de·pos·i·to·ries

de·pot

de·prave
  dep·ra·va·tion
  de·praved·
  de·prav·i·ty

dep·re·cate
  dep·re·cat·ing·ly

dep·re·ca·tion
dep·re·ca·to·ry

de·pre·ci·ate

de·pre·ci·a·tion

dep·re·da·tion

de·press
de·press·ing
de·press·ing·ly

de·pres·sant

de·pres·sion
also De·pres·sion

de·pres·sive

de·prive
de·priv·a·ble
de·priv·al
dep·ri·va·tion

depth
in-depth

dep·u·ta·tion

de·pute

dep·u·tize

dep·u·ty
pl. dep·u·ties

De Quin·cey

de·rail
de·rail·ment

de·rail·leur

de·range
de·range·ment

Der·by (*city, horse race*)

der·by (*hat, any competition*)
pl. der·bies

de·reg·u·late
de·reg·u·la·tion

der·e·lict

der·e·lic·tion

de·ride
de·rid·ing·ly

de ri·gueur

de·ri·sion

de·ri·sive
de·ri·sive·ly
de·ri·sive·ness

de·ri·so·ry

der·i·va·tion
der·i·va·tion·al

de·riv·a·tive
de·riv·a·tive·ly

de·rive
de·riv·a·ble

der·ma·ti·tis

der·ma·tol·o·gy
der·ma·to·lòg·i·cal
der·ma·tol·o·gist

der·mis
also der·ma
der·mal

der·o·gate
de·rog·a·tive

de·rog·a·to·ry
de·rog·a·to·ri·ly

der·rick

der·ri·ere
also der·ri·ère

der·rin·ger

der·vish

de Sade

de·sal·i·nate
de·sal·i·na·tion

des·cant

Des·cartes

de·scend
de·scend·ent

de·scend·ant

de·scen·sion

de·scent (*going down*; see DISSENT)

de·scribe
de·scrib·a·ble
de·scrib·er

de·scrip·tion
de·scrip·tive

de·scry
de·scries, de·scried

des·e·crate
des·e·cra·tion
des·e·cra·tor

de·seg·re·gate
de·seg·re·ga·tion

de·sen·si·tize
de·sen·si·ti·za·tion

de·sert (*abandon*; see DESSERT)
de·sert·er
de·ser·tion

des·ert (*barren land*)

de·serve
de·serv·ed·ly
de·serving

des·ic·cate
des·ic·ca·tion
des·ic·ca·tive
des·ic·ca·tor

de·sid·er·a·tum
pl. de·sid·er·a·ta

de·sign

des·ig·nate
des·ig·na·tion
des·ig·na·tor

de·sign·ing
de·sign·ing·ly

de·sir·a·ble
de·sir·a·bil·i·ty
de·sir·a·ble·ness
de·sir·a·bly

de·sire

de·sir·ous

de·sist

desk

desk·top

Des Moines

des·o·late
des·o·late·ly
des·o·late·ness

des·o·la·tion

de So·to

de·spair
de·spair·ing·ly

des·patch
var. of dis·patch

des·per·a·do
pl. des·per·a·does *or*
des·per·a·dos

des·per·ate
des·per·ate·ly
des·per·ate·ness
des·per·a·tion

des·pi·ca·ble
des·pi·ca·bly

de·spise

de·spite

de·spoil
de·spoil·er
de·spo·li·a·tion

de·spond·ent
de·spond·ence
de·spond·en·cy
de·spond·ent·ly

des·pot
des·pot·ic
des·pot·i·cal·ly
des·pot·ism

des·sert (*sweet food; see*
DESERT)

des·ti·na·tion

des·tine

des·ti·ny
pl. des·ti·nies

des·ti·tute
des·ti·tu·tion

de·stroy

de·stroy·er

de·struct

de·struc·tion
de·struct·i·bil·i·ty
de·struct·i·ble
de·struc·tive
de·struc·tive·ly
de·struc·tive·ness

des·ue·tude

des·ul·to·ry
des·ul·to·ri·ly
des·ul·to·ri·ness

de·tach
de·tach·a·ble
de·tach·ed·ly

de·tach·ment

de·tail

de·tain
de·tain·ee
de·tain·ment

de·tect
de·tect·a·ble
de·tect·a·bly
de·tec·tion

de·tec·tive

dé·tente

de·ten·tion

de·ter
de·terred, de·ter·ring
de·ter·ment

de·ter·gent

de·te·ri·o·rate
de·te·ri·o·ra·tion

de·ter·mi·nant

de·ter·mi·nate

de·ter·mi·na·tion

de·ter·mine
de·ter·min·a·ble

de·ter·mined
de·ter·mined·ly
de·ter·mined·ness

de·ter·rent
de·ter·rence

de·test
de·test·a·ble
de·test·er

de·throne
de·throne·ment

det·o·nate
det·o·na·tion
det·o·na·tive
det·o·na·tor

de·tour

de·tox·i·fy
de·tox·i·fi·ca·tion

de·tract
de·trac·tion
de·trac·tive
de·trac·tor

det·ri·ment
det·ri·men·tal

de·tri·tus
de·tri·tal

De·troit

deuce

deu·te·ri·um

deut·sche mark
also Deut·sche·mark

De Va·le·ra

de·val·ue
de·val·ues, de·val·ued,
de·val·u·ing
de·val·u·a·tion

dev·as·tate
dev·as·tat·ing
dev·as·tat·ing·ly

dev•as•ta•tion
dev•as•ta•tor

de•vel•op
de•vel•op•er

de•vel•op•ment
de•vel•op•men•tal
de•vel•op•men•tal•ly

de•vi•ant
de•vi•ance
de•vi•an•cy

de•vi•ate
de•vi•a•tion
de•vi•a•tor
de•vi•a•to•ry

de•vice

dev•il
dev•iled, dev•il•ing;
dev•illed, dev•il•ling
dev•il•ish

dev•il•ment

dev•il•ry
also dev•il•try
pl. dev•il•ries

de•vi•ous
de•vi•ous•ly
de•vi•ous•ness

de•vise
de•vis•a•ble
de•vis•ee
de•vis•er
de•vi•sor

de•void

de•volve
de•volve•ment

De•vo•ni•an

de•vote

de•vot•ed
de•vot•ed•ly
de•vot•ed•ness

dev•o•tee

de•vo•tion
de•vo•tion•al

de•vour
de•vour•ing•ly

de•vout
de•vout•ly
de•vout•ness

dew (*vapor; see* DO, DUE)
dew•y
dew•i•er, dew•i•est

dew•ber•ry
pl. dew•ber•ries

dew•claw

dew•drop

Dew•ey

dew•lap

dex•ter•i•ty

dex•ter•ous
also dex•trous
dex•ter•ous•ly

dex•trose

Dha•ka

dho•ti
pl. dho•tis

di•a•be•tes
di•a•bet•ic

di•a•bol•ic
also di•a•bol•i•cal
di•a•bol•i•cal•ly

di•a•crit•ic
di•a•crit•i•cal

di•a•dem

di•aer•e•sis
also di•er•e•sis
pl. di•aer•e•ses

Di•a•ghi•lev

di•ag•nose
di•ag•nos•a•ble

di•ag•no•sis
pl. di•ag•no•ses

di•ag•nos•tic
di•ag•nos•ti•cal•ly
di•ag•nos•ti•cian

di•ag•nos•tics

di•ag•o•nal
di•ag•o•nal•ly

di•a•gram
di•a•gramed, di•a•
gram•ing; di•a•
grammed, di•a•gram•
ming
di•a•gram•mat•ic
di•a•gram•mat•i•cal•ly

di•al
di•al•er

di•a•lect
di•a•lec•tal
di•a•lec•tol•o•gy
di•a•lec•tol•o•gist

di•a•lec•tic

di•a•logue
also di•a•log

di•al•y•sis
pl. di•al•y•ses

di•am•e•ter
di•am•e•tral

di•a•met•ri•cal
also di•a•met•ric
di•a•met•ri•cal•ly

di•a•mond

di•a•mond•back

Di•a•mond Head

di•a•per

di•aph•a•nous
di•aph•a•nous•ly

di•a•phragm
di•a•phrag•mat•ic

di•a•rist
di•a•ris•tic

di•ar•rhe•a
di•ar•rhe•al
di•ar•rhe•ic

di·a·ry
  pl. di·a·ries

Di·as
  also Di·az

Di·as·po·ra
  also di·as·po·ra

di·a·stase
  di·a·sta·sic
  di·a·stat·ic

di·as·to·le
  di·as·tol·ic

di·a·ther·my

di·a·tom
  di·a·to·ma·ceous

di·a·tom·ic

di·a·ton·ic

di·a·tribe

dib·ble

dibs

dice

dic·ey
  dic·i·er, dic·i·est

di·chot·o·my
  pl. di·chot·o·mies
  di·cho·tom·ic
  di·chot·o·mize
  di·chot·o·mous

dick

Dick·ens

dick·er
  dick·er·er

dick·ey
  also dick·y
  pl. dick·eys *or* dick·ies

Dick·in·son

dic·ta

dic·tate
  dic·ta·tion

dic·ta·tor
  dic·ta·tor·ship

dic·ta·to·ri·al
  dic·ta·to·ri·al·ly

dic·tion

dic·tion·ar·y
  pl. dic·tion·ar·ies

dic·tum
  pl. dic·ta *or* dic·tums

did

di·dac·tic
  di·dac·ti·cal·ly
  di·dac·ti·cism

did·dle
  did·dler

did·dly

Di·de·rot

did·n't

die (*perish*; see DYE)
  dies, died, dy·ing
  pl. dies *or* dice

die·hard

di·er·e·sis
  var. of di·aer·e·sis

die·sel

di·et
  di·e·ta·ry
  di·et·er

di·e·tet·ic
  di·e·tet·i·cal·ly

di·e·tet·ics

di·e·ti·tian
  also di·e·ti·cian

dif·fer

dif·fer·ence

dif·fer·ent
  dif·fer·ent·ly

dif·fer·en·tial
  dif·fer·en·tial·ly

dif·fer·en·ti·ate
  dif·fer·en·ti·a·tion

dif·fi·cult

dif·fi·cul·ty
  pl. dif·fi·cul·ties

dif·fi·dent
  dif·fi·dence
  dif·fi·dent·ly

dif·fuse
  dif·fuse·ly
  dif·fuse·ness
  dif·fus·i·ble
  dif·fu·sion
  dif·fu·sive

dig
  dig·ging; *past and past*
  part. dug
  dig·ger

di·gest
  di·gest·i·ble
  di·gest·i·bil·i·ty

di·ges·tion
  di·ges·tive

di·git

dig·i·tal
  dig·it·al·ly

dig·i·tal·is

dig·i·tize
  dig·i·ti·za·tion

dig·ni·fied

dig·ni·fy
  dig·ni·fies, dig·ni·fied

dig·ni·tar·y
  pl. dig·ni·tar·ies

dig·ni·ty
  pl. dig·ni·ties

di·graph
  di·graph·ic

di·gress
  di·gres·sion

Di·jon

dike
  also dyke

di·lap·i·dat·ed

dil·a·ta·tion

di·late
  di·la·tion

dil·a·to·ry
  dil·a·to·ri·ly
  dil·a·to·ri·ness

di·lem·ma

dil·et·tante
  pl. dil·et·tantes *or* dil·
    et·tan·ti
  dil·et·tan·tish
  dil·et·tan·tism

dil·i·gent
  dil·i·gence
  dil·i·gent·ly

dill

dil·ly·dal·ly
  dil·ly·dal·lies, dil·ly·
    dal·lied

di·lute
  di·lut·er
  di·lu·tion

dim
  dim·mer, dim·mest
  dimmed, dim·ming
  dim-wit·ted
  dim·ly
  dim·mish
  dim·ness

Di·Mag·gi·o

dime

di·men·sion
  di·men·sion·al
  di·men·sion·less

di·min·ish
  di·min·ish·a·ble

di·min·u·en·do
  pl. di·min·u·en·dos

dim·i·nu·tion

di·min·u·tive

dim·mer

dim·ple
  dim·ply

dim sum
  also dim sim

dim·wit

din

dine (*eat;* see DYNE)

din·er

di·nette

ding

din·ghy (*small boat*)
  pl. din·ghies

din·go
  pl. din·goes

din·gy (*shabby*)
  din·gi·er, din·gi·est
  din·gi·ly
  din·gi·ness

din·ky
  din·ki·er, din·ki·est

din·ner

din·ner·ware

di·no·saur
  di·no·sau·ri·an

dint

di·o·cese
  di·oc·e·san

Di·o·cle·tian

di·ode

Di·og·e·nes

Di·o·ny·si·us I

di·o·ram·a
  di·o·ram·ic

di·ox·ide

dip
  dipped, dip·ping

diph·the·ri·a
  diph·the·ri·al
  diph·the·rit·ic
  diph·the·roid

diph·thong
  diph·thon·gal

dip·lod·o·cus

di·plo·ma
  pl. di·plo·mas
  di·plo·maed

di·plo·ma·cy

dip·lo·mat
  dip·lo·mat·ic

di·pole

dip·so·ma·ni·a
  dip·so·ma·ni·ac

dip·stick

dip·tych

dire
  dire·ly
  dire·ness

di·rect
  di·rect·ness

di·rec·tion
  di·rec·tion·al
  di·rec·tion·al·i·ty
  di·rec·tion·al·ly
  di·rec·tion·less

di·rec·tive

di·rect·ly

di·rec·tor
  di·rec·to·ri·al
  di·rec·tor·ship

di·rec·tor·ate

di·rec·to·ry
pl. di·rec·to·ries

dirge
dirge·ful

dir·i·gi·ble

dirk

dirn·dl

dirt

dirt·y
dirt·i·er, dirt·i·est
dirt·ies, dirt·ied
dirt·i·ly
dirt·i·ness

dis
var. of diss

dis·a·bil·i·ty
pl. dis·a·bil·i·ties

dis·a·ble
dis·a·ble·ment

dis·a·buse

dis·ad·van·tage
dis·ad·van·ta·geous

dis·ad·van·taged

dis·af·fect·ed
dis·af·fect·ed·ly
dis·af·fec·tion

dis·a·gree
dis·a·grees, dis·a·
greed, dis·a·gree·ing
dis·a·gree·ment

dis·a·gree·a·ble
dis·a·gree·a·ble·ness
dis·a·gree·a·bly

dis·al·low
dis·al·low·ance

dis·ap·pear
dis·ap·pear·ance

dis·ap·point
dis·ap·point·ed
dis·ap·point·ing
dis·ap·point·ingly
dis·ap·point·ment

dis·ap·pro·ba·tion

dis·ap·prove
dis·ap·prov·al
dis·ap·prov·ing
dis·ap·prov·ingly

dis·arm
dis·arm·ing
dis·arm·ing·ly

dis·ar·ma·ment

dis·ar·range
dis·ar·range·ment

dis·ar·ray

dis·as·so·ci·ate
dis·as·so·ci·a·tion

dis·as·ter
dis·as·trous
dis·as·trous·ly

dis·a·vow
dis·a·vow·al

dis·band
dis·band·ment

dis·bar
dis·barred, dis·bar·ring
dis·bar·ment

dis·be·lieve
dis·be·lief
dis·be·liev·ing
dis·be·liev·ing·ly

dis·burse
dis·burs·al
dis·burse·ment

disc
var. of disk

dis·card

dis·cern
dis·cern·i·ble
dis·cern·i·bly

dis·cern·ing
dis·cern·ing·ly
dis·cern·ment

dis·charge
dis·charge·a·ble
dis·charg·er

dis·ci·ple

dis·ci·pli·nar·i·an

dis·ci·pline
dis·ci·plin·a·ble
dis·ci·pli·nal
dis·ci·plin·ar·y

dis·claim

dis·claim·er

dis·close
dis·clos·er
dis·clo·sure

dis·co
pl. dis·cos
dis·coes, dis·coed

dis·cog·ra·phy
pl. dis·cog·ra·phies
dis·cog·ra·pher

dis·col·or
dis·col·or·a·tion

dis·com·fit
dis·com·fi·ture

dis·com·fort

dis·com·mode
dis·com·mo·di·ous

dis·com·pose
dis·com·po·sure

dis·con·cert
dis·con·cert·ing

dis·con·nect
dis·con·nec·tion

dis·con·nect·ed

dis·con·so·late
dis·con·so·late·ly

dis·con·tent
dis·con·tent·ment

dis·con·tin·ue
dis·con·tin·u·ance
dis·con·tin·u·a·tion

dis•con•tin•u•ous
dis•con•ti•nu•i•ty
dis•con•tin•u•ous•ly

dis•cord
dis•cord•ance
dis•cord•an•cy
dis•cord•ant
dis•cord•ant•ly

dis•co•theque

dis•count
dis•count•a•ble
dis•coun•ter

dis•coun•te•nance

dis•cour•age
dis•cour•age•ment
dis•cour•ag•ing•ly

dis•course

dis•cour•te•ous
dis•cour•te•ous•ly
dis•cour•te•ous•ness
dis•cour•te•sy

dis•cov•er
dis•cov•er•a•ble
dis•cov•er•er

dis•cov•er•y
pl. dis•cov•er•ies

dis•cred•it

dis•cred•it•a•ble
dis•cred•it•a•bly

dis•creet (*prudent*; see
DISCRETE)
dis•creet•er, dis•creet•
est
dis•creet•ly
dis•creet•ness

dis•crep•an•cy
pl. dis•crep•an•cies
dis•crep•ant

dis•crete (*separate*; see
DISCREET)
dis•crete•ly
dis•crete•ness

dis•cre•tion
dis•cre•tion•ary

dis•crim•i•nate
dis•crim•i•nate•ly
dis•crim•i•na•tion
dis•crim•i•na•to•ry

dis•crim•i•nat•ing

dis•cur•sive
dis•cur•sive•ly
dis•cur•sive•ness

dis•cus (*thrown disk*)
pl. dis•cus•es

dis•cuss (*talk about*)
dis•cuss•a•ble
dis•cus•sant
dis•cuss•er
dis•cus•sion

dis•dain
dis•dain•ful

dis•ease

dis•em•bark
dis•em•bar•ka•tion

dis•em•bow•el
dis•em•bow•el•ment

dis•en•chant
dis•en•chant•ing•ly
dis•en•chant•ment

dis•en•cum•ber

dis•en•fran•chise
var. of dis•fran•chise

dis•en•gage
dis•en•gage•ment

dis•en•tan•gle
dis•en•tan•gle•ment

dis•fa•vor

dis•fig•ure
dis•fig•ure•ment

dis•fran•chise
also dis•en•fran•chise
dis•fran•chise•ment

dis•gorge
dis•gorge•ment

dis•grace
dis•grace•ful
dis•grace•ful•ly

dis•grun•tled
dis•grun•tle•ment

dis•guise

dis•gust
dis•gust•ed•ly
dis•gust•ing

dish
dish•ful
pl. dish•fuls
dish•like

dis•har•mo•ny
dis•har•mo•ni•ous

dis•heart•en
dis•heart•en•ing•ly

di•shev•eled
di•shev•el
di•shev•el•ment

dis•hon•est
dis•hon•est•ly
dis•hon•es•ty

dis•hon•or

dis•hon•or•a•ble
dis•hon•or•a•ble•ness
dis•hon•or•a•bly

dish•pan

dish•wash•er

dis•il•lu•sion
dis•il•lu•sion•ment

dis•in•cline

dis•in•fect
dis•in•fect•ant
dis•in•fec•tion

dis•in•for•ma•tion

dis•in•gen•u•ous
dis•in•gen•u•ous•ly
dis•in•gen•u•ous•ness

dis•in•her•it
dis•in•her•i•tance

dis·in·te·grate
dis·in·te·gra·tion
dis·in·te·gra·tor

dis·in·ter
dis·in·terred, dis·in·
ter·ring
dis·in·ter·ment

dis·in·ter·est·ed
dis·in·ter·est
dis·in·ter·est·ed·ly
dis·in·ter·est·ed·ness

dis·joint
dis·joint·ed·ly
dis·joint·ed·ness

disk
also disc

disk·ette

dis·like
dis·lik·a·ble
also dis·like·a·ble.

dis·lo·cate
dis·lo·ca·tion

dis·lodge
dis·lodg·ment
also dis·lodge·ment

dis·loy·al
dis·loy·al·ist
dis·loy·al·ly
dis·loy·al·ty

dis·mal
dis·mal·ly

dis·man·tle

dis·may

dis·mem·ber
dis·mem·ber·ment

dis·miss
dis·mis·sal

dis·mis·sive
dis·mis·sive·ly
dis·mis·sive·ness

dis·mount

Dis·ney

dis·o·be·di·ent
dis·o·be·di·ence
dis·o·be·di·ent·ly

dis·o·bey
dis·o·bey·er

dis·o·blige

dis·or·der

dis·or·der·ly
dis·or·der·li·ness

dis·or·gan·ize
dis·or·gan·i·za·tion

dis·o·ri·ent

dis·own

dis·par·age
dis·par·age·ment
dis·par·ag·ing·ly

dis·pa·rate
dis·pa·rate·ly
dis·pa·rate·ness

dis·par·i·ty
pl. dis·par·i·ties

dis·pas·sion·ate
dis·pas·sion·ate·ly
dis·pas·sion·ate·ness

dis·patch
also des·patch
dis·patch·er

dis·pel
dis·pelled, dis·pel·ling
dis·pel·ler

dis·pen·sa·ble
dis·pen·sa·bil·i·ty

dis·pen·sa·ry
pl. dis·pen·sa·ries

dis·pen·sa·tion
dis·pen·sa·tion·al

dis·pense
dis·pens·er

dis·perse
dis·pers·a·ble
dis·pers·al

dis·pers·er
dis·pers·i·ble
dis·per·sion
dis·per·sive

dis·pir·it
dis·pir·it·ed·ly
dis·pir·it·ed·ness
dis·pir·it·ing·ly

dis·place

dis·place·ment

dis·play
dis·play·er

dis·please
dis·plea·sure

dis·port

dis·pos·a·ble

dis·pos·al

dis·pose

dis·po·si·tion

dis·pos·sess
dis·pos·ses·sion

dis·pro·por·tion
dis·pro·por·tion·al
dis·pro·por·tion·al·ly

dis·pro·por·tion·ate
dis·pro·por·tion·ate·ly
dis·pro·por·tion·ate·
ness

dis·prove

dis·put·a·ble
dis·put·a·bly

dis·pu·ta·tion

dis·pu·ta·tious

dis·pute
dis·pu·tant
dis·put·er

dis·qual·i·fy
dis·qual·i·fies, dis·
qual·i·fied
dis·qual·i·fi·ca·tion

dis·qui·et
  dis·qui·et·ing
  dis·qui·et·ing·ly

dis·qui·si·tion
  dis·qui·si·tion·al

Dis·rae·li

dis·re·gard
  dis·re·gard·ful
  dis·re·gard·ful·ly

dis·re·pair

dis·rep·u·ta·ble
  dis·rep·u·ta·bly

dis·re·pute

dis·re·spect
  dis·re·spect·ful
  dis·re·spect·ful·ly

dis·robe

dis·rupt
  dis·rup·tion
  dis·rup·tive
  dis·rup·tive·ly

diss

dis·sat·is·fy
  dis·sat·is·fies, dis·sat·
  is·fied
  dis·sat·is·fac·tion

dis·sect
  dis·sec·tion

dis·sem·ble

dis·sem·i·nate
  dis·sem·i·na·tion

dis·sen·sion

dis·sent (*disagree*; see
  DESCENT)
  dis·sent·er
  dis·sent·ing
  dis·sent·ing·ly

dis·ser·ta·tion

dis·serv·ice

dis·si·dent
  dis·si·dence

dis·sim·i·lar
  dis·sim·i·lar·i·ty
  pl. dis·sim·i·lar·i·ties

dis·sim·u·late

dis·si·pate

dis·si·pa·tion

dis·so·ci·ate
  dis·so·ci·a·tive

dis·so·lute

dis·so·lu·tion

dis·solve
  dis·solv·a·ble

dis·so·nant
  dis·so·nance

dis·suade
  dis·sua·sion
  dis·sua·sive

dis·taff

dis·tance

dis·tant
  dis·tant·ly

dis·taste
  dis·taste·ful
  dis·taste·ful·ly
  dis·taste·ful·ness

dis·tem·per

dis·tend
  dis·ten·sion

dis·till
  dis·til·late
  dis·til·la·tion
  dis·till·er

dis·till·er·y
  pl. dis·till·er·ies

dis·tinct
  dis·tinct·ly

dis·tinc·tion

dis·tinc·tive
  dis·tinc·tive·ly
  dis·tinc·tive·ness

dis·tin·guish
  dis·tin·guish·a·ble

dis·tin·guished

dis·tort
  dis·tor·tion

dis·tract
  dis·tract·ed
  dis·tract·ed·ly
  dis·tract·ing

dis·trac·tion

dis·trait
  fem. dis·traite

dis·traught

dis·tress
  dis·tress·ful

dis·tressed

dis·trib·u·te
  dis·tri·bu·tion

dis·trib·u·tor

dis·trict

dis·trust
  dis·trust·ful
  dis·trust·ful·ly

dis·turb
  dis·tur·bing

dis·turb·ance

dis·u·ni·ty

dis·use

ditch

dith·er
  dith·er·er

dit·sy
  also dit·zy
  dit·si·er, dit·si·est; dit·
  zi·er, dit·zi·est
  ditz

dit•to
  pl. dit•tos
  dit•toes, dit•toed

dit•ty
  pl. dit•ties

di•u•ret•ic

di•ur•nal
  di•ur•nal•ly

di•va
  pl. di•vas *or* di•ve

di•van

dive
  dived *or* dove
  dive-bomb
  div•er

di•verge
  di•ver•gence
  di•ver•gen•cy
  di•ver•gent
  di•ver•gent•ly

di•vers (*several*)

di•verse (*varied*)
  di•verse•ly

di•ver•si•fy
  di•ver•si•fies, di•ver•
    si•fied
  di•ver•si•fi•ca•tion

di•ver•sion
  di•ver•sion•ar•y

di•ver•si•ty
  pl. di•ver•si•ties

di•vert

di•ver•tic•u•li•tis

di•ver•tic•u•lum
  pl. di•ver•tic•u•la

di•vest
  di•vest•i•ture
  di•vest•ment

di•vide

div•i•dend

div•i•na•tion

di•vine
  di•vin•er, di•vin•est
  di•vine•ly

di•vin•i•ty
  pl. di•vin•i•ties

di•vis•i•ble
  di•vis•i•bil•i•ty

di•vi•sion
  di•vi•sion•al

di•vi•sive
  di•vi•sive•ly
  di•vi•sive•ness

di•vi•sor

di•vorce (*separation*)

di•vor•cé (*man*)

di•vor•cée (*woman*)

div•ot

di•vulge
  di•vul•gence

div•vy
  div•vies, div•vied

Dix•ie

Dix•ie•land

diz•zy
  diz•zi•er, diz•zi•est
  diz•zi•ly
  diz•zi•ness

djel•la•ba
  also djel•la•bah, jel•
    la•ba

Dji•bou•ti

Dni•pro•pe•trovsk

do (*musical note*; see DOE,
    DOUGH)
  also doh

do (*perform*; see DEW,
    DUE)
  does; *past* did; *past part.*
    done

pl. dos *or* do's
do-it-your•self
do•a•ble

Do•ber•man
  in full Do•ber•man pin•
    scher

doc (*doctor*; see DOCK)

do•cent

doc•ile
  doc•ile•ly
  do•cil•i•ty

dock (*pier*; see DOC)

dock•et

dock•hand

dock•side

dock•yard

doc•tor

doc•tor•al

doc•tor•ate

doc•tri•naire

doc•trine
  doc•tri•nal

doc•u•dra•ma

doc•u•ment

doc•u•men•ta•ry
  pl. doc•u•men•ta•ries

doc•u•men•ta•tion

dod•der
  dod•der•ing

do•dec•a•gon

do•dec•a•hed•ron
  do•dec•a•he•dral

dodge
  dodg•er

Dodg•son

do•do
  pl. do•does *or* do•dos

doe (*animal*; see DO, DOUGH)

do•er

does

does•n't

doff

dog
dogged, dog•ging
dog-eared
dog-eat-dog

dog•catch•er

dog•fight

dog•fish
pl. same *or* dog•fish•es

dog•ged
dog•ged•ly
dog•ged•ness

dog•ger•el

dog•gy
also dog•gie
pl. dog•gies
dog•gi•ness

dog•house

do•gie

dog•ma

dog•mat•ic
dog•mat•i•cal•ly

dog•ma•tism
dog•ma•tist

do-good•er

dog•wood

Do•ha

doi•ly
also doy•ley
pl. doi•lies *or* doi•leys

do•ing

Dol•by

dol•drums

Dole (*proper name*)

dole (*deal out, unemployment benefits*)

dole•ful
dole•ful•ly
dole•ful•ness

doll

dol•lar

doll•house

dol•lop

dol•ly
pl. dol•lies
dol•lies, dol•lied

dol•men

do•lo•mite

do•lor
dol•or•ous
dol•or•ous•ly

dol•phin

dolt
dolt•ish

do•main

dome
dome•like

do•mes•tic
do•mes•ti•cal•ly

do•mes•ti•cate
do•mes•ti•ca•tion

do•mes•tic•i•ty

dom•i•cile
also dom•i•cil

dom•i•nant
dom•i•nance
dom•i•nant•ly

dom•i•nate
dom•i•na•tion
dom•i•na•tor

dom•i•neer
dom•i•neer•ing•ly

Dom•i•ni•ca

Dom•i•ni•can Re•pub•lic

do•min•ion

dom•i•no
pl. dom•i•noes *or* dom•i•nos

don
donned, don•ning

do•nate
do•na•tor

do•na•tion

done (*past part. of do*; see DUN)

Do•netsk

Don Juan

don•key
pl. don•keys

don•ny•brook

do•nor

Don Riv•er

don't

do•nut
var. of dough•nut

doo•dad

doo•dle
doo•dler

doom

dooms•day

door
door-to-door
doored

door•bell

door•knob

door•man
pl. door•men

door•mat

door•step

door•stop

door•way

doo•zy
pl. doo•zies
also doo•zie

dope

dope•y
also dop•y
dop•i•er, dop•i•est
dop•i•ly
dop•i•ness

Dop•pler ra•dar

Dor•ic

dork
dork•y

dor•mant
dor•man•cy

dor•mer

dor•mi•to•ry
pl. dor•mi•to•ries

dor•mouse
pl. dor•mice

dor•sal
dor•sal•ly

Dort•mund

do•ry
pl. do•ries

DOS

dos•age

dose

dos•si•er

dot
dot•ted, dot•ting

dot•age

do•tard

dote
dot•ing•ly

dou•ble
dou•ble-blind
dou•ble-cross
dou•ble-deal•er
dou•ble-deal•ing
dou•ble-deck•er
dou•ble-talk
dou•bler
dou•bly

dou•ble en•ten•dre

dou•blet

dou•bloon

doubt
doub•ter
doubt•ing•ly

doubt•ful
doubt•ful•ly

doubt•less
doubt•less•ly

douche

dough (*flour and water;*
see DO, DOE)
dough•y

dough•boy

dough•nut
also do•nut

dough•ty
dough•ti•er, dough•
ti•est
dough•ti•ly
dough•ti•ness

Doug•las fir

dour
dour•ly
dour•ness

douse (*throw water over;*
see DOWSE)

dove

dove (*bird*)

Do•ver

dove•tail

dow•a•ger

dow•dy
dow•di•er, dow•di•est
dow•di•ly
dow•di•ness

dow•el

dow•er

down
down•most
down•y
down•i•er, down•i•est
down-and-out
down-to-earth

down•beat

down•cast

down•er

down•fall

down•grade

down•heart•ed
down•heart•ed•ly

down•hill

down•load

down•play

down•pour

down•right

down•shift

down•size
down•sized,
down•siz•ing

Down's syn•drome
also Down syn•drome

down•stage

down•stairs

down•state

down•stream

down•time

down•town

down·trod·den

down·turn

down·ward
also down·wards
down·ward·ly

down·wind

dow·ry
pl. dow·ries

dowse (*search for
underground water*; see
DOUSE)
dows·er

dox·ol·o·gy
pl. dox·ol·o·gies
dox·o·log·i·cal

doze
doz·er

doz·en
pl. doz·en

drab
drab·ber, drab·best
drab·ly
drab·ness

drach·ma
pl. drach·mas *or* drach·
mai *or* drach·mae

dra·co·ni·an
also dra·con·ic

draft
draft·ee
draft·er

drafts·man
pl. drafts·men
drafts·man·ship

draft·y
draft·i·er, draft·i·est
draft·i·ly
draft·i·ness

drag
dragged, drag·ging

drag·net

drag·on

drag·on·fly
pl. drag·on·flies

dra·goon

drain
drain·er

drain·age

drain·pipe

drake

dram

dra·ma
dra·mat·ic

dra·mat·ics

dram·a·tist

dram·a·tize
dram·a·ti·za·tion

drank

drape

dra·per·y
pl. dra·per·ies

dras·tic
dras·ti·cal·ly

draw
past drew; *past part.*
drawn

draw·back

draw·bridge

draw·er
draw·er·ful
pl. draw·er·fuls

draw·ing

draw·ing room

drawl

drawn

draw·string

dray

dread

dread·ful
dread·ful·ly

dread·locks

dread·nought

dream
past and *past part.*
dreamed *or* dreamt
dream·like

dream·er

dream·land

dream·y
dream·i·er, dream·i·est
dream·i·ly
dream·i·ness

drear·y
drear·i·er, drear·i·est
drear·i·ly
drear·i·ness

dredge

dregs

drench

Dres·den

dress

dres·sage

dress·er

dress·ing

dress·y
dress·i·er, dress·i·est
dress·i·ness

drew

drib·ble
drib·bler
drib·bly

dribs and drabs

dried

dri·er
also dry·er

dri·est

drift
drift•age

drift•er

drift•wood

drill

dri•ly
var. of dry•ly

drink
past drank; *past part.*
drunk
drink•a•ble
drink•er

drip
dripped, drip•ping
drip-dry
drip-dries, drip-dried

drive
past drove; *past part.*
driv•en
drive-by
drive-in
driv•a•ble

driv•el
driv•el•er

driv•en

driv•er

drive•way

driz•zle
driz•zly

droll
droll•er•y
pl. droll•er•ies
drol•ly
droll•ness

drom•e•dar•y
pl. drom•e•dar•ies

drone

drool

droop
droop•y

drop
dropped, drop•ping
drop-leaf
drop•let

drop•out

drop•per

drop•pings

drop•sy
pl. drop•sies

dro•soph•i•la

dross

drought
drought•y

drove

drown

drowse

drow•sy
drow•si•er, drow•si•est
drow•si•ly
drow•si•ness

drub
drubbed, drub•bing
drub•bing

drudge
drudg•er•y

drug
drugged, drug•ging

drug•gist

drug•store

Dru•id
Dru•id•ism
Dru•id•ic

drum
drummed, drum•ming
drum•mer

drum•stick

drunk

drunk•ard

drunk•en
drunk•en•ly
drunk•en•ness

drupe
dru•pa•ceous

dry
dri•er; dri•est
dries, dried
dry-clean
dry•ly, dri•ly
dry•ness

dry•ad

dry•wall

du•al (*twofold*; see DUEL)
du•al•i•ty
du•al•ize
du•al•ly

dub
dubbed, dub•bing

Du•bai

du•bi•e•ty
pl. du•bi•e•ties

du•bi•ous
du•bi•ous•ly

Dub•lin
Dub•lin•er

dub•ni•um

Du•buque

du•cal

du•cat

duch•ess

duch•y
pl. duch•ies

duck
pl. same *or* ducks

duck•bill
also duck-billed plat•
y•pus

duck•ling

duck•y

duct

duc•tile
  duc•til•i•ty

dud

dude

dudg•eon

due (*owed, fitting*; see DEW, DO)

du•el (*contest*; see DUAL)
  du•el•er
  du•el•ist

du•et
  du•et•tist

duf•fel
  also duf•fle

duf•fer

dug

du•gong
  pl. same *or* du•gongs

dug•out

Duis•burg

du jour

duke

duke•dom

dul•cet

dul•ci•mer

dull
  dull•ness
  dul•ly

dull•ard

Du•luth

du•ly

Du Mau•ri•er

dumb
  dumb•ly
  dumb•ness

dumb•bell

dumb•found
  also dum•found

dumb•wait•er

dum•my
  pl. dum•mies

dump
  dump•ing

dump•ling

dumps

Dump•ster

dump•y
  dump•i•er, dump•i•est
  dump•i•ness

dun (*color, demand for payment*; see DONE)
  dunned, dun•ning

Dun•can

dunce

Dun•dee

dune

dung

dun•ga•ree

dun•geon

dunk

Duns Sco•tus

du•o
  pl. du•os

du•o•dec•i•mal

du•o•de•num
  du•o•de•nal

dupe
  dup•a•ble
  dup•er

du•ple

du•plex

du•pli•cate
  du•pli•ca•ble

du•pli•ca•tion
  dup•li•ca•tor

du•plic•i•ty
  du•plic•i•tous

du Pont

du•ra•ble
  du•ra•bil•i•ty

du•ra ma•ter

Du•ran•go

Du•rant

du•ra•tion
  du•ra•tion•al

Dur•ban

du•ress

Dur•ham

dur•ing

du•rum

Du•shan•be

dusk

dusk•y
  dusk•i•er, dusk•i•est
  dusk•i•ly
  dusk•i•ness

Düs•sel•dorf

dust

Dust Bowl

dust•pan

dust•y
  dust•i•er, dust•i•est
  dust•i•ly
  dust•i•ness

Dutch

du•ti•a•ble

du•ti•ful
  du•ti•ful•ly

du•ty
  pl. du•ties

du•vet

Dvo•ák

dwarf
pl. dwarfs *or* dwarves
dwarf•ish

dweeb

dwell
past and *past part.*
dwelled *or* dwelt
dwell•er

dwell•ing

dwin•dle

dye (*color*; see DIE)
dye•ing
dye•a•ble

dy•ing

Dyl•an

dy•nam•ic
dy•nam•i•cal•ly

dy•nam•ics

dy•na•mism
dy•na•mist

dy•na•mite

dy•na•mo
pl. dy•na•mos

dy•nas•ty
pl. dy•nas•ties
dy•nas•tic
dy•nas•ti•cal•ly

dyne (*unit of force*; see
DINE)

dys•en•ter•y
dys•en•ter•ic

dys•func•tion
dys•func•tion•al

dys•lex•i•a
dys•lex•ic

dys•pep•sia
dys•pep•tic

dys•pha•sia

dys•pro•si•um

dys•tro•phy
dys•troph•ic

E

each

ea·ger
  ea·ger·ly
  ea·ger·ness

ea·gle
  ea·gle-eyed

ea·glet

ear
  eared

ear·ache

ear·drum

ear·ful
  pl. ear·fuls

Ear·hart

earl
  earl·dom

ear·lobe

ear·ly
  ear·li·er, ear·li·est
  ear·li·ness

ear·mark

ear·muff

earn (*obtain, deserve;*
  see URN)

ear·nest
  ear·nest·ly
  ear·nest·ness

earn·ings

ear·phone

ear·ring

ear·shot

ear·split·ting

earth
  also Earth

earth-shat·ter·ing
earth·ward
earth·wards

earth·en

earth·en·ware

earth·ling

earth·ly

earth·quake

earth·work

earth·worm

earth·y
  earth·i·er, earth·i·est
  earth·i·ness

ear·wig

ease

ea·sel

ease·ment

eas·i·ly

east

east·bound

Eas·ter

east·er·ly
  pl. east·er·lies

east·ern
  east·ern·most

east·ern·er
  also East·ern·er

East·man

east·ward
  also east·wards

eas·y
  eas·i·er, eas·i·est
  eas·i·ness

eas·y·go·ing

eat
  past ate; *past part.* eat·
  en
  eat·a·ble
  eat·er

eat·er·y
  pl. eat·er·ies

eats

eau de co·logne

eaves

eaves·drop
  eaves·dropped, eaves·
  drop·ping
  eaves·drop·per

ebb

eb·on·y
  pl. eb·on·ies

e·bul·lient
  e·bul·lience
  e·bul·lien·cy
  e·bul·lient·ly

ec·cen·tric
  ec·cen·tri·cal·ly
  ec·cen·tric·i·ty
  pl. ec·cen·tric·i·ties

ec·cle·si·as·tic

ec·cle·si·as·ti·cal
  ec·cle·si·as·ti·cal·ly

ech·e·lon

ech·e·ve·ri·a

e·chi·no·derm

ech·o
  pl. ech·oes *or* ech·os
  ech·oes, ech·oed

e·cho·ic
  ech·o·ism

ech·o·lo·ca·tion

é·clair

é·clat

ec·lec·tic
ec·lec·ti·cal·ly
ec·lec·ti·cism

e·clipse

e·clip·tic

ec·logue

E·co

e·col·o·gy
ec·o·log·i·cal
ec·o·log·i·cal·ly
e·col·o·gist

ec·o·nom·ic

ec·o·nom·ics

e·con·o·mist

e·con·o·mize
e·con·o·mi·za·tion
e·con·o·miz·er

e·con·o·my
pl. e·con·o·mies

ec·o·sys·tem

ec·ru

ec·sta·sy
pl. ec·sta·sies
ec·stat·ic
ec·stat·i·cal·ly

ec·to·morph
ec·to·mor·phic

ec·top·ic

ec·to·plasm

Ec·ua·dor
Ec·ua·dor·an or Ec·
ua·do·ri·an

ec·u·men·i·cal
ec·u·men·i·cal·ism or
ec·u·me·nism
ec·u·men·i·cal·ly

ec·ze·ma

E·dam

Ed·dy (proper name)

ed·dy (whirlpool)
pl. ed·dies
ed·dies, ed·died

e·del·weiss

e·de·ma
e·dem·a·tose
e·dem·a·tous

E·den

edge
edge·less
edg·er

edge·wise

edg·ing

edg·y
edg·i·er, edg·i·est
edg·i·ly
edg·i·ness

ed·i·ble
ed·i·bil·i·ty

e·dict

ed·i·fice

ed·i·fy
ed·i·fies, ed·i·fied
ed·i·fi·ca·tion

Ed·in·burgh

Ed·i·son

ed·it

e·di·tion

ed·i·tor
ed·i·tor·ship

ed·i·to·ri·al
ed·i·to·ri·al·ize
ed·i·to·ri·al·ly

Ed·mon·ton

ed·u·cate
ed·u·ca·ble
ed·u·ca·bil·i·ty

ed·u·ca·tive
ed·u·ca·tor

ed·u·cat·ed

ed·u·ca·tion
ed·u·ca·tion·al
ed·u·ca·tion·al·ly

e·duce
e·duc·i·ble
e·duc·tion
e·duc·tive

Ed·ward

Ed·wards

eel
eel·like
eel·y

e'er
var. of ev·er

ee·rie
ee·ri·er, ee·ri·est
ee·ri·ly
ee·ri·ness

ef·face
ef·face·ment

ef·fect (result; see
AFFECT)

ef·fec·tive
ef·fec·tive·ly
ef·fec·tive·ness

ef·fec·tu·al
ef·fec·tu·al·ly

ef·fec·tu·ate
ef·fec·tu·a·tion

ef·fem·i·nate
ef·fem·i·na·cy
ef·fem·i·nate·ly

ef·fer·vesce
ef·fer·ves·cence
ef·fer·ves·cent

ef·fete
ef·fete·ness

ef·fi·ca·cious
ef·fi·ca·cious·ly
ef·fi·ca·cy

ef·fi·cient
ef·fi·cien·cy
ef·fi·cient·ly

ef·fi·gy
pl. ef·fi·gies

ef·flu·ence

ef·fluent

ef·flu·vi·um
pl. ef·flu·vi·a

ef·fort
ef·fort·less
ef·fort·less·ly
ef·fort·less·ness

ef·fron·ter·y
pl. ef·fron·ter·ies

ef·fuse
ef·fu·sive
ef·fu·sive·ly
ef·fu·sive·ness

ef·fu·sion

e·gal·i·tar·i·an
e·gal·i·tar·i·an·ism

egg
egg·y
egg·i·er, egg·i·est

egg·head

egg·nog

egg·plant

egg·shell

e·go
pl. e·gos

e·go·cen·tric
e·go·cen·tri·cal·ly
e·go·cen·tric·i·ty

e·go·ism
e·go·ist
e·go·is·tic
e·go·is·ti·cal

e·go·ma·ni·a
e·go·ma·ni·ac
e·go·ma·ni·a·cal

e·go·tism
e·go·tist
e·go·tis·tic
e·go·tis·ti·cal
e·go·tis·ti·cal·ly

e·gre·gious
e·gre·gious·ly
e·gre·gious·ness

e·gress
e·gres·sion

e·gret

E·gypt
E·gyp·tian

Eich·mann

ei·der

ei·der·down

Eif·fel

eight (*number*; see ATE)

eight·een
eight·eenth

eighth

eight·y
pl. eight·ies
eight·y-first, -sec·ond,
etc.
eight·y-one, -two, etc.
eight·i·eth

Ein·stein

ein·stein·i·um

Eir·e

Ei·sen·how·er

Ei·sen·staedt

ei·ther
ei·ther-or

e·jac·u·late
e·jac·u·la·tion

e·jac·u·la·tor
e·jac·u·la·to·ry

e·ject
e·jec·tion
e·jec·tor

eke

e·lab·o·rate
e·lab·o·rate·ly
e·lab·o·rate·ness
e·lab·o·ra·tion
e·lab·o·ra·tive
e·lab·o·ra·tor

é·lan

e·land

e·lapse

e·las·tic
e·las·ti·cal·ly
e·las·tic·i·ty
e·las·ti·cize

e·late
e·lat·ed·ly
e·lat·ed·ness
e·la·tion

El·ba

el·bow

el·bow·room

El·brus, Mount

El Cid

el·der

el·der·ber·ry
pl. el·der·ber·ries

eld·er·ly

eld·est

e·lect

e·lec·tion

e·lec·tion·eer

e·lec·tive
e·lec·tive·ly

e·lec·tor

e·lec·tor·al
  e·lec·tor·al·ly

e·lec·tor·ate

e·lec·tric
  e·lec·tri·cal
  e·lec·tri·cal·ly

e·lec·tri·cian

e·lec·tric·i·ty

e·lec·tri·fy
  e·lec·tri·fies, e·lec·tri·
  fied
  e·lec·tri·fi·ca·tion
  e·lec·tri·fi·er

e·lec·tro·car·di·o·
  gram

e·lec·tro·car·di·o·
  graph

e·lec·tro·cute
  e·lec·tro·cu·tion

e·lec·trode

e·lec·tro·en·ceph·a·lo·
  gram

e·lec·tro·en·ceph·a·lo·
  graph

e·lec·trol·y·sis
  e·lec·tro·lyt·ic
  e·lec·tro·lyt·i·cal
  e·lec·tro·lyt·i·cal·ly

elec·tro·lyte

e·lec·tro·lyze
  e·lec·tro·lyz·er

e·lec·tro·mag·net
  e·lec·tro·mag·net·ic
  e·lec·tro·mag·net·ism

e·lec·tro·mo·tive

e·lec·tron

e·lec·tron·ic

e·lec·tron·ics

e·lec·tro·plate
  e·lec·tro·plat·er

e·lec·tro·shock

el·ee·mos·y·nar·y

el·e·gant
  el·e·gance
  el·e·gant·ly

el·e·gi·ac
  el·e·gi·a·cal·ly

el·e·gy
  pl. el·e·gies

el·e·ment

el·e·men·tal

el·e·men·ta·ry
  el·e·men·tar·i·ly

el·e·phant
  pl. same *or* el·e·phants

el·e·phan·ti·a·sis

el·e·phan·tine

el·e·vate

el·e·va·tion

el·e·va·tor

e·lev·en

e·lev·enth

elf
  pl. elves
  elf·in
  elf·ish
  elv·ish

El·gar

El Gi·za

El Gre·co

E·li·a

e·lic·it (*draw out*; see
  ILLICIT)
  e·lic·i·ta·tion
  e·lic·i·tor

e·lide

el·i·gi·ble
  el·i·gi·bil·i·ty

e·lim·i·nate
  e·lim·i·na·tion
  e·lim·i·na·tor

El·i·ot

e·li·sion

e·lite

e·lit·ism
  e·lit·ist

e·lix·ir

E·liz·a·beth

E·liz·a·be·than

elk
  pl. same *or* elks

elk·hound

ell

El·ling·ton

el·lipse
  el·lip·tic
  also el·lip·ti·cal
  el·lip·ti·cal·ly

el·lip·sis
  pl. el·lip·ses

El·lis

El·lis Is·land

elm

El Mon·te

El Ni·ño

el·o·cu·tion
  el·o·cu·tion·ar·y
  el·o·cu·tion·ist

e·lon·gate
  e·lon·ga·tion

e·lope
  e·lope·ment

el·o·quence
  el·o·quent
  el·o·quent·ly

El Pas•o

El Sal•va•dor
Sal•va•do•ran *or* Sal•
va•do•ri•an

else

else•where

e•lu•ci•date
e•lu•ci•da•tion
e•lu•ci•da•tive
e•lu•ci•da•tor

e•lude
e•lu•sion
e•lu•so•ry

e•lu•sive
e•lu•sive•ly
e•lu•sive•ness

el•ver

elves

em (*unit of measurement;*
see 'EM)

'em (*them;* see EM)

e•ma•ci•ate
e•ma•ci•a•tion

E-mail
also e-mail

em•a•nate
em•a•na•tion

e•man•ci•pate
e•man•ci•pa•tion
e•man•ci•pa•tor
e•man•ci•pa•to•ry

e•mas•cu•late
e•mas•cu•la•tion
e•mas•cu•la•tor
e•mas•cu•la•to•ry

em•balm
em•balm•er

em•bank•ment

em•bar•go
pl. em•bar•goes
em•bar•goes,
em•bar•goed

em•bark
em•bar•ka•tion

em•bar•rass
em•bar•rass•ing
em•bar•rass•ing•ly
em•bar•rass•ment

em•bas•sy
pl. em•bas•sies

em•bat•tle

em•bed
also im•bed
em•bed•ded, em•bed•
ding

em•bel•lish
em•bel•lish•ment

em•ber

em•bez•zle
em•bez•zle•ment
em•bez•zler

em•bit•ter

em•bla•zon

em•blem
em•blem•at•ic
em•blem•at•i•cal
em•blem•at•i•cal•ly

em•bod•y
em•bod•ies, em•bod•
ied
em•bod•i•ment

em•bold•en

em•bol•ism

em•boss

em•bou•chure

em•brace
em•brace•a•ble

em•broi•der
em•broi•der•er

em•broi•der•y
pl. em•broi•der•ies

em•broil
em•broil•ment

em•bry•o
pl. em•bry•os
em•bry•on•ic

em•bry•ol•o•gy
em•bry•ol•o•gist

em•cee
em•cees, em•ceed

e•mend
e•men•da•tion

em•er•ald

e•merge
e•mer•gence
e•mer•gent

e•mer•gen•cy
pl. e•mer•gen•cies

e•mer•i•tus

Em•er•son

em•er•y

e•met•ic

em•i•grate
em•i•grant
em•i•gra•tion

é•mi•gré
also e•mi•gré

em•i•nence

em•i•nent
em•i•nent•ly

e•mir
e•mir•ate

em•is•sar•y
pl. em•is•sar•ies

e•mit
e•mit•ted, e•mit•ting
e•mis•sion

e•mol•lient
e•mol•lience

e•mol•u•ment

e·mote

e·mo·tion

e·mo·tion·al
em·o·tion·al·ism
e·mo·tion·al·ly

em·pa·thize

em·pa·thy
em·pa·thet·ic
em·pa·thet·i·cal·ly

Em·ped·o·cles

em·per·or

em·pha·sis
pl. em·pha·ses

em·pha·size

em·phat·ic
em·phat·i·cal·ly

em·phy·se·ma

em·pire

em·pir·i·cal
also em·pir·ic
em·pir·i·cal·ly
em·pir·i·cism
em·pir·i·cist

em·place·ment

em·ploy
em·ploy·a·ble
em·ploy·a·bil·i·ty
em·ploy·er

em·ploy·ee
also em·ploy·e

em·ploy·ment

em·po·ri·um
pl. em·po·ri·ums or
em·po·ri·a

em·pow·er
em·pow·er·ment

em·press

emp·ty
emp·ti·er, emp·ti·est

emp·ties, emp·tied
pl. emp·ties
emp·ti·ly
emp·ti·ness

em·py·re·an

e·mu

em·u·late
em·u·la·tion
em·u·la·tive
em·u·la·tor

e·mul·si·fi·er

e·mul·si·fy
e·mul·si·fies, e·mul·
si·fied
e·mul·si·fi·ca·tion

e·mul·sion
e·mul·sive

en

en·a·ble
en·a·bler

en·act
en·act·ment
en·ac·tor

e·nam·el

en·am·or

en·camp
en·camp·ment

en·cap·su·late
en·cap·su·la·tion

en·case
en·case·ment

en·ceph·a·li·tis
en·ceph·a·lit·ic

en·ceph·a·lo·gram

en·ceph·a·lo·graph

en·chant
en·chant·ed·ly
en·chant·ing
en·chant·ing·ly
en·chant·ment

en·chi·la·da

en·cir·cle
en·cir·cle·ment

en·clave

en·close

en·clo·sure

en·code
en·cod·er

en·co·mi·um
pl. en·co·mi·ums or en·
co·mi·a
en·co·mi·ast
en·co·mi·as·tic

en·com·pass
en·com·pass·ment

en·core

en·coun·ter

en·cour·age
en·cour·age·ment
en·cour·ag·ing
en·cour·ag·ing·ly

en·croach
en·croach·ment

en·crust
en·crust·ment

en·crypt
en·cryp·tion

en·cum·ber
en·cum·brance

en·cyc·li·cal

en·cy·clo·pe·di·a
also en·cy·clo·pae·di·a

en·cy·clo·pe·dic
also en·cy·clo·pae·dic

end

en·dan·ger
en·dan·ger·ment

en·dear
en·dear·ing
en·dear·ing·ly
en·dear·ment

en·deav·or

en·dem·ic
  en·dem·i·cal·ly

end·ing

en·dive

end·less
  end·less·ly
  end·less·ness

end·most

en·do·crine

en·do·cri·nol·o·gy
  en·do·crin·o·log·i·cal
  en·do·cri·nol·o·gist

en·do·morph
  en·do·mor·phic
  en·do·mor·phy

en·dor·phin

en·dorse
  en·dors·a·ble
  en·dor·see
  en·dorse·ment
  en·dors·er

en·dow
  en·dow·er
  en·dow·ment

en·due

en·dur·ance

en·dure
  en·dur·a·bil·i·ty
  en·dur·a·ble
  en·dur·ing·ly

end·ways

en·e·ma

en·e·my
  pl. en·e·mies

en·er·gize
  en·er·giz·er

en·er·gy
  pl. en·er·gies
  en·er·get·ic
  en·er·get·i·cal·ly

en·er·vate
  en·er·va·tion

en·fee·ble
  en·fee·ble·ment

en·fi·lade

en·fold

en·force
  en·force·a·ble
  en·force·a·bil·i·ty
  en·forc·ed·ly
  en·force·ment
  en·forc·er

en·fran·chise
  en·fran·chise·ment

en·gage

en·gaged

en·gage·ment

en·gag·ing
  en·gag·ing·ly

En·gels

en·gen·der

en·gine

en·gi·neer

en·gi·neer·ing

Eng·land

Eng·lish

Eng·lish·man
  pl. Eng·lish·men; *fem.*
  Eng·lish·wom·an, *pl.*
  Eng·lish·wom·en

en·gorge
  en·gorge·ment

en·grave
  en·grav·er

en·grav·ing

en·gross
  en·gross·ing

en·gulf
  en·gulf·ment

en·hance
  en·hance·ment
  en·hanc·er

e·nig·ma
  en·ig·mat·ic
  en·ig·mat·i·cal
  en·ig·mat·i·cal·ly

en·join
  en·join·ment

en·joy
  en·joy·a·ble
  en·joy·er
  en·joy·ment

en·large
  en·large·ment

en·larg·er

en·light·en

en·light·en·ment
  also En·light·en·ment

en·list
  en·list·ment

en·liv·en
  en·liv·en·ment

en masse

en·mesh
  en·mesh·ment

en·mi·ty
  pl. en·mi·ties

en·ne·ad

En·ni·us

en·no·ble
  en·no·ble·ment

en·nui

e·nol·o·gy
  e·no·log·i·cal
  e·nol·o·gist

e·nor·mi·ty
  pl. e·nor·mi·ties

e·nor·mous
  e·nor·mous·ly
  e·nor·mous·ness

e·nough

en·plane

en·quire
  var. of in·quire

en·quir·y
  var. of in·quir·y

en·rage
  en·rage·ment

en·rap·ture

en·rich
  en·rich·ment

en·roll
  also en·rol
  en·rolled, en·rol·ling
  en·roll·ee
  en·roll·er
  en·roll·ment
  en·rol·ment

en route

En·sche·de

en·sconce

en·sem·ble

en·shrine
  en·shrine·ment

en·shroud

en·sign

en·slave
  en·slave·ment
  en·slav·er

en·snare
  en·snare·ment

en·sue

en·sure

en·tail
  en·tail·ment

en·tan·gle
  en·tan·gle·ment

en·tente

en·ter

en·ter·prise

en·ter·pris·ing
  en·ter·pris·ing·ly

en·ter·tain
  en·ter·tain·er
  en·ter·tain·ing

en·ter·tain·ment

en·thrall
  en·thrall·ment

en·throne
  en·throne·ment

en·thuse

en·thu·si·asm
  en·thu·si·ast
  en·thu·si·as·tic
  en·thu·si·as·ti·cal·ly

en·tice
  en·tice·ment
  en·tic·er
  en·tic·ing·ly

en·tire

en·tire·ly

en·tire·ty
  pl. en·tire·ties

en·ti·tle
  en·ti·tle·ment

en·ti·ty
  pl. en·ti·ties

en·tomb
  en·tomb·ment

en·to·mol·o·gy
  en·to·mo·log·i·cal
  en·to·mol·o·gist

en·tou·rage

en·trails

en·trance
  en·trance·ment
  en·tranc·ing
  en·tranc·ing·ly

en·trant

en·trap
  en·trapped, en·trap·
    ping
  en·trap·per

en·trap·ment

en·treat
  en·treat·ing·ly
  en·treat·y
  pl. en·treat·ies

en·trée
  also en·tree

en·trench
  en·trench·ment

en·tre·pre·neur
  en·tre·pre·neur·i·al
  en·tre·pre·neur·i·al·ly
  en·tre·pre·neur·ship

en·tro·py
  en·tro·pic
  en·tro·pi·cal·ly

en·trust
  en·trust·ment

en·try
  pl. en·tries

en·twine

e·nu·mer·ate
  e·nu·mer·a·ble
  e·nu·mer·a·tion
  e·nu·mer·a·tive
  e·nu·mer·a·tor

e·nun·ci·ate
  e·nun·ci·a·tion
  e·nun·ci·a·tive
  e·nun·ci·a·tor

en·u·re·sis

en·vel·op (*to surround*)
  en·vel·op·ment

en·ve·lope (*paper covering*)

En·ver Pa·sha

en·vi·a·ble
en·vi·a·bly

en·vi·ous
en·vi·ous·ly

en·vi·ron·ment
en·vi·ron·men·tal
en·vi·ron·men·tal·ly

en·vi·ron·men·tal·ist
en·vi·ron·men·tal·ism

en·vi·rons

en·vis·age

en·vi·sion

en·voy
en·voy·ship

en·vy
pl. en·vies
en·vies, en·vied
en·vi·er

en·wrap
en·wrapped, en·wrap·ping

en·zyme
en·zy·mat·ic

e·on
also ae·on

e·o·sin

ep·au·let
also ep·au·lette

é·pée
é·pée·ist

e·phem·er·al
e·phem·er·al·i·ty
e·phem·er·al·ly

ep·ic
ep·i·cal
ep·i·cal·ly

ep·i·cene

ep·i·cen·ter
ep·i·cen·tral

ep·i·cure

Ep·i·cu·re·an
also ep·i·cu·re·an
Ep·i·cu·re·an·ism

E·pi·cu·rus

ep·i·dem·ic
ep·i·dem·i·cal·ly

ep·i·de·mi·ol·o·gy
ep·i·de·mi·o·log·i·cal
ep·i·de·mi·ol·o·gist

ep·i·der·mis
ep·i·der·mal
ep·i·der·mic
ep·i·der·moid

ep·i·du·ral

ep·i·glot·tis
ep·i·glot·tal
ep·i·glot·tic

ep·i·gram
ep·i·gram·mat·ic
ep·i·gram·mat·i·cal·ly
ep·i·gram·ma·tist
ep·i·gram·ma·tize

ep·i·graph
ep·i·graph·ic
ep·i·graph·i·cal
e·pig·ra·phy

ep·i·lep·sy

ep·i·lep·tic

ep·i·logue
also ep·i·log

ep·i·neph·rine
also ep·i·neph·rin

e·piph·a·ny
pl. e·piph·a·nies
also E·piph·a·ny
ep·i·phan·ic

ep·i·phyte
ep·i·phyt·ic

e·pis·co·pa·cy
pl. e·pis·co·pa·cies

e·pis·co·pal
e·pis·co·pal·ism

E·pis·co·pa·lian
E·pis·co·pa·lian·ism

e·pis·co·pate

e·pi·si·ot·o·my
pl. e·pi·si·ot·o·mies

ep·i·sode
ep·i·sod·ic
ep·i·sod·i·cal·ly

e·pis·tle
also E·pis·tle

e·pis·to·lar·y

ep·i·taph

ep·i·the·li·um
pl. ep·i·the·li·a *or* ep·i·the·li·ums
ep·i·the·li·al

ep·i·thet
ep·i·thet·ic
ep·i·thet·i·cal
ep·i·thet·i·cal·ly

e·pit·o·me

e·pit·o·mize
e·pit·o·mi·za·tion

ep·och
ep·och·al

ep·ode

ep·o·nym

ep·ox·y

ep·si·lon

Ep·som

eq·ua·ble
eq·ua·bil·i·ty
eq·ua·bly

e·qual
e·qual·i·ty
e·qual·ly

e·qual·ize
  e·qual·i·za·tion

e·qua·nim·i·ty

e·quate
  e·quat·a·ble

e·qua·tion
  e·qua·tion·al

e·qua·tor
  e·qua·to·ri·al

E·qua·to·ri·al Guin·ea

e·ques·tri·an
  fem. e·ques·tri·enne
  e·ques·tri·an·ism

e·qui·dis·tant
  e·qui·dis·tant·ly

e·qui·lat·er·al

e·qui·lib·ri·um
  pl. e·qui·lib·ri·ums *or*
  e·qui·lib·ri·a

e·quine

e·qui·nox
  e·qui·noc·tial

e·quip
  e·quipped, e·quip·ping
  e·quip·per

e·quip·ment

e·qui·poise

eq·ui·ta·ble
  eq·ui·ta·bly

eq·ui·ta·tion

eq·ui·ty
  pl. eq·ui·ties

e·quiv·a·lent
  e·quiv·a·lence
  e·quiv·a·len·cy
  e·quiv·a·lent·ly

e·quiv·o·cal
  e·quiv·o·cal·i·ty
  e·quiv·o·cal·ly

e·quiv·o·cate
  e·quiv·o·ca·cy
  e·quiv·o·ca·tion
  e·quiv·o·ca·tor
  e·quiv·o·ca·to·ry

e·ra

e·rad·i·cate
  e·rad·i·ca·ble
  e·rad·i·ca·tion
  e·rad·i·ca·tor

e·rase
  e·ras·a·ble
  e·ra·sure

e·ras·er

E·ras·mus

er·bi·um

ere (*before*; see AIR, HEIR)

e·rect
  e·rect·a·ble
  e·rec·tion
  e·rect·ly
  e·rect·ness
  e·rec·tor

e·rec·tile

Er·furt

erg

er·go

er·go·nom·ics
  er·go·nom·ic
  er·gon·o·mist

er·got

E·rie

Er·in

Er·i·tre·a

er·mine
  pl. same *or* er·mines

erne
  also ern

Ernst

e·rode
  e·rod·i·ble

e·rog·e·nous

e·ro·sion
  e·ro·sive

e·rot·ic
  e·rot·i·cal·ly

e·rot·i·ca

e·rot·i·cism

err

er·rand

er·rant
  er·ran·cy
  er·rant·ry

er·rat·ic
  er·rat·i·cal·ly

er·ra·tum
  pl. er·ra·ta

er·ro·ne·ous
  er·ro·ne·ous·ly
  er·ro·ne·ous·ness

er·ror
  er·ror·less

er·satz

Erse

erst·while

e·ruc·ta·tion

er·u·dite
  er·u·dite·ly
  er·u·di·tion

e·rupt (*break out, eject
  lava;* see IRRUPT)
  e·rup·tion
  e·rup·tive

e·ryth·ro·cyte

es·ca·late
  es·ca·la·tion

es·ca·la·tor

es·ca·pade

es·cape
  es·cap·er

es·cap·ee

es·cape·ment

es·cap·ism
  es·cap·ist

es·car·got

es·ca·role

es·carp·ment
  also es·carp

es·cheat

es·chew
  es·chew·al

Es·con·di·do

es·cort

es·cri·toire

es·crow

es·cutch·eon
  es·cutch·eoned

Es·fa·han
  also Is·fa·han

e·soph·a·gus
  pl. e·soph·a·gi
  e·soph·a·ge·al

es·o·ter·ic
  es·o·ter·i·cal
  es·o·ter·i·cal·ly
  es·o·ter·i·cism
  es·o·ter·i·cist

es·pa·drille

es·pal·ier

es·pe·cial

es·pe·cial·ly

Es·pe·ran·to

es·pi·o·nage

es·pla·nade

es·pous·al

es·pouse
  es·pous·er

es·pres·so
  also ex·pres·so
  pl. es·pres·sos

es·prit

es·sprit de corps

es·py
  es·pies, es·pied

es·quire

es·say
  es·say·ist

Es·sen

es·sence

es·sen·tial
  es·sen·ti·al·i·ty
  es·sen·tial·ly
  es·sen·tial·ness

es·tab·lish

es·tab·lish·ment

es·tate

es·teem

es·ter

es·ti·ma·ble
  es·ti·ma·bly

es·ti·mate
  es·ti·ma·tion
  es·ti·ma·tor

Es·to·ni·a
  Es·to·ni·an

es·top
  es·topped, es·top·ping

es·trange
  es·trange·ment

es·tro·gen

es·trus
  es·trous

es·tu·ar·y
  pl. es·tu·ar·ies

e·ta

et·cet·er·a

etch
  etch·er

etch·ing

e·ter·nal
  e·ter·nal·ly

e·ter·ni·ty
  pl. e·ter·ni·ties

eth·ane

eth·a·nol

Eth·el·red

e·ther
  e·ther·ic

e·the·re·al
  e·the·re·al·ly

eth·ic

eth·i·cal
  eth·i·cal·ly

eth·ics
  eth·i·cist

E·thi·o·pi·a
  E·thi·o·pi·an

eth·nic
  eth·ni·cal·ly
  eth·nic·i·ty

eth·no·cen·tric
  eth·no·cen·tri·cal·ly
  eth·no·cen·tric·i·ty
  eth·no·cen·trism

eth·nol·o·gy
  eth·no·log·ic
  eth·no·log·i·cal
  eth·nol·o·gist

e·thos

eth·yl

eth·yl·ene

e·ti·ol·o·gy
  e·ti·o·log·ic
  e·ti·o·log·i·cal
  e·ti·o·log·i·cal·ly

et·i·quette

Et·na, Mount
  also Aet·na

E·trus·can

é·tude

e·tui

et·y·mol·o·gy
  pl. et·y·mol·o·gies
  et·y·mo·log·i·cal
  et·y·mo·log·i·cal·ly
  et·y·mol·o·gist

eu·ca·lyp·tus
  pl. eu·ca·lyp·ti *or* eu·
  ca·lyp·tus·es

Eu·cha·rist
  Eu·cha·ris·tic

eu·chre

Eu·clid

eu·clid·e·an
  also Eu·clid·e·an

Eu·gene

eu·gen·ics
  eu·gen·ic
  eu·gen·i·cal·ly
  eu·gen·i·cist
  eu·ge·nist

Eu·gé·nie

eu·kar·y·ote
  eu·kar·y·ot·ic

eu·lo·gize
  eu·lo·gist
  eu·lo·gis·tic
  eu·lo·gis·ti·cal·ly

eu·lo·gy
  pl. eu·lo·gies

eu·nuch

eu·phe·mism
  eu·phe·mist
  eu·phe·mis·tic
  eu·phe·mis·ti·cal·ly
  eu·phe·mize

eu·pho·ny
  pl. eu·pho·nies
  eu·phon·ic
  eu·pho·ni·ous
  eu·pho·ni·ous·ly

eu·pho·ri·a
  eu·phor·ic
  eu·phor·i·cal·ly

Eu·phra·tes

Eur·a·sian

eu·re·ka

Eu·rip·i·des

Eu·rope

Eu·ro·pe·an

eu·ro·pi·um

Eu·sta·chian tube

eu·tha·na·sia

e·vac·u·ate
  e·vac·u·ant
  e·vac·u·a·tion
  e·vac·u·a·tor

e·vade
  e·vad·a·ble
  e·vad·er

e·val·u·ate
  e·val·u·a·tion
  e·val·u·a·tive
  e·val·u·a·tor

ev·a·nes·cent
  ev·a·nes·cence
  ev·a·nes·cent·ly

e·van·gel·i·cal
  e·van·gel·i·cal·ism
  e·van·gel·i·cal·ly

e·van·ge·list
  e·van·ge·lism
  e·van·ge·lis·tic

e·van·ge·lize
  e·van·ge·li·za·tion
  e·van·ge·liz·er

Ev·ans

Ev·ans·ton

Ev·ans·ville

e·vap·o·rate
  e·vap·o·ra·ble
  e·vap·o·ra·tion
  e·vap·o·ra·tive
  e·vap·o·ra·tor

e·va·sion

e·va·sive
  e·va·sive·ly
  e·va·sive·ness

Eve (*proper name*)

eve (*evening*)

e·ven
  e·ven·er, e·ven·est
  e·ven·ly

e·ven·hand·ed
  e·ven·hand·ed·ly
  e·ven·hand·ed·ness

eve·ning

e·ven·song

e·vent

e·vent·ful
  e·vent·ful·ly
  e·vent·ful·ness

e·ven·tide

e·ven·tu·al
  e·ven·tu·al·ly

e·ven·tu·al·i·ty
  pl. e·ven·tu·al·i·ties

e·ven·tu·ate
  e·ven·tu·a·tion

ev·er

Ev·er·est, Mount

Ev·er·glades

ev·er·green

ev·er·last·ing
ev·er·last·ing·ly

ev·er·more

e·vert
e·ver·sion

eve·ry

eve·ry·bod·y

eve·ry·day

eve·ry·one

eve·ry·thing

eve·ry·where

e·vict
e·vic·tion
e·vic·tor

ev·i·dence

ev·i·dent

ev·i·dent·ly

e·vil
e·vil·ly
e·vil·ness

e·vil·do·er
e·vil·do·ing

e·vince
e·vin·ci·ble
e·vin·cive

e·vis·cer·ate
e·vis·cer·a·tion

ev·o·ca·tive
e·voc·a·tive·ly
e·voc·a·tive·ness

e·voke
ev·o·ca·tion
e·vok·er

ev·o·lu·tion
ev·o·lu·tion·ar·y

ev·o·lu·tion·ist
ev·o·lu·tion·ism
ev·o·lu·tion·is·tic

e·volve
e·volv·a·ble
e·volve·ment

ewe (*animal*; see YEW, YOU)

ew·er

ex

ex·ac·er·bate
ex·ac·er·ba·tion

ex·act
ex·ac·ti·tude
ex·act·ness
ex·ac·tor

ex·act·ing
ex·act·ing·ly
ex·act·ing·ness

ex·ac·tion

ex·act·ly

ex·ag·ger·ate
ex·ag·ger·at·ed·ly
ex·ag·ger·at·ing·ly
ex·ag·ger·a·tion
ex·ag·ger·a·tor

ex·alt
ex·al·ta·tion
ex·alt·ed·ly
ex·alt·ed·ness
ex·alt·er

ex·am

ex·am·i·na·tion

ex·am·ine
ex·am·in·a·ble
ex·am·i·nee
ex·am·in·er

ex·am·ple

ex·as·per·ate
ex·as·per·at·ing·ly
ex·as·per·a·tion

ex ca·the·dra

ex·ca·vate
ex·ca·va·tion
ex·ca·va·tor

ex·ceed

ex·ceed·ing·ly

ex·cel
ex·celled, ex·cel·ling

ex·cel·lence

Ex·cel·len·cy
pl. Ex·cel·len·cies

ex·cel·lent
ex·cel·lent·ly

ex·cel·si·or

ex·cept

ex·cept·ing

ex·cep·tion

ex·cep·tion·a·ble
ex·cep·tion·a·bly

ex·cep·tion·al
ex·cep·tion·al·ly

ex·cerpt
ex·cerpt·i·ble
ex·cerp·tion

ex·cess
ex·ces·sive
ex·ces·sive·ly
ex·ces·sive·ness

ex·change
ex·change·a·ble
ex·change·a·bil·i·ty
ex·chang·er

ex·cheq·uer

ex·cise
ex·ci·sion

ex·cit·a·ble
ex·cit·a·bil·i·ty
ex·cit·a·bly

ex·cite
ex·cit·ant
ex·ci·ta·tion
ex·cit·ed·ly
ex·cit·ed·ness
ex·cite·ment

ex·cit·ing
  ex·cit·ing·ly

ex·claim

ex·cla·ma·tion

ex·clam·a·to·ry

ex·clude
  ex·clud·a·ble
  ex·clud·er
  ex·clu·sion

ex·clu·sive
  ex·clu·sive·ly
  ex·clu·sive·ness
  ex·clu·siv·i·ty

ex·com·mu·ni·cate
  ex·com·mu·ni·ca·tion
  ex·com·mu·ni·ca·tor

ex-con

ex·co·ri·ate
  ex·co·ri·a·tion

ex·cre·ment
  ex·cre·men·tal

ex·cres·cence
  ex·cres·cent

ex·cre·ta

ex·crete
  ex·cre·tion
  ex·cre·tive
  ex·cre·to·ry

ex·cru·ci·ate
  ex·cru·ci·at·ing·ly

ex·cul·pate
  ex·cul·pa·tion
  ex·cul·pa·to·ry

ex·cur·sion
  ex·cur·sion·al
  ex·cur·sion·ar·y
  ex·cur·sion·ist

ex·cur·sive
  ex·cur·sive·ly
  ex·cur·sive·ness

ex·cuse
  ex·cus·a·ble
  ex·cus·a·bly

ex·e·cra·ble
  ex·e·cra·bly

ex·e·crate
  ex·e·cra·tion
  ex·e·cra·tive
  ex·e·cra·to·ry

ex·e·cute
  ex·e·cut·a·ble
  ex·e·cu·tion

ex·e·cu·tion·er

ex·ec·u·tive
  ex·ec·u·tive·ly

ex·ec·u·tor
  fem. ex·ec·u·trix , *pl.*
    ex·ec·u·tri·ces *or* ex·
    ec·u·trix·es
  ex·ec·u·to·ri·al

ex·e·ge·sis
  pl. ex·e·ge·ses
  ex·e·gete
  ex·e·get·ic
  ex·e·get·i·cal

ex·em·plar

ex·em·pla·ry
  ex·em·pla·ri·ness

ex·em·pli·fy
  ex·em·pli·fies, ex·em·
    pli·fied
  ex·em·pli·fi·ca·tion

ex·empt
  ex·emp·tion

ex·er·cise
  ex·er·cis·er

ex·ert
  ex·er·tion

ex·hale
  ex·ha·la·tion

ex·haust
  ex·haust·i·ble
  ex·haust·i·bil·i·ty
  ex·haus·ti·bly

ex·haus·tion

ex·haus·tive
  ex·haus·tive·ly
  ex·haus·tive·ness

ex·hib·it
  ex·hib·i·tor

ex·hi·bi·tion

ex·hi·bi·tion·ism
  ex·hi·bi·tion·ist
  ex·hi·bi·tion·is·tic
  ex·hi·bi·tion·is·ti·cal·
    ly

ex·hil·a·rate
  ex·hil·a·rant
  ex·hil·a·rat·ing·ly
  ex·hil·a·ra·tion
  ex·hil·a·ra·tive

ex·hort
  ex·hor·ta·tion
  ex·hort·a·tive
  ex·hort·a·to·ry
  ex·hort·er

ex·hume
  ex·hu·ma·tion

ex·i·gen·cy
  pl. ex·i·gen·cies
  also ex·i·gence
  ex·i·gent

ex·ig·u·ous
  ex·i·gu·i·ty
  ex·ig·u·ous·ly
  ex·ig·u·ous·ness

ex·ile

ex·ist

ex·is·tence
  ex·ist·ent

ex·is·ten·tial
  ex·is·ten·tial·ly

ex·is·ten·tial·ism
  ex·is·ten·tial·ist

ex·it

ex·o·dus
  also Ex·o·dus

ex of·fi·cio

ex·on·er·ate
  ex·on·er·a·tion
  ex·on·er·a·tive

ex·or·bi·tant
  ex·or·bi·tance
  ex·or·bi·tant·ly

ex·or·cize
  ex·or·cism
  ex·or·cist

ex·o·skel·e·ton
  ex·o·skel·e·tal

ex·o·sphere

ex·o·ter·ic

ex·ot·ic
  ex·ot·i·cal·ly
  ex·ot·i·cism

ex·pand
  ex·pand·a·ble
  ex·pand·er
  ex·pan·si·ble
  ex·pan·si·bil·i·ty

ex·panse

ex·pan·sion
  ex·pan·sion·ism
  ex·pan·sion·ist
  ex·pan·sion·is·tic

ex·pan·sive
  ex·pan·sive·ly
  ex·pan·sive·ness

ex·pa·ti·ate
  ex·pa·ti·a·tion
  ex·pa·ti·a·to·ry

ex·pa·tri·ate
  ex·pa·tri·a·tion

ex·pect

ex·pec·tan·cy
  pl. ex·pec·tan·cies

ex·pec·tant
  ex·pec·tant·ly

ex·pec·ta·tion

ex·pec·to·rant

ex·pec·to·rate
  ex·pec·to·ra·tion
  ex·pec·to·ra·tor

ex·pe·di·ent
  ex·pe·di·ence
  ex·pe·di·en·cy
  ex·pe·di·ent·ly

ex·pe·dite
  ex·pe·dit·er

ex·pe·di·tion
  ex·pe·di·tion·ar·y
  ex·pe·di·tion·ist

ex·pe·di·tious
  ex·pe·di·tious·ly
  ex·pe·di·tious·ness

ex·pel
  ex·pelled, ex·pel·ling
  ex·pel·la·ble
  ex·pel·lee
  ex·pel·ler

ex·pend

ex·pend·a·ble
  ex·pend·a·bil·i·ty
  ex·pend·a·bly

ex·pen·di·ture

ex·pense

ex·pen·sive
  ex·pen·sive·ly

ex·pe·ri·ence
  ex·pe·ri·en·tial

ex·pe·ri·enced

ex·per·i·ment
  ex·per·i·men·ta·tion
  ex·per·i·ment·er

ex·per·i·men·tal
  ex·per·i·men·tal·ism
  ex·per·i·men·tal·ist
  ex·per·i·men·tal·ly

ex·pert
  ex·pert·ly
  ex·pert·ness

ex·per·tise

ex·pi·ate
  ex·pi·a·ble
  ex·pi·a·to·ry
  ex·pi·a·tion
  ex·pi·a·tor

ex·pire
  ex·pi·ra·tion
  ex·pi·ra·to·ry
  ex·pi·ry

ex·plain
  ex·plain·a·ble
  ex·plain·er

ex·pla·na·tion

ex·plan·a·tory

ex·ple·tive

ex·pli·ca·ble

ex·pli·cate
  ex·pli·ca·tion
  ex·pli·ca·tive
  ex·pli·ca·tor
  ex·pli·ca·to·ry

ex·plic·it
  ex·plic·it·ly
  ex·plic·it·ness

ex·plode
  ex·plod·er

ex·ploit
  ex·ploi·ta·tion
  ex·ploit·a·tive
  ex·ploit·er
  ex·ploit·ive

ex·plore
  ex·plo·ra·tion
  ex·plor·a·tive
  ex·plor·a·to·ry
  ex·plor·er

ex·plo·sion

ex·plo·sive
  ex·plo·sive·ly
  ex·plo·sive·ness

ex·po·nent

ex·po·nen·tial
ex·po·nen·tial·ly

ex·port
ex·port·a·ble
ex·port·a·bil·i·ty
ex·por·ta·tion
ex·port·er

ex·pose
ex·pos·er

ex·po·sé

ex·po·si·tion
ex·po·si·tion·al

ex post fac·to

ex·pos·tu·late
ex·pos·tu·la·tion

ex·po·sure

ex·pound
ex·pound·er

ex·press
ex·press·er
ex·press·i·ble
ex·press·ly

ex·pres·sion
ex·pres·sion·less
ex·pres·sion·less·ly

ex·pres·sion·ism
ex·pres·sion·ist
ex·pres·sion·is·tic
ex·pres·sion·is·ti·cal·ly

ex·pres·sive
ex·pres·sive·ly
ex·pres·sive·ness
ex·pres·siv·i·ty

ex·press·way

ex·pro·pri·ate
ex·pro·pri·a·tion
ex·pro·pri·a·tor

ex·pul·sion
ex·pul·sive

ex·punge
ex·punc·tion
ex·pung·er

ex·pur·gate
ex·pur·ga·tion
ex·pur·ga·tor

ex·qui·site
ex·quis·ite·ly
ex·quis·ite·ness

ex·tant

ex·tem·po·ra·ne·ous
ex·tem·po·ra·ne·ous·ly

ex·tem·po·re

ex·tem·po·rize
ex·tem·po·ri·za·tion

ex·tend
ex·tend·a·ble
ex·tend·a·bil·i·ty
ex·tend·ible
ex·tend·i·bil·i·ty
ex·ten·si·ble
ex·ten·si·bil·i·ty

ex·ten·sion
ex·ten·sion·al

ex·ten·sive
ex·ten·sive·ly
ex·ten·sive·ness

ex·ten·sor

ex·tent

ex·ten·u·ate
ex·ten·u·a·tion

ex·te·ri·or

ex·ter·mi·nate
ex·ter·mi·na·tion
ex·ter·mi·na·tor

ex·ter·nal
ex·ter·nal·ly

ex·ter·nal·ize
ex·ter·nal·i·za·tion

ex·tinct

ex·tinc·tion

ex·tin·guish
ex·tin·guish·a·ble
ex·tin·guish·er

ex·tir·pate
ex·tir·pa·tion
ex·tir·pa·tor

ex·tol
ex·tolled, ex·tol·ling
ex·tol·ler
ex·tol·ment

ex·tort

ex·tor·tion
ex·tor·tion·ate
ex·tor·tion·er
ex·tor·tion·ist

ex·tra

ex·tract
ex·tract·a·ble
ex·tract·a·bil·i·ty

ex·trac·tion

ex·tra·cur·ric·u·lar

ex·tra·dite
ex·tra·di·tion

ex·tra·mar·i·tal
ex·tra·mar·i·tal·ly

ex·tra·ne·ous
ex·tra·ne·ous·ly
ex·tra·ne·ous·ness

ex·tra·or·di·nar·y
ex·tra·or·di·nar·i·ly

ex·trap·o·late
ex·trap·o·la·tion
ex·trap·o·la·tor

ex·tra·sen·so·ry

ex·tra·ter·res·tri·al

ex·trav·a·gant
ex·trav·a·gance
ex·trav·a·gant·ly

ex·trav·a·gan·za

ex·treme
  ex·treme·ly
  ex·treme·ness

ex·trem·ist
  ex·trem·ism

ex·trem·i·ty
  pl. ex·trem·i·ties

ex·tri·cate
  ex·tri·ca·ble
  ex·tri·ca·tion

ex·trin·sic
  ex·trin·si·cal·ly

ex·tro·vert
  ex·tro·ver·sion
  ex·tro·vert·ed

ex·trude
  ex·tru·sion
  ex·tru·sive

ex·u·ber·ant
  ex·u·ber·ance
  ex·u·ber·ant·ly

ex·ude
  ex·u·date
  ex·u·da·tion
  ex·u·da·tive

ex·ult
  ex·ul·ta·tion
  ex·ult·ant
  ex·ult·ant·ly

ex·urb
  ex·ur·ban
  ex·ur·ban·ite

ex·ur·bi·a

eye (*organ of sight*; see
  AYE)
  eyes, eyed, eye·ing *or*
  ey·ing
  eye-catch·ing
  eye-o·pen·er

eye·ball

eye·brow

eye·ful
  pl. eye·fuls

eye·glass

eye·lash

eye·let (*small hole*; see
  ISLET)

eye·lid

eye·lin·er

eye·piece

eye·sight

eye·sore

eye·tooth

eye·wash

eye·wit·ness

ey·rie
  var. of aer·ie

F

fa

Fa·ber·gé

fa·ble
fa·bler

fab·ric

fab·ri·cate
fab·ri·ca·tor

fab·ri·ca·tion

fab·u·lous
fab·u·lous·ly
fab·u·lous·ness

fa·çade

face
face-lift
 also face-lift·ing
faced
fac·ing

face·less
face·less·ly
face·less·ness

fac·et
fac·et·ed

fa·ce·tious
fa·ce·tious·ly
fa·ce·tious·ness

fa·cial
fa·cial·ly

fa·cile
fac·ile·ly
fac·ile·ness

fa·cil·i·tate
fa·cil·i·ta·tion
fa·cil·i·ta·tive
fa·cil·i·ta·tor

fa·cil·i·ty
 pl. fa·cil·i·ties

fac·ing

fac·sim·i·le

fact

fac·tion

fac·tious
fac·tious·ly
fac·tious·ness

fac·ti·tious
fac·ti·tious·ly
fac·ti·tious·ness

fac·toid

fac·tor
fac·tor·a·ble

fac·to·ri·al
fac·to·ri·al·ly

fac·to·ry
 pl. fac·to·ries

fac·to·tum

fac·tu·al
fac·tu·al·i·ty
fac·tu·al·ly

fac·ul·ty
 pl. fac·ul·ties

fad
fad·dish
fad·dish·ly
fad·dist

fade
fade·less
fad·er

Faer·oe Is·lands

fag·got (derogatory term
 for homosexual; see
 FAGOT)

fag·ot (bundle of sticks;
 see FAGGOT)

Fahd

Fahr·en·heit

fa·ience

fail
fail-safe

fail·ing

fail·ure

fain (willing; see FEIGN)

faint (weak, giddy; see
 FEINT)
faint-heart·ed
faint·ly
faint·ness

fair (equitable, bazaar;
 see FARE)
fair·ish
fair·ness

Fair·banks

Fair·field

fair·ing

fair·ly

fair·way

fair·y (imaginary being;
 see FERRY)
 pl. fair·ies
fairy·like

Fai·sa·la·bad

fait ac·com·pli

faith

faith·ful
faith·ful·ly
faith·ful·ness

faith·less
faith·less·ly
faith·less·ness

fa·ji·tas

fake
fak·er
fak·er·y

fal·con

Falk·land Is·lands

fall
past fell; *past part.* fall·en

Fal·la

fal·la·cy
pl. fal·la·cies
fal·la·cious
fal·la·cious·ly

fal·li·ble
fal·li·bil·i·ty
fal·li·bly

Fal·lo·pi·an tube

fall·out

fal·low
fal·low·ness

false
false·ly
false·ness
fal·si·ty
pl. fal·si·ties

false·hood

fal·set·to
pl. fal·set·tos

fal·si·fy
fal·si·fies, fal·si·fied
fal·si·fi·a·ble
fal·si·fi·a·bil·i·ty
fal·si·fi·ca·tion

fal·ter
fal·ter·er
fal·ter·ing·ly

fame

famed

fa·mil·ial

fa·mil·iar
fa·mil·i·ar·i·ty
fa·mil·iar·ly

fa·mil·iar·ize
fa·mil·iar·i·za·tion

fam·i·ly
pl. fam·i·lies

fam·ine

fam·ish

fa·mous
fa·mous·ly
fa·mous·ness

fan *(device)*
fanned, fan·ning
fan·like
fan·ner

fan *(person)*
fan·dom

fa·nat·ic
fa·nat·i·cal
fa·nat·i·cal·ly
fa·nat·i·cism

fan·ci·er

fan·ci·ful
fan·ci·ful·ly
fan·ci·ful·ness

fan·cy
pl. fan·cies
fan·ci·er, fan·ci·est
fan·cies, fan·cied
fan·cy-free
fan·ci·ly
fan·ci·ness

fan·dan·go
pl. fan·dan·goes *or* fan·dan·gos

fan·fare

fang
fanged
fang·less

fan·ny
pl. fan·nies

fan·ta·size
fan·ta·sist

fan·tas·tic
also fan·tas·ti·cal
fan·tas·ti·cal·ly

fan·ta·sy
pl. fan·ta·sies

far
far·ther, far·thest *or* fur·ther, fur·thest
far-fetched
far-flung

far·ad

Far·a·day

far·a·way

farce

far·ci·cal
far·ci·cal·i·ty
far·ci·cal·ly

fare *(price, food, to get on; see* FAIR*)*

fare·well

Far·go

fa·ri·na
far·i·na·ceous

farm
farm·a·ble
farm·er
farm·ing

farm·house

farm·land

far·o *(card game; see* PHARAOH*)*

Fa·rouk

far·ra·go
pl. far·ra·goes
far·rag·i·nous

Far·ra·gut

far·ri·er
far·ri·er·y

far·row

far·see·ing

far·sight·ed
far·sight·ed·ly
far·sight·ed·ness

fart

far·ther
also fur·ther
far·ther·most

far·thest
also furth·est

far·thing

fas·ces

fas·cia

fas·ci·nate
fas·ci·nat·ed
fas·ci·nat·ing
fas·ci·nat·ing·ly
fas·ci·na·tion
fas·ci·na·tor

Fas·cism
Fas·cist
also fas·cist
Fa·scis·tic
also fa·scis·tic

fash·ion
fash·ion·er

fash·ion·a·ble
fash·ion·a·bly

fast (*quick*)

fast (*refrain from eating*)
fast·er

fast·en
fas·ten·er

fast·en·ing

fas·tid·i·ous
fas·tid·i·ous·ly
fas·tid·i·ous·ness

fast·ness

fat
fat·ter, fat·test
fat·less
fat·ly
fat·ness
fat·tish

fa·tal
fa·tal·ly

fa·tal·ism
fa·tal·ist
fa·tal·is·tic
fa·tal·is·ti·cal·ly

fa·tal·i·ty
pl. fa·tal·i·ties

fate (*destiny*; see FÊTE)

fate·ful
fate·ful·ly
fate·ful·ness

fa·ther
fa·ther-in-law
pl. fa·thers-in-law
fa·ther·hood
fa·ther·less
fa·ther·like

fa·ther·land

fa·ther·ly
fa·ther·li·ness

fath·om
pl. fath·om *or* fath·oms
fath·om·a·ble
fath·om·less

fa·tigue
fa·tigues, fa·tigued, fa·tigu·ing
fat·i·ga·ble
fat·i·ga·bil·i·ty
fa·tigue·less

fat·ten

fat·ty
fat·ti·er, fat·ti·est
fat·ti·ly
fat·ti·ness

fat·u·ous
fa·tu·i·ty
pl. fa·tu·i·ties
fat·u·ous·ly
fat·u·ous·ness

fat·wa

fau·cet

Faulk·ner

fault

fault·find·ing

fault·less
fault·less·ly
fault·less·ness

fault·y
fault·i·er, fault·i·est
fault·i·ly
fault·i·ness

faun (*Roman deity*; see FAWN)

fau·na
pl. fau·nas *or* fau·nae
fau·nal
fau·nist
fau·nis·tic

Fau·ré

Faust
also Faus·tus

faux

faux pas
pl. same

fa·vor
fa·vor·er

fa·vor·a·ble
fa·vor·a·ble·ness
fa·vor·a·bly

fa·vor·ite

fa·vor·it·ism

fawn (*flatter*; see FAUN)
fawn·er
fawn·ing
fawn·ing·ly

fawn (*young deer*; see FAUN)

fax

Fay·ette·ville

faze (*disconcert*; see
    PHASE)

fe·al·ty
    pl. fe·al·ties

fear
    fear·less
    fear·less·ly
    fear·less·ness

fear·ful
    fear·ful·ly
    fear·ful·ness

fear·some
    fear·some·ly
    fear·some·ness

fea·si·ble
    fea·si·bil·i·ty
    fea·si·bly

feast
    feast·er

feat (*achievement*; see
    FEET)

feath·er
    feath·ered
    feath·er·less
    feath·er·y
    feath·er·i·ness

feath·er·bed·ding

feath·er·weight

fea·ture
    fea·tured
    fea·ture·less

fe·brile
    fe·bril·i·ty

Feb·ru·ar·y
    pl. Feb·ru·ar·ies

fe·ces
    fe·cal

feck·less
    feck·less·ly
    feck·less·ness

fe·cund
    fe·cun·di·ty

fed

fed·er·al
    fed·er·al·ism
    fed·er·al·ist
    fed·er·al·ize
    fed·er·al·i·za·tion
    fed·er·al·ly

fed·er·ate
    fed·er·a·tive

fed·er·a·tion
    fed·er·a·tion·ist

fe·do·ra

fee

fee·ble
    fee·ble·ness
    fee·blish
    fee·bly

fee·ble·mind·ed
    fee·ble·mind·ed·ly
    fee·ble·mind·ed·ness

feed
    past and *past part.* fed
    feed·a·ble
    feed·er

feed·back

feel
    past and *past part.* felt

feel·er

feel·ing
    feel·ing·less
    feel·ing·ly

feet (*plural of foot*; see
    FEAT)

feign (*to pretend*; see
    FAIN)

feint (*mock attack*; see
    FAINT)

feld·spar
    also fel·spar
    feld·spath·ic
    feld·spath·oid

fe·lic·i·tate
    fe·lic·i·ta·tion

fe·lic·i·tous
    fe·lic·i·tous·ly
    fe·lic·i·tous·ness

fe·lic·i·ty
    pl. fe·lic·i·ties

fe·line
    fe·lin·i·ty

fell
    fell·er

fel·low

fel·low·ship

fel·on

fe·lo·ni·ous
    fe·lo·ni·ous·ly

fel·o·ny
    pl. fel·o·nies

felt
    felt·y

fe·male
    fe·male·ness

fem·i·nine
    fem·i·nine·ly
    fem·i·nine·ness
    fem·i·nin·i·ty

fem·i·nism
    fem·i·nist

femme fa·tale
    pl. femmes fa·tales

fe·mur
    pl. fe·murs *or* fem·o·ra
    fem·o·ral

fen
    fen·ny

fence
    fence·less
    fenc·er

fenc·ing

fend

fend·er

fen·nel

fe·ral

Fer·ber

Fer·di·nand

fer·ment
  fer·ment·a·ble
  fer·ment·er

fer·men·ta·tion
  fer·men·ta·tive

Fer·mi

fer·mi·um

fern
  pl. same *or* ferns
  fern·er·y
  pl. fern·er·ies
  fern·less
  fern·y

fe·ro·cious
  fe·ro·cious·ly
  fe·ro·cious·ness

fe·roc·i·ty
  pl. fe·roc·i·ties

Fer·ra·ra

fer·ret
  fer·ret·er
  fer·ret·y

fer·ric

Fer·ris wheel

fer·rous

fer·rule

fer·ry (*ship*; see FAIRY)
  pl. fer·ries
  fer·ries, fer·ried
  fer·ry·man
  pl. fer·ry·men

fer·tile
  fer·til·i·ty

fer·til·ize
  fer·ti·liz·a·ble
  fer·ti·li·za·tion

fer·til·iz·er

fer·vent
  fer·ven·cy
  fer·vent·ly

fer·vid
  fer·vid·ly

fer·vor

fes·tal
  fes·tal·ly

fes·ter

fes·ti·val

fes·tive
  fes·tive·ly
  fes·tive·ness

fes·tiv·i·ty
  pl. fes·tiv·i·ties

fes·toon
  fes·toon·er·y

fet·a

fetch
  fetch·er

fetch·ing
  fetch·ing·ly

fête (*celebration*; see
  FATE)

fet·id
  also foet·id
  fet·id·ly
  fet·id·ness

fe·tish
  fet·ish·ism
  fet·ish·ist
  fet·ish·is·tic

fet·lock

fet·ter

fet·tle

fe·tus
  fe·tal

feud

feu·dal
  feu·dal·ism
  feu·dal·ist
  feu·dal·is·tic
  feu·dal·ly

fe·ver
  fe·vered

fe·ver·ish
  fe·ver·ish·ly
  fe·ver·ish·ness

few

fey
  fey·ly
  fey·ness

Fez (*city*)
  also Fès

fez (*hat*)
  pl. fez·zes
  fezzed

fi·an·cé
  fem. fi·an·cée

fi·as·co
  pl. fi·as·cos

fi·at

fib
  fibbed, fib·bing
  fib·ber
  fib·ster

fi·ber
  fi·bered
  fi·ber·less
  fi·bri·form

fi·ber·board

fi·ber·glass

fi·bril
  fi·bril·lar
  fi·bril·lar·y

fi·broid

fi·bro·sis
  fi·brot·ic

fib·u·la
  pl. fib·u·lae *or* fib·u·las
  fib·u·lar

fiche
  pl. same *or* fich·es

fick·le
fick·le·ness
fick·ly

fic·tion
fic·tion·al
fic·tion·al·ize
fic·tion·al·i·za·tion
fic·tion·al·ly

fic·ti·tious
fic·ti·tious·ly
fic·ti·tious·ness

fid·dle

fid·dler

fid·dle·stick

fi·del·i·ty

fid·get
fid·get·y
fidg·et·i·ness

fi·du·ci·ar·y
pl. fi·du·ci·ar·ies

fie

Fied·ler

fief

fief·dom

field

field·er

Field·ing

Fields

field·work
field·work·er

fiend
fiend·ish
fiend·ish·ly
fiend·ish·ness
fiend·like

fierce
fierc·er, fierc·est
fierce·ly
fierce·ness

fi·er·y
fi·er·i·er, fi·er·i·est
fi·er·i·ly
fi·er·i·ness

fi·es·ta

fife
fif·er

fif·teen
fif·teenth

fifth
fifth·ly

fif·ty
pl. fif·ties
fif·ty-fif·ty
fif·ti·eth

fig

fight
past and past part.
fought

fight·er

fig·ment

fig·u·ra·tive
fig·u·ra·tive·ly
fig·ur·a·tive·ness

fig·ure
fig·ure·less

fig·ure·head

fig·u·rine

Fi·ji
Fi·ji·an

fil·a·ment
fil·a·men·ta·ry
fil·a·ment·ed
fil·a·men·tous

fil·bert

filch
filch·er

file (folder; see PHIAL)
fil·er

fi·let
var. of fil·let

fi·let mi·gnon
pl. fi·lets mi·gnons

fil·i·al
fil·i·al·ly

fil·i·bus·ter

fil·i·gree
also fil·a·gree
fil·i·greed

fil·ing

Fil·i·pi·no
pl. Fil·i·pi·nos; fem.
Fil·i·pi·na, pl. Fil·i·
pi·nas

fill

fill·er

fil·let
also fi·let
fil·let·er

fill·ing

fil·lip
fil·liped, fil·lip·ing

Fill·more

fil·ly
pl. fil·lies

film

film·mak·er

film·strip

film·y
film·i·er, film·i·est
film·i·ly
film·i·ness

fil·ter (strainer, to purify;
see PHILTER)

filth
filth·i·ly
filth·i·ness
filth·y
filth·i·er, filth·i·est

fil·trate
fil·tra·tion

fin
fin·less
finned

fi·na·gle
fi·na·gler

fi·nal
fi·nal·ly

fi·na·le

fi·nal·ist

fi·nal·i·ty
pl. fi·nal·i·ties

fi·na·lize
fi·na·li·za·tion

fi·nance
fi·nan·cial
fi·nan·cial·ly

fi·nan·cier

finch

find
past and *past part.* found
find·a·ble

find·ing

fine (*excellent, thin, sharp*)
fine-tune
fine·ly
fine·ness

fine (*money paid as penalty*)
fin·a·ble

fin·er·y

fi·nesse

fin·ger
fin·gered
fin·ger·less

fin·ger·ing

fin·ger·nail

fin·ger·print

fin·ger·tip

fin·i·al

fin·ick·y
fin·ick·i·ness

fi·nis

fin·ish
fin·ish·er

fi·nite
fi·nite·ly
fi·nite·ness
fin·i·tude

Fin·land
Finn
Finn·ish

fiord
var. of fjord

fir (*tree;* see FUR)
fir·ry

fire
fire·less
fir·er

fire·arm

fire·ball

fire·bomb

fire·brand

fire·break

fire·crack·er

fire·fight·er

fire·fly
pl. fire·flies

fire·man
pl. fire·men

fire·place

fire·plug

fire·proof

fire·side

fire·wa·ter

fire·wood

fire·work

fir·ing

firm
firm·ly
firm·ness

fir·ma·ment
fir·ma·men·tal

first
first-born
first-class
first-rate

first·hand

first·ly

firth
also frith

fis·cal
fis·cal·ly

fish
pl. same *or* fish·es
fish·like

fish·er·man
pl. fish·er·men

fish·er·y
pl. fish·er·ies

fish·hook

fish·ing

fish·net

fish·tail

fish·y
fish·i·er, fish·i·est
fish·i·ly
fish·i·ness

fis·sile
fis·sil·i·ty

fis·sion

fis·sure

fist
fist·ed
fist·ful
pl. fist·fuls

fist·i·cuffs

fis·tu·la
pl. fis·tu·las *or* fis·tu·lae
fis·tu·lar
fis·tu·lous

fit
fit•ter, fit•test
fit•ted, fit•ting
fit•ly
fit•ness
fit•ter

fit•ful
fit•ful•ly
fit•ful•ness

fit•ting
fit•ting•ly
fit•ting•ness

Fitz•ger•ald

five

fix
fix•a•ble
fix•ed•ly
fix•ed•ness
fix•er

fix•ate

fix•a•tion

fix•a•tive

fix•ings

fix•i•ty

fix•ture

fizz

fiz•zle

fizz•y
fizz•i•er, fizz•i•est
fizz•i•ly
fizz•i•ness

fjord
also fiord

flab

flab•ber•gast

flab•by
flab•bi•er, flab•bi•est
flab•bi•ly
flab•bi•ness

flac•cid
flac•cid•i•ty
flac•cid•ly

flag
flagged, flag•ging
flag•ger
flag•stone

flag•el•late
flag•el•la•tion
flag•el•la•tor

flag•el•lum
pl. fla•gel•la
fla•gel•lar
fla•gel•li•form

flag•on

flag•pole

fla•grant
fla•gran•cy
fla•grant•ly

flag•ship

flag•stone

flail

flair (talent; see FLARE)

flak
also flack

flake

flak•y
flak•i•er, flak•i•est
flak•i•ly
flak•i•ness

flam•boy•ant
flam•boy•ance
flam•boy•an•cy
flam•boy•ant•ly

flame
flame•less
flame•like

fla•men•co
pl. fla•men•cos

flame•proof

flame•throw•er

flam•ing

fla•min•go
pl. fla•min•gos or fla•min•goes

flam•ma•ble
flam•ma•bil•i•ty

flan

Flan•ders

flange
flange•less

flank

flan•nel
flan•nel•ly

flan•nel•ette

flap
flapped, flap•ping
flap•py

flap•jack

flap•per

flare (broaden, blaze; see FLAIR)
flare-up

flash

flash•back

flash•ing

flash•light

flash•y
flash•i•er, flash•i•est
flash•i•ly
flash•i•ness

flask

flat
flat•ter, flat•test
flat•ly
flat•ness
flat•tish

flat•fish

flat•foot
pl. flat•foots or flat•feet

flat·foot·ed
flat·-foot·ed·ly
flat·-foot·ed·ness

flat·i·ron

flat·ten
flat·ten·er

flat·ter
flat·ter·er
flat·ter·ing
flat·ter·ing·ly

flat·ter·y
pl. flat·ter·ies

flat·u·lent
flat·u·lence
flat·u·len·cy
flat·u·lent·ly

flat·ware

flat·worm

Flau·bert

flaunt
flaunt·er
flaunt·y

flau·tist

fla·vor
fla·vor·ful
fla·vor·less
fla·vor·some

fla·vor·ing

flaw
flawed
flaw·less
flaw·less·ly
flaw·less·ness

flax

flax·en

flay
flay·er

flea (*insect*; see FLEE)

fleck

fled

fledg·ling

flee (*to run away*; see
FLEA)
past and *past part.* fled
fle·er

fleece
fleece·a·ble
fleeced

fleec·y
fleec·i·er, fleec·i·est
fleec·i·ly
fleec·i·ness

fleet
fleet·ly
fleet·ness

fleet·ing
fleet·ing·ly

Flem·ing

Flem·ish

flesh
flesh·less

flesh·ly
flesh·li·er, flesh·li·est
flesh·li·ness

flesh·y
flesh·i·er, flesh·i·est
flesh·i·ness

Fletch·er

fleur-de-lis
also fleur-de-lys
pl. fleur-de-lis, fleurs-
de-lys

flew (*past of fly*; see FLU,
FLUE)

flex

flex·i·ble
flex·i·bil·i·ty
flex·i·bly

flex·or

flex·time
also flex·i·time

flick

flick·er

fli·er
also fly·er

flight

flight·less

flight·y
flight·i·er, flight·i·est
flight·i·ly
flight·i·ness

flim·sy
flims·i·er, flims·i·est
flim·si·ly
flim·si·ness

flinch
flinch·er
flinch·ing·ly

fling
past and *past part.* flung
fling·er

flint
flint·y
flint·i·er, flint·i·est
flint·i·ly
flint·i·ness

flip
flipped, flip·ping

flip-flop
flip-flopped, flip-flop·
ping

flip·pant
flip·pan·cy
flip·pant·ly

flip·per

flirt
flir·ta·tion
flir·ta·tious
flir·ta·tious·ly
flirt·y
flirt·i·er, flirt·i·est

flit
flit·ted, flit·ting
flit·ter

float
  float·a·ble
  float·a·bil·i·ty

float·ing
  float·ing·ly

floc·cu·lent
  floc·cu·lence

flock

floe (*floating ice*; see
  FLOW)

flog
  flogged, flog·ging
  flog·ger

flood

flood·gate

flood·light

flood·plain

flood·wa·ter

floor
  floor·less

floor·board

floor·ing

flop
  flopped, flop·ping

flop·py
  flop·pi·er, flop·pi·est
  pl. flop·pies
  flop·pi·ly
  flop·pi·ness

flo·ra
  pl. flo·ras *or* flo·rae

flo·ral
  flo·ral·ly

Flor·ence
  Italian Fi·ren·ze
  Flor·en·tine

flo·res·cence (*state of
  blooming*; see
  FLUORESCENCE)

flo·ri·cul·ture

flor·id
  flo·rid·i·ty
  flor·id·ly
  flor·id·ness

Flor·i·da
  Flo·rid·i·an

flor·in

flo·rist
  flo·ris·try

floss

floss·y
  floss·i·er, floss·i·est

flo·ta·tion
  also float·a·tion

flo·til·la

flot·sam

flounce

floun·der
  floun·der·er

flour (*ground grain*; see
  FLOWER)
  flour·y
  flour·i·er, flour·i·est
  flour·i·ness

flour·ish
  flour·ish·er
  flour·ish·y

flout

flow (*stream*; see FLOE)

flow·er (*bloom*; see
  FLOUR)
  flow·ered
  flow·er·less
  flow·er·like

flow·er·pot

flow·er·y
  flow·er·i·ness

flow·ing
  flow·ing·ly

flown

flu (*illness*; see FLEW,
  FLUE)

fluc·tu·ate
  fluc·tu·a·tion

flue (*vent*; see FLEW, FLU)

flu·ent
  flu·en·cy
  flu·ent·ly

fluff

fluff·y
  fluff·i·er, fluff·i·est
  fluff·i·ly
  fluff·i·ness

flu·gel·horn

flu·id
  flu·id·i·fy
  flu·id·i·fies, flu·id·i·
  fied
  flu·id·i·ty
  flu·id·ly
  flu·id·ness

fluke
  fluk·y
  fluk·i·er, fluk·i·est

flume

flum·mox

flung

flunk

flun·ky
  also flun·key
  pl. flun·kies *or* flun·keys

fluo·resce

fluo·res·cence (*light
  radiation*; see
  FLORESCENCE)

fluo·res·cent

fluor·i·date
  fluor·i·da·tion

fluor·ide

fluor·i·nate

fluor·ine

fluo·rite

fluor·o·car·bon

fluor·o·scope

flur·ry
 pl. flur·ries
 flur·ries, flur·ried

flush
 flush·er

flus·ter

flute
 flute·like
 flut·ing
 flut·ist
 flut·y

flut·ter
 flut·ter·er
 flut·ter·y

flu·vi·al

flux

fly (*move through the air*)
 flies; *past* flew; *past part.* flown
 pl. flies
 fly·a·ble

fly (*insect, fish bait*)
 pl. flies
 fly-fish

fly·ing

fly·leaf
 pl. fly·leaves

fly·pa·per

fly·trap

fly·weight

fly·wheel

f-num·ber
 also f-stop

foal

foam
 foam·less
 foam·y
 foam·i·er, foam·i·est

fob
 fobbed, fob·bing

fo·cal

Foch

fo'c's'le
 var. of fore·cas·tle

fo·cus
 pl. fo·cus·es *or* fo·ci
 fo·cused, fo·cus·ing;
  fo·cussed, fo·cus·sing
 fo·cus·er

fod·der

foe

fog
 fogged, fog·ging

fo·gey
 var. of fo·gy

fog·gy
 fog·gi·er, fog·gi·est
 fog·gi·ly
 fog·gi·ness

fog·horn

fo·gy
 also fo·gey
 pl. fo·gies *or* fo·geys
 fo·gy·ish

foi·ble

foil

foist

fold
 fold·a·ble

fold·er

fo·li·age

fo·lic ac·id

fo·li·o
 pl. fo·li·os

folk
 pl. folk *or* folks

folk·lore
 folk·lor·ic
 folk·lor·ist
 folk·lor·is·tic

folk·sy
 folk·si·er, folk·si·est
 folk·si·ness

fol·li·cle
 fol·lic·u·lar
 fol·lic·u·late

fol·low
 fol·low-through
 fol·low-up

fol·low·er

fol·low·ing

fol·ly
 pl. fol·lies

fo·ment
 fo·men·ta·tion
 fo·ment·er

fond
 fond·ly
 fond·ness

Fon·da

fon·dant

fon·dle
 fon·dler

fon·due

font
 font·al

fon·ta·nel
 also fon·ta·nelle

Fon·teyn

food

food·stuff

fool

fool·har·dy
 fool·har·di·er, fool·har·di·est
 fool·har·di·ly
 fool·har·di·ness

fool·ish
 fool·ish·ly
 fool·ish·ness

fool·proof

foot
 pl. feet *or* foot
 foot·ed
 foot·less

foot·age

foot·ball
 foot·ball·er

foot·bridge

foot·fall

foot·hill

foot·hold

foot·ing

foot·lights

foot·lock·er

foot·loose

foot·note

foot·path

foot·print

foot·race

foot·step

foot·stool

foot·wear

foot·work

fop
 fop·per·y
 fop·pish
 fop·pish·ly
 fop·pish·ness

for (*preposition*; see FORE, FOUR)

for·age
 for·ag·er

for·ay

for·bade
 also for·bad

for·bear (*abstain*)
 past for·bore; *past part.* for·borne

for·bear (*ancestor*)
 var. of fore·bear

for·bear·ance

for·bid
 for·bid·ding; *past* for·bade *or* for·bad; *past part.* for·bid·den
 for·bid·dance

for·bid·ding
 for·bid·ding·ly

for·bore

for·borne

force
 force·a·ble
 forc·er

forced

force·ful
 force·ful·ly
 force·ful·ness

force ma·jeure

for·ceps
 pl. same

for·ci·ble
 for·ci·ble·ness
 for·ci·bly

Ford (*proper name, automobile*)

ford (*water crossing*)
 ford·a·ble
 ford·less

fore (*front part*; see FOR, FOUR)

fore·arm

fore·bear
 also for·bear

fore·bode

fore·bod·ing
 fore·bod·ing·ly

fore·cast
 past and past part. fore·cast *or* fore·cast·ed
 fore·cast·er

fore·cas·tle
 also fo'c's'le

fore·close
 fore·clo·sure

fore·fa·ther

fore·fin·ger

fore·foot
 pl. fore·feet

fore·front

fore·go
 fore·goes; *past* fore·went; *past part.* fore·gone

fore·go·ing

fore·gone

fore·ground

fore·hand
 also fore·hand·ed

fore·head

for·eign
 for·eign·ness

for·eign·er

fore·leg

fore·lock

fore·man
 pl. fore·men

fore·mast

fore·most

fo•ren•sic
  fo•ren•si•cal•ly

fore•play

fore•run•ner

fore•see
  past fore•saw; *past part.*
    fore•seen
  fore•see•a•ble
  fore•se•er

fore•shad•ow

fore•short•en

fore•sight
  fore•sight•ed
  fore•sight•ed•ly
  fore•sight•ed•ness

fore•skin

for•est
  for•est•er

fore•stall
  fore•stall•er
  fore•stall•ment

for•est•ry

fore•taste

fore•tell
  past and past part. fore•
    told
  fore•tell•er

fore•thought

for•ev•er

fore•warn
  fore•warn•er

fore•went

fore•wom•an
  pl. fore•wom•en

fore•word (*preface*; see
  FORWARD)

for•feit
  for•feit•a•ble
  for•feit•er
  for•fei•ture

for•gath•er
  also fore•gath•er

for•gave

forge
  forge•a•ble
  forg•er

forg•er•y
  pl. forg•er•ies

for•get
  for•get•ting; *past* for•
    got; *past part.* for•got•
    ten *or* for•got
  for•get-me-not
  for•get•ta•ble
  for•get•ter

for•get•ful
  for•get•ful•ly
  for•get•ful•ness

for•give
  past for•gave; *past part.*
    for•giv•en
  for•giv•a•ble
  for•giv•a•bly
  for•give•ness
  for•giv•er

for•giv•ing
  for•giv•ing•ly

for•go
  also fore•go
  for•goes; *past* for•went;
    past part. for•gone

for•got

for•got•ten

fork

forked

fork•lift

for•lorn
  for•lorn•ly
  for•lorn•ness

form
  form•less
  form•less•ly

for•mal
  for•mal•ly

form•al•de•hyde

for•ma•lin

for•mal•ism
  for•mal•ist
  for•mal•is•tic

for•mal•i•ty
  pl. for•mal•i•ties

for•mal•ize
  for•mal•i•za•tion

for•mat
  for•mat•ted, for•mat•
    ting

for•ma•tion
  for•ma•tion•al

form•a•tive
  form•a•tive•ly

for•mer

for•mer•ly

For•mi•ca

for•mi•da•ble
  for•mi•da•ble•ness
  for•mi•da•bly

for•mu•la
  pl. for•mu•las *or* for•
    mu•lae
  for•mu•la•ic
  for•mu•lar•ize
  for•mu•lize

for•mu•late
  for•mu•la•tion

for•ni•cate
  for•ni•ca•tion
  for•ni•ca•tor

for•sake
  past for•sook; *past part.*
    for•sak•en
  for•sak•en•ness
  for•sak•er

for•sooth

For•ster

for·swear
past for·swore; past part.
for·sworn

For·syth

for·syth·i·a

fort (fortified building; see
FORTE)

Fort Col·lins

for·te (loud, loudly)

forte (strength, talent; see
FORT)

forth (forward; see
FOURTH)

forth·com·ing

forth·right
forth·right·ly
forth·right·ness

forth·with

for·ti·fy
for·ti·fies, for·ti·fied
for·ti·fi·a·ble
for·ti·fi·ca·tion
for·ti·fi·er

for·tis·si·mo

for·ti·tude

Fort Lau·der·dale

fort·night
fort·night·ly

for·tress

for·tu·i·tous
for·tu·i·tous·ly
for·tu·i·tous·ness
for·tu·i·ty

for·tu·nate
for·tu·nate·ly

for·tune
for·tune-tell·er
for·tune-tell·ing

Fort Wayne

Fort Worth

for·ty
pl. for·ties
for·ti·eth

fo·rum

for·ward (in front; see
FOREWORD)
also for·wards
for·ward·er
for·ward·ly
for·ward·ness

for·went

fos·sil
fos·sil·ize
fos·sil·i·za·tion

Fos·ter (proper name)

fos·ter (encourage, bring
up)
fos·ter·age
fos·ter·er

Fou·cault

fought

foul (vile, violation; see
FOWL)
foul-up
foul·ly
foul·ness

found
found·er
found·er·ship

foun·da·tion
foun·da·tion·al

found·er

found·ling

found·ry
pl. found·ries

fount

foun·tain
foun·tained

four (number; see FOR,
FORE)

four·fold

four·some

four·square

four·teen
four·teenth

fourth (next after third;
see FORTH)
fourth·ly

fowl (birds; see FOUL)
pl. same or fowls
fowl·er

Fowles

fox
pl. fox·es
fox·ing
fox·like

fox·glove

fox·hole

fox·hound

fox·trot
fox·trot·ted, fox·trot·
ting

fox·y
fox·i·er, fox·i·est
fox·i·ly
fox·i·ness

foy·er

fra·cas
pl. same

frac·tion
frac·tion·al
frac·tion·ar·y
frac·tion·ize

frac·tious
frac·tious·ly
frac·tious·ness

frac·ture

frag·ile
frag·ile·ly
fra·gil·i·ty

frag·ment
frag·men·tal
frag·men·ta·tion
frag·ment·ize

frag·men·tar·y
frag·men·tar·i·ly

Fra·go·nard

fra·grance
fra·gran·cy
fra·grant
fra·grant·ly

frail
frail·ly
frail·ness

frail·ty
pl. frail·ties

frame
frame-up
fram·a·ble
also frame·a·ble
frame·less
fram·er

frame·work

franc (*monetary unit; see* FRANK)

France

fran·chise
fran·chi·see
fran·chis·er
also fran·chi·sor

fran·ci·um

Franck

Fran·co

fran·gi·ble

Frank (*proper name, member of ancient people*)
Frank·ish

frank (*candid; see* FRANC)
frank·a·ble
frank·er
frank·ly
frank·ness

Frank·en·stein

Frank·fort (*American city*)

Frank·furt (*city in Germany*)
also Frank·furt am Main
also Frank·furt an der Oder
Frank·furt·er (*person from Frankfurt*)

frank·furt·er (*hot dog*)

frank·in·cense

Frank·lin

Frank·lin stove

fran·tic
fran·ti·cal·ly
fran·tic·ly

Franz Jo·sef

frap·pé

frat

fra·ter·nal
fra·ter·nal·ism
fra·ter·nal·ly

fra·ter·ni·ty
pl. fra·ter·ni·ties

frat·er·nize
frat·er·ni·za·tion

frat·ri·cide
frat·ri·cid·al

Frau
pl. Frau·en

fraud

fraud·u·lent
fraud·u·lence
fraud·u·lent·ly

fraught

Fräu·lein

fray

Fra·zer

fraz·zle

freak
freak·ish
freak·ish·ly
freak·ish·ness

freak·y
freak·i·er, freak·i·est
freak·i·ly
freak·i·ness

freck·le
freck·ly

Fred·er·ick

Fred·er·ic·ton

free
fre·er; fre·est
free-for-all
free-hand·ed
free-hand·ed·ly
free-hand·ed·ness
free-stand·ing
free·ly
free·ness

free·bie

free·boot·er
free·boot

free·born

freed·man
pl. freed·men

free·dom

free·hand

free·hold
free·hold·er

free·lance
also free·lanc·er

free·load·er
free·load

free·style

free·think·er
free·think·ing

Free·town

free·way

freeze (ice, immobilize;
    see FRIEZE)
    past froze; past part.
    fro•zen
    freeze-dry
    freeze-dries, freeze-
    dried
    freez•a•ble
    fro•zen•ly

freez•er

freight

freight•er

Fre•mont (city)

Fré•mont (proper name)

French
    French•man
    pl. French•men
    French•wom•an
    pl. French•wom•en
    French•ness

fre•net•ic
    fre•net•i•cal•ly

fren•zy
    pl. fren•zies
    fren•zies, fren•zied
    fren•zied•ly

fre•quen•cy
    pl. fre•quen•cies

fre•quent
    fre•quen•ta•tion
    fre•quent•er
    fre•quent•ly

fres•co
    pl. fres•cos or fres•coes
    fres•coed

fresh
    fresh•ly
    fresh•ness

fresh•en

fresh•man
    pl. fresh•men

fresh•wa•ter

Fres•no

fret (worry)
    fret•ted, fret•ting

fret (ridge on guitar)
    fret•less

fret•ful
    fret•ful•ly
    fret•ful•ness

fret•work

Freud
    Freud•i•an
    Freud•i•an•ism

fri•a•ble
    fri•a•bil•i•ty

fri•ar (monk; see FRYER)
    fri•ar•ly

fric•as•see
    fric•as•sees, fric•as•
    seed

fric•a•tive

fric•tion
    fric•tion•al
    fric•tion•less

Fri•day

fridge

Frie•dan

Fried•man

friend
    friend•less

friend•ly
    friend•li•er, friend•li•
    est
    friend•li•ness

friend•ship

fri•er
    var. of fry•er

frieze (sculpted band; see
    FREEZE)

frig•ate

fright

fright•en
    fright•en•ing
    fright•en•ing•ly

fright•ful
    fright•ful•ly

frig•id
    fri•gid•i•ty
    frig•id•ly
    frig•id•ness

fri•jo•les

frill
    frilled
    frill•er•y
    frill•i•ness
    frill•y
    frill•i•er, frill•i•est

fringe
    fringe•less
    fring•y

frip•per•y
    pl. frip•per•ies

Fris•bee (trademark)

frisk
    frisk•er

frisk•y
    frisk•i•er, frisk•i•est
    frisk•i•ly
    frisk•i•ness

frit•ter

friv•o•lous
    fri•vol•i•ty
    pl. fri•vol•i•ties
    friv•o•lous•ly
    friv•o•lous•ness

frizz
    friz•zi•ness
    friz•zy
    friz•zi•er, friz•zi•est

friz•zle

fro

frock

frog (amphibian)

frog (*coat fastener*)
frogged
frog•ging

frog•man
pl. frog•men

frol•ic
frol•icked, frol•ick•ing
frol•ick•er

frol•ic•some
frol•ic•some•ly

from

frond
frond•age
fron•dose

front
front•less
front•ward
front•wards

front•age

fron•tal
front•al•ly

fron•tier
fron•tier•less

fron•tiers•man
pl. fron•tiers•men

fron•tis•piece

frost
frost•less

frost•bite

frost•ing

frost•y
frost•i•er, frost•i•est
frost•i•ly
frost•i•ness

froth
froth•i•ly
froth•i•ness
froth•y
froth•i•er, froth•i•est

frown
frown•er
frown•ing•ly

frow•zy
also frow•sy
frow•zi•er, frow•zi•est
frow•zi•ness

froze

fro•zen

fruc•ti•fy
fruc•ti•fies, fruc•ti•fied

fruc•tose

fru•gal
fru•gal•i•ty
fru•gal•ly
fru•gal•ness

fruit
fruit•ed

fruit•cake

fruit•ful
fruit•ful•ly
fruit•ful•ness

fru•i•tion

fruit•less
fruit•less•ly
fruit•less•ness

fruit•y
fruit•i•er, fruit•i•est
fruit•i•ly
fruit•i•ness

frump
frump•ish
frump•ish•ly

frump•y
frump•i•er, frump•i•est
frump•i•ly
frump•i•ness

frus•trate
frus•trat•ed•ly
frus•trat•er
frus•trat•ing
frus•trat•ing•ly
frus•tra•tion

fry
fries, fried
pl. fries

Frye

fry•er (*person who fries;*
see FRIAR)
also fri•er

Fu•ad

fuch•sia

fud•dle

fud•dy-dud•dy
pl. fud•dy-dud•dies

fudge

Fueh•rer
var. of Füh•rer

fu•el
fu•eled, fu•el•ing

Fuen•tes

fu•gi•tive
fu•gi•tive•ly

fugue
fu•gal

Füh•rer
also Fueh•rer

Fu•ji, Mount

Fu•ku•o•ka

Ful•bright

ful•crum
pl. ful•cra *or* ful•crums

ful•fill
ful•filled, ful•fill•ing
ful•fill•a•ble
ful•fill•er
ful•fill•ment

full
full-blood•ed
full-blown
full-fledged
full-scale
full-time
full•ness

full·back

Ful·ler

Ful·ler·ton

ful·mi·nate
ful·mi·na·tion
ful·mi·na·to·ry

ful·some
ful·some·ly
ful·some·ness

Ful·ton

fum·ble
fum·bler
fum·bling·ly

fume
fume·less
fum·ing·ly

fu·mi·gate
fu·mi·gant
fu·mi·ga·tion
fu·mi·ga·tor

fun

Fu·na·fu·ti

fu·nam·bu·list

func·tion
func·tion·less

func·tion·al
func·tion·al·i·ty
func·tion·al·ly

func·tion·ar·y
pl. func·tion·ar·ies

fund
fund-rais·er
fund-rais·ing

fun·da·men·tal
fun·da·men·tal·ly

fun·da·men·tal·ism
fun·da·men·tal·ist

Fun·dy, Bay of

fu·ner·al
fu·ner·ar·y

fu·ne·re·al
fu·ne·re·al·ly

fun·gi·cide
fun·gi·cid·al

fun·gus
pl. fun·gi *or* fun·gus·es
fun·gal
fun·gi·form
fun·giv·or·ous
fun·gous

fu·nic·u·lar

funk

funk·y
funk·i·er, funk·i·est
funk·i·ly
funk·i·ness

fun·nel
fun·neled, fun·nel·ing;
fun·nelled, fun·nel·
ling
fun·nel·like

fun·ny
fun·ni·er, fun·ni·est
fun·ni·ness

fur (*animal pelt; see* FIR)
fur·less

fur·be·low

fur·bish
fur·bish·er

fu·ri·ous
fu·ri·ous·ly

furl
furl·a·ble

fur·long

fur·lough

fur·nace

fur·nish
fur·nished

fur·nish·ings

fur·ni·ture

fu·ror

fur·ri·er

fur·row
fur·row·less
fur·row·y

fur·ry
fur·ri·er, fur·ri·est
fur·ri·ness

fur·ther
fur·ther·er
fur·ther·most

fur·ther·ance

fur·ther·more

fur·thest
var. of far·thest

fur·tive
fur·tive·ly
fur·tive·ness

fu·ry
pl. fu·ries

fuse (*melt by heat, circuit protection*)

fuse (*device to ignite explosive*)
also fuze
fuse·less

fu·se·lage

Fu·shun

fus·i·ble
fu·si·bil·i·ty

fu·sil·ier
also fu·si·leer

fu·sil·lade

fu·sion
fu·sion·al

fuss
fuss·er

fuss·budg·et

fuss·y
fuss·i·er, fuss·i·est
fuss·i·ly
fuss·i·ness

fus•ty
  fus•ti•er, fus•ti•est
  fus•ti•ly
  fus•ti•ness

fu•tile
  fu•tile•ly
  fu•til•i•ty

fu•ton

fu•ture
  fu•ture•less

fu•tur•ist

fu•tur•is•tic
  fu•tur•is•ti•cal•ly

fu•tu•ri•ty
  pl. fu•tu•ri•ties

fuze
  var. of fuse

fuzz

fuzz•y
  fuzz•i•er, fuzz•i•est
  fuzz•i•ly
  fuzz•i•ness

G

gab
  gab·ber
  gab·by
  gab·bi·er, gab·bi·est

gab·ar·dine
  also gab·er·dine

gab·ble
  gab·bler

Ga·ble (*proper name*)

ga·ble (*wall under roof*)
  ga·bled

Ga·bon
  Gab·o·nese

Ga·bo·ro·ne

gad
  gad·ded, gad·ding

gad·a·bout

Gad·da·fi

gad·fly
  pl. gad·flies

gadg·et
  gadg·e·teer
  gadg·et·ry
  gadg·et·y

gad·o·lin·i·um

Gael·ic

gaff (*stick for fishing; see* GAFFE)

gaffe (*blunder; see* GAFF)

gaf·fer

gag
  gagged, gag·ging

ga·ga

Ga·ga·rin

Gage

gag·gle

gai·e·ty
  also gay·e·ty

gai·ly

gain
  gain·a·ble
  gain·er
  gain·ings

Gaines·ville

gain·ful
  gain·ful·ly
  gain·ful·ness

gain·say
  past and past part. gain·said
  gain·say·er

Gains·bor·ough

gait (*step; see* GATE)

gai·ter
  gait·ered

gal

ga·la

ga·lac·tic

Ga·lá·pa·gos Is·lands

gal·ax·y
  pl. gal·ax·ies

Gal·braith

gale

Ga·len

Gal·i·lee

Gal·i·le·o

gall (*impudence; see* GAUL)
  gall·ing
  gall·ing·ly

gal·lant
  gal·lant·ly

gal·lant·ry
  pl. gal·lant·ries

gall·blad·der
  also gall blad·der

gal·le·on

gal·ler·i·a

gal·ler·y
  pl. gal·ler·ies
  gal·ler·ied

gal·ley
  pl. gal·leys

Gal·lic
  Gal·li·cize

gal·li·um

gal·li·vant

gal·lon
  gal·lon·age

gal·lop
  gal·loped, gal·lop·ing
  gal·lop·er

gal·lows

gall·stone

ga·lore

ga·losh

Gals·wor·thy

ga·lumph

gal·van·ic
  gal·van·i·cal·ly

gal·va·nize
  gal·va·ni·za·tion
  gal·va·niz·er

gal·va·nom·e·ter
  gal·va·no·met·ric

Gal•ves•ton

Ga•ma

Gam•bi•a, the

gam•bit

gam•ble (*wager*; see
  GAMBOL)
  gam•bler

gam•bol (*frolic*; see
  GAMBLE)
  gam•boled, gam•bol•
  ing; gam•bolled, gam•
  bol•ling

gam•brel

game
  game•ly
  game•ster

game•cock
  also game•fowl

game•keep•er

games•man•ship

ga•mete
  ga•met•ic

gam•in (*boy*)

ga•mine (*girl, slender*)

gam•ma

gam•ut

gam•y
  gam•i•er, gam•i•est
  gam•i•ly
  gam•i•ness

gan•der

Gan•dhi

gang

Gan•ges

gang•land

gan•gling

gan•gli•on
  pl. gan•gli•a *or* gan•
  gli•ons

gan•gli•ar
gan•gli•on•ic

gan•gly
  gan•gli•er, gan•gli•est

gang•plank

gan•grene
  gan•gre•nous

gang•ster
  gang•ster•ism

gang•way

gan•net

gant•let
  var. of gaunt•let

gan•try
  pl. gan•tries

gap
  gapped
  gap•py

gape
  gap•ing•ly

ga•rage

garb

gar•bage

gar•ble
  gar•bler

Gar•bo

Gar•cí•a Lor•ca

Gar•cí•a Már•quez

gar•den
  gar•den•er
  gar•den•ing

gar•de•nia

Gard•ner

Gar•field

gar•gan•tu•an

gar•gle

gar•goyle

Gar•i•bal•di

gar•ish
  gar•ish•ly
  gar•ish•ness

Gar•land (*proper name*)

gar•land (*wreath of
  flowers*)

gar•lic
  gar•lick•y

gar•ment

gar•ner

gar•net

gar•nish
  gar•nish•ment

gar•nish•ee
  gar•nish•ees, gar•nish•
  eed

ga•rotte
  var. of gar•rote

gar•ret

Gar•ri•son (*proper name*)

gar•ri•son (*stationed
  troops*)

gar•rote
  also ga•rotte, gar•rotte

gar•ru•lous
  gar•ru•li•ty
  gar•ru•lous•ly
  gar•ru•lous•ness

gar•ter

Gar•vey

Gar•y

gas
  pl. gas•es
  gas•es, gassed, gas•sing

gas•e•ous
  gas•e•ous•ness

gash

gas•ket

gas·o·line

gasp

gas·sy
gas·si·er, gas·si·est
gas·si·ness

gas·tric

gas·tri·tis

gas·tron·o·my
gas·tro·nom·ic
gas·tro·nom·i·cal
gas·tro·nom·i·cal·ly

gas·tro·pod

gate (*barrier;* see GAIT)

gate·crash·er
gate·crash

gate·fold

gate·house

Gates

gate·way

gath·er
gath·er·er

gath·er·ing

ga·tor
also ga·ter

Ga·tun

gauche
gauche·ly
gauche·ness

gau·che·rie

gau·cho
pl. gau·chos

gaud·y
gaud·i·er, gaud·i·est
gaud·i·ly
gaud·i·ness

gauge
also gage
gauge·a·ble
gaug·er

Gau·guin

Gaul (*European region;*
see GALL)
Gaul·ish

Gaulle (*proper name*)

gaunt
gaunt·ly
gaunt·ness

gaunt·let (*glove*)

gaunt·let (*punishment, as
in "run the gauntlet"*)
also gant·let

Gau·ta·ma

gauze

gauz·y
gauz·i·er, gauz·i·est
gauz·i·ly
gauz·i·ness

gave

gav·el

ga·votte

gawk
gawk·ish

gawk·y
gawk·i·er, gawk·i·est
gawk·i·ly
gawk·i·ness

gay
gay·ness

gay·e·ty
var. of gai·e·ty

Ga·za Strip

gaze
gaz·er

ga·ze·bo
pl. ga·ze·bos *or*
ga·ze·boes

ga·zelle

ga·zette

gaz·et·teer

gaz·pa·cho
pl. gaz·pa·chos

Gdansk

Gdy·nia

gear

gear·shift

gear·wheel

geck·o
pl. geck·os *or* geck·oes

gee
also gee whiz

geek

geese

gee·zer

Geh·rig

Gei·ger count·er

Gei·sel

gei·sha
pl. same *or* gei·shas

gel (*colloidal suspension;*
see JELL)
gelled, gel·ling
ge·la·tion

gel·a·tin
also gel·a·tine
ge·lat·i·nize
ge·lat·i·ni·za·tion

ge·lat·i·nous
ge·lat·i·nous·ly

geld

geld·ing

gem
gem·like
gem·my

Gem·i·ni

gem·stone

gen·darme

gen·der

gene

ge·ne·al·o·gy
  pl. ge·ne·al·o·gies
  ge·ne·a·log·i·cal
  ge·ne·a·log·i·cal·ly
  ge·ne·al·o·gist

gen·er·al
  gen·er·al·ist
  gen·er·al·ness

gen·er·a·lis·si·mo
  pl. gen·er·a·lis·si·mos

gen·er·al·i·ty
  pl. gen·er·al·i·ties

gen·er·al·ize
  gen·er·al·i·za·tion
  gen·er·al·iz·er

gen·er·al·ly

gen·er·ate
  gen·er·a·ble

gen·er·a·tion
  gen·er·a·tion·al

gen·er·a·tive

gen·er·a·tor

ge·ner·ic
  ge·ner·i·cal·ly

gen·er·ous
  gen·er·os·i·ty
  gen·er·ous·ly

gen·e·sis
  also Gen·e·sis

ge·net·ic
  ge·net·i·cal·ly

ge·net·ics
  ge·net·i·cist

Ge·ne·va

Gen·ghis Khan

gen·i·al
  ge·ni·al·i·ty
  ge·nial·ly

ge·nie
  pl. ge·nii or ge·nies

gen·i·tal

gen·i·ta·li·a

gen·i·tive
  gen·i·ti·val
  gen·i·ti·val·ly

ge·nius
  pl. gen·ius·es or
  ge·ni·i
  pl. gen·ius·es

Gen·o·a

gen·o·cide
  gen·o·ci·dal

gen·re

gent

gen·teel
  gen·teel·ly
  gen·teel·ness

gen·tian

Gen·tile

gen·til·i·ty

gen·tle
  gen·tler, gen·tlest
  gen·tle·ness
  gen·tly

gen·tle·man
  pl. gen·tle·men
  gen·tle·man·li·ness
  gen·tle·man·ly

gen·tri·fi·ca·tion
  gen·tri·fy
  gen·tri·fies, gen·tri·fied

gen·try

gen·u·flect
  gen·u·flec·tion
  gen·u·flec·tor

gen·u·ine
  gen·u·ine·ly
  gen·u·ine·ness

ge·nus
  pl. gen·er·a

ge·o·cen·tric
  ge·o·cen·tri·cal·ly

ge·ode
  ge·o·dic

ge·o·de·sic
  also ge·o·det·ic

ge·od·e·sy
  ge·od·e·sist

ge·o·graph·ic
  also ge·o·graph·i·cal
  ge·o·graph·i·cal·ly

ge·o·graph·i·cal
  var. of ge·o·graph·ic

ge·og·ra·phy
  ge·og·ra·pher

ge·ol·o·gy
  ge·o·log·ic
  ge·o·log·i·cal
  ge·o·log·i·cal·ly
  ge·ol·o·gist

ge·o·met·ric
  also ge·o·met·ri·cal
  ge·o·met·ri·cal·ly

ge·om·e·try
  ge·om·e·tri·cian

ge·o·phys·ics
  ge·o·phys·i·cal
  ge·o·phys·i·cist

George·town

Geor·gia
  Geor·gian

ge·o·syn·chro·nous

ge·ra·ni·um

ger·bil

ger·i·at·ric

ger·i·at·rics
  ger·i·a·tri·cian

germ
germ•y

Ger•man
Ger•man•ic

ger•mane
ger•mane•ly
ger•mane•ness

ger•ma•ni•um

Ger•ma•ny

ger•mi•cide
ger•mi•cid•al

ger•mi•nal
ger•mi•nal•ly

ger•mi•nate
ger•mi•na•tion
ger•mi•na•tor

Ge•ron•i•mo

ger•on•tol•o•gy
ge•ron•to•log•i•cal
ger•on•tol•o•gist

ger•ry•man•der
ger•ry•man•der•er

Gersh•win

ger•und

gest (*story*; see JEST)

Ge•sta•po

ges•tate

ges•ta•tion

ges•tic•u•late
ges•tic•u•la•tion
ges•tic•u•la•tive
ges•tic•u•la•tor
ges•tic•u•la•tory

ges•ture
ges•tur•al
ges•tur•er

ge•sund•heit

get
get•ting; *past* got; *past
part.* got *or* got•ten

get-to•geth•er

get-up

get•ta•ble

get•a•way

Get•ty

Get•tys•burg

gew•gaw

gey•ser

Gha•na
Gha•na•ian, Ghan•i•an

ghast•ly
ghast•li•er, ghast•li•
est
ghast•li•ness

ghee

Ghent

gher•kin

ghet•to
pl. ghet•tos

ghost
ghost•like

ghost•ly
ghost•li•er, ghost•li•
est
ghost•li•ness

ghost•write
ghost•writ•er

ghoul
ghoul•ish
ghoul•ish•ly
ghoul•ish•ness

gi•ant
gi•ant•ism
gi•ant•like

gib•ber

gib•ber•ish

gib•bet

Gib•bon (*proper name*)

gib•bon (*ape*)

gib•bous
gib•bos•i•ty
gib•bous•ly
gib•bous•ness

gibe (*jeer*; see JIBE)
also jibe
gib•er

gib•lets

Gi•bral•tar

Gib•ran

gid•dy
gid•di•er, gid•di•est
gid•di•ly
gid•di•ness

Gide

Giel•gud

gift

gift•ed
gift•ed•ly
gift•ed•ness

gig

gig•a•bit

gig•a•byte

gi•gan•tic
gi•gan•tesque
gi•gan•ti•cal•ly

gig•gle
gig•gler
gig•gly
gig•gli•er, gig•gli•est
gig•gli•ness

gig•o•lo
pl. gig•o•los

Gi•jón

Gil•bert

gild (*embellish*; see
GUILD)
past part. gild•ed *or* gilt
gild•er
gild•ing

gill

Gil·les·pie

gilt (*golden*; see GUILT)
gilt-edged

gim·bals

gim·crack
gim·crack·er·y
gim·crack·y

gim·let

gim·mick
gim·mick·ry
gim·mick·y

gin (*alcohol*)

gin (*machine to process cotton*)
ginned, gin·ning
gin·ner

gin·ger
gin·ger·y

gin·ger·bread

gin·ger·ly
gin·ger·li·ness

ging·ham

gin·gi·va
pl. gin·gi·vae
gin·gi·val

gin·gi·vi·tis

Ging·rich

gink·go
also ging·ko
pl. gink·gos *or* gink·goes

Gins·berg

gin·seng

Gior·gio·ne

Giot·to

Gip·sy
var. of Gyp·sy

gi·raffe
pl. same *or* gi·raffes

gird
past and *past part.* gird·ed *or* girt

gird·er

gir·dle

girl
girl·hood
girl·ish
girl·ish·ly
girl·ish·ness

girl·friend

girt

girth

Gis·card d'Es·taing

Gish

gist

give
past gave; *past part.* giv·en
giv·a·ble, give·a·ble
giv·er

giv·en

Gi·za

giz·mo
also gis·mo
pl. giz·mos

giz·zard

gla·cé

gla·cial
gla·cial·ly

gla·cier

glad
glad·der, glad·dest
glad-hand
glad·ly
glad·ness

glad·den

glade

glad·i·a·tor
glad·i·a·tor·i·al

gla·di·o·lus
pl. gla·di·o·li *or* gla·di·o·lus·es

Glad·stone

glam·or·ize
also glam·our·ize
glam·or·i·za·tion

glam·our
also glam·or
glam·or·ous
glam·or·ous·ly

glance
glanc·ing·ly

gland

glan·du·lar

glare
glar·y

glar·ing
glar·ing·ly

Glas·gow
Glas·we·gian

glas·nost

glass
glass·ful
pl. glass·fuls
glass·like

glass·ware

glass·y
glas·si·er, glas·si·est
also glas·sie
glass·i·ly
glass·i·ness

glau·co·ma

glaze
glaz·er
glaz·y

gla·zier
gla·zier·y

gleam

glean
glean•er
glean•ings

Glea•son

glee

glee•ful
glee•ful•ly
glee•ful•ness

glen

Glen•dale

Glen•dow•er
also Glyn•dwr

Glenn

glib

glide
glid•ing•ly

glid•er

glim•mer
glim•mer•ing•ly

glimpse

glint

glis•san•do
pl. glis•san•di *or* glis•
san•dos

glis•ten

glitch

glit•ter
glit•ter•y

glitz
glitz•y
glitz•i•er, glitz•i•est

gloam•ing

gloat
gloat•ing•ly

glob

glob•al
glob•al•ly

globe
globe-trot•ter
globe-trot•ting
globe•like

glob•u•lar
glob•u•lar•ly

glob•ule

glock•en•spiel

gloom

gloom•y
gloom•i•er, gloom•i•est
gloom•i•ly
gloom•i•ness

glo•ri•fy
glo•ri•fies; glo•ri•fied
glo•ri•fi•ca•tion

glo•ri•ous
glo•ri•ous•ly

glo•ry
pl. glo•ries

gloss

glos•sa•ry
pl. glos•sa•ries

glos•so•la•li•a

gloss•y
gloss•i•er, gloss•i•est
pl. gloss•ies
gloss•i•ly
gloss•i•ness

glot•tal

glot•tis

Glouces•ter

glove

glow
glow•ing•ly

glow•er
glow•er•ing•ly

glow•worm

glu•cose

glue
glues, glued, glu•ing
or glue•ing
glue•like
glue•y
glu•i•er, glu•i•est
glu•ey•ness

glum
glum•mer, glum•mest
glum•ly
glum•ness

glut
glut•ted, glut•ting

glu•ten

glu•te•us
pl. glu•te•i
glu•te•al

glu•ti•nous
glu•ti•nous•ly
glu•ti•nous•ness

glut•ton
glut•ton•ous
glut•ton•ous•ly

glut•ton•y

glyc•er•in
also glyc•er•ol, glyc•
er•ine

gly•co•gen
gly•co•gen•ic

G-man
pl. G-men

gnarl

gnarled
also gnarl•y

gnash

gnat

gnaw
past part. gnawed *or*
gnawn
gnaw•ing
gnaw•ing•ly

gneiss

gnoc•chi

gnome

gnom·ic

gnu (*animal*; see KNEW, NEW)

go
past went; *past part.* gone
pl. goes
go·a·head
go·be·tween

goad

goal

goal·keep·er
goal·ie

goat

goa·tee

goat·herd

goat·skin

gob

gob·ble (*eat hurriedly*)
gob·bler

gob·ble (*turkey sound*)

gob·ble·dy·gook
also gob·ble·de·gook

Go·bi

gob·let

gob·lin

god
also God
god·less
god·less·ness
god·like

god·child

God·dard

god·daugh·ter

god·dess

god·fa·ther

god·for·sak·en
also God·for·sak·en

god·head
also God·head

Go·di·va

god·ly
god·li·ness

god·mo·ther

god·par·ent

god·send

god·son

Go·du·nov

Goeb·bels

Goe·ring

Goe·the

go·fer

gog·gle

Go·gol

go·ing

goi·ter

gold

gold·en

gold·en·rod

gold·finch

gold·fish

Gol·ding

Gold·smith (*proper name*)

gold·smith (*person who works with gold*)

go·lem

golf
golf·er

Go·li·ath

gol·ly

Gom·pers

go·nad
go·nad·al

gon·do·la

gon·do·lier

gone

gon·er

gong

gon·or·rhea
gon·or·rhe·al

goo

good
bet·ter, best

good-bye
also good·bye, good-by, good·by
pl. good-byes

good-hu·mored
good·-hu·mored·ly

good·ly
good·li·er, good·li·est
good·li·ness

Good·man

good-na·tured
good·-na·tured·ly

good·ness

good·will

good·y
also good·ie
pl. good·ies
good·y-good·y

Good·year

goo·ey
goo·i·er, goo·i·est
goo·ey·ness
also goo·i·ness.

goof

goof·ball

goof·y
goof·i·er, goof·i·est
goof·i·ness

goon

goose
  pl. geese

goose·ber·ry
  pl. goose·ber·ries

go·pher

Gor·ba·chev

Gor·di·an knot

Gor·di·mer

Gor·don

Gore (*proper name*)

gore (*blood, pierce*)

gorge

gor·geous
  gor·geous·ly

gor·gon
  gor·go·ni·an

Gor·gon·zo·la

go·ril·la (*animal;* see
  GUERRILLA)

Gor·ky

gorse

gor·y
  gor·i·er, gor·i·est
  gor·i·ly
  gor·i·ness

gosh

gos·ling

gos·pel
  also Gospel

gos·sa·mer

gos·sip
  gos·siped, gos·sip·ing
  gos·sip·mon·ger
  gos·sip·y

got

Gö·te·borg
  also Goth·en·burg

Goth

Goth·ic

Got·land

got·ten

gouache

Gou·da

gouge

gou·lash

Gou·nod

gourd
  gourd·ful
  pl. gourd·fuls

gour·mand
  gour·mand·ism

gour·met

gout
  gout·y

gov·ern
  gov·ern·a·ble

gov·er·nance

gov·er·ness

gov·ern·ment
  gov·ern·ment·al

gov·er·nor
  gov·er·nor·ship

gown

goy
  pl. goy·im *or* goys
  goy·ish, *also* goy·isch

Go·ya

grab
  grabbed, grab·bing
  grab·ber

grace

grace·ful
  grace·ful·ly
  grace·ful·ness

grace·less

gra·cious
  gra·cious·ly
  gra·cious·ness

gra·date

gra·da·tion
  gra·da·tion·al

grade

gra·di·ent

grad·u·al
  grad·u·al·ly

grad·u·al·ism
  grad·u·a·list
  grad·u·al·is·tic

grad·u·ate
  grad·u·a·tion

graf·fi·ti
  sing. graf·fi·to

graft

Gra·ham (*proper name*)

gra·ham (*grain;* see
  GRAM)

gra·ham crack·er

Gra·hame

Grail

grain
  grain·y

gram (*unit of weight;* see
  GRAHAM)

gram·mar
  gram·mar·i·an
  gram·mat·i·cal
  gram·mat·i·cal·ly

gram·o·phone

Gra·na·da

gran·a·ry
  pl. gran·a·ries

grand
  grand·ly
  grand·ness

grand·child
  pl. grand·chil·dren

Grand Cou·lee Dam

grand·dad·dy
  also gran·dad·dy
  pl. grand·dad·dies

grand·daugh·ter

gran·dee

gran·deur

grand·fa·ther
  grand·fa·ther·ly

gran·dil·o·quent
  gran·dil·o·quence
  gran·dil·o·quent·ly

gran·di·ose
  gran·di·ose·ly
  gran·di·os·i·ty

grand·mo·ther
  grand·moth·er·ly

grand·pa·rent

grand·son

grand·stand

grange

gran·ite

gran·ny
  also gran·nie
  pl. gran·nies

gra·no·la

Grant (*proper name*)

grant (*allow, gift*)
  gran·tee
  grant·er
  gran·tor

gran·u·lar
  gran·u·lar·i·ty

gran·u·late
  gran·u·la·tion

gran·ule

grape

grape·fruit
  pl. same

grape·vine

graph

graph·ic
  graph·i·cal·ly

graph·ics

graph·ite

gra·phol·o·gy
  graph·ol·o·gist

grap·nel

grap·ple

grasp

grasp·ing

Grass (*proper name*)

grass (*plant*)
  grass·y
  gras·si·er, gras·si·est

grass·hop·per

grass·land

grate (*shred; see* GREAT)
  grat·er

grate (*metal frame in fireplace; see* GREAT)

grate·ful
  grate·ful·ly
  grate·ful·ness

grat·i·fy
  grat·i·fies, grat·i·fied
  grat·i·fi·ca·tion

grat·ing (*harsh sounding*)
  grat·ing·ly

grat·ing (*metal framework*)

grat·is

grat·i·tude

gra·tu·i·tous
  gra·tu·i·tous·ly
  gra·tu·i·tous·ness

gra·tu·i·ty
  pl. gra·tu·i·ties

grave
  grave·ly

grav·el

grav·el·ly

Graves

grave·stone

grave·yard

grav·i·tate

grav·i·ta·tion
  grav·i·ta·tion·al

grav·i·ty

gra·vy
  pl. gra·vies

gray
  also grey
  gray·ish
  gray·ness

Graz

graze

grease

grease·paint

greas·y
  greas·i·er, greas·i·est
  greas·i·ly
  greas·i·ness

great (*considerable; see* GRATE)
  great·ly
  great·ness

Great Brit·ain

Great·er An·til·les

Great·er Sun·da Is·lands

grebe

Gre·co, El

Gre·co-Ro·man

Greece
  Gre·cian
  Greek

greed

greed·y
  greed·i·er, greed·i·est
  greed·i·ly
  greed·i·ness

Gree·ley

green
  green-eyed
  green·ish
  green·ly
  green·ness

green·back

Greene

green·er·y

green·gro·cer

green·horn

green·house

Green·land
  Green·land·ic

green·room

Greens·bo·ro

greens·keep·er

Green·span

green·sward

Green·wich

green·y

Greer

greet
  greet·er

greet·ing

gre·gar·i·ous
  gre·gar·i·ous·ly
  gre·gar·i·ous·ness

Gre·go·ri·an

Greg·o·ry

grem·lin

Gre·na·da

gre·nade

gren·a·dine

Gre·no·ble

Gren·ville

grew

grey
  var. of gray

grey·hound

grid
  grid·ded

grid·dle

grid·i·ron

grid·lock
  grid·locked

grief

Grieg

griev·ance

grieve

griev·ous
  griev·ous·ly

grif·fin
  also gryph·on, grif·fon

Grif·fith

grill (broil, question; see
  GRILLE)
  grill·ing

grille (grating; see GRILL)
  also grill

grill·work

grim
  grim·mer, grim·mest
  grim·ly
  grim·ness

grim·ace

grime

Grimm

grin
  grinned, grin·ning

grind
  past and past part.
  ground

grind·er

grind·stone

grip (clutch; see GRIPPE)
  gripped, grip·ping

gripe

grippe (influenza; see
  GRIP)

gris·ly (gruesome; see
  GRIZZLY)
  gris·li·er, gris·li·est
  gris·li·ness

grist

gris·tle
  gris·tly

grit
  grit·ted, grit·ting
  grit·ty
  grit·ti·er, grit·ti·est
  grit·ti·ness

grits

griz·zled

griz·zly (gray, bear; see
  GRISLY)
  griz·zli·er, griz·zli·est
  pl. griz·zlies

groan
  groan·er
  groan·ing·ly

gro·cer

gro·cer·y
  pl. gro·cer·ies

grog

grog·gy
grog·gi·er, grog·gi·est
grog·gi·ly
grog·gi·ness

groin

grom·met
also grum·met

Gro·my·ko

Gro·ning·en

groom

groove

groov·y
groov·i·er, groov·i·est
groov·i·ness

grope

Gro·pi·us

gros·grain

gross
pl. same
gross·ly
gross·ness

gro·tesque
gro·tesque·ly
gro·tesque·ness

grot·to
pl. grot·toes *or* grot·tos

grouch
grouch·y

ground (*surface*)

ground (*past and past
part. of* grind)

ground·break·ing

ground·ing

ground·less

ground·ling

grounds·keep·er

ground·swell

ground·water

ground·work

group
group·ing

group·ie

grouse (*bird*)
pl. same

grouse (*complain*)

grout
grout·er

grove

grov·el
grov·eled, grov·el·ing;
grov·elled, grov·el·
ling
grov·el·er
grov·el·ing

grow
past grew; *past part.*
grown
grown-up
grow·er

growl

growth

Groz·ny

grub
grubbed, grub·bing

grub·by
grub·bi·er, grub·bi·est
grub·bi·ly
grub·bi·ness

grub·stake

grudge
grudg·ing

gru·el

gru·el·ing
gru·el·ing·ly

grue·some
grue·some·ly
grue·some·ness

gruff
gruff·ly
gruff·ness

grum·ble
grum·bler
grum·bling
grum·bling·ly

grump·y
grump·i·er, grump·i·
est
grump·i·ly
grump·i·ness

grunge
grun·gy

grunt

Gru·yère

gua·ca·mo·le

Gua·da·la·ja·ra

Gua·dal·ca·nal

Gua·da·lu·pe (*Mexico*)

Gua·de·loupe (*West
Indies*)

Guam
Gua·ma·ni·an

Gua·na·jua·to

gua·no
pl. gua·nos

Guan·tá·na·mo

Gua·ra·ni

guar·an·tee (*warranty,
assurance*)
guar·an·tees, guar·an·
teed

guar·an·tor

guar·an·ty (*security*)
pl. guar·an·ties

guard

guard·ed
guard·ed·ly

guard·i·an
guard·i·an·ship

guard·rail

Gua•te•ma•la
  Gua•te•ma•lan

gua•va

Guay•a•quil

gu•ber•na•to•ri•al

Guern•sey

Guer•re•ro

guer•ril•la (*insurgent*;
  see GORILLA)
  also gue•ril•la

guess

guess•work

guest

Gue•va•ra

guff

guf•faw

guid•ance

guide

guide•book

guide•line

guild (*association*; see
  GILD)

guild•er

guile
  guile•ful
  guile•less

guil•lo•tine

guilt (*culpability*; see
  GILT)
  guilt•less

guilt•y
  guilt•i•er, guilt•i•est
  guilt•i•ly
  guilt•i•ness

Guin•ea (*place*)

guin•ea (*gold coin*)

Guin•ea-Bis•sau

Guin•ness

guise

gui•tar
  gui•tar•ist

Gui•yang

Gu•ja•ra•ti
  pl. Gu•ja•ra•tis

gulch

gulf

gull

gul•let

gul•li•ble
  gul•li•bil•i•ty
  gul•lib•ly

gull•y
  pl. gull•ies
  gull•ies, gull•ied

gulp

gum
  gummed, gum•ming
  gum•my
  gum•mi•er, gum•mi•est

gum•bo
  pl. gum•bos

gum•drop

gump•tion

gum•shoe

gun
  gunned, gun•ning

gun•boat

gun•fight
  gun•fight•er

gun•fire

gung-ho

gunk

gun•man
  pl. gun•men

gun•met•al

gun•nel
  var. of gun•wale

gun•ner

gun•ner•y

gun•ny
  pl. gun•nies

gun•pow•der

gun•run•ner
  gun•run•ning

gun•shot

gun•smith

gun•wale
  also gun•nel

gup•py
  pl. gup•pies

gur•gle

gu•ru

gush
  gush•ing
  gush•y

gush•er

gus•set
  gus•set•ed

gust
  gust•y

Gus•tav•us A•dol•phus

gus•to
  pl. gus•toes

gut
  gut•ted, gut•ting

Gut•en•berg

Guth•rie

gut•less

gut•sy
  gut•si•er, gut•si•est
  gut•si•ness

gut•ter

gut•ter•snipe

gut·tur·al
  gut·tur·al·ly

guy

Guy·a·na

guz·zle
  guz·zler

Gyan·dzha

gybe
  var. of jibe

gym

gym·na·si·um
  pl. gym·na·si·ums *or*
  gym·na·si·a

gym·nas·tics
  gym·nast
  gym·nas·tic
  gym·nas·ti·cal·ly

gym·no·sperm

gy·ne·col·o·gy
  gy·ne·co·log·i·cal
  gy·ne·col·o·gist

gyp
  gypped, gyp·ping

gyp·sum

Gyp·sy
  also Gip·sy
  pl. Gyp·sies

gy·rate
  gy·ra·tion
  gy·ra·tor
  gy·ra·to·ry

gy·ro
  pl. gy·ros

gy·ro·scope
  gy·ro·scop·ic
  gy·ro·scop·i·cal·ly

H

ha
   also hah

Haar·lem (*Holland*)

ha·be·as cor·pus

hab·er·dash·er
   hab·er·dash·er·y
   pl. hab·er·dash·er·ies

ha·bil·i·ment

hab·it
   hab·it-form·ing

hab·it·a·ble
   hab·it·a·bil·i·ty

hab·i·tat

hab·i·ta·tion

ha·bit·u·al
   ha·bit·u·al·ly

ha·bit·u·ate
   ha·bit·u·a·tion

ha·bit·u·é

ha·ček
   also há·ček

ha·ci·en·da

hack

hack·er

hack·le

hack·ney
   pl. hack·neys

hack·neyed

hack·saw

had

had·dock
   pl. same

Ha·des
   Ha·de·an

haf·ni·um

haft

hag

Hag·ga·dah

hag·gard
   hag·gard·ness

hag·gis

hag·gle
   hag·gler

Hague, The

hah
   var. of ha

ha ha

Hai·fa

hai·ku
   pl. same

hail (*frozen rain, welcome*;
   see HALE)

Hai·le Se·las·sie

hail·stone

hail·storm

Hai·phong

hair (*tresses*; see HARE)
   hair-rais·ing
   hair·less
   hair·like

hair·ball
   also hair ball

hair·brush

hair·cut

hair·do
   pl. hair·dos

hair·dress·er
   hair·dress·ing

hair·line

hair·net

hair·piece

hair·pin

hair·split·ting

hair·style
   hair·styl·ing
   hair·styl·ist

hair·y (*shaggy*; see
   HARRY)
   hair·i·er, hair·i·est
   hair·i·ness

Hai·ti
   Hai·tian

hajj

hake

Hak·luyt

hal·berd
   also hal·bert

hal·cy·on

Hale (*proper name*)

hale (*hearty*; see HAIL)

Ha·ley

half
   pl. halves
   half-baked
   half-life
   half-mast
   half-time
   half-truth

half·back

half·heart·ed
   half·heart·ed·ly
   half·heart·ed·ness

half·pen·ny
   also ha'penny
   pl. half·pen·nies *or* half·pence

half•tone

half•way

half•wit
half•wit•ted

hal•i•but
pl. same

Hal•i•fax

hal•i•to•sis

hall (*vestibule,
auditorium*; see HAUL.)

Hal•le

hal•le•lu•jah
var. of al•le•lu•ia

Hal•ley (*astronomer*)

hall•mark

hal•low

Hal•low•een
also Hal•low•e'en

hal•lu•ci•nate

hal•lu•ci•na•tion
hal•lu•ci•na•to•ry

hal•lu•ci•no•gen
hal•lu•ci•no•gen•ic

hall•way

ha•lo
pl. ha•loes, ha•los
ha•loes, ha•loed

ha•lo•gen
ha•lo•gen•ic

Hals

Hal•sey

halt
halt•ing•ly

halt•er

halve (*split*; see HAVE)

halves

hal•yard

ham
hammed, ham•ming

Ham•a•dan

Ham•burg (*city*; see
HOMBURG)

ham•burg•er

Ham•il•ton

ham•let

Ham•mar•skjold

ham•mer

ham•mer•head

Ham•mer•stein

ham•mer•toe

Ham•mett

ham•mock

Ham•mu•ra•bi

ham•per

Hamp•ton

ham•ster

ham•string
past and *past part.* ham•
strung *or* ham•
stringed

Ham•sun

Han•cock

hand
hand-me-down

hand•bag

hand•ball

hand•bill

hand•book

hand•cart

hand•cuff

Han•del

hand•ful
pl. hand•fuls

hand•gun

hand•i•cap
hand•i•capped, hand•
i•cap•ping
hand•i•capped

hand•i•craft

hand•i•work

hand•ker•chief
pl. hand•ker•chiefs *or*
hand•ker•chieves

han•dle

han•dle•bar

han•dler

hand•made

hand•out

hand•rail

hand•set

hand•shake

hand•some (*attractive*;
see HANSOM)
hand•som•er, hand•
som•est
hand•some•ly

hand•spring

hand•stand

hand•work
hand•worked

hand•writ•ing
hand•writ•ten

Han•dy (*proper name*)

hand•y (*convenient*)
hand•i•er, hand•i•est
hand•i•ly
hand•i•ness

hand•y•man
  pl. hand•y•men

hang
  past and *past part.* hung
  hang-up

hang•ar (*building*; see HANGER)

hang•dog

hang•er (*person or thing that hangs*; see HANGAR)
  hang•er-on
  pl. hang•ers-on

hang•ing

hang•man
  pl. hang•men

hang•nail

hang•out

hang•over

hank

han•ker
  han•ker•ing

Hanks

han•ky-pan•ky

Han•ni•bal

Ha•noi

Han•o•ver

han•som (*carriage*; see HANDSOME)

Ha•nuk•kah
  also Cha•nuk•kah

hap•haz•ard
  hap•haz•ard•ly

hap•less
  hap•less•ly
  hap•less•ness

hap•pen

hap•pen•ing

hap•py
  hap•pi•er, hap•pi•est
  hap•py-go-luck•y
  hap•pi•ly
  hap•pi•ness

ha•ra-ki•ri
  also ha•ri-ka•ri

ha•rangue

Ha•ra•re

ha•rass
  ha•rass•ment *or*
  ha•rass•ment

Har•bin

har•bin•ger

har•bor

hard
  hard-boiled
  hard-core
  hard-lin•er
  hard-nosed
  hard-pressed
  hard•ness

hard•back

hard•ball

hard•bit•ten

hard•cov•er

hard•en
  hard•en•ing

hard•head•ed
  hard•head•ed•ly
  hard•head•ed•ness

hard-heart•ed
  hard-heart•ed•ly
  hard-heart•ed•ness

har•di•hood

Har•ding

hard•ly

hard•ship

hard•top

hard•ware

hard•wood

hard•work•ing

Har•dy (*proper name*)

hard•y (*robust*)
  hard•i•er, hard•i•est
  har•di•ly
  har•di•ness

hare (*animal*; see HAIR)

hare•brained

hare•lip

har•em

ha•ri-ka•ri
  var. of ha•ra-ki•ri

hark

har•le•quin

Har•lem (*New York*)

har•lot
  har•lot•ry

harm

harm•ful
  harm•ful•ly
  harm•ful•ness

harm•less
  harm•less•ly
  harm•less•ness

har•mon•ic
  har•mon•i•cal•ly

har•mon•i•ca

har•mo•ni•ous
  har•mo•ni•ous•ly

har•mo•nize
  har•mo•ni•za•tion

har•mo•ny
  pl. har•mo•nies

Harms•worth

har•ness

harp
  harp•ist

har•poon

harp•si•chord
harp•si•chord•ist

har•py
pl. har•pies

har•ri•dan

har•ri•er

Har•ris

Har•ris•burg

Har•ri•son

har•row

har•row•ing

har•ry (ravage, harass;
see HAIRY)
har•ries, har•ried

harsh
harsh•ly
harsh•ness

Hart (proper name)

hart (deer; see HEART)

Hart•ford

har•um-scar•um

har•vest
har•ves•ter

Har•vey

has

has-been

hash

hash•ish

has•n't

hasp

has•si•um

has•sle

has•sock

haste

hast•en

hast•y
hast•i•er, hast•i•est
hast•i•ly
hast•i•ness

hat

hatch (door)

hatch (emerge from the
egg, devise)
hatch•er•y

hatch•back

hatch•et

hatch•way

hate

hate•ful
hate•ful•ly
hate•ful•ness

Hath•a•way

ha•tred

hat•ter

haugh•ty
haugh•ti•er, haugh•
ti•est
haugh•ti•ly
haugh•ti•ness

haul (pull, transport; see
HALL)
haul•er

haunch

haunt

haunt•ing
haunt•ing•ly

Haupt•mann

Hau•sa
pl. same or Hau•sas

haute cou•ture

haute cui•sine

Ha•van•a

have (possess; see HALVE)
past and past part. had
have-not

Ha•vel

ha•ven

have•n't

hav•er•sack

hav•oc

Ha•wai•i
Ha•wai•ian

hawk (bird, person
advocating war)
hawk-eyed
hawk•ish
hawk•ish•ly
hawk•ish•ness

hawk (sell goods)
hawk•er

Hawke (proper name)

Hawk•ing

haw•ser

haw•thorn (shrub)

Haw•thorne (proper
name)

Hay (proper name)

hay (dried grass; see HEY)

Hay•dn

Hayes

hay•stack

Hay•ward

hay•wire

haz•ard
haz•ard•ous

haze

ha•zel

ha•zel•nut

haz·y
  haz·i·er, haz·i·est
  ha·zi·ly
  ha·zi·ness

H-bomb

he
  he-man
  pl. he-men

head
  head-on

head·ache
  head·ach·y

head·board

head·dress

head·er

head·hunt·ing
  head·hunt
  head·hunt·er

head·ing

head·land

head·light

head·line
  head·lin·er

head·long

head·mas·ter
  fem. head·mis·tress

head·phone

head·quar·ters

head·rest

head·room

head·set

head·stone

head·strong

head·wa·ter

head·way

head·word

head·y
  head·i·er, head·i·est
  head·i·ly
  head·i·ness

heal (*mend*; see HEEL, HELL)
  heal·er

health

health·ful
  health·ful·ly
  health·ful·ness

health·y
  health·i·er, health·i·est
  health·i·ly
  health·i·ness

heap

hear (*perceive sound*; see HERE)
  past and *past part.* heard
  hear·er

hear·ing

hear·ken

hear·say

hearse

Hearst

heart (*organ, core*; see HART)
  heart-rend·ing
  heart-to-heart

heart·ache

heart·beat

heart·break
  heart·break·er
  heart·break·ing
  heart·bro·ken

heart·burn

heart·en
  heart·en·ing

heart·felt

hearth

heart·i·ly

heart·land

heart·less
  heart·less·ly

heart·sick

heart·throb

heart·warm·ing

heart·y
  heart·i·er, heart·i·est
  heart·i·ly
  heart·i·ness

heat
  heat·ing

heat·ed
  heat·ed·ly

heat·er

Heath (*proper name*)

heath (*uncultivated land*)

hea·then

hea·ther
  hea·ther·y

heat·stroke

heat·wave

heave
  past and *past part.*
  heaved *or* hove

heav·en
  heav·en·ward

heav·en·ly

heav·y
  heav·i·er, heav·i·est
  pl. heav·ies
  heav·y-du·ty
  heav·y-heart·ed
  heav·i·ly
  heav·i·ness
  heav·y·ish

heav·y-hand·ed
  heav·y-hand·ed·ly
  heav·y-hand·ed·ness

heav·y·set

heav·y·weight

He·bra·ic

He·brew

Heb·ri·des

heck

heck·le
heck·ler

hec·tare

hec·tic
hec·ti·cal·ly

hec·tor

he'd (*he had, he would*;
see HEED)

hedge

hedge·hog

he·do·nism
he·don·ist
he·don·is·tic

heed (*attend to*; see HE'D)
heed·ful
heed·less
heed·less·ly

hee-haw

heel (*part of foot*; see
HEAL, HE'LL)

heft·y
heft·i·er, heft·i·est
heft·i·ly
heft·i·ness

He·gel

he·ge·mo·ny

he·gi·ra
also he·ji·ra, He·gi·ra,
or He·ji·ra

Hei·deg·ger

Hei·del·berg

heif·er

Hei·fetz

height

height·en

Heim·lich ma·neu·ver

Hei·ne

hei·nous

Heinz

heir (*inheritor*; see AIR,
ERE)

heir·ess

heir·loom

heist

held

Hel·e·na

he·li·cal

hel·i·ces

he·li·cop·ter

he·li·o·cen·tric

he·li·o·trope

hel·i·port

he·li·um

he·lix
pl. he·li·ces

hell

he'll (*he will, he shall*; see
HEAL, HEEL)

hel·la·cious

hel·le·bore

Hel·le·nism
Hel·len·ic
Hel·len·ist

Hel·len·is·tic

Hel·ler

hell·hole

hel·lish

hel·lish·ly
hel·lish·ness

Hell·man

hel·lo
pl. hel·los

helm

hel·met
hel·met·ed

helms·man
pl. helms·men

help
help·er

help·ful
help·ful·ly
help·ful·ness

help·ing

help·less
help·less·ly
help·less·ness

help·mate

Hel·sin·ki

hel·ter-skel·ter

hem (*cloth border*)
hemmed, hem·ming

hem (*clearing of the throat*)
also a·hem
hemmed, hem·ming

he·ma·tol·o·gy
he·ma·tol·o·gist

Hem·ing·way

hem·i·sphere
hem·i·spher·ic
hem·i·spher·i·cal

hem·line

hem·lock

he·mo·glo·bin

he·mo·phil·i·a
he·mo·phil·ic

he·mo·phil·i·ac

hem·or·rhage

hem·or·rhoid
  hem·or·rhoi·dal

hemp

hem·stitch

hen

hence

hence·forth
  also hence·for·ward

hench·man
  pl. hench·men

Hen·drix

hen·na

hen·peck

Hen·ry

Hen·son

hep
  var. of hip

he·pat·ic

hep·a·ti·tis

Hep·burn

hep·ta·gon
  hep·tag·o·nal

hep·tath·lon

her

Her·a·cli·tus

He·rak·li·on
  also I·rák·li·on

her·ald
  her·ald·ic

her·ald·ry

herb
  her·ba·ceous
  herb·al
  herb·al·ist

her·bi·cide

her·bi·vore
  her·biv·o·rous

Her·cu·le·an

Her·cu·les

herd
  herd·er

herds·man
  pl. herds·men

here (*this place*; see HEAR)

here·a·bouts
  also here·a·bout

here·af·ter

here·by

he·red·i·tar·y

he·red·i·ty

here·in

her·e·sy
  pl. her·e·sies

her·e·tic
  he·ret·i·cal

here·to·fore

here·up·on

here·with

her·i·tage

herk·y-jerk·y

her·maph·ro·dite
  her·maph·ro·dit·ic

her·met·ic
  her·met·i·cal·ly

her·mit
  her·mit·ic

her·mit·age

Her·mo·si·llo

her·ni·a
  pl. her·ni·as *or* her·
  ni·ae
  her·ni·at·ed

he·ro
  pl. he·roes

Her·od

He·rod·o·tus

he·ro·ic
  her·o·i·cal·ly

her·o·in (*drug*; see
  HEROINE)

her·o·ine (*woman*; see
  HEROIN)

her·o·ism

her·on

her·pes
  her·pes zos·ter

her·pe·tol·o·gy
  her·pe·to·log·i·cal
  her·pe·tol·o·gist

Her·rick

her·ring

her·ring·bone

hers

her·self

hertz
  pl. same

Her·zl

he's

He·si·od

hes·i·tant
  hes·i·tance
  hes·i·tan·cy
  hes·i·tant·ly

hes·i·tate
  hes·i·ta·tion

Hess

Hes·se

het·er·o·dox
  het·er·o·dox·y

het•er•o•ge•ne•ous
het•er•o•ge•ne•i•ty

het•er•o•sex•u•al
het•er•o•sex•u•al•i•ty
het•er•o•sex•u•al•ly

heu•ris•tic
heu•ris•ti•cal•ly

hew (*chop*; see HUE)
past part. hewn *or*
hewed

hex

hex•a•dec•i•mal
also hex

hex•a•gon
hex•ag•o•nal

hex•a•gram

hex•am•e•ter

hey (*expression calling
attention*; see HAY)

hey•day

Hey•er•dahl

Hi•a•le•ah

hi•a•tus
pl. hi•a•tus•es

hi•ba•chi

hi•ber•nate
hi•ber•na•tion

Hi•ber•ni•an

hi•bis•cus

hic•cup
also hic•cough

hick

Hick•ok

hick•o•ry
pl. hick•o•ries

hid

Hi•dal•go

hid•den

hide (*conceal*)
past hid; *past part.* hid•
den
hide-and-seek
hide-out
hid•den
hid•er

hide (*skin*)

hide•a•way

hide•bound

hid•e•ous
hid•e•ous•ly
hid•e•ous•ness

hi•er•ar•chy
pl. hi•er•ar•chies
hi•er•ar•chi•cal

hi•er•o•glyph•ic

hi-fi
pl. hi-fis

hig•gle•dy-pig•gle•dy

high
high-flown
high-lev•el
high-oc•cu•pan•cy
high-pitched
high-pow•ered
high-rise
high-spir•it•ed
high-strung

high•ball

high•boy

high•brow

high•fa•lu•tin
also high•fa•lu•ting

high-hand•ed
high•-hand•ed•ly
high•-hand•ed•ness

high•land
also the High•lands
high•land•er
also High•land•er

high•light

high•ly

high-mind•ed
high•-mind•ed•ly
high•-mind•ed•ness

high•ness

high•way

high•way•man
pl. high•way•men

hi•jack
hi•jack•er

hike
hik•er

hi•lar•i•ous
hi•lar•i•ous•ly
hi•lar•i•ty

hill
hil•li•ness
hill•y

Hil•la•ry

hill•bil•ly
pl. hill•bil•lies

hill•side

hill•top

hilt

Hil•ton

him (*objective case of he*;
see HYMN)

Him•a•la•yas
Him•a•lay•an

Himm•ler

him•self

hind

Hin•de•mith

Hin•den•burg

hin•der

Hin•di

hind•most

hind·quar·ters

hin·drance

hind·sight

Hin·du
  Hin·du·ism

Hin·du Kush

Hin·du·sta·ni

hinge

hint

hin·ter·land

hip (*fruit of a rose*)
  also hep

hip (*part of body*)

hip (*stylish, aware*)
  also hep
  hip·per, hip·pest

hip·bone

hip·pie
  also hip·py
  pl. hip·pies

hip·po
  pl. hip·pos

hip·po·cam·pus
  pl. hip·po·cam·pi

Hip·poc·ra·tes

Hip·po·crat·ic oath

hip·po·drome

hip·po·pot·a·mus
  pl. hip·po·pot·a·mus·
  es *or* hip·po·pot·a·mi

hip·py
  var. of hip·pie

hire
  hir·a·ble
  also hire·a·ble
  hir·er

hire·ling

Hi·ro·hi·to

Hi·ro·shi·ma

hir·sute
  hir·sut·ism

his

His·pan·ic

His·pan·io·la

hiss

his·ta·mine

his·tol·o·gy

his·to·ri·an

his·tor·ic

his·tor·i·cal
  his·tor·i·cal·ly

his·to·ric·i·ty

his·tor·i·og·ra·phy
  his·tor·i·og·ra·pher
  his·tor·i·o·graph·ic
  his·tor·i·o·graph·i·cal

his·to·ry
  pl. his·to·ries

his·tri·on·ic

hit
  hit·ting; *past* and *past*
  part. hit

hitch

Hitch·cock

hitch·hike
  hitch·hiker

hith·er

hith·er·to

Hit·ler

Hit·tite

hive

hives

hoa·gie
  also hoa·gy
  pl. hoa·gies

hoar (*frost*; see WHORE)

hoard (*stockpile*; see
  HORDE)
  hoard·er
  hoard·ing

hoarse (*husky*; see
  HORSE)
  hoarse·ly
  hoarse·ness

hoar·y
  hoar·i·er, hoar·i·est

hoax

Hobbes

hob·ble

hob·by
  pl. hob·bies
  hob·by·ist

hob·by·horse

hob·gob·lin

hob·nail

hob·nob
  hob·nobbed, hob·nob·
  bing

ho·bo
  pl. ho·boes *or* ho·bos

Ho Chi Minh

hock

hock·ey

ho·cus-po·cus
  ho·cus-po·cused,
  ho·cus-po·cus·ing;
  ho·cus-po·cussed,
  ho·cus-po·cus·sing

hod

hodge·podge

Hodg·kin's dis·ease

hoe
  hoes, hoed, hoe·ing

hog
  hogged, hog•ging
  hog•gish

Ho•garth

hogs•head

hog•wash

hoi pol•loi

hoist

hoi•ty-toi•ty

hok•ey
  also hok•y
  hok•i•er, hok•i•est
  hok•ey•ness

Hok•kai•do

ho•kum

Hol•bein

hold
  past and *past part.* held
  hold•er

hold•ing

hold•up

hole (*cavity, puncture;*
  see WHOLE)
  hol•ey (*having holes;*
  see HOLY, WHOLLY)

hol•i•day

ho•li•ness

Hol•ins•hed

ho•lism
  ho•lis•tic
  ho•lis•ti•cal•ly

Hol•land

hol•lan•daise sauce

hol•ler

hol•low
  hol•low•ly
  hol•low•ness

hol•low•ware

hol•ly
  pl. hol•lies

hol•ly•hock

Hol•ly•wood

Holmes

hol•mi•um

ho•lo•caust
  also the Ho•lo•caust

ho•lo•gram

ho•lo•graph

ho•log•ra•phy
  hol•o•graph•ic

Holst

hol•ster

ho•ly (*sacred;* see *holey*
  [HOLE], WHOLLY)
  ho•li•er, ho•li•est
  ho•li•er-than-thou

hom•age

Hom•burg (*hat;* see
  HAMBURG)
  also hom•burg

home
  home•like

home•boy

home•com•ing

home•grown

home•land

home•less
  home•less•ness

home•ly
  home•li•er, home•li•est
  home•li•ness

home•made

home•maker

ho•me•op•a•thy
  ho•me•o•path
  ho•me•o•path•ic

Ho•mer
  Ho•mer•ic

home•sick
  home•sick•ness

home•spun

home•stead

home•style

home•ward
  also home•wards

home•work

hom•ey
  also hom•y
  hom•i•er, hom•i•est
  hom•ey•ness
  also hom•i•ness

ho•mi•cide
  ho•mi•ci•dal

hom•i•ly
  pl. hom•i•lies
  hom•i•let•ic

hom•i•nid

hom•i•noid

hom•i•ny

ho•mo•ge•ne•ous
  ho•mo•ge•ne•i•ty
  ho•mo•ge•ne•ous•ly

ho•mog•en•ize

hom•o•graph

ho•mol•o•gous

hom•o•nym

ho•mo•pho•bi•a
  ho•mo•phobe
  ho•mo•pho•bic

ho•mo•phone

Ho•mo sa•pi•ens

ho•mo•sex•u•al
  ho•mo•sex•u•al•i•ty

hom•y
  var. of hom•ey

hon•cho
  pl. hon•chos

Hon•du•ras
  Hon•du•ran

hone

Ho•neck•er

hon•est
  hon•es•ty

hon•est•ly

hon•ey
  pl. hon•eys

hon•ey•comb

hon•ey•dew

hon•eyed
  also hon•ied

hon•ey•moon
  hon•ey•moon•er

hon•ey•suck•le

Hong Kong

Ho•ni•a•ra

honk

honk•y-tonk

Hon•o•lu•lu

hon•or

hon•or•a•ble
  hon•or•a•bly

hon•o•rar•i•um
  pl. hon•o•rar•i•ums *or*
  hon•o•rar•i•a

hon•or•ar•y

hon•or•if•ic
  hon•or•if•i•cal•ly

Hon•shu

hooch

hood

hood•lum

hood•wink

hoo•ey

hoof
  pl. hoofs *or* hooves

hook

hoo•kah

hooked

hook•er

hook•up

hook•worm

hook•y
  also hook•ey

hoo•li•gan
  hoo•li•gan•ism

hoop

hoop•la

hoo•ray

hoot

Hoo•ver

hooves

hop (*jumping step*)
  hopped, hop•ping

hop (*plant*)

hope

hope•ful

hope•ful•ly

hope•less
  hope•less•ly
  hope•less•ness

Ho•pi

Hop•kins

Hop•per (*proper name*)

hop•per (*tapering
  container, insect*)

hop•scotch

Hor•ace

horde (*large group;* see
  HOARD)

hore•hound

ho•ri•zon

hor•i•zon•tal
  hor•i•zon•tal•ly

hor•mone
  hor•mon•al

horn

horn•blende

hor•net

horn•pipe

horn•y
  horn•i•er, horn•i•est
  horn•i•ness

ho•rol•o•gy
  ho•ro•log•i•cal

hor•o•scope

Hor•o•witz

hor•ren•dous
  hor•ren•dous•ly

hor•ri•ble
  hor•ri•bly

hor•rid

hor•rif•ic
  hor•rif•i•cal•ly

hor•ri•fy
  hor•ri•fies, hor•ri•fied
  hor•ri•fy•ing

hor•ror

hors d'oeuvre
  pl. same or hors
  d'oeuvres

horse (*animal;* see
  HOARSE)

horse•back

horse·fly
 pl. horse·flies

horse·hair

horse·man
 pl. horse·men

horse·play

horse·pow·er
 pl. same

horse·rad·ish

horse·shoe

horse·tail

horse·whip
 horse·whipped, horse·
 whip·ping

horse·wom·an
 pl. horse·wom·en

hors·y
 also hors·ey
 hors·i·er, hors·i·est

hor·ti·cul·ture
 hor·ti·cul·tur·al
 hor·ti·cul·tur·ist

ho·san·na

hose

ho·sier·y

hos·pice

hos·pi·ta·ble
 hos·pi·ta·bly

hos·pi·tal

hos·pi·tal·i·ty

hos·pi·tal·ize
 hos·pi·tal·i·za·tion

host

hos·tage

hos·tel (*lodging*; see
 HOSTILE)

hos·tel·ry
 pl. hos·tel·ries

host·ess

hos·tile (*antagonistic*; see
 HOSTEL)
 hos·tile·ly

hos·til·i·ty
 pl. hos·til·i·ties

hot
 hot·ter, hot·test
 hot-blood·ed
 hot-tem·pered
 hot·ly
 hot·ness

hot·bed

hot·cake

ho·tel

ho·tel·ier

hot·head
 hot·head·ed
 hot·head·ed·ness

hot·house

Hou·di·ni

hound

hour (*60 minutes*; see
 OUR)

hour·glass

hour·ly

house

house·boat

house·break·ing
 house·break·er

house·bro·ken

house·coat

house·dress

house·fly

house·hold
 house·hold·er

house·hus·band

house·keep·er

house·keep·ing

house·maid

house·plant

house·wares

house·warm·ing

house·wife
 pl. house·wives
 house·wife·ly

house·work

hous·ing

Hous·man

Hous·ton

hove

hov·el

hov·er

hov·er·craft
 pl. same

how

how·dah

Howe

How·ells

how·ev·er

how·it·zer

howl

howl·er

how·so·ev·er

Hox·ha

hoy·den

Huang River

hub

hub·bub

hub·by
 pl. hub·bies

hu·bris
 hu·bris·tic**

huck·le·ber·ry
  pl. huck·le·ber·ries

huck·ster

hud·dle

Hud·son

hue (*shade*; see HEW)

hue and cry

huff
  huff·y

hug
  hugged, hug·ging

huge
  huge·ly

Hughes

Hu·go

Hu·gue·not

huh

hu·la
  also hu·la-hu·la

hulk

hulk·ing

Hull (*proper name, place*)

hull (*shell*)

hul·la·ba·loo
  pl. hul·la·ba·loos

hum
  hummed, hum·ming

hu·man

hu·mane
  hu·mane·ly
  hu·mane·ness

hu·man·ism
  hu·man·ist
  hu·man·is·tic

hu·man·i·tar·i·an
  hu·man·i·tar·i·an·ism

hu·man·i·ty
  pl. hu·man·i·ties

hu·man·ize
  hu·man·i·za·tion

hu·man·kind

hu·man·ly

hum·ble
  hum·ble·ness
  hum·bly

hum·bug
  hum·bugged, hum·bug·ging

hum·ding·er

hum·drum

Hume

hu·mer·us (*bone*; see HUMOROUS)
  pl. hu·mer·i
  hu·mer·al

hu·mid

hu·mid·i·fy
  hu·mid·i·fies, hu·mid·i·fied
  hu·mid·i·fi·ca·tion
  hu·mid·i·fi·er

hu·mid·i·ty
  pl. hu·mid·i·ties

hu·mi·dor

hu·mil·i·ate
  hu·mil·i·at·ing
  hu·mil·i·a·tion

hu·mil·i·ty

hum·ming·bird

hum·mock

hum·mus

hu·mon·gous
  also hu·mun·gous

hu·mor
  hu·mor·ist

hu·mor·less
  hu·mor·less·ly
  hu·mor·less·ness

hu·mor·ous (*amusing*; see HUMERUS)
  hu·mor·ous·ly

hump

hump·back
  hump·backed

Hum·per·dinck

hu·mus

Hun

hunch

hunch·back
  hunch·backed

hun·dred
  pl. hun·dreds *or* hun·dred
  hun·dred·fold
  hun·dredth

hun·dred·weight
  pl. same *or* hun·dred·weights

hung

Hun·ga·ry
  Hun·gar·i·an

hun·ger
  hun·gry
  hun·gri·er, hun·gri·est
  hun·gri·ly

hunk
  hunk·y
  hunk·i·er, hunk·i·est

hunt
  hunt·er
  hunt·ress
  hunt·ing
  hunts·man
  pl. hunts·men

Hun·ting·ton

Hunts·ville

hur•dle
hur•dler

hur•dy-gur•dy
pl. hur•dy-gur•dies

hurl

hur•ly-bur•ly

Hu•ron

hur•rah
also hur•ray

hur•ri•cane

hur•ry
pl. hur•ries
hur•ries, hur•ried
hur•ried•ly

hurt
past and past part. hurt

hurt•ful
hurt•ful•ly

hur•tle

hus•band

hus•band•ry

hush

hush-hush

husk

husk•y (*dog*)
pl. husk•ies

husk•y (*hoarse, brawny*)
husk•i•er, husk•i•est
husk•i•ly
husk•i•ness

Hus•sein
also Hu•sain

Hus•serl

hus•sy
pl. hus•sies

hus•tings

hus•tle
hus•tler

hut

hutch

Hutch•in•son

Hux•ley

hy•a•cinth

hy•brid
hy•brid•ism

hy•brid•ize
hy•brid•i•za•tion

Hy•der•a•bad

hy•dra

hy•dran•gea

hy•drant

hy•drate
hy•dra•tion

hy•drau•lic
hy•drau•li•cal•ly

hy•drau•lics

hy•dro•car•bon

hy•dro•chlo•ric ac•id

hy•dro•dy•nam•ics
hy•dro•dy•nam•ic

hy•dro•e•lec•tric
hy•dro•e•lec•tric•i•ty

hy•dro•foil

hy•dro•gen
hy•dro•gen•ous

hy•drog•e•nate
hy•drog•en•a•tion

hy•drol•o•gy
hy•drol•o•gist

hy•drol•y•sis

hy•dro•lyze

hy•drom•e•ter

hy•dro•pho•bi•a
hy•dro•pho•bic

hy•dro•plane

hy•dro•pon•ics
hy•dro•pon•ic
hy•dro•pon•i•cal•ly

hy•dro•sphere

hy•dro•ther•a•py

hy•drous

hy•drox•ide

hy•e•na

hy•giene
hy•gi•en•ic
hy•gi•en•i•cal•ly

hy•gien•ist

hy•grom•e•ter

hy•men

hymn (*song;* see HIM)

hym•nal

hype

hy•per

hy•per•ac•tive
hy•per•ac•tiv•i•ty

hy•per•bo•la
pl. hy•per•bo•las *or* hy•
per•bo•lae
hy•per•bol•ic

hy•per•bo•le
hy•per•bol•ic
hy•per•bol•i•cal

hy•per•crit•i•cal
hy•per•crit•i•cal•ly

hy•per•gly•ce•mi•a

hy•per•sen•si•tive
hy•per•sen•si•tiv•i•ty

hy•per•ten•sion
hy•per•ten•sive

hy•per•text

hy•per•ther•mi•a
hy•per•ther•mic

hy·per·thy·roid·ism
  hy·per·thy·roid

hy·per·ven·ti·la·tion

hy·phen

hy·phen·ate
  hy·phen·a·tion

hyp·no·sis

hyp·no·ther·a·py

hyp·not·ic
  hyp·not·i·cal·ly

hyp·no·tism
  hyp·no·tist

hyp·no·tize

hy·po
  pl. hy·pos

hy·po·al·ler·gen·ic

hy·po·chon·dri·a
  hy·po·chon·dri·ac
  hy·po·chon·dri·a·cal

hy·poc·ri·sy
  pl. hy·poc·ri·sies

hy·po·crite
  hy·po·crit·i·cal
  hy·po·crit·i·cal·ly

hy·po·der·mic

hy·po·gly·ce·mi·a
  hy·po·gly·ce·mic

hy·po·ten·sion
  hy·po·ten·sive

hy·pot·e·nuse

hy·po·thal·a·mus
  pl. hy·po·thal·a·mi
  hy·po·thal·a·mic

hy·po·ther·mi·a

hy·poth·e·sis
  pl. hy·poth·e·ses
  hy·poth·e·size

hy·po·thet·i·cal
  hy·po·thet·i·cal·ly

hy·po·thy·roid·ism
  hy·po·thy·roid

hys·ter·ec·to·my
  pl. hys·ter·ec·to·mies

hys·te·ri·a

hys·ter·ic

hys·ter·i·cal
  hys·ter·i·cal·ly

I

i•amb

i•am•bic

I•ba•dan

I•be•ri•an Pen•in•su•la
  also I•ber•i•a

i•bex
  pl. same *or* i•bex•es

i•bis
  pl. same *or* i•bis•es

Ibn Sa•ud

Ib•sen

i•bu•pro•fen

ice
  ice-skate
  ice-skat•er

ice•berg

ice•box

ice•break•er

ice floe

Ice•land
  Ice•land•er
  Ice•land•ic

i•chor

ich•thy•ol•o•gy
  ich•thy•o•log•i•cal
  i•ch•thy•ol•o•gist

i•ci•cle

ic•ing

ick•y

i•con
  i•con•ic

i•con•o•clast
  i•con•o•clasm
  i•con•o•clas•tic
  i•con•o•clas•ti•cal•ly

i•co•nog•ra•phy
  pl. i•co•nog•ra•phies
  i•co•nog•ra•pher
  i•con•o•graph•ic
  i•con•o•graph•i•cal
  i•con•o•graph•i•cal•ly

i•cy
  i•ci•er, i•ci•est
  i•ci•ly
  i•ci•ness

id

I•da•ho
  I•da•ho•an

i•de•a
  i•de•a•less

i•de•al
  i•de•al•ly

i•de•al•ism
  i•de•al•ist
  i•de•al•is•tic
  i•de•al•is•ti•cal•ly

i•de•al•ize
  i•de•al•i•za•tion

i•dée fixe
  pl. i•dées fixes

i•den•ti•cal
  i•den•ti•cal•ly

i•den•ti•fi•ca•tion

i•den•ti•fy
  i•den•ti•fies, i•den•ti•
    fied
  i•den•ti•fi•a•ble

i•den•ti•ty
  pl. i•den•ti•ties

id•e•o•gram

id•e•o•logue

id•e•ol•o•gy
  pl. id•e•ol•o•gies
  i•de•o•log•i•cal
  i•de•o•log•i•cal•ly
  i•de•ol•o•gist

ides

id•i•o•cy
  pl. id•i•o•cies

id•i•om
  id•i•o•mat•ic
  i•di•o•mat•i•cal•ly

id•i•o•syn•cra•sy
  pl. id•i•o•syn•cra•sies
  id•i•o•syn•crat•ic
  id•i•o•syn•crat•i•cal•ly

id•i•ot
  id•i•ot•ic
  id•i•ot•i•cal•ly

i•dle (*lazy, unused*; see
  IDOL, IDYLL)
  i•dler, i•dlest
  i•dle•ness
  i•dler
  i•dly

i•dol (*graven image*; see
  IDLE, IDYLL)

i•dol•a•try

i•dol•ize
  i•dol•i•za•tion
  i•dol•iz•er

i•dyll (*literary term*; see
  IDLE, IDOL)
  also i•dyl
  i•dyl•list
  i•dyl•lize

i•dyl•lic
  i•dyl•li•cal•ly

if

if•fy
  if•fi•er, if•fi•est

ig•loo

Ig·na·tius

ig·ne·ous

ig·nite
　ig·nit·a·ble
　ig·nit·a·bil·i·ty
　ig·nit·i·ble
　ig·nit·i·bil·i·ty

ig·ni·tion

ig·no·ble
　ig·no·bler, ig·no·blest
　ig·no·bil·i·ty
　ig·no·bly

ig·no·min·i·ous
　ig·no·min·i·ous·ly

ig·no·mi·ny

ig·no·ra·mus
　pl. ig·no·ra·mus·es *or*
　ig·no·ra·mi

ig·no·rance
　ig·no·rant
　ig·no·rant·ly

ig·nore
　ig·nor·er

i·gua·na

I·guas·sú Falls

Ikh·na·ton

il·e·os·to·my
　pl. il·e·os·to·mies

il·e·um (*part of the
　intestine*; see ILIUM)
　pl. il·e·a
　il·e·ac

il·i·um (*bone in the pelvis*;
　see ILEUM)
　pl. il·i·a

ilk

I'll (*I shall, I will*; see
　AISLE, ISLE)

ill
　ill-ad·vised
　ill-bred

ill-fat·ed
ill-fa·vored
ill-got·ten
ill-man·nered
ill-na·tured
ill-tem·pered
Ill-treat
ill-use

il·le·gal
　il·le·gal·i·ty
　pl. il·le·gal·i·ties
　il·le·gal·ly

il·leg·i·ble
　il·leg·i·bil·i·ty
　il·leg·i·bly

il·le·git·i·mate
　il·le·git·i·ma·cy
　il·le·git·i·mate·ly

il·lib·er·al
　il·lib·er·al·i·ty
　pl. il·lib·er·al·i·ties
　il·lib·er·al·ly

il·li·cit (*unlawful*; see
　ELICIT)
　il·li·cit·ly
　il·li·cit·ness

il·lim·it·a·ble

Il·li·nois
　Il·li·nois·an *or*
　Il·li·noi·an

il·lit·er·ate
　il·lit·er·a·cy

ill·ness

il·log·i·cal
　il·log·i·cal·i·ty
　pl. il·log·i·cal·i·ties
　il·log·i·cal·ly

il·lu·mi·nate
　il·lu·mi·nat·ing
　il·lu·mi·na·tion
　il·lu·mi·na·tive
　il·lu·mi·na·tor

il·lu·mi·na·ti

il·lu·mine

il·lu·sion (*deception,
　fantasy*; see
　ALLUSION)
　il·lu·sion·al
　il·lu·sive

il·lu·sion·ist

il·lu·so·ry
　il·lu·so·ri·ly
　il·lu·so·ri·ness

il·lus·trate
　il·lus·tra·tor

il·lus·tra·tion
　il·lus·tra·tion·al

il·lus·tra·tive
　il·lus·tra·tive·ly

il·lus·tri·ous
　il·lus·tri·ous·ly
　il·lus·tri·ous·ness

I'm

im·age

i·mag·i·nar·y
　i·mag·i·nar·i·ly

i·mag·i·na·tion

i·mag·i·na·tive
　i·mag·i·na·tive·ly
　i·mag·i·na·tive·ness

i·mag·ine
　i·mag·in·a·ble
　i·mag·in·er

i·mag·in·ings

i·ma·go
　pl. i·ma·goes *or* i·ma·
　gi·nes

i·mam
　i·mam·ate

im·bal·ance

im·be·cile
　im·be·cil·ic
　im·be·cil·i·ty
　pl. im·be·cil·i·ties

im·bed
  var. of em·bed

im·bibe
  im·bib·er

im·bro·glio
  pl. im·bro·glios

im·bue
  im·bues, im·bued, im·bu·ing

im·i·tate
  im·i·ta·ble
  im·i·ta·tor

im·i·ta·tion
  im·i·ta·tive·ly

im·mac·u·late
  im·mac·u·late·ly
  im·mac·u·late·ness

im·ma·nent
  im·ma·nence
  im·ma·nen·cy

im·ma·te·ri·al
  im·ma·te·ri·al·ly

im·ma·ture
  im·ma·ture·ly
  im·ma·tu·ri·ty

im·mea·sur·a·ble
  im·mea·sur·a·bil·i·ty
  im·mea·sur·a·bly

im·me·di·ate
  im·me·di·a·cy
  im·me·di·ate·ly
  im·me·di·ate·ness

im·me·mo·ri·al

im·mense
  im·mense·ly
  im·mense·ness
  im·men·si·ty

im·merse
  im·mer·sion

im·mi·grant

im·mi·grate
  im·mi·gra·tion

im·mi·nent
  im·mi·nence
  im·mi·nent·ly

im·mo·bile
  im·mo·bil·i·ty

im·mo·bi·lize
  im·mo·bi·li·za·tion

im·mod·er·ate
  im·mod·er·ate·ly
  im·mod·er·a·tion

im·mod·est
  im·mod·est·ly
  im·mod·es·ty

im·mo·late
  im·mo·la·tion

im·mor·al
  im·mo·ral·i·ty
  pl. im·mo·ral·i·ties
  im·mor·al·ly

im·mor·tal
  im·mor·tal·i·ty
  im·mor·tal·ize

im·mov·a·ble
  im·mov·a·bil·i·ty
  im·mov·a·bly

im·mune

im·mu·ni·ty
  pl. im·mu·ni·ties

im·mu·nize
  im·mu·ni·za·tion
  im·mu·niz·er

im·mu·nol·o·gy
  im·mu·no·log·ic
  im·mu·no·log·i·cal
  im·mu·nol·o·gist

im·mu·no·sup·pressed

im·mu·no·sup·pres·sion
  im·mu·no·sup·pres·sant
  im·mu·no·sup·pres·sive

im·mu·no·ther·a·py

im·mure

im·mu·ta·ble
  im·mu·ta·bil·i·ty
  im·mu·ta·bly

imp

im·pact
  im·pac·tion

im·pair
  im·pair·ment

im·pa·la
  pl. same

im·pale
  im·pale·ment

im·pal·pa·ble
  im·pal·pa·bil·i·ty
  im·pal·pa·bly

im·pan·el
  im·pan·el·ment

im·part
  im·part·a·ble

im·par·tial
  im·par·ti·al·i·ty
  im·par·tial·ly

im·pass·a·ble (*dense, inaccessible*; see IMPASSIBLE)
  im·pass·a·bil·i·ty
  im·pass·a·bly

im·passe

im·pas·si·ble (*impassive*; see IMPASSABLE)
  im·pas·si·bil·i·ty
  im·pas·si·bly

im·pas·sioned

im·pas·sive
  im·pas·sive·ly
  im·pas·sive·ness
  im·pas·siv·i·ty

im·pas·to

im·pa·tient
  im·pa·tience
  im·pa·tient·ly

im·peach
  im·peach·a·ble
  im·peach·ment

im·pec·ca·ble
  im·pec·ca·bly

im·pe·cu·ni·ous
  im·pe·cu·ni·ous·ness

im·ped·ance

im·pede

im·ped·i·ment
  im·ped·i·men·tal

im·ped·i·men·ta

im·pel
  im·pelled, im·pel·ling
  im·pel·lent
  im·pel·ler

im·pend
  im·pend·ing

im·pen·e·tra·ble
  im·pen·e·tra·bil·i·ty
  im·pen·e·tra·ble·ness
  im·pen·e·tra·bly

im·pen·i·tent
  im·pen·i·tence
  im·pen·i·tent·ly

im·per·a·tive
  im·per·a·ti·val
  im·per·a·tive·ly

im·per·cep·ti·ble
  im·per·cep·ti·bil·i·ty
  im·per·cep·ti·bly

im·per·fect
  im·per·fect·ly

im·per·fec·tion

im·pe·ri·al
  im·pe·ri·al·ly

im·pe·ri·al·ism
  im·pe·ri·al·ist
  im·pe·ri·al·is·tic
  im·pe·ri·al·is·ti·cal·ly

Im·pe·ri·al Val·ley

im·per·il

im·pe·ri·ous
  im·pe·ri·ous·ly
  im·pe·ri·ous·ness

im·per·ish·a·ble
  im·per·ish·a·bil·i·ty
  im·per·ish·a·bly

im·per·ma·nent
  im·per·ma·nence
  im·per·ma·nen·cy
  im·per·ma·nent·ly

im·per·me·a·ble
  im·per·me·a·bil·i·ty

im·per·mis·si·ble

im·per·son·al
  im·per·son·al·ly

im·per·son·ate
  im·per·son·a·tion
  im·per·son·a·tor

im·per·ti·nent
  im·per·ti·nence
  im·per·ti·nent·ly

im·per·turb·a·ble
  im·per·turb·a·bil·i·ty
  im·per·turb·a·bly

im·per·vi·ous
  im·per·vi·ous·ly
  im·per·vi·ous·ness

im·pe·ti·go

im·pet·u·ous
  im·pet·u·os·i·ty
  im·pet·u·ous·ly
  im·pet·u·ous·ness

im·pe·tus

im·pi·et·y
  pl. im·pi·et·ies

im·pinge
  im·pinge·ment
  im·ping·er

im·pi·ous
  im·pi·ous·ly
  im·pi·ous·ness

imp·ish
  imp·ish·ly
  imp·ish·ness

im·pla·ca·ble
  im·pla·ca·bil·i·ty
  im·plac·a·bly

im·plant
  im·plan·ta·tion

im·plau·si·ble
  im·plau·si·bil·i·ty
  im·plau·si·bly

im·ple·ment
  im·ple·men·ta·tion

im·pli·cate

im·pli·ca·tion

im·plic·it
  im·plic·it·ly
  im·plic·it·ness

im·plode
  im·plo·sion
  im·plo·sive

im·plore
  im·plor·ing
  im·plor·ing·ly

im·ply
  im·plies, im·plied
  im·plied

im·po·lite
  im·po·lite·ly
  im·po·lite·ness

im·pol·i·tic
  im·pol·i·tic·ly

im·pon·der·a·ble
  im·pon·der·a·bil·i·ty
  im·pon·der·a·bly

im·port
  im·port·a·ble
  im·por·ta·tion
  im·port·er

im·por·tant
  im·por·tance
  im·por·tant·ly

im·por·tu·nate
  im·por·tu·nate·ly
  im·por·tu·ni·ty

im·por·tune

im·pose
  im·po·si·tion

im·pos·ing
  im·pos·ing·ly

im·pos·si·ble
  im·pos·si·bil·i·ty
  im·pos·si·bly

im·post

im·pos·tor
  also im·pos·ter

im·pos·ture

im·po·tent
  im·po·tence
  im·po·ten·cy
  im·po·tent·ly

im·pound
  im·pound·a·ble
  im·pound·er
  im·pound·ment

im·pov·er·ish
  im·pov·er·ish·ment

im·prac·ti·ca·ble
  im·prac·ti·ca·bil·i·ty
  im·prac·ti·ca·bly

im·prac·ti·cal
  im·prac·ti·cal·i·ty
  im·prac·ti·cal·ly

im·pre·cate

im·pre·ca·tion

im·pre·cise
  im·pre·cise·ly
  im·pre·ci·sion

im·preg·na·ble
  im·preg·na·bil·i·ty
  im·preg·na·bly

im·preg·nate
  im·preg·na·tion

im·pre·sa·ri·o
  pl. im·pre·sa·ri·os

im·press
  im·press·i·ble

im·pres·sion

im·pres·sion·a·ble
  im·pres·sion·a·bil·i·ty
  im·pres·sion·a·bly

im·pres·sion·ism
  im·pres·sion·ist
  im·pres·sion·is·tic

im·pres·sive
  im·pres·sive·ly
  im·pres·sive·ness

im·pri·ma·tur

im·print

im·pris·on
  im·pris·on·ment

im·prob·a·ble
  im·prob·a·bil·i·ty
  im·prob·a·bly

im·promp·tu

im·prop·er
  im·prop·er·ly

im·pro·pri·e·ty
  pl. im·pro·pri·e·ties

im·prove
  im·prov·a·ble
  im·prove·ment

im·prov·i·dent
  im·prov·i·dence
  im·prov·i·dent·ly

im·pro·vise
  im·pro·vi·sa·tion
  im·pro·vi·sa·tion·al
  im·pro·vi·ser

im·pru·dent
  im·pru·dence
  im·pru·dent·ly

im·pu·dent
  im·pu·dence
  im·pu·dent·ly

im·pugn
  im·pugn·a·ble

im·pulse

im·pul·sion

im·pul·sive
  im·pul·sive·ly
  im·pul·sive·ness

im·pu·ni·ty

im·pure
  im·pure·ly
  im·pure·ness

im·pu·ri·ty
  pl. im·pu·ri·ties

im·pute
  im·put·a·ble
  im·pu·ta·tion
  im·pu·ta·tive

in (*preposition*; see INN)

in·a·bil·i·ty

in ab·sen·tia

in·ac·ces·si·bil·i·ty

in·ac·ces·si·ble

in·ac·ces·si·bly

in·ac·cu·ra·cy

in·ac·cu·rate

in·ac·cu·rate·ly

in·ac·tive

in·ac·tiv·i·ty

in·ad·e·qua·cy

in·ad·e·quate

in·ad·e·quate·ly

in·ad·mis·si·ble

in·ad·ver·tent
  in·ad·ver·tence
  in·ad·ver·ten·cy
  in·ad·ver·tent·ly

in·ad·vis·a·ble

in·a·lien·a·ble
in·a·lien·a·bly

in·am·o·ra·to
pl. in·am·o·ra·tos
fem. in·am·o·ra·ta

in·ane
in·ane·ly
in·an·i·ty
pl. in·an·i·ties

in·an·i·mate

in·ap·pli·ca·ble

in·ap·pro·pri·ate

in·ap·pro·pri·ate·ly

in·apt

in·ar·gu·a·ble

in·ar·gu·a·bly

in·ar·tic·u·late
in·ar·tic·u·late·ly
in·ar·tic·u·late·ness

in·ar·tis·tic

in·as·much

in·at·ten·tive

in·au·di·ble

in·au·di·bly

in·au·gu·ral

in·au·gu·rate
in·au·gu·ra·tion
in·au·gu·ra·tor
in·au·gu·ra·to·ry

in·aus·pi·cious

in·aus·pi·cious·ly

in·board

in·born

in·bred

in·breed·ing
in·breed
past and *past part.* in·
bred

In·ca
In·can

in·cal·cu·la·ble
in·cal·cu·la·bil·i·ty
in·cal·cu·la·bly

in·can·des·cent
in·can·des·cence
in·can·des·cent·ly

in·can·ta·tion
in·can·ta·tion·al

in·ca·pa·ble

in·ca·pac·i·tate
in·ca·pac·i·ta·tion

in·ca·pac·i·ty
pl. in·ca·pac·i·ties

in·car·cer·ate
in·car·cer·a·tion
in·car·cer·a·tor

in·car·nate

in·car·na·tion

in·cau·tious

in·cen·di·ar·y
pl. in·cen·di·ar·ies
in·cen·di·ar·ism

in·cense

in·cen·tive

in·cep·tion

in·ces·sant
in·ces·san·cy
in·ces·sant·ly
in·ces·sant·ness

in·cest

in·ces·tu·ous
in·ces·tu·ous·ly

inch

in·cho·ate
in·cho·ate·ly
in·cho·ate·ness
in·cho·a·tive

In·chon

in·ci·dence

in·ci·dent

in·ci·den·tal

in·ci·den·tal·ly

in·cin·er·ate
in·cin·er·a·tion
in·cin·er·a·tor

in·cip·i·ent
in·cip·i·ence
in·cip·i·en·cy
in·cip·i·ent·ly

in·cise

in·ci·sion

in·ci·sive
in·ci·sive·ly
in·ci·sive·ness

in·ci·sor

in·cite
in·cite·ment
in·cit·er

in·ci·vil·i·ty

in·clem·ent
in·clem·en·cy
pl. in·clem·en·cies
in·clem·ent·ly

in·cli·na·tion

in·cline
in·clin·er

in·clude
in·clud·a·ble
in·clud·i·ble
in·clu·sion

in·clu·sive
in·clu·sive·ly
in·clu·sive·ness

in·cog·ni·to
pl. in·cog·ni·tos

in·co·her·ent
in·co·her·ence
in·co·her·en·cy
pl. in·co·her·en·cies
in·co·her·ent·ly

in·com·bus·ti·ble

in·come

in·com·ing

in·com·men·su·ra·ble

in·com·mu·ni·ca·ble

in·com·mu·ni·ca·do

in·com·pa·ra·ble
in·com·pa·ra·bil·i·ty
in·com·pa·ra·ble·ness
in·com·pa·ra·bly

in·com·pat·i·ble
in·com·pat·i·bil·i·ty
in·com·pat·i·bly

in·com·pe·tent
in·com·pe·tence
in·com·pe·ten·cy
in·com·pe·tent·ly

in·com·plete
in·com·plete·ly
in·com·plete·ness

in·com·pre·hen·si·ble

in·com·pre·hen·si·bly

in·con·ceiv·a·ble
in·con·ceiv·a·bly

in·con·clu·sive
in·con·clu·sive·ly
in·con·clu·sive·ness

in·con·gru·ous
in·con·gru·i·ty
pl. in·con·gru·i·ties
in·con·gru·ous·ly

in·con·se·quen·tial
in·con·se·quen·tial·i·ty
pl. in·con·se·quen·tial·
i·ties
in·con·se·quen·tial·ly

in·con·sid·er·a·ble
in·con·sid·er·a·bly

in·con·sid·er·ate
in·con·sid·er·ate·ly
in·con·sid·er·a·tion

in·con·sist·ent
in·con·sist·en·cy
pl. in·con·sist·en·cies
in·con·sist·ent·ly

in·con·sol·a·ble
in·con·sol·a·bly

in·con·spic·u·ous
in·con·spic·u·ous·ly
in·con·spic·u·ous·ness

in·con·stant
in·con·stan·cy
pl. in·con·stan·cies
in·con·stant·ly

in·con·test·a·ble
in·con·test·a·bil·i·ty
in·con·test·a·bly

in·con·ti·nent
in·con·ti·nence
in·con·ti·nent·ly

in·con·tro·vert·i·ble
in·con·tro·vert·i·bly

in·con·ven·ience

in·con·ven·ient
in·con·ven·ient·ly

in·cor·po·rate
in·cor·po·ra·tion
in·cor·po·ra·tor

in·cor·po·re·al
in·cor·po·re·al·i·ty
in·cor·po·re·al·ly

in·cor·rect

in·cor·rect·ly

in·cor·ri·gi·ble
in·cor·ri·gi·bil·i·ty
in·cor·ri·gi·ble·ness
in·cor·ri·gi·bly

in·cor·rupt·i·ble
in·cor·rupt·i·bil·i·ty
in·cor·rupt·i·bly

in·crease
in·creas·a·ble

in·creas·er
in·creas·ing·ly

in·cred·i·ble
in·cred·i·ble·ness
in·cred·i·bly

in·cred·u·lous
in·cre·du·li·ty
in·cred·u·lous·ly

in·cre·ment
in·cre·ment·al

in·crim·i·nate
in·crim·i·na·tion
in·crim·i·na·to·ry

in·crus·ta·tion

in·cu·bate

in·cu·ba·tion

in·cu·ba·tor

in·cu·bus
pl. in·cu·bi *or* in·cu·
bus·es

in·cul·cate
in·cul·ca·tion
in·cul·ca·tor

in·cum·ben·cy
pl. in·cum·ben·cies

in·cum·bent

in·cu·nab·u·lum
pl. in·cu·nab·u·la

in·cur
in·curred, in·cur·ring
in·cur·ra·ble

in·cur·a·ble

in·cur·a·bly

in·cu·ri·ous
in·cu·ri·os·i·ty
in·cu·ri·ous·ly
in·cu·ri·ous·ness

in·cur·sion
in·cur·sive

in·debt·ed
  in·debt·ed·ness

in·de·cent
  in·de·cen·cy
  pl. in·de·cen·cies
  in·de·cent·ly

in·de·ci·pher·a·ble

in·de·ci·sion

in·de·ci·sive
  in·de·ci·sive·ly
  in·de·ci·sive·ness

in·dec·o·rous

in·dec·o·rous·ly

in·deed

in·de·fat·i·ga·ble
  in·de·fat·i·ga·bil·i·ty
  in·de·fat·i·ga·bly

in·de·fen·si·ble
  in·de·fen·si·bil·i·ty
  in·de·fen·si·bly

in·de·fin·a·ble

in·de·fin·a·bly

in·def·i·nite
  in·def·i·nite·ly
  in·def·i·nite·ness

in·del·i·ble
  in·del·i·bil·i·ty
  in·del·i·bly

in·del·i·cate
  in·del·i·ca·cy
  pl. in·del·i·ca·cies
  in·del·i·cate·ly

in·dem·ni·fy
  in·dem·ni·fies, in·dem·
    ni·fied
  in·dem·ni·fi·ca·tion
  in·dem·ni·fi·er

in·dem·ni·ty
  pl. in·dem·ni·ties

in·dent
  in·dent·er

in·den·ta·tion

in·den·tion

in·den·ture
  in·den·ture·ship

In·de·pend·ence *(city)*

in·de·pend·ence *(state
  of being independent)*

in·de·pen·dent
  in·de·pen·dent·ly

in·des·crib·a·ble
  in·des·crib·a·bly

in·de·struc·ti·ble
  in·de·struc·ti·bil·i·ty
  in·de·struc·ti·bly

in·de·ter·min·a·ble
  in·de·ter·min·a·bly

in·de·ter·mi·nate
  in·de·ter·mi·nate·ly

in·dex
  pl. in·dex·es *or* in·di·ces
  in·dex·a·tion
  in·dex·er

In·di·a

in·di·a ink
  also In·dia ink

In·di·an

In·di·an·a
  In·di·an·an

In·di·an·ap·o·lis

in·di·cate
  in·di·ca·tion

in·dic·a·tive
  in·dic·a·tive·ly

in·di·ca·tor

in·di·ces

in·dict *(accuse;* see
  INDITE)
  in·dict·a·ble
  in·dict·er
  in·dict·ment

in·dif·fer·ent
  in·dif·fer·ence
  in·dif·fer·ent·ly

in·dig·e·nous
  in·dig·e·nous·ly

in·di·gent
  in·di·gence

in·di·gest·i·ble
  in·di·gest·i·bly

in·di·ges·tion
  in·di·ges·tive

in·dig·nant
  in·dig·nant·ly

in·dig·na·tion

in·dig·ni·ty
  pl. in·dig·ni·ties

in·di·go
  pl. in·di·gos

in·di·rect
  in·di·rect·ly
  in·di·rect·ness

in·dis·cern·i·ble

in·dis·creet
  in·dis·creet·ly

in·dis·cre·tion

in·dis·crim·i·nate
  in·dis·crim·i·nate·ly

in·dis·pens·a·ble
  in·dis·pen·sa·bil·i·ty
  in·dis·pen·sa·bly

in·dis·posed
  in·dis·po·si·tion

in·dis·put·a·ble

in·dis·put·a·bly

in·dis·sol·u·ble
  in·dis·sol·u·bil·i·ty
  in·dis·sol·u·bly

in·dis·tinct

in·dis·tinct·ly

in·dis·tin·guish·a·ble

in·dite (*write*; see
  INDICT)

in·di·um

in·di·vid·u·al

in·di·vid·u·al·ism
  in·di·vid·u·al·ist
  in·di·vid·u·al·is·tic
  in·di·vid·u·al·is·ti·
    cal·ly

in·di·vid·u·al·i·ty
  pl. in·di·vid·u·al·i·ties

in·di·vid·u·al·ize
  in·di·vid·u·al·i·za·tion

in·di·vid·u·al·ly

in·di·vis·i·ble

In·do·chi·na

in·doc·tri·nate
  in·doc·tri·na·tion
  in·doc·tri·na·tor

In·do-Eu·ro·pe·an

in·do·lent
  in·do·lence
  in·do·lent·ly

in·dom·i·ta·ble
  in·dom·i·ta·bil·i·ty
  in·dom·i·ta·bly

In·do·ne·sia
  In·do·ne·sian

in·door

in·doors

in·dorse
  var. of en·dorse

in·du·bi·ta·ble
  in·du·bi·ta·bly

in·duce
  in·duc·er
  in·duc·i·ble

in·duce·ment

in·duct
  in·duc·tee

in·duc·tance

in·duc·tion

in·due
  var. of en·due

in·dulge
  in·dulg·er

in·dul·gence

in·dul·gent
  in·dul·gent·ly

In·dus Riv·er

in·dus·tri·al
  in·dus·tri·al·ly

in·dus·tri·al·ism

in·dus·tri·al·ist

in·dus·tri·al·ize
  in·dus·tri·a·li·za·tion

in·dus·tri·ous
  in·dus·tri·ous·ly
  in·dus·tri·ous·ness

in·dus·try
  pl. in·dus·tries

in·e·bri·ate
  in·e·bri·a·tion
  in·e·bri·e·ty

in·ed·i·ble

in·ed·u·ca·ble

in·ef·fa·ble
  in·ef·fa·bil·i·ty
  in·ef·fa·bly

in·ef·fec·tive

in·ef·fec·tive·ly

in·ef·fec·tu·al
  in·ef·fec·tu·al·i·ty
  in·ef·fec·tu·al·ly
  in·ef·fec·tu·al·ness

in·ef·fi·ca·cy

in·ef·fi·cient
  in·ef·fi·cien·cy
  in·ef·fi·cient·ly

in·e·las·tic

in·el·e·gant
  in·el·e·gance
  in·el·e·gant·ly

in·el·i·gi·ble

in·e·luc·ta·ble
  in·e·luc·ta·bly

in·ept
  in·ep·ti·tude
  in·ept·ly
  in·ept·ness

in·e·qual·i·ty
  pl. in·e·qual·i·ties

in·eq·ui·ta·ble

in·eq·ui·ty

in·ert
  in·ert·ly
  in·ert·ness

in·er·tia
  in·er·tial

in·es·cap·a·ble
  in·es·cap·a·bil·i·ty
  in·es·cap·a·bly

in·es·ti·ma·ble
  in·es·ti·ma·bly

in·ev·i·ta·ble
  in·ev·i·ta·bil·i·ty
  in·ev·i·ta·ble·ness
  in·ev·i·ta·bly

in·ex·act

in·ex·cus·a·ble
  in·ex·cus·a·bly

in·ex·haust·i·ble
  in·ex·haust·i·bly

in·ex·o·ra·ble
  in·ex·o·ra·bil·i·ty
  in·ex·o·ra·bly

in·ex·pe·di·ence

in·ex·pe·di·ent

in·ex·pen·sive

in·ex·pen·sive·ly

in·ex·pe·ri·ence
  in·ex·pe·ri·enced

in·ex·pert
  in·ex·pert·ly

in·ex·pi·a·ble
  in·ex·pi·a·bly

in·ex·pli·ca·ble
  in·ex·pli·ca·bly

in·ex·press·i·ble
  in·ex·press·i·bly

in·ex·tin·guish·a·ble

in ex·tre·mis

in·ex·tri·ca·ble
  in·ex·tri·ca·bly

in·fal·li·ble
  in·fal·li·bil·i·ty
  in·fal·li·bly

in·fa·mous
  in·fa·mous·ly
  in·fa·my
  pl. in·fa·mies

in·fan·cy
  pl. in·fan·cies

in·fant

in·fan·ti·cide
  in·fan·ti·cid·al

in·fan·tile
  in·fan·til·i·ty
  pl. in·fan·til·i·ties

in·fan·try
  pl. in·fan·tries
  in·fan·try·man
  pl. in·fan·try·men

in·farct
  in·farc·tion

in·fat·u·ate
  in·fat·u·at·ed
  in·fat·u·a·tion

in·fect
  in·fec·tor

in·fec·tion

in·fec·tious
  in·fec·tious·ly

in·fe·lic·i·ty
  pl. in·fe·lic·i·ties

in·fer
  in·ferred, in·fer·ring
  in·fer·a·ble

in·fer·ence
  in·fer·en·tial
  in·fer·en·tial·ly

in·fe·ri·or
  in·fe·ri·or·i·ty

in·fer·nal
  in·fer·nal·ly

in·fer·no
  pl. in·fer·nos

in·fer·tile

in·fer·til·i·ty

in·fest
  in·fes·ta·tion

in·fi·del

in·fi·del·i·ty
  pl. in·fi·del·i·ties

in·field
  in·field·er

in·fight·ing
  in·fight·er

in·fil·trate
  in·fil·tra·tion
  in·fil·tra·tor

in·fi·nite
  in·fi·nite·ly
  in·fi·nite·ness

in·fin·i·tes·i·mal
  in·fin·i·tes·i·mal·ly

in·fin·i·tive
  in·fin·i·tiv·al

in·fin·i·tude

in·fin·i·ty
  pl. in·fin·i·ties

in·firm
  in·firm·i·ty
  pl. in·firm·i·ties
  in·firm·ly

in·fir·ma·ry
  pl. in·fir·ma·ries

in fla·gran·te de·lic·to

in·flame

in·flam·ma·ble
  in·flam·ma·bil·i·ty
  in·flam·ma·bly

in·flam·ma·tion

in·flam·ma·to·ry

in·flat·a·ble

in·flate
  in·flat·ed·ly
  in·flat·ed·ness
  in·flat·er
  in·fla·tor

in·fla·tion
  in·fla·tion·ar·y

in·flect
  in·flec·tive

in·flec·tion
  in·flec·tion·al

in·flex·i·ble
  in·flex·i·bil·i·ty
  in·flex·i·bly

in·flict

in·flo·res·cence

in·flu·ence
  in·flu·enc·er

in·flu·en·tial
  in·flu·en·tial·ly

in·flu·en·za

in·flux

in·fo

in·fo·mer·cial

in·form
in·form·ant
in·form·er

in·for·mal
in·for·mal·i·ty
pl. in·for·mal·i·ties
in·for·mal·ly

in·for·ma·tics

in·for·ma·tion
in·for·ma·tion·al

in·for·ma·tive
also in·for·ma·to·ry
in·for·ma·tive·ly

in·formed

in·fo·tain·ment

in·fra

in·frac·tion
in·fract
in·frac·tor

in·fra dig

in·fra·red

in·fra·struc·ture

in·fre·quent
in·fre·quen·cy
in·fre·quent·ly

in·fringe
in·fringe·ment
in·fring·er

in·fu·ri·ate
in·fu·ri·at·ing
in·fu·ri·at·ing·ly

in·fuse
in·fus·er
in·fu·sion
in·fu·sive

Inge

in·ge·nious
in·ge·ni·ous·ly
in·ge·ni·ous·ness

in·ge·nue
also in·gé·nue

in·ge·nu·i·ty

in·gen·u·ous
in·gen·u·ous·ly
in·gen·u·ous·ness

in·gest
in·ges·tion
in·ges·tive

In·gle·wood

in·glo·ri·ous
in·glo·ri·ous·ly

in·got

in·grained

in·grate

in·gra·ti·ate
in·gra·ti·at·ing
in·gra·ti·at·ing·ly
in·gra·ti·a·tion

in·grat·i·tude

in·gre·di·ent

In·gres

in·gress
in·gres·sion

in·grow·ing
in·grown

in·gui·nal
in·gui·nal·ly

in·hab·it
in·hab·i·ta·ble
in·hab·it·ant

in·hal·ant

in·hale
in·ha·la·tion

in·hal·er

in·here

in·her·ent
in·her·ence
in·her·ent·ly

in·her·it
in·her·it·a·ble
in·her·i·tor

in·her·i·tance

in·hib·it
in·hib·i·tive
in·hib·i·tor
in·hib·i·to·ry

in·hi·bi·tion

in·hos·pi·ta·ble
in·hos·pi·ta·bly

in·house

in·hu·man
in·hu·man·i·ty
pl. in·hu·man·i·ties
in·hu·man·ly

in·hu·mane

in·im·i·cal
in·im·i·cal·ly

in·im·i·ta·ble
in·im·i·ta·bil·i·ty
in·im·i·t·ably

in·iq·ui·ty
pl. in·iq·ui·ties
in·iq·ui·tous
in·iq·ui·tous·ly

in·i·tial
in·i·tial·ly

in·i·tial·ism

in·i·tial·ize
in·i·tial·i·za·tion

in·i·ti·ate
in·i·ti·a·tion
in·i·ti·a·tor
in·i·ti·a·to·ry

in·i·ti·a·tive

in·ject
in·ject·a·ble
in·jec·tor

in·jec·tion

in·ju·di·cious

in•junc•tion
  in•junc•tive

in•jure
  in•jured
  in•jur•er

in•ju•ri•ous
  in•ju•ri•ous•ly
  in•ju•ri•ous•ness

in•ju•ry
  pl. in•ju•ries

in•jus•tice

ink
  ink-jet

ink•ling

ink•well

ink•y
  ink•i•er, ink•i•est
  ink•i•ness

in•laid

in•land
  in•land•er

in-law

in•lay
  past and *past part.* in•laid
  in•lay•er

in•let

in-line

in lo•co pa•ren•tis

in•mate

in me•mo•ri•am

in•most

inn (*hotel*; see IN)

in•nards

in•nate
  in•nate•ly
  in•nate•ness

in•ner
  in•ner•most

in•ning

inn•keep•er

in•no•cent
  in•no•cence
  in•no•cen•cy
  in•no•cent•ly

in•noc•u•ous
  in•noc•u•ous•ly
  in•noc•u•ous•ness

in•no•vate
  in•no•va•tion
  in•no•va•tion•al
  in•no•va•tor
  in•no•va•tive
  in•no•va•tive•ness

Inns•bruck

in•nu•en•do
  pl. in•nu•en•dos *or* in•nu•en•does

in•nu•mer•a•ble
  in•nu•mer•a•bly

in•nu•mer•ate
  in•nu•mer•a•cy

in•oc•u•late
  in•oc•u•la•ble
  in•oc•u•la•tion

in•of•fen•sive
  in•of•fen•sive•ly
  in•of•fen•sive•ness

in•op•er•a•ble
  in•op•er•a•bil•i•ty
  in•op•er•a•bly

in•op•er•a•tive

in•op•por•tune

in•op•por•tune•ly

in•or•di•nate
  in•or•di•nate•ly

in•or•gan•ic
  in•or•gan•i•cal•ly

in•pa•tient

in•put
  in•put•ting; *past* and *past part.* in•put•ted *or* in•put•ted
  in•put•ter

in•quest

in•qui•e•tude

in•quire
  in•quir•er

in•qui•ry
  pl. in•qui•ries

in•qui•si•tion
  in•qui•si•tion•al
  in•qui•si•tor

in•qui•si•tive
  in•qui•si•tive•ly
  in•qui•si•tive•ness

in re

in•road

in•sane
  in•sane•ly
  in•san•i•ty
  pl. in•san•i•ties

in•sa•tia•ble
  in•sa•tia•bil•i•ty
  in•sa•tia•bly

in•scribe
  in•scrib•a•ble
  in•scrib•er

in•scrip•tion
  in•scrip•tion•al
  in•scrip•tive

in•scru•ta•ble
  in•scru•ta•bil•i•ty
  in•scru•ta•ble•ness
  in•scru•ta•bly

in•sect
  in•sec•tile

in•sec•ti•cide
  in•sec•ti•cid•al

in•sec•ti•vore
  in•sec•ti•vor•ous

in·se·cure
  in·se·cure·ly
  in·se·cur·i·ty

in·sem·i·nate
  in·sem·i·na·tion
  in·sem·i·na·tor

in·sen·sate
  in·sen·sate·ly

in·sen·si·ble
  in·sen·si·bil·i·ty
  in·sen·si·bly

in·sen·si·tive
  in·sen·si·tive·ly
  in·sen·si·tive·ness
  in·sen·si·tiv·i·ty

in·sen·ti·ent
  in·sen·tience

in·sep·a·ra·ble
  in·sep·a·ra·bly

in·sert
  in·sert·a·ble
  in·sert·er

in·ser·tion

in·set
  in·set·ting; *past* and
  past part. in·set

in·shore

in·side

in·sid·er

in·sid·i·ous
  in·sid·i·ous·ly
  in·sid·i·ous·ness

in·sight
  in·sight·ful
  in·sight·ful·ly

in·sig·ni·a

in·sig·nif·i·cance

in·sig·nif·i·cant
  in·sig·ni·fi·cance
  in·sig·ni·fi·cant·ly

in·sin·cere
  in·sin·cere·ly

in·sin·cer·i·ty
  pl. in·sin·cer·i·ties

in·sin·u·ate
  in·sin·u·a·tion
  in·sin·u·a·tive
  in·sin·u·a·tor

in·sip·id
  in·sip·id·i·ty
  in·sip·id·ly
  in·sip·id·ness

in·sist
  in·sist·er
  in·sist·ing·ly

in·sis·tent
  in·sis·tence
  in·sis·ten·cy
  in·sis·tent·ly

in si·tu

in·so·bri·e·ty

in·so·far as

in·sole

in·so·lent
  in·so·lence
  in·so·lent·ly

in·sol·u·ble
  in·sol·u·bil·i·ty
  in·sol·u·bly

in·solv·a·ble

in·sol·vent
  in·sol·ven·cy

in·som·ni·a
  in·som·ni·ac

in·so·much

in·sou·ci·ant
  in·sou·ci·ance
  in·sou·ci·ant·ly

in·spect
  in·spec·tion

in·spec·tor
  in·spec·tor·ate
  in·spec·to·ri·al
  in·spec·tor·ship

in·spi·ra·tion
  in·spi·ra·tion·al

in·spire
  in·spir·a·to·ry
  in·spir·ed·ly
  in·spir·er
  in·spir·ing
  in·spir·ing·ly

in·sta·bil·i·ty
  pl. in·sta·bil·i·ties

in·stall
  in·stalled, in·stall·ing
  in·stal·la·tion
  in·stall·er

in·stall·ment

in·stance

in·stant

in·stan·ta·ne·ous
  in·stan·ta·ne·ous·ly

in·stant·ly

in·stead

in·step

in·sti·gate
  in·sti·ga·tion
  in·sti·ga·tive
  in·sti·ga·tor

in·still
  in·stilled, in·still·ing
  in·stil·la·tion
  in·still·er
  in·still·ment

in·stinct
  in·stinc·tive
  in·stinc·tu·al
  in·stinc·tu·al·ly

in·sti·tute

in·sti·tu·tion
  in·sti·tu·tion·al
  in·sti·tu·tion·al·ism
  in·sti·tu·tion·al·ly

in·sti·tu·tion·al·ize
in·sti·tu·tion·al·i·za·tion

in·struct

in·struc·tion
in·struc·tion·al

in·struc·tive
in·struc·tive·ly
in·struc·tive·ness

in·struc·tor
fem. in·struc·tress

in·stru·ment

in·stru·men·tal
in·stru·men·tal·ist
in·stru·men·tal·i·ty
in·stru·men·tal·ly

in·stru·men·ta·tion

in·sub·or·di·nate
in·sub·or·din·ate·ly
in·sub·or·di·na·tion

in·sub·stan·tial
in·sub·stan·ti·al·i·ty
in·sub·stan·tial·ly

in·suf·fer·a·ble

in·suf·fi·cient

in·suf·fi·cient·ly

in·su·lar
in·su·lar·ism
in·su·lar·i·ty
in·su·lar·ly

in·su·late
in·su·la·tion
in·su·la·tor

in·su·lin

in·sult
in·sult·er
in·sult·ing·ly

in·su·per·a·ble
in·su·per·a·bil·i·ty
in·su·per·a·bly

in·sup·port·a·ble
in·sup·port·a·bly

in·sup·press·i·ble

in·sur·ance

in·sure
in·sur·a·ble
in·sur·a·bil·i·ty

in·sured

in·sur·er

in·sur·gent
in·sur·gence
in·sur·gen·cy
pl. in·sur·gen·cies

in·sur·mount·a·ble

in·sur·rec·tion
in·sur·rec·tion·ar·y
in·sur·rec·tion·ist

in·sus·cep·ti·ble

in·tact
in·tact·ness

in·ta·glio
pl. in·ta·glios
in·ta·glioes, in·ta·
glioed

in·take

in·tan·gi·ble
in·tan·gi·bil·i·ty
in·tan·gi·bly

in·te·ger

in·te·gral
in·teg·ral·ly

in·te·grate
in·teg·ra·ble
in·teg·ra·bil·i·ty
in·te·gra·tion

in·teg·ri·ty

in·teg·u·ment
in·teg·u·ment·al
in·teg·u·men·ta·ry

in·tel·lect

in·tel·lec·tu·al
in·tel·lec·tu·al·i·ty

in·tel·lec·tu·a·lize
in·tel·lec·tu·al·ly

in·tel·li·gence

in·tel·li·gent
in·tel·li·gent·ly

in·tel·li·gent·si·a

in·tel·li·gi·ble
in·tel·li·gi·bil·i·ty
in·tel·li·gi·bly

in·tem·per·ate
in·tem·per·ance
in·tem·per·ate·ly
in·tem·per·ate·ness

in·tend

in·tend·ed

in·tense
in·tens·er, in·tens·est
in·tense·ly
in·tense·ness

in·ten·si·fy
in·ten·si·fies, in·ten·
si·fied
in·ten·si·fi·ca·tion

in·ten·si·ty
pl. in·ten·si·ties

in·ten·sive
in·ten·sive·ly
in·ten·sive·ness

in·tent
in·tent·ly
in·tent·ness

in·ten·tion
in·ten·tioned

in·ten·tion·al
in·ten·tion·al·ly

in·ter
in·terred, in·ter·ring

in·ter·act
in·ter·ac·tant
in·ter·ac·tion

in·ter·ac·tive
  in·ter·ac·tive·ly

in·ter a·li·a

in·ter·breed
  past and *past part.* in·ter·bred

in·ter·cede
  in·ter·ced·er

in·ter·cept
  in·ter·cep·tion
  in·ter·cep·tive
  in·ter·cep·tor

in·ter·ces·sion
  in·ter·ces·sion·al
  in·ter·ces·sor
  in·ter·ces·so·ry

in·ter·change
  in·ter·change·a·ble
  in·ter·change·a·bly

in·ter·com

in·ter·com·mu·ni·ca·tion

in·ter·con·nect
  in·ter·con·nec·tion

in·ter·con·ti·nen·tal
  in·ter·con·ti·nen·tal·ly

in·ter·course

in·ter·de·nom·i·na·tion·al
  in·ter·de·nom·i·na·tion·al·ly

in·ter·de·part·ment·al
  in·ter·de·part·men·tal·ly

in·ter·de·pend
  in·ter·de·pend·ence
  in·ter·de·pend·en·cy
  in·ter·de·pend·ent

in·ter·dict
  in·ter·dic·tion
  in·ter·dic·to·ry

in·ter·dis·ci·plin·ar·y

in·ter·est
  in·ter·est·ed·ly

in·ter·est·ing
  in·ter·est·ing·ly

in·ter·face

in·ter·fere
  in·ter·fer·er
  in·ter·fer·ing
  in·ter·fer·ing·ly

in·ter·fer·ence

in·ter·fer·on

in·ter·fuse
  in·ter·fu·sion

in·ter·im

in·te·ri·or
  in·te·ri·or·ize
  in·te·ri·or·ly

in·ter·ject
  in·ter·jec·to·ry

in·ter·jec·tion
  in·ter·jec·tion·al

in·ter·lace
  in·ter·lace·ment

in·ter·lard

in·ter·leave

in·ter·lin·e·ar

in·ter·lin·ing

in·ter·lock
  in·ter·lock·er

in·ter·loc·u·tor
  in·ter·lo·cu·tion

in·ter·loc·u·to·ry

in·ter·lop·er
  in·ter·lope

in·ter·lude

in·ter·mar·ry
  in·ter·mar·ries, in·ter·mar·ried
  in·ter·mar·riage

in·ter·me·di·ar·y
  pl. in·ter·me·di·ar·ies

in·ter·me·di·ate
  in·ter·me·di·a·cy
  in·ter·me·di·ate·ly
  in·ter·me·di·a·tion
  in·ter·me·di·a·tor

in·ter·ment

in·ter·mez·zo
  pl. in·ter·mez·zi *or* in·ter·mez·zos

in·ter·mi·na·ble
  in·ter·mi·na·bly

in·ter·min·gle

in·ter·mis·sion

in·ter·mit·tent
  in·ter·mit·tence
  in·ter·mit·ten·cy
  in·ter·mit·tent·ly

in·ter·mix

in·tern
  in·tern·ment
  in·tern·ship

in·ter·nal
  in·ter·nal·i·ty
  in·ter·nal·ize
  in·ter·nal·i·za·tion
  in·ter·nal·ly

in·ter·na·tion·al
  in·ter·na·tion·al·i·ty
  in·ter·na·tion·al·ize
  in·ter·na·tion·al·ly

in·ter·na·tion·al·ism
  in·ter·na·tion·al·ist

in·ter·ne·cine

in·tern·ee

In·ter·net

in·tern·ist

in·ter·per·son·al
  in·ter·per·son·al·ly

in·ter·plan·e·tar·y

in·ter·play

In·ter·pol

in·ter·po·late
in·ter·po·la·tion
in·ter·po·la·tive
in·ter·po·la·tor

in·ter·pose
in·ter·po·si·tion

in·ter·pret
in·ter·pret·a·ble
in·ter·pret·a·bil·i·ty
in·ter·pre·ta·tion
in·ter·pre·ta·tion·al
in·ter·pre·ta·tive
in·ter·pre·tive
in·ter·pre·tive·ly

in·ter·pret·er

in·ter·ra·cial
in·ter·ra·cial·ly

in·ter·reg·num
pl. in·ter·reg·nums *or*
in·ter·reg·na

in·ter·re·late
in·ter·re·la·tion
in·ter·re·la·tion·ship

in·ter·ro·gate
in·ter·ro·ga·tion
in·ter·ro·ga·tor

in·ter·rog·a·tive
in·ter·rog·a·tive·ly

in·ter·rog·a·to·ry

in·ter·rupt
in·ter·rupt·er
in·ter·rup·tion
in·ter·rup·tive

in·ter·sect

in·ter·sec·tion
in·ter·sec·tion·al

in·ter·ses·sion

in·ter·sperse
in·ter·sper·sion

in·ter·state

in·ter·stel·lar

in·ter·stice
in·ter·sti·tial

in·ter·twine

in·ter·val
in·ter·val·lic

in·ter·vene
in·ter·ven·er
in·ter·ve·nor

in·ter·ven·tion

in·ter·view
in·ter·view·ee
in·ter·view·er

in·ter·weave
past in·ter·wove; *past
part.* in·ter·wo·ven

in·tes·tate
in·tes·ta·cy

in·tes·tine
in·tes·tin·al

in·ti·ma·cy

in·ti·mate (*familiar,
personal*)
in·ti·mate·ly

in·ti·mate (*imply*)
in·ti·mat·er
in·ti·ma·tion

in·ti·mi·date
in·ti·mi·da·tion
in·ti·mi·da·tor

in·to

in·tol·er·a·ble
in·tol·er·a·bly

in·tol·er·ant
in·tol·er·ance
in·tol·er·ant·ly

in·to·na·tion
in·to·na·tion·al

in·tone
in·ton·er

in to·to

in·tox·i·cant

in·tox·i·cate
in·tox·i·ca·tion

in·tox·i·cat·ing
in·tox·i·cat·ing·ly

in·trac·ta·ble
in·trac·ta·bil·i·ty
in·trac·ta·ble·ness
in·trac·ta·bly

in·tra·mu·ral
in·tra·mu·ral·ly

in·tra·mus·cu·lar

in·tran·si·gent
in·tran·si·gence
in·tran·si·gen·cy
in·tran·si·gent·ly

in·tran·si·tive
in·tran·si·tive·ly
in·tran·si·tiv·i·ty

in·tra·u·ter·ine

in·tra·ve·nous
in·tra·ve·nous·ly

in·trep·id
in·tre·pid·i·ty
in·trep·id·ly

in·tri·cate
in·tri·ca·cy
pl. in·tri·ca·cies
in·tri·cate·ly

in·trigue
in·trigues, in·trigued,
in·trigu·ing
in·tri·guer
in·tri·guing
in·tri·guing·ly

in·trin·sic
in·trin·si·cal·ly

in·tro·duce
in·tro·duc·er
in·tro·duc·i·ble

in·tro·duc·tion

in·tro·duc·to·ry

in·tro·spec·tion
  in·tro·spec·tive
  in·tro·spec·tive·ly
  in·tro·spec·tive·ness

in·tro·vert
  also in·tro·vert·ed
  in·tro·ver·sion
  in·tro·ver·sive
  in·tro·vert·ed
  in·tro·ver·tive

in·trude
  in·trud·ing·ly
  in·tru·sion

in·trud·er

in·tru·sive
  in·tru·sive·ly
  in·tru·sive·ness

in·trust
  var. of en·trust

in·tu·bate
  in·tu·ba·tion

in·tu·i·tion
  in·tu·i·tion·al

in·tu·i·tive
  in·tu·i·tive·ly
  in·tu·i·tive·ness

In·u·it
  also In·nu·it
  pl. same *or* In·u·its

in·un·date
  in·un·da·tion

in·ure
  in·ure·ment

in u·ter·o

in va·cu·o

in·vade
  in·vad·er

in·va·lid (*sick person*)
  in·va·lid·ism

in·val·id (*void, false*)
  in·val·id·ly

in·val·i·date
  in·val·i·da·tion

in·val·u·a·ble
  in·val·u·a·bly

in·var·i·a·ble

in·var·i·a·bly

in·va·sion
  in·va·sive

in·vec·tive

in·veigh

in·vei·gle
  in·vei·gle·ment

in·vent
  in·vent·a·ble
  in·ven·tor

in·ven·tion

in·ven·tive
  in·ven·tive·ly
  in·ven·tive·ness

in·ven·to·ry
  pl. in·ven·to·ries
  in·ven·to·ries, in·ven·
    to·ried

in·verse
  in·verse·ly

in·ver·sion
  in·ver·sive

in·vert
  in·vert·er
  in·vert·i·ble
  in·vert·i·bil·i·ty

in·ver·te·brate

in·vest
  in·vest·a·ble
  in·vest·i·ble
  in·ves·tor

in·ves·ti·gate
  in·ves·ti·ga·tion
  in·ves·ti·ga·tive
  in·ves·ti·ga·tor
  in·ves·ti·ga·to·ry

in·ves·ti·ture

in·vest·ment

in·vet·er·ate
  in·vet·er·a·cy
  in·vet·er·ate·ly

in·vid·i·ous
  in·vid·i·ous·ly
  in·vid·i·ous·ness

in·vig·o·rate
  in·vig·or·at·ing
  in·vig·or·a·tion
  in·vig·or·a·tive
  in·vig·or·a·tor

in·vin·ci·ble
  in·vin·ci·bil·i·ty
  in·vin·ci·ble·ness
  in·vin·ci·bly

in·vi·o·la·ble
  in·vi·o·la·bil·i·ty
  in·vi·o·la·bly

in·vi·o·late
  in·vi·o·late·ly

in·vis·i·ble
  in·vis·i·bil·i·ty
  in·vis·i·bly

in·vi·ta·tion

in·vite
  in·vit·er

in·vit·ing
  in·vit·ing·ly

in vi·tro

in·vo·ca·tion
  in·vo·ca·to·ry

in·voice

in·voke
  in·vo·ca·ble
  in·vok·er

in·vol·un·tar·y
  in·vol·un·tar·i·ly

in·vo·lu·tion
  in·vo·lu·tion·al

in•volve
  in•volve•ment

in•vul•ner•a•ble
  in•vul•ner•a•bil•i•ty
  in•vul•ner•a•bly

in•ward
  also in•wards

in•ward•ly

i•o•dide

i•o•dine

i•on
  i•on•ic

Io•nes•co

I•o•ni•an Sea

I•on•ic

i•on•ize
  i•on•iz•a•ble
  i•on•i•za•tion
  i•on•iz•er

i•on•o•sphere
  i•on•o•spher•ic

i•o•ta

I•o•wa
  I•o•wan

ip•e•cac

ip•so fac•to

Ips•wich

I•ran
  I•ra•ni•an

I•raq
  I•ra•qi
  pl. I•ra•qis

i•ras•ci•ble
  i•ras•ci•bil•i•ty
  i•ras•ci•bly

i•rate
  i•rate•ly
  i•rate•ness

Ir•bid

ire
  ire•ful

Ire•land
  I•rish

ir•i•des•cent
  ir•i•des•cence
  ir•i•des•cent•ly

i•rid•i•um

i•ris

irk

irk•some
  irk•some•ly
  irk•some•ness

Ir•kutsk

i•ron
  i•ron•er
  i•ron•ing
  i•ron•less
  i•ron•like

i•ron•clad

i•ron•ic
  also i•ron•i•cal
  i•ron•i•cal•ly

i•ron•stone

i•ron•ware

i•ro•ny
  pl. i•ro•nies

Ir•o•quois
  pl. same
  Ir•o•quoi•an

ir•ra•di•ate
  ir•ra•di•a•tion
  ir•ra•di•a•tive

ir•ra•tion•al
  ir•ra•tion•al•i•ty
  ir•ra•tion•al•ly

ir•rec•on•cil•a•ble
  ir•rec•on•cil•a•bly

ir•re•cov•er•a•ble
  ir•re•cov•er•a•bly

ir•re•deem•a•ble
  ir•re•deem•a•bly

ir•re•duc•i•ble
  ir•re•duc•i•bly

ir•re•fut•a•ble
  ir•re•fut•a•bil•i•ty
  ir•re•fut•a•bly

ir•re•gard•less

ir•reg•u•lar
  ir•reg•u•lar•i•ty
  pl. ir•reg•u•lar•i•ties
  ir•reg•u•lar•ly

ir•rel•e•vant
  ir•rel•e•vance
  ir•rel•e•van•cy
  ir•rel•e•vant•ly

ir•re•li•gious
  ir•re•li•gious•ly

ir•re•me•di•a•ble
  ir•re•me•di•a•bly

ir•rep•a•ra•ble
  ir•rep•a•ra•bly

ir•re•place•a•ble
  ir•re•place•a•bly

ir•re•press•i•ble
  ir•re•press•i•bil•i•ty
  ir•re•press•i•bly

ir•re•proach•a•ble
  ir•re•proach•a•bil•i•ty
  ir•re•proach•a•bly

ir•re•sist•i•ble
  ir•re•sist•i•bil•i•ty
  ir•re•sist•i•bly

ir•res•o•lute
  ir•res•o•lute•ly
  ir•res•o•lute•ness
  ir•res•o•lu•tion

ir•re•spec•tive
  ir•re•spec•tive•ly

ir•re•spon•si•ble
  ir•re•spon•si•bil•i•ty
  ir•re•spon•si•bly

ir·re·triev·a·ble
  ir·re·triev·a·bly

ir·rev·er·ent
  ir·rev·er·ence
  ir·rev·er·ent·ly

ir·re·vers·i·ble
  ir·re·vers·i·bil·i·ty
  ir·re·vers·i·bly

ir·re·vo·ca·ble
  ir·re·vo·ca·bil·i·ty
  ir·re·vo·ca·bly

ir·ri·gate
  ir·ri·ga·ble
  ir·ri·ga·tion
  ir·ri·ga·tor

ir·ri·ta·ble
  ir·ri·ta·bil·i·ty
  ir·ri·ta·bly

ir·ri·tant
  ir·ri·tan·cy

ir·ri·tate
  ir·ri·tat·ed·ly
  ir·ri·tat·ing
  ir·ri·tat·ing·ly
  ir·ri·ta·tion
  ir·ri·ta·tive
  ir·ri·ta·tor

ir·rupt (*enter violently*;
  see ERUPT)
  ir·rup·tion

Ir·vine

Ir·ving

is·chi·um
  pl. is·chi·a
  is·chi·al

Is·fa·han
  also Es·fa·han,
  Is·pa·han

Ish·er·wood

i·sin·glass

Is·lam
  Is·lam·ic

Is·lam·a·bad

is·land

is·land·er

isle (*island*; see AISLE,
  I'LL)

is·let (*small island*; see
  EYELET)

ism

isn't

i·so·bar
  i·so·bar·ic

i·so·late
  i·so·lat·a·ble
  i·so·lat·ed
  i·so·la·tion
  i·so·la·tor

i·so·la·tion·ism
  i·so·la·tion·ist

i·so·mer
  i·so·mer·ic
  i·som·er·ism
  i·som·er·ize

i·so·met·ric
  i·so·met·ri·cal·ly

i·so·met·rics

i·sos·ce·les

i·so·ton·ic
  i·so·ton·i·cal·ly

i·so·tope
  i·so·top·ic
  i·so·top·i·cal·ly

Is·ra·el
  Is·rae·li

Is·ra·el·ite

is·sue
  is·sues, is·sued,
    is·su·ing
  is·su·a·ble
  is·su·ance
  is·sue·less
  is·su·er

Is·tan·bul

isth·mus

i·tal·ic

i·tal·i·cize
  i·tal·i·ci·za·tion

It·a·ly
  I·tal·ian
  I·tal·ian·ate

itch

itch·y
  itch·i·er, itch·i·est
  itch·i·ness

it'd

i·tem

i·tem·ize
  i·tem·i·za·tion
  i·tem·iz·er

it·er·ate
  it·er·a·tion
  it·er·a·tive

i·tin·er·ant

i·tin·er·ar·y
  pl. i·tin·er·ar·ies

it'll

its (*of it*)

it's (*it is, it has*)

it·self

it·ty-bit·ty
  also it·sy-bit·sy

I've

Ives

i·vo·ry
  pl. i·vo·ries
  i·vo·ried

I·vo·ry Coast
  I·vo·ri·an

i·vy
  pl. i·vies

I·wo Ji·ma

Iz·mir

J

jab
 jabbed, jab•bing

jab•ber

ja•bot

jack
 jack-in-the-box
 jack-in-the-pul•pit
 jack-of-all-trades
 jack-o'-lan•tern

jack•al

jack•ass

jack•daw

jack•et

jack•ham•mer

jack•knife
 pl. jack•knives
 jack•knifed, jack•knif•
  ing

jack•pot

jack•rab•bit

Jack•son

Ja•co•be•an

Jac•quard

Ja•cuz•zi

jade

jad•ed
 jad•ed•ly
 jad•ed•ness

jag
 jag•ged, jag•ging
 jag•ger

jag•ged
 jag•ged•ly
 jag•ged•ness

ja•guar

jai a•lai

jail

jail•break

jail•er

Ja•kar•ta

Ja•la•pa

ja•la•pe•ño

Ja•lis•co

ja•lop•y
 pl. ja•lop•ies

jal•ou•sie

jam (wedge, block, fruit
  preserve; see JAMB)
 jammed, jam•ming
 jam-packed
 jam•mer

Ja•mai•ca

jamb (architectural term;
  see JAM)

jam•ba•lay•a

jam•bo•ree

James

jan•gle

jan•i•tor
 jan•i•to•ri•al

Jan•u•ar•y
 pl. Jan•u•ar•ies

Ja•pan (country)
 Jap•a•nese
 pl. same

ja•pan (varnish)
 ja•panned, ja•pan•ning

jape
 jap•er•y

jar (container)
 jar•ful
 pl. jar•fuls

jar (jolt)
 jarred, jar•ring

jar•di•niere
 also jar•di•nière

jar•gon
 jar•gon•is•tic
 jar•gon•ize

jas•mine
 also jes•sa•mine

jas•per

jaun•dice

jaunt

jaunt•y
 jaunt•i•er, jaunt•i•est
 jaunt•i•ly
 jaunt•i•ness

Ja•va
 Jav•a•nese
 pl. same

jav•e•lin

jaw

jaw•bone

jaw•break•er

jay

jay•walk
 jay•walk•er

jazz
 jazz•er

jazz•y
 jazz•i•er, jazz•i•est
 jazz•i•ly
 jazz•i•ness

jeal•ous
 jeal•ous•ly

jeal•ou•sy
 pl. jeal•ou•sies

jeans

Jeep

jeer
jeer•ing•ly

Jef•fer•son
Jef•fer•so•ni•an

je•had
var. of ji•had

Je•ho•vah

je•june
je•june•ly

je•ju•num

jell (congeal; see GEL)

jel•ly
pl. jel•lies
jel•lies, jel•lied
jel•ly•like

jel•ly•fish
pl. same or jel•ly•fish•es

Je•na

jeop•ar•dize

jeop•ar•dy

jer•e•mi•ad

Jer•e•mi•ah

jerk
jerk•er

jer•kin

jer•ky
jerk•i•er, jerk•i•est
jerk•i•ly
jerk•i•ness

Jer•sey (place, cow)

jer•sey (shirt)
pl. jer•seys

Je•ru•sa•lem

jest (joke; see GEST)
jest•ful

jest•er

Jes•u•it

Je•sus

jet
jet•ted, jet•ting
jet-pro•pelled
jet-set•ter

jet•sam

jet•ti•son

jet•ty
pl. jet•ties

Jew

jew•el (gem; see JOULE)
jew•el•like

jew•el•er

jew•el•ry

Jew•ish
Jew•ish•ness

Jew•ry
pl. Jew•ries

Jez•e•bel

jib
jibbed, jib•bing

jibe (sail's movement,
agree; see GIBE)

Jid•da

jif•fy

jig
jigged, jig•ging

jig•ger

jig•gle
jig•gly

jig•saw

ji•had
also je•had

jil•lion

jilt

jim crow
also Jim Crow
jim crow•ism

jim•my
pl. jim•mies
jim•mies, jim•mied

jin•gle
jin•gly
jin•gli•er, jin•gli•est

jin•go
pl. jin•goes
jin•go•ism
jin•go•ist
jin•go•is•tic

jin•ni
also jinn
pl. jinn or jinns

jinx

jit•ney

jit•ter
jit•ter•y
jit•ter•i•ness

jit•ter•bug
jit•ter•bugged, jit•ter•
bug•ging

jive
jiv•er

Joan

job
jobbed, job•bing
job-shar•ing

job•ber

jock

jock•ey
pl. jock•eys

jock•strap

jo•cose
jo•cose•ly
jo•cos•i•ty
pl. jo•cos•i•ties

joc·u·lar
joc·u·lar·i·ty
pl. joc·u·lar·i·ties
joc·u·lar·ly

jo·cund
jo·cun·di·ty
pl. jo·cun·di·ties
jo·cund·ly

Jodh·pur

jodh·purs

Joe Blow

jog
jogged, jog·ging
jog·ger

Jo·han·nes·burg

john

John Bull

Johns

John·son

joie de vivre

join
join·a·ble

join·er
join·er·y

joint
joint·less
joint·ly

joist
joist·ed

jo·jo·ba

joke
jok·ing·ly
jok·i·ly

jok·er

Jo·li·et

jol·li·ty
pl. jol·li·ties

jol·ly
jol·li·er, jol·li·est
jol·lies, jol·lied

jol·li·ly
jol·li·ness

jolt

Jo·nah

Jones

Jung

jon·quil

Jon·son

Jor·dan
Jor·da·ni·an

Jo·se·phus

josh
josh·er

jos·tle

jot
jot·ted, jot·ting

joule (*unit of work or
energy*; see JEWEL)

jounce

jour·nal

jour·nal·ism
jour·nal·ist
jour·nal·is·tic

jour·ney
pl. jour·neys
jour·neys, jour·neyed

jour·ney·man
pl. jour·ney·men

joust
joust·er

Jove

jo·vi·al
jo·vi·al·i·ty
jo·vi·al·ly

jowl
jowl·y

joy
joy·less

joy·less·ly
joy·ous
joy·ous·ly

Joyce

joy·ful
joy·ful·ly
joy·ful·ness

joy·ride
past joy·rode; *past part.*
joy·rid·den
joy·rid·er

joy·stick

Juan Car·los

Juan de Fu·ca, Strait of

ju·bi·lant
ju·bi·lance
ju·bi·lant·ly

ju·bi·lee

Ju·da·ism
Ju·da·ic
Ju·da·ist

Ju·das

judge
judge·like
judge·ship

judg·ment
also judge·ment

judg·men·tal
also judge·men·tal
judg·men·tal·ly

ju·di·ca·ture

ju·di·cial
ju·di·cial·ly

ju·di·ci·ar·y
pl. ju·di·ci·ar·ies

ju·di·cious
ju·di·cious·ly
ju·di·cious·ness

ju·do
ju·do·ist

jug
jug•ful
pl. jug•fuls

jug•ger•naut

jug•gle
jug•gler

jug•u•lar

juice
juice•less

juic•er

juic•y
juic•i•er, juic•i•est
juic•i•ly
juic•i•ness

ju•jit•su
also jiu•jit•su

ju•jube

juke•box

ju•lep

ju•li•enne

Jul•ius

Ju•ly
pl. Ju•lys

jum•ble
jumb•ly

jum•bo
pl. jum•bos

jump

jump•er

jump•suit

jump•y
jump•i•er, jump•i•est
jump•i•ly
jump•i•ness

jun•co
pl. jun•cos *or* jun•coes

junc•tion

junc•ture

June

Ju•neau

Jung
Jung•i•an

Jung•frau

jun•gle

jun•ior

ju•ni•per

junk

jun•ket
jun•ket•ing

junk•ie

junk•yard

jun•ta

Ju•pi•ter

Jur•as•sic

ju•rid•i•cal
ju•rid•i•cal•ly

ju•ris•dic•tion
ju•ris•dic•tion•al

ju•ris•pru•dence
ju•ris•pru•dent

ju•rist

ju•ror

ju•ry
pl. ju•ries

ju•ry-rigged

just
just•ly
just•ness

jus•tice

jus•ti•fy
jus•ti•fies, jus•ti•fied
jus•ti•fi•a•ble
jus•ti•fi•a•bly
jus•ti•fi•ca•tion
jus•ti•fi•er

Jus•tin•i•an

jut
jut•ted, jut•ting

jute

Ju•ve•nal

ju•ve•nile

jux•ta•pose
jux•ta•po•si•tion

K

ka·bob

ka·bu·ki

Ka·bul

Kaf·ka

Ka·go·shi·ma

kai·ser

Ka·la·ha·ri

Kal·a·ma·zoo

kale

ka·lei·do·scope
ka·lei·do·scop·ic

Ka·li·nin

Ka·li·nin·grad

Kamchatka

Ka·me·ha·me·ha

ka·mi·ka·ze

Kam·pa·la

Kam·pu·che·a

Kan·din·sky

kan·ga·roo

Ka·no

Kan·pur

Kan·sa

Kan·sas
Kan·san

Kant

Kao·hsiung

ka·o·lin
ka·o·lin·ic

ka·pok

Ka·po·si's sar·co·ma

kap·pa

ka·put

Ka·ra·chi

ka·ra·o·ke

ka·rat (*measure of purity of gold;* see CARAT, CARET, CARROT)

ka·ra·te

Karl-Marx-Stadt

Karls·ruh·e

kar·ma
kar·mic

Kath·man·du
also Katmandu

Ka·to·wi·ce

ka·ty·did

Kau·nas

Ka·wa·ba·ta

Ka·wa·sa·ki

kay·ak

kayo
pl. kay·os
kay·oed, kay·o·ing

Kay·se·ri

Ka·zakh·stan
Ka·zakh

ka·zoo

ke·a

Keats

keel

keel·haul

Kee·lung
also Chi·lung

keen (*eager, sharp*)
keen·ly
keen·ness

keen (*funeral song*)
keen·er

keep
past and *past part.* kept

keep·er

keep·ing

keep·sake

kees·hond

keg

keis·ter

Kel·ler

Kel·ly

kelp

kel·vin

Kem·pis, Thomas à

kempt

ken

ken·do

Ken·ne·dy

ken·nel
ken·neled, ken·nel·ing; ken·nelled, ken·nel·ling

Ken·tuck·y
Ken·tuck·i·an

Ken·ya

Ken·yat·ta

kep·i
pl. kep·is

Kep·ler

kept

ker·a·tin

ker·chief
ker·chiefed

kerf

Kern

ker·nel (*grain, core*; see
COLONEL)

ker·o·sene

Ker·ou·ac

kes·trel

ketch

ketch·up
also cat·sup

ke·tone
ke·ton·ic

ke·to·sis

ket·tle
ket·tle·ful
pl. ket·tle·fuls

ket·tle·drum

Kew·pie

key (*opener, scale*; see
QUAY)
pl. keys
keys, keyed

key·board
key·board·er
key·board·ist

key·hole

Keynes
Keynes·i·an

key·note

key·pad

key·punch
key·punch·er

key·stone

key·stroke

key·word

kha·ki
pl. kha·kis

khan (*ruler*; see CON)
khan·ate

Khar·kiv
formerly Khar·kov

Khar·toum

Khmer

Kho·mei·ni

Khru·shchev

kib·ble

kib·butz (*communal
settlement*)

kib·itz (*offer advice*)
kib·itz·er

ki·bosh

kick
kick-start

Kick·a·poo

kick·back

kick·off

kick·stand

kid (*young goat*)

kid (*tease*)
kid·ded, kid·ding
kid·der
kid·ding·ly

Kidd (*proper name*)

kid·die
pl. kid·dies

kid·nap
kid·napped, kid·nap·
ping *or* kid·naped,
kid·nap·ing
kid·nap·per

kid·ney
pl. kid·neys

kiel·ba·sa

Kier·ke·gaard

Ki·ev

Ki·ga·li

Ki·lau·e·a

Kil·i·man·ja·ro, Mount

kill

kill·deer

kill·er

kill·ing

kill·joy

Kil·mer

kiln

ki·lo
pl. ki·los

kil·o·byte

kil·o·cy·cle

kil·o·gram

kil·o·hertz

kil·o·li·ter

kil·o·me·ter
kil·o·met·ric

kil·o·ton

kil·o·watt

kil·o·watt-hour

kilt

kil·ter

Kim Il Sung

ki·mo·no
pl. ki·mo·nos

kin

kind

kin·der·gar·ten

kind·heart·ed
kind·heart·ed·ly
kind·heart·ed·ness

kin·dle
  kin·dler

kin·dling

kind·ly
  kind·li·er, kind·li·est
  kind·li·ness

kind·ness

kin·dred

ki·ne·mat·ics
  ki·ne·mat·ic
  ki·ne·mat·i·cal·ly

kin·e·scope

kin·es·thet·ic

ki·net·ic
  ki·net·i·cal·ly

ki·net·ics

kin·folk
  also kin·folks, kins·folk

king
  king-size or king-sized
  king·ly
  king·li·ness
  king·ship

king·dom

king·fish·er

king·pin

Kings·ton

Kings·town

kink

kink·y
  kink·i·er, kink·i·est
  kink·i·ly
  kink·i·ness

kins·folk
  var. of kin·folk

Kin·sha·sa

kin·ship

kins·man
  pl. kins·men; fem. kins·
  wom·an, pl. kins·
  wom·en

ki·osk

Ki·o·wa

Kip·ling

kip·per

Ki·ri·ba·ti

kirk

Kir·kuk

Ki·shi·nev
  also Chi·si·nau,
  Ki·shi·nyov

kis·met

kiss
  kiss·a·ble

Kis·sin·ger

kit

Ki·ta·kyu·shu

kitch·en

Kitch·e·ner

kitch·en·ette

kitch·en·ware

kite

kith

kitsch

kit·ten

kit·ten·ish
  kit·ten·ish·ly

kit·ty
  pl. kit·ties

kit·ty-cor·ner
  var. of ca·ter·cor·nered

ki·wi
  pl. ki·wis

Klee

klep·to·ma·ni·a
  klep·to·ma·ni·ac

klutz
  klutz·y

knack

knap·sack

knave (rogue, jack; see
  NAVE)
  knav·er·y
  pl. knav·er·ies
  knav·ish
  knav·ish·ly

knead (manipulate; see
  NEED)
  knead·a·ble
  knead·er

knee
  knees, kneed, knee·
  ing
  knee-deep
  knee-jerk

knee·cap

kneel
  past and past part. knelt
  or kneeled

knell

knelt

knew (past of know; see
  GNU, NEW)

knick·ers

knick·knack

knife
  pl. knives
  knife·like
  knif·er

knight (military rank,
  title; see NIGHT)
  knight-er·rant
  knight·hood
  knight·like
  knight·ly

knit (*make a garment;*
  see NIT)
  knit•ting; *past* and *past
  part.* knit•ted *or* knit
  knit•ter

knit•ting

knives

knob
  knob•by
  knob•like

knock
  knock-kneed
  knock-knees

knock•er

knock•out

knock•wurst

knoll

knot (*bond, bunch;* see
  NOT)
  knot•ted, knot•ting
  knot•ter

knot•hole

knot•ty
  knot•ti•er, knot•ti•est
  knot•ti•ly
  knot•ti•ness

know (*comprehend;* see
  NO)
  past knew; *past part.*
  known
  know-how
  know-it-all
  know•a•ble
  know•er

know•ing
  know•ing•ly

knowl•edge

knowl•edge•a•ble
  knowl•edge•a•bly

known

Knox

Knox•ville

knuck•le

knuck•le•ball

knuck•le•head

knurl
  knurl•ed

Knut

ko•a•la

Ko•be

Ko•blenz
  also Co•blenz

Ko•di•ak

Kohl

kohl•ra•bi
  pl. kohl•ra•bies

Köln

Kol•we•zi

Kon•ya

kook
  kook•i•ness
  kook•y
  kook•i•er, kook•i•est

kook•a•bur•ra

ko•peck
  also ko•pek, co•peck

Ko•ran
  Ko•ran•ic

Ko•re•a
  Ko•re•an

Kos•ci•us•ko

ko•sher

Kos•suth

kow•tow

kraal

Kra•ka•to•a
  also Kra•ka•tau

Kra•ków
  also Cra•cow

Kras•no•yarsk

krem•lin
  also the Krem•lin

krill

Kroc

kro•na
  pl. kro•nor

kro•ne
  pl. kro•ner

Kru•ger•rand
  also kru•ger•rand

kryp•ton

Kua•la Lum•pur

Ku•blai Khan

ku•dos

Ku Klux Klan

Ku•ma•mo•to

Ku•ma•si

kum•quat
  also cum•quat

kung fu

K'ung Fu-tzu

Kurd
  Kurd•ish

Ku•wait
  Ku•wai•ti

kvetch
  kvetch•er

Kwang•ju

Kyo•to

Kyr•gyz•stan

Kyu•shu

L

la

lab

la·bel
la·beled, la·bel·ing or
la·belled, la·bel·ling
la·bel·er

la·bi·al

la·bi·um
pl. la·bi·a

la·bor
la·bor-in·ten·sive

lab·o·ra·to·ry
pl. lab·o·ra·to·ries

la·bor·er

la·bo·ri·ous
la·bo·ri·ous·ly

Lab·ra·dor

lab·y·rinth
lab·y·rin·thi·an
lab·y·rin·thine

lac (*resin*; see LACK)

lace

lac·er·ate
lac·er·a·tion

lach·ry·mal
also lac·ri·mal

lach·ry·mose
lach·ry·mose·ly

lack (*want*; see LAC)
lack·ing

lack·a·dai·si·cal
lack·a·dai·si·cal·ly

lack·ey
pl. lack·eys

lack·lus·ter

la·con·ic
la·con·i·cal·ly

lac·quer

lac·ri·mal
var. of lach·ry·mal

la·crosse

lac·tate

lac·ta·tion

lac·te·al

lac·tic

lac·tose

la·cu·na
pl. la·cu·nae *or* la·cu·
nas

lac·y
lac·i·er, lac·i·est
lac·i·ly
lac·i·ness

lad

lad·der

lade (*to load*; see LAID)
past part. lad·en

la-di-da
also la-de-da

la·dle
la·dle·ful
pl. la·dle·fuls
la·dler

La·do·ga, Lake

la·dy
pl. la·dies
la·dy-in-wait·ing
la·dy-kill·er

la·dy·bug

la·dy·fin·ger

la·dy·like

la·dy·ship

La·fa·yette
also La Fa·yette

La·Fol·lette

La Fon·taine

lag
lagged, lag·ging
lag·ger

la·ger

lag·gard
lag·gard·ly

lag·ging

la·gniappe

la·goon

La·hore

laid (*past of* lay; see LADE)

la·i·cize

lain (*past part. of* lie; see
LANE)

lair

lais·sez-faire
also lais·ser-faire

la·it·y

lake

Lake·wood

lal·ly·gag
var. of lol·ly·gag

lam (*flight*; see LAMB)

la·ma (*Buddhist monk*;
see LLAMA)

la·ma·ser·y
pl. la·ma·ser·ies

La Ma·tan·za

La·maze meth·od

Lamb (*proper name*)

lamb (*young sheep*; see LAM)

lam·ba·da

lam·baste
also lam·bast

lamb·da

lam·bent
lam·ben·cy
lam·bent·ly

lame
lame·ly
lame·ness

la·mé

lame·brain
lame·brained

la·ment
lam·en·ta·tion

la·men·ta·ble
la·men·ta·bly

lam·i·nate
lam·i·na·tion
lam·i·na·tor

lamp

lamp·black

lam·poon
lam·poon·er
lam·poon·ist

lamp·post

lam·prey
pl. lam·preys

lamp·shade

lance

lanc·er

lan·cet

land

lan·dau

land·ed

land·fall

land·fill

land·form

land·ing

land·la·dy
pl. land·la·dies

land·locked

land·lord

land·lub·ber

land·mark

land·mass

land·own·er
land·own·ing

land·scape

land·slide

lane (*road*; see LAIN)

Lang·land

lan·gous·tine

lan·guage

lan·guid
lan·guid·ly
lan·guid·ness

lan·guish

lan·guor
lan·guor·ous
lan·guor·ous·ly

lan·gur

lank

lank·y
lank·i·er, lank·i·est
lank·i·ly
lank·i·ness

lan·o·lin

Lan·sing

lan·tern

lan·tha·nide

lan·tha·num

lan·yard

La·os
La·o·tian

Lao-tse
also Lao-tsze, Lao-tsu

lap (*fold, use one's tongue to drink*; see LAPP)
lapped, lap·ping
lap-weld

lap (*part of seated body* see LAPP)
lap·ful
pl. lap·fuls

La Paz

lap·dog

la·pel
la·pelled *or* la·peled

lap·i·dar·y
pl. lap·i·dar·ies

lap·is laz·u·li

La Pla·ta

Lapp (*northern Scandinavian*; see LAP)

lapse

lap·top

lap·wing

lar·board

lar·ce·ny
pl. lar·ce·nies
lar·ce·nist
lar·ce·nous

larch

lard

lar·der

La·re·do

large
large•ness
larg•ish

large•ly

lar•gesse
also lar•gess

lar•go
pl. lar•gos

lar•i•at

lark

lark•spur

La Roche•fou•cauld

La•rousse

lar•va
pl. lar•vae
lar•val

lar•yn•gi•tis

lar•ynx
pl. la•ryn•ges *or* lar•
ynx•es

la•sa•gna
also la•sa•gne

La Salle

las•civ•i•ous
las•civ•i•ous•ly
las•civ•i•ous•ness

Las Cru•ces

lase

la•ser

lash

Las Pal•mas

lass

Las•sa fe•ver

las•sie

las•si•tude

las•so
pl. las•sos *or* las•soes
las•soes, las•soed
las•so•er

last
last-ditch

last•ing
last•ing•ly

last•ly

Las Ve•gas

Lat•a•ki•a

latch

latch•key
pl. latch•keys

late
late•ness

late•com•er

la•teen

late•ly

la•tent
la•ten•cy
la•tent•ly

lat•er•al
lat•er•al•ly

la•tex
pl. lat•i•ces *or* la•tex•es

lath
pl. laths

lathe

lath•er
lath•er•y

Lat•in

La•ti•no
pl. La•ti•nos; *fem.* La•
ti•na, *pl.* La•ti•nas

lat•ish

lat•i•tude
lat•i•tu•di•nal
lat•i•tu•di•nal•ly

la•trine

lat•ter
lat•ter-day

lat•tice
lat•ticed
lat•tic•ing

lat•tice•work

Lat•vi•a
Lat•vi•an

laud

laud•a•ble
laud•a•bil•i•ty
laud•a•bly

lau•da•num

laud•a•to•ry

laugh
laugh•er

laugh•a•ble
laugh•a•bly

laugh•ing
laugh•ing•ly

laugh•ing•stock

laugh•ter

launch

launch•pad

laun•der
laun•der•er

Laun•dro•mat
(*trademark*)

laun•dry
pl. laun•dries

lau•re•ate
lau•re•ate•ship

lau•rel

Lau•sanne

la•va

la•vage

La•val

lav•a•lierc

lav•a•to•ry
  pl. lav•a•to•ries

lave

lav•en•der

lav•ish
  lav•ish•ly
  lav•ish•ness

law
  law-a•bid•ing

law•break•er
  law•break•ing

law•ful
  law•ful•ly
  law•ful•ness

law•giv•er

law•less
  law•less•ly
  law•less•ness

law•mak•er

law•man
  pl. law•men

lawn

Law•rence

law•ren•ci•um

law•suit

law•yer
  law•yer•ly

lax
  lax•i•ty
  lax•ly
  lax•ness

lax•a•tive

lay (*put*; see LEI)
  past and *past part.* laid

lay•a•bout

Lay•a•mon

lay•er
  lay•ered

lay•ette

lay•man
  pl. lay•men; *fem.* lay•
  wom•an, *pl.* lay•wom•
  en

lay•off

lay•out

lay•o•ver

laze

la•zy
  la•zi•er, la•zi•est
  la•zi•ly
  la•zi•ness

la•zy•bones
  pl. same

lea (*meadow*; see LEE)
  also ley

leach (*to filter*; see
  LEECH)
  leach•er

lead (*direct, guide*)
  past and *past part.* led
  lead-in

lead (*metal*; see LED)

lead•en
  lead•en•ly
  lead•en•ness

lead•er
  lead•er•ship

lead•ing

leaf
  pl. leaves
  leaf•age
  leafed
  leaf•less
  leaf•less•ness
  leaf•like
  leaf•y
  leaf•i•er, leaf•i•est

leaf•let

league (*association*)
  leagues, leagued,
  leagu•ing

league (*measure of
  distance*)

leak (*accidental hole*; see
  LEEK)
  leak•y
  leak•i•er, leak•i•est

leak•age

Lea•key

lean (*incline*; see LIEN)
  past and *past part.*
  leaned *or* leant
  lean-to
  pl. lean-tos

lean (*thin*; see LIEN)
  lean•ly
  lean•ness

lean•ing

leap
  past and *past part.*
  leaped *or* leapt
  leap•er

leap•frog
  leap•frogged, leap•
  frog•ging

Lear

learn
  past and *past part.*
  learned *or* learnt
  learn•a•ble
  learn•er

learn•ed
  learn•ed•ly
  learn•ed•ness

learn•ing

lease
  leas•a•ble
  leas•er

lease•hold
  lease•hold•er

leash

least

leath•er
  leath•er•y

leath•er•back

leath·er·ette

leath·er·neck

leave
  past and *past part.* left
  leav·er

leav·en

leaves

leav·ings

Leb·a·non
  Leb·a·nese

lech

lech·er
  lech·er·ous
  lech·er·ous·ly
  lech·er·ous·ness
  lech·er·y

lec·i·thin

lec·tern

lec·ture
  lec·tur·er

led (*past of lead [direct,*
  guide]; see LEAD
  [metal])

ledge
  ledged

led·ger

Lee

lee (*shelter; see* LEA)

leech (*bloodsucking worm;*
  see LEACH)

Leeds

leek (*onionlike plant; see*
  LEAK)

leer
  leer·ing·ly

leer·y
  leer·i·er, leer·i·est

lees

lee·ward

lee·way

left
  left-hand
  left-wing
  left-wing·er

left-hand·ed
  left-hand·ed·ly
  left-hand·ed·ness
  left-hand·er

left·ism
  left·ist

left·most

left·o·ver

left·y
  pl. left·ies

leg
  leg-of-mut·ton
  leg·ged

leg·a·cy
  pl. leg·a·cies

le·gal
  le·gal·ly

le·gal·ese

le·gal·ism
  le·gal·ist
  le·gal·is·tic
  le·gal·is·ti·cal·ly

le·gal·i·ty
  pl. le·gal·i·ties

le·gal·ize
  le·gal·i·za·tion

leg·ate
  leg·ate·ship

leg·a·tee

le·ga·tion

le·ga·to
  pl. le·ga·tos

le·ga·tor

leg·end

leg·end·ar·y
  leg·end·ar·i·ly

leg·er·de·main

leg·ging
  also leg·gin

leg·gy
  leg·gi·er, leg·gi·est
  leg·gi·ness

Leg·horn

leg·i·ble
  leg·i·bil·i·ty
  leg·i·bly

le·gion

le·gion·naire

leg·is·late

leg·is·la·tion

leg·is·la·tive
  leg·is·la·tive·ly

leg·is·la·tor

leg·is·la·ture

le·git

le·git·i·mate
  le·git·i·ma·cy
  le·git·i·mate·ly
  le·git·i·ma·tion

le·git·i·ma·tize

le·git·i·mize
  le·git·i·mi·za·tion

leg·room

leg·ume

le·gu·mi·nous

Le Ha·vre

lei (*garland; see* LAY)

Leib·niz

Leices·ter

Lei·den

Leip·zig

lei·sure

lei·sure·ly
  lei·sure·li·ness

lei·sure·wear

leit·mo·tiv
  also leit·mo·tif

Le·man, Lake

Le Mans

lem·ming

lem·on
  lem·on·y

lem·on·ade

le·mur

Len·a·pe

lend
  past and past part. lent
  lend·a·ble
  lend·er
  lend·ing

L'En·fant

length

length·en
  length·en·er

length·wise

length·y
  length·i·er, length·i·est
  length·i·ly
  length·i·ness

le·ni·ent
  le·ni·ence
  le·ni·en·cy
  le·ni·ent·ly

Le·nin

Le·nin·grad

Len·non

le·no
  pl. le·nos

lens
  lensed
  lens·less

Lent (*season*)
  Lent·en

lent (*past of lend*)

len·til

len·to

Le·o
  pl. Le·os

Le·ón

Le·o·nar·do da Vin·ci

le·o·nine

leop·ard
  fem. leop·ard·ess

le·o·tard

lep·er

lep·i·dop·ter·ous
  lep·i·dop·ter·an
  lep·i·dop·ter·ist

lep·re·chaun

lep·ro·sy
  lep·rous

Ler·ner

les·bi·an
  les·bi·an·ism

lese-maj·es·ty
  also lèse-maj·es·té

le·sion

Le·so·tho

less

less·ee

less·en (*make or become less;* see LESSON)

Les·seps

less·er

Less·er An·til·les

les·son (*amount of teaching;* see LESSEN)

les·sor

lest

let
  let·ting; *past and past part.* let

let·down

le·thal
  le·thal·ly

leth·ar·gy
  le·thar·gic
  le·thar·gi·cal·ly

let's

let·ter
  let·ter-per·fect
  let·ter-qual·i·ty
  let·ter·er
  let·ter·less

let·tered

let·ter·head

let·ter·ing

let·ter·press

let·tuce

let·up

leu·ke·mi·a
  leu·ke·mic

leu·ko·cyte
  leu·ko·cyt·ic

Le·vant, the

lev·ee (*embankment;* see LEVY)

lev·el
  lev·el·ly
  lev·el·ness

lev·el·head·ed
  lev·el·head·ed·ly
  lev·el·head·ed·ness

lev·er

lev·er·age

le·vi·a·than

Le·vis

lev·i·tate
  lev·i·ta·tion
  levi·ta·tor

Lev·it·town

lev·i·ty

lev·y (*impose payment;*
  see LEVEE)
  lev·ies, lev·ied
  pl. lev·ies
  lev·i·a·ble

lewd
  lewd·ly
  lewd·ness

Lew·is

lex·i·cal
  lex·i·cal·ly

lex·i·cog·ra·phy
  lex·i·cog·ra·pher
  lex·i·co·graph·ic
  lex·i·co·graph·i·cal
  lex·i·co·graph·i·cal·ly

lex·i·col·o·gy
  lex·i·co·log·i·cal
  lex·i·co·log·i·cal·ly
  lex·i·col·o·gist

lex·i·con

Lex·ing·ton

li·a·bil·i·ty
  pl. li·a·bil·i·ties

li·a·ble

li·aise

li·ai·son

li·ar (*person who tells a
  lie;* see LYRE)

lib

li·ba·tion

li·bel
  li·beled, li·bel·ing *or*
  li·belled, li·bel·ling
  li·bel·er
  li·bel·ous

lib·er·al
  lib·er·al·ism
  lib·er·al·ist
  lib·er·al·is·tic
  lib·er·al·i·ty
  lib·er·al·ly

lib·er·al·ize
  lib·er·al·i·za·tion

lib·er·ate
  lib·er·a·tion
  lib·er·a·tor

Li·be·ri·a
  Li·be·ri·an

lib·er·tar·i·an
  lib·er·tar·i·an·ism

lib·er·tine
  lib·er·tin·ism

lib·er·ty
  pl. lib·er·ties

li·bid·i·nous
  li·bid·i·nous·ly

li·bi·do
  pl. li·bi·dos
  li·bid·i·nal
  li·bid·i·nal·ly

Li·bra

li·brar·i·an
  li·brar·i·an·ship

li·brar·y
  pl. li·brar·ies

li·bret·to
  pl. li·bret·tos *or* li·bret·
  ti
  li·bret·tist

Li·bre·ville

Lib·y·a
  Lib·y·an

lice

li·cense
  li·cens·a·ble
  li·cens·er
  li·cen·sor

li·cen·see

li·cen·ti·ate

li·cen·tious
  li·cen·tious·ly
  li·cen·tious·ness

li·chee
  var. of li·tchi

li·chen

lic·it
  lic·it·ly

lick
  lick·er (*one who licks;*
  see LIQUOR)

lick·e·ty-split

lick·ing

lic·o·rice

lid
  lid·ded
  lid·less

lie (*recline;* see LYE)
  ly·ing; *past* lay; *past
  part.* lain

lie (*untruth;* see LYE)
  lies, lied, ly·ing

Liech·ten·stein
  Liech·ten·stein·er

liege

Li·ège

lien (*right over another's
  property;* see LEAN)

lieu

lieu·ten·ant
  lieu·ten·an·cy
  pl. lieu·ten·an·cies

life
pl. lives
life-and-death
life-size
also life-sized
life-sup•port

life•blood

life•boat

life•guard

life•less
life•less•ly
life•less•ness

life•like

life•line

life•long

lif•er

life•sav•er
life•sav•ing

life•style

life•time

life•work

lift
lift•a•ble
lift•er

lift•off

lig•a•ment

lig•a•ture

li•ger

light (*illumination*)
past lit; *past part.* lit *or*
light•ed
light-year
light•ish
light•ness

light (*not heavy*)
past and *past part.* lit
or light•ed
light•er-than-air
light-fin•gered
light-foot•ed
light-head•ed

light-head•ed•ness
light•ish
light•ly
light•ness

light•bulb

light•en

light•er

light•heart•ed
light•heart•ed•ly
light•heart•ed•ness

light•house

light•ing

light•ning

light•ship

light•weight

lig•nite
lig•nit•ic

lik•a•ble
also like•a•ble
lik•a•ble•ness
lik•a•bly

like
like-mind•ed
like-mind•ed•ness

like•a•ble
var. of lik•a•ble

like•li•hood

like•ly
like•li•ness

lik•en

like•ness

like•wise

lik•ing

li•lac

Lille

lil•li•pu•tian
also Lil•li•pu•tian

Li•long•we

lilt

lil•y
pl. lil•ies
lil•y-liv•ered
lil•y-white
lil•ied

Li•ma

li•ma bean

limb (*arm;* see LIMN)
limbed
limb•less

lim•ber
lim•ber•ness

lim•bo
pl. lim•bos

lime
lim•y
lim•i•er, lim•i•est

lime•light

lim•er•ick

lime•stone

lim•ey
also Lim•ey
pl. lim•eys

lim•it
lim•it•a•ble
lim•i•ta•tion
lim•it•er
lim•it•less

lim•it•ed
lim•it•ed•ness

limn (*paint;* see LIMB)
lim•ner

lim•o
pl. lim•os

Li•moges

lim•ou•sine

limp (*lame walk*)

limp (*not stiff*)
limp•ly
limp•ness

lim·pet

lim·pid
  lim·pid·i·ty
  lim·pid·ly
  lim·pid·ness

lin·age

linch·pin

Lin·coln

Lind·bergh

lin·den

Lind·say

line

lin·e·age

lin·e·al
  lin·e·al·ly

lin·e·a·ment

lin·e·ar
  lin·e·ar·i·ty
  lin·e·ar·ize
  lin·e·ar·ly

line·man
  pl. line·men

lin·en

lin·er

lines·man
  pl. lines·men

line·up

lin·ger
  lin·ger·er
  lin·ger·ing
  lin·ger·ing·ly

lin·ge·rie

lin·go
  pl. lin·goes

lin·gua fran·ca
  pl. lin·gua fran·cas *or*
  lin·guae fran·cae

lin·gual
  lin·gual·ly

lin·guine
  also lin·gui·ni

lin·guist

lin·guis·tic
  lin·guis·ti·cal·ly

lin·guis·tics

lin·i·ment

lin·ing

link

link·age

links (*golf course;* see
  LYNX)

link·up

Lin·nae·us

lin·net

li·no·le·um

lin·seed

lint
  lint·y

lin·tel

Linz

li·on
  fem. li·on·ess

li·on·heart
  li·on·heart·ed

li·on·ize
  li·on·i·za·tion
  li·on·iz·er

lip
  lip·less
  lip·like
  lipped

lip·gloss

lip·id

lip·o·suc·tion

lip·read·ing
  lip·read
  lip·read·er

lip·stick

liq·ue·fy
  liq·ue·fies, liq·ue·fied
  liq·ue·fa·cient
  liq·ue·fac·tion
  liq·ue·fi·er

li·queur

liq·uid
  liq·uid·ly

liq·ui·date
  liq·ui·da·tion
  liq·ui·da·tor

li·quid·i·ty
  pl. li·quid·i·ties

liq·uid·ize

liq·uor (*drink;* see *licker*
  [LICK])

li·ra
  pl. li·re *or* li·ras

Lis·bon

lisle

lisp
  lisp·er
  lisp·ing·ly

lis·some
  also lis·som
  lis·some·ly
  lis·some·ness

list
  list·ing

lis·ten
  lis·ten·er

Lis·ter

list·less
  list·less·ly
  list·less·ness

Liszt

lit

lit·a·ny
  pl. lit·a·nies

li·tchi
  also li·chee, ly·chee

li·ter

lit·er·a·cy

lit·er·al
  lit·er·al·ize
  lit·er·al·ly
  lit·er·al·ness

lit·er·ar·y
  lit·er·ar·i·ness

lit·er·ate
  lit·er·ate·ly

lit·e·ra·ti

lit·er·a·ture

lithe
  lithe·ly
  lithe·ness
  lithe·some

lith·i·um

lith·o·graph

li·thog·ra·phy
  li·thog·ra·pher
  li·tho·graph·ic
  li·tho·graph·i·cal·ly

lith·o·sphere
  lith·o·spher·ic

Lith·u·a·ni·a
  Lith·u·a·ni·an

lit·i·gant

lit·i·gate
  lit·i·ga·tion
  lit·i·ga·tor

li·ti·gious
  li·ti·gious·ly
  li·ti·gious·ness

lit·mus

lit·ter

lit·ter·bug

lit·tle
  lit·tler, lit·tlest; less *or*
  les·ser; least
  lit·tle·ness

Lit·tle Rock

lit·to·ral

lit·ur·gy
  pl. lit·ur·gies
  li·tur·gi·cal
  li·tur·gi·cal·ly

liv·a·ble
  also live·a·ble
  liv·a·bil·i·ty

live

live·a·ble
  var. of liv·a·ble

live·li·hood

live·long

live·ly
  live·li·er, live·li·est
  live·li·ness

liv·en

liv·er

Liv·er·pool
  Liv·er·pud·li·an

liv·er·wurst

liv·er·y
  pl. liv·er·ies

lives

live·stock

liv·id
  li·vid·i·ty
  liv·id·ly
  liv·id·ness

liv·ing

Liv·ing·stone

Li·vo·ni·a

Li·vor·no

Liv·y

liz·ard

Lju·blja·na

lla·ma (*animal*; see LAMA)

lla·no
  pl. lla·nos

Lla·no Es·ta·ca·do

Lloyd George

Lloyd Web·ber

load (*burden*; see LODE)

load·ed

load·stone
  var. of lode·stone

loaf
  pl. loaves

loaf·er

loam
  loam·y
  loam·i·ness

loan (*money lent*; see LONE)

loath

loathe
  loath·er
  loath·ing

loath·some
  loath·some·ly
  loath·some·ness

loaves

lob
  lobbed, lob·bing

lob·by
  pl. lob·bies
  lob·bies, lob·bied
  lob·by·er
  lob·by·ist

lobe
  lo·bar
  lobed

lo·bel·ia

lo·bot·o·my
  pl. lo·bot·o·mies

lob·ster

lo·cal
  lo·cal·ly

lo·cale

lo·cal·i·ty
  pl. lo·cal·i·ties

lo·cal·ize
  lo·cal·i·za·tion

lo·cate

lo·ca·tion

loch (*lake*; see LOCK)

Loch Ness

lo·ci

lock (*fastener*; see LOCH)
  lock·a·ble

Locke

lock·er

lock·et

lock·jaw

lock·out

lock·smith

lock·up

lo·co
  pl. lo·cos *or* lo·coes

lo·co·mo·tion

lo·co·mo·tive

lo·co·weed

lo·cus
  pl. lo·ci

lo·cust

lo·cu·tion

lode (*vein of mineral*; see
  LOAD)

lo·den

lode·star

lode·stone
  also load·stone

lodge

lodg·er

lodg·ing

Lódz

lo·ess

Loewe

loft

loft·y
  loft·i·er, loft·i·est
  loft·i·ly
  loft·i·ness

log
  logged, log·ging

lo·gan·ber·ry
  pl. lo·gan·ber·ries

log·a·rithm
  log·a·rith·mic
  log·a·rith·mi·cal·ly

log·book

loge

log·ger

log·ger·head

log·ging

log·ic
  lo·gi·cian

log·i·cal
  log·i·cal·i·ty
  log·i·cal·ly

lo·gis·tics
  lo·gis·tic
  lo·gis·ti·cal
  lo·gis·ti·cal·ly

log·jam

lo·go
  pl. lo·gos

lo·go·type

log·rolling
  log·roll
  log·roll·er

lo·gy

loin

loin·cloth

loi·ter
  loi·ter·er

loll
  loll·er

lol·li·pop

lol·ly·gag
  also lal·ly·gag
  lol·ly·gagged, lol·ly·
  gag·ging

Lo·mas de Za·mo·ra

Lo·mé

Lon·don

lone (*solitary*; see LOAN)

lone·ly
  lone·li·er, lone·li·est
  lone·li·ness

lon·er

lone·some
  lone·some·ly
  lone·some·ness

long
  long·er; long·est
  long-dis·tance
  long-drawn (*or* long-
  drawn-out)
  long-faced
  long-lived
  long-play·ing
  long-range
  long-run·ning
  long-sleeved

long-stand•ing
long-suf•fer•ing
long-term
long•ish

lon•gev•i•ty

Long•fel•low

long•hair

long•hand

long•horn

long•ing
long•ing•ly

lon•gi•tude

lon•gi•tu•di•nal
lon•gi•tu•di•nal•ly

long•shore•man
pl. long•shore•men

long•time

long•wind•ed
long-wind•ed•ly
long-wind•ed•ness

loo•fah
also luf•fa

look
look-a•like
look-see

look•er

look•ing glass

look•out

loom

loon

loon•y
pl. loon•ies
loon•i•er, loon•i•est
loon•i•ness

loop

loop•hole

loop•y
loop•i•er, loop•i•est

loose
loose-leaf
loose•ly
loose•ness

loos•en
loos•en•er

loot (*money;* see LUTE)
loot•er

lop (*cut*)
lopped, lop•ping
lop•per

lop (*hang limply*)
lopped, lop•ping
lop-eared
lop•py

lope

lop•sid•ed
lop•sid•ed•ly
lop•sid•ed•ness

lo•qua•cious
lo•qua•cious•ly
lo•qua•cious•ness
lo•quac•i•ty

lord

lord•ly
lord•li•er, lord•li•est
lord•li•ness

lord•ship

lore

lor•gnette

lor•i•keet

lo•ris
pl. same

Los An•ge•les
An•ge•le•no
Los An•ge•le•no
Los An•ge•le•an

lose
past and *past part.* lost
los•a•ble
los•er

loss

lost

lot

lo•thar•i•o

lo•tion

lot•ter•y
pl. lot•ter•ies

lot•to

lo•tus
lo•tus-eat•er

loud
loud•ly
loud•ness

loud•mouth
loud-mouthed

loud•speak•er

Lou Gehr•ig's dis•ease

Lou•is

Lou•ise, Lake

Lou•i•si•an•a
Lou•i•si•an•an
Lou•i•si•an•i•an

Lou•is Phi•lippe

Lou•is•ville
Lou•is•vill•ian

lounge
loung•er

Lourdes

Lou•ren•ço Mar•ques

louse
pl. lice *or* lous•es

lous•y
lous•i•er, lous•i•est
lous•i•ly
lous•i•ness

lout
lout•ish

lou•ver
lou•vered

lov•age

love
  lov•a•ble
  love•a•ble
  love•less

love•bird

love•lorn

love•ly
  love•li•er, love•li•est
  pl. love•lies
  love•li•ness

love•mak•ing

lov•er

love•sick
  love•sick•ness

lov•ing
  lov•ing•ly
  lov•ing•ness

low
  low-ball
  low-class
  low-cut
  low-down
  low-grade
  low-key
  low-ly•ing
  low-pitched
  low•ish
  low•ness

low•born

low•brow
  low•browed

Low•ell

low•er
  low•er-class
  low•er•most

low•er•case

low•land
  low•land•er

low•ly
  low•li•er, low•li•est
  low•li•ness

lox

loy•al
  loy•al•ly
  loy•al•ty

loy•al•ist
  loy•al•ism

loz•enge

Lu•an•da

lub•ber
  lub•ber•ly

Lub•bock

Lü•beck

Lu•blin

lu•bri•cant

lu•bri•cate
  lu•bri•ca•tion
  lu•bri•ca•tive
  lu•bri•ca•tor

Lu•bum•ba•shi

lu•cid
  lu•cid•i•ty
  lu•cid•ly
  lu•cid•ness

Lu•ci•fer

luck
  luck•less

luck•i•ly

Luck•now

luck•y
  luck•i•er, luck•i•est
  luck•i•ness

lu•cra•tive
  lu•cra•tive•ly
  lu•cra•tive•ness

lu•cre

Lu•cre•tius

lu•di•crous
  lu•di•crous•ly
  lu•di•crous•ness

luff

luf•fa
  var. of loo•fah

lug
  lugged, lug•ging

Lu•gansk

luge

Lu•ger

lug•gage

lug•ger

lug•sail

lu•gu•bri•ous
  lu•gu•bri•ous•ly
  lu•gu•bri•ous•ness

luke•warm
  luke•warm•ly
  luke•warm•ness

lull

lul•la•by
  pl. lul•la•bies

lu•lu

lum•ba•go

lum•bar

lum•ber (*move slowly*)
  lum•ber•ing

lum•ber (*timber*)
  lum•ber•er
  lum•ber•ing

lum•ber•jack
  also lum•ber•man , *pl.*
  lum•ber•men

lu•mi•nar•y
  pl. lu•mi•nar•ies

lu•mi•nes•cence
  lu•mi•nes•cent

lu•mi•nous
  lu•mi•nos•i•ty
  lu•mi•nous•ly
  lu•min•ous•ness

lum·mox

lump
  lump·y

lu·na·cy
  pl. lu·na·cies

lu·na moth

lu·nar

lu·nate

lu·na·tic

lunch
  lunch·er

lunch·box

lunch·eon

lunch·eon·ette

lung

lunge

lu·pine

lu·pus

lurch

lure
  lur·ing
  lur·ing·ly

lu·rid
  lu·rid·ly
  lu·rid·ness

lurk
  lurk·er

Lu·sa·ka

lus·cious
  lus·cious·ly
  lus·cious·ness

lush (*alcoholic*)

lush (*luxurious*)
  lush·ly
  lush·ness

lust
  lust·ful
  lust·ful·ly
  lust·ful·ness

lus·ter
  lus·ter·less
  lus·trous
  lus·trous·ly
  lus·trous·ness

lust·y
  lust·i·er, lust·i·est
  lust·i·ly
  lust·i·ness

lute (*instrument*; see
  LOOT)

lu·te·ti·um

Lu·ther

Lu·ther·an
  Lu·ther·an·ism

lutz

Lux·em·bourg
  Lux·em·bourg·er
  Lux·em·bourg·i·an

lux·u·ri·ant
  lux·u·ri·ance
  lux·u·ri·ant·ly

lux·u·ri·ate

lux·u·ri·ous
  lux·u·ri·ous·ly
  lux·u·ri·ous·ness

lux·u·ry
  pl. lux·u·ries

Lviv
  also Lvov

Ly·all·pur

ly·ce·um

ly·chee
  var. of li·tchi

Ly·cra

Ly·cur·gus

Lyd·i·a
  Lyd·i·an

lye (*alkaline*; see LIE)

ly·ing

Lyl·y

Lyme dis·ease

lymph
  lym·phoid
  lym·phous

lym·phat·ic

lym·pho·ma
  pl. lym·pho·mas *or* lym·
  pho·ma·ta

lynch
  lynch·er
  lynch·ing

Lynn

lynx (*animal*; see LINKS)

Ly·on

ly·on·naise

Ly·ons
  also Ly·on

lyre (*instrument*; see
  LIAR)

lyre·bird

lyr·ic

lyr·i·cal
  lyr·i·cal·ly

lyr·i·cism

lyr·i·cist

ly·ser·gic ac·id

M

ma'am

Maas·tricht

ma·ca·bre
also ma·ca·ber

mac·ad·am
mac·ad·am·ize

mac·a·da·mi·a

mac·a·ro·ni

mac·a·roon

Mac·Ar·thur

Ma·cau

Ma·cau·lay

ma·caw

Mac·beth

Mac·ca·be·us

Mac·Don·ald

Mace (*trademark*)
mace

mace

Mac·e·do·ni·a
Mac·e·do·ni·an

mac·er·ate
mac·er·a·tion
mac·er·a·tor

Mach
also mach

ma·chet·e

Mach·i·a·vel·li

Mach·i·a·vel·li·an
Mach·i·a·vel·li·an·ism

mach·i·nate
mach·i·na·tion
mach·i·na·tor

ma·chine
ma·chine-read·a·ble

ma·chin·er·y
pl. ma·chin·er·ies

ma·chin·ist

ma·chis·mo

ma·cho

Mac·ken·zie

mack·er·el
pl. same or mack·er·els

mack·i·naw

mack·in·tosh
also mac·in·tosh

Mac·Leish

Mac·mil·lan

Ma·con

mac·ra·mé

mac·ro·bi·ot·ic

mac·ro·cosm
mac·ro·cos·mic
mac·ro·cos·mi·cal·ly

ma·cron

mac·ro·scop·ic
mac·ro·scop·i·cal·ly

mad
mad·der, mad·dest
mad·ness

Mad·a·gas·car
Ma·da·gas·can

mad·am

mad·ame
pl. mes·dames

mad·cap

mad·den
mad·den·ing
mad·den·ing·ly

mad·der

made (*past of make*; see
MAID)

Ma·dei·ra

mad·e·moi·selle
pl. mad·e·moi·selles or
mes·de·moi·selles

mad·house

Mad·i·son

mad·ly

mad·man
pl. mad·men

Ma·don·na

Ma·dras (*city*)

ma·dras (*fabric*)

Ma·drid
Mad·ri·le·ni·an

mad·ri·gal
mad·ri·gal·ist

mad·wom·an
pl. mad·wom·en

mael·strom

maes·tro
pl. maes·tri or maes·tros

Mae·ter·linck

Ma·fi·a
Ma·fi·o·so

mag·a·zine

Mag·de·burg

Ma·gel·lan

ma·gen·ta

mag·got
mag·got·y

ma·gi

mag·ic
mag·i·cal
mag·i·cal·ly

ma·gi·cian

mag·is·te·ri·al
mag·is·te·ri·al·ly

mag·is·trate
mag·is·tra·cy

mag·ma
pl. mag·ma·ta or mag·
mas
mag·mat·ic

Mag·na Car·ta
also Mag·na Char·ta

mag·nan·i·mous
mag·na·nim·i·ty
mag·nan·i·mous·ly

mag·nate (wealthy
person; see MAGNET)

mag·ne·sia
mag·ne·sian

mag·ne·si·um

mag·net (device; see
MAGNATE)

mag·net·ic
mag·net·i·cal·ly

mag·net·ism

mag·net·ize
mag·net·iz·a·ble
mag·net·i·za·tion
mag·net·iz·er

mag·ne·to
pl. mag·ne·tos

mag·nif·i·cent
mag·nif·i·cence
mag·nif·i·cent·ly

mag·ni·fy
mag·ni·fies, mag·ni·
fied
mag·ni·fi·ca·tion
mag·ni·fi·er

mag·ni·tude

mag·no·lia

mag·num
pl. mag·nums

mag·num o·pus

mag·pie

Ma·gritte

ma·gus
pl. ma·gi
(the Ma·gi)

Mag·yar

Ma·hal·la al-Ku·bra

ma·ha·ra·ja
also ma·ha·ra·jah

ma·ha·ra·ni
also ma·ha·ra·nee

ma·ha·ri·shi

ma·hat·ma

Mah·fouz

Ma·hi·can
also Mo·hi·can

mah·jongg
also mah·jong

Mah·ler

ma·hog·a·ny
pl. ma·hog·a·nies

ma·hout

maid (servant; see MADE)

maid·en
maid·en·hood
maid·en·ish
maid·en·like
maid·en·ly

maid·en·hair

maid·en·head

maid·serv·ant

mail (armor; see MALE)
mailed

mail (letters, etc.; see
MALE)

mail·bag

mail·box

Mail·er

mail·man
pl. mail·men

maim

Mai·mon·i·des

main (principal; see
MAINE, MANE)

Maine (U.S. state; see
MAIN, MANE)
Main·er

main·frame

main·land
main·land·er

main·line
main·lin·er

main·ly

main·mast

main·sail

main·spring

main·stay

main·stream

main·tain
main·tain·er
main·tain·a·ble
main·tain·a·bil·i·ty

main·te·nance

Mainz

maî·tre d'hô·tel
pl. maî·tres d'hô·tel
maître d'
pl. maî·tres d'

maize (*corn*; see MAZE)

ma·jes·tic
  ma·jes·ti·cal·ly

maj·es·ty
  pl maj·es·ties

ma·jol·i·ca
  also ma·iol·i·ca

Ma·jor (*proper name*)

ma·jor (*important*)
  ma·jor·ship

ma·jor·do·mo
  pl. ma·jor·do·mos

ma·jor·i·ty
  pl. ma·jor·i·ties

Ma·ju·ro

make
  make-be·lieve
  mak·a·ble
  mak·er

make·shift

make·up

mak·ing

ma·ko
  pl. ma·kos

Ma·la·bo

mal·ad·just·ed
  mal·ad·just·ment

mal·a·droit
  mal·a·droit·ly
  mal·a·droit·ness

mal·a·dy
  pl. mal·a·dies

Má·la·ga

Mal·a·gas·y

ma·laise

Mal·a·mud

mal·a·mute
  also mal·e·mute

Ma·lang

mal·a·prop·ism
  also mal·a·prop

ma·lar·i·a
  ma·lar·i·al
  ma·lar·i·an
  ma·lar·i·ous

ma·lar·key

Ma·la·wi

Ma·lay
  Ma·lay·an

Ma·lay·a

Mal·a·ya·lam

Ma·lay·sia
  Ma·lay·sian

Mal·colm X

mal·con·tent

Mal·dives
  Mal·div·i·an

Ma·le

male (*masculine*; see MAIL)
  male·ness

mal·e·dic·tion
  mal·e·dic·tive
  mal·e·dic·to·ry

mal·e·fac·tor
  mal·e·fac·tion

ma·lev·o·lent
  ma·lev·o·lence
  ma·lev·o·lent·ly

mal·fea·sance
  mal·fea·sant

mal·for·ma·tion
  mal·formed

mal·func·tion

Ma·li
  Ma·li·an

mal·ice

ma·li·cious
  ma·li·cious·ly
  ma·li·cious·ness

ma·lign
  ma·lign·er
  ma·lig·ni·ty
  pl. ma·lig·ni·ties
  ma·lign·ly

ma·lig·nant
  ma·lig·nan·cy
  pl. ma·lig·nan·cies
  ma·lig·nant·ly

ma·lin·ger
  ma·lin·ger·er

Ma·li·now·ski

mall (*shopping center*; see MAUL)

mal·lard
  pl. same *or* mal·lards

Mal·lar·mé

mal·le·a·ble
  mal·le·a·bil·i·ty
  mal·le·a·bly

mal·let

mal·low

Mal·mö

mal·nour·ished
  mal·nour·ish·ment

mal·nu·tri·tion

mal·o·dor·ous

Mal·o·ry

mal·prac·tice

Mal·raux

malt

Mal·ta

Mal·tese
  pl. same

Mal·thus

mal·treat
mal·treat·er
mal·treat·ment

Mal·vi·nas, Is·las

ma·ma

mam·ba

mam·bo
pl. mam·bos

mam·ma
var. of ma·ma

mam·mal
mam·ma·li·an
mam·mal·o·gy

mam·ma·ry

mam·mog·ra·phy

mam·mon
also Mam·mon
mam·mon·ism
mam·mon·ist

mam·moth

man
pl. men
manned, man·ning
man-hour
man-made
man-of-war
man·less

man·a·cle

man·age

man·age·a·ble
man·age·a·bil·i·ty
man·age·a·bly

man·age·ment

man·ag·er
man·a·ge·ri·al
man·a·ge·ri·al·ly
man·ag·er·ship

Ma·na·gua

Ma·na·ma

ma·ña·na

Ma·náos

man·a·tee

Man·ches·ter
Man·cu·ni·an

man·da·la

Man·da·lay

man·da·mus

man·da·rin
man·da·rin·ate

man·date
man·da·tor

man·da·to·ry
man·da·to·ri·ly

Man·de·la

man·di·ble
man·dib·u·lar

man·do·lin
man·do·lin·ist

man·drake

man·drel (shaft; see
MANDRILL)

man·drill (baboon; see
MANDREL)

mane (hair; see MAIN,
MAINE)
maned
mane·less

ma·nège
also ma·nege

Ma·net

ma·neu·ver
ma·neu·ver·a·ble
ma·neu·ver·a·bil·i·ty
ma·neu·ver·er

man·ful
man·ful·ly
man·ful·ness

man·ga·nese

mange

man·ger

man·gle (hack, mutilate)
man·gler

man·gle (machine)

man·go
pl. man·goes or
man·gos

man·grove

man·gy
man·gi·er, man·gi·est
man·gi·ly
man·gi·ness

man·han·dle

Man·hat·tan (place)

man·hat·tan (drink)

man·hole

man·hood

man·hunt

ma·ni·a

ma·ni·ac
ma·ni·a·cal
ma·ni·a·cal·ly

man·ic
man·ic-de·pres·sive
man·i·cal·ly

ma·ni·cot·ti
pl. same

man·i·cure
man·i·cur·ist

man·i·fest (cargo list)

man·i·fest (obvious)
man·i·fes·ta·tion
man·i·fest·ly

man·i·fes·to
pl. man·i·fes·tos or
man·i·fes·toes

man·i·fold

man·i·kin (dwarf; see
MANNEQUIN)
also man·ni·kin

Ma·nil·a
  also Ma·nil·la, ma·nil·a

ma·nip·u·late
  ma·nip·u·la·ble
  ma·nip·u·la·tion
  ma·nip·u·la·tive
  ma·nip·u·la·tor

Man, Isle of
  Manx

Man·i·to·ba

man·kind

man·ly
  man·li·er, man·li·est
  man·li·ness

Mann

man·na

manned

man·ne·quin (*dummy*;
  see MANIKIN)

man·ner (*behavior*; see
  MANOR)
  man·ner·less

man·nered

man·ner·ism
  man·ner·ist
  man·ner·is·tic

man·ner·ly
  man·ner·li·ness

Mann·heim

man·ni·kin
  var. of man·i·kin

man·nish
  man·nish·ly
  man·nish·ness

ma·nom·e·ter
  man·o·met·ric

man·or (*large house*; see
  MANNER)
  ma·no·ri·al

man·pow·er

man·qué

Man Ray

man·sard

manse

man·serv·ant
  pl. men·serv·ants

Mans·field

man·sion

man·slaugh·ter

man·tel (*fireplace area*;
  see MANTLE)

man·tel·piece

man·til·la

man·tis
  pl. same *or* man·tis·es

man·tis·sa

man·tle (*cloak*; see
  MANTEL)

man·tra

man·u·al
  man·u·al·ly

man·u·fac·ture
  man·u·fac·tur·er

man·u·mit
  man·u·mit·ted, man·
  u·mit·ting
  man·u·mis·sion

ma·nure

man·u·script

Manx

man·y
  more; most

Mao·ism
  Mao·ist

Mao·ri
  pl. same *or* Mao·ris

Mao Ze·dong
  also Mao Tse-tung

map
  mapped, map·ping
  map·less
  map·per

ma·ple

Ma·pu·to

mar
  marred, mar·ring

mar·a·bou
  also mar·a·bout

ma·ra·ca

Mar·a·cai·bo

Ma·ra·cay

mar·a·schi·no
  pl. mar·a·schi·nos

Ma·rat

Ma·ra·thi
  also Mah·rat·ti

mar·a·thon
  mar·a·thon·er

ma·raud
  ma·raud·er

mar·ble
  mar·bly

March (*month*)

march (*walk*)
  march·er

Mar·ci·a·no

Mar·co·ni

Mar·co Po·lo

Mar·cos

Mar·cus Au·re·li·us

Mar·cu·se

Mar·di Gras

ma·re (*area on moon*)
  pl. ma·ri·a *or* ma·res

mare (*female horse, etc.*)

mar·ga·rine

mar·ga·ri·ta

mar·gin
 mar·gin·al
 mar·gin·al·ly

mar·gi·na·li·a

mar·gin·al·ize
 mar·gin·al·i·za·tion

Mar·gre·the II

ma·ri·a·chi

Mar·i·an·a Trench

Ma·rie An·toi·nette

Ma·rie de Mé·di·cis

mar·i·gold

ma·ri·jua·na
 also ma·ri·hua·na

ma·rim·ba

ma·ri·na

mar·i·nade

ma·ri·na·ra

mar·i·nate
 mar·i·na·tion

ma·rine

mar·i·ner

mar·i·on·ette

mar·i·tal
 mar·i·tal·ly

mar·i·time

Mar·i·time Prov·in·ces

Ma·ri·u·pol

mar·jo·ram

mark

Mark An·to·ny

mark·down

marked
 mark·ed·ly
 mark·ed·ness

mark·er

mar·ket
 mar·ket·a·bil·i·ty
 mar·ket·a·ble
 mar·ket·er

mar·ket·ing

mar·ket·place

Mark·ham

mark·ing

marks·man
 pl. marks·men; *fem.*
 marks·wom·an, *pl.*
 marks·wom·en
 marks·man·ship

mark·up

Marl·bor·ough

mar·lin

Mar·lowe

mar·ma·lade

Mar·ma·ra, Sea of

mar·mo·set

mar·mot

ma·roon

Mar·quand

marque

mar·quee (*sign; see*
 MARQUIS)

mar·quess

mar·que·try
 also mar·que·te·rie

Mar·quette

Már·quez

mar·quis (*nobleman; see*
 MARQUEE)

mar·quise

Mar·ra·kesh

mar·riage
 mar·riage·a·bil·i·ty
 mar·riage·a·ble

mar·ried

mar·row

mar·ry (*wed; see* MARY,
 MERRY)
 mar·ries, mar·ried

Mars

Mar·seilles

marsh
 marsh·y
 marsh·i·er, marsh·i·est
 marsh·i·ness

mar·shal (*officer; see*
 MARTIAL)
 mar·shal·er

Mar·shall

marsh·mal·low

mar·su·pi·al

mart

Mar·tel

mar·ten (*animal; see*
 MARTIN)

Mar·tha's Vine·yard

Mar·tial (*proper name*)

mar·tial (*warlike; see*
 MARSHAL)
 mar·tial·ly

Mar·tian

mar·tin (*bird; see*
 MARTEN)

mar·ti·net

mar·ti·ni

Mar·ti·nique

mar·tyr
mar·tyr·dom

mar·vel
mar·vel·er

mar·vel·ous
mar·vel·ous·ly

Marx

Marx·ism
Marx·ist

Mar·y (*proper name;* see MARRY, MERRY)

Mar·y·land
Mar·y·land·er

mar·zi·pan

Ma·sa·ryk

mas·car·a

mas·cot

mas·cu·line
mas·cu·line·ly
mas·cu·lin·i·ty

Mase·field

ma·ser

Ma·se·ru

mash
mash·er

Mash·an·tuck·et

mask (*cover;* see MASQUE)
mask·er

mas·och·ism
mas·och·ist
mas·och·is·tic
mas·och·is·ti·cal·ly

ma·son
also Ma·son

Ma·son-Dix·on line

Ma·son·ic

ma·son·ry
also Ma·son·ry)

masque (*entertainment;* see MASK)
mas·quer

mas·quer·ade
mas·quer·ad·er

mass (*lot, quantity, people*)
mass-mar·ket
mass-pro·duce
mass·less

mass (*religious service*)
also Mass

Mas·sa·chu·set (*Native American tribe*)
also Mas·sa·chu·sett

Mas·sa·chu·setts (*state*)

mas·sa·cre

mas·sage
mas·sag·er

mas·seur
fem. mas·seuse

mas·sive
mas·sive·ly
mas·sive·ness

mast (*nuts*)

mast (*pole for sails*)
mast·ed

mas·tec·to·my
pl. mas·tec·to·mies

mas·ter
mas·ter·dom
mas·ter·hood
mas·ter·less

mas·ter·ful
mas·ter·ful·ly
mas·ter·ful·ness

mas·ter·ly
mas·ter·li·ness

mas·ter·mind

mas·ter·piece

Mas·ters

mas·ter·stroke

mas·ter·work

mas·ter·y

mast·head

mas·ti·cate
mas·ti·ca·tion
mas·ti·ca·tor

mas·tiff

mas·to·don

mas·toid

mas·tur·bate
mas·tur·ba·tion
mas·tur·ba·tor

mat
mat·ted, mat·ting

mat·a·dor

Mat·a·mo·ros

match (*contest*)
match·a·ble

match (*flammable stick*)

match·box

match·less
match·less·ly

match·mak·er
match·mak·ing

match·stick

mate
mate·less

ma·te·ri·al
ma·te·ri·al·i·ty

ma·te·ri·al·ism
ma·te·ri·al·ist
ma·te·ri·al·is·tic
ma·te·ri·al·is·ti·cal·ly

ma·te·ri·al·ize
ma·te·ri·al·i·za·tion

ma·te·ri·al·ly

ma·té·ri·el
also ma·te·ri·el

ma•ter•nal
  ma•ter•nal•ism
  ma•ter•nal•is•tic
  ma•ter•nal•ly

ma•ter•ni•ty

math

math•e•mat•i•cal
  math•e•mat•i•cal•ly

math•e•mat•ics
  math•e•ma•ti•cian

mat•i•née
  also mat•i•nee

mat•ins

Ma•tisse

ma•tri•arch
  ma•tri•ar•chal
  ma•tri•ar•chy

ma•tri•ces

mat•ri•cide
  mat•ri•cid•al

ma•tric•u•late
  ma•tric•u•la•tion

mat•ri•mo•ny
  pl. mat•ri•mo•nies
  mat•ri•mo•ni•al
  mat•ri•mo•ni•al•ly

ma•trix
  pl. ma•tri•ces *or* ma•
  trix•es

ma•tron
  ma•tron•ly

matte
  also matt, mat

mat•ter

Mat•ter•horn

mat•ter-of-fact
  mat•ter-of-fact•ly
  mat•ter-of-fact•ness

mat•ting

mat•tock

mat•tress

ma•ture
  ma•tur•er, ma•tur•est
  ma•ture•ly
  ma•ture•ness
  ma•tu•ri•ty

mat•zo
  also mat•zoh; *pl.* mat•
  zos *or* mat•zohs *or*
  mat•zoth

maud•lin

Maugham

Mau•i

maul (*beat*; see MALL)
  maul•er

Mau•na Lo•a

maun•der

Mau•pas•sant

Mau•riac

Mau•ri•ta•ni•a

Mau•ri•tius

mau•so•le•um
  pl. mau•so•le•ums *or*
  mau•so•le•a

mauve
  mauv•ish

mav•er•ick

maw

mawk•ish
  mawk•ish•ly
  mawk•ish•ness

max•i
  pl. max•is

max•il•la
  pl. max•il•lae *or*
  max•il•las
  max•il•lar•y

max•im

Max•i•mil•ian

max•i•mize
  max•i•mi•za•tion
  max•i•miz•er

max•i•mum
  pl. max•i•ma *or*
  max•i•mums
  max•i•mal
  max•i•mal•ly

May (*month*)

may (*verb*)

Ma•ya
  pl. same *or* Ma•yas
  Ma•yan

Ma•ya•güez

may•be

May•day

may•flow•er

may•fly
  pl. may•flies

may•hem

may•on•naise

may•or
  may•or•al

may•or•al•ty
  pl. may•or•al•ties

may•pole

Maz•a•rin

Ma•za•tlán

maze (*puzzle*; see MAIZE)
  ma•zy
  ma•zi•er, ma•zi•est

ma•zur•ka

Mba•bane

Mboy•a

Mc•Al•len

Mc•Car•thy

Mc•Cart•ney

Mc•Clel•lan

Mc·Cor·mick

Mc·Kin·ley

Mc·Lu·han

Mead (*proper name*)

mead (*beverage*)

mead·ow
  mead·ow·y

mea·ger
  mea·ger·ly
  mea·ger·ness

meal

meal·y
  meal·i·er, meal·i·est
  meal·i·ness

mean (*average*; see MIEN)

mean (*cruel*; see MIEN)
  mean·ly
  mean·ness

mean (*intend*; see MIEN)
  past and *past part.*
  meant

me·an·der
  me·an·drous

mean·ie
  also mean·y
  pl. mean·ies

mean·ing
  mean·ing·ly

mean·ing·ful
  mean·ing·ful·ly
  mean·ing·ful·ness

mean·ing·less
  mean·ing·less·ly
  mean·ing·less·ness

means

meant

mean·time

mean·while

mean·y
  var. of mean·ie

mea·sles

mea·sly
  mea·sli·er, mea·sli·est

meas·ure
  meas·ur·a·ble
  meas·ur·a·bly
  meas·ure·less

meas·ured
  meas·ured·ly

meas·ure·ment

meat (*flesh*; see MEET, METE)
  meat·i·ness
  meat·less
  meat·y
  meat·i·er, meat·i·est

Mec·ca

me·chan·ic

me·chan·i·cal
  me·chan·i·cal·ly

me·chan·ics

mech·an·ism

mech·a·nize
  mech·a·ni·za·tion
  mech·a·niz·er

med·al (*award*; see MEDDLE, METAL, METTLE)
  med·aled
  me·dal·lic

med·al·ist

me·dal·lion

Me·dan

med·dle (*interfere*; see MEDAL, METAL, METTLE)
  med·dler

med·dle·some
  med·dle·some·ly
  med·dle·some·ness

Me·del·lín

me·di·a

me·di·al
  me·di·al·ly

me·di·an
  me·di·an·ly

me·di·ate
  me·di·a·tion
  me·di·a·tor
  me·di·a·to·ry

med·ic

Med·i·caid

med·i·cal
  med·i·cal·ly

Med·i·care

med·i·cate
  med·i·ca·tion
  med·i·ca·tive

Med·i·ci

me·dic·i·nal
  me·dic·i·nal·ly

med·i·cine

me·di·e·val
  also me·di·ae·val
  me·di·e·val·ism
  me·di·e·val·ist
  me·di·e·val·ly

Me·di·na

me·di·o·cre
  me·di·oc·ri·ty

med·i·tate
  med·i·ta·tion
  med·i·ta·tor

med·i·ta·tive
  med·i·ta·tive·ly
  med·i·ta·tive·ness

Med·i·ter·ra·ne·an

me•di•um
  pl. me•di•a or
    me•di•ums
  me•di•um•is•tic
  me•di•um•ship

med•ley
  pl. med•leys

me•dul•la
  me•dul•la ob•long•a•ta

meek
  meek•ly
  meek•ness

meer•schaum

meet (encounter; see
  MEAT, METE)
  past and past part. met
  meet•er

meet•ing

meg•a•bucks

meg•a•byte

meg•a•hertz

meg•a•lith
  meg•a•lith•ic

meg•a•lo•ma•ni•a
  meg•a•lo•ma•ni•ac
  meg•a•lo•ma•ni•a•cal

meg•a•lop•o•lis
  meg•a•lo•pol•i•tan

meg•a•phone

meg•a•ton

meg•a•watt

Mei•ji Ten•no

mei•o•sis
  mei•ot•ic
  mei•ot•i•cal•ly

Me•ir

meit•ne•ri•um

Mek•nès

Me•kong

mel•a•mine

mel•an•cho•li•a

mel•an•chol•y
  pl. mel•an•chol•ies
  mel•an•chol•ic

Mel•a•ne•sia

Mel•a•ne•sian

mé•lange

mel•a•nin

mel•a•no•ma

Mel•ba

Mel•bourne

meld

me•lee
  also mê•lée

mel•lif•lu•ous
  mel•lif•lu•ence
  mel•lif•lu•ent
  mel•lif•lu•ous•ly
  mel•lif•lu•ous•ness

Mel•lon

mel•low
  mel•low•ly
  mel•low•ness

me•lod•ic
  me•lod•i•cal•ly

me•lo•di•ous
  me•lo•di•ous•ly
  me•lo•di•ous•ness

mel•o•dra•ma
  mel•o•dra•mat•ic
  mel•o•dra•mat•i•cal•
    ly
  mel•o•dram•a•tist
  mel•o•dram•a•tize

mel•o•dy
  pl. mel•o•dies

mel•on

melt
  melt•a•ble
  melt•er
  melt•ing•ly

melt•down

Mel•ville

mem•ber
  mem•bered
  mem•ber•less

mem•ber•ship

mem•brane
  mem•bra•nous

me•men•to
  pl. me•men•tos or
    me•men•toes

me•men•to mo•ri
  pl. same

mem•o
  pl. mem•os

mem•oir
  mem•oir•ist

mem•o•ra•bil•i•a

mem•o•ra•ble
  mem•o•ra•bil•i•ty
  mem•o•ra•bly

mem•o•ran•dum
  pl. mem•o•ran•da or
    mem•o•ran•dums

me•mo•ri•al

mem•o•rize
  mem•o•ri•za•tion
  mem•o•riz•er

mem•o•ry
  pl. mem•o•ries

Mem•phis

men

men•ace
  men•ac•er
  men•ac•ing
  men•ac•ing•ly

mé•nage

me•nag•er•ie

Me•nan•der

men•ar•che

Men·ci·us

Menck·en

mend
  mend·a·ble
  mend·er

men·da·cious
  men·da·cious·ly
  men·da·cious·ness
  men·dac·i·ty
  pl. men·dac·i·ties

Men·del

men·de·le·vi·um

Men·del·ism
  Men·de·li·an

Men·dels·sohn

men·di·cant
  men·di·can·cy
  men·dic·i·ty

Me·nes

men·folk

Meng-tzu
  also Meng·zi

me·ni·al
  me·ni·al·ly

men·in·gi·tis
  men·in·git·ic

me·ninx
  pl. me·nin·ges
  me·nin·ge·al

me·nis·cus
  pl. me·nis·ci *or*
  me·nis·cus·es
  me·nis·coid

men·o·pause
  men·o·pau·sal

me·nor·ah

Me·not·ti

men·ses

men·stru·al

men·stru·ate
  men·stru·a·tion

men·su·ra·tion

mens·wear

men·tal
  men·tal·ly

men·tal·i·ty
  pl. men·tal·i·ties

men·thol
  men·tho·lat·ed

men·tion
  men·tion·a·ble

men·tor

men·u

Men·u·hin

me·ow

mer·can·tile

Mer·ca·tor

mer·ce·nar·y
  pl. mer·ce·nar·ies

mer·cer·ize
  mer·cer·i·za·tion

mer·chan·dise
  mer·chan·dis·a·ble
  mer·chan·dis·er

mer·chant

mer·chant·man
  pl. mer·chant·men

mer·ci·ful
  mer·ci·ful·ly
  mer·ci·ful·ness

mer·ci·less
  mer·ci·less·ly
  mer·ci·less·ness

mer·cu·ri·al
  mer·cu·ri·al·ism
  mer·cu·ri·al·i·ty
  mer·cu·ri·al·ly

mer·cu·ry
  mer·cu·ric
  mer·cu·rous

mer·cy
  pl. mer·cies

mere
  mer·est
  mere·ly

Mer·e·dith

mer·e·tri·cious
  mer·e·tri·cious·ly
  mer·e·tri·cious·ness

mer·gan·ser

merge

merg·er

Mé·ri·da

me·rid·i·an

me·ringue

me·ri·no
  pl. me·ri·nos

mer·it

mer·i·toc·ra·cy
  pl. mer·i·toc·ra·cies

mer·i·to·ri·ous
  mer·i·to·ri·ous·ly
  mer·i·to·ri·ous·ness

mer·maid

mer·ri·ment

mer·ry (*happy*; see
  MARRY, MARY)
  mer·ri·er, mer·ri·est
  mer·ri·ly
  mer·ri·ness

mer·ry-go-round

mer·ry·mak·ing
  mer·ry·mak·er

Mer·sin

me·sa

mes·cal

mes·ca·line
  also mes·ca·lin

mes·dames
  sing. mad·ame

mes·de·moi·selles
  sing. mad·e·moi·selle

mesh

Me·shed

mes·mer·ize
  mes·mer·ic
  mes·mer·ism
  mes·mer·ist
  mes·mer·i·za·tion
  mes·mer·iz·er
  mes·mer·iz·ing·ly

mes·o·morph
  mes·o·mor·phic

me·son
  mes·ic
  me·son·ic

Mes·o·po·ta·mi·a

mes·o·sphere

Mes·o·zo·ic

mes·quite

mess

mes·sage

mes·sen·ger

Mes·si·ah
  Mes·si·ah·ship
  Mes·si·an·ic
  Mes·si·a·nism

mes·sieurs
  sing. mon·sieur

Mes·si·na

mess·y
  mess·i·er, mess·i·est
  mess·i·ly
  mess·i·ness

met

me·tab·o·lism
  met·a·bol·ic
  met·a·bol·i·cal·ly

me·tab·o·lize
  me·tab·o·liz·a·ble

met·a·car·pus
  pl. met·a·car·pi
  met·a·car·pal

Met·air·ie

met·al (*iron, etc.*; see
  MEDAL, MEDDLE,
  METTLE)

met·a·lan·guage

me·tal·lic
  me·tal·li·cal·ly

met·al·lur·gy
  met·al·lur·gic
  met·al·lur·gi·cal
  met·al·lur·gi·cal·ly
  met·al·lur·gist

met·a·mor·phic
  met·a·mor·phism

met·a·mor·phose

met·a·mor·pho·sis
  pl. met·a·mor·pho·ses

met·a·phor
  met·a·phor·ic
  met·a·phor·i·cal
  met·a·phor·i·cal·ly

met·a·phys·i·cal
  met·a·phys·i·cal·ly

met·a·phys·ics
  met·a·phy·si·cian

me·tas·ta·sis
  pl. me·tas·ta·ses
  me·tas·ta·size
  met·a·stat·ic

met·a·tar·sus
  pl. met·a·tar·si
  met·a·tar·sal

me·tath·e·sis
  pl. me·tath·e·ses
  met·a·thet·ic
  met·a·thet·i·cal

mete (*distribute*; see
  MEAT, MEET)

me·te·or

me·te·or·ic
  me·te·or·i·cal·ly

me·te·or·ite
  me·te·or·it·ic

me·te·or·oid

me·te·or·ol·o·gy
  me·te·or·o·log·i·cal
  me·te·or·o·log·i·cal·ly
  me·te·or·ol·o·gist

me·ter
  me·ter·age

meth·a·done
  also meth·a·don

meth·ane

meth·a·nol

me·thinks
  past me·thought

meth·od

me·thod·i·cal
  also me·thod·ic
  me·thod·i·cal·ly

Meth·od·ist
  Meth·od·ism
  Meth·od·is·tic

meth·od·ol·o·gy
  pl. meth·od·ol·o·gies
  meth·od·o·log·i·cal
  meth·od·o·log·i·cal·ly
  meth·od·ol·o·gist

meth·yl
  me·thyl·ic

me·tic·u·lous
  me·tic·u·lous·ly
  me·tic·u·lous·ness

mé·tier
  also me·tier

me·ton·y·my
  met·o·nym·ic
  met·o·nym·i·cal

met·ric

met·ri·cal
  met·ri·cal·ly

met·ro
  pl. met·ros

met·ro·nome
  met·ro·nom·ic

me·trop·o·lis
  met·ro·pol·i·tan

Met·ter·nich

met·tle (*courage*; see
  MEDAL, MEDDLE,
  METAL)
  met·tled
  met·tle·some

Metz

mew

mewl

mews (*street*; see MUSE)

Mex·i·cal·i

Mex·i·co
  Mex·i·can

me·zu·zah
  also me·zu·za; *pl.* me·
  zu·zas; *also* me·zu·
  zot *or* me·zu·zoth

mez·za·nine

mez·zo

mez·zo-so·pran·o

Mi·am·i

mi·as·ma
  pl. mi·as·mas *or* mi·
  as·ma·ta

mi·ca
  mi·ca·ceous

mice

Mi·chael

Mich·ael·mas

Mi·chel·an·ge·lo

Miche·ner

Mich·i·gan
  Mich·i·gan·der
  Mich·i·gan·ite

Mi·cho·a·cán

Mick·ey Finn

mi·crobe
  mi·cro·bi·al
  mi·cro·bic

mi·cro·bi·ol·o·gy
  mi·cro·bi·o·log·i·cal
  mi·cro·bi·o·log·i·cal·ly
  mi·cro·bi·ol·o·gist

mi·cro·brew·er·y

mi·cro·chip

mi·cro·com·put·er

mi·cro·cosm
  mi·cro·cos·mic
  mi·cro·cos·mi·cal·ly

mi·cro·dot

mi·cro·ec·o·nom·ics

mi·cro·e·lec·tron·ics

mi·cro·fiche
  pl. same *or* mi·cro·
  fich·es

mi·cro·film

mi·cro·light

mi·crom·e·ter
  mi·crom·e·try

mi·cron

Mi·cro·ne·sia
  Mi·cro·ne·sian

mi·cro·or·gan·ism

mi·cro·phone
  mi·cro·phon·ic

mi·cro·proc·es·sor

mi·cro·scope

mi·cro·scop·ic
  mi·cro·scop·i·cal
  mi·cro·scop·i·cal·ly

mi·cros·co·py
  mi·cros·co·pist

mi·cro·sec·ond

mi·cro·sur·ger·y
  mi·cro·sur·gi·cal

mi·cro·wave

Mi·das

mid·day

mid·dle
  mid·dle-aged
  mid·dle-class
  mid·dle-of-the-road

mid·dle·brow

mid·dle·man
  pl. mid·dle·men

mid·dle·weight

mid·dling
  mid·dling·ly

midge

midg·et

Mid·land (*city*)

mid·land (*interior*)
  mid·land·er

mid·night

mid·riff

mid·ship·man
  pl. mid·ship·men

mid·ships

midst

mid·sum·mer

mid·way

Mid·west

mid·wife
  pl. mid·wives
  mid·wife·ry

mid·win·ter

mien (*bearing*; see MEAN)

Mies van der Rohe

miff

might (*power*; see MITE)

might·y
might·i·er, might·
i·est
might·i·ly
might·i·ness

mi·graine

mi·grant

mi·grate
mi·gra·tion
mi·gra·tion·al
mi·gra·tor
mi·gra·to·ry

mi·ka·do
pl. mi·ka·dos

mike

mil (*measure*; see MILL)

mi·la·dy
pl. mi·la·dies

Mi·lan
Mil·an·ese

milch

mild
mild·ish
mild·ly
mild·ness

mil·dew
mil·dew·y

mile

mile·age

mile·post

mil·er

mile·stone

mi·lieu
pl. mi·lieus *or* mi·lieux

mil·i·tant
mil·i·tan·cy
mil·i·tant·ly

mil·i·ta·rism
mil·i·ta·rist
mil·i·ta·ris·tic
mil·i·ta·ris·ti·cal·ly

mil·i·ta·rize
mil·i·ta·ri·za·tion

mil·i·tar·y
mil·i·tar·i·ly
mil·i·tar·i·ness

mil·i·tate

mi·li·tia
mi·li·tia·man
pl. mi·li·tia·men

milk
milk·er

milk·maid

milk·man
pl. milk·men

milk·sop

milk·y
milk·i·er, milk·i·est
milk·i·ness

Mill (*proper name*; see MIL)

mill (*grind*; see MIL)
mill·a·ble
mill·er

Mil·lay

mil·len·ni·um
pl. mil·len·ni·a *or*
mil·len·ni·ums
mil·len·ni·al
mil·len·ni·al·ist

Mil·ler

Mil·let (*proper name*)

mil·let (*grass*)

mil·li·gram

mil·li·li·ter

mil·li·me·ter

mil·li·ner
mil·li·ner·y

mil·lion
mil·lion·fold
mil·lionth

mil·lion·aire
fem. mil·lion·air·ess

mil·li·pede
also mil·le·pede

mil·li·sec·ond

mill·race

mill·stone

mill·wright

Milne

mi·lord

milt

Mil·ton

Mil·wau·kee

mime
mim·er

mim·e·o·graph

mi·met·ic
mi·met·i·cal·ly

mim·ic
mim·icked, mim·
ick·ing
mim·ick·er
mim·ic·ry

mi·mo·sa

min·a·ret
min·a·ret·ed

min·a·to·ry

mince
minc·er
minc·ing·ly

mince·meat

mind
mind-bog·gling
mind-read

mind·ed

mind·ful
  mind·ful·ly
  mind·ful·ness

mind·less
  mind·less·ly
  mind·less·ness

mind·set

mine (*belonging to the speaker*)

mine (*excavation*)
  min·ing

mine·field

min·er (*one who mines; see* MINOR)

min·er·al

min·er·al·o·gy
  min·er·al·og·i·cal
  min·er·al·o·gist

min·e·stro·ne

mine·sweep·er

min·gle
  min·gler

min·i
  pl. min·is

min·i·a·ture
  min·i·a·tur·ist

min·i·a·tur·ize
  min·i·a·tur·i·za·tion

min·i·bike

min·i·cam

min·i·com·put·er

min·i·ma

min·i·mal
  min·i·mal·ism
  min·i·mal·ist
  min·i·mal·ly

min·i·mize
  min·i·mi·za·tion
  min·i·miz·er

min·i·mum
  pl. min·i·ma

min·ion

min·i·ser·ies

min·i·skirt

min·is·ter
  min·is·te·ri·al
  min·is·te·ri·al·ly

min·is·tra·tion
  min·is·trant

min·is·try
  pl. min·is·tries

min·i·van

mink

Min·ne·ap·o·lis

Min·ne·so·ta
  Min·ne·so·tan

min·now

Mi·no·an

mi·nor (*lesser; see* MINER)

mi·nor·i·ty
  pl. mi·nor·i·ties

min·ox·i·dil

Minsk

min·strel

mint (*flavor*)
  mint·y
  mint·i·er, mint·i·est

mint (*place money is coined*)
  mint·age

min·u·et

Min·u·it

mi·nus

mi·nus·cule
  mi·nus·cu·lar

mi·nute (*tiny part*)
  mi·nut·est
  mi·nute·ly

min·ute (*sixty seconds*)

min·ute·man
  pl. min·ute·men

mi·nu·ti·a
  pl. mi·nu·ti·ae

minx

mir·a·cle

mi·rac·u·lous
  mi·rac·u·lous·ly
  mi·rac·u·lous·ness

mi·rage

mire

Mi·ró

mir·ror

mirth
  mirth·ful
  mirth·ful·ly
  mirth·ful·ness
  mirth·less
  mirth·less·ly
  mirth·less·ness

mis·ad·ven·ture

mis·a·lign
  mis·a·lign·ment

mis·an·thrope
  also mis·an·thro·pist
  mis·an·throp·ic
  mis·an·throp·i·cal
  mis·an·throp·i·cal·ly
  mis·an·thro·py

mis·ap·ply
  mis·ap·plies, mis·ap·plied
  mis·ap·pli·ca·tion

mis·ap·pre·hend
  mis·ap·pre·hen·sion
  mis·ap·pre·hen·sive

mis·ap·pro·pri·ate
  mis·ap·pro·pri·a·tion

mis·be·got·ten

mis·be·have
  mis·be·hav·ior

mis·car·riage

mis·car·ry
  mis·car·ries, mis·
  car·ried

mis·cast
  past and *past part.*
  mis·cast

mis·ceg·e·na·tion

mis·cel·la·ne·ous
  mis·cel·la·ne·ous·ly

mis·cel·la·ny
  pl. mis·cel·la·nies

mis·chance

mis·chief

mis·chie·vous
  mis·chie·vous·ly
  mis·chie·vous·ness

mis·ci·ble
  mis·ci·bil·i·ty

mis·con·ceive
  mis·con·ceiv·er
  mis·con·cep·tion

mis·con·duct

mis·con·strue
  mis·con·struc·tion

mis·count

mis·cre·ant

mis·deal
  past and *past part.* mis·
  dealt

mis·deed

mis·de·mean·or

mis·di·rect
  mis·di·rec·tion

mis·do·ing

mi·ser
  mi·ser·li·ness
  mi·ser·ly

mis·er·a·ble
  mis·er·a·ble·ness
  mis·er·a·bly

mis·er·y
  pl. mis·er·ies

mis·fire

mis·fit

mis·for·tune

mis·giv·ing

mis·gov·ern
  mis·gov·ern·ment

mis·guide
  mis·guid·ance
  mis·guid·ed·ly
  mis·guid·ed·ness

mis·han·dle

mis·hap

mis·hear
  past and *past part.*
  mis·heard

mish·mash

mis·in·form
  mis·in·for·ma·tion

mis·in·ter·pret
  mis·in·ter·pre·ta·tion
  mis·in·ter·pret·er

mis·judge
  mis·judg·ment

mis·lay
  past and *past part.*
  mis·laid

mis·lead
  past and *past part.*
  mis·led
  mis·lead·er

mis·lead·ing
  mis·lead·ing·ly

mis·man·age
  mis·man·age·ment

mis·match

mis·no·mer

mi·sog·y·ny
  mi·sog·y·nist
  mi·sog·y·nous

mis·place
  mis·place·ment

mis·print

mis·pri·sion

mis·pro·nounce
  mis·pro·nun·ci·a·tion

mis·quote
  mis·quo·ta·tion

mis·read
  past and *past part.*
  mis·read

mis·rep·re·sent
  mis·rep·re·sen·ta·tion
  mis·rep·re·sen·ta·tive

mis·rule

miss (*fail to hit*)
  miss·a·ble

miss (*girl*)

mis·sal (*book*; see
  MISSILE)

mis·shap·en
  mis·shap·en·ly
  mis·shap·en·ness

mis·sile (*weapon*; see
  MISSAL)
  mis·sile·ry

miss·ing

mis·sion

mis·sion·ar·y
  pl. mis·sion·ar·ies

mis·sis
  var. of mis·sus

Mis·sis·sau·ga

Mis·sis·sip·pi

mis·sive

Mis·sour·i
  Mis·sour·i·an

mis·spell
  past and *past part.* mis·
  spelled *or* mis·spelt

mis·spend
  past and *past part.* mis·
  spent

mis·state
  mis·state·ment

mis·step

mis·sus
  also mis·sis

mist
  mist·like

mis·take
  past mis·took; *past part.*
  mis·tak·en
  mis·tak·a·ble
  mis·tak·a·bly

mis·tak·en
  mis·tak·en·ly

mis·ter

mis·time

mis·tle·toe

mis·took

mis·treat
  mis·treat·ment

mis·tress

mis·tri·al

mis·trust

mis·trust·ful
  mis·trust·ful·ly
  mis·trust·ful·ness

mist·y
  mist·i·er, mist·i·est
  mist·i·ly
  mist·i·ness

mis·un·der·stand
  past and *past part.* mis·
  un·der·stood

mis·un·der·stand·ing

mis·use
  mis·us·er

Mitch·ell

mite (*small thing*; see
  MIGHT)
  mit·y

mi·ter
  mi·tered

Mit·ford

Mith·ri·da·tes

mit·i·gate
  mit·i·ga·ble
  mit·i·ga·tion
  mit·i·ga·tor
  mit·i·ga·to·ry

mi·to·sis
  mi·tot·ic

mi·tral

mitt

mit·ten
  mit·tened

Mit·ter·rand

mix
  mix-up
  mix·a·ble

mixed
  mixed-up

mix·er

mix·ture

miz·zen·mast

mne·mon·ic
  mne·mon·i·cal·ly

moan (*sound*; see *mown*
  [MOW])
  moan·er
  moan·ing·ly

moat (*ditch*; see MOTE)

mob
  mobbed, mob·bing
  mob·ber

Mo·bile (*city*)

mo·bile (*movable*)
  mo·bil·i·ty

mo·bi·lize
  mo·bi·liz·a·ble
  mo·bi·li·za·tion
  mo·bi·liz·er

mob·ster

Mo·bu·tu Se·se Se·ko

moc·ca·sin

mo·cha

mock
  mock-up
  mock·a·ble
  mock·er
  mock·ing·ly

mock·er·y
  pl. mock·er·ies

mock·ing·bird

mod

mod·al
  mod·al·ly

mode (*fashion*; see *mowed*
  [MOW])

mod·el
  mod·el·er

mo·dem

Mo·de·na

mod·er·ate
  mod·er·ate·ly
  mod·er·ate·ness
  mod·er·a·tion

mod·er·a·tor

mod·ern
  mo·der·ni·ty
  mod·ern·ly
  mod·ern·ness

mod•ern•ism
  mod•ern•ist
  mod•ern•is•tic
  mod•ern•is•ti•cal•ly

mod•ern•ize
  mod•ern•i•za•tion
  mod•ern•iz•er

mod•est
  mod•est•ly
  mod•es•ty

Mo•des•to

mod•i•cum

mod•i•fi•er

mod•i•fy
  mod•i•fies, mod•i•fied
  mod•i•fi•a•ble
  mod•i•fi•ca•tion

Mo•di•glia•ni

mod•ish
  mod•ish•ly
  mod•ish•ness

mod•u•late
  mod•u•la•tion
  mod•u•la•tor

mod•ule
  mod•u•lar
  mod•u•lar•i•ty

mo•dus op•e•ran•di
  pl. mo•di op•e•ran•di

mo•dus vi•ven•di
  pl. mo•di vi•ven•di

Mo•ga•di•shu

mo•gul

mo•hair

Mo•ha•ve

Mo•hawk

Mo•he•gan

Mo•hi•can
  var. of Ma•hi•can

moi•e•ty
  pl. moi•e•ties

moire

moiré

moist
  moist•ly
  moist•ness

moist•en

mois•ture
  mois•ture•less

mois•tur•ize
  mois•tur•iz•er

Mo•ja•ve
  var. of Mo•ha•ve

mo•lar

mo•las•ses

mold
  mold•a•ble
  mold•er

mold•er

mold•ing

Mol•do•va

mold•y
  mold•i•er, mold•i•est
  mold•i•ness

mole
  mo•lar
  mo•lar•i•ty

mol•e•cule
  mo•lec•u•lar

mole•hill

mole•skin

mo•lest
  mo•les•ta•tion
  mo•lest•er

Mo•lière

mol•li•fy
  mol•li•fies, mol•li•fied
  mol•li•fi•ca•tion
  mol•li•fi•er

mol•lusk
  mol•lus•kan *or* mol•
  lus•can
  mol•lusk•like

mol•ly•cod•dle

Mol•nár

Mo•lo•ka•i

molt
  molt•er

mol•ten

Mo•luc•cas

mo•lyb•de•num

mom

Mom•ba•sa

mo•ment

mo•men•tar•y
  mo•men•tar•i•ly
  mo•men•tar•i•ness

mo•men•tous
  mo•men•tous•ly
  mo•men•tous•ness

mo•men•tum
  pl. mo•men•ta

mom•ma
  var. of ma•ma

Momm•sen

mom•my
  pl. mom•mies

Mon•a•co
  Mon•a•can
  Mon•e•gasque

mon•arch
  mo•nar•chic
  mo•nar•chi•cal

mon•ar•chism
  mon•ar•chist

mon•ar•chy
  pl. mon•ar•chies
  mo•nar•chi•al

mon·as·ter·y
  pl. mon·as·ter·ies

mo·nas·tic
  mo·nas·ti·cal·ly
  mo·nas·ti·cism

Mön·chen·glad·bach

Mon·dale

Mon·day

Mon·dri·an

Mo·net

mon·e·tar·y
  mon·e·tar·i·ly

mon·ey
  pl. mon·eys *or* mon·ies
  mon·ey-grub·ber
  mon·ey-grub·bing
  mon·ey·less

mon·ey·bags

mon·eyed

mon·ey·mak·er
  mon·ey·mak·ing

mon·ger

Mon·go·li·a
  Mon·go·li·an

mon·gol·ism

Mon·gol·oid

mon·goose
  pl. mon·goos·es *or*
  mon·geese

mon·grel
  mon·grel·ism
  mon·grel·ize
  mon·grel·i·za·tion

mon·i·ker
  also mon·ick·er

mon·i·tor
  mon·i·to·ri·al

monk
  monk·ish

mon·key
  pl. mon·keys
  mon·keyed
  mon·key·ish

mon·key·shine

mon·o

mon·o·chro·mat·ic
  mon·o·chro·mat·i·cal·ly

mon·o·chrome
  mon·o·chro·mic

mon·o·cle
  mon·o·cled

mon·o·clo·nal

mon·o·cot·y·le·don
  mon·o·cot·y·le·don·ous

mon·oc·u·lar
  mon·oc·u·lar·ly

mo·nog·a·my
  mo·nog·a·mist
  mo·nog·a·mous
  mo·nog·a·mous·ly

mon·o·gram
  mon·o·gram·mat·ic
  mon·o·grammed

mon·o·graph
  mo·nog·ra·pher
  mon·o·graph·ic

mon·o·lin·gual

mon·o·lith
  mon·o·lith·ic

mon·o·logue
  also monolog
  mon·o·log·ic
  mon·o·log·i·cal
  mon·o·log·ist
  also mon·o·logu·ist

mon·o·ma·ni·a
  mon·o·ma·ni·ac
  mon·o·ma·ni·a·cal

mon·o·nu·cle·o·sis

mon·o·phon·ic
  mon·o·phon·i·cal·ly

mo·nop·o·list
  mo·nop·o·lis·tic

mo·nop·o·lize
  mo·nop·o·li·za·tion
  mo·nop·o·liz·er

mo·nop·o·ly
  pl. mo·nop·o·lies

mon·o·rail

mon·o·so·di·um glu·ta·mate

mon·o·syl·la·ble
  mon·o·syl·lab·ic
  mon·o·syl·lab·i·cal·ly

mon·o·the·ism
  mon·o·the·ist
  mon·o·the·is·tic
  mon·o·the·is·ti·cal·ly

mon·o·tone

mo·not·o·nous
  mo·not·o·nous·ly
  mo·not·o·nous·ness

mo·not·o·ny

Mon·roe

Mon·ro·vi·a

mon·sieur
  pl. mes·sieurs

Mon·si·gnor
  pl. Mon·si·gnors *or*
  Mon·si·gno·ri

mon·soon
  mon·soon·al

mon·ster

mon·strance

mon·strous
  mon·stros·i·ty
  mon·strous·ly
  mon·strous·ness

mon·tage

Mon·taigne

Mon·tan·a
  Mon·tan·an

Mont·calm

Mon·te·ne·gro
  Mon·te·ne·grin

Mon·te·rey (*California*)

Mon·ter·rey (*Mexico*)

Mon·tes·quieu

Mon·tes·so·ri

Mon·te·ver·di

Mon·te·vi·de·o

Mon·te·zu·ma II

Mont·gom·er·y

month

month·ly
  pl. month·lies

Mont·pel·ier (*Vermont*)

Mont·pel·lier (*France*)

Mont·re·al

Mont·ser·rat

mon·u·ment

mon·u·men·tal
  mon·u·men·tal·i·ty
  mon·u·men·tal·ly

moo
  moos, mooed
  pl. moos

mooch
  mooch·er

mood

mood·swing

mood·y
  mood·i·er, mood·i·est
  mood·i·ly
  mood·i·ness

Moon

moon
  moon·less

moon·beam

moon·light
  moon·light·ed
  moon·light·er

moon·lit

moon·scape

moon·shine

moon·shot

moon·stone

moon·struck

moor (*attach a boat, etc.,
to something*)
  moor·age

moor (*open uncultivated
land*)
  moor·ish

Moor (*people*)
  Moor·ish

Moore (*proper name*)

moor·ing

moose (*animal*; see
MOUSSE)
  pl. same

moot

mop
  mopped, mop·ping

mope
  mop·er
  mop·i·ly
  mop·i·ness
  mop·y
  mop·i·er, mop·i·est

mo·ped (*motorbike*)

mo·raine
  mo·rain·al

mor·al
  mor·al·ly

mo·rale

mor·al·ist
  mor·al·is·tic
  mor·al·is·ti·cal·ly

mo·ral·i·ty
  pl. mo·ral·i·ties

mor·al·ize
  mor·al·i·za·tion
  mor·al·iz·er
  mor·al·iz·ing·ly

mo·rass

mor·a·to·ri·um
  pl. mor·a·to·ri·ums *or*
  mor·a·to·ri·a

mor·bid
  mor·bid·i·ty
  mor·bid·ly
  mor·bid·ness

mor·dant
  mor·dan·cy
  mor·dant·ly

More (*proper name*)

more (*further*)

Mo·re·lia

Mo·re·los

Mo·re·no Val·ley

more·o·ver

mo·res

Mor·gan

morgue

mor·i·bund
  mor·i·bun·di·ty

Mo·ri·sot

Mor·mon
  Mor·mon·ism

morn (*morning*; see
MOURN)

morn·ing

Mo·roc·co (*city*)
  Mo·roc·can

mo·roc·co (*leather*)
  pl. mo·roc·cos

mo·ron
  mo·ron·ic
  mo·ron·i·cal·ly

Mo·rón (*city*)

Mo·ro·ni

mo·rose
  mo·rose·ly
  mo·rose·ness

morph
  morph·ing

mor·pheme
  mor·phe·mic
  mor·phe·mi·cal·ly

mor·phine

mor·phol·o·gy
  mor·pho·log·i·cal
  mor·pho·log·i·cal·ly
  mor·phol·o·gist

Mor·ris

Mor·ri·son

mor·row

Morse

mor·sel

mor·tal
  mor·tal·ly

mor·tal·i·ty
  pl. mor·tal·i·ties

mor·tar
  mor·tar·less

mor·tar·board

mort·gage
  mort·gage·a·ble

mort·ga·gee

mort·ga·gor
  also mort·gag·er

mor·ti·cian

mor·ti·fy
  mor·ti·fies, mor·ti·fied
  mor·ti·fi·ca·tion
  mor·ti·fy·ing
  mor·ti·fy·ing·ly

mor·tise
  also mor·tice

mor·tu·ar·y
  pl. mor·tu·ar·ies

mo·sa·ic (*patterned picture*)
  mo·sa·i·cist

Mo·sa·ic (*relating to Moses*)

Mos·cow

Mo·ses

mo·sey
  mo·seys, mo·seyed

Mos·lem
  var. of Mus·lim

mosque

mos·qui·to
  pl. mos·qui·toes *or* mos·qui·tos

moss
  moss·i·ness
  moss·like
  moss·y
  moss·i·er, moss·i·est

most

most·ly

Mo·sul

mote (*speck;* see MOAT)

mo·tel

moth
  moth-eat·en
  moth·y
  moth·i·er, moth·i·est

moth·ball

moth·er
  moth·er-in-law
  pl. moth·ers-in-law
  moth·er-of-pearl
  moth·er·hood
  moth·er·less
  moth·er·like

moth·er·board

moth·er·land

moth·er·ly
  moth·er·li·ness

Mo·ther Te·re·sa

mo·tif

mo·tile
  mo·til·i·ty

mo·tion
  mo·tion·less

mo·ti·vate
  mo·ti·va·tion
  mo·ti·va·tion·al
  mo·ti·va·tion·al·ly

mo·tive
  mo·tive·less

mot·ley
  mot·li·er, mot·li·est

mo·to·cross

mo·tor

mo·tor·bike

mo·tor·bus

mo·tor·cade

mo·tor·cy·cle
  mo·tor·cy·clist

mo·tor·ist

mo·tor·ize
  mo·tor·i·za·tion

Mott

mot·tle

mot·to
  pl. mot·toes *or* mot·tos

mound

mount
  mount·a·ble
  mount·er

moun·tain
moun·tain·y

moun·tain·eer
moun·tain·eer·ing

moun·tain·ous

Mount·bat·ten

moun·te·bank

Moun·tie

mount·ing

mourn (*grieve*; see MORN)
mourn·er

mourn·ful
mourn·ful·ly
mourn·ful·ness

mourn·ing

mouse
pl. mice
mouse·like
mous·er

mousse (*dessert*; see MOOSE)

Mous·sorg·sky
also Mus·sorg·sky,
Mus·org·sky

mous·tache
var. of mus·tache

mous·y
mous·i·er, mous·i·est
mous·i·ly
mous·i·ness

mouth
pl. mouths
mouthed
mouth·er
mouth·less

mouth·ful
pl. mouth·fuls

mouth·piece

mouth·wash

mouth·wa·ter·ing

mou·ton

mov·a·ble
also move·a·ble
mov·a·bil·i·ty
mov·a·ble·ness
mov·a·bly

move
mov·er

move·a·ble
var. of mov·a·ble

move·ment

mov·ie

mov·ie·dom

mow
past part. mowed (see MODE) *or* mown (see MOAN)
mow·a·ble
mow·er

Mo·zam·bique
Mo·zam·bi·can

Mo·zart

moz·za·rel·la

mu

much
much·ly

mu·ci·lage
mu·ci·lag·i·nous

muck
muck·i·ness
muck·y
muck·i·er, muck·i·est

muck·rake
muck·rak·er
muck·rak·ing

mu·cous
mu·cos·i·ty

mu·cus

mud

mud·dy
mud·di·er, mud·di·est
mud·dies, mud·died
mud·di·ly
mud·di·ness

mu·ez·zin

muff

muf·fin

muf·fle

muf·fler

muf·ti

mug
mugged, mug·ging
mug·ger
mug·ful
pl. mug·fuls

Mu·ga·be

mug·gy
mug·gi·er, mug·gi·est
mug·gi·ness

Mu·ham·mad
also Mo·ham·med, Ma·hom·et

Muir

mu·ja·hi·din
also mu·ja·he·din, mu·ja·he·deen

mu·lat·to
pl. mu·lat·toes *or* mu·lat·tos

mul·ber·ry
pl. mul·ber·ries

mulch

mulct

mule (*animal*)
mul·ish
mul·ish·ly
mul·ish·ness

mule (*slipper, shoe*)

mu·le·teer

mull

mul·lah

mul·let

mul·li·ga·taw·ny

mul·lion
also mun·nion
mul·lioned

Mul·tan

mul·ti·cul·tur·al
mul·ti·cul·tur·al·ism
mul·ti·cul·tur·al·ly

mul·ti·eth·nic

mul·ti·fac·et·ed

mul·ti·far·i·ous
mul·ti·far·i·ous·ly
mul·ti·far·i·ous·ness

mul·ti·lat·er·al
mul·ti·lat·er·al·ly

mul·ti·lin·gual
mul·ti·lin·gual·ly

mul·ti·me·di·a

mul·ti·na·tion·al
mul·ti·na·tion·al·ly

mul·ti·ple
mul·ti·ple-choice

mul·ti·plex
mul·ti·plex·er
also mul·ti·plex·or

mul·ti·pli·cand

mul·ti·pli·ca·tion
mul·ti·pli·ca·tive

mul·ti·plic·i·ty
pl. mul·ti·plic·i·ties

mul·ti·pli·er

mul·ti·ply
mul·ti·plies, mul·ti·
plied

mul·ti·proc·ess·ing

mul·ti·ra·cial
mul·ti·ra·cial·ly

mul·ti·tude

mul·ti·tu·di·nous
mul·ti·tu·di·nous·ly
mul·ti·tu·di·nous·ness

mum

mum·ble
mum·bler

mum·bo jum·bo
pl. mum·bo jum·bos

mum·mer

mum·mer·y
pl. mum·mer·ies

mum·mi·fy
mum·mi·fies, mum·
mi·fied
mum·mi·fi·ca·tion

mum·my
pl. mum·mies

mumps

munch

munch·ies

mun·dane
mun·dane·ly
mun·dane·ness

Mu·nich

mu·nic·i·pal
mu·nic·i·pal·ize
mu·nic·i·pal·ly

mu·nic·i·pal·i·ty
pl. mu·nic·i·pal·i·ties

mu·nif·i·cent
mu·nif·i·cence
mu·nif·i·cent·ly

mu·ni·tion

Mun·ro

Mün·ster

mu·on

mu·ral
mu·ral·ist

Mu·rat

Mur·cia

mur·der
mur·der·er
mur·der·ess

mur·der·ous
mur·der·ous·ly

Mur·doch

murk

murk·y
murk·i·er, murk·i·est
murk·i·ly
murk·i·ness

Mur·mansk

mur·mur
mur·mur·er
mur·mur·ing·ly
mur·mur·ous

Mur·ray

Mus·cat (*city*)

mus·cat (*grape*)
also mus·ca·tel

mus·cle (*motive organ;*
see MUSSEL)
mus·cle-bound
mus·cled
mus·cle·less

mus·cu·lar
mus·cu·lar·i·ty

mus·cu·la·ture

mus·cu·lo·skel·e·tal

Muse (*goddess;* see MEWS)

muse (*think;* see MEWS)

mu·se·um

mush
mush•y
mush•i•er, mush•i•est
mush•i•ly
mush•i•ness

mush•room

mu•sic

mu•si•cal
mu•si•cal•i•ty
mu•si•cal•ize
mu•si•cal•ly
mu•si•cal•ness

mu•si•cian
mu•si•cian•ly
mu•si•cian•ship

mu•si•col•o•gy
mu•si•col•o•gist
mu•si•co•log•i•cal

musk
musk•y
musk•i•er, musk•i•est
musk•i•ness

mus•kel•lunge

mus•ket

mus•ket•eer

musk•rat

Mus•lim
also Mos•lem

mus•lin

muss
muss•y

mus•sel (*shellfish*; see
  MUSCLE)

Mus•so•li•ni

Mus•sorg•sky
var. of Mous•sorg•sky

must

mus•tache
also mous•tache
mus•tached

mus•tang

mus•tard

mus•ter

must•n't

mus•ty
mus•ti•er, mus•ti•est
must•i•ly
mus•ti•ness

mu•ta•ble
mu•ta•bil•i•ty

mu•ta•gen
mu•ta•gen•ic
mu•ta•gen•e•sis

mu•tant

mu•ta•tion
mu•tate
mu•ta•tion•al
mu•ta•tion•al•ly

mute
mute•ly
mute•ness

mu•ti•late
mu•ti•la•tion
mu•ti•la•tive
mu•ti•la•tor

mu•ti•ny
pl. mu•ti•nies
mu•ti•nies, mu•ti•nied
mu•ti•neer
mu•ti•nous
mu•ti•nous•ly

mutt

mut•ter
mut•ter•er
mut•ter•ing•ly

mut•ton
mut•ton•y

mu•tu•al
mu•tu•al•i•ty
mu•tu•al•ly

muu•muu

Mu•zak

muz•zle
muz•zler

my•al•gi•a
my•al•gic

My•an•mar

My•ce•nae•an

my•col•o•gy
my•co•log•i•cal
my•co•log•i•cal•ly
my•col•o•gist

my•e•lin
my•e•li•na•tion

my•e•li•tis

My•lar (*trademark*)

my•nah
also my•na, mi•na

my•o•pia
my•op•ic
my•op•i•cal•ly

myr•i•ad

My•ron

myrrh
myrrh•ic
myrrh•y

myr•tle

my•self

My•sore

mys•te•ri•ous
mys•te•ri•ous•ly
mys•te•ri•ous•ness

mys•ter•y
pl. mys•ter•ies

mys•tic
mys•ti•cism

mys•ti•cal
mys•ti•cal•ly

mys·ti·fy
  mys·ti·fies, mys·ti·fied
  mys·ti·fi·ca·tion

mys·tique

myth
  myth·ic

myth·i·cal
myth·i·cal·ly

my·thol·o·gy
  pl. my·thol·o·gies
  myth·o log·ic
  myth·o·log·i·cal

myth·o·log·i·cal·ly
my·thol·o·gist
my·thol·o·gize

Myu·ko·la·yiv

N

nab
nabbed, nab•bing

na•bob

Na•bo•kov

na•cho
pl. na•chos

na•cre
na•cre•ous

Na•der (proper name)

na•dir (lowest point)

nag
nagged, nag•ging

Na•ga•no

Na•ga•sa•ki

Na•go•ya

Nag•pur

Na•hua•tl

nai•ad
pl. nai•ads or nai•ades

nail

Nai•ro•bi

na•ive
also na•ïve
na•ïve•ly
na•ïve•té

na•ked
na•ked•ly
na•ked•ness

nam•by-pam•by
pl. nam•by-pam•bies

name
name•a•ble

name•less

name•ly

name•sake

Na•mib•i•a
Na•mib•i•an

Nam•po

Nam•pu•la

Nan•chang

Nan•cy

Nan•jing

nan•ny
pl. nan•nies

Nantes

Nan•tuck•et

nap
napped, nap•ping

na•palm

nape

naph•tha

naph•tha•lene

nap•kin

Na•ples

Na•po•le•on
Na•po•le•on•ic

narc
also nark

nar•cis•sism
nar•cis•sist
nar•cis•sis•tic

nar•cis•sus
pl. nar•cis•si or nar•cis•sus•es

nar•co•lep•sy
nar•co•lep•tic

nar•cot•ic

Nar•ra•gan•sett

nar•rate
nar•ra•tion
nar•ra•tor

nar•ra•tive

nar•row
nar•row•er, nar•row•est
nar•row•ly
nar•row•ness

nar•row-mind•ed
nar•row-mind•ed•ness

nar•whal

nar•y

na•sal
na•sal•i•ty
na•sal•ize
na•sal•i•za•tion
na•sal•ly

nas•cent
nas•cen•cy

Nash

Nash•u•a

Nash•ville

Nas•sau

Nas•ser

nas•tur•tium

nas•ty
nas•ti•er, nas•ti•est
nas•ti•ly
nas•ti•ness

na•tal

na•ta•to•ri•um

Natch•ez

na•tion
na•tion•hood

na•tion•al
na•tion•al•ly

na·tion·al·ism
  na·tion·al·ist
  na·tion·al·is·tic

na·tion·al·i·ty
  pl. na·tion·al·i·ties

na·tion·al·ize
  na·tion·al·i·za·tion

na·tion·wide

na·tive

na·tiv·i·ty
  pl. na·tiv·i·ties

nat·ty
  nat·ti·er, nat·ti·est
  nat·ti·ly

nat·u·ral
  nat·u·ral·ness

nat·u·ral·ism
  nat·u·ral·is·tic

nat·u·ral·ist

nat·u·ral·ize
  nat·u·ral·i·za·tion

nat·u·ral·ly

na·ture

na·tured

naught

naugh·ty
  naugh·ti·er, naugh·
    ti·est
  naugh·ti·ly
  naugh·ti·ness

Na·u·ru

nau·se·a

nau·se·ate
  nau·se·at·ing

nau·seous

nau·ti·cal
  naut·i·cal·ly

nau·ti·lus
  pl. nau·ti·lus·es *or* nau·
    ti·li

Nav·a·jo
  pl. Nav·a·jos
  also Nav·a·ho
  pl. Nav·a·hos

na·val (*of the navy; see*
    NAVEL)

nave (*part of a church;*
    see KNAVE)

na·vel (*belly button; see*
    NAVAL)

nav·i·ga·ble
  nav·i·ga·bil·i·ty

nav·i·gate
  nav·i·ga·tor

nav·i·ga·tion

na·vy
  pl. na·vies

nay (*negative vote; see*
    NÉE, NEIGH)
  nay·say·er

Na·ya·rit

Na·zi
  pl. Na·zis
  Na·zism

N'Dja·me·na

Ndo·la

Ne·an·der·thal
  also Ne·an·der·tal

neap

Ne·a·pol·i·tan

near
  near·ish
  near·ness

near·by

near·ly

near·sight·ed
  near·sight·ed·ness

neat
  neat·ly
  neat·ness

neat·en

Ne·bras·ka
  Ne·bras·kan

Neb·u·chad·nez·zar

neb·u·la
  pl. neb·u·lae *or* ne·
    bu·las
  neb·u·lar

neb·u·lous

nec·es·sar·y
  pl. nec·es·sar·ies
  nec·es·sar·i·ly

ne·ces·si·tate

ne·ces·si·ty
  pl. ne·ces·si·ties

neck

neck·er·chief

neck·lace

neck·line

neck·tie

nec·ro·man·cy
  nec·ro·man·cer

nec·ro·phil·i·a
  also nec·ro·phil·y
  nec·ro·phile
  nec·ro·phil·ic
  ne·croph·i·lism

ne·cro·sis
  ne·crot·ic

nec·tar
  nec·tar·ous

nec·tar·ine

née (*born; see* NAY,
    NEIGH)
  also nee

need (*require; see* KNEAD)

need·ful
  need·ful·ly

nee·dle

nee·dle·point

need·less
  need·less·ly
  need·less·ness

nee·dle·work

needs

need·y
  need·i·er, need·i·est
  need·i·ness

ne'er
  ne'er-do-well

ne·far·i·ous
  ne·far·i·ous·ly
  ne·far·i·ous·ness

ne·gate

ne·ga·tion
  neg·a·to·ry

neg·a·tive
  neg·a·tive·ly
  neg·a·tiv·i·ty

neg·a·tiv·ism

Neg·ev

ne·glect
  ne·glect·ful
  ne·glect·ful·ly

neg·li·gee
  also neg·li·gée,
  nég·li·gé

neg·li·gence
  neg·li·gent
  neg·li·gent·ly

neg·li·gi·ble
  neg·li·gi·bly

ne·go·ti·ate
  ne·go·tia·ble
  ne·go·ti·a·tion
  ne·go·ti·a·tor

Ne·gro
  pl. Ne·groes
  Ne·groid

Neh·ru

neigh (*whinny*; see NAY, NÉE)

neigh·bor

neigh·bor·hood

neigh·bor·ly
  neigh·bor·li·ness

nei·ther

Nel·son

nem·a·tode

nem·e·sis
  pl. nem·e·ses

ne·o·clas·si·cal
  also ne·o·clas·sic
  ne·o·clas·si·cism

ne·o·co·lo·ni·al·ism

ne·o·dym·i·um

Ne·o·lith·ic
  also ne·o·lith·ic

ne·ol·o·gism

ne·on

ne·o·phyte

ne·o·prene

Ne·pal
  Ne·pa·lese

Ne·pal·i
  pl. same *or* Ne·pal·is;
  also Ne·pal·ese

neph·ew

ne·phrit·ic

ne·phri·tis

ne plus ul·tra

nep·o·tism

Nep·tune

nep·tu·ni·um

nerd
  also nurd
  nerd·y

Ne·ro

nerve
  nerve-rack·ing
  also nerve-wrack·ing

nerve·less
  nerve·less·ly
  nerve·less·ness

nerv·ous
  nerv·ous·ly
  nerv·ous·ness

nerv·y
  nerv·i·er, nerv·i·est

nest

nes·tle

nest·ling

net
  net·ted, net·ting

Net·an·ya·hu

neth·er

Neth·er·lands
  Neth·er·land·er

ne·tsu·ke
  pl. same *or* ne·tsu·kes

net·ting

net·tle

net·tle·some

net·work

Ne·tza·hual·có·yotl

neu·ral

neu·ral·gia
  neu·ral·gic

neu·ri·tis
  neu·rit·ic

neu·rol·o·gy
  neu·ro·log·i·cal
  neu·rol·o·gist

neu•ron
also neu•rone
neu•ron•ic

neu•ro•sis
pl. neu•ro•ses

neu•ro•sur•ger•y
neu•ro•sur•geon
neu•ro•sur•gi•cal

neu•rot•ic
neu•rot•i•cal•ly

neu•ter

neu•tral
neu•tral•i•ty
neu•tral•ly

neu•tral•ize
neu•tral•iz•er

neu•tri•no
pl. neu•tri•nos

neu•tron

Ne•vad•a
Ne•vad•an
Ne•vad•i•an

nev•er

nev•er•more

nev•er•the•less

ne•vus
pl. ne•vi

new (*recent*; see GNU,
    KNEW)
new•ish
new•ness

New•ark

New Bed•ford

new•born

New Bruns•wick

New Cal•e•do•ni•a

New•cas•tle

new•com•er

New Del•hi

new•el

New Eng•land

new•fan•gled

New•found•land
New•found•lander

New Guin•ea

New Hamp•shire
New Hamp•shir•ite
New Hamp•shire•man

New Ha•ven

New Jer•sey
New Jer•sey•ite
New Jer•sey•an

new•ly

New•man

New Mex•i•co
New Mex•i•can

New Or•le•ans
New Or•lea•ni•an

New•port News

news

news•cast
news•cast•er

news•deal•er

news•let•ter

news•pa•per

news•print

news•stand

news•week•ly

news•wor•thy

news•y
news•i•er, news•i•est

newt

New•ton

New York
New York•er

New Zea•land
New Zea•land•er

next

nex•us
pl. same

Nez Per•cé
also Nez Per•ce

Ngo Dinh Diem

ni•a•cin

Ni•ag•a•ra

Nia•mey

nib

nib•ble

nibs

ni•cad

Nic•a•ra•gua
Nic•a•ra•guan

Nice (*city*)

nice
nice•ly
nice•ness

ni•ce•ty
pl. ni•ce•ties

niche

nick

nick•el
nick•el-and-dime

nick•el•o•de•on

Nick•laus

nick•name

Nic•o•si•a

nic•o•tine

nic•o•tin•ic ac•id

nic•ti•tate

Nie•buhr

niece

Nie·tzsche

nif·ty
 nif·ti·er, nif·ti·est

Ni·ger
 Ni·ge·ri·en

Ni·ge·ri·a
 Ni·ge·ri·an

Ni·ger

nig·gard·ly
 nig·gard·li·ness

nig·gle
 nig·gling

nigh

night (*darkness; see*
 KNIGHT)

night·cap

night·club

night·fall

night·gown

night·hawk

Night·in·gale (*proper
 name*)

night·in·gale (*bird*)

night·life

night·ly

night·mare
 night·mar·ish

night·shirt

night·spot

night·stick

night·time

ni·hil·ism
 ni·hil·ist
 ni·hil·is·tic

Ni·jin·sky

Ni·ko·la·yev

nil

Nile

nim·ble
 nim·bler, nim·blest
 nim·bly

nim·bus
 pl. nim·bi *or* nim·bus·
 es

Nîmes

Nim·itz

nin·com·poop

nine
 ninth

nine·fold

nine·teen
 nine·teenth

nine·ty
 pl. nine·ties
 nine·ti·eth

nin·ja

nin·ny
 pl. nin·nies

ninth

ni·o·bi·um

nip
 nipped, nip·ping

nip·per

nip·ple

nip·py
 nip·pi·er, nip·pi·est

nir·va·na

ni·sei
 also Ni·sei

nit (*insect; see* KNIT)

ni·ter

nit·pick
 nit·pick·er
 nit·pick·ing

ni·trate
 ni·tra·tion

ni·tric

ni·tro·gen
 ni·trog·e·nous

ni·tro·glyc·er·in
 also ni·tro·glyc·er·ine

ni·trous ox·ide

nit·ty-grit·ty

nit·wit

nix

Nix·on

Nkru·mah

no (*a negative; see* KNOW)
 pl. noes *or* nos (*see*
 NOSE)

no (*not any; see* KNOW)
 no-brain·er
 no-fault
 no-go
 no-no
 no-win

No·bel

No·bel·ist

no·bel·i·um

no·bil·i·ty
 pl. no·bil·i·ties

no·ble
 no·bler, nob·lest
 no·ble·ness

no·ble·man
 pl. no·ble·men

no·blesse o·blige

no·ble·wom·an
 pl. no·ble·wom·en

no·bod·y
 pl. no·bod·ies

noc·tur·nal

noc·turne

nod
nod·ded, nod·ding

node
nod·al

nod·ule
nod·u·lar

No·el

nog·gin

noise

noise·less
noise·less·ly

noi·some

nois·y
nois·i·er, nois·i·est
nois·i·ness

no·mad
no·mad·ic

nom de plume
pl. noms de plume

Nome

no·men·cla·ture

nom·i·nal
nom·i·nal·ly

nom·i·nate
nom·i·na·tion
nom·i·na·tor

nom·i·na·tive

nom·i·nee

non·a·bra·sive

non·ab·sor·bent

non·a·bu·sive

non·ad·dic·tive

non·ad·he·sive

non·ad·just·a·ble

non·a·ge·nar·i·an

non·ag·gres·sion

non·a·gon

non·al·co·hol·ic

non·a·ligned
non·a·lign·ment

non·al·ler·gic

non·am·big·u·ous

non·be·liev·er

non·bel·lig·er·ent
non·bel·lig·er·en·cy

non·black

non·can·cer·ous

nonce

non·cha·lant
non·cha·lance
non·cha·lant·ly

non-Chris·tian

non·cler·i·cal

non·com

non·com·bat·ant

non·com·bus·ti·ble

non·com·mis·sioned

non·com·mit·tal

non·com·pli·ance

non com·pos men·tis

non·con·duc·tor

non·con·form·ist
non·con·form·i·ty

non·con·struc·tive

non·con·ta·gious

non·con·tro·ver·sial

non·de·duct·i·ble

**non·de·nom·i·na·
tion·al**

non·de·script

non·drink·er

non·dry·ing

none (*not any*; see NUN)

non·ef·fec·tive

non·en·ti·ty
pl. non·en·ti·ties

non·es·sen·tial

none·the·less

non·e·vent

non·ex·ist·ence

non·ex·ist·ent

non·ex·plo·sive

non·fat·ten·ing

non·fer·rous

non·fic·tion

non·flam·ma·ble

non·greas·y

non·haz·ard·ous

non·he·red·i·tar·y

non·his·tor·i·cal

non·hu·man

non·i·den·ti·cal

non·in·clu·sive

non·in·fec·tious

non·in·flam·ma·to·ry

non·in·fla·tion·ar·y

non·in·flect·ed

non·in·te·grat·ed

**non·in·ter·change·
a·ble**

non·in·ter·fer·ence

non·in·ter·ven·tion

non·in·tox·i·cat·ing

non·ir·ri·tat·ing

non·lin·e·ar

non·mag·net·ic

non·ma·lig·nant

non·mem·ber

non·mi·gra·to·ry

non·mil·i·tant

non·mil·i·tar·y

non·nar·cot·ic

non·ne·go·ti·a·ble

non·ob·jec·tive

non·ob·lig·a·to·ry

non·ob·serv·ant

non·of·fi·cial

non·or·gan·ic

non·pa·reil

non·par·ti·san

non·pay·ing

non·pay·ment

non·per·ish·a·ble

non·plus
   non·plussed, non·plus·
   sing *or* non·plused,
   non·plus·ing

non·poi·son·ous

non·po·lit·i·cal

non·pol·lut·ing

non·po·rous

non·prac·tic·ing

non·pro·duc·tive

non·pro·fes·sion·al

non·prof·it

non·prof·it·a·ble

non·pro·lif·er·a·tion

non·pub·lic

non·ra·cial

non·re·ac·tive

non·re·cip·ro·cal

non·re·cip·ro·cat·ing

non·re·cur·ring

non·re·deem·a·ble

non·re·fill·a·ble

non·re·new·a·ble

non·rep·re·sen·ta·
   tion·al

non·res·i·dent
   non·res·i·den·tial

non·re·sis·tance

non·re·sis·tant

non·re·turn·a·ble

non·rhyth·mic

non·sal·a·ried

non·sci·en·tif·ic

non·sea·son·al

non·sec·tar·i·an

non·sense
   non·sen·si·cal
   non·sen·si·cal·ly

non se·qui·tur

non·sex·ist

non·sex·u·al

non·skid

non·slip

non·smok·er

non·smok·ing

non·spe·cif·ic

non·stain·ing

non·start·er

non·stick

non·stop

non·swim·mer

non·tar·nish·ing

non·tax·a·ble

non·tech·ni·cal

non·think·ing

non·threat·en·ing

non·tox·ic

non·trans·fer·a·ble

non·un·ion

non·us·er

non·ven·om·ous

non·ver·bal

non·vi·o·lence
   non·vi·o·lent

non·vir·u·lent

non·vo·cal

non·vot·er

non·white

non·work·ing

noo·dle

nook

noon

no one

noose

nor

Nor·dic

nor'east·er

Nor·folk

norm

nor·mal
  nor·mal·cy
  nor·mal·i·ty
  nor·mal·i·za·tion
  nor·mal·ize

nor·mal·ly

Nor·man

nor·ma·tive

Norse
  Norse·man
  pl. Norse·men

north

North A·mer·i·ca
  North A·mer·i·can

North·amp·ton

North Car·o·li·na
  North Car·o·lin·i·an

North Da·ko·ta
  North Da·ko·tan

north·east

north·east·er
  also nor'east·er

north·er·ly

north·ern
  north·ern·most

north·er·ner

North·ern Ire·land

North·ern Mar·i·an·a Is·lands

North Ko·re·a

north·west

North·west Ter·ri·to·ries

Nor·way
  Nor·we·gian

Nor·wich

nose (part of the face; see noes, nos[NO])

nose·bleed

nose·dive

nose·gay

nosh

nos·tal·gia
  nos·tal·gic
  nos·tal·gi·cal·ly

Nos·tra·da·mus

nos·tril

nos·trum

nos·y
  also nos·ey
  nos·i·er, nos·i·est
  nos·i·ly
  nos·i·ness

not (negative; see KNOT)

no·ta be·ne

no·ta·ble
  no·ta·bil·i·ty
  no·ta·bly

no·ta·rize

no·ta·ry
  pl. no·ta·ries
  no·tar·i·al

no·ta·ry pub·lic
  pl. no·ta·ries pub·lic

no·ta·tion

notch

note

note·book

note·paper

note·wor·thy

noth·ing

noth·ing·ness

no·tice

no·tice·a·ble
  no·tice·a·bly

no·ti·fy
  no·ti·fies, no·ti·fied
  no·ti·fi·ca·tion

no·tion

no·tion·al
  no·tion·al·ly

no·to·ri·e·ty

no·to·ri·ous
  no·to·ri·ous·ly

Not·ting·ham

not·with·stand·ing

Nouak·chott

nou·gat

nought
  var. of naught

noun

nour·ish
  nour·ish·ing

nour·ish·ment

nou·veau riche
  pl. nou·veaux riches

no·va
  pl. no·vas or no·vae

No·va Sco·tia
  No·va Sco·tian

nov·el

nov·el·ette

nov·el·ist

no·vel·la
  pl. no·vel·las or no·vel·le

nov·el·ty
  pl. nov·el·ties

No·vem·ber

no·ve·na

Nov·go·rod

nov·ice

no·vi·ti·ate
  also no·vi·ci·ate

no·vo·caine
  also No·vo·cain
  (*trademark*)

No·vo·si·birsk

now

now·a·days

no·where

no·wise

nox·ious

Noyes

noz·zle

nu·ance

nub
  nub·by

Nu·bi·an

nu·bile
  nu·bil·i·ty

nu·cle·ar

nu·cle·ate

nu·cle·ic ac·id

nu·cle·o·lus
  pl. nu·cle·o·li

nu·cle·on

nu·cle·us
  pl. nu·cle·i

nude
  nu·di·ty

nudge

nud·ist
  nud·ism

nu·di·ty

Nue·vo La·re·do

Nue·vo Le·ón

nu·ga·to·ry

nug·get

nui·sance

nuke

Nu·ku·a·lo·fa

null

nul·li·fy
  nul·li·fies, nul·li·fied
  nul·li·fi·ca·tion

numb
  numb·ness

num·ber

num·ber·less

numb·skull
  var. of num·skull

nu·mer·a·ble

nu·mer·al

nu·mer·ate
  nu·mer·a·cy

nu·mer·a·tor

nu·mer·i·cal
  also nu·mer·ic
  nu·mer·i·cal·ly

nu·mer·ol·o·gy
  pl. nu·mer·ol·o·gies

nu·mer·ous

nu·mi·nous

nu·mis·mat·ics
  nu·mis·mat·ic
  nu·mis·ma·tist

num·skull

nun (*religious woman;* see
  NONE)

nun·ci·o
  pl. nun·ci·os

nun·ner·y
  pl. nun·ner·ies

nup·tial

nurd
  var. of nerd

Nu·rem·berg

Nu·re·yev

nurse
  nurse-prac·ti·tion·er

nurse·maid

nur·ser·y
  pl. nur·ser·ies

nur·ser·y·man
  pl. nur·ser·y·men

nurs·ing

nur·ture
  nur·tur·er

nut

nut·case

nut·crack·er

nut·hatch

nut·meg

nu·tri·a

nu·tri·ent

nu·tri·ment

nu·tri·tion
  nu·tri·tion·al
  nu·tri·tion·ist

nu·tri·tious

nuts

nut·shell

nut•ty
  nut•ti•er, nut•ti•est
  nut•ti•ness
nuz•zle

Nya•sa
ny•lon
nymph

nym•pho•ma•ni•a
nym•pho•ma•ni•ac

O

oaf
  pl. oafs
  oaf·ish
  oaf·ish·ly
  oaf·ish·ness

O·a·hu

oak
  oak·en

Oak·land

oa·kum

oar (*paddle*; see O'ER, OR, ORE)

oar·lock

oars·man
  pl. oars·men; *fem.* oars·wom·an, *pl.* oars·wom·en
  oars·man·ship

o·a·sis
  pl. o·a·ses

oat
  oat·en

oat·cake

oath
  pl. oaths

oat·meal

Oa·xa·ca

ob·bli·ga·to
  pl. ob·bli·ga·tos

ob·du·rate
  ob·du·ra·cy

o·be·di·ent
  o·be·di·ence
  o·be·di·ent·ly

o·bei·sance
  o·bei·sant

ob·e·lisk

o·bese
  o·be·si·ty

o·bey

ob·fus·cate
  ob·fus·ca·tion

o·bit·u·ar·y
  pl. o·bit·u·ar·ies

ob·ject
  ob·jec·tor

ob·jec·ti·fy
  ob·jec·ti·fies, ob·jec·ti·fied

ob·jec·tion

ob·jec·tion·a·ble
  ob·jec·tion·a·bly

ob·jec·tive
  ob·jec·tive·ly
  ob·jec·tive·ness
  ob·jec·tiv·i·ty

ob·jet d'art
  pl. ob·jets d'art

ob·la·tion

ob·li·gate

ob·li·ga·tion

o·blig·a·to·ry
  o·blig·a·to·ri·ly

o·blige

o·blig·ing
  o·blig·ing·ly

o·blique
  o·blique·ly
  o·blique·ness

ob·lit·er·ate
  ob·lit·er·a·tion

ob·liv·i·on

ob·liv·i·ous
  ob·liv·i·ous·ly
  ob·liv·i·ous·ness

ob·long

ob·lo·quy

ob·nox·ious
  ob·nox·ious·ly
  ob·nox·ious·ness

o·boe
  o·bo·ist

ob·scene
  ob·scene·ly
  ob·scen·i·ty

ob·scu·rant·ism
  ob·scu·rant·ist

ob·scure
  ob·scure·ly
  ob·scu·ri·ty

ob·se·quies

ob·se·qui·ous
  ob·se·qui·ous·ly
  ob·se·qui·ous·ness

ob·serv·ance

ob·serv·ant
  ob·serv·ant·ly

ob·ser·va·tion
  ob·ser·va·tion·al

ob·serv·a·to·ry
  pl. ob·serv·a·to·ries

ob·serve
  ob·serv·a·ble
  ob·serv·er

ob·sess
  ob·ses·sive-com·pul·sive
  ob·ses·sive
  ob·ses·sive·ly
  ob·ses·sive·ness

ob·ses·sion
  ob·ses·sion·al
  ob·ses·sion·al·ly

ob·sid·i·an

ob·so·les·cent
  ob·so·les·cence

ob·so·lete

ob·sta·cle

ob·stet·rics
  ob·stet·ric
  ob·ste·tri·cian

ob·sti·nate
  ob·sti·na·cy
  ob·sti·nate·ly

ob·strep·er·ous
  ob·strep·er·ous·ly
  ob·strep·er·ous·ness

ob·struct
  ob·struc·tive
  ob·struc·tive·ness
  ob·struc·tor

ob·struc·tion
  ob·struc·tion·ist

ob·tain
  ob·tain·a·ble
  ob·tain·ment

ob·trude
  ob·tru·sion
  ob·tru·sive
  ob·tru·sive·ly
  ob·tru·sive·ness

ob·tuse
  ob·tuse·ly
  ob·tuse·ness

ob·verse

ob·vi·ate
  ob·vi·a·tion

ob·vi·ous
  ob·vi·ous·ly
  ob·vi·ous·ness

oc·a·ri·na

O'Ca·sey

oc·ca·sion

oc·ca·sion·al
  oc·ca·sion·al·ly

Oc·ci·dent
  oc·ci·den·tal

oc·ci·put
  oc·cip·i·tal

oc·clude
  oc·clu·sion
  oc·clu·sive

oc·cult

oc·cu·pant
  oc·cu·pan·cy
  pl. oc·cu·pan·cies

oc·cu·pa·tion
  oc·cu·pa·tion·al

oc·cu·py
  oc·cu·pies, oc·cu·pied

oc·cur
  oc·curred, oc·cur·ring

oc·cur·rence

o·cean
  o·ce·an·ic

o·cea·nar·i·um
  pl. o·cea·nar·i·ums or
  o·cea·nar·i·a

O·ce·an·i·a

o·cea·nog·ra·phy
  o·cea·nog·ra·pher
  o·cea·no·graph·ic
  o·cea·no·graph·i·cal

O·cean·side

oc·e·lot

o·cher
  also o·chre
  o·cher·ous

o'clock

O'Con·nell

O'Con·nor

oc·ta·gon
  oc·tag·o·nal

oc·ta·he·dron
  pl. oc·ta·he·drons or
  oc·ta·he·dra
  oc·ta·he·dral

oc·tane

oc·tave

Oc·ta·vi·an

oc·ta·vo
  pl. oc·ta·vos

oc·tet
  also oc·tette

Oc·to·ber

oc·to·ge·nar·i·an

oc·to·pus
  pl. oc·to·pus·es, oc·to·
  pi

oc·u·lar

oc·u·list

OD
  OD's, OD'd, OD'ing

odd
  odd·ly
  odd·ness

odd·ball

odd·i·ty
  pl. odd·i·ties

odds
  odds-on

ode

O·den·se

O·der Riv·er

O·des·sa

O·dets

o·di·ous
  o·di·ous·ly
  o·di·ous·ness

o·di·um

o·dom·e·ter

o·dor
  o·dor·less

o·dor·ant

o·dor·ous

o·dor·if·er·ous

od·ys·sey
  pl. od·ys·seys

Oed·i·pus
  Oed·i·pal
  also oed·i·pal

oe·no·phile

o'er (*over*; see OAR, OR, ORE)

oeu·vre

of

off
  off-key
  off-line
  off-load
  off-peak
  off-road
  off-season
  off-white

of·fal (*waste products*; see AWFUL)

off·beat

Of·fen·bach

of·fend
  of·fend·er
  of·fend·ing

of·fense

of·fen·sive
  of·fen·sive·ly
  of·fen·sive·ness

of·fer

of·fer·ing

of·fer·to·ry
  pl. of·fer·to·ries

off·hand
  off·hand·ed
  off·hand·ed·ly
  off·hand·ed·ness

of·fice

of·fi·cer

of·fi·cial
  of·fi·cial·dom
  of·fi·cial·ly

of·fi·ci·ate
  of·fi·ci·a·tion
  of·fi·ci·a·tor

of·fi·cious
  of·fi·cious·ly
  of·fi·cious·ness

off·ing

off·screen

off·set
  off·set·ting; *past and past part.* off·set

off·shoot

off·shore

off·side

off·spring
  pl. same

off·stage

oft

of·ten
  of·ten·er, of·ten·est

Og·bo·mo·sho

o·gle
  o·gler

O·gle·thorpe

o·gre
  fem. o·gress
  o·gre·ish

O'Hig·gins

O·hi·o
  O·hi·o·an

ohm

oil
  oil·er

oil·cloth

oil·skin

oil·stone

oil·y
  oil·i·er, oil·i·est
  oil·i·ness

oint·ment

O·jib·wa

OK
  also o·kay
  pl. OKs
  OK's, OK'd, OK'ing

O·ka·ya·ma

O·kee·cho·bee, Lake

O'Keeffe

O·ke·fe·no·kee Swamp

o·key·doke
  also o·key·do·key

O·khotsk

O·ki·na·wa

O·kla·ho·ma
  O·kla·ho·man

o·kra

old
  old·er, old·est
  old-boy
  old-time
  old-tim·er
  old·ish

old·en

Old Faith·ful

old-fash·ioned

old·ie

o·le·ag·i·nous

o•le•an•der

o•le•o•mar•ga•rine

ol•fac•to•ry

ol•i•garch

ol•i•gar•chy
  pl. ol•i•gar•chies
  ol•i•gar•chic
  ol•i•gar•chi•cal

ol•ive

O•liv•i•er

Ol•mec

Olm•sted

O•lym•pi•a

O•lym•pi•ad

O•lym•pi•an

O•lym•pic

O•lym•pus

O•ma•ha

O•man

O•mar Khay•yám

om•buds•man
  pl. om•buds•men

Om•dur•man

o•me•ga

om•e•lette
  also om•e•let

o•men

om•i•cron

om•i•nous
  om•i•nous•ly

o•mis•sion

o•mit
  o•mit•ted, o•mit•ting

om•ni•bus

om•nip•o•tent
  om•nip•o•tence

om•ni•pres•ent
  om•ni•pres•ence

om•nis•cient
  om•nis•cience

om•niv•o•rous
  om•ni•vore
  om•niv•o•rous•ly

Omsk

on
  on-line
  on-screen

O•nas•sis

once
  once-o•ver

on•co•gene

on•col•o•gy

on•com•ing

one
  one-horse
  one-on-one
  one-sid•ed
  one-way

O•nei•da

one•ness

on•er•ous
  on•er•ous•ness

one•self

one•time

on•go•ing

on•ion
  on•ion•y

on•look•er
  on•look•ing

on•ly

on•o•mas•tics

on•o•mat•o•poe•ia
  on•o•mat•o•poe•ic
  o•no•mat•o•po•et•ic

On•on•da•ga

on•rush

on•set

on•shore

on•side

on•slaught

on•stage

On•tar•i•o

on•to

on•tog•e•ny

on•tol•o•gy

o•nus
  pl. o•nus•es

on•ward
  also on•wards

on•yx

oo•dles

oo•long

oops

ooze
  ooz•y

o•pal
  o•pal•es•cence
  o•pal•es•cent

o•paque
  o•paqu•er, o•paqu•est
  o•pac•i•ty
  o•paque•ly
  o•paque•ness

op art

o•pen
  o•pen-end•ed
  o•pen-faced
  o•pen-heart•ed
  o•pen-heart sur•ger•y
  o•pen-mind•ed
  o•pen•er
  o•pen•ly
  o•pen•ness

o•pen•hand•ed

o•pen•ing

o•pen•work

op•er•a (*drama set to music*)
op•er•at•ic
op•er•at•i•cal•ly

o•pe•ra (*pl. of opus*)

op•er•a•ble

op•er•ate

op•er•a•tion

op•er•a•tion•al
op•er•a•tion•al•ly

op•er•a•tive

op•er•a•tor

op•er•et•ta

oph•thal•mic

oph•thal•mol•o•gy
oph•thal•mol•o•gist

o•pi•ate

o•pine

o•pin•ion

o•pin•ion•at•ed

o•pi•um

O•por•to
also Pôr•to

o•pos•sum

op•po•nent

op•por•tune

op•por•tun•ism
op•por•tun•ist
op•por•tun•is•tic
op•por•tun•is•ti•cal•ly

op•por•tu•ni•ty
pl. op•por•tu•ni•ties

op•pos•a•ble

op•pose
op•pos•er

op•po•site

op•po•si•tion

op•press
op•pres•sion
op•pres•sor

op•pres•sive
op•pres•sive•ly
op•pres•sive•ness

op•pro•bri•ous

op•pro•bri•um

opt

op•tic

op•ti•cal
op•ti•cal•ly

op•ti•cian

op•tics

op•ti•mal

op•ti•mism
op•ti•mist
op•ti•mis•tic
op•ti•mis•ti•cal•ly

op•ti•mize
op•ti•mi•za•tion

op•ti•mum
pl. op•ti•ma *or* op•ti•mums

op•tion

op•tion•al
op•tion•al•ly

op•tom•e•try
op•tom•e•trist

op•u•lent
op•u•lence

o•pus
pl. o•pe•ra *or* o•pus•es

or (*alternatively*; see OAR, O'ER, ORE)

or•a•cle
o•rac•u•lar

o•ral (*by the mouth*; see AURAL)
o•ral•ly

O•ran

Or•ange (*proper name*)

or•ange (*fruit*)

o•rang•u•tan

O•ran•je•stad

o•rate

o•ra•tion

or•a•tor

or•a•to•ri•o
pl. or•a•to•ri•os

or•a•to•ry
pl. or•a•to•ries
or•a•tor•i•cal

orb

or•bit
or•bit•al
or•bit•er

or•ca

or•chard

or•ches•tra
or•ches•tral

or•ches•trate
or•ches•tra•tion

or•chid

or•dain

or•deal

or•der

or•der•ly
pl. or•der•lies
or•der•li•ness

or·di·nal

or·di·nance

or·di·nar·y
  or·di·nar·i·ly
  or·di·nar·i·ness

or·di·nate

or·di·na·tion

ord·nance

or·dure

ore (metal; see OAR, O'ER, OR)

o·reg·a·no

Or·e·gon
  Or·e·go·ni·an

or·gan
  or·gan·ist

or·gan·dy
  also or·gan·die
  pl. or·gan·dies

or·gan·elle

or·gan·ic
  or·gan·i·cal·ly

or·gan·ism

or·gan·i·za·tion
  or·gan·i·za·tion·al

or·gan·ize
  or·gan·iz·er

or·gan·za

or·gasm
  or·gas·mic

or·gi·as·tic

or·gy
  pl. or·gies

o·ri·el

o·ri·ent
  also the O·ri·ent

o·ri·en·tal
  also O·ri·en·tal

o·ri·en·ta·tion
  o·ri·en·ta·tion·al

o·ri·en·teer·ing

or·i·fice

o·ri·ga·mi

or·i·gin

o·rig·i·nal
  o·rig·i·nal·i·ty
  o·rig·i·nal·ly

o·rig·i·nate
  o·rig·i·na·tion
  o·rig·i·na·tive
  o·rig·i·na·tor

O-ring

o·ri·ole

Ork·ney Is·lands

Or·lan·do

Or·lé·ans

Or·lon (trademark)

or·mo·lu

or·na·ment
  or·na·men·tal
  or·na·men·ta·tion

or·nate
  or·nate·ly
  or·nate·ness

or·ner·y
  or·ner·i·ness

or·ni·thol·o·gy
  or·ni·tho·log·i·cal
  or·ni·thol·o·gist

o·ro·tund

or·phan

or·phan·age

or·rer·y
  pl. or·rer·ies

or·tho·don·tics
  also or·tho·don·tia
  or·tho·don·tic
  or·tho·don·tist

or·tho·dox
  or·tho·dox·y

or·thog·ra·phy
  pl. or·thog·ra·phies
  or·tho·graph·ic

or·tho·pe·dics
  also or·tho·pae·dics
  or·tho·pe·dic
  or·tho·pe·dist

or·thot·ics

O·sage

O·sa·ka

os·cil·late
  os·cil·la·tion
  os·cil·la·tor

os·cil·lo·scope

os·cu·late

Osh·kosh

o·sier

Os·lo

os·mi·um

os·mo·sis
  os·mot·ic

os·prey
  pl. os·preys

os·si·fy
  os·si·fies, os·si·fied
  os·si·fi·ca·tion

os·so bu·co
  also os·so buc·co

os·su·ar·y
  pl. os·su·ar·ies

os·ten·si·ble
  os·ten·si·bly

os·ten·sive

os•ten•ta•tion
  os•ten•ta•tious
  os•ten•ta•tious•ly

os•te•o•ar•thri•tis
  os•te•o•ar•thrit•ic

os•te•op•a•thy
  os•te•o•path

os•te•o•po•ro•sis

os•tra•cize
  os•tra•cism

O•stra•va

os•trich

oth•er

oth•er•wise

oth•er•world•ly

o•ti•ose

o•ti•tis

Ot•ta•wa

ot•ter

ot•to•man

Oua•ga•dou•gou

ouch

ought (*expressing duty;* see AUGHT)

Oui•ja (*trademark*)

ounce

our (*of us;* see HOUR)

ours

our•selves

oust

oust•er

out

out•age

out•back

out•bal•ance

out•board

out•break

out•build•ing

out•burst

out•cast

out•class

out•come

out•crop

out•cry
  pl. out•cries

out•dat•ed

out•dis•tance

out•do

out•door

out•doors

out•er
  out•er•most

out•field
  out•field•er

out•fit
  out•fit•ted, out•fit•ting

out•fit•ter

out•flank

out•fox

out•go•ing

out•grow
  past out•grew; *past part.*
  out•grown

out•growth

out•house

out•ing

out•land•ish
  out•land•ishly
  out•land•ish•ness

out•last

out•law

out•lay

out•let

out•line

out•live

out•look

out•ly•ing

out•ma•neu•ver

out•mod•ed

out•pa•tient

out•place•ment

out•post

out•pour•ing

out•put
  out•put•ting; *past and*
  past part. out•put *or*
  out•put•ted

out•rage

out•ra•geous
  out•ra•geous•ly

ou•tré

out•rid•er

out•rig•ger

out•right
  out•right•ness

out•run
  out•run•ning; *past* out•
  ran; *past part.* out•run

out•sell
  past and past part. out•
  sold

out•set

out•shine
  past and past part. out•
  shone

out•side

out•sid•er

out•size

out•skirts

out•smart

out•spo•ken
  out•spo•ken•ly
  out•spo•ken•ness

out•spread

out•stand•ing
  out•stand•ing•ly

out•sta•tion

out•strip
  out•stripped, out•strip•
  ping

out•take

out•vote

out•ward
  also out•wards
  out•ward•ly

out•wear
  past out•wore; *past part.*
  out•worn

out•weigh

out•wit
  out•wit•ted, out•wit•
  ting

o•va

o•val

o•va•ry
  pl. o•va•ries
  o•var•i•an

o•va•tion

ov•en

o•ver
  o•ver-the-count•er

o•ver•a•bun•dance

o•ver•a•bun•dant

over•a•chieve
  o•ver•a•chieve•ment
  o•ver•a•chiev•er

o•ver•act

o•ver•act•ive

o•ver•all

o•ver•anx•ious

o•ver•arm

o•ver•awe

o•ver•bal•ance

o•ver•bear•ing

o•ver•bite

o•ver•blown

o•ver•board

o•ver•book

o•ver•bur•den

o•ver•came

o•ver•cast

o•ver•cau•tious

o•ver•charge

o•ver•coat

o•ver•come
  past o•ver•came; *past
  part.* o•ver•come

o•ver•con•fi•dence

o•ver•con•fi•dent

o•ver•cook

o•ver•crit•i•cal

o•ver•crowd

o•ver•crowd•ed

o•ver•crowd•ing

o•ver•de•vel•op

o•ver•do
  3rd sing. present o•ver•
  does; *past* o•ver•did;
  past part. o•ver•done

o•ver•dose

o•ver•draft

o•ver•draw
  past o•ver•drew; *past
  part.* o•ver•drawn

o•ver•drive

o•ver•dub
  o•ver•dubbed, o•ver•
  dub•bing

o•ver•due

o•ver•ea•ger

o•ver•eat

o•ver•em•pha•size

o•ver•en•thu•si•asm

o•ver•en•thu•si•as•tic

o•ver•en•thu•si•as•ti•
  cal•ly

o•ver•es•ti•mate
  o•ver•es•ti•ma•tion

o•ver•ex•cite

o•ver•ex•cite•ment

o•ver•ex•ert

o•ver•ex•er•tion

o•ver•ex•pose
  o•ver•ex•po•sure

o•ver•ex•tend

o•ver•fa•mil•iar

o•ver•feed

o•ver•flow

o•ver•fond

o•ver•full

o•ver•gen•er•ous

o•ver•grown

o•ver•hand

o•ver•hang
  past and past part.
  o•ver•hung

o•ver•haul

o•ver•head

o•ver•hear
 past and *past part.*
 o•ver•heard

o•ver•heat

o•ver•in•dulge

o•ver•in•dul•gence

o•ver•in•dul•gent

o•ver•in•flate

o•ver•in•fla•tion

o•ver•joyed

o•ver•kill

o•ver•land

o•ver•lap
 o•ver•lapped, o•ver•
 lap•ping

o•ver•lay
 past and *past part.*
 o•ver•laid

o•ver•leaf

o•ver•load

o•ver•look

o•ver•lord

o•ver•ly

o•ver•mas•ter

o•ver•much

o•ver•night

o•ver•par•tic•u•lar

o•ver•pass

o•ver•pay

o•ver•play

o•ver•pop•u•lat•ed
 o•ver•pop•u•la•tion

o•ver•pow•er
 o•ver•pow•er•ing
 o•ver•pow•er•ing•ly

o•ver•price

o•ver•print

o•ver•pro•duce
 o•ver•pro•duc•tion

o•ver•pro•tec•tive

o•ver•qual•i•fied

o•ver•rate

o•ver•reach

o•ver•re•act
 o•ver•re•ac•tion

o•ver•re•fined

o•ver•ride
 past o•ver•rode; *past
 part.* o•ver•rid•den

o•ver•ripe

o•ver•rule

o•ver•run
 o•ver•run•ning; *past*
 o•ver•ran; *past part.*
 o•ver•run

o•ver•seas

o•ver•see
 o•ver•sees; *past* o•ver•
 saw; *past part.* o•ver•
 seen
 o•ver•se•er

o•ver•sell

o•ver•sen•si•tive

o•ver•sen•si•tive•ness

o•ver•sen•si•tiv•i•ty

o•ver•shad•ow

o•ver•shoe

o•ver•shoot
 past and *past part.*
 o•ver•shot

o•ver•sight

o•ver•sim•pli•fy
 o•ver•sim•pli•fies,
 o•ver•sim•pli•fied
 o•ver•sim•pli•fi•ca•tion

o•ver•size
 also o•ver•sized

o•ver•sleep
 past and *past part.*
 o•ver•slept

o•ver•spe•cial•ize
 o•ver•spe•cial•i•za•tion

o•ver•spend

o•ver•spill

o•ver•spread

o•ver•state
 o•ver•state•ment

o•ver•stay

o•ver•steer

o•ver•step
 o•ver•stepped, o•ver•
 step•ping

o•ver•stim•u•late

o•ver•stock

o•ver•strung

o•ver•stuff

o•ver•sup•ply

o•vert
 o•vert•ly

o•ver•take
 past o•ver•took; *past
 part.* o•ver•tak•en

o•ver•tax

o•ver•throw
 past o•ver•threw; *past
 part.* o•ver•thrown

o•ver•time

o•ver•tire

o•ver•tone

o•ver•ture

o•ver•turn

o·ver·use

o·ver·view

o·ver·weight

o·ver·whelm
  o·ver·whelm·ing

o·ver·wind

o·ver·work

o·ver·wrought

o·vi·duct

O·vie·do

o·vine

o·vip·a·rous

o·void

o·vo·vi·vip·a·rous
  o·vo·vi·vi·par·i·ty

ov·u·late
  ov·u·la·tion

ov·ule
  ov·u·lar

o·vum
  pl. o·va

owe

ow·ing

owl
  owl·ish

owl·et

own
  own·er
  own·er·ship

ox
  pl. ox·en

ox·bow

Ox·ford

ox·i·da·tion

ox·ide

ox·i·dize
  ox·i·diz·er

Ox·nard

ox·tail

ox·y·a·cet·y·lene

ox·y·gen

ox·y·gen·ate
  ox·y·gen·a·tion

ox·y·mo·ron

oys·ter

O·zark

o·zone
  o·zone-friend·ly

P

pa

Pab·lum (*trademark*)

pab·u·lum

pace
  paced (*past of pace;* see
    PASTE)
  pac·er

pace·mak·er

pace·set·ter

Pa·chu·ca

pach·y·derm

pach·y·san·dra

pa·cif·ic
  pa·cif·i·cal·ly

Pa·cif·ic O·cean

pac·i·fi·er

pac·i·fism
  pac·i·fist

pac·i·fy
  pac·i·fies, pac·i·fied
  pac·i·fi·ca·tion

pack
  pack·a·ble
  pack·er

pack·age
  pack·ag·er

pack·ag·ing

pack·et

pack·ing

pact

pad
  pad·ded, pad·ding

Pa·dang

pad·ding

pad·dle
  pad·dler

pad·dle·ball

pad·dock

pad·dy
  pl. pad·dies

pad·lock

pa·dre

Pad·u·a

pae·an (*hymn;* see PEON)

pa·el·la

pa·gan
  pa·gan·ish
  pa·gan·ism
  pa·gan·ize

page

pag·eant

pag·eant·ry
  pl. pag·eant·ries

pag·er

pag·i·nate
  pag·i·na·tion

pa·go·da

Pa·go Pa·go

paid

pail (*bucket;* see PALE)
  pail·ful
  pl. pail·fuls

pain (*hurt;* see PANE)
  pain·ful
  pain·ful·ly
  pain·ful·ness

pain·kill·er
  pain·kill·ing

pain·less
  pain·less·ly
  pain·less·ness

pains·tak·ing
  pains·tak·ing·ly

paint
  paint·a·ble

paint·er

paint·ing

pair (*two;* see PARE, PEAR)

Pais·ley
  also pais·ley

Pai·ute
  also Pi·ute

pa·ja·mas

Pa·ki·stan
  Pa·ki·stan·i

pal

pal·ace

pal·at·a·ble
  pal·at·a·bil·i·ty
  pal·at·a·ble·ness
  pal·at·a·bly

pal·a·tal
  pal·a·tal·ize
  pal·a·tal·i·za·tion
  pal·a·tal·ly

pal·ate (*taste;* see
  PALETTE, PALLET)

pa·la·tial
  pa·la·tial·ly

Pa·lat·i·nate

pal·a·tine
  also Palatine

pa·lav·er

pale (*white;* see PAIL)
  pale·ly

pale·ness
pal·ish

pale·face

Pa·lem·bang

pa·le·og·ra·phy
pa·le·og·ra·pher
pa·le·o·graph·ic
pa·le·o·graph·i·cal
pa·le·o·graph·i·cal·ly

pa·le·o·lith·ic

pa·le·on·tol·o·gy
pa·le·on·to·log·i·cal
pa·le·on·tol·o·gist

Pa·le·o·zo·ic

Pa·ler·mo

Pal·es·tine
Pal·es·tin·i·an

pal·ette (*artist's board*;
   see PALATE, PALLET)

pal·frey

pal·i·mo·ny

pa·limp·sest

pal·in·drome
pal·in·drom·ic
pa·lin·dro·mist

pal·ing

pal·i·sade

pall (*covering*; see PAWL)

pal·la·di·um
   pl. pal·la·di·a

pall·bear·er

pal·let (*bed*; see PALATE,
   PALETTE)

pal·let (*platform*; see
   PALATE, PALETTE)
   pal·let·ize

pal·li·ate
   pal·li·a·tion
   pal·li·a·tive

pal·li·a·tive·ly
pal·li·a·tor

pal·lid
   pal·lid·ly
   pal·lid·ness

pal·lor

palm (*part of hand*)
   pal·mar
   palmed
   palm·ful
   pl. palm·fuls

palm (*tree*)
   pal·ma·ceous

Pal·ma
   also Pal·ma de Ma·
   llor·ca

pal·mate

pal·met·to

palm·ist·ry
   palm·ist

palm·y
   palm·i·er, palm·i·est

Pal·o Al·to

pal·o·mi·no

pal·pa·ble
   pal·pa·bil·i·ty
   pal·pa·bly

pal·pate
   pal·pa·tion

pal·pi·tate
   pal·pi·tant
   pal·pi·ta·tion

pal·sy
   pl. pal·sies
   pal·sies, pal·sied

pal·try
   pal·tri·er, pal·tri·est
   pal·tri·ness

pam·pas

pam·per
   pam·per·er

pam·phlet
   pam·phlet·eer

Pam·plo·na

pan
   panned, pan·ning
   pan·ful
   pl. pan·fuls
   pan·like

pan·a·ce·a
   pan·a·ce·an

pa·nache

Pan·a·ma (*country*)
   Pa·na·ma·ni·an

pan·a·ma (*hat*)

pan·cake

Pan·chi·ao

pan·chro·mat·ic

pan·cre·as
   pan·cre·at·ic
   pan·cre·a·ti·tis

pan·da

pan·dem·ic

pan·de·mo·ni·um

pan·der
   also pan·der·er

Pan·do·ra

pane (*glass*; see PAIN)

pan·e·gy·ric
   pan·e·gy·ri·cal

pan·el

pan·el·ing

pan·el·ist

pang

pan·han·dle
   pan·han·dler

pan·ic
  pan·icked, pan·ick·ing
  pan·ic-strick·en
  pan·ic-struck
  pan·ick·y

pan·nier

pan·o·ply
  pl. pan·o·plies
  pan·o·plied

pan·o·ra·ma
  pan·o·ram·ic
  pan·o·ram·i·cal·ly

pan·sy
  pl. pan·sies

pant
  pant·ing·ly

pan·ta·loon

pan·the·ism
  pan·the·ist
  pan·the·is·tic
  pan·the·is·ti·cal
  pan·the·is·ti·cal·ly

pan·the·on

pan·ther

pant·ies

pan·to·mime
  pan·to·mim·ic

pan·try
  pl. pan·tries

pants

pant·suit
  also pants suit

pant·yhose
  also pant·y hose

pant·y·waist

pap
  pap·py

pa·pa

pa·pa·cy
  pl. pa·pa·cies

Pap·a·go

pa·pal
  pa·pal·ly

pa·paw
  var. of paw·paw

pa·pa·ya

pa·per
  pa·per·er
  pa·per·less
  pa·per·y

pa·per·back

pa·per·bound

pa·per·boy
  fem. pa·per·girl

pa·per·weight

pa·per·work

pa·pier mâ·ché

pa·pil·la
  pl. pa·pil·lae
  pap·il·lar·y
  pap·il·lose

pa·poose

pa·pri·ka

Pap smear

Pap·u·a New Guin·ea

pa·py·rus
  pl. pa·py·ri

par

par·a-a·mi·no·ben·zo·ic acid

par·a·ble

pa·rab·o·la

par·a·bol·ic
  par·a·bol·i·cal·ly

par·a·chute
  par·a·chut·ist

pa·rade
  pa·rad·er

par·a·digm
  par·a·dig·mat·ic
  par·a·dig·mat·i·cal·ly

par·a·dise
  also Par·a·dise
  par·a·di·sa·i·cal

par·a·dox
  par·a·dox·i·cal
  par·a·dox·i·cal·ly

par·af·fin

par·a·gon

par·a·graph
  par·a·graph·ic

Par·a·guay
  Par·a·guay·an

par·a·keet

par·a·le·gal

par·al·lax
  par·al·lac·tic

par·al·lel
  par·al·lel·ism

par·al·lel·o·gram

pa·ral·y·sis
  pl. pa·ral·y·ses
  par·a·lyt·ic
  par·a·lyt·i·cal·ly

par·a·lyze
  par·a·ly·za·tion
  par·a·lyz·ing·ly

Par·a·mar·i·bo

par·a·me·ci·um

par·a·med·ic

par·a·med·i·cal

pa·ram·e·ter
  pa·ra·met·ric
  pa·ram·e·trize

par·a·mil·i·tar·y

par·a·mount
  par·a·mount·ly

par·a·mour

par·a·noi·a
par·a·noi·ac
par·a·noid

par·a·nor·mal
par·a·nor·mal·ly

par·a·pet
par·a·pet·ed

par·a·pher·na·lia

par·a·phrase
par·a·phras·tic

par·a·ple·gi·a
par·a·ple·gic

par·a·psy·chol·o·gy
par·a·psy·cho·log·i·cal
par·a·psy·chol·o·gist

par·a·quat

par·a·site
par·a·sit·ic
par·a·sit·i·cal
par·a·sit·i·cal·ly
par·a·si·tol·o·gy
par·a·si·tol·o·gist

par·a·sol

par·a·sym·pa·thet·ic

par·a·thy·roid

par·a·troops
par·a·troop·er

par·boil

par·cel

parch

Par·chee·si (*trademark*)

parch·ment

par·don
par·don·a·ble
par·don·a·bly

pare (*trim*; see PAIR, PEAR)
par·er

par·ent
pa·ren·tal
pa·ren·tal·ly
par·ent·hood

par·ent·age

pa·ren·the·sis
pl. pa·ren·the·ses

par·en·thet·ic
par·en·thet·i·cal
par·en·thet·i·cal·ly

par·ent·ing

pa·re·ve

par ex·cel·lence

par·fait

pa·ri·ah

pa·ri·e·tal

par·i·mu·tu·el

par·ing

Par·is
Pa·ri·sian

par·ish (*church area*; see PERISH)

pa·rish·ion·er

par·i·ty

park

par·ka

Par·kin·son's dis·ease
also Par·kin·son·ism

Par·kin·son's law

park·way

par·lance

par·lay

par·ley

par·lia·ment

par·lia·men·tar·i·an

par·lia·men·ta·ry

par·lor

Par·ma

Par·me·san

par·mi·gia·na
also par·mi·gia·no

pa·ro·chi·al
pa·ro·chi·al·ism
pa·ro·chi·al·ly

par·o·dy
pl. par·o·dies
par·o·dies, par·o·died
pa·rod·ic
par·o·dist

pa·role
pa·rol·ee

par·ox·ysm
par·ox·ys·mal

par·quet

par·quet·ry

par·ri·cide
par·ri·ci·dal

par·rot

par·ry
pl. par·ries
par·ries, par·ried

parse
pars·er

par·sec

par·si·mo·ny
par·si·mo·ni·ous
par·si·mo·ni·ous·ly

pars·ley

pars·nip

par·son
par·son·i·cal

par·son·age

part
part-time
part-tim·er

par•take
  past par•took; *past part.*
  par•taken
  par•tak•a•ble
  par•tak•er

par•terre

par•the•no•gen•e•sis
  par•the•no•ge•net•ic
  par•the•no•ge•net•i•
  cal•ly

par•tial
  par•ti•al•i•ty
  par•tial•ly

par•tic•i•pate
  par•tic•i•pa•tion
  par•tic•i•pant
  par•tic•i•pa•tor
  par•tic•i•pa•to•ry

par•ti•ci•ple
  par•ti•cip•i•al
  par•ti•cip•i•al•ly

par•ti•cle

par•ti•cle•board

par•ti•col•ored

par•tic•u•lar
  par•tic•u•lar•i•ty

par•tic•u•lar•ize
  par•tic•u•lar•i•za•tion

par•tic•u•lar•ly

par•tic•u•late

part•ing

par•ti•san
  also par•ti•zan
  par•ti•san•ship

par•ti•tion
  par•ti•tioned
  par•ti•tion•er
  par•ti•tion•ist

par•ti•tive

part•ly

part•ner
  part•ner•less
  part•ner•ship

par•took

par•tridge
  pl. same *or* par•tridg•es

par•tu•ri•tion

par•ty
  pl. par•ties
  par•ties, par•tied

par•ve•nu
  fem. par•ve•nue

Pas•a•de•na

pas•chal

pa•sha
  also pa•cha

pass
  past part. passed (*see*
  PAST)
  pass•er

pass•a•ble
  pass•a•bly

pas•sage

pas•sage•way

pass•book

pas•sé

pas•sen•ger

pas•ser•by
  pl. pas•sers•by

pas•sim

pass•ing
  pass•ing•ly

pas•sion
  pas•sion•less

pas•sion•ate
  pas•sion•ate•ly

pas•sive
  pas•sive•ly
  pas•sive•ness
  pas•siv•i•ty

pass•key

Pass•o•ver

pass•port

pass•word

past (*gone by;* see *passed*
  [PASS])

pas•ta

paste (*glue;* see *paced*
  [PACE])
  past•ing

paste•board

pas•tel
  pas•tel•ist

pas•tern

pas•teur•ize
  pas•teur•i•za•tion
  pas•teur•iz•er

pas•tiche

pas•tille
  also pas•til

pas•time

pas•tor
  pas•tor•ate
  pas•tor•ship

pas•to•ral
  pas•to•ral•ism
  pas•to•ral•ly

pas•tra•mi

pas•try
  pl. pas•tries

pas•tur•age

pas•ture

past•y
  past•i•er, past•i•est
  past•i•ly
  past•i•ness

pat (*known thoroughly*)
  pat•ly
  pat•ness

pat (*touch*)
  pat•ted, pat•ting

patch
  patch•er

patch•ou•li

patch•work

patch•y
  patch•i•er, patch•i•est
  patch•i•ly
  patch•i•ness

pate (*head*)

pâ•té (*food paste*)

pâ•té de foie gras
  pl. pâ•tés de foie gras

pa•tel•la
  pl. pa•tel•lae
  pa•tel•lar
  pa•tel•late

pat•ent
  pa•ten•cy
  pat•ent•a•ble
  pat•ent•ly

pa•ter•nal
  pa•ter•nal•ly

pa•ter•nal•ism
  pa•ter•nal•ist
  pa•ter•nal•is•tic
  pa•ter•nal•is•ti•cal•ly

pa•ter•ni•ty

pa•ter•nos•ter

Pat•er•son

path
  pl. paths
  path•less

pa•thet•ic
  pa•thet•i•cal•ly

path•o•gen
  path•o•gen•ic

path•o•log•i•cal
  path•o•log•i•cal•ly

pa•thol•o•gy
  pa•thol•o•gist

pa•thos

path•way

pa•tience

pa•tient
  pa•tient•ly

pa•ti•na
  pl. pa•ti•nas
  pat•i•nat•ed
  pat•i•na•tion

pat•i•o

Pat•na

pa•tois
  pl. same

pa•tri•arch
  pa•tri•ar•chal
  pa•tri•ar•chal•ly

pa•tri•arch•ate

pa•tri•ar•chy
  pl. pa•tri•ar•chies

pa•tri•cian

pat•ri•cide

pat•ri•mo•ny
  pl. pat•ri•mo•nies
  pat•ri•mo•ni•al

pa•tri•ot
  pa•tri•ot•ic
  pa•tri•ot•i•cal•ly
  pa•tri•o•tism

pa•trol
  pa•trolled, pa•trol•ling
  pa•trol•ler

pa•trol•man
  pl. pa•trol•men

pa•tron
  fem. pa•tron•ess

pa•tron•age

pa•tron•ize
  pa•tron•i•za•tion

pa•tron•iz•er
pa•tron•iz•ing
pa•tron•iz•ing•ly

pat•ro•nym•ic

pat•sy
  pl. pat•sies

pat•ter

pat•tern

pat•ty
  pl. pat•ties

pau•ci•ty

paunch
  paunch•y
  paunch•i•er, paunch•
    i•est
  paunch•i•ness

pau•per
  pau•per•ism
  pau•per•ize
  pau•per•i•za•tion

pause

pave
  pav•er
  pav•ing

pave•ment

pa•vil•ion

Pav•lo•vi•an

paw

pawl (*lever;* see PALL)

pawn

pawn•brok•er
  pawn•brok•ing

Paw•nee

pawn•shop

paw•paw
  also pa•paw

pay
  past and *past part.* paid
  pay•ee
  pay•er

pay·a·ble

pay·day

pay·load

pay·mas·ter

pay·ment

pay·off

pay·o·la

pay·roll

pea

peace (*quiet*; see PIECE)

peace·a·ble
  peace·a·ble·ness
  peace·a·bly

peace·ful
  peace·ful·ly
  peace·ful·ness

peace·mak·er
  peace·mak·ing

peace·time

peach
  peach·y
  peach·i·er, peach·i·est
  peach·i·ness

pea·coat

pea·cock

pea·fowl

pea·hen

pea jack·et

peak (*top*; see PEEK, PIQUE)
  peaked
  peak·i·ness

peal (*ring*; see PEEL)

pea·nut

pear (*fruit*; see PAIR, PARE)

pearl (*gem*; see PURL)
  pearl·er
  pearl·y

Pearl Har·bor

peas·ant
  peas·ant·ry
  pl. peas·ant·ries

peat
  peat·y

peat·bog

peat·moss

peb·ble
  peb·bly

pe·can

pec·ca·dil·lo
  pl. pec·ca·dil·loes *or*
  pec·ca·dil·los

peck

pec·tin
  pec·tic

pec·to·ral

pec·u·late
  pec·u·la·tion
  pec·u·la·tor

pe·cu·liar
  pe·cu·liar·ly

pe·cu·li·ar·i·ty
  pl. pe·cu·li·ar·i·ties

pe·cu·ni·ar·y
  pe·cu·ni·ar·i·ly

ped·a·gogue
  also ped·a·gog
  ped·a·gog·ic
  ped·a·gog·i·cal
  ped·a·gog·i·cal·ly
  ped·a·gog·ism
  also ped·a·gogu·ism

ped·a·go·gy
  ped·a·gog·ics

ped·al (*foot lever*; see PEDDLE)

ped·ant
  pe·dan·tic
  pe·dan·ti·cal·ly
  ped·ant·ry
  pl. ped·ant·ries

ped·dle (*sell*; see PEDAL)
  ped·dler
  ped·dler·y

ped·er·as·ty
  ped·er·ast

ped·es·tal

pe·des·tri·an
  pe·des·tri·an·ism
  pe·des·tri·an·ize

pe·di·at·rics
  pe·di·at·ric
  pe·di·a·tri·cian

ped·i·cure

ped·i·gree
  ped·i·greed

ped·i·ment
  ped·i·men·tal
  ped·i·ment·ed

pe·dom·e·ter

pe·dun·cle
  pe·dun·cu·lar
  pe·dun·cu·late

peek (*look*; see PEAK, PIQUE)

peel (*skin*; see PEAL)
  peel·er

peel·ing

peen

peep

peep·hole

peer (*look*; see PIER)

peer (*person*; see PIER)
  fem. peer·ess
  peer·age
  peer·less

peeve

peev·ish
  pee·vish·ly
  pee·vish·ness

peg
  pegged, peg·ging

peg·board

peign·oir

pe·jo·ra·tive
  pe·jo·ra·tive·ly

Pe·king
  also Bei·jing

Pe·king·ese
  also Pe·kin·ese
  pl. same

pe·koe

pe·lag·ic

pelf

pel·i·can

pel·la·gra
  pel·la·grous

pel·let
  pel·let·ize

pell-mell

pel·lu·cid
  pel·lu·cid·i·ty
  pel·lu·cid·ly

pelt (*hide*)
  pelt·ry

pelt (*strike repeatedly*)

pel·vic

pel·vis
  pl. pel·vis·es *or* pel·ves

pen
  penned, pen·ning

pe·nal
  pe·nal·ly

pe·nal·ize
  pe·nal·i·za·tion

pen·al·ty
  pl. pen·al·ties

pen·ance

pen·chant

pen·cil
  pen·ciled, pen·cil·ing;
  pen·cilled, pen·cil·
  ling
  pen·cil·er

pend·ant (*jewel*; see
  PENDENT)
  also pend·ent

pend·ent (*hanging*; see
  PENDANT)
  also pend·ant
  pen·den·cy

pend·ing

pen·du·lous
  pen·du·lous·ly

pen·du·lum

pen·e·trate
  pen·e·tra·ble
  pen·e·tra·bil·i·ty
  pen·e·trant
  pen·e·trat·ing·ly
  pen·e·tra·tion
  pen·e·tra·tive
  pen·e·tra·tor

pen·guin

pen·i·cil·lin

pen·in·su·la
  pen·in·su·lar

pe·nis
  pl. pe·nis·es *or* pe·nes
  pe·nile

pen·i·tent
  pen·i·tence
  pen·i·ten·tial
  pen·i·ten·tial·ly
  pen·i·tent·ly

pen·i·ten·tia·ry
  pl. pen·i·ten·tia·ries

pen·knife

pen·light

pen·man·ship

pen·nant

pen·ni·less
  pen·ni·less·ly
  pen·ni·less·ness

pen·non
  pen·noned

Penn·syl·va·nia
  Penn·syl·va·nian

pen·ny
  pl. pen·nies
  pen·ny-pinch·er
  pen·ny-pinch·ing

pen·ny·weight

Pe·nob·scot

pe·nol·o·gy
  pe·no·log·i·cal
  pe·nol·o·gist

Pen·sa·co·la

pen·sion
  pen·sion·a·ble
  pen·sion·er
  pen·sion·less

pen·sive
  pen·sive·ly
  pen·sive·ness

pent

pen·ta·cle

pen·ta·gon
  pen·tag·o·nal

pen·ta·gram

pen·tam·e·ter

Pen·ta·teuch
  Pen·ta·teuch·al

pen·tath·lon
  pen·tath·lete

Pen·te·cost
Pen·te·cos·tal
also pen·te·cos·tal
Pen·te·cos·tal·ism
Pen·te·cos·tal·ist

pent·house

Pen·to·thal (*trademark*)

pen·ul·ti·mate

pen·um·bra
pl. pen·um·brae *or* pen·um·bras
pen·um·bral

pe·nu·ri·ous
pe·nu·ri·ous·ly
pe·nu·ri·ous·ness

pen·u·ry
pl. pen·u·ries

pe·on (*drudge*; see PAEON)
pe·on·age

pe·o·ny
pl. pe·o·nies

peo·ple

Pe·o·ri·a

pep
pepped, pep·ping

pep·per

pep·per·corn

pep·per·mint
pep·per·mint·y

pep·per·o·ni

pep·per·y
pep·per·i·ness

pep·py
pep·pi·er, pep·pi·est
pep·pi·ly
pep·pi·ness

pep·sin

pep·tic

Pe·quot

per (*for, by*; see PURR)

per·ad·ven·ture

per·am·bu·late
per·am·bu·la·tion
per·am·bu·la·to·ry

per an·num

per·cale

per cap·i·ta

per·ceive
per·ceiv·a·ble
per·ceiv·er

per·cent
also per cent

per·cent·age

per·cen·tile

per·cep·ti·ble
per·cep·ti·bil·i·ty
per·cep·ti·bly

per·cep·tion
per·cep·tion·al
per·cep·tu·al
per·cep·tu·al·ly

per·cep·tive
per·cep·tive·ly
per·cep·tive·ness
per·cep·tiv·i·ty

per·cep·tu·al

perch (*fish*)
pl. same *or* perch·es

perch (*roost*)

per·chance

per·cip·i·ent

per·co·late
per·co·la·tion

per·co·la·tor

per·cus·sion
per·cus·sion·ist
per·cus·sive
per·cus·sive·ly
per·cus·sive·ness

per di·em

per·di·tion

per·e·gri·nate
per·e·gri·na·tion
per·e·gri·na·tor

per·e·grine

pe·remp·to·ry
pe·remp·to·ri·ly
pe·remp·to·ri·ness

per·en·ni·al
per·en·ni·al·ly

per·e·stroi·ka

per·fect
per·fect·er
per·fect·i·ble
per·fect·i·bil·i·ty
per·fect·ly
per·fect·ness

per·fec·ta

per·fec·tion

per·fec·tion·ism
per·fec·tion·ist

per·fi·dy
per·fid·i·ous
per·fid·i·ous·ly

per·fo·rate
per·fo·ra·tion
per·fo·ra·tive
per·fo·ra·tor

per·force

per·form
per·form·a·ble
per·form·er
per·form·ing

per·for·mance

per·form·ing arts

per·fume
per·fum·y

per·fum·er
per·fum·er·y
pl. per·fum·er·ies

per·func·to·ry
  per·func·to·ri·ly
  per·func·to·ri·ness

per·go·la

per·haps

per·i·car·di·um
  pl. per·i·car·di·a
  per·i·car·di·ac
  per·i·car·di·al
  per·i·car·di·tis

per·i·gee
  per·i·ge·an

per·i·he·li·on
  pl. per·i·he·li·a

per·il

per·il·ous
  per·il·ous·ly
  per·il·ous·ness

pe·rim·e·ter

per·i·ne·um
  per·i·ne·al

pe·ri·od

pe·ri·od·ic
  pe·ri·o·dic·i·ty

pe·ri·od·i·cal
  pe·ri·od·i·cal·ly

per·i·o·don·tics
  per·i·o·don·tal
  per·i·o·don·tist

per·i·pa·tet·ic
  per·i·pa·tet·i·cal·ly
  per·i·pa·tet·i·cism

pe·riph·er·al
  pe·riph·er·al·ly

pe·riph·er·y
  pl. pe·riph·er·ies

pe·riph·ra·sis
  pl. pe·riph·ra·ses
  per·i·phras·tic
  per·i·phras·ti·cal·ly

per·i·scope
  per·i·scop·ic
  per·i·scop·i·cal·ly

per·ish (*be destroyed*; see PARISH)

per·ish·a·ble
  per·ish·a·bil·i·ty
  per·ish·a·ble·ness

per·i·to·ne·um
  pl. per·i·to·ne·ums *or*
  per·i·to·ne·a
  per·i·to·ne·al

per·i·to·ni·tis

per·i·wig
  per·i·wigged

per·i·win·kle

per·jure
  per·jur·er

per·ju·ry
  pl. per·ju·ries
  per·ju·ri·ous

perk

perk·y
  perk·i·er, perk·i·est
  perk·i·ly
  perk·i·ness

Perm (*city*)

perm (*permanent*)

per·ma·frost

per·ma·nent
  per·ma·nence
  per·ma·nen·cy
  per·ma·nent·ly

per·me·a·ble

per·me·ate
  per·me·ance
  per·me·ant
  per·me·a·tion
  per·me·a·tor

per·mis·si·ble
  per·mis·si·bil·i·ty
  per·mis·si·bly

per·mis·sion

per·mis·sive
  per·mis·sive·ly
  per·mis·sive·ness

per·mit
  per·mit·ted, per·mit·
  ting
  per·mit·tee
  per·mit·ter

per·mu·ta·tion
  per·mu·ta·tion·al

per·ni·cious
  per·ni·cious·ly
  per·ni·cious·ness

per·o·ra·tion

Pe·rot

per·ox·ide

per·pen·dic·u·lar
  per·pen·dic·u·lar·i·ty
  per·pen·dic·u·lar·ly

per·pe·trate
  per·pe·tra·tion
  per·pe·tra·tor

per·pet·u·al
  per·pet·u·al·ly

per·pet·u·ate
  per·pet·u·ance
  per·pet·u·a·tion
  per·pet·u·a·tor

per·pe·tu·i·ty
  pl. per·pe·tu·i·ties

per·plex
  per·plex·ed·ly
  per·plex·ing
  per·plex·ing·ly

per·plex·i·ty
  pl. per·plex·i·ties

per·qui·site

Per·ry

per se

per•se•cute
  per•se•cu•tion
  per•se•cu•tor
  per•se•cu•to•ry

per•se•vere
  per•se•ver•ance

Per•shing

Per•sia
  Per•sian

per•si•flage

per•sim•mon

per•sist

per•sist•ent
  per•sist•ence
  per•sist•en•cy
  per•sist•ent•ly

per•snick•et•y

per•son

per•so•na
  pl. per•so•nae

per•son•a•ble
  per•son•a•ble•ness
  per•son•a•bly

per•son•age

per•son•al

per•son•al•i•ty
  pl. per•son•al•i•ties

per•son•al•ize
  per•son•al•i•za•tion

per•son•al•ly

per•so•na non gra•ta

per•son•i•fy
  per•son•i•fies, per•son•i•fied
  per•son•i•fi•ca•tion
  per•son•i•fi•er

per•son•nel

per•spec•tive
  per•spec•tiv•al
  per•spec•tive•ly

per•spi•ca•cious
  per•spi•ca•cious•ly
  per•spi•cac•i•ty

per•spic•u•ous
  per•spi•cu•i•ty
  per•spic•u•ous•ly
  per•spic•u•ous•ness

per•spi•ra•tion
  per•spi•ra•to•ry

per•spire

per•suade
  per•suad•a•ble
  per•suad•a•bil•i•ty
  per•sua•si•ble

per•sua•sion

per•sua•sive
  per•sua•sive•ly
  per•sua•sive•ness

pert
  pert•ly
  pert•ness

per•tain

Perth

per•ti•na•cious
  per•ti•na•cious•ly
  per•ti•nac•i•ty

per•ti•nent
  per•ti•nence
  per•ti•nen•cy
  per•ti•nent•ly

per•turb
  per•turb•a•ble
  per•tur•ba•tion
  per•tur•ba•tive
  per•turb•ing•ly

per•tus•sis

Pe•ru
  Pe•ru•vi•an

pe•ruke

pe•ruse
  pe•rus•al
  pe•rus•er

per•vade
  per•va•sion

per•va•sive
  per•va•sive•ly
  per•va•sive•ness

per•verse
  per•verse•ly
  per•verse•ness
  per•ver•si•ty
  pl. per•ver•si•ties

per•ver•sion

per•vert
  per•ver•sive
  per•vert•ed•ly
  per•vert•er

Pe•sha•war

Pesh•kov

pes•ky
  pes•ki•er, pes•ki•est
  pesk•i•ly
  pesk•i•ness

pe•so

pes•si•mism
  pes•si•mist
  pes•si•mis•tic
  pes•si•mis•ti•cal•ly

pest

pes•ter
  pes•ter•er

pes•ti•cide
  pes•ti•cid•al

pes•tif•er•ous

pes•ti•lence

pes•ti•lent
  pes•ti•lent•ly

pes•ti•len•tial
  pes•ti•len•tial•ly

pes•tle

pes•to

pet
  pet·ted, pet·ting
  pet·ter

Pé·tain

pet·al
  pet·al·ine
  pet·alled
  pet·al·like
  pet·al·oid

pe·tard

pe·ter

Pe·ter·sen

Pe·ter·son

pet·it four
  pl. pet·its fours

pe·tite

pe·ti·tion
  pe·ti·tion·a·ble
  pe·ti·tion·ar·y
  pe·ti·tion·er

pet·it point

Pe·trarch
  Pe·trarch·an

pet·rel (bird; see PETROL)

Pe·tri dish

pet·ri·fy
  pet·ri·fies, pet·ri·fied
  pet·ri·fac·tion

pet·ro·chem·i·cal

pet·ro·dol·lar

pet·rol (gasoline; see
  PETREL)

pe·tro·le·um

pet·ti·coat
  pet·ti·coat·ed
  pet·ti·coat·less

pet·ti·fog
  pet·ti·fogged, pet·ti·
  fog·ging
  pet·ti·fog·ger

pet·ti·fog·ger·y
  pet·ti·fog·ging

pet·tish
  pet·tish·ly
  pet·tish·ness

pet·ty
  pet·ti·er, pet·ti·est
  pet·ti·ly
  pet·ti·ness

pet·u·lant
  pet·u·lance
  pet·u·lant·ly

pe·tu·nia

pew
  pew·less

pew·ter
  pew·ter·er

pe·yo·te

phag·o·cyte
  phag·o·cyt·ic

pha·lanx
  pl. pha·lanx·es or pha·
  lan·ges

phal·lus
  pl. phal·li or phal·lus·es
  phal·lic
  phal·li·cal·ly
  phal·li·cism

phan·tasm
  phan·tas·mal
  phan·tas·mic

phan·tas·ma·go·ri·a
  phan·tas·ma·gor·ic
  phan·tas·ma·gor·i·cal

phan·tom

Phar·aoh (ruler; see
  FARO)
  Phar·a·on·ic

Phar·i·see
  also phar·i·see
  Phar·i·sa·ic
  Phar·i·sa·i·cal
  Phar·i·sa·ism

phar·ma·ceu·ti·cal
  phar·ma·ceu·ti·cal·ly
  phar·ma·ceu·tics

phar·ma·cist

phar·ma·col·o·gy
  phar·ma·co·log·i·cal
  phar·ma·co·log·i·cal·ly
  phar·ma·col·o·gist

phar·ma·co·poe·ia
  phar·ma·co·poe·ial

phar·ma·cy
  pl. phar·ma·cies

phar·ynx
  pl. pha·ryn·ges
  pha·ryn·gal
  pha·ryn·ge·al
  phar·yn·gi·tis

phase (stage; see FAZE)
  pha·sic

pheas·ant

phe·no·bar·bi·tal

phe·nol
  phe·no·lic

phe·nom·e·nal
  phe·nom·e·nal·ly

phe·nom·e·non
  pl. phe·nom·e·na

pher·o·mone
  pher·o·mo·nal

phi

phi·al (vial; see FILE)

Phid·i·as

Phil·a·del·phi·a

phi·lan·der
  phi·lan·der·er

phil·an·throp·ic
  phil·an·throp·i·cal·ly

phi·lan·thro·py
  phi·lan·thro·pist
  phi·lan·thro·pize

phi•lat•e•ly
  phil•a•tel•ic
  phil•a•tel•i•cal•ly
  phi•lat•e•list

phil•har•mon•ic

phi•lip•pic

Phil•ip•pines

Phil•is•tine
  phil•is•tin•ism

Phil•lips

phil•o•den•dron
  pl. phil•o•den•drons *or*
  phil•o•den•dra

phi•lol•o•gy
  phil•o•lo•gi•an
  phi•lol•o•gist
  phil•o•log•i•cal
  phil•o•log•i•cal•ly

phi•los•o•pher

phil•o•soph•i•cal
  also phil•o•soph•ic
  phil•o•soph•i•cal•ly

phi•los•o•phize
  phi•los•o•phiz•er

phi•los•o•phy
  pl. phi•los•o•phies

phil•ter (*potion;* see
  FILTER)

phle•bi•tis
  phle•bit•ic

phlegm
  phlegm•y

phleg•mat•ic
  phleg•mat•i•cal•ly

phlo•em

phlox

Phnom Penh

pho•bi•a
  pho•bic

phoe•be

Phoe•nix (*city*)

phoe•nix (*bird*)

phone

pho•neme
  pho•ne•mic
  pho•ne•mics

pho•net•ic
  pho•net•i•cal•ly
  pho•net•i•cize

pho•net•ics
  pho•ne•ti•cian

phon•ic
  phon•i•cal•ly

pho•no•graph

pho•nol•o•gy
  pho•no•log•i•cal
  pho•no•log•i•cal•ly
  pho•nol•o•gist

pho•ny
  also pho•ney
  pho•ni•er, pho•ni•est
  pl. pho•nies *or* pho•neys
  pho•ni•ly
  pho•ni•ness

phos•gene

phos•phate
  phos•phat•ic

phos•phor

phos•pho•res•cence
  phos•pho•resce
  phos•pho•res•cent

phos•pho•rus
  phos•phor•ic
  phos•pho•rous

pho•to
  pho•to-op

pho•to•cop•y
  pl. pho•to•cop•ies
  pho•to•cop•ies, pho•
  to•cop•ied
  pho•to•cop•i•er

pho•to•e•lec•tric
  pho•to•e•lec•tric•i•ty

pho•to•fin•ish•ing

pho•to•gen•ic
  pho•to•gen•i•cal•ly

pho•to•graph
  pho•tog•ra•pher
  pho•to•graph•i•cal•ly

pho•to•graph•ic

pho•tog•ra•phy

pho•ton

pho•to•sen•si•tive
  pho•to•sen•si•tiv•i•ty

Pho•to•stat (*trademark*)
  also pho•to•stat
  pho•to•stat•ted, pho•
  to•stat•ting
  pho•to•stat•ic

pho•to•syn•the•sis
  pho•to•syn•the•size
  pho•to•syn•thet•ic
  pho•to•syn•thet•i•cal•ly

phrase
  phras•al
  phras•ing

phra•se•ol•o•gy
  pl. phra•se•ol•o•gies
  phra•se•o•log•i•cal

phre•nol•o•gy
  phren•o•log•i•cal
  phre•nol•o•gist

phy•lac•ter•y
  pl. phy•lac•ter•ies

phy•lum
  pl. phy•la

phys•i•cal
  phys•i•cal•i•ty
  phys•i•cal•ly
  phys•i•cal•ness

phy•si•cian

phys•ics
  phys•i•cist

phys·i·og·no·my
 pl. phys·i·og·no·mies
 phys·i·og·nom·ic
 phys·i·og·nom·i·cal
 phys·i·og·nom·i·cal·ly
 phys·i·og·nom·ist

phy·si·og·ra·phy
 phys·i·og·ra·pher
 phys·i·o·graph·ic
 phys·i·o·graph·i·cal
 phys·i·o·graph·i·cal·ly

phys·i·o·log·i·cal
 also phys·i·o·log·ic
 phys·i·o·log·i·cal·ly

phys·i·ol·o·gy
 phys·i·ol·o·gist

phys·i·o·ther·a·py

phy·sique

pi (Greek letter; see PIE)

Pi·af

Pia·get

pi·a ma·ter

pi·a·nis·si·mo
 pl. pi·a·nis·si·mos or
 pi·a·nis·si·mi

pi·an·ist

pi·an·o
 pl. pi·an·os

pi·an·o·forte

pi·az·za

pi·broch

pi·ca

pi·ca·dor

pic·a·resque

Pi·cas·so

pic·a·yune

pic·ca·lil·li
 pl. pic·ca·lil·lis

pic·co·lo

pick
 pick·a·ble
 pick·er

pick·ax
 also pick·axe

pick·er·el

pick·et
 also pic·quet, piq·uet
 pick·et·er

Pick·ett

pick·ings

pick·le

pick·pock·et

pick·up

pick·y
 pick·i·er, pick·i·est
 pick·i·ness

pic·nic
 pic·nicked, pic·nick·
 ing
 pic·nick·er
 pic·nick·y

pic·to·graph
 also pic·to·gram
 pic·to·graph·ic
 pic·tog·ra·phy

pic·to·ri·al
 pic·to·ri·al·ly

pic·ture

pic·tur·esque
 pic·tur·esque·ly
 pic·tur·esque·ness

pid·dle
 pid·dler

pid·gin (language; see
 PIGEON)

pie (baked dish; see PI)

pie·bald

piece (portion; see PEACE)
 piec·er

pièce de ré·sis·tance
 pl. pièces de ré·sis·
 tance

piece·meal

pied

pied-à-terre
 pl. pieds-à-terre

pier (dock; see PEER)

Pierce (proper name)

pierce (puncture)
 pierc·er
 pierc·ing·ly

pie·ro·gi
 also pi·ro·gi
 pl. same or pie·ro·gies

Pierre

pi·e·ty
 pl. pi·e·ties

pig
 pig·gish
 pig·gish·ly
 pig·gish·ness
 pig·let
 pig·like

pi·geon (bird; see
 PIDGIN)
 pi·geon-toed

pi·geon·hole

pig·gy
 also pig·gie
 pig·gi·er, pig·gi·est

pig·gy·back
 also pick·a·back

pig·head·ed
 pig·head·ed·ly
 pig·head·ed·ness

pig·ment
 pig·men·tar·y

pig·men·ta·tion

pig·my
 var. of pyg·my

pig·pen

pig·skin

pig·sty
  pl. pig·sties

pig·tail
  pig·tailed

pike (*fish*)
  pl. same

pike (*weapon*)

Pikes Peak

pi·laf
  also pi·laff, pi·law,
  pi·lau

pi·las·ter
  pi·las·tered

Pi·late (*proper name;* see
  PILOT)

pil·chard

pile

piles

pile·up

pil·fer
  pil·fer·age
  pil·fer·er

pil·grim

pil·grim·age

pil·ing

pill

pil·lage
  pil·lag·er

pil·lar
  pil·lared

pill·box

pil·lo·ry
  pl. pil·lo·ries
  pil·lo·ries, pil·lo·ried

pil·low
  pil·low·y

pil·low·case

pi·lot (*aviator;* see
  PILATE)
  pi·lot·age
  pi·lot·less

pi·lot·house

Pi·ma

pi·mien·to
  also pi·men·to

pimp

pim·ple
  pim·pled
  pim·ply

pin
  pinned, pin·ning

pi·na co·la·da
  also pi·ña co·la·da

pin·a·fore

pi·ña·ta

pin·ball

pince-nez
  pl. same

pin·cers

pinch
  pinch-hit

pin·cush·ion

Pin·dar

pine (*tree*)
  pin·er·y
  pl. pin·er·ies

pine (*yearn*)

pin·e·al

pine·ap·ple

ping

Ping-Pong (*trademark*)

pin·head

pin·hole

pin·ion

pink (*color*)
  pink·ish
  pink·ly
  pink·ness
  pink·y

pink (*pierce*)

Pink·er·ton

pin·na·cle

pin·nate
  pin·nat·ed
  pin·nate·ly
  pin·na·tion

Pi·no·chet U·gar·te

pi·noch·le

pin·point

pin·prick

pin·stripe

pint
  pint-sized
  also pint-size

Pin·ter

pin·up

pin·wheel

Pin·yin

pi·o·neer

pi·ous
  pi·ous·ly
  pi·ous·ness

pip

pipe
  pipe·ful
  pl. pipe·fuls
  pipe·less

pipe dream

pipe·fit·ter

pipe·fit·ting

pipe·line

pi·pette

pip·ing

pip·it

pip·pin

pip·squeak

pi·quant
  pi·quan·cy
  pi·quant·ly

pique (*irritation*; see
  PEAK, PEEK)
  piques, piqued, piqu·
  ing

pi·ra·cy
  pl. pi·ra·cies

Pi·rae·us

Pi·ran·del·lo

pi·ra·nha

pi·rate
  pi·rat·ic
  pi·rat·i·cal
  pi·rat·i·cal·ly

pir·ou·ette

Pi·sa

pis·ca·to·ry

Pis·ces

Pi·sis·tra·tus

Pis·sar·ro (*French proper
  name*; see PIZARRO)

pis·tach·i·o

pis·til (*part of flower*; see
  PISTOL)
  pis·til·late

pis·tol (*gun*; see PISTIL)
  pis·tol-whip
  pis·tol-whipped, pis·
  tol-whip·ping

pis·ton

pit
  pit·ted, pit·ting

pi·ta
  also pit·ta

pit-a-pat
  also pit·ter-pat·ter

pitch (*slant*)

pitch (*tar-like substance*)
  pitch-black
  pitch-dark

pitch·blende

pitch·er (*ballplayer*)

pitch·er (*container for
  liquid*)
  pitch·er·ful
  pl. pitch·er·fuls

pitch·fork

pitch·man

pit·e·ous
  pit·e·ous·ly
  pit·e·ous·ness

pit·fall

pith
  pith·less

pith·y
  pith·i·er, pith·i·est
  pith·i·ly
  pith·i·ness

pit·i·a·ble
  pit·i·a·ble·ness
  pit·i·a·bly

pit·i·ful
  pit·i·ful·ly
  pit·i·ful·ness

pit·i·less
  pit·i·less·ly

pi·ton

Pitt

pit·tance

pit·ter-pat·ter
  var. of pit-a-pat

Pitts·burgh

pi·tu·i·tar·y
  pl. pi·tu·i·tar·ies

pit·y
  pl. pit·ies
  pit·ies, pit·ied
  pit·y·ing
  pit·y·ing·ly

Piu·ra

Pi·ute
  var. of Pia·ute

piv·ot
  piv·ot·al

pix·el

pix·ie
  also pix·y
  pl. pix·ies

Pi·zar·ro (*Spanish proper
  name*; see PISSARRO)

piz·za

piz·ze·ri·a

piz·zi·ca·to

plac·ard

pla·cate
  pla·cat·ing·ly
  pla·ca·tion
  pla·ca·to·ry

place
  place-name
  place·less
  place·ment

pla·ce·bo

pla·cen·ta
  pl. pla·cen·tae *or* pla·
  cen·tas
  pla·cen·tal

plac·er

plac·id
  pla·cid·i·ty

plac·id·ly
plac·id·ness

plack·et

pla·gia·rism
pla·gia·rist
pla·gia·ris·tic

pla·gia·rize
pla·gia·riz·er

plague
plagues, plagued,
plagu·ing
plague·some

plaid
plaid·ed

plain (*simple*; see PLANE)
plain·ly
plain·ness

plain·clothes·man

plain·song

plaint

plain·tiff

plain·tive
plain·tive·ly
plain·tive·ness

plait (*braid*; see PLATE)

plan
planned, plan·ning
plan·ner
plan·ning

Planck

plane (*level, airplane*; see
PLAIN)

plan·et
plan·e·tar·y
plan·e·tol·o·gy

plan·e·tar·i·um
pl. plan·e·tar·i·ums or
plan·e·tar·i·a

plan·gent
plan·gen·cy

plank

plank·ing

plank·ton
plank·ton·ic

Pla·no

plant
plant·a·ble
plant·let
plant·like

Plan·tag·e·net

plan·tain

plan·ta·tion

plant·er

plaque

plas·ma
also plasm
plas·mat·ic
plas·mic

plas·ter
plas·ter·er
plas·ter·y

plas·ter·board

plas·tic
plas·tic·al·ly
plas·tic·i·ty
plas·ti·cize
plas·ti·ci·za·tion
plas·ti·ciz·er

plate (*dish*; see PLAIT)
plate·ful
pl. plate·fuls
plate·less
plat·er

pla·teau
pl. pla·teaux *or* pla·
teaus

plate·let

plat·en

plat·form

Plath

plat·i·num

plat·i·tude
plat·i·tu·di·nize
plat·i·tu·di·nous

Pla·to

Pla·ton·ic
Pla·ton·i·cal·ly

Pla·to·nism
Pla·to·nist

pla·toon

plat·ter

plat·y·pus

plau·dit

plau·si·ble
plau·si·bil·i·ty
plau·si·bly

Plau·tus

play
play-by-play
play-off
play·a·ble
play·a·bil·i·ty

play·act
play·act·ing
play·ac·tor

play·back

play·bill

play·boy

play·er

play·ful
play·ful·ly
play·ful·ness

play·go·er

play·ground

play·house

play·ing card

play·mate

play·pen

play·thing

play•wright

pla•za

plea

plead
past and *past part.*
plead•ed *or* pled
plead•a•ble
plead•er
plead•ing
plead•ing•ly

pleas•ant
pleas•ant•er, pleas•ant•est
pleas•ant•ly
pleas•ant•ness

pleas•ant•ry
pl. pleas•ant•ries

please
pleased
pleas•ing
pleas•ing•ly

pleas•ur•a•ble
pleas•ur•a•ble•ness
pleas•ur•a•bly

pleas•ure

pleat

plebe

ple•be•ian
ple•be•ian•ism

pleb•i•scite

plec•trum
pl. plec•trums *or* plec•tra

pled

pledge
pledge•a•ble
pledg•er
pledg•or

ple•na•ry

plen•i•po•ten•ti•ar•y
pl. plen•i•po•ten•ti•ar•ies

plen•i•tude

plen•te•ous
plen•te•ous•ly
plen•te•ous•ness

plen•ti•ful
plen•ti•ful•ly
plen•ti•ful•ness

plen•ty

ple•o•nasm
ple•o•nas•tic
ple•o•nas•ti•cal•ly

pleth•o•ra
ple•thor•ic
ple•thor•i•cal•ly

pleu•ra
pl. pleu•rae
pleu•ral (*of the pleura;* see PLURAL)

pleu•ri•sy
pleu•rit•ic

Plex•i•glas (*trademark*)

plex•us
pl. same *or* plex•us•es
plex•i•form

pli•a•ble
pli•a•bil•i•ty
pli•a•ble•ness
pli•a•bly

pli•ant
pli•an•cy
pli•ant•ly

pli•ers

plight

plinth

Plin•y

plod
plod•ded, plod•ding
plod•der
plod•ding•ly

Plo•es•ti

plop
plopped, plop•ping

plot
plot•ted, plot•ting
plot less
plot•ter

plov•er

plow
also plough
plow•a•ble
plow•er

plow•share

ploy

pluck
pluck•er
pluck•less

pluck•y
pluck•i•er, pluck•i•est
pluck•i•ly
pluck•i•ness

plug
plugged, plug•ging
plug•ger

plum (*fruit;* see PLUMB)

plum•age
plum•aged

plumb (*ball;* see PLUM)

plumb•er

plumb•ing

plume
plume•less
plume•like
plum•er•y
plum•y
plum•i•er, plum•i•est

plum•met

plump
plump•ish
plump•ly
plump•ness

plun·der
  plun·der·er

plunge

plung·er

plu·per·fect

plu·ral (*more than one*;
  see *pleural* [PLEURA])
  plu·ral·ly

plu·ral·ism
  plu·ral·ist
  plu·ral·is·tic
  plu·ral·is·ti·cal·ly

plu·ral·i·ty
  pl. plu·ral·i·ties

plus

plush
  plush·ly
  plush·ness

Plu·tarch

Plu·to

plu·toc·ra·cy
  pl. plu·toc·ra·cies
  plu·to·crat
  plu·to·crat·ic
  plu·to·crat·i·cal·ly

plu·to·ni·um

plu·vi·al
  plu·vi·ous

ply (*layer*)
  pl. plies

ply (*use, work*)
  plies, plied

Plym·outh

ply·wood

pneu·mat·ic
  pneu·mat·i·cal·ly
  pneu·ma·tic·i·ty

pneu·mo·nia
  pneu·mon·ic

poach
  poach·er

Po·ca·hon·tas

pock
  also pock·mark
  pock·marked
  pock·y

pock·et
  pock·et·a·ble
  pock·et·less

pock·et·book

pod

Pod·go·ri·ca

po·di·a·try
  po·di·a·trist

po·di·um
  pl. po·di·ums *or* po·di·a

Poe

po·em

po·e·sy

po·et
  fem. po·et·ess

po·et·ic
  also po·et·i·cal
  po·et·i·cal·ly

po·et·ics

po·et·ry

po·grom

poign·ant
  poign·ance
  poign·an·cy
  poign·ant·ly

poin·set·ti·a

point
  point-blank

Point Bar·row

point·ed
  point·ed·ly
  point·ed·ness

Pointe-Noire

point·er

poin·til·lism
  poin·til·list
  poin·til·list·ic

point·less
  point·less·ly
  point·less·ness

poise

poised

poi·son
  poi·son·er
  poi·son·ous
  poi·son·ous·ly

poke

pok·er (*card game*)
  pok·er-faced

pok·er (*metal rod*)

pok·y
  pok·i·er, pok·i·est
  pok·i·ly
  pok·i·ness

Po·land
  Po·lish

po·lar

po·lar·i·ty
  pl. po·lar·i·ties

po·lar·ize
  po·lar·iz·a·ble
  po·lar·i·za·tion
  po·lar·iz·er

pole (*end of imaginary
  line through earth;* see
  POLL)
  pole·ward
  pole·wards

pole (*rod;* see POLL)
  pole-vault·er

Pole (*Polish person*)

pole·cat

po·lem·ic
  po·lem·i·cal

po•lem•i•cal•ly
po•lem•i•cist
po•lem•i•cize

pol•em•ics

pole•star

po•lice

po•lice•man
pl. po•lice•men; *fem.*
po•lice•wom•an, *pl.*
po•lice•wom•en

pol•i•cy
pl. pol•i•cies

pol•i•cy•hold•er

po•li•o

po•li•o•my•e•li•tis

pol•ish
pol•ish•able
pol•ish•er

Po•lit•bu•ro
also po•lit•bu•ro

po•lite
po•lit•er, po•lit•est
po•lite•ly
po•lite•ness

pol•i•tesse

pol•i•tic
pol•i•ticked, pol•i•tick•
ing

po•lit•i•cal
po•lit•i•cal•ly

pol•i•ti•cian

po•lit•i•cize
po•lit•i•ci•za•tion

po•lit•i•co
pl. po•lit•i•cos

pol•i•tics

pol•i•ty
pl. pol•i•ties

Polk

pol•ka
pol•kas, pol•kaed *or*
pol•ka'd, pol•ka•ing

poll (*vote*; see POLE)
poll•ster

pol•len
pol•len•less

pol•li•nate
pol•li•na•tion
pol•li•na•tor

Pol•lock

pol•lute
pol•lu•tant
pol•lut•er
pol•lu•tion

po•lo (*sport*)

po•lo•naise

po•lo•ni•um

Pol Pot

pol•ter•geist

pol•troon
pol•troon•er•y

pol•y•an•dry
pol•y•an•drous

pol•y•chro•mat•ic
pol•y•chro•ma•tism

pol•y•chrome
pol•y•chrom•ous

pol•y•es•ter

pol•y•eth•yl•ene

po•lyg•a•my
po•lyg•a•mist
po•lyg•a•mous

pol•y•glot
pol•y•glot•tal
pol•y•glot•tic

pol•y•gon
po•lyg•o•nal

pol•y•graph

pol•y•he•dron
pl. pol•y•he•dra
pol•y•he•dral
pol•y•he•dric

pol•y•math
pol•y•math•ic

pol•y•mer

Pol•y•ne•sia
Pol•y•ne•sian

pol•y•no•mi•al

pol•yp

po•lyph•o•ny
pl. po•lyph•o•nies
pol•y•phon•ic
pol•y•phon•i•cal•ly
po•lyph•o•nous

pol•y•pro•pyl•ene

pol•y•sac•cha•ride

pol•y•sty•rene

pol•y•syl•lab•ic
pol•y•syl•lab•i•cal•ly
pol•y•syl•la•ble

pol•y•tech•nic

pol•y•the•ism
pol•y•the•ist
pol•y•the•is•tic

pol•y•un•sat•u•rat•ed

pol•y•u•re•thane

pol•y•vi•nyl chlo•ride

po•made

po•man•der

pome•gran•ate

pom•mel

Po•mo•na

pomp

Pom•pa•no Beach

Pom•pey

Pom•pi•dou

pom·pom
  also pom·pon

pomp·ous
  pom·pos·i·ty
  pl. pom·pos·i·ties
  pomp·ous·ly
  pomp·ous·ness

Pon·ce

Ponce de Le·ón

pon·cho
  pl. pon·chos

pond

pon·der

pon·der·ous
  pon·der·ous·ly
  pon·der·ous·ness

pon·gee

pon·iard

Pont·char·train, Lake

Pon·ti·ac

pon·tiff

pon·tif·i·cal
  pon·tif·i·cal·ly

pon·tif·i·cate

pon·toon

po·ny
  pl. po·nies

po·ny·tail

poo·dle

pooh-pooh

pool

Poo·na

poop

poor (*needy;* see PORE, POUR)

poor·ly

pop (*sound, drink*)
  popped, pop·ping

pop (*popular*)

pop·corn

Pope (*proper name*)

pope (*pontiff*)

pop·in·jay

pop·lar

pop·lin

Po·po·cat·e·petl

pop·o·ver

pop·py
  pl. pop·pies

pop·py·cock

Pop·si·cle (*trademark*)

pop·u·lace (*people;* see POPULOUS)

pop·u·lar
  pop·u·lar·ism
  pop·u·lar·i·ty
  pop·u·lar·ly

pop·u·lar·ize
  pop·u·lar·i·za·tion
  pop·u·lar·iz·er

pop·u·late

pop·u·la·tion

pop·u·list
  pop·u·lism
  pop·u·lis·tic

pop·u·lous (*inhabited;* see POPULACE)
  pop·u·lous·ly

Po·que·lin

por·ce·lain
  por·ce·la·ne·ous

porch
  porched
  porch·less

por·cine

por·cu·pine

pore (*hole, examine;* see POUR)

pork

pork·y
  pork·i·er, pork·i·est

porn

por·nog·ra·phy
  por·nog·ra·pher
  por·no·graph·ic
  por·no·graph·i·cal·ly

po·rous
  po·ros·i·ty
  po·rous·ly

por·phy·ry
  pl. por·phy·ries
  por·phy·rit·ic

por·poise

por·ridge

por·rin·ger

Porsche

port

port·a·ble
  port·a·bil·i·ty
  port·a·bly

por·tage

por·tal

Port-au-Prince

port·cul·lis

por·tend

por·tent

por·ten·tous
  por·ten·tous·ly

Por·ter (*proper name*)

por·ter (*attendant*)
  por·ter·age

por·ter·house

port·fo·li·o
  pl. port·fo·li·os

port•hole

por•ti•co
 pl. por•ti•coes *or* por•
 ti•cos

por•tiere
 also por•tière

por•tion

Port•land

port•ly
 port•li•er, port•li•est
 port•li•ness

port•man•teau
 pl. port•man•teaus *or*
 port•man•teaux

Port Mores•by

Pôr•to
 var. of O•por•to

Pôr•to A•le•gre

Port-of-Spain

Por•to No•vo

por•trait

por•trait•ist

por•trai•ture

por•tray
 por•tray•able
 por•tray•al
 por•tray•er

Port Sa•id

Ports•mouth

Por•tu•gal
 Por•tu•guese
 pl. same

pose

po•seur
 fem. po•seuse

posh
 posh•ly
 posh•ness

pos•it

po•si•tion
 po•si•tion•al
 po•si•tion•er

pos•i•tive
 pos•i•tive•ly
 pos•i•tive•ness
 pos•i•tiv•i•ty

pos•i•tron

pos•se

pos•sess
 pos•ses•sor

pos•ses•sion
 pos•ses•sion•less

pos•ses•sive
 pos•ses•sive•ly
 pos•ses•sive•ness

pos•si•bil•i•ty
 pl. pos•si•bil•i•ties

pos•si•ble

pos•si•bly

pos•sum

post (*mail*)
 post-haste

post (*pole, position*)

post•age

post•al

post•card

post•er

pos•te•ri•or
 pos•te•ri•or•i•ty
 pos•te•ri•or•ly

pos•ter•i•ty

post•grad•u•ate

post•hu•mous
 post•hu•mous•ly

post•man
 pl. post•men; *fem.* post•
 wom•an, *pl.* post•
 wom•en

post•mark

post•mas•ter

post•mod•ern
 post•mod•ern•ism
 post•mod•ern•ist

post•mor•tem

post•na•tal

post•paid

post•pone
 post•pon•able
 post•pone•ment
 post•pon•er

post•script

pos•tu•late
 pos•tu•la•tion

pos•ture
 pos•tur•al
 pos•tur•er
 pos•tur•ing

po•sy
 pl. po•sies

pot
 pot•ted, pot•ting
 pot-roast
 pot•ful
 pl. pot•fuls

po•ta•ble
 po•ta•bil•i•ty

pot•ash

po•tas•si•um
 po•tas•sic

po•ta•to
 pl. po•ta•toes

pot•bel•ly
 pot•bel•lies
 pot•bel•lied

pot•boil•er

po·tent
  po·tence
  po·ten·cy
  po·tent·ly

po·ten·tate

po·ten·tial
  po·ten·ti·al·i·ty
  po·ten·tial·ly

poth·er

pot·herb

pot·hole

po·tion

pot·luck

Po·to·mac Riv·er

pot·pour·ri

Pots·dam

pot·sherd

pot·shot

pot·tage

Pot·ter (*proper name*)

pot·ter (*maker of pottery*)

pot·ter·y
  pl. pot·ter·ies

pot·ty
  pl. pot·ties

pouch
  pouched
  pouch·y

poul·tice

poul·try

pounce
  pounc·er

Pound (*proper name*)

pound (*enclosure*)

pound (*hit*)
  pound·er

pound (*weight*)
  pound·age

pour (*flow*; see PORE)
  pour·a·ble
  pour·er

pout
  pout·er
  pout·ing·ly
  pout·y

pov·er·ty
  pov·er·ty-strick·en

pow·der
  pow·der·y

Pow·ell

pow·er
  pow·ered

pow·er·boat

pow·er·ful
  pow·er·ful·ly
  pow·er·ful·ness

pow·er·house

pow·er·less
  pow·er·less·ly
  pow·er·less·ness

Pow·ha·tan

pow·wow

pox

Poz·nan

prac·ti·ca·ble
  prac·ti·ca·bil·i·ty
  prac·ti·ca·bly

prac·ti·cal
  prac·ti·cal·i·ty
  pl. prac·ti·cal·i·ties

prac·ti·cal·ly

prac·tice
  prac·tic·er

prac·ti·tion·er

Prae·to·ri·an Guard
  also prae·to·ri·an guard

prag·mat·ic
  prag·mat·i·cal·ly

prag·ma·tism
  prag·ma·tist
  prag·ma·tis·tic

Prague

Prai·a

prai·rie

praise
  praise·ful
  prais·er

praise·wor·thy
  praise·wor·thi·ly
  praise·wor·thi·ness

pra·line

prance
  pranc·er

prank
  prank·ish

prank·ster

pra·se·o·dym·i·um

prate
  prat·er
  prat·ing

prat·tle
  prat·tler
  prat·tling

prawn

prax·is
  pl. prax·es *or* prax·is·es

Prax·it·e·les

pray (*say prayers*; see
  PREY)

prayer
  prayer·ful

preach
  preach·a·ble
  preach·er

pre·am·ble

pre·ar·range

Pre·cam·bri·an

pre·can·cer·ous
  pre·can·cer·ous·ly

pre·car·i·ous
  pre·car·i·ous·ly
  pre·car·i·ous·ness

pre·cau·tion
  pre·cau·tion·ary

pre·cede

prec·e·dence
  also prec·e·den·cy

prec·e·dent

pre·cept
  pre·cep·tive

pre·cep·tor
  fem. pre·cep·tress
  pre·cep·to·ri·al

pre·ces·sion

pre·cinct

pre·ci·os·i·ty

pre·cious
  pre·cious·ly
  pre·cious·ness

prec·i·pice

pre·cip·i·tate
  pre·cip·i·tate·ly
  pre·cip·i·tate·ness
  pre·cip·i·ta·tor

pre·cip·i·ta·tion

pre·cip·i·tous
  pre·cip·i·tous·ly
  pre·cip·i·tous·ness

pré·cis
  pl. same

pre·cise
  pre·cise·ness

pre·cise·ly

pre·ci·sion
  pre·ci·sion·ism
  pre·ci·sion·ist

pre·clude
  pre·clu·sion
  pre·clu·sive

pre·co·cious
  pre·co·cious·ly
  pre·coc·i·ty

pre·cog·ni·tion
  pre·cog·ni·tive

pre·con·ceive

pre·con·cep·tion

pre·con·di·tion

pre·cur·sor

pre·date

pred·a·tor

pred·a·to·ry
  pred·a·to·ri·ly

pre·de·cease

pred·e·ces·sor

pre·des·tine
  pre·des·ti·na·tion

pre·de·ter·mine
  pre·de·ter·mi·na·ble
  pre·de·ter·mi·nate
  pre·de·ter·mi·na·tion

pre·dic·a·ment

pred·i·cate
  pred·i·ca·tion

pred·i·ca·tive
  pred·i·ca·tive·ly

pre·dict
  pre·dic·tive
  pre·dic·tive·ly
  pre·dic·tor

pre·dict·a·ble
  pre·dict·a·bil·i·ty
  pre·dict·a·bly

pre·dic·tion

pre·di·lec·tion

pre·dis·pose
  pre·dis·po·si·tion

pre·dom·i·nant
  pre·dom·i·nance
  pre·dom·i·nant·ly

pre·dom·i·nate

pree·mie

pre·em·i·nent
  pre·em·i·nence
  pre·em·i·nent·ly

pre·empt
  pre·emp·tor
  pre·emp·to·ry

pre·emp·tion

pre·emp·tive

preen
  preen·er

pre·ex·is·tence

pre·fab

pre·fab·ri·cate
  pre·fab·ri·ca·tion

pref·ace
  pref·a·to·ri·al
  pref·a·to·ry

pre·fect
  pre·fec·to·ri·al

pre·fec·ture
  pre·fec·tur·al

pre·fer
  pre·ferred, pre·fer·ring

pref·er·a·ble
  pref·er·a·bly

pref·er·ence
  pref·er·en·tial
  pref·er·en·tial·ly

pre·fer·ment

pre·fig·ure
  pre·fig·u·ra·tion
  pre·fig·ur·a·tive

pre·fix
  pre·fix·ion

preg·nan·cy
  pl. preg·nan·cies

preg·nant
  preg·nant·ly

pre·heat

pre·hen·sile

pre·his·tor·ic
  pre·his·tor·i·cal·ly
  pre·his·to·ry

pre·judge
  pre·judg·ment

prej·u·dice

prej·u·di·cial
  prej·u·di·cial·ly

prel·ate

pre·lim·i·nar·y
  pl. pre·lim·i·nar·ies

prel·ude

pre·mar·i·tal

pre·ma·ture
  pre·ma·ture·ly

pre·med·i·tate
  pre·med·i·ta·tion

pre·men·stru·al
  pre·men·stru·al·ly

pre·mier (*person, first;*
  see PREMIERE)

pre·miere (*showing;* see
  PREMIER)
  also pre·mière

prem·ise

pre·mi·um

prem·o·ni·tion
  pre·mon·i·to·ry

pre·oc·cu·py
  pre·oc·cu·pies, pre·oc·
  cu·pied
  pre·oc·cu·pa·tion

pre·or·dain

prep

pre·paid

prep·a·ra·tion

pre·pa·ra·to·ry

pre·pare
  pre·par·er

pre·par·ed·ness

pre·pay
  past and *past part.* pre·
  paid
  pre·pay·a·ble
  pre·pay·ment

pre·pon·der·ant
  pre·pon·der·ance
  pre·pon·der·ant·ly

pre·pon·der·ate

prep·o·si·tion
  prep·o·si·tion·al
  prep·o·si·tion·al·ly

pre·pos·sess
  pre·pos·ses·sion

pre·pos·ter·ous
  pre·pos·ter·ous·ly

prep·py
  also prep·pie
  pl. prep·pies
  prep·pi·er, prep·pi·est

pre·req·ui·site

pre·rog·a·tive

pres·age

Pres·by·te·ri·an
  Pres·by·te·ri·an·ism

pre·school
  pre·school·er

pre·scient
  pre·science
  pre·scient·ly

pre·scribe
  pre·scrib·er

pre·scrip·tion

pre·scrip·tive
  pre·scrip·tive·ly
  pre·scrip·tive·ness
  pre·scrip·tiv·ism
  pre·scrip·tiv·ist

pres·ence

pre·sent (*introduce*)
  pre·sent·er

pres·ent (*now*)
  pres·ent-day

pre·sent·a·ble
  pre·sent·a·bil·i·ty
  pre·sent·a·bly

pres·en·ta·tion
  pres·en·ta·tion·al

pre·sen·ti·ment

pres·ent·ly

pres·er·va·tion

pre·serv·a·tive

pre·serve
  pre·serv·a·ble
  pre·serv·er

pre·shrunk

pre·side

pres·i·den·cy
  pl. pres·i·den·cies

pres·i·dent
  pres·i·den·tial
  pres·i·den·tial·ly

Pres·ley

press

press·ing
  press·ing·ly

pres•sure

pres•sur•ize
pres•sur•i•za•tion

pres•ti•dig•i•ta•tor
pres•ti•dig•i•ta•tion

pres•tige

pres•ti•gious
pres•ti•gious•ly
pres•ti•gious•ness

pres•to

pre•sum•a•bly

pre•sume
pre•sum•a•ble
pre•sum•ed•ly

pre•sump•tion

pre•sump•tive
pre•sump•tive•ly

pre•sump•tu•ous
pre•sump•tu•ous•ly
pre•sump•tu•ous•ness

pre•sup•pose
pre•sup•po•si•tion

pre•tend

pre•tend•er

pre•tense

pre•ten•sion

pre•ten•tious
pre•ten•tious•ly
pre•ten•tious•ness

pret•er•it
also pret•er•ite

pre•ter•nat•u•ral
pre•ter•nat•u•ral•ly

pre•text

Pre•to•ri•a

pret•ti•fy
pret•ti•fies, pret•ti•fied
pret•ti•fi•er

pret•ty
pret•ti•er, pret•ti•est

pret•ties, pret•tied
pret•ti•ly
pret•ti•ness
pret•ty•ish

pret•zel

pre•vail
pre•vail•ing•ly

prev•a•lent
prev•a•lence
prev•a•lent•ly

pre•var•i•cate
pre•var•i•ca•tion
pre•var•i•ca•tor

pre•vent
pre•vent•a•ble
also pre•vent•i•ble
pre•vent•er
pre•ven•tion

pre•ven•tive
also pre•vent•a•tive
pre•ven•tive•ly

pre•view

Prev•in

pre•vi•ous
pre•vi•ous•ly

prey (victim; see PRAY)
prey•er

Price (proper noun)

price (cost)
priced
pric•er

price•less
price•less•ly
price•less•ness

pric•ey
also pric•y
pric•i•er, pric•i•est
pric•i•ness

prick

prick•er

prick•le

prick•ly
prick•li•er, prick•li•est
prick•li•ness

pric•y
var. of pric•ey

pride (conceit; see pried
[PRY])
pride•ful
pride•ful•ly
pride•less

priest
priest•hood
priest•like

priest•ess

Priest•ley (proper name)

priest•ly (of a priest)
priest•li•ness

prig
prig•gish
prig•gish•ly
prig•gish•ness

prim
prim•mer, prim•mest
prim•ly
prim•ness

pri•ma bal•le•ri•na

pri•ma•cy
pl. pri•ma•cies

pri•ma don•na
pl. pri•ma don•nas
pri•ma don•na-ish

pri•ma fa•cie

pri•mal
pri•mal•ly

pri•mar•y
pl. pri•mar•ies
pri•mar•i•ly

pri•mate
pri•ma•tial
pri•ma•tol•o•gy

pri•ma•ver•a

prime

prim·er

pri·me·val
  pri·me·val·ly

prim·i·tive
  prim·i·tive·ly
  prim·i·tive·ness

pri·mo·gen·i·ture
  pri·mo·gen·i·tal

pri·mor·di·al
  pri·mor·di·al·ly

primp

prim·rose

prince
  prince·like

Prince Ed·ward Is·land

prince·ly
  prince·li·er, prince·
  li·est
  prince·li·ness

prin·cess

Prince Wil·liam Sound

prin·ci·pal (*chief*; see
  PRINCIPLE)

prin·ci·pal·i·ty
  pl. prin·ci·pal·i·ties

prin·ci·pal·ly

prin·ci·ple (*truth*; see
  PRINCIPAL)

prin·ci·pled

print
  print·a·ble
  print·less

print·er

print·ing

print·out

pri·or
  pri·or·ate
  pri·or·ess

pri·or·i·ty
  pl. pri·or·i·ties
  pri·or·i·tize
  pri·or·i·ti·za·tion

pri·o·ry
  pl. pri·o·ries

prism
  pris·mat·ic
  pris·mat·i·cal·ly

pris·on

pris·on·er

pris·sy
  pris·si·er, pris·si·est
  pris·si·ly
  pris·si·ness

pris·tine

pri·va·cy

pri·vate
  pri·vate·ly

pri·va·tion

pri·va·tize
  pri·va·ti·za·tion

priv·et

priv·i·lege
  priv·i·leged

priv·y
  pl. priv·ies
  priv·i·ly

prize (*open*)
  also prise

prize (*value highly*)

prize·fight
  prize·fight·er

prize·win·ner
  prize·win·ning

pro (*for*)
  pl. pros (see PROSE)
  pro-choice
  pro-life

pro (*professional*)
  pl. pros (see *prose*)

pro·ac·tive
  pro·ac·tion
  pro·ac·tive·ly

prob·a·bil·ism

prob·a·bil·i·ty
  pl. prob·a·bil·i·ties

prob·a·ble
  prob·a·bly

pro·bate

pro·ba·tion
  pro·ba·tion·al
  pro·ba·tion·ar·y

pro·ba·tion·er

probe
  probe·a·ble
  prob·er
  prob·ing·ly

pro·bi·ty

prob·lem

prob·lem·at·ic
  also prob·lem·at·i·cal
  prob·lem·at·i·cal·ly

pro·bos·cis

pro·ce·dure
  pro·ce·dur·al
  pro·ce·dur·al·ly

pro·ceed

pro·ceed·ing

pro·ceeds

proc·ess (*course of action*)

pro·cess (*walk*)
  pro·cess·a·ble

pro·ces·sion

pro·ces·sion·al

proc·es·sor

pro·claim
  pro·claim·er
  proc·la·ma·tion

pro•cliv•i•ty
  pl. pro•cliv•i•ties

pro•cras•ti•nate
  pro•cras•ti•na•tion
  pro•cras•ti•na•tor

pro•cre•ate
  pro•cre•ant
  pro•cre•a•tive
  pro•cre•a•tion
  pro•cre•a•tor

Pro•crus•tes
  Pro•crus•te•an

proc•tor
  proc•to•ri•al

pro•cure
  pro•cur•a•ble
  pro•cure•ment

pro•cur•er

prod
  prod•ded, prod•ding
  prod•der

prod•i•gal
  prod•i•gal•i•ty
  prod•i•gal•ly

pro•di•gious
  pro•di•gious•ly

prod•i•gy
  pl. prod•i•gies

pro•duce
  pro•duc•i•ble

pro•duc•er

prod•uct

pro•duc•tion
  pro•duc•tion•al

pro•duc•tive
  pro•duc•tive•ly
  pro•duc•tive•ness

pro•duc•tiv•i•ty

pro•fane
  pro•fa•na•tion
  pro•fane•ly
  pro•fan•er

pro•fan•i•ty
  pl. pro•fan•i•ties

pro•fess

pro•fessed
  pro•fess•ed•ly

pro•fes•sion

pro•fes•sion•al
  pro•fes•sion•al•ism
  pro•fes•sion•al•ly

pro•fes•sor
  pro•fes•so•ri•al
  pro•fes•so•ri•al•ly
  pro•fes•sor•ship

prof•fer

pro•fi•cient
  pro•fi•cien•cy
  pro•fi•cient•ly

pro•file
  pro•fil•er

prof•it (*gain;* see
  PROPHET)
  prof•it•a•bil•i•ty
  prof•it•a•ble
  prof•it•a•bly
  prof•it•less

prof•it•eer

prof•li•gate
  prof•li•ga•cy
  prof•li•gate•ly

pro for•ma

pro•found
  pro•found•er, pro•
   found•est
  pro•found•ly
  pro•found•ness
  pro•fun•di•ty
  pl. pro•fun•di•ties

pro•fuse
  pro•fuse•ly
  pro•fuse•ness
  pro•fu•sion

pro•gen•i•tor
  pro•gen•i•to•ri•al

prog•e•ny

pro•ges•ter•one

prog•no•sis
  pl. prog•no•ses

prog•nos•tic
  prog•nos•ti•cal•ly

prog•nos•ti•cate
  prog•nos•ti•ca•tion
  prog•nos•ti•ca•tive
  prog•nos•ti•ca•tor

pro•gram
  pro•grammed, pro•
   gram•ming *or* pro•
   gramed, pro•gram•ing
  pro•gram•ma•ble
  pro•gram•mat•ic
  pro•gram•mat•i•cal•ly
  pro•gram•mer *or*
   pro•gram•er

prog•ress (*improvement*)

pro•gress (*move forward*)

pro•gres•sion
  pro•gres•sion•al

pro•gres•sive
  pro•gres•sive•ly
  pro•gres•sive•ness
  pro•gres•siv•ism

pro•hib•it
  pro•hib•it•er
  pro•hib•i•tor

pro•hi•bi•tion
  pro•hi•bi•tion•ist

pro•hib•i•tive
  pro•hib•i•tive•ly
  pro•hib•i•tive•ness

proj•ect (*undertaking*)

pro•ject (*jut out, forecast*)

pro•jec•tile

pro•jec•tion
  pro•jec•tion•ist

pro•jec•tor

Pro•ko•fiev

pro•lapse
also pro•lap•sus

pro•le•gom•e•non
pl. pro•le•gom•e•na

pro•le•tar•i•at
pro•le•tar•i•an
pro•le•tar•i•an•ism

pro•lif•er•ate
pro•lif•er•a•tion

pro•lif•ic
pro•lif•i•ca•cy
pro•lif•i•cal•ly

pro•lix
pro•lix•i•ty
pro•lix•ly

pro•logue
also pro•log

pro•long
pro•lon•ga•tion
pro•long•ed•ly
pro•long•er

prom

prom•e•nade

Pro•me•the•an

pro•me•thi•um

prom•i•nent
prom•i•nence
prom•i•nen•cy
prom•i•nent•ly

pro•mis•cu•ous
prom•is•cu•i•ty
pro•mis•cu•ous•ly

prom•ise
prom•is•er

prom•is•ing
prom•is•ing•ly

prom•is•so•ry

pro•mo
pl. pro•mos

prom•on•to•ry
pl. prom•on•to•ries

pro•mote
pro•mot•able
pro•mot•a•bil•i•ty
pro•mo•tion
pro•mo•tion•al

pro•mot•er

prompt
prompt•ing
promp•ti•tude
prompt•ly
prompt•ness

prompt•er

prom•ul•gate
prom•ul•ga•tion
prom•ul•ga•tor

pro•nate

prone
prone•ness

prong
pronged

pro•noun

pro•nounce
pro•nounce•a•ble
pro•nounce•ment
pro•nounc•er

pro•nounced
pro•nounc•ed•ly

pron•to

pro•nun•ci•a•tion

proof
proof•less

proof•read
past and past part.
proof•read
proof•read•er
proof•read•ing

prop
propped, prop•ping

prop•a•gan•da
prop•a•gan•dist
prop•a•gan•dize

prop•a•gate
prop•a•ga•tion
prop•a•ga•tive
prop•a•ga•tor

pro•pane

pro•pel
pro•pelled, pro•pel•ling
pro•pel•lant
pro•pel•lent

pro•pel•ler

pro•pen•si•ty
pl. pro•pen•si•ties

prop•er
prop•er•ness

prop•er•ly

prop•er•tied

prop•er•ty
pl. prop•er•ties

proph•e•cy
pl. proph•e•cies

proph•e•sy
proph•e•sies, proph•
e•sied
proph•e•si•er

proph•et (*religious seer,*
see PROFFIT)
fem. proph•et•ess

pro•phet•ic
pro•phet•i•cal
pro•phet•i•cal•ly

pro•phy•lac•tic

pro•phy•lax•is
pl. pro•phy•lax•es

pro•pin•qui•ty

pro•pi•ti•ate
pro•pi•ti•a•tion
pro•pi•ti•a•tor

pro•pi•ti•a•to•ry

pro·pi·tious
pro·pi·tious·ly
pro·pi·tious·ness

prop·jet

pro·po·nent

pro·por·tion
pro·por·tioned
pro·por·tion·less
pro·por·tion·ate
pro·por·tion·ate·ly

pro·por·tion·al
pro·por·tion·al·i·ty
pro·por·tion·al·ly

pro·pos·al

pro·pose
pro·pos·er

prop·o·si·tion
prop·o·si·tion·al

pro·pound
pro·pound·er

pro·pri·e·tar·y

pro·pri·e·tor
fem. pro·pri·e·tress
pro·pri·e·to·ri·al
pro·pri·e·to·ri·al·ly
pro·pri·e·tor·ship

pro·pri·e·ty
pl. pro·pri·e·ties

pro·pul·sion
pro·pul·sive

pro ra·ta

pro·rate
pro·ra·tion

pro·sa·ic
pro·sa·i·cal·ly

pro·sce·ni·um
pl. pro·sce·ni·ums *or*
pro·sce·ni·a

pro·scribe
pro·scrip·tion
pro·scrip·tive

prose (*language*; see *pros*
[PRO])

pros·e·cute
pros·e·cut·a·ble
pros·e·cu·tion
pros·e·cu·tor
pros·e·cu·to·ri·al

pros·e·lyte
pros·e·lyt·ism

pros·e·lyt·ize
pros·e·lyt·iz·er

pros·o·dy
pro·sod·ic
pros·o·dist

pros·pect
pros·pec·tor

pro·spec·tive
pro·spec·tive·ly

pro·spec·tus

pros·per

pros·per·i·ty

pros·per·ous
pros·per·ous·ly
pros·per·ous·ness

pros·tate
pros·tat·ic

pros·the·sis
pl. pros·the·ses
pros·thet·ic
pros·thet·i·cal·ly

pros·ti·tute
pros·ti·tu·tion
pros·ti·tu·tor

pros·trate
pros·tra·tion

pros·y
pros·i·er, pros·i·est
pros·i·ly
pros·i·ness

prot·ac·tin·i·um

pro·tag·o·nist

pro·te·an

pro·tect

pro·tec·tion
pro·tec·tion·ist

pro·tec·tive
pro·tec·tive·ly
pro·tec·tive·ness

pro·tec·tor
pro·tec·tor·al

pro·tec·tor·ate

pro·té·gé
fem. pro·té·gée

pro·tein
pro·tein·a·ceous

pro tem

pro tem·po·re

Prot·er·o·zo·ic

pro·test
pro·test·er
pro·test·ing·ly
pro·tes·tor

Prot·es·tant
Prot·es·tant·ism
Prot·es·tant·ize

prot·es·ta·tion

pro·thon·e·tar·y

pro·to·col

pro·to·lan·guage

pro·ton
pro·ton·ic

pro·to·plasm
pro·to·plas·mal
pro·to·plas·mat·ic
pro·to·plas·mic

pro·to·type
pro·to·typ·ic
pro·to·typ·i·cal
pro·to·typ·i·cal·ly

pro·to·zo·an
also pro·to·zo·on
pl. pro·to·zo·a *or* pro·
to·zo·ans
pro·to·zo·ic
pro·to·zo·al

pro•tract
  pro•tract•ed•ly
  pro•tract•ed•ness

pro•trac•tor

pro•trude
  pro•tru•sion
  pro•tru•sive

pro•tu•ber•ant
  pro•tu•ber•ance

proud
  proud•ly
  proud•ness

Prou•dhon

Proust

prove
  past part. proved *or*
  prov•en
  prov•a•ble
  prov•a•bil•i•ty
  prov•a•bly

prov•e•nance

Pro•ven•çal

prov•en•der

prov•erb

pro•ver•bi•al
  pro•ver•bi•al•ly

pro•vide
  pro•vid•er

pro•vid•ed

Prov•i•dence (*city*)

prov•i•dence (*divine care*)
  also Providence

prov•i•dent
  prov•i•dent•ly

prov•i•den•tial
  prov•i•den•tial•ly

prov•ince

pro•vin•cial
  pro•vin•cial•ism
  pro•vin•ci•al•i•ty
  pro•vin•cial•ly

pro•vi•sion
  pro•vi•sion•er

pro•vi•sion•al
  pro•vi•sion•al•ly

pro•vi•so
  pl. pro•vi•sos

Pro•vo

prov•o•ca•tion

pro•voc•a•tive
  pro•voc•a•tive•ly
  pro•voc•a•tive•ness

pro•voke
  pro•vok•a•ble
  pro•vok•ing•ly

pro•vo•lo•ne

pro•vost

prow

prow•ess

prowl
  prowl•er

prox•i•mate
  prox•i•mate•ly

prox•im•i•ty

prox•y
  pl. prox•ies

prude
  prud•er•y
  pl. prud•er•ies
  prud•ish
  prud•ish•ly
  prud•ish•ness

pru•dent
  pru•dence
  pru•dent•ly

pru•den•tial
  pru•den•tial•ly

prune (*dried plum*)

prune (*trim*)
  prun•er

pru•ri•ent
  pru•ri•ence
  pru•ri•en•cy
  pru•ri•ent•ly

Prus•sia
  Prus•sian

pry
  pries, pried (see PRIDE)
  pry•ing
  pry•ing•ly

psalm
  also Psalm
  psalm•ist

psal•ter

p's and q's

pseu•do•nym

psi

pso•ri•a•sis

psst
  also pst

psych
  also psyche

psy•che

psy•che•del•ic
  psy•che•del•i•cal•ly

psy•chi•a•try
  psy•chi•at•ric
  psy•chi•at•ri•cal
  psy•chi•at•ri•cal•ly
  psy•chi•a•trist

psy•chic
  psy•chi•cal
  psy•chi•cal•ly

psy•cho
  pl. psy•chos

psy•cho•a•nal•y•sis
  psy•cho•an•a•lyze
  psy•cho•an•a•lyst

psy·cho·an·a·lyt·ic
psy·cho·an·a·lyt·i·
cal·ly

psy·cho·bab·ble
psy·cho·bab·bler

psy·cho·log·i·cal
psy·cho·log·i·cal·ly

psy·chol·o·gy
pl. psy·chol·o·gies
psy·chol·o·gist
psy·chol·o·gize

psy·cho·path
psy·cho·path·ic
psy·cho·path·i·cal·ly

psy·cho·pa·thol·o·gy
psy·cho·path·o·log·i·
cal

psy·cho·sis
pl. psy·cho·ses

psy·cho·so·mat·ic
psy·cho·so·mat·i·cal·ly

psy·cho·ther·a·py
psy·cho·ther·a·peu·tic
psy·cho·ther·a·pist

psy·chot·ic
psy·chot·i·cal·ly

ptar·mi·gan

pter·o·dac·tyl

Ptol·e·my

pto·maine

pub

pu·ber·ty

pu·bes
pl. same

pu·bes·cence
pu·bes·cent

pu·bic

pu·bis
pl. pu·bes

pub·lic
pub·lic-ad·dress
pub·lic·ly

pub·li·can

pub·li·ca·tion

pub·li·cist

pub·lic·i·ty

pub·li·cize

pub·lish
pub·lish·a·ble

pub·lish·er

Puc·ci·ni

puce

puck (*hockey disk*)

puck (*sprite*)
puck·ish
puck·ish·ly

puck·er
puck·er·y

pud·ding

pud·dle
pud·dler
pud·dly

pu·den·dum
pl. pu·den·da

pudg·y
pudg·i·er, pudg·i·est
pudge
pudg·i·ly
pudg·i·ness

Pue·bla

Pueb·lo (*city*)

pueb·lo (*dwelling*)
pl. pueb·los

pu·er·ile
pu·er·ile·ly
pu·er·il·i·ty
pl. pu·er·il·i·ties

Puer·to Ri·co
Puer·to Ri·can

puff

puff·ball

puf·fin

puff·y
puff·i·er, puff·i·est
puff·i·ly
puff·i·ness

pug
pug-nosed

Pu·get Sound

pu·gil·ist
pu·gil·ism
pu·gil·is·tic

pug·na·cious
pug·na·cious·ly
pug·nac·i·ty

puis·sance

puke
puk·ey

Pu·las·ki

pul·chri·tude
pul·chri·tu·di·nous

pule

Pu·litz·er

pull

pul·let

pul·ley
pl. pul·leys

Pull·man (*trademark*)

pull·o·ver

pul·mo·nar·y
pul·mo·nate

pulp
pulp·er
pulp·less
pulp·y
pulp·i·ness

pul·pit

pul·sar

pul·sate
  pul·sa·tion
  pul·sa·tor
  pul·sa·to·ry

pulse
  pulse·less

pul·ver·ize
  pul·ver·i·za·tion
  pul·ver·iz·er

pu·ma

pum·ice

pum·mel
  also pom·mel

pump

pum·per·nick·el

pump·kin

pun
  punned, pun·ning
  pun·ning·ly
  pun·ster

punch (*hit*)
  punch-drunk
  punch·er

punch (*tool, beverage*)

punch·y
  punch·i·er, punch·i·est

punc·til·i·o
  pl. punc·til·i·os

punc·til·i·ous
  punc·til·i·ous·ly
  punc·til·i·ous·ness

punc·tu·al
  punc·tu·al·i·ty
  punc·tu·al·ly

punc·tu·ate

punc·tu·a·tion

punc·ture

pun·dit
  pun·dit·ry

pun·gent
  pun·gen·cy
  pun·gent·ly

pun·ish
  pun·ish·a·ble
  pun·ish·er
  pun·ish·ing

pun·ish·ment

pu·ni·tive
  also pu·ni·to·ry
  pu·ni·tive·ly

punk
  punk·y

pun·ster

punt
  punt·er

pu·ny
  pu·ni·er, pu·ni·est
  pu·ni·ly
  pu·ni·ness

pup

pu·pa
  pl. pu·pae
  pu·pal

pu·pil (*part of eye*)
  pu·pil·lar
  pu·pil·lar·y

pu·pil (*student*)

pup·pet
  pup·pet·eer
  pup·pet·ry

pup·py
  pl. pup·pies
  pup·py·hood
  pup·py·ish

pur·blind
  pur·blind·ness

pur·chase
  pur·chas·a·ble
  pur·chas·er

pur·dah

pure
  pure·ness

pure·bred

pu·rée
  pu·rées, pu·réed

pure·ly

pur·ga·tive

pur·ga·to·ry
  pl. pur·ga·to·ries
  pur·ga·to·ri·al

purge
  purg·er

pu·ri·fy
  pu·ri·fies, pu·ri·fied
  pu·ri·fi·ca·tion
  pu·rif·i·ca·to·ry
  pu·ri·fi·er

pur·ist
  pur·ism
  pu·ris·tic

pu·ri·tan
  also Pu·ri·tan
  pu·ri·tan·ism

pu·ri·tan·i·cal
  pu·ri·tan·i·cal·ly

pu·ri·ty

purl (*stitch*; see PEARL)

pur·lieu

pur·loin
  pur·loin·er

pur·ple
  pur·plish

pur·port
  pur·port·ed·ly

pur·pose
  pur·pose·ful·ly
  pur·pose·ful·ness
  pur·pose·less
  pur·pose·ly

pur·pos·ive
pur·pos·ive·ly
pur·pos·ive·ness

purr (*cat sound; see* PER)

purse

purs·er

pur·su·ance

pur·su·ant
pur·su·ant·ly

pur·sue
pur·sues, pur·sued,
pur·su·ing
pur·su·er

pur·suit

pu·ru·lent
pu·ru·lence
pu·ru·len·cy
pu·ru·lent·ly

pur·vey
pur·vey·ance
pur·vey·or

pur·view

pus

Pu·san

push
push-up

push·er

push·ing

Push·kin

push·o·ver

push·y
push·i·er, push·i·est
push·i·ly
push·i·ness

pu·sil·lan·i·mous
pu·sil·la·nim·i·ty
pu·sil·lan·i·mous·ly

puss·y
pl. puss·ies
also puss, puss·y·cat

puss·y·foot
puss·y·foot·er

pus·tule
pus·tu·lar
pus·tu·lous

put
put·ting; *past and past
part.* put
put-on
put·ter

pu·ta·tive
pu·ta·tive·ly

pu·tre·fy
pu·tre·fies, pu·tre·fied
pu·tre·fa·cient
pu·tre·fac·tion
pu·tre·fac·tive

pu·tres·cent
pu·tres·cence

pu·trid
pu·trid·ly

putsch

putt
putt·er (*golf club*)

put·ter (*busy oneself*)
put·ter·er

put·ty
pl. put·ties
put·ties, put·tied

putz

puz·zle
puz·zle·ment
puz·zling·ly

puz·zler

pyg·my
pl. pyg·mies
also pig·my
pl. pig·mies
pyg·mae·an *or* pyg·
me·an

py·lon

Pyong·yang

py·or·rhe·a

pyr·a·mid
py·ram·i·dal
py·ram·i·dal·ly
pyr·a·mid·ic
also pyr·a·mid·i·cal
pyr·a·mid·i·cal·ly

pyre

Pyr·e·nees

Py·rex (*trademark*)

py·rite

py·rites
py·rit·ic
py·ri·tous

py·ro·ma·ni·a
py·ro·ma·ni·ac

py·ro·tech·nics
py·ro·tech·nic
py·ro·tech·ni·cal

pyr·rhic

Py·thag·o·ras

**Py·thag·o·re·an
the·o·rem**

py·thon

pyx
also pix

Q

Qa·dha·fi
also Gad·da·fi

Qa·tar
Qa·tar·i

Qing·dao
also Tsing·tao

Qom

qua

quack (*charlatan*)
quack·er·y
quack·ish

quack (*duck sound*)

quad

quad·ran·gle
quad·ran·gu·lar

quad·rant

quad·rat·ic

quad·ri·ceps

quad·ri·lat·er·al

quad·rille

quad·ri·ple·gia
quad·ri·ple·gic

quad·riv·i·um

quad·ru·ped
quad·ru·ped·al

quad·ru·ple
quad·rup·ly

quad·ru·plet

quad·ru·pli·cate

quaff

quag·mire

quail
pl. same *or* quails

quaint
quaint·ly
quaint·ness

quake
quak·y
quak·i·er, quak·i·est

Quak·er
Quak·er·ish
Quak·er·ism

qual·i·fi·ca·tion

qual·i·fy
qual·i·fies, qual·i·fied
qual·i·fi·er

qual·i·ta·tive
qual·i·ta·tive·ly

qual·i·ty
pl. qual·i·ties

qualm

quan·da·ry
pl. quan·da·ries

quan·ti·fy
quan·ti·fies, quan·ti·fied
quan·ti·fi·a·ble
quan·ti·fi·ca·tion
quan·ti·fi·er

quan·ti·ta·tive
quan·ti·ta·tive·ly

quan·ti·ty
pl. quan·ti·ties

quan·tum
pl. quan·ta

quar·an·tine

quark

quar·rel
quar·rel·er

quar·rel·some
quar·rel·some·ly
quar·rel·some·ness

quar·ry (*place to dig stone*)
pl. quar·ries
quar·ries, quar·ried

quar·ry (*prey*)
pl. quar·ries

quart

quar·ter

quar·ter·back

quar·ter·deck

quar·ter·fi·nal

quar·ter·ly
pl. quar·ter·lies

quar·ter·mas·ter

quar·tet

quar·tile

quar·to
pl. quar·tos

quartz

qua·sar

quash

quat·er·na·ry

quat·rain

qua·ver
qua·ver·ing·ly
qua·ver·y

quay (*landing; see* KEY)
quay·age

quea·sy
quea·si·er, quea·si·est
quea·si·ly
quea·si·ness

Que·bec
Que·beck·er
Que·bec·ois

Quech•ua
Quech•uan

queen
queen•less
queen•like
queen-size

queen•ly
queen•li•er, queen•
li•est
queen•li•ness

Queens

queer
queer•ish
queer•ly
queer•ness

quell
quell•er

quench
quench•a•ble
quench•er
quench•less

Que•ré•ta•ro

quer•u•lous
quer•u•lous•ly
quer•u•lous•ness

que•ry
pl. que•ries
que•ries, que•ried

quest
quest•er
quest•ing•ly

ques•tion
ques•tion•er
ques•tion•ing•ly
ques•tion•less

ques•tion•a•ble
ques•tion•a•ble•ness
ques•tion•a•bly

ques•tion•naire

queue (*line*; see CUE)
queues, queued, queu•
ing *or* queue•ing

Que•zon Cit•y

quib•ble
quib•bler
quib•bling
quib•bling•ly

quiche

quick
quick-tem•pered
quick•ly
quick•ness

quick•en

quick•ie

quick•lime

quick•sand

quick•sil•ver

quick-wit•ted
quick-wit•ted•ness

quid pro quo

qui•es•cent
qui•es•cence
qui•es•cent•ly

qui•et
qui•et•er, qui•et•est
qui•et•ly
qui•et•ness

qui•e•tude

qui•e•tus

quill

Quil•mes

quilt
quilt•er
quilt•ing

quince

qui•nine

Quin•ta•na Ro•o

quin•tes•sence
quin•tes•sen•tial
quin•tes•sen•tial•ly

quin•tet

quin•tile

quin•tu•ple

quin•tu•plet

quip
quipped, quip•ping
quip•ster

quire (*paper*; see CHOIR)

quirk
quirk•ish
quirk•y
quirk•i•er, quirk•i•est
quirk•i•ly
quirk•i•ness

quis•ling

quit
quit•ting; *past and past
part.* quit *or* quit•ted

quite

Qui•to

quits

quit•ter

quiv•er (*arrow holder*)

quiv•er (*tremble*)
quiv•er•ing•ly
quiv•er•y

quix•ot•ic
quix•ot•i•cal•ly

quiz
pl. quiz•zes

quiz•zi•cal
quiz•zi•cal•ly

**quod e•rat de•mon•
stran•dum**

quod vi•de

quoin (*cornerstone*; see
COIN)

quoit

quon•dam

Quon•set hut
(*trademark*)

quo·rum
quo·ta
quot·a·ble
quo·ta·tion

quote
quoth
quo·tid·i·an
quo·tient

QWERTY

R

Ra·bat

rab·bet (*channel*; see
RABBIT)

rab·bi
  pl. rab·bis
  rab·bin·i·cal

rab·bit (*animal*; see
RABBET)

rab·ble
  rab·ble-rous·er

Rab·e·lais
  Rab·e·lai·si·an

rab·id
  rab·id·i·ty
  rab·id·ly
  rab·id·ness

ra·bies

Ra·bin

rac·coon

race
  rac·er

race·horse

ra·ceme

race·track

race·way

Rach·ma·ni·noff

ra·cial
  ra·cial·ly

Ra·cine

rac·ism
  rac·ist

rack (*framework*; see
WRACK)

rack·et (*for tennis, etc.*)
  also rac·quet

rack·et (*noise*)

rack·et·eer
  rack·et·eer·ing

rac·on·teur
  fem. rac·on·teuse

rac·quet
  var. of rack·et

rac·quet·ball

rac·y
  rac·i·er, rac·i·est
  rac·i·ly
  rac·i·ness

rad

ra·dar

ra·di·al
  ra·di·al·ly

ra·di·ant
  ra·di·ance
  ra·di·ant·ly

ra·di·ate

ra·di·a·tion
  ra·di·a·tion·al
  ra·di·a·tion·al·ly

ra·di·a·tor

rad·i·cal
  rad·i·cal·ism
  rad·i·cal·ly

ra·dic·chi·o
  pl. ra·dic·chi·os

rad·i·ces

ra·di·i

ra·di·o
  pl. ra·di·os
  ra·di·oed

ra·di·o·ac·tive
  ra·di·o·ac·tive·ly

ra·di·o·ac·tiv·i·ty

ra·di·ol·o·gy
  ra·di·o·log·ic
  ra·di·o·log·i·cal
  ra·di·ol·o·gist

ra·di·om·e·ter
  ra·di·om·e·try

ra·di·os·co·py
  ra·di·o·scop·ic

ra·di·o·ther·a·py
  ra·di·o·ther·a·peu·tic
  ra·di·o·ther·a·pist

rad·ish

ra·di·um

ra·di·us
  pl. ra·di·i *or* ra·di·us·es

ra·dix
  pl. rad·i·ces *or* ra·dix·es

ra·don

raf·fi·a

raf·fish
  raf·fish·ly
  raf·fish·ness

raf·fle

raft

raf·ter

rag
  ragged, rag·ging

rag·a·muf·fin

rage

rag·ged
  rag·ged·ly
  rag·ged·ness
  rag·ged·y

rag·gle-tag·gle

rag·ing

rag·lan

ra·gout

rag·pick·er

rag·tag

rag·time

rag·weed

rah

raid (*attack; see rayed* [RAY])
raid·er

rail
rail·er
rail·ing

rail·ing

rail·ler·y
pl. rail·ler·ies

rail·road

rail·way

rai·ment

rain (*drops of water; see* REIGN, REIN)
rain·y
rain·i·er, rain·i·est

rain·bow

rain·coat

rain·drop

rain·fall

Rai·nier, Mt.

rain·proof

rain·storm

rain·water

raise (*elevate; see* RAZE)

rai·sin
rai·sin·y

rai·son d'ê·tre
pl. rai·sons d'ê·tre

raj

ra·ja
also ra·jah

rake
rak·er

rak·ish
rak·ish·ly
rak·ish·ness

rale

Ra·leigh (*city*)

Ra·leigh (*proper name*)
also Ra·legh

ral·ly
ral·lies, ral·lied
pl. ral·lies
ral·li·er

ram
rammed, ram·ming

Ram·a·dan

ram·ble
ram·bling

ram·bler

ram·bunc·tious
ram·bunc·tious·ly
ram·bunc·tious·ness

ram·e·kin

ram·i·fi·ca·tion

ram·i·fy

ramp

ram·page
ram·pag·er

ram·pant
ram·pan·cy
ram·pant·ly

ram·part

ram·rod

Ram·ses
also Ram·e·ses

ram·shack·le

ran

ranch
ranch·er

Ran·cho Cu·ca·mon·ga

ran·cid
ran·cid·i·ty

ran·cor
ran·cor·ous
ran·cor·ous·ly

Rand (*proper name*)

rand (*leather strip, coin*)

ran·dom
ran·dom-ac·cess
ran·dom·ly
ran·dom·ness

ran·dy
ran·di·er, ran·di·est
ran·di·ly
ran·di·ness

rang

range

rang·er

Ran·goon
also Yan·gon

rang·y
rang·i·er, rang·i·est

ra·ni
also ra·nee

rank (*foul-smelling*)
rank·ness

rank (*position*)

ran·kle

ran·sack
ran·sack·er

ran·som

rant

rap (*tapping sound; see* WRAP)
rapped (*see* RAPT, *wrapped* [WRAP]), rap·ping
rap·per

ra•pa•cious
  ra•pa•cious•ly
  ra•pa•cious•ness
  ra•pac•i•ty

rape
  rap•ist

Raph•a•el

rap•id
  rap•id-fire
  ra•pid•i•ty
  rap•id•ly
  rap•id•ness

Rap•id Cit•y

ra•pi•er

rap•ine

rap•port

rap•proche•ment

rap•scal•lion

rapt (*absorbed*; see *rapped*
  [RAP], *wrapped*
  [WRAP])
  rapt•ly
  rapt•ness

rap•tor
  rap•to•ri•al

rap•ture
  rap•tur•ous
  rap•tur•ous•ly

rare
  rar•er, rar•est
  rare•ness

rare•bit

rar•e•fy
  rar•e•fies, rar•e•fied
  rar•e•fac•tion
  rar•e•fac•tive

rare•ly

rar•ing

rar•i•ty
  pl. rar•i•ties

ras•cal
  ras•cal•ly

rash
  rash•ly
  rash•ness

rash•er

rasp
  rasp•ing•ly
  rasp•y

rasp•ber•ry
  pl. rasp•ber•ries

Ra•spu•tin

Ras•ta•far•i•an
  Ras•ta•far•i•an•ism

rat
  rat•ted, rat•ting

ra•ta•tou•ille

ratch•et

rate

rath•er

rat•i•fy
  rat•i•fies, rat•i•fied
  rat•i•fi•ca•tion
  rat•i•fi•er

rat•ing

ra•ti•o
  pl. ra•ti•os

ra•tion

ra•tion•al
  ra•tion•al•i•ty
  ra•tion•al•ly

ra•tion•ale

ra•tion•al•ism
  ra•tion•al•ist

ra•tion•al•ize
  ra•tion•al•i•za•tion

rat•line
  also rat•lin

rat•tan

rat•tle

rat•tle•snake

rat•tling

rat•ty
  rat•ti•er, rat•ti•est
  rat•ti•ness

rau•cous
  rau•cous•ly
  rau•cous•ness

raun•chy
  raun•chi•er, raun•chi•
    est
  raun•chi•ly
  raun•chi•ness

rav•age

rave

Ra•vel (*proper name*)

rav•el (*entangle*)

ra•ven

rav•en•ing

Ra•ven•na

rav•en•ous
  rav•en•ous•ly
  rav•en•ous•ness

ra•vine
  ra•vined

rav•ing
  rav•ing•ly

rav•i•o•li

rav•ish
  rav•ish•er
  rav•ish•ment

rav•ish•ing
  rav•ish•ing•ly

raw
  raw•ish
  raw•ly
  raw•ness

Ra·wal·pin·di

raw·boned

raw·hide

Ray (*proper name*)

ray (*beam; see* RE)
  rayed (*see* RAID)

ray·on

raze (*destroy; see* RAISE)

ra·zor

ra·zor·back

razz

raz·zle-daz·zle

razz·ma·tazz
  also raz·za·ma·tazz

re (*musical note; see* RAY)

re·ab·sorb

re·ac·cept

re·ac·cus·tom

reach
  reach·a·ble

re·ac·quaint

re·ac·quire

re·act

re·ac·tion
  re·ac·tion·ist

re·ac·tion·ar·y
  pl. re·ac·tion·ar·ies

re·ac·ti·vate
  re·ac·ti·va·tion

re·ac·tive
  re·ac·tiv·i·ty

re·ac·tor

read (*interpret; see* REED)
  past and *past part.* read
  (*see* RED)
  read-on·ly
  read-write

read·a·ble
  read·a·bil·i·ty
  read·a·bly

re·a·dapt

re·ad·ap·ta·tion

re·ad·dress

read·er

read·er·ship

read·i·ly

Read·ing (*proper name*)

read·ing (*interpretation*)

re·ad·just

re·ad·just·ment

re·ad·mis·sion

re·ad·mit

re·a·dopt

read·out

read·y
  read·i·er, read·i·est
  read·ies, read·ied
  read·y-made
  read·y-to-wear
  read·i·ness

re·af·firm

re·af·fir·ma·tion

Rea·gan

re·a·gent

re·al (*genuine; see* REEL)
  re·al-time
  re·al·ness

re·a·lign

re·a·lign·ment

re·al·ism
  re·al·ist

re·al·is·tic
  re·al·is·ti·cal·ly

re·al·i·ty
  pl. re·al·i·ties

re·al·ize
  re·al·iz·a·ble
  re·al·i·za·tion
  re·al·iz·er

re·al·lo·cate

re·al·lo·ca·tion

re·al·ly

realm

Re·al·tor (*trademark*)

re·al·ty

ream

re·an·i·mate
  re·an·i·ma·tion

reap

reap·er

re·ap·pear

re·ap·pear·ance

re·ap·pli·ca·tion

re·ap·ply

re·ap·point

re·ap·point·ment

rear (*back part*)

rear (*cultivate*)
  rear·er

re·arm

re·ar·ma·ment

rear·most

re·ar·range
  re·ar·range·ment

rear·ward
  also rear·wards

rea·son
  rea·son·ing

rea·son·a·ble
  rea·son·a·ble·ness
  rea·son·a·bly

re·as·sem·ble

re·as·sem·bly

re·as·sess

re·as·sess·ment

re·as·sign

re·as·sign·ment

re·as·sure
  re·as·sur·ance
  re·as·sur·ing
  re·as·sur·ing·ly

re·a·wak·en

re·bate
  re·bat·a·ble
  re·bat·er

reb·el
  re·belled, re·bel·ling

re·bel·lion

re·bel·lious
  re·bel·lious·ly
  re·bel·lious·ness

re·bind

re·birth
  re·born

re·bound
  re·bound·er

re·buff

re·build

re·buke
  re·buk·er
  re·buk·ing·ly

re·bus

re·but
  re·but·ted, re·but·ting
  re·but·ment
  re·but·ta·ble
  re·but·tal

re·cal·ci·trant
  re·cal·ci·trance
  re·cal·ci·trant·ly

re·call
  re·call·a·ble

re·cant
  re·can·ta·tion
  re·cant·er

re·cap
  re·capped, re·cap·ping

re·ca·pit·u·late
  re·ca·pit·u·la·tive
  re·ca·pit·u·la·to·ry

re·ca·pit·u·la·tion

re·cede

re·ceipt

re·ceive
  re·ceiv·a·ble

re·ceiv·er

re·ceiv·er·ship

re·cent
  re·cent·ly

re·cep·ta·cle

re·cep·tion

re·cep·tion·ist

re·cep·tive
  re·cep·tive·ly
  re·cep·tiv·i·ty

re·cess

re·ces·sion
  re·ces·sion·ar·y

re·ces·sion·al

re·ces·sive
  re·ces·sive·ly
  re·ces·sive·ness

re·charge

re·charge·a·ble

re·cher·ché

re·cid·i·vist
  re·cid·i·vism
  re·cid·i·vis·tic

Re·ci·fe

re·ci·pe

re·cip·i·ent

re·cip·ro·cal
  re·cip·ro·cal·i·ty
  re·cip·ro·cal·ly

re·cip·ro·cate
  re·cip·ro·ca·tion
  re·cip·ro·ca·tor

rec·i·proc·i·ty

re·cit·al

rec·i·ta·tion

rec·i·ta·tive

re·cite
  re·cit·er

reck·less
  reck·less·ly
  reck·less·ness

reck·on

re·claim
  re·claim·a·ble
  re·claim·er
  rec·la·ma·tion

re·clas·si·fi·ca·tion

re·clas·si·fy

re·cline
  re·clin·a·ble

re·clin·er

rec·luse
  re·clu·sion
  re·clu·sive

rec·og·ni·tion

re·cog·ni·zance

rec·og·nize
  rec·og·niz·a·ble
  rec·og·niz·a·bil·i·ty
  rec·og·niz·a·bly
  rec·og·niz·er

re•coil

rec•ol•lect
rec•ol•lec•tion

re•com•bi•nant

re•com•mence

re•com•mence•ment

rec•om•mend
rec•om•men•da•tion

rec•om•pense

rec•on•cile
rec•on•cil•a•ble
rec•on•cile•ment
rec•on•cil•er
rec•on•cil•i•a•tion
rec•on•cil•i•a•to•ry

rec•on•dite
rec•on•dite•ly
rec•on•dite•ness

re•con•di•tion
re•con•di•tion•er

re•con•nais•sance

re•con•nect

re•con•nec•tion

re•con•noi•ter

re•con•sid•er
re•con•sid•er•a•tion

re•con•sti•tute
re•con•sti•tu•tion

re•con•struct
re•con•struct•i•ble
also re•con•struct•a•ble
re•con•struc•tion
re•con•struc•tive

re•con•vene

re•con•ver•sion

re•con•vert

rec•ord (*account*)

re•cord (*take down*)
re•cord•a•ble

re•cord•er

re•cord•ing

re•count

re•coup
re•coup•a•ble
re•coup•ment

re•course

re•cov•er
re•cov•er•a•ble
re•cov•er•a•bil•i•ty
re•cov•er•y

rec•re•ant
rec•re•an•cy
rec•re•ant•ly

rec•re•a•tion
rec•re•a•tion•al
rec•re•a•tion•al•ly

re•crim•i•nate
re•crim•i•na•tion
re•crim•i•na•to•ry

re•cru•des•cence

re•cruit
re•cruit•ment

rec•ta

rec•tal
rec•tal•ly

rec•tan•gle
rec•tan•gu•lar

rec•ti•fy
rec•ti•fies, rec•ti•fied
rec•ti•fi•a•ble
rec•ti•fi•ca•tion
rec•ti•fi•er

rec•ti•lin•e•ar
also rec•ti•lin•e•al
rec•ti•lin•e•ar•i•ty
rec•ti•lin•e•ar•ly

rec•ti•tude

rec•to
pl. rec•tos

rec•tor

rec•to•ry
pl. rec•to•ries

rec•tum
pl. rec•tums *or* rec•ta

re•cum•bent
re•cum•ben•cy
re•cum•bent•ly

re•cu•per•ate
re•cu•per•a•tion
re•cu•per•a•tive

re•cur
re•curred, re•cur•ring

re•cur•rent
re•cur•rence
re•cur•rent•ly

re•cy•cle
re•cy•cla•ble

red (*color; see* read
[READ])
red-blood•ed
red-eye
red-faced
red-hand•ed
red-hot
red-let•ter day
red•dish
red•ness

red•cap

red•coat

red•den

re•dec•o•rate
re•dec•o•ra•tion

re•deem
re•deem•a•ble

re•deem•er

re•de•fine

re•demp•tion
re•demp•tive

re·de·vel·op
  re·de·vel·op·er
  re·de·vel·op·ment

red·head

re·dis·cov·er

re·dis·trib·ute

re·dis·tri·bu·tion

re·dis·trict·ing

red·neck

re·do
  3rd sing. present re·does;
    past re·did; *past part.*
    re·done

red·o·lent
  red·o·lence
  red·o·lent·ly

re·dou·ble

re·doubt

re·doubt·a·ble
  re·doubt·a·bly

re·dound

re·draft

re·draw

re·dress
  re·dress·er
  also re·dres·sor

re·duce
  re·duc·er
  re·duc·i·ble
  re·duc·i·bil·i·ty
  re·duc·tion

re·dun·dant
  re·dun·dan·cy
  pl. re·dun·dan·cies
  re·dun·dant·ly

re·du·pli·cate
  re·du·pli·ca·tion

red·wood

Reed (*proper name*)

reed (*stalk;* see READ)

reed·y
  reed·i·er, reed·i·est
  reed·i·ness

reef

reef·er

reek (*smell;* see WREAK)

reel (*winding device,
  dance;* see REAL)
  reel·er

re·e·lect

re·e·lec·tion

re·em·bark

re·e·merge

re·em·pha·size

re·em·ploy

re·em·ploy·ment

re·en·act
  re·en·act·ment

re·en·ter

re·en·try
  pl. re·en·tries

re·es·tab·lish

re·es·tab·lish·ment

re·e·val·u·ate

re·ex·am·i·na·tion

re·ex·am·ine

ref

re·fec·to·ry
  pl. re·fec·to·ries

re·fer
  re·ferred, re·fer·ring
  re·fer·a·ble
  re·fer·ral
  re·fer·rer

ref·er·ee
  ref·er·ees, ref·er·eed

ref·er·ence
  ref·er·en·tial

ref·er·en·dum
  pl. ref·er·en·dums *or*
    ref·er·en·da

re·fill
  re·fill·a·ble

re·fi·nance

re·fine
  re·fin·a·ble
  re·fined
  re·fine·ment

re·fin·er·y
  pl. re·fin·er·ies

re·fit
  re·fit·ted, re·fit·ting
  re·fit·ment

re·flect

re·flec·tion
  re·flec·tion·al

re·flec·tive
  re·flec·tive·ly
  re·flec·tive·ness

re·flec·tor

re·flex

re·flex·ive
  re·flex·ive·ly
  re·flex·ive·ness

re·fo·cus

re·for·est
  re·for·est·a·tion

re·form
  re·form·a·ble

re·for·mat

ref·or·ma·tion

re·for·ma·to·ry
  pl. re·for·ma·to·ries

re·form·er

re·for·mu·late

re•for•mu•la•tion

re•fract
re•frac•tion
re•frac•tive

re•frac•tor

re•frac•to•ry
re•frac•to•ri•ly

re•frain

re•fresh
re•fresh•er
re•fresh•ing
re•fresh•ing•ly

re•fresh•ment

re•frig•er•ant

re•frig•er•ate
re•frig•er•a•tion
re•frig•er•a•tive

re•frig•er•a•tor

ref•uge

ref•u•gee

re•fund
re•fund•a•ble

re•fur•bish
re•fur•bish•ment

re•fur•nish

ref•use (*garbage*)

re•fuse (*say no*)
re•fus•a•ble
re•fus•al

re•fute
re•fut•a•ble
ref•u•ta•tion
re•fut•er

re•gain

re•gal
re•gal•ly

re•gale
re•gale•ment

re•ga•li•a

re•gard

re•gard•ing

re•gard•less
re•gard•less•ly

re•gat•ta

re•gen•cy
pl. re•gen•cies

re•gen•er•ate
re•gen•er•a•tion
re•gen•er•a•tive
re•gen•er•a•tive•ly
re•gen•er•a•tor

re•gent

reg•gae

reg•i•cide
reg•i•cid•al

re•gime
also ré•gime

reg•i•men

reg•i•ment
reg•i•ment•al
reg•i•ment•ed
reg•i•men•ta•tion

Re•gi•na

re•gion
re•gion•al
re•gion•al•ly

reg•is•ter
reg•is•tra•ble

reg•is•trar

reg•is•tra•tion

reg•is•try
pl. reg•is•tries

re•gress
re•gres•sion
re•gres•sive
re•gres•sive•ly

re•gret
re•gret•ted, re•gret•
ting

re•gret•ful
re•gret•ful•ly
re•gret•ta•ble
re•gret•ta•bly

re•group
re•group•ment

re•grow

reg•u•lar
reg•u•lar•i•ty
reg•u•lar•ize
reg•u•lar•i•za•tion
reg•u•lar•ly

reg•u•late
reg•u•la•tive
reg•u•la•tor
reg•u•la•to•ry

reg•u•la•tion

re•gur•gi•tate
re•gur•gi•ta•tion

re•hab

re•ha•bil•i•tate
re•ha•bil•i•ta•tion
re•ha•bil•i•ta•tive

re•hash

re•hears•al

re•hearse

re•heat

Rehn•quist

Reich

reign (*rule*; see RAIN,
REIN)

re•im•burse
re•im•burs•a•ble
re•im•burse•ment
re•im•burs•er

re•im•pose

Reims

rein (*strap*; see RAIN,
REIGN)

re·in·car·na·tion
re·in·car·nate

rein·deer
pl. same *or* reindeers

re·in·fect

re·in·force
re·in·force·ment
re·in·forc·er

re·in·oc·u·late

re·in·sert

re·in·state
re·in·state·ment

re·in·sure
re·in·sur·ance
re·in·sur·er

re·in·ter·pret

re·in·ter·pre·ta·tion

re·in·vest

re·in·vest·ment

re·is·sue

re·it·er·ate
re·it·er·a·tion
re·it·er·a·tive

re·ject
re·ject·er
also re·jec·tor
re·jec·tion

re·joice
re·joic·ing·ly

re·join

re·join·der

re·ju·ve·nate
re·ju·ve·na·tion
re·ju·ve·na·tor

re·kin·dle

re·lapse

re·late
re·lat·a·ble

re·lat·ed

re·la·tion
re·la·tion·al

re·la·tion·ship

rel·a·tive
rel·a·tive·ly

rel·a·tiv·i·ty

re·lax
re·lax·a·tion
re·lax·er

re·lax·ant

re·lay

re·learn

re·lease
re·leas·a·ble

rel·e·gate
rel·e·ga·tion

re·lent

re·lent·less
re·lent·less·ly
re·lent·less·ness

rel·e·vant
rel·e·vance
rel·e·van·cy
rel·e·vant·ly

re·li·a·ble
re·li·a·bil·i·ty
re·li·a·bly

re·li·ance
re·li·ant

rel·ic

re·lief

re·lieve
re·liev·a·ble
re·lieved
re·liev·er

re·light

re·li·gion

re·lig·i·os·i·ty

re·li·gious
re·li·gious·ly

re·lin·quish
re·lin·quish·ment

rel·ish

re·live

re·load

re·lo·cate
re·lo·ca·tion

re·luc·tant
re·luc·tance
re·luc·tant·ly

re·ly
re·lies, re·lied

re·main

re·main·der

re·mains

re·make
past and *past part.*
re·made

re·mand

re·mark

re·mark·a·ble
re·mark·a·ble·ness
re·mark·a·bly

Re·marque

re·match

Rem·brandt

re·me·di·al
re·me·di·al·ly

rem·e·dy
pl. rem·e·dies
rem·e·dies, rem·e·died

re·mem·ber

re·mem·brance

re·mind

re·mind·er

rem·i·nisce

rem·i·nis·cence

rem·i·nis·cent
  rem·i·nis·cent·ly

re·miss

re·mis·sion
  re·mis·sive

re·mit
  re·mit·ted, re·mit·ting
  re·mit·ta·ble
  re·mit·tal
  re·mit·ter

re·mit·tance

rem·nant

re·mod·el

re·mon·strate
  re·mon·strance
  re·mon·strant
  re·mon·stra·tion
  re·mon·stra·tive
  re·mon·stra·tor

re·morse
  re·morse·ful
  re·morse·ful·ly
  re·morse·less

re·mote
  re·mot·er, re·mot·est
  re·mote·ly
  re·mote·ness

re·move
  re·mov·a·ble
  re·mov·a·bil·i·ty
  re·mov·al

re·mu·ner·ate
  re·mu·ner·a·tion
  re·mu·ner·a·tive

Ren·ais·sance
  also ren·ais·sance

re·nal

re·name

re·nas·cent
  re·nas·cence

Re·nault

rend
  past and past part. rent

ren·der
  ren·der·ing

ren·dez·vous
  pl. same
  ren·dez·vouses, ren·
    dez·voused, ren·dez·
    vous·ing

ren·di·tion

ren·e·gade

re·nege
  re·neg·er

re·ne·go·ti·ate

re·ne·go·ti·a·tion

re·new
  re·new·a·ble
  re·new·al
  re·new·er

Rennes

ren·net

Re·no

Re·noir

re·nom·i·nate

re·nounce
  re·nounce·a·ble
  re·nounce·ment

ren·o·vate
  ren·o·va·tion
  ren·o·va·tor

re·nown
  re·nowned

rent (*lease*)
  rent·er

rent (*rip*)

rent·al

re·num·ber

re·nun·ci·a·tion

re·oc·cu·pa·tion

re·oc·cu·py

re·oc·cur

re·o·pen

re·or·ga·nize

re·or·i·ent

re·or·i·en·tate
  re·or·i·en·ta·tion

rep

re·paid

re·pair
  re·pair·a·ble
  re·pair·er

re·pair·man
  pl. re·pair·men

rep·a·ra·ble
  rep·a·ra·bil·i·ty
  rep·a·ra·bly

rep·a·ra·tion
  re·par·a·tive

rep·ar·tee

re·past

re·pa·tri·ate
  re·pa·tri·a·tion

re·pay
  past and past part. re·
    paid
  re·pay·a·ble
  re·pay·ment

re·peal
  re·peal·a·ble

re·peat
  re·peat·a·ble
  re·peat·a·bil·i·ty
  re·peat·ed·ly

re·pel
  re·pelled, re·pel·ling
  re·pel·lent
  re·pel·ler

re·pent
  re·pent·ance

re•pent•ant
re•pent•er

re•per•cus•sion
re•per•cus•sive

rep•er•toire

rep•er•to•ry
pl rep•er•to•ries

rep•e•ti•tion
rep•e•ti•tious
rep•e•ti•tious•ly
re•pet•i•tive
re•pet•i•tive•ly

re•place
re•place•a•ble
re•place•ment
re•plac•er

re•play

re•plen•ish
re•plen•ish•ment

re•plete
re•plete•ness
re•ple•tion

rep•li•ca
rep•li•cate
rep•li•ca•tion

re•ply
re•plies, re•plied
pl. re•plies
re•pli•er

re•pop•u•late

re•port
re•port•ed•ly

re•port•age

re•port•er

re•pose

re•pos•i•to•ry
pl. re•pos•i•to•ries

re•pos•sess
re•pos•ses•sion
re•pos•ses•sor

rep•re•hend
rep•re•hen•sion

rep•re•hen•si•ble
rep•re•hen•si•bil•i•ty
rep•re•hen•si•bly

rep•re•sent
rep•re•sent•a•ble

rep•re•sen•ta•tion
rep•re•sen•ta•tion•al

rep•re•sen•ta•tive

re•press
re•press•er
also re•pres•sor
re•pres•si•ble
re•pres•sion
re•pres•sive
re•pres•sive•ly

re•prieve

rep•ri•mand

re•print

re•pris•al

re•prise

re•proach
re•proach•a•ble
re•proach•er
re•proach•ful
re•proach•ful•ly
re•proach•ing•ly

rep•ro•bate

re•proc•ess

re•pro•duce
re•pro•duc•er
re•pro•duc•i•ble
re•pro•duc•i•bil•i•ty

re•pro•duc•tion
re•pro•duc•tive
re•pro•duc•tive•ly

re•pro•gram

re•pro•gram•ma•ble

re•proof

re•prove
re•prov•er
re•prov•ing•ly

rep•tile
rep•til•i•an

re•pub•lic

re•pub•li•can
re•pub•li•can•ism

re•pub•lish

re•pu•di•ate
re•pu•di•a•tion
re•pu•di•a•tor

re•pug•nance
also re•pug•nan•cy
re•pug•nant

re•pulse

re•pul•sion

re•pul•sive
re•pul•sive•ly
re•pul•sive•ness

rep•u•ta•ble
rep•u•ta•bly

rep•u•ta•tion

re•pute
re•put•ed•ly

re•quest
re•quest•er

req•ui•em

re•quire
re•quir•er
re•quire•ment

req•ui•site

req•ui•si•tion
req•ui•si•tion•er

re•quite
re•quit•al

re•read

re•re•cord

re•re•lease

re•route

re·run
re·run·ning; *past* re·ran; *past part.* re·run

re·sale

re·sched·ule

re·scind
re·scind·a·ble
re·scind·ment
re·scis·sion

res·cue
res·cues, res·cued, res·cu·ing
res·cu·a·ble
res·cu·er

re·seal

re·seal·a·ble

re·search
re·search·a·ble
re·search·er

re·sell

re·sem·blance

re·sem·ble

re·sent
re·sent·ful
re·sent·ful·ly
re·sent·ment

res·er·va·tion

re·serve
re·serv·a·ble
re·serv·er

re·served
re·serv·ed·ly
re·serv·ed·ness

re·serv·ist

res·er·voir

re·set
re·set·ting; *past* and *past part.* re·set
re·set·ta·ble

re·set·tle

re·shape

re·shuf·fle

re·side

res·i·dence

res·i·den·cy
pl. res·i·den·cies

res·i·dent

res·i·den·tial
res·i·den·tial·ly

re·sid·u·al
re·sid·u·al·ly

res·i·due

re·sign

res·ig·na·tion

re·signed
re·sign·ed·ly
re·sign·ed·ness

re·sil·i·ent
re·sil·i·ence
re·sil·i·en·cy
re·sil·i·ent·ly

res·in
res·in·ous

re·sist
re·sist·ant
re·sist·er
re·sist·i·ble
re·sist·i·bil·i·ty

re·sist·ance

re·sis·tor

res·o·lute
res·o·lute·ly
res·o·lute·ness

res·o·lu·tion

re·solve
re·solv·a·ble
re·solv·a·bil·i·ty
re·solv·er

re·solved

res·o·nant
res·o·nance
res·o·nant·ly

res·o·nate
res·o·na·tor

re·sorb
re·sorb·ence
re·sorb·ent
re·sorp·tion

re·sort

re·sound

re·sound·ing
re·sound·ing·ly

re·source
re·source·ful
re·source·ful·ly
re·source·ful·ness

re·spect
re·spect·er

re·spect·a·ble
re·spect·a·bil·i·ty
re·spect·a·bly

re·spect·ful
re·spect·ful·ly
re·spect·ful·ness

re·spect·ing

re·spec·tive
re·spec·tive·ly

res·pi·ra·tion

res·pi·ra·tor

re·spire
res·pi·ra·to·ry

res·pite

re·splend·ent
re·splend·ence
re·splend·en·cy
re·splend·ent·ly

re·spond

re·spond·ent

re·sponse

re·spon·si·bil·i·ty
   pl. re·spon·si·bil·i·ties

re·spon·si·ble
   re·spon·si·bly

re·spon·sive
   re·spon·sive·ly
   re·spon·sive·ness

re·spon·so·ry

rest (*be still*; see WREST)

re·state

res·tau·rant

res·tau·ra·teur

rest·ful
   rest·ful·ly
   rest·ful·ness

res·ti·tu·tion

res·tive
   res·tive·ly
   res·tive·ness

rest·less
   rest·less·ly
   rest·less·ness

re·stock

res·to·ra·tion

re·stor·a·tive
   re·stor·a·tive·ly

re·store
   re·stor·a·ble
   re·stor·er

re·strain
   re·strain·a·ble
   re·strain·er

re·straint

re·strict
   re·strict·ed·ly
   re·strict·ed·ness
   re·stric·tion

re·stric·tive
   re·stric·tive·ly
   re·stric·tive·ness

re·string

re·struc·ture

re·style

re·sult
   re·sult·ant

re·sume (*begin again*)
   re·sum·a·ble

ré·su·mé (*summary*)
   also re·su·mé, re·su·me

re·sump·tion
   re·sump·tive

re·sur·face

re·sur·gent
   re·sur·gence

res·ur·rect

res·ur·rec·tion
   res·ur·rec·tion·al

re·sus·ci·tate
   re·sus·ci·ta·tion
   re·sus·ci·ta·tive
   re·sus·ci·ta·tor

re·tail
   re·tail·er

re·tain
   re·tain·a·ble

re·tain·er

re·take
   past re·took; *past part.*
   re·tak·en

re·tal·i·ate
   re·tal·i·a·tion
   re·tal·i·a·tor
   re·tal·i·a·to·ry

re·tard
   re·tard·ant
   re·tar·da·tion

re·tard·ed

retch (*vomit*; see
   WRETCH)

re·tell

re·ten·tion
   re·ten·tive
   re·ten·tive·ly

ret·i·cence
   ret·i·cent
   ret·i·cent·ly

re·tic·u·late
   re·tic·u·late·ly
   re·tic·u·la·tion

ret·i·cule

ret·i·na
   pl. ret·i·nas *or* ret·i·nae
   ret·i·nal

ret·i·nue

re·tire
   re·tired
   re·tir·ee
   re·tire·ment
   re·tir·er

re·tir·ing
   re·tir·ing·ly

re·took

re·tort

re·touch

re·trace

re·tract
   re·tract·a·ble
   re·trac·tion
   re·trac·tive

re·trac·tile
   re·trac·til·i·ty

re·tread
   past re·trod; *past part.*
   re·trod·den

re·treat

re·trench
   re·trench·ment

ret·ri·bu·tion
   re·trib·u·tive
   re·trib·u·to·ry

re·trieve
  re·triev·a·ble
  re·triev·al

re·triev·er

ret·ro

ret·ro·ac·tive
  ret·ro·ac·tive·ly
  ret·ro·ac·tiv·i·ty

ret·ro·fit
  ret·ro·fit·ted, ret·ro·
  fit·ting

ret·ro·grade

ret·ro·gress
  ret·ro·gres·sion
  ret·ro·gres·sive
  ret·ro·gres·sive·ly

ret·ro-rock·et

ret·ro·spect
  ret·ro·spec·tion

ret·ro·spec·tive
  ret·ro·spec·tive·ly

ret·ro·vi·rus

re·try
  re·tries, re·tried
  re·tri·al

re·turn
  re·turn·a·ble

re·turn·ee

re·type

re·un·ion (*gathering*)

Ré·u·nion (*proper name*)

re·u·nite

re·up·hol·ster

re·use
  re·us·a·ble

rev
  revved, rev·ving

re·vamp

re·veal
  re·veal·ing·ly

rev·eil·le

rev·el
  rev·el·er
  rev·el·ry
  pl. rev·el·ries

rev·e·la·tion
  rev·e·la·tion·al

re·venge
  re·venge·ful
  re·venge·ful·ly
  re·veng·er

rev·e·nue

re·ver·ber·ate
  re·ver·ber·ant
  re·ver·ber·ant·ly
  re·ver·ber·a·tion
  re·ver·ber·a·tive
  re·ver·ber·a·tor
  re·ver·ber·a·to·ry

Re·vere (*proper name*)

re·vere (*hold in respect*)
  rev·er·ence
  rev·er·ent
  rev·er·en·tial
  rev·er·en·tial·ly

rev·er·end

rev·er·ie

re·verse
  re·ver·sal
  re·vers·er
  re·vers·i·ble
  re·vers·i·bil·i·ty
  re·vers·i·bly

re·vert

re·view (*appraisal*; see
  REVUE)
  re·view·a·ble
  re·view·er

re·vile
  re·vile·ment
  re·vil·er
  re·vil·ing

re·vise
  re·vis·a·ble
  re·vis·er
  re·vi·sion
  re·vi·so·ry

re·vi·sion·ism
  re·vi·sion·ist

re·vis·it

re·vi·tal·ize

re·viv·al
  re·viv·al·ism
  re·viv·al·ist
  re·viv·al·is·tic

re·vive
  re·viv·a·ble

re·viv·i·fy
  re·viv·i·fies, re·viv·i·
  fied
  re·viv·i·fi·ca·tion

re·voke
  re·vo·ca·ble
  re·vo·ca·bil·i·ty
  rev·o·ca·tion
  re·vok·er

re·volt

re·volt·ing
  re·volt·ing·ly

rev·o·lu·tion
  rev·o·lu·tion·ar·y
  rev·o·lu·tion·ism
  rev·o·lu·tion·ist

rev·o·lu·tion·ize

re·volve

re·volv·er

re·vue (*entertainment*; see
  REVIEW)

re·vul·sion

re·ward

re·ward·ing
  re·ward·ing·ly

re•wind
past and past part.
re•wound
re•wind•er

re•wire

re•word

re•work

re•write
past re•wrote, *past part.*
re•writ•ten

Reye's syn•drome

Rey•kja•vik

Reyn•olds

rhap•so•dize

rhap•so•dy
pl. rhap•so•dies
rhap•sod•ic
rhap•sod•i•cal

rhe•a

Rhee

rhe•ni•um

rhe•o•stat
rhe•o•stat•ic

rhe•sus

rhet•o•ric
rhe•tor•i•cal
rhe•tor•i•cal•ly

rheu•ma•tism
rheu•mat•ic
rheu•mat•i•cal•ly

rheu•ma•toid

Rh fac•tor

Rhine Riv•er

rhine•stone

rhi•ni•tis

rhi•no
pl. same *or* rhi•nos

rhi•noc•er•os
pl. same *or* rhi•noc•er•
os•es

rhi•zome

rho

Rhode Is•land
Rhode Is•land•er

Rhodes

Rho•de•sia

rho•di•um

rho•do•den•dron

rhom•boid
rhom•boi•dal

rhom•bus
pl. rhom•bus•es *or*
rhom•bi

Rhone Riv•er

rhu•barb

rhyme (*poetry*; see RIME)
rhym•er

rhythm
rhyth•mic
rhyth•mi•cal
rhyth•mi•cal•ly
rhythm•less

rib
ribbed, rib•bing
rib•less

rib•ald

rib•bon
rib•boned

ri•bo•fla•vin

ri•bo•nu•cle•ic ac•id

rice
ric•er

rich
rich•ly
rich•ness

Rich•ard•son

Rich•e•lieu

rich•es

Rich•mond

Rich•ter scale

rich•els

rick•et•y
rick•et•i•ness

Rick•o•ver

rick•sha
also rick•shaw

ric•o•chet
ric•o•cheted; ric•o•
chet•ing

ri•cot•ta

rid
rid•ding; *past and past
part.* rid

rid•dance

rid•dle
rid•dler

Ride (*proper name*)

ride (*travel on*)
past rode; *past part.*
rid•den
rid•a•ble

rid•er
rid•er•less

ridge
ridg•y

ridge•pole

rid•i•cule

ri•dic•u•lous
ri•dic•u•lous•ly
ri•dic•u•lous•ness

rid•ing

rife
rife•ness

riff

rif•fle

riff-raff

ri·fle

ri·fle·man
pl. ri·fle·men

ri·fling

rift

rig
rigged, rig·ging

Ri·ga

rig·ger (one who rigs; see
RIGOR)

rig·ging

right (true; see RITE,
WRIGHT, WRITE)
right-hand
right-hand·ed
right-mind·ed
right-think·ing
right-to-die
right-to-life
right-to-work
right-wing
right-wing·er
right·a·ble
right·ly
right·ness

right·eous
right·eous·ly
right·eous·ness

right·ful
right·ful·ly

right·ism
right·ist

right·most

rig·id
ri·gid·i·ty
rig·id·ly
rig·id·ness

rig·ma·role
also rig·a·ma·role

rig·or (strictness; see
RIGGER)

rig·or·ous
rig·or·ous·ly
rig·or·ous·ness

rile

rill

rim
rimmed, rim·ming
rim·less

rime (frost; see RHYME)

Rim·i·ni

Rim·sky-Kor·sa·kov

rind

ring (sound; see WRING)
past rang; past part.
rung
ringed
ring·er (athlete; see
WRINGER)
ring·ing
ring·ing·ly

ring·lead·er

ring·let

ring·mas·ter

ring·side

ring·worm

rink

rinse
rins·er
rins·ing

Ri·o de Ja·nei·ro

Ri·o Gran·de

ri·ot
ri·ot·er
ri·ot·ous

rip
ripped, rip·ping
rip-off

ri·par·i·an

ripe
ripe·ly
ripe·ness

rip·en

ri·poste

rip·ple
rip·ply

rip-roar·ing
rip-roar·ing·ly

rip·saw

rip·snort·er
rip·snort·ing
rip·snort·ing·ly

rip·tide

rise
past rose; past part.
ris·en

ris·er

ris·i·ble

ris·ing

risk
risk·i·ly
risk·i·ness
risk·y

ris·qué

rite (ceremony; see RIGHT,
WRIGHT, WRITE)

rit·u·al
rit·u·al·ism
rit·u·al·ist
rit·u·al·is·tic
rit·u·al·is·ti·cal·ly
rit·u·al·i·za·tion
rit·u·al·ize
rit·u·al·ly

ritz·y
ritz·i·er, ritz·i·est
ritz·i·ly
ritz·i·ness

ri·val
ri·val·ry
pl. ri·val·ries

rive
past rived; past part.
riv·en

riv·er

Ri·ve·ra

riv·er·side

riv·et
  riv·et·er

riv·u·let

Ri·yadh

roach

road (*street*; see RODE)

road·bed

road·block

road·house

road·run·ner

road·side

road·ster

road·way

road·work

roam
  roam·er

roan

Ro·a·noke

roar
  roar·er

roar·ing

roast

roast·er

roast·ing

rob
  robbed, rob·bing
  rob·ber
  rob·ber·y
  pl. rob·ber·ies

Rob·bins

robe

Robe·son

Robes·pierre

rob·in

Rob·in·son

ro·bot
  ro·bot·ic
  ro·bot·ize

ro·bot·ics

ro·bust
  ro·bust·er, ro·bust·est
  ro·bust·ly
  ro·bust·ness

Roch·es·ter

rock
  rock-bot·tom

rock·a·bil·ly

Rock·e·fel·ler

rock·er

rock·et

rock·et·ry

Rock·ford

rock·y
  rock·i·er, rock·i·est
  rock·i·ly
  rock·i·ness

Rock·y Moun·tains

ro·co·co

rod
  rod·less
  rod·like

rode (*past of ride*; see
  ROAD)

ro·dent

ro·de·o
  pl. ro·de·os

Rodg·ers

Ro·din

roe (*deer*; see ROW)
  pl. same *or* roes (see
  ROSE)

roe (*fish eggs*; see ROW)

roe·buck
  pl. same *or* roe·bucks

Roent·gen (*proper name*)

roent·gen (*unit of
  radiation*)

rog·er

Rog·ers

rogue
  ro·guer·y
  ro·guish
  ro·guish·ly
  ro·guish·ness

roil

roist·er
  roist·er·er
  roist·er·ing
  roist·er·ous

role (*actor's part*; see
  ROLL)
  also rôle

roll (*turn, bread*; see
  ROLE)
  roll-top
  roll·a·ble

roll·a·way

roll·er

Rol·ler·blade
  (*trademark*)

rol·lick

roll·over

Röl·vaag

ro·ly-po·ly

ro·maine

Ro·man
  also ro·man (*type*)

Ro·man Cath·o·lic
  Ro·man Ca·thol·i·cism

ro·mance
  also Ro·mance
  (*languages*)

Ro·ma·ni·a
  also Ru·ma·ni·a
  Ro·ma·ni·an
  also Ru·ma·ni·an

Ro·ma·no

Ro·mansh

ro·man·tic
  ro·man·ti·cal·ly

ro·man·ti·cism
  also Ro·man·ti·cism)
  ro·man·ti·cist
  also Ro·man·ti·cist

ro·man·ti·cize
  ro·man·ti·ci·za·tion

Rom·a·ny

Rom·berg

Rome

Ro·me·o
  pl. Ro·me·os

Rom·mel

romp

romp·er

ron·do

Rönt·gen
  var. of Roent·gen

rood (*crucifix; see* RUDE)

roof
  pl. roofs
  roofed
  roof·er

roof·ing

roof·top

rook

rook·er·y
  pl. rook·er·ies

rook·ie

room
  room·er (*one who rooms;*
    see RUMOR)
  room·ful
  pl. room·fuls

room·mate

room·y
  room·ier, room·i·est
  room·i·ly
  room·i·ness

Roo·se·velt

roost

roost·er

root (*dig, cheer*)
  root·er

root (*part of a plant*)
  root·ed·ness
  root·less
  root·let

rope

Roque·fort

ror·qual

Ror·schach test

ro·sa·ceous

Ro·sa·ri·o

ro·sa·ry
  pl. ro·sa·ries

rose (*flower; see* roes
  [ROE])

ro·sé (*wine*)

ro·se·ate

Ro·seau

rose·bud

rose·mar·y

ro·sette

rose·wood

Rosh Ha·sha·nah
  also Rosh Ha·sha·na

ros·in
  ros·in·y

Ross

Ros·set·ti

Ros·si·ni

Ros·tand

ros·ter

Ros·tock

Ro·stov

ros·trum
  pl. ros·tra *or* ros·trums

ros·y
  ros·i·er, ros·i·est
  ros·i·ly
  ros·i·ness

rot
  rot·ted, rot·ting

ro·ta·ry
  pl. ro·ta·ries

ro·tate
  ro·tat·a·ble
  ro·ta·tion
  ro·ta·tive
  ro·ta·tor
  ro·ta·to·ry

rote (*repetition; see* wrote
  [WRITE])

rot·gut

Roth

Roth·schild

ro·tis·ser·ie

ro·tor

ro·to·til·ler
  ro·to·till

rot·ten
  rot·ten·er, rot·ten·est
  rot·ten·ly
  rot·ten·ness

Rot·ter·dam

Rott·wei·ler

ro·tund
  ro·tun·di·ty
  ro·tund·ly

ro·tun·da

rou·é

Rou·en

rouge

rough (*uneven*; see RUFF)
  rough-hewn
  rough·ly
  rough·ness

rough·age

rough·en

rough·house

rough·neck

rough·shod

rou·lette

round
  round·ish
  round·ness

round·a·bout

roun·de·lay

round·house

round·ly

round·up

round·worm

rouse
  rous·a·ble
  rous·er
  rous·ing
  rous·ing·ly

Rous·seau

roust·a·bout

rout

route

rou·tine

rove
  rov·ing

row (*succession, quarrel*; see ROE)

row (*propel a boat*; see ROE)
  row·er

row·boat

row·dy
  row·di·er, row·di·est
  pl. row·dies
  row·di·ly
  row·di·ness
  row·dy·ism

row·el

roy·al
  roy·al·ly

roy·al·ist

roy·al·ism

roy·al·ty
  pl. roy·al·ties

rub
  rubbed, rub·bing

rub·ber
  rub·ber-stamp
  rub·ber·y
  rub·ber·i·ness

rub·ber·ize

rub·ber·neck

rub·bish
  rub·bish·y

rub·ble
  rub·bly

rube

ru·bel·la

Ru·bens

ru·bi·cund

ru·bid·i·um

Ru·bin·stein

ru·ble

ru·bric
  ru·bri·cal

ru·by
  pl. ru·bies

ruck·sack

ruck·us

rud·der

rud·dy
  rud·di·er, rud·di·est
  rud·di·ly
  rud·di·ness

rude (*impolite*; see ROOD)
  rude·ly
  rude·ness

ru·di·ment
  ru·di·men·ta·ry

rue
  rues, rued, ru·ing
  rue·ful
  rue·ful·ly
  rue·ful·ness

ruff (*collar*; see ROUGH)

ruf·fi·an
  ruf·fi·an·ism

ruf·fle

ru·fous

rug

rug·by

rug·ged
  rug·ged·ly
  rug·ged·ness

ru·in
  ru·in·a·tion
  ru·in·ous
  ru·in·ous·ly

rule

rul·er
  rul·er·ship

rul·ing

rum

Ru·ma·ni·a
var. of Ro·ma·ni·a
Ru·ma·ni·an
var. of Ro·ma·ni·an

rum·ba
rum·bas, rum·baed,
rum·ba·ing

rum·ble
rum·bler

ru·mi·nant

ru·mi·nate
ru·mi·na·tion
ru·mi·na·tive
ru·mi·na·tive·ly
ru·mi·na·tor

rum·mage
rum·mag·er

rum·my

ru·mor (*gossip*; see *roomer*
[ROOM])

rump

rum·ple
rum·ply

rum·pus

run
run·ning; *past* ran; *past
part.* run
run-down
run-in
run-of-the-mill
run-through

run·a·bout

run·a·round

run·a·way

run·down

rune
ru·nic

rung (*step of a ladder*; see
WRUNG)
runged
rung·less

rung (*past part. of ring*;
see WRUNG)

run·nel

run·ner
run·ner-up
pl. run·ners-up

run·ning

run·ny
run·ni·er, run·ni·est

run·off

runt
runt·y

run·way

ru·pee

rup·ture
rup·tur·a·ble

ru·ral
ru·ral·ly

ruse

rush (*hurry*)
rush·er
rush·ing·ly

rush (*plant*)
rush·y

Rush·die

Rush·more, Mt.

rusk

Rus·kin

Rus·sell

rus·set
rus·set·y

Rus·sia
Rus·sian

rust

rus·tic
rus·ti·cal·ly
rus·tic·i·ty

rus·ti·cate
rus·ti·ca·tion

rus·tle
rus·tler

rust·proof

rust·y
rust·i·er, rust·i·est
rust·i·ly
rust·i·ness

rut
rut·ted, rut·ting
rut·ty

ru·ta·ba·ga

Ruth

ru·the·ni·um

Ruth·er·ford

ruth·er·for·di·um

ruth·less
ruth·less·ly
ruth·less·ness

Rwan·da
Rwan·dan

rye (*grain*; see WRY)

Ryle

S

Saa·ri·nen

Sab·bath

sab·bat·i·cal

sa·ber

Sa·bin

sa·ble

sab·ot

sab·o·tage
sab·o·teur

Sac
var. of Sauk

sac (membranous bag; see
SACK)

sac·cha·rin (sweetener;
see SACCHARINE)

sac·cha·rine (sugary;
see SACCHARIN)

sac·er·do·tal
sac·er·do·tal·ly

sa·chem

sa·chet (perfume; see
SASHAY)

sack (bag; see SAC)
sack·ful
pl. sack·fuls

sack·cloth

sac·ra·ment
sac·ra·men·tal

Sac·ra·men·to

sa·cred
sa·cred·ly
sa·cred·ness

sac·ri·fice
sac·ri·fi·cial
sac·ri·fi·cial·ly

sac·ri·lege
sac·ri·le·gious
sac·ri·le·gious·ly

sac·ris·ty
sac·ris·tan

sac·ro·il·i·ac

sac·ro·sanct
sac·ro·sanc·ti·ty

sac·rum
pl. sac·ra or sac·rums

sad
sad·der, sad·dest
sad·ly
sad·ness

sad·den

sad·dle

sad·dle·bag

Sad·du·cee
Sad·du·ce·an

sa·dism
sa·dist
sa·dis·tic
sa·dis·ti·cal·ly

sa·do·mas·o·chism
sa·do·mas·o·chist
sa·do·mas·o·chis·tic

sa·fa·ri
pl. sa·fa·ris

safe
safe-con·duct
safe-de·pos·it box
safe·ly
safe·ness

safe·crack·er

safe·guard

safe·keep·ing

safe·ty
pl. safe·ties
safe·ty-de·pos·it box

saf·flow·er

saf·fron

sag
sagged, sag·ging
sag·gy

sa·ga

sa·ga·cious
sa·ga·cious·ly
sa·gac·i·ty

sag·a·more

sage (herb)
sag·y

sage (wise)
sage·ly

sage·brush

Sag·it·tar·i·us
Sag·it·tar·i·an

sa·go
pl. sa·gos

sa·gua·ro
pl. sa·gua·ros

Sa·har·a Des·ert

Sa·hel

sa·hib

said

Sai·gon

sail (navigate; see SALE)
sail·a·ble
sailed
sail·less

sail·board
sail·board·er
sail·board·ing

sail·boat

sail•cloth

sail•fish

sail•or
sail•or•ly

sail•plane

saint
saint•hood
saint•like
saint•ly
saint•li•er, saint•li•est

St. Ber•nard

St. Chris•to•pher–Ne•
vis

St. Hel•ens, Mt.

St. Kitts–Ne•vis

St. Law•rence Riv•er

St. Lou•is

St. Lu•cia

St. Paul

St. Pe•ters•burg

St. Vin•cent and the
Gren•a•dines

Sa•kai

sake (benefit)

sa•ke (rice wine)

Sa•kha•lin

sa•laam

sal•a•ble
also sale•a•ble
sal•a•bil•i•ty

sa•la•cious
sa•la•cious•ly
sa•la•cious•ness
sa•lac•i•ty

sal•ad

Sal•a•man•ca

sal•a•man•der

sa•la•mi
pl. sa•la•mis

sal•a•ry
pl. sal•a•ries
sal•a•ries, sal•a•ried

sale (selling; see SAIL)

sale•a•ble
var. of sal•a•ble

Sa•lem

Sa•ler•no

sales•clerk

sales•girl

sales•la•dy
pl. sales•la•dies

sales•man
pl. sales•men; fem.
sales•wom•an, pl.
sales•wom•en

sales•man•ship

sales•per•son

sales•room

sal•i•cyl•ic ac•id
sa•lic•y•late

sa•li•ent
sa•li•ence
sa•li•en•cy
sa•li•ent•ly

Sa•li•nas

sa•line
sa•lin•i•ty
sal•i•ni•za•tion

sa•li•va
sal•i•var•y

sal•i•vate
sal•i•va•tion

sal•low
sal•low•er, sal•low•est
sal•low•ness

sal•ly
pl. sal•lies
sal•lies, sal•lied

salm•on
pl. same or salm•ons
salm•on•y

sal•mo•nel•la
pl. sal•mo•nel•lae

sa•lon

Sa•lon•i•ka

sa•loon

sal•sa

salt

salt•cel•lar

Sal•ti•llo

sal•tine

Salt Lake Cit•y

Sal•ton Sea

salt•pe•ter

salt•shak•er

salt•wa•ter

salt•y
salt•i•er, salt•i•est
salt•i•ness

sa•lu•bri•ous
sa•lu•bri•ous•ly
sa•lu•bri•ous•ness

sa•lu•ki
also Sa•lu•ki
pl. sa•lu•kis

sal•u•tar•y

sal•u•ta•tion
sal•u•ta•tion•al

sal•u•ta•to•ry
pl. sa•lu•ta•to•ries
sa•lu•ta•to•ri•an

sa•lute
sa•lut•er

Sal•va•dor

sal·vage
  sal·vage·a·ble
  sal·vag·er

sal·va·tion

salve

sal·ver

sal·vo
  pl. sal·voes *or* sal·vos

Salz·burg

Sa·ma·ra

Sa·mar·i·a

Sa·mar·i·tan
  Sa·mar·i·tan·ism

sa·mar·i·um

Sam·ar·kand

sam·ba
  sam·bas, sam·baed,
  sam·ba·ing

same
  same·ness

Sa·mo·a
  Sa·mo·an

sam·o·var

Sam·o·yed

sam·pan

sam·ple

sam·pler

Sam·son

sam·u·rai
  pl. same

Sa·naa

San An·dre·as Fault

San An·to·ni·o

san·a·to·ri·um
  pl. san·a·to·ri·ums *or*
  san·a·to·ri·a

San Ber·nar·di·no

San Bue·na·ven·tu·ra

sanc·ti·fy
  sanc·ti·fies, sanc·ti·fied
  sanc·ti·fi·ca·tion
  sanc·ti·fi·er

sanc·ti·mo·ni·ous
  sanc·ti·mo·ni·ous·ly
  sanc·ti·mo·ni·ous·ness
  sanc·ti·mo·ny

sanc·tion
  sanc·tion·able

sanc·ti·ty
  pl. sanc·ti·ties

sanc·tu·ar·y
  pl. sanc·tu·ar·ies

sanc·tum
  pl. sanc·tums *or* sanc·ta

sand
  sand·er

san·dal

san·dal·wood

sand·bag
  sand·bagged, sand·
  bag·ging
  sand·bag·ger

sand·bar

sand·blast
  sand·blast·er

sand·box

sand·hog

San Di·e·go

sand·lot

sand·man

sand·pa·per

sand·pip·er

sand·stone

sand·storm

sand·wich

sand·y
  sand·i·er, sand·i·est
  sand·i·ness

sane (*not* suzy; see
  SEINE)
  sane·ly
  sane·ness

San Fran·cis·co
  San Fran·cis·can

sang

sang-froid

san·gri·a

san·gui·nar·y
  san·gui·nar·i·ly

san·guine
  san·guine·ly
  san·guine·ness

san·i·tar·i·um
  pl. san·i·tar·i·ums *or*
  san·i·tar·i·a

san·i·tar·y
  san·i·tar·i·an
  san·i·tar·i·ly

san·i·ta·tion

san·i·tize
  san·i·tiz·er

san·i·ty

San Joa·quin Val·ley

San Jo·se (*California*)

San Jo·sé (*Costa Rica*)

San Juan

San Jus·to

sank

San Lu·is Po·to·sí

San Ma·ri·no
  San Mar·i·nese

sans

San Sal·va·dor

San·skrit

sans ser·if
  also sans-ser·if

San·ta An·a

San·ta Bar·ba·ra

San·ta Cat·a·li·na

San·ta Cla·ra

San·ta Cla·ri·ta

San·ta Claus

San·ta Cruz

San·ta Fe

San·ta Mon·i·ca

San·ta Ro·sa

San·ti·a·go

San·to Do·min·go

San·to To·mé de Gua·
  ya·na

São Pau·lo

São To·mé and Prín·
  ci·pe

sap
  sapped, sap·ping

sap·id
  sa·pid·i·ty

sa·pi·ent
  sa·pi·ence
  sa·pi·ent·ly

sap·ling

sap·phire

Sap·po·ro

sap·py
  sap·pi·er, sap·pi·est
  sap·pi·ly
  sap·pi·ness

sap·ro·phyte
  sap·ro·phyt·ic

Sar·a·cen

Sar·a·gos·sa
  also Za·ra·go·za

Sa·ra·je·vo

Sar·a·so·ta

sar·casm
  sar·cas·tic
  sar·cas·ti·cal·ly

sar·co·ma
  pl. sar·co·mas *or* sar·
    co·ma·ta
  sar·co·ma·to·sis

sar·coph·a·gus
  pl. sar·coph·a·gi

sar·dine

Sar·din·i·a

sar·don·ic
  sar·don·i·cal·ly

sa·ri
  also sa·ree
  pl. sa·ris *or* sa·rees

sa·rong

sar·sa·pa·ril·la

sar·to·ri·al
  sar·to·ri·al·ly

sash
  sashed

sa·shay (*walk*; see
  SACHET)

Sas·katch·e·wan

Sas·ka·toon

sass

sas·sa·fras

Sa·tan

sa·tan·ic
  sa·tan·i·cal·ly

Sa·tan·ism
  Sa·tan·ist

satch·el

sate

sa·teen

sat·el·lite

sa·ti·ate

sa·ti·e·ty

sat·in
  sat·in·ized
  sat·in·y

sat·in·wood

sat·ire
  sa·tir·ic
  sa·tir·i·cal
  sa·tir·i·cal·ly
  sat·i·rist

sat·i·rize
  sat·i·ri·za·tion

sat·is·fac·tion

sat·is·fac·to·ry
  sat·is·fac·to·ri·ly

sat·is·fy
  sat·is·fies, sat·is·fied
  sat·is·fi·a·ble
  sat·is·fy·ing

sa·trap

sat·u·rate
  sat·u·ra·ble
  sat·u·rant
  sat·u·ra·tion

Sat·ur·day

Sat·urn
  Sa·tur·ni·an

sat·ur·nine

sa·tyr

sauce
  sauce·less

sauce·pan
  sauce·pan·ful
  pl. sauce·pan·fuls

sau·cer
sau·cer·ful
pl. sau·cer·fuls
sau·cer·less

sau·cy
sau·ci·er, sau·ci·est
sau·ci·ly
sau·ci·ness

Sau·di
pl. Sau·dis

Sau·di A·ra·bi·a
Sau·di *or* Sau·di A·ra·bi·an

sau·er·kraut

Sauk
also Sac

sau·na

saun·ter
saun·ter·er

sau·ri·an

sau·sage

sau·té
sau·téed *or* sau·téd

Sau·terne (*California wine*)
also sau·terne

Sau·ternes (*French region*)

sav·age
sav·age·ly
sav·age·ry
pl. sav·age·ries

sa·van·na
also sa·van·nah

Sa·van·nah

sa·vant
fem. sa·vante

save (*rescue*)
sav·a·ble
also save·a·ble
sav·er (*one who saves;*
see SAVOR)

save (*unless*)

sav·ing

sav·ior
also sav·iour

sa·voir faire

sa·vor (*enjoy;* see *saver*
[SAVE])
sa·vor·less

sa·vor·y (*appetizing*)
sa·vor·i·ly
sa·vor·i·ness

sa·vor·y (*herb*)
pl. sa·vor·ies

sav·vy
sav·vi·er, sav·vi·est

saw
past part. sawed *or* sawn
saw·like

saw·dust

saw·horse

saw·mill

sawn

saw·tooth

saw·yer

sax
sax·ist

Sax·on

sax·o·phone
sax·o·phon·ic
sax·o·phon·ist

say
3rd sing. present says;
past and *past part.* said
say-so
say·a·ble
say·er

say·ing

scab
scabbed, scab·bing
scab·by

scab·bi·er, scab·bi·est
scab·bi·ness
scab·like

scab·bard

sca·bies

scab·rous
scab·rous·ly
scab·rous·ness

scaf·fold
scaf·fold·er

scaf·fold·ing

scal·a·wag
also scal·ly·wag

scald
scald·er

scale (*measuring device, climb*)
scal·er

scale (*on fish*)

sca·lene

scal·lion

scal·lop
also scol·lop
scal·loped, scal·lop·ing
scal·lop·er

scalp
scalp·er

scal·pel

scam

scam·per

scam·pi

scan
scanned, scan·ning
scan·na·ble

scan·dal
scan·dal·ous
scan·dal·ous·ly

scan·dal·ize

scan·dal·mon·ger

Scan·di·na·vi·a
Scan·di·na·vi·an

scan·di·um

scan·ner

scan·sion

scant
scant·ly
scant·ness

scant·y
scant·i·er, scant·i·est
scant·i·ly
scant·i·ness

scape·goat
scape·goat·er

scap·u·la
pl. scap·u·lae or scap·
u·las

scar
scarred, scar·ring
scar·less

scar·ab

Scar·bor·ough

scarce
scarce·ness

scarce·ly

scar·ci·ty
pl. scar·ci·ties

scare
scar·er

scare·crow

scarf
pl. scarfs or scarves
scarfed

scar·i·fy
scar·i·fies, scar·i·fied
scar·i·fi·ca·tion

scar·let

scarp

scar·y
scar·i·er, scar·i·est
scar·i·ly

scat
scat·ted, scat·ting

scathe

scath·ing

scat·o·log·i·cal

scat·ter
scat·ter·er

scat·ter·brain
scat·ter·brained

scav·enge

scav·en·ger

sce·nar·i·o
pl. sce·nar·i·os
sce·nar·ist

scene (place, incident; see
SEEN)

sce·ner·y

sce·nic
sce·ni·cal·ly

scent (smell; see CENT,
SENT)

scep·ter
scep·tered

sched·ule
sched·ul·er

sche·mat·ic
sche·mat·i·cal·ly

scheme
schem·er
schem·ing

Sche·nec·ta·dy

scher·zo
pl. scher·zos or scher·zi

Schil·ler

schism
schis·mat·ic

schist

schiz·oid

schiz·o·phre·ni·a
schiz·o·phren·ic

schle·miel

schlep
also schlepp
schlepped, schlep·ping
schlep·per

Schles·in·ger

Schlie·mann

schlock

schmaltz
schmaltz·y
schmaltz·i·er,
schmaltz·i·est

schmuck

schnapps

schnau·zer

schnit·zel

schol·ar
schol·ar·ly
schol·ar·li·ness

schol·ar·ship

scho·las·tic
scho·las·ti·cal·ly
scho·las·ti·cism

Schön·berg
also Schoen·berg

school

school·boy

school·child

school·girl

school·house

school·ing

school·marm
also school·ma'am
school·marm·ish

school·mas·ter
  school·mas·ter·ly

school·mis·tress

school·room

school·teach·er
  school·teach·ing

schoo·ner

Scho·pen·hau·er

Schrö·ding·er

Schu·bert

Schulz

Schu·mann

schuss

Schuyl·kill Riv·er

schwa

Schwarz·kopf

Schweit·zer

sci·at·ic

sci·at·i·ca

sci·ence

sci·en·tif·ic
  sci·en·tif·i·cal·ly

sci·en·tist

sci-fi

Scil·ly Is·lands

scim·i·tar

scin·til·la

scin·til·late
  scin·til·la·tion

sci·on
  also ci·on

Scip·i·o

scis·sors

scle·ro·sis
  scle·rot·ic

scoff
  scoff·er
  scoff·ing·ly

scoff·law

scold
  scold·er
  scold·ing

sconce

scone

scoop
  scoop·er
  scoop·ful
  pl. scoop·fuls

scoot

scoot·er

scope

scor·bu·tic
  scor·bu·ti·cal·ly

scorch
  scorch·er
  scorch·ing·ly

score
  pl. same *or* scores

score·board

scorn
  scorn·ful
  scorn·ful·ly
  scorn·ful·ness

Scor·pi·o
  pl. Scor·pi·os
  Scor·pi·an

scor·pi·on

Scot

scotch (*crush*)

Scotch (*var. of Scottish
  or Scots*)
  Scotch whis·ky

Scot·land

Scots

Scots·man
  pl. Scots·men; *fem.*
  Scots·wom·an, *pl.*
  Scots·wom·en

Scott

Scot·tie

Scot·tish
  Scot·tish·ness

Scotts·dale

scoun·drel

scour
  scour·er

scourge
  scourg·er

scout
  scout·er
  scout·ing

scout·mas·ter

scow

scowl
  scowl·er

scrab·ble

scrag·gly

scram
  scrammed, scram·
  ming

scram·ble

scram·bler

Scran·ton

scrap
  scrapped, scrap·ping
  scrap·per

scrap·book

scrape
  scrap·er

scrap·py
  scrap·pi·er, scrap·
  pi·est
  scrap·pi·ly
  scrap·pi·ness**

scratch
scratch•er
scratch•i•ly
scratch•i•ness
scratch•y

scrawl
scrawl•y

scrawn•y
scrawn•i•er,
scrawn•i•est
scrawn•i•ness

scream

screech
screech•er
screech•y
screech•i•er, screech•
i•est

screed

screen
screen•er

screen•play

screen•writ•er

screw

screw•ball

screw•driv•er

screw•y
screw•i•er, screw•i•est
screw•i•ness

scrib•ble
scrib•bler
scrib•bly

scribe

scrim

scrim•mage
scrim•mag•er

scrimp
scrimp•y

scrim•shaw

scrip

script

scrip•ture

script•writ•er
script•writ•ing

scrod

scrof•u•la
scrof•u•lous

scroll

scro•tum
pl. scro•ta or scro•tums
scro•tal

scrounge
scroung•er

scrub (brushwood)
scrub•by

scrub (scour)
scrubbed, scrub•bing
scrub•ber

scruff

scruff•y
scruff•i•er, scruff•i•est
scruff•i•ly
scruff•i•ness

scrump•tious
scrump•tious•ly
scrump•tious•ness

scrunch

scru•ple

scru•pu•lous
scru•pu•los•i•ty
scru•pu•lous•ly
scru•pu•lous•ness

scru•ti•nize
scru•ti•niz•er

scru•ti•ny
pl. scru•ti•nies

scu•ba
pl. scu•bas

scuff

script

scull (oar; see SKULL)

scul•ler•y
pl. scul•ler•ies

sculpt
also sculp

sculp•tor
fem. sculp•tress

sculp•ture
sculp•tur•al
sculp•tur•al•ly
sculp•tur•esque

scum
scummed, scum•ming
scum•my
scum•mi•er, scum•mi•
est

scum•bag

scup•per

scur•ril•ous
scur•ril•ous•ly
scur•ril•ous•ness

scur•ry
scur•ries, scur•ried
pl. scur•ries

scur•vy

scut•tle

scut•tle•butt

scuz•zy

scythe

sea (ocean; see SEE)

sea•bed

sea•board

Sea•borg

sea•borg•i•um

sea•coast

sea•far•er
sea•far•ing

sea•food

sea•go•ing

sea•gull

seal (*close*)
  seal•a•ble

seal (*animal*)
  seal•er

seal•ant

seal•skin

seam (*joint;* see SEEM)
  seam•er
  seam•less

sea•man (*sailor,* see
  SEMEN)
  pl. sea•men
  sea•man•like
  sea•man•ly

sea•man•ship

seam•stress

seam•y
  seam•i•er, seam•i•est
  seam•i•ness

sé•ance
  also se•ance

sea•plane

sea•port

sear

search
  search•a•ble
  search•er
  search•ing•ly

search•light

sea•scape

sea•shell

sea•shore

sea•sick
  sea•sick•ness

sea•side

sea•son
  sea•son•er

sea•son•a•ble
  sea•son•a•ble•ness
  sea•son•a•bly

sea•son•al
  sea•son•al•ly

sea•son•ing

seat

seat•ing

Se•at•tle

sea•ward
  also sea•wards

sea•way

sea•weed

sea•wor•thy
  sea•wor•thi•ness

se•ba•ceous

seb•or•rhe•a

sec

se•cant

se•cede
  se•ced•er

se•ces•sion
  se•ces•sion•ism
  se•ces•sion•ist

se•clude

se•clu•sion
  se•clu•sion•ist
  se•clu•sive

sec•ond
  sec•ond-guess
  sec•ond-rate

sec•ond•ar•y
  pl. sec•ond•ar•ies
  sec•ond•ar•i•ly

sec•ond•hand

sec•ond•ly

se•cre•cy

se•cret
  se•cret•ly

sec•re•tar•i•at

sec•re•tar•y
  pl. sec•re•tar•ies
  sec•re•tar•i•al

se•crete (*conceal*)

se•crete (*produce by
  secretion*)
  se•cre•tor

se•cre•tion

se•cre•tive
  se•cre•tive•ly
  se•cre•tive•ness

sect

sec•tar•i•an
  sec•tar•i•an•ism

sec•tion

sec•tion•al
  sec•tion•al•ism
  sec•tion•al•ist
  sec•tion•al•ize
  sec•tion•al•ly

sec•tor

sec•u•lar
  sec•u•lar•ism
  sec•u•lar•ize
  sec•u•lar•i•za•tion
  sec•u•lar•ly

se•cure
  se•cur•a•ble
  se•cure•ly
  se•cure•ment

se•cu•ri•ty
  pl. se•cu•ri•ties

se•dan

se•date (*put under
  sedation*)

se•date (*tranquil*)
  se•date•ly
  se•date•ness

se·da·tion

sed·a·tive

sed·en·tar·y

Se·der

sedge
  sedg·y

sed·i·ment
  sed·i·men·ta·ry
  sed·i·men·ta·tion

se·di·tion
  se·di·tious
  se·di·tious·ly

se·duce
  se·duc·er
  se·duc·i·ble
  se·duc·tion
  se·duc·tive
  se·duc·tive·ly
  se·duc·tress

sed·u·lous
  se·du·li·ty
  sed·u·lous·ly
  sed·u·lous·ness

se·dum

see (*perceive*; see SEA)
  past saw; *past part.* seen
  see-through

seed (*kernel*; see CEDE)
  seed·less

seed·ling

seed·y
  seed·i·er, seed·i·est
  seed·i·ly
  seed·i·ness

see·ing

seek
  past and *past part.*
  sought
  seek·er

seem (*appear to be*; see
  SEAM)

seem·ing
  seem·ing·ly

seem·ly
  seem·li·er, seem·li·est
  seem·li·ness

seen (*past part. of see*;
  see SCENE)

seep
  seep·age

seer

seer·suck·er

see·saw

seethe
  seeth·ing·ly

seg·ment
  seg·men·tal
  seg·men·tal·ly
  seg·men·tar·y
  seg·men·ta·tion

Se·go·vi·a

seg·re·gate
  seg·re·ga·ble
  seg·re·ga·tive

seg·re·ga·tion
  seg·re·ga·tion·al
  seg·re·ga·tion·ist

se·gue
  se·gues, se·gued,
  se·gue·ing

sei·gneur
  also sei·gnior
  sei·gneu·ri·al
  sei·gnio·ri·al

Seine (*river*)

seine (*net*; see SANE)

seis·mic
  seis·mal
  seis·mi·cal
  seis·mi·cal·ly

seis·mo·graph
  seis·mo·graph·ic
  seis·mo·graph·i·cal

seis·mol·o·gy
  seis·mo·log·i·cal
  seis·mo·log·i·cal·ly
  seis·mol·o·gist

seize
  seiz·a·ble
  seiz·er
  sei·zure

sel·dom

se·lect
  se·lec·ta·ble

se·lec·tion
  se·lec·tive
  se·lec·tive·ly
  se·lec·tiv·ity

se·le·ni·um

Se·leu·cus

self
  pl. selves

self-a·base·ment

self-ab·sorbed

self-ab·sorp·tion

self-a·buse

self-ad·dressed

self-ad·just·ing

self-ag·gran·dize·ment
  self-ag·gran·diz·ing

self-ap·point·ed

self-as·ser·tion

self-as·sur·ance

self-as·sured

self-a·ware
  self-a·ware·ness

self-cen·tered
  self-cen·tered·ly
  self-cen·tered·ness

self-clean·ing

self-com·pla·cent

self-con·fessed

self-con·fi·dence

self-con·fi·dent

self-con·scious
  self-con·scious·ly
  self-con·scious·ness

self-con·tained
  self-con·tain·ment

self-con·trol
  self-con·trolled

self-crit·i·cal

self-crit·i·cism

self-de·cep·tion
  self-de·ceit
  self-de·ceiv·er
  self-de·ceiv·ing
  self-de·cep·tive

self-de·feat·ing

self-de·fense
  self-de·fen·sive

self-de·lu·sion

self-de·ni·al
  self-de·ny·ing

self-de·struct

self-de·ter·mi·na·tion
  self-de·ter·mined
  self-de·ter·min·ing

self-dis·ci·pline
  self-dis·ci·plined

self-doubt

self-ed·u·cat·ed

self-ef·fac·ing
  self-ef·face·ment
  self-ef·fac·ing·ly

self-em·ployed
  self-em·ploy·ment

self-es·teem

self-ev·i·dent
  self-ev·i·dence
  self-ev·i·dent·ly

self-ex·am·i·na·tion

self-ex·plan·a·to·ry

self-ex·pres·sion
  self-ex·pres·sive

self-fer·ti·li·za·tion

self-ful·fill·ing

self-gov·ern·ing

self-gov·ern·ment

self-help

self-im·age

self-im·posed

self-im·prove·ment

self-in·crim·i·na·tion

self-in·duced

self-in·dul·gent
  self-in·dul·gence
  self-in·dul·gent·ly

self-in·flict·ed

self-in·ter·est
  self-in·ter·est·ed

self·ish
  self·ish·ly
  self·ish·ness

self-jus·ti·fi·ca·tion

self-know·ledge

self·less
  self·less·ly
  self·less·ness

self-love

self-made

self-mo·ti·vat·ed

self-mo·ti·va·tion

self-per·pet·u·at·ing

self-pit·y
  self-pit·y·ing
  self-pit·y·ing·ly

self-pol·li·nat·ing

self-pol·li·na·tion

self-por·trait

self-pos·sessed
  self-pos·ses·sion

self-pres·er·va·tion

self-pro·claimed

self-pro·pelled
  self-pro·pel·ling

self-pro·tec·tion

self-reg·u·lat·ing
  self-reg·u·la·tion
  self-reg·u·la·to·ry

self-re·li·ance
  self-re·li·ant
  self-re·li·ant·ly

self-re·proach

self-re·spect
  self-re·spect·ing

self-re·straint
  self-re·strained

self-right·eous
  self-right·eous·ly
  self-right·eous·ness

self-sac·ri·fice
  self-sac·ri·fic·ing

self·same

self-seek·ing
  self-seek·er

self-serv·ice

self-start·er

self-styled

self-suf·fi·cient
  self-suf·fi·cien·cy
  self-suf·fi·cient·ly

self-sup·port·ing
self-sup·port

self-sus·tain·ing

self-taught

self-willed
self-will

self-worth

sell (*offer for sale*; see
CELL)
past and *past part.* sold
sell·a·ble
sell·er (*one who sells*;
see CELLAR)

sell·out

selt·zer

sel·vage
also sel·vedge

se·man·tic
se·man·ti·cal·ly

se·man·tics
se·man·ti·cist

sem·a·phore
sem·a·phor·ic

Se·ma·rang

sem·blance

se·men (*fluid*; see
SEAMAN)

se·mes·ter

sem·i
pl. sem·is

sem·i·an·nu·al

sem·i·cir·cle
sem·i·cir·cu·lar

sem·i·co·lon

sem·i·con·duc·tor
sem·i·con·duct·ing

sem·i·con·scious

sem·i·fi·nal
sem·i·fi·nal·ist

sem·i·nal
sem·i·nal·ly

sem·i·nar

sem·i·nar·y
pl. sem·i·nar·ies
sem·i·nar·i·an

Sem·i·nole

se·mi·ot·ics
se·mi·ot·ic
se·mi·ot·i·cal
se·mi·o·ti·cian

sem·i·per·me·a·ble

sem·i·pre·cious

sem·i·pro·fes·sion·al

sem·i·skilled

Sem·ite
Sem·i·tism

Se·mit·ic

sem·i·tone

sem·i·trail·er

sen·ate

sen·a·tor
sen·a·to·ri·al

send
past and *past part.* sent
send-off
send·a·ble
send·er

Sen·dai

Sen·e·ca
Sen·e·can

Sen·e·gal
Sen·e·gal·ese

se·nile
se·nil·i·ty

sen·ior
sen·ior·i·ty

sen·na

Sen·nach·er·ib

se·ñor
pl. se·ñor·es

se·ño·ra

se·ño·ri·ta

sen·sa·tion

sen·sa·tion·al
sen·sa·tion·al·ism
sen·sa·tion·al·ize
sen·sa·tion·al·ly

sense

sense·less
sense·less·ly
sense·less·ness

sen·si·bil·i·ty
pl. sen·si·bil·i·ties

sen·si·ble
sen·si·ble·ness
sen·si·bly

sen·si·tive
sen·si·tive·ly
sen·si·tive·ness
sen·si·tiv·i·ty

sen·si·tize
sen·si·ti·za·tion
sen·si·tiz·er

sen·sor (*device*; see
CENSER, CENSOR)

sen·so·ry
sen·so·ri·ly

sen·su·al
sen·su·al·ism
sen·su·al·ist
sen·su·al·i·ty
sen·su·al·ly

sen·su·ous

sent (*past of send*; see
CENT, SCENT)

sen·tence

sen·ten·tious
sen·ten·tious·ly
sen·ten·tious·ness

sen·tient
sen·tience
sen·tient·ly

sen·ti·ment

sen·ti·men·tal
sen·ti·men·tal·ism
sen·ti·men·tal·ist
sen·ti·men·tal·i·ty
sen·ti·men·tal·ize
sen·ti·men·tal·ly

sen·ti·nel

sen·try
pl. sen·tries

Seoul (*city*; see SOL, SOLE, SOUL)

se·pal

sep·a·ra·ble
sep·a·ra·bil·i·ty
sep·a·ra·ble·ness
sep·a·ra·bly

sep·a·rate
sep·a·rate·ly
sep·a·rate·ness
sep·a·ra·tive

sep·a·ra·tion

sep·a·rat·ist
sep·a·ra·tism

sep·a·ra·tor

se·pi·a

sep·sis

Sep·tem·ber

sep·tet
also sep·tette

sep·tic

sep·ti·ce·mi·a
sep·ti·ce·mic

sep·tu·a·ge·nar·i·an

Sep·tu·a·gint

sep·tum
pl. sep·ta

sep·ul·cher
also sep·ul·chre
se·pul·chral

se·quel

se·quence
se·quen·tial
se·quen·tial·ly

se·ques·ter

se·quin
se·quined

se·quoi·a (*tree*; see SEQUOYA)

Se·quoy·a (*proper name*; see SEQUOIA)

se·ragl·io
pl. se·ragl·ios

se·ra·pe

ser·aph
pl. ser·a·phim *or* ser·aphs
se·raph·ic
se·raph·i·cal·ly

Ser·bi·a
Serb *or* Ser·bi·an

Ser·bo-Cro·at
also Ser·bo-Cro·a·tian

ser·e·nade
ser·e·nad·er

ser·en·dip·i·ty
ser·en·dip·i·tous
ser·en·dip·i·tous·ly

se·rene
se·ren·er, se·ren·est
se·rene·ly
se·ren·i·ty

serf (*laborer*; see SURF)
serf·dom

serge (*fabric*; see SURGE)

ser·geant
ser·gean·cy
pl. ser·gean·cies

se·ri·al (*in a series*; see CEREAL)
se·ri·al·ly

se·ri·al·ize
se·ri·al·i·za·tion

se·ries
pl. same

ser·if

se·ri·ous
se·ri·ous·ly
se·ri·ous·ness

ser·mon
ser·mon·ize
ser·mon·iz·er

se·rous

ser·pent

ser·pen·tine

ser·rate
ser·ra·tion

ser·ried

se·rum
pl. se·ra *or* se·rums

serv·ant

serve

serv·er

serv·ice

serv·ice·a·ble
serv·ice·a·bil·i·ty
serv·ice·a·bly

serv·ice·man
pl. serv·ice·men

serv·ice·wom·an
pl. serv·ice·wom·en

ser·vile
ser·vile·ly
ser·vil·i·ty

serv·ing

ser·vi·tude

ser•vo
  pl. ser•vos

ser•vo•mech•an•ism

ses•a•me

ses•qui•cen•ten•ni•al

ses•sion (*assembly*; see
  CESSION)

set

set•back

Se•ton

set•tee

set•ter

set•ting

set•tle
  set•tler

set•tle•ment

set•up

Seu•rat

Seuss

Se•vas•to•pol

sev•en
  sev•enth

sev•en•teen
  sev•en•teenth

sev•en•ty
  pl, sev•en•ties
  sev•en•ti•eth
  sev•en•ty•fold

sev•er
  sev•er•a•ble

sev•er•al
  sev•er•al•ly

sev•er•ance

se•vere
  se•vere•ly
  se•ver•i•ty

Se•ville

sew (*stitch*; see SO, SOW)
  past part. sewn *or* sewed
  sew•er

sew•age

Sew•ard

sew•er (*drain*; see *suer*
  [SUE])

sew•er•age

sew•ing

sex

sex•a•ge•nar•i•an

sex•ism
  sex•ist

sex•ol•o•gy
  sex•o•log•i•cal
  sex•ol•o•gist

sex•tant

sex•tet
  also sex•tette

sex•ton

sex•tu•plet

sex•u•al
  sex•u•al•i•ty
  sex•u•al•ly

sex•y
  sex•i•er, sex•i•est
  sex•i•ly
  sex•i•ness

Sey•chelles

shab•by
  shab•bi•er, shab•bi•est
  shab•bi•ly
  shab•bi•ness

shack

shack•le

shad
  pl. same *or* shads

shade
  shade•less

shad•ing

shad•ow
  shad•ow•er
  shad•ow•less
  shad•ow•y

shad•ow•box
  shad•ow•box•ing

shad•y
  shad•i•er, shad•i•est
  shad•i•ly
  shad•i•ness

shaft

shag
  shagged, shag•ging

shag•gy
  shag•gi•er, shag•gi•est
  shag•gi•ly
  shag•gi•ness

shah

shake
  past shook; *past part.*
  shak•en
  shak•a•ble
  also shake•a•ble

shake•down

Shak•er (*religion*)
  Shak•er•ism

shak•er (*thing that shakes*)

Shake•speare

Shake•spear•e•an
  also Shake•spear•i•an

shak•y
  shak•i•er, shak•i•est
  shak•i•ly
  shak•i•ness

shale
  shal•y

Sha•li•kash•vi•li

shall
  3rd sing. present shall;
  past should

shal·lot

shal·low
shal·low·ly
shal·low·ness

shalt

sham
shammed, sham·ming
sham·mer

sham·ble

sham·bles

shame
shame·ful
shame·ful·ly
shame·ful·ness

shame·faced

shame·less
shame·less·ly
shame·less·ness

sham·poo
sham·poos, sham·
pooed

sham·rock

Shang·hai (*city*)

shang·hai (*seize*)
shang·hais, shang·
haied, shang·hai·ing

shank
shanked

Shan·kar

shan·ty (*hut*; see
CHANTEY)
pl. shan·ties

shape
shap·a·ble
also shape·a·ble
shaped
shape·less
shape·less·ly
shape·less·ness
shap·er

shape·ly
shape·li·er, shape·li·est
shape·li·ness

shard

share
share·a·ble
also shar·a·ble
shar·er

share·crop·per

share·hold·er

share·ware

shark

shark·skin

sharp
sharp-wit·ted
sharp·ly
sharp·ness

sharp·en
sharp·en·er

sharp·er

sharp·shoot·er
sharp·shoot·ing

shat·ter
shat·ter·ing
shat·ter·ing·ly
shat·ter-proof

shave
past part. shaved *or* (*as
adj.*) shav·en

shav·er

shav·ing

Shaw

shawl
shawled

Shaw·nee

she
obj. her; *poss.* her; *pl.*
they

sheaf
pl. sheaves

shear (*cut*; see SHEER)
past sheared, shore;
past part. shorn *or*
sheared
shear·er

sheath
pl. sheaths
sheath·less

sheathe

sheave

she·bang

shed (*drop*)
shed·ding; *past and
past part.* shed
shed·der

shed (*outbuilding*)

she'd

sheen

sheep
pl. same

sheep·dog

sheep·fold

sheep·ish
sheep·ish·ly
sheep·ish·ness

sheep·skin

sheer (*steep*; see SHEAR)
sheer·ly
sheer·ness

sheet

sheet·ing

Shef·field

sheikh
also sheik
sheikh·dom

shek·el

shelf
pl. shelves
shelved
shelf·ful
pl. shelf·fuls

she'll

shell
shell-shocked
shelled
shell-less
shell-like

shel·lac
shel·lacked,
shel·lack·ing

Shel·ley

shell·fish

shel·ter

shelve
shelv·er
shelv·ing

shelves

she·nan·i·gan

Shen·yang

shep·herd
fem. shep·herd·ess

sher·bet

Sher·i·dan

sher·iff

Sher·man

Sher·pa
pl. same *or* Sher·pas

sher·ry
pl. sher·ries

she's

Shet·land

Shev·ard·na·dze

Shi·ah
also Shi·a

shib·bo·leth

shield
shield·less

shi·er

shi·est

shift
shift·a·ble
shift·er

shift·less
shift·less·ly
shift·less·ness

shift·y
shift·i·er, shift·i·est
shift·i·ly
shift·i·ness

Shi·ko·ku

shill

shil·le·lagh

shil·ling

shil·ly-shal·ly
shil·lies, shil·lied

shim
shimmed, shim·ming

shim·mer
shim·mer·ing·ly
shim·mer·y

shin

shin·bone

shin·dig

shine
past and *past part.* shone
or shined
shin·ing·ly

shin·er

shin·gle

shin·gles

Shin·to
Shin·to·ism
Shin·to·ist

shin·y
shin·i·er, shin·i·est
shin·i·ly
shin·i·ness

ship
shipped, ship·ping
ship·pa·ble

ship·board

ship·build·er
ship·build·ing

ship·mate

ship·ment

ship·per

ship·ping

ship·shape

ship·wreck

ship·wright

ship·yard

Shi·raz

shire

shirk
shirk·er

shirr
shirr·ing

shirt

shirt·sleeve

shirt·tail

shirt·waist

shish ke·bab

shiv·er
shiv·er·er
shiv·er·ing·ly
shiv·er·y

shoal

shock
shock·a·ble

shock·er

shock·ing
shock·ing·ly

shock·proof

shod

shod·dy
shod·di·er, shod·di·est
pl. shod·dies
shod·di·ly
shod·di·ness

shoe (*footwear;* see SHOO)
shoes, shoe·ing; *past
and past part.* shod
shoe·less

shoe·horn

shoe·lace

shoe·mak·er
shoe·mak·ing

shoe·string

sho·far
pl. sho·fars *or* sho·froth

sho·gun
sho·gun·ate

shone (*past of shine;* see
SHOWN)

shoo (*drive away;* see
SHOE)
shoos, shooed

shook

shoot (*fire a gun;* see
CHUTE)
past and past part. shot
shoot-out
shoot·er
shoot·ing

shop
shopped, shop·ping
shop·per

shop·keep·er
shop·keep·ing

shop·lift·er
shop·lift
shop·lift·ing

shop·ping

shop·worn

shore (*coast*)
shore·less
shore·ward
shore·wards

shore (*support*)
shor·ing

shore·line

shorn

short
short-cir·cuit
short-list
short-lived
short-or·der
short-wind·ed
short·ish
short·ness

short·age

short·bread

short·cake

short·change

short·com·ing

short·en

short·en·ing

short·fall

short·hand

short·hand·ed

short·horn

short·list

short·ly

shorts

short·sight·ed
short·sight·ed·ly
short·sight·ed·ness

short·stop

short-term

short·wave

short·y
also short·ie
pl. short·ies

Sho·sho·ne
also Sho·sho·ni

Sho·sta·ko·vich

shot
pl. same *or* shots
shot-put·ter
shot·proof

shot·gun

should

shoul·der
shoul·dered

should·n't

shout
shout·er

shove

shov·el
shov·el·ful
pl. shov·el·fuls

show
show-off

Sho·wa

show·case

show·down

show·er
show·er·y

show·girl

show·ing

show·man
pl. show·men
show·man·ship

shown (*past part. of show;*
see SHONE)

show·piece

show·place

show·room

show·stop·per

show•y
show•i•er, show•i•est
show•i•ly
show•i•ness

shrank

shrap•nel

shred
shred•ded, shred•ding
shred•der

Shreve•port

shrew
shrew•ish

shrewd
shrewd•ly
shrewd•ness

shriek
shriek•er

shrift

shrike

shrill
shril•ly
shrill•ness

shrimp
pl. same *or* shrimps
shrimp•er

shrine

shrink
past shrank; *past part.*
shrunk *or* shrunk•en
shrink-wrap
shrink-wrapped,
shrink-wrap•ping
shrink•a•ble
shrink•er
shrink•proof

shrink•age

shrive
past shrove; *past part.*
shriv•en

shriv•el

shroud
shroud•less

Shrove Tues•day

shrub
shrub•by

shrub•ber•y
pl. shrub•ber•ies

shrug
shrugged, shrug•ging

shtick

Shub•ra al-Khay•mah

shuck
shuck•er

shud•der
shud•der•ing•ly
shud•der•y

shuf•fle
shuf•fler

shuf•fle•board

shun
shunned, shun•ning

shunt
shunt•er

shush

shut
shut•ting; *past and past
part.* shut
shut-eye
shut-in

shut•down

shut•ter

shut•tle

shut•tle•cock

shy
shy•er, shy•est *or* shi•
er, shi•est
shies, shied
shy•ly
shy•ness

shy•ster

shroud
Si•am

Si•a•mese
pl. same

Si•an
also Xi•an

Si•be•li•us

sib•i•lant
sib•i•lance

sib•ling

sib•yl
sib•yl•line

sic (*as written*; see SICK)

sic (*urge to attack*; see
SICK)
sicced, sic•cing *or*
sicked, sick•ing

Sic•i•ly

sick (*ill*; see SIC)
sick•ish

sick•bay

sick•bed

sick•en
sick•en•ing•ly

sick•le

sick•ly
sick•li•er, sick•li•est
sick•li•ness

sick•ness

Sid•dhart•ha

side
side•less

side•board

side•burns

side•car

side•kick

side•light

side•line

side·long

si·de·re·al

side·sad·dle

side·show

side·split·ting

side·step
  side·stepped, side·step·
  ping
  side·step·per

side·swipe

side·track

side·walk

side·wall

side·ways
  also side·wise

sid·ing

si·dle

Si·don

siege

Sie·mens

si·er·ra

Si·er·ra Le·o·ne
  Si·er·ra Le·o·ne·an

si·es·ta

sieve
  sieve·like

sift
  sift·er

sigh

sight (*vision*; see CITE,
  SITE)
  sight-read
  past and *past part.* sight-
  read
  sight·er

sight·ed

sight·less
  sight·less·ly
  sight·less·ness

sight·ly
  sight·li·ness

sight·se·er
  sight·see
  sight·see·ing

sig·ma

sign (*indication*; see SINE)
  sign·a·ble
  sign·er

sig·nal
  sig·nal·er *or* sig·nal·ler

sig·nal·man
  pl. sig·nal·men

sig·na·to·ry
  pl. sig·na·to·ries

sig·na·ture

sign·board

sig·net (*seal*; see
  CYGNET)

sig·nif·i·cant
  sig·nif·i·cance
  sig·nif·i·cant·ly

sig·ni·fy
  sig·ni·fies, sig·ni·fied
  sig·ni·fi·ca·tion
  sig·ni·fier

si·gnor
  pl. si·gno·ri

si·gno·ra

si·gno·ri·na

sign·post

Si·kor·sky

si·lage

si·lence

si·lenc·er

si·lent
  si·lent·ly

sil·hou·ette

sil·i·ca

sil·i·cate

sil·i·con

sil·i·cone

Sil·i·con Val·ley

silk
  silk-screen
  silk·like

silk·worm

silk·y
  silk·i·er, silk·i·est
  silk·i·ly
  silk·i·ness

sill

Sills

sil·ly
  sil·li·er, sil·li·est
  pl. sil·lies
  sil·li·ness

si·lo
  pl. si·los
  si·loes, si·loed

silt
  silt·y

sil·ver

sil·ver·fish
  pl. same *or* sil·ver·
  fish·es

sil·ver·smith
  sil·ver·smith·ing

sil·ver·ware

sil·ver·y

sim·i·an

sim·i·lar
  sim·i·lar·i·ty
  pl. sim·i·lar·i·ties
  sim·i·lar·ly

sim·i·le

si·mil·i·tude

Si·mi Val·ley

sim·mer

Si·mon

si·mo·ny

sim·per
sim·per·ing·ly

sim·ple

sim·ple·mind·ed
sim·ple·mind·ed·ly
sim·ple·mind·ed·ness

sim·ple·ton

sim·plic·i·ty

sim·pli·fy
sim·pli·fies, sim·pli·fied
sim·pli·fi·ca·tion

sim·plis·tic
sim·plis·ti·cal·ly

sim·ply

sim·u·late
sim·u·la·tion
sim·u·la·tor

si·mul·ta·ne·ous
si·mul·ta·ne·ous·ly

sin
sinned, sin·ning
sin·ful
sin·ful·ly
sin·ful·ness
sin·less
sin·less·ly
sin·less·ness
sin·ner

Si·na·lo·a

Si·na·tra

since

sin·cere
sin·cer·er, sin·cer·est
sin·cere·ly
sin·cer·i·ty

Sin·clair

sine (*mathematical ratio*; see SIGN)

si·ne·cure

si·ne qua non

sin·ew
sin·ew·less
sin·ew·y

sing
past sang; *past part.* sung
sing·a·ble
sing·er

Sin·ga·pore
Sin·ga·po·re·an

singe
singe·ing

Sing·er

sin·gle
sin·gle-breast·ed
sin·gle-hand·ed
sin·gle-hand·ed·ly
sin·gle-mind·ed
sin·gle·ness
sin·gly

sin·gle·ton

sing·song
past and *past part.* sing·songed

sin·gu·lar
sin·gu·lar·i·ty
pl. sin·gu·lar·i·ties
sin·gu·lar·ly

Sin·ha·lese
also Sin·gha·lese
pl. same

sin·is·ter

sink (*descend, basin*; see SYNC)
past sank *or* sunk; *past part.* sunk *or* sunk·en

sink·a·ble
sink·age

sink·er

sin·u·ous
sin·u·ous·ly
sin·u·ous·ness

si·nus

si·nus·i·tis

Sioux (*proper name*; see SUE)
pl. same
Siou·an

sip
sipped, sip·ping
sip·per

si·phon
also sy·phon
si·phon·age

sir

sire

si·ren

sir·loin

si·roc·co
pl. si·roc·cos

sir·up
var. of syr·up

sis

si·sal

sis·sy
pl. sis·sies
sis·si·er, sis·si·est
sis·si·fied
sis·sy·ish

sis·ter
sis·ter-in-law
pl. sis·ters-in-law
sis·ter·hood
sis·ter·less
sis·ter·ly
sis·ter·li·ness

Sis·y·phe·an

sit
  sit•ting; *past* and *past part.* sat
  sit-down
  sit-in
  sit-up
  sit•ter

si•tar
  si•tar•ist

sit•com

site (*location*; see CITE, SIGHT)

sit•ting

sit•u•ate

sit•u•a•tion
  sit•u•a•tion•al

six
  six-gun
  six-pack
  six-shoot•er

six•teen
  six•teenth

sixth

six•ty
  pl. six•ties
  six•ti•eth
  six•ty•fold

siz•a•ble
  also size•a•ble
  siz•a•bly

size (*dimension*)
  siz•er

size (*stiffening material*)
  also siz•ing

siz•zle
  siz•zler
  siz•zling

skate (*fish*)
  pl. same *or* skates

skate (*roller or ice skate*)
  skat•er

skate•board
  skate•board•er

ske•dad•dle

skeet

skein

skel•e•ton
  skel•e•tal
  skel•e•tal•ly
  skel•e•ton•ize

skep•tic
  skep•ti•cal
  skep•ti•cal•ly
  skep•ti•cism

sketch

sketch•y
  sketch•i•er, sketch•i•est
  sketch•i•ly
  sketch•i•ness

skew

skew•er

ski
  pl. skis *or* ski
  skis, skied; ski•ing
  ski•a•ble
  ski•er

skid
  skid•ded, skid•ding

skiff

skill
  skilled
  skill•ful
  skill•ful•ly
  skill•ful•ness

skil•let

skim
  skimmed, skim•ming
  skim•mer

skimp

skimp•y
  skimp•i•er, skimp•i•est
  skimp•i•ly
  skimp•i•ness

skin
  skinned, skin•ning
  skin-deep
  skin•less
  skin•like
  skinned

skin•flint

skin•head

Skin•ner

skin•ny
  skin•ni•er, skin•ni•est
  skin•ny-dip•ping
  skin•ni•ness

skin•tight

skip
  skipped, skip•ping

skip•per

skirl

skir•mish
  skir•mish•er

skirt
  skirt•ed
  skirt•less

skit

skit•tish
  skit•tish•ly
  skit•tish•ness

skiv•vy
  pl. skiv•vies

Skop•je

skul•dug•ger•y
  also skull•dug•ger•y

skulk
  skulk•er

skull (*head*; see SCULL)
  skulled

skull•cap

skunk

sky
  pl. skies
  sky-high

sky•box

sky•cap

sky•div•ing
  sky•dive
  sky•div•er

Skye

sky•jack
  sky•jack•er

sky•light

sky•line

sky•rock•et

sky•scrap•er

sky•ward
  also sky•wards

sky•writ•ing

slab
  slabbed, slab•bing

slack
  slack•ly
  slack•ness

slack•en

slack•er

slag
  slag•gy
  slag•gi•er, slag•gi•est

slain

slake

sla•lom

slam
  slammed, slam•ming

slan•der
  slan•der•er
  slan•der•ous
  slan•der•ous•ly

slang
  slang•i•ly

slang•i•ness
slang•y
slang•i•er, slang•i•est

slant

slap
  slapped, slap•ping

slap•dash

slap•hap•py

slap•stick

slash
  slash•er

slat

slate
  slat•y

slath•er

slat•tern

slaugh•ter
  slaugh•ter•er

slaugh•ter•house

Slav
  Slav•ism

slave

slav•er

slav•er•y

Slav•ic

slav•ish
  slav•ish•ly
  slav•ish•ness

slay (*kill*; see SLEIGH)
  past slew; *past part.* slain
  slay•er

sleaze

slea•zy
  slea•zi•er, slea•zi•est
  slea•zi•ly
  slea•zi•ness

sled
  sled•ded, sled•ding

sledge

sledge•ham•mer

sleek
  sleek•ly
  sleek•ness

sleep
  past and *past part.* slept
  sleep•less
  sleep•less•ly
  sleep•less•ness

sleep•er

sleep•walk
  sleep•walk•er
  sleep•walk•ing

sleep•y
  sleep•i•er, sleep•i•est
  sleep•i•ly
  sleep•i•ness

sleet
  sleet•y

sleeve
  sleeved
  sleeve•less

sleigh (*sled*; see SLAY)

sleight (*dexterity*; see SLIGHT)

slen•der
  slen•der•er, slen•der•est
  slen•der•ly
  slen•der•ness

slept

sleuth

slew (*change position*; see SLOUGH)
  also slue

slew (*large quantity, past of slay*; see SLOUGH)

slice
  slice•a•ble
  slic•er

slick
slick•ly
slick•ness

slick•er

slide
past and past part. slid
slid•er

slight (*small;* see
SLEIGHT)
slight•ing•ly
slight•ish
slight•ly
slight•ness

slim
slim•mer, slim•mest
slimmed, slim•ming
slim•ly
slim•ness

slime
slim•i•ly
slim•i•ness
slim•y
slim•i•er, slim•i•est

sling
past and past part. slung

sling•shot

slink
past and past part. slunk

slink•y
slink•i•er, slink•i•est
slink•i•ly
slink•i•ness

slip
slipped, slip•ping
slip-on

slip•cov•er

slip•knot

slip•page

slip•per

slip•per•y
slip•per•i•ness

slip•shod

slip-up

slit
slit•ting; *past and past
part.* slit
slit•ter

slith•er
slith•er•y

sliv•er

slob
slob•bish

slob•ber
slob•ber•y

sloe (*fruit;* see SLOW)

slog
slogged, slog•ging
slog•ger

slo•gan

sloop

slop
slopped, slop•ping

slope

slop•py
slop•pi•er, slop•pi•est
slop•pi•ly
slop•pi•ness

slosh

sloshed

slot
slot•ted, slot•ting

sloth
sloth•ful
sloth•ful•ly
sloth•ful•ness

slouch
slouch•y
slouch•i•er, slouch•i•
est

slough (*cast off*)

slough (*swamp;* see
SLEW)

Slo•vak

Slo•va•ki•a

slov•en
slov•en•ly
slov•en•li•ness

Slo•ve•ni•a
Slo•ve•ni•an

slow (*not fast;* see SLOE)
slow•ish
slow•ly
slow•ness

slow•down

sludge
sludg•y

slue (*var. of slew;* see also
SLOUGH)

slug
slugged, slug•ging
slug•ger

slug•gard
slug•gard•ly
slug•gard•li•ness

slug•gish
slug•gish•ly
slug•gish•ness

sluice

slum
slummed, slum•ming
slum•my
slum•mi•er, slum•mi•
est
slum•mi•ness

slum•ber
slum•ber•er
slum•ber•ous

slump

slung

slunk

slur
slurred, slur•ring

slurp

slur•ry
  pl. slur•ries

slush
  slush•y
  slush•i•er, slush•i•est
  slush•i•ness

slut
  slut•tish
  slut•tish•ness

sly
  sli•er, sli•est *or* sly•er,
    sly•est
  sly•ly
  also sli•ly
  sly•ness

smack

smack•er

small
  small•ish
  small•ness

small-mind•ed
  small-mind•ed•ly
  small-mind•ed•ness

small•pox

smart
  smart-ass
  smart•ing•ly
  smart•ly
  smart•ness

smart•en

smash

smash•ing
  smash•ing•ly

smash•up

smat•ter•ing

smear
  smear•er
  smear•y
  smear•i•er, smear•i•est

smell
  past and past part.
    smelled *or* smelt
  smell•a•ble

smell•er
smell-less

smell•y
  smell•i•er, smell•i•est
  smell•i•ness

smelt (*extract metal*)
  smelt•er

smelt (*fish*)
  pl. same *or* smelts

smelt (*smelled*)

Sme•ta•na

smid•gen
  also smid•gin

smile
  smile•less
  smil•er
  smil•ing•ly

smirch

smirk
  smirk•er
  smirk•ing•ly
  smirk•y
  smirk•i•ly

smite
  past smote; *past part.*
    smit•ten
  smit•er

Smith (*proper name*)

smith (*metal worker*)

smith•er•eens

smith•y
  pl. smith•ies

smit•ten

smock

smock•ing

smog
  smog•gy
  smog•gi•er, smog•gi•
    est

smoke
  smok•a•ble
  also smoke•a•ble
  smoke•less
  smok•er
  smok•i•ly
  smok•i•ness
  smok•y
  smok•i•er, smok•i•est

smoke•stack

smol•der

Smo•lensk

Smol•lett

smooch
  smooch•er
  smooch•y
  smooch•i•er, smooch•
    i•est

smooth
  smooth-tongued
  smooth•a•ble
  smooth•er
  smooth•ish
  smooth•ly
  smooth•ness

smooth•ie

smor•gas•bord

smote

smoth•er

smudge
  smudge•less
  smudg•i•ly
  smudg•i•ness
  smudg•y
  smudg•i•er, smudg•i•
    est

smug
  smug•ger, smug•gest
  smug•ly
  smug•ness

smug•gle
  smug•gler
  smug•gling

smut
smut•ty
smut•ti•er, smut•ti•est
smut•ti•ly
smut•ti•ness

Smuts

Smyr•na

snack

snaf•fle

snag
snagged, snag•ging
snag•gy

snail
snail•like

snake
snake•like

Snake Riv•er

snak•y
snak•i•ly
snak•i•ness

snap
snapped, snap•ping
snap•pa•ble
snap•per
snap•ping•ly
snap•pish

snap•drag•on

snap•py
snap•pi•er, snap•pi•est
snap•pi•ly
snap•pi•ness

snap•shot

snare
snar•er

snarl (*growl*)
snarl•er
snarl•ing•ly
snarl•y
snarl•i•er, snarl•i•est

snarl (*tangle*)
snarl•y
snarl•i•er, snarl•i•est

snatch
snatch•er

snaz•zy
snaz•zi•er, snaz•zi•est
snaz•zi•ly
snaz•zi•ness

sneak
sneak•i•ly
sneak•ing•ly
sneak•i•ness
sneak•y
sneak•i•er, sneak•i•est

sneak•er

sneer
sneer•er
sneer•ing•ly

sneeze
sneez•er
sneez•y

snick•er
snick•er•ing•ly

snide
snide•ly
snide•ness

sniff
sniff•er
sniff•ing•ly

snif•fle
snif•fler
sniff•ly

snif•ter

snig•ger
snig•ger•er
snig•ger•ing•ly

snip
snipped, snip•ping

snipe
pl. same *or* snipes
snip•er

snip•pet

snip•py
snip•pi•er, snip•pi•est
also snip•pet•y

snip•pi•ly
snip•pi•ness

snit

snitch

sniv•el
sniv•el•er
sniv•el•ing
sniv•el•ing•ly

snob
snob•ber•y
pl. snob•ber•ies
snob•bish
snob•bish•ly
snob•bish•ness
snob•by
snob•bi•er, snob•bi•est

snood

snoop
snoop•er
snoop•y

snoot

snooze
snooz•er
snooz•y
snooz•i•er, snooz•i•est

snore
snor•er

snor•kel
snor•kel•er

snort

snot

snot•ty
snot•ti•er, snot•ti•est
snot•ti•ly
snot•ti•ness

snout
snout•ed
snout•like
snout•y

snow
snow•less
snow•like

snow•ball

snow•blow•er

snow•board
snow•board•er

snow•bound

snow•drift

snow•drop

snow•fall

snow•flake

snow•man
pl. snow•men

snow•mo•bile

snow•plow

snow•shoe
snow•sho•er

snow•storm

snow•y
snow•i•er, snow•i•est
snow•i•ly

snub
snubbed, snub•bing
snub•ber

snuff

snuff•box

snug
snug•ger, snug•gest
snug•ly
snug•ness

snug•gle

so (to that extent; see SEW,
SOW)
so-called

so
var. of sol

soak
soak•age
soak•er
soak•ing

so-and-so
pl. so-and-sos

soap
soap•i•ly
soap•i•ness
soap•less
soap•like
soap•y
soap•i•er, soap•i•est

soap•box

soap•stone

soar (fly; see SORE)
soar•er
soar•ing•ly

sob
sobbed, sob•bing
sob•ber
sob•bing•ly

so•ber
so•ber•er, so•ber•est
so•ber•ing•ly
so•ber•ly

so•bri•e•ty

so•bri•quet
also sou•bri•quet

soc•cer

so•cia•ble
so•cia•bil•i•ty
so•cia•ble•ness
so•cia•bly

so•cial
so•cial•ly

so•cial•ism
so•cial•ist
so•cial•is•tic

so•cial•ite

so•cial•ize
so•cial•i•za•tion

so•ci•e•ty
pl. so•ci•e•ties
so•ci•e•tal
so•ci•e•tal•ly

So•ci•e•ty Is•lands

so•ci•o•ec•o•nom•ic

so•ci•ol•o•gy
so•ci•o•log•i•cal
so•ci•o•log•i•cal•ly
so•ci•ol•o•gist

so•ci•o•path
so•ci•o•path•ic

sock
pl. socks or sox

sock•et

Soc•ra•tes
So•crat•ic

sod

so•da

so•dal•i•ty

sod•den
sod•den•ly

so•di•um

sod•om•y
sod•om•ite
sod•om•ize

so•fa

sof•fit

So•fi•a

soft
soft-boiled
soft-ped•al
soft-soap
soft-spo•ken
soft•ish
soft•ly
soft•ness

soft•ball

soft•cov•er

soft•en
soft•en•er

soft•heart•ed
soft•heart•ed•ness

soft•ware

soft•y
  also soft•ie
  pl. soft•ies

sog•gy
  sog•gi•er, sog•gi•est
  sog•gi•ly
  sog•gi•ness

soil
  soil•less

soi•rée
  also soi•ree

so•journ
  so•journ•er

sol (*musical note;* see
  SEOUL, SOLE, SOUL)
  also so

sol•ace

so•lar

so•lar•i•um
  pl. so•lar•i•ums *or* so•
  lar•i•a

sold

sol•der
  sol•der•er

sol•dier
  sol•dier•ly

sole (*shoe part;* see SEOUL,
  SOL, SOUL)

sole (*only;* see SEOUL,
  SOL, SOUL))
  sole•ly

sol•e•cism
  sol•e•cist
  sol•e•cis•tic

sol•emn
  sol•emn•ly
  sol•emn•ness

so•lem•ni•ty
  pl. so•lem•ni•ties

sol•em•nize
  sol•em•ni•za•tion

so•le•noid

so•lic•it
  so•lic•i•ta•tion

so•lic•i•tor

so•lic•i•tous
  so•lic•i•tous•ly

so•lic•i•tude

sol•id
  sol•id•er, sol•id•est
  sol•id-state
  sol•id•ly

sol•i•dar•i•ty

so•lid•i•fy
  so•lid•i•fies, so•lid•i•
  fied
  so•lid•i•fi•ca•tion
  so•lid•i•fi•er

so•lid•i•ty

sol•i•dus
  pl. sol•i•di

so•lil•o•quy
  pl. so•lil•o•quies
  so•lil•o•quist
  so•lil•o•quize

sol•i•taire

sol•i•tar•y
  sol•i•tar•i•ly

sol•i•tude

so•lo
  pl. so•los *or* so•li
  so•loes, so•loed
  so•lo•ist

Sol•o•mon Is•lands

So•lon

sol•stice
  sol•sti•tial

sol•u•ble
  sol•u•bil•i•ty

sol•ute

so•lu•tion

solve
  solv•a•ble
  solv•er

sol•vent
  sol•ven•cy

Sol•zhe•ni•tsyn

So•ma•li•a
  So•ma•li
  pl. same *or* So•ma•lis
  So•ma•li•an

so•mat•ic
  so•mat•i•cal•ly

som•ber
  som•ber•ly
  som•ber•ness

som•bre•ro
  pl. som•bre•ros

some (*unspecified amount;*
  see SUM)

some•bod•y
  pl. some•bod•ies

some•day

some•how

some•one

some•place

som•er•sault
  also sum•mer•sault

some•thing

some•time

some•times

some•what

some•where

som•nam•bu•lism
  som•nam•bu•list

som•no•lent
  som•no•lence
  som•no•lent•ly

son (*child;* see SUN)
  son-in-law
  pl. sons-in-law
  son•less
  son•ship

so•nar

so•na•ta

Sond•heim

song
song•less

song•bird

son•ic

son•net

son•ny (*term of address*;
  see SUNNY)

son•o•gram

So•no•ra

So•no•ran Des•ert

so•no•rous
  so•nor•i•ty
  so•no•rous•ly
  so•no•rous•ness

Son•tag

soon
  soon•ish

soot

soothe
  sooth•er
  sooth•ing
  sooth•ing•ly

sooth•say•er

soot•y
  soot•i•er, soot•i•est
  soot•i•ly
  soot•i•ness

sop
  sopped, sop•ping

soph•ism

soph•ist
  so•phis•tic
  so•phis•ti•cal

so•phis•ti•cate
  so•phis•ti•ca•tion

so•phis•ti•cat•ed

soph•ist•ry
  pl. soph•ist•ries

Soph•o•cles

soph•o•more
  soph•o•mor•ic

sop•o•rif•ic
  sop•o•rif•er•ous
  sop•o•rif•i•cal•ly

sop•py
  sop•pi•er, sop•pi•est

so•pran•o
  pl. so•pran•os *or* so•
  pran•i

sor•bet

sor•cer•er
  fem. sor•cer•ess
  sor•cer•y
  pl. sor•cer•ies

sor•did
  sor•did•ly
  sor•did•ness

sore (*painful*; see SOAR)
  sore•ness

sore•ly

sor•ghum

so•ror•i•ty
  pl. so•ror•i•ties

sor•rel

sor•row
  sor•row•er
  sor•row•ing

sor•row•ful
  sor•row•ful•ly
  sor•row•ful•ness

sor•ry
  sor•ri•er, sor•ri•est
  sor•ri•ly

sort
  sort•a•ble

sort•er
sort•ing

sor•tie

SOS
  pl. SOSs

sot

sot•to vo•ce

sou•bri•quet
  var. of so•bri•quet

souf•flé

sought

soul (*spirit*; see SEOUL,
  SOL, SOLE)

soul•ful
  soul•ful•ly
  soul•ful•ness

soul•less
  soul•less•ly
  soul•less•ness

sound (*healthy*)
  sound•ly
  sound•ness

sound (*noise*)
  sound•less
  sound•less•ly
  sound•less•ness

sound (*plumb depth*)
  sound•er

sound•ing

sound•proof

sound•track

soup

soup•çon

soup•y
  soup•i•er, soup•i•est
  soup•i•ness

sour
  sour•ish
  sour•ly
  sour•ness

source

sour·puss

Sou·sa

souse

Sou·ter

south
south·east
south·east·er·ly
south·east·ern
south·west
south·west·er·ly
south·west·ern

South Af·ri·ca
South Af·ri·can

South A·mer·i·ca
South A·mer·i·can

South·amp·ton

South Car·o·li·na
South Car·o·lin·i·an

South Da·ko·ta
South Da·ko·tan

south·east·er

south·er·ly
pl. south·er·lies

south·ern
south·ern·er
south·ern·most

Sou·they

South Ko·re·a

south·paw

South Pole

south·ward
also south·wards

south·west·er

sou·ve·nir

sou'west·er

sov·er·eign
sov·er·eign·ty
pl. sov·er·eign·ties

so·vi·et
also So·vi·et

sow (pig)

sow (plant; see SEW, SO)
past sowed; past part.
sown or sowed
sow·er
sow·ing

So·we·to

sox
var. of socks

soy
also soy·a

soy·bean

So·yin·ka

spa

space
spac·er

space·craft

space·man
pl. space·men; fem.
space·wom·an, pl.
space·wom·en

space·ship

space·suit

spac·ey
also spac·y
spac·i·er, spac·i·est

spa·cial
var. of spa·tial

spa·cious
spa·cious·ly
spa·cious·ness

spade
spade·ful
pl. spade·fuls

spade·work

spa·ghet·ti

Spain
Span·iard
Span·ish

span
spanned, span·ning

span·drel

span·gle
span·gly

span·iel

Span·ish

spank

spank·ing

spar
sparred, spar·ring

spare
spare·ly
spare·ness
spar·er

spare·ribs

spar·ing
spar·ing·ly

spark
spark·less
spark·y

spar·kle
spar·kly

spar·kler

spar·row

sparse
sparse·ly
sparse·ness
spar·si·ty

Spar·ta·cus

Spar·tan
also spar·tan

spasm

spas·mod·ic
spas·mod·i·cal·ly

spas·tic
spas·ti·cal·ly
spas·tic·i·ty

spat

spate

spathe

spa·tial
also spa·cial
spa·ti·al·i·ty
spa·tial·ly

spat·ter

spat·u·la

spawn
spawn·er

spay

speak
past spoke; *past part.*
spok·en
speak·a·ble

speak·eas·y
pl. speak·eas·ies

speak·er

speak·er·phone

spear

spear·head

spear·mint

spec

spe·cial
spe·cial·ly
spe·cial·ness

spe·cial·ist
spe·cial·ism

spe·cial·ize
spe·cial·i·za·tion

spe·cial·ty
pl. spe·cial·ties

spe·cie

spe·cies
pl. same

spe·cif·ic
spe·cif·i·cal·ly
spec·i·fic·i·ty

spec·i·fi·ca·tion

spec·i·fy
spec·i·fies, spec·i·fied
spec·i·fi·er

spec·i·men

spe·cious
spe·ci·os·i·ty
spe·cious·ly
spe·cious·ness

speck
speck·less

speck·le

specs

spec·ta·cle

spec·ta·cles

spec·tac·u·lar
spec·tac·u·lar·ly

spec·ta·tor

spec·ter

spec·tral
spec·tral·ly

spec·trom·e·ter
spec·tro·met·ric
spec·trom·e·try

spec·tro·scope
spec·tro·scop·ic
spec·tro·scop·i·cal
spec·tros·co·py

spec·trum
pl. spec·tra

spec·u·late
spec·u·la·tion
spec·u·la·tor

spec·u·la·tive
spec·u·la·tive·ly

spec·u·lum
pl. spec·u·la *or* spec·u·lums

sped

speech
speech·ful

speech·less
speech·less·ly
speech·less·ness

speed
past and *past part.* sped
or speed·ed
speed·er

speed·boat

speed·om·e·ter

speed·way

speed·y
speed·i·er, speed·i·est
speed·i·ly
speed·i·ness

spe·le·ol·o·gy
spe·le·o·log·i·cal
spe·le·ol·o·gist

spell
past and *past part.*
spelled *or* spelt
spell·a·ble

spell·bind
past and *past part.*
spell·bound
spell·bind·er
spell·bind·ing·ly

spel·ler

spel·ling

spe·lunk·er
spe·lunk·ing

spend
past and *past part.* spent
spend·a·ble
spend·er

spend·thrift

Spen·ser

sperm
  pl. same *or* sperms

sper·ma·to·zo·on
  pl. sper·ma·to·zo·a
  sper·ma·to·zo·an

sper·mi·cide
  sper·mi·cid·al

spew
  spew·er

sphag·num

sphere
  spher·i·cal

spher·oid
  sphe·roi·dal

sphinc·ter

sphinx
  also Sphinx
  pl. sphinx·es *or* sphin·
  ges

**sphyg·mo·ma·nom·e·
  ter**

spice
  spic·y

spick-and-span
  also spic-and-span

spi·der

spi·der·y

spiel
  spiel·er

spif·fy
  spif·fi·er, spif·fi·est
  spif·fi·ly

spig·ot

spike
  spik·i·ly
  spik·i·ness
  spik·y
  spik·i·er, spik·i·est

spill
  past and past part.
  spilled *or* spilt
  spil·ler

spill·age

spill·way

spin
  spin·ning; *past and past
  part.* spun
  spin·ner

spi·na bif·i·da

spin·ach

spi·nal

spin·dle

spin·dly
  spin·dli·er, spin·dli·est

spine
  spine-chil·ling
  spine-tin·gling
  spined

spine·less
  spine·less·ly
  spine·less·ness

spin·et

spin·ner·et

spin·ning

Spi·no·za

spin·ster
  spin·ster·hood
  spin·ster·ish

spin·y
  spin·i·er, spin·i·est
  spin·i·ness

spi·ral
  spi·ral·ly

spire

spi·re·a
  also spi·rae·a

spir·it

spir·it·ed
  spir·it·ed·ly
  spir·it·ed·ness

spir·it·less
  spir·it·less·ly

spir·i·tu·al
  spir·i·tu·al·i·ty
  spir·i·tu·al·ly
  spir·i·tu·al·ness

spir·i·tu·al·ism
  spir·i·tu·al·ist

spir·i·tu·ous

spi·ro·chete
  also spi·ro·chaete

spit (*expectorate*)
  spit·ting; *past and past
  part.* spat *or* spit
  spit·ter

spit (*skewer*)
  spit·ted, spit·ting

spite

spite·ful
  spite·ful·ly
  spite·ful·ness

spit·fire

spit·tle

spit·toon

splash

splash·down

splash·y
  splash·i·er, splash·i·est

splat
  splat·ted, splat·ting

splat·ter

splay

spleen
  spleen·ful

splen·did
  splen·did·ly

splen·dor

sple·net·ic
  sple·net·i·cal·ly

splice
  splic·er

splint

splin·ter
  splin·ter·y

split
  split·ting; *past and past part.* split
  split-lev·el
  split·ter

splotch
  splotch·y

splurge

splut·ter
  splut·ter·er
  splut·ter·ing·ly

Spock

spoil
  past and past part. spoiled *or* spoilt
  spoil·age
  spoil·er

Spo·kane

spoke

spo·ken

spokes·man
  pl. spokes·men; *fem.* spokes·wom·an, *pl.* spokes·wom·en

spokes·per·son
  pl. spokes·per·sons *or* spokes·peo·ple

spo·li·a·tion

spon·dee
  spon·da·ic

sponge
  sponge·a·ble
  sponge·like
  spong·er
  spon·gi·form

spong·y
  spong·i·er, spong·i·est
  spong·i·ness

spon·sor
  spon·so·ri·al
  spon·sor·ship

spon·ta·ne·ous
  spon·ta·ne·i·ty
  spon·ta·ne·ous·ly

spoof

spook

spook·y
  spook·i·er, spook·i·est
  spook·i·ly
  spook·i·ness

spool

spoon
  spoon·er
  spoon·ful
  pl. spoon·fuls

spoon·bill

spoo·ner·ism

spoon·feed
  past and past part. spoon·fed

spo·rad·ic
  spo·rad·i·cal·ly

spore

sport
  sport·er

sport·ing
  sport·ing·ly

sport·ive

sports·man
  pl. sports·men; *fem.* sports·wom·an, *pl.* sports·wom·en
  sports·man·like
  sports·man·ly
  sports·man·ship

sports·wear

sport·y
  sport·i·er, sport·i·est
  sport·i·ly
  sport·i·ness

spot
  spot·ted, spot·ting
  spot·ter

spot·less
  spot·less·ly
  spot·less·ness

spot·light
  past and past part. spot·light·ed *or* spot·lit

spot·ty
  spot·ti·er, spot·ti·est
  spot·ti·ly
  spot·ti·ness

spouse

spout
  spout·er
  spout·less

sprain

sprang

sprat

sprawl
  sprawl·ing·ly

spray
  spray·a·ble
  spray·er

spread
  past and past part. spread
  spread-ea·gle
  spread·a·ble
  spread·er

spread·sheet

spree

sprig

spright·ly
  spright·li·er, spright·li·est
  spright·li·ness

spring
past sprang *or* sprung;
past part. sprung
spring·less
spring·like

spring·board

Spring·field

spring·time

spring·y
spring·i·er, spring·i·est
spring·i·ly
spring·i·ness

sprin·kle
sprin·kler

sprin·kling

sprint
sprint·er

sprite

spritz·er

sprock·et

sprout

spruce

sprung

spry
spry·er, spry·est
spry·ly
spry·ness

spud

spume
spum·y
spum·i·er, spum·i·est

spun

spunk

spunk·y
spunk·i·er, spunk·i·est
spunk·i·ly

spur
spurred, spur·ring

spu·ri·ous
spu·ri·ous·ly
spu·ri·ous·ness

spurn
spurn·er

spurt

sput·nik
also Sput·nik

sput·ter
sput·ter·er

spu·tum
pl. spu·ta

spy
pl. spies
spies, spied
spy·ing

spy·glass

squab

squab·ble
squab·bler

squad

squad·ron

squal·id
squa·lid·i·ty
squal·id·ly
squal·id·ness

squall
squal·ly

squa·lor

squan·der
squan·der·er

Squan·to

square
square·ly
square·ness
squar·ish

squash (*crush*)
squash·y
squash·i·er, squash·i·
est

squash·i·ly
squash·i·ness

squash (*plant*)
pl. same *or* squash·es

squat
squat·ted, squat·ting
squat·ter, squat·test

squat·ter

squaw

squawk
squawk·er

squeak
squeak·er
squeak·i·ly
squeak·i·ness
squeak·y
squeak·i·er, squeak·i·
est

squeal
squeal·er

squeam·ish
squeam·ish·ly
squeam·ish·ness

squee·gee

squeeze
squeez·er

squelch
squelch·er
squelch·y

squib

squid

squig·gle
squig·gly

squint
squint·er
squint·y

squire

squirm
squirm·er
squirm·y
squirm·i·er, squirm·i·
est

squir·rel

squirt
squirt·er

squish
squish·y
squish·i·er, squish·i·est

Sri Lan·ka
Sri Lan·kan

stab
stabbed, stab·bing
stab·ber

sta·bil·i·ty

sta·bi·lize
sta·bi·li·za·tion

sta·bi·liz·er

sta·ble (*horse barn*)
sta·ble·ful
pl. sta·ble·fuls

sta·ble (*steady*)
sta·bler, sta·blest
sta·ble·ness
sta·bly

stac·ca·to

stack
stack·a·ble
stack·er

sta·di·um
pl. sta·di·ums *or* sta·
di·a

staff
pl. staffs *or* staves
also stave; *pl.* staffs *or*
staves
staffed

stag

stage

stage·coach

stage·craft

stage·hand

stag·fla·tion

stag·ger
stag·ger·er

stag·ger·ing
stag·ger·ing·ly

stag·ing

stag·nant
stag·nan·cy
stag·nant·ly

stag·nate
stag·na·tion

staid
staid·ly
staid·ness

stain
stain·a·ble
stain·er

stain·less

stair (*step*; see STARE)

stair·case

stair·way

stair·well

stake (*stick, wager*; see
STEAK)
stak·er

stake·out

sta·lac·tite

sta·lag·mite

stale
stal·er, stal·est
stale·ness

stale·mate

Sta·lin

Sta·lin·grad

stalk (*pursue*)
stalk·er

stalk (*stem*)
stalked
stalk·y

stall

stal·lion

stal·wart
stal·wart·ly

sta·men

Stam·ford

stam·i·na

stam·mer
stam·mer·er
stam·mer·ing·ly

stamp
stamp·er

stam·pede
stam·ped·er

stance

stanch
also staunch

stan·chion

stand
past and *past part.* stood
stand·er

stand·ard
stand·ard-bear·er

stand·ard·ize
stand·ard·i·za·tion

stand·by
pl. stand·bys

stand·ing

Stan·dish

stand·off·ish
stand·off·ish·ly
stand·off·ish·ness

stand·pipe

stand·point

stand·still

Stan·i·slav·sky

stank

Stan•ley

Stan•ton

stan•za

sta•ple
staplen

star (*celestial body; see*
STARR)
starred, star•ring
star-span•gled
star•dom
star•less
star•like

star•board

starch
starch•er

starch•y
starch•i•er, starch•i•est
starch•i•ly
starch•i•ness

stare (*gaze; see* STAIR)
star•er

star•fish

star•gaz•er

stark
stark•ly
stark•ness

star•let

star•light

star•ling

star•lit

Starr (*proper name; see*
STAR)

star•ry
star•ri•er, star•ri•est
star•ry-eyed
star•ri•ness

start

start•er

star•tle

star•tling
star•tling•ly

starve
star•va•tion

stash

state
stat•a•ble
stat•ed•ly

state•hood

state•less
state•less•ness

state•ly
state•li•er, state•li•est
state•li•ness

state•ment

Stat•en Is•land

state•room

states•man
pl. states•men; *fem.*
states•wom•an, *pl.*
states•wom•en
states•man•like
states•man•ship

stat•ic
stat•i•cal•ly

sta•tion

sta•tion•ar•y (*unmoving;*
see STATIONERY)

sta•tion•er

sta•tion•er•y (*writing*
paper; see
STATIONARY)

sta•tis•tic

sta•tis•tics
sta•tis•ti•cal
sta•tis•ti•cal•ly
stat•is•ti•cian

stat•u•ar•y
pl. stat•u•ar•ies

stat•ue

stat•u•esque
stat•u•esque•ness

stat•u•ette

stat•ure
stat•ured

sta•tus

sta•tus quo

stat•ute

stat•u•to•ry
stat•u•to•ri•ly

staunch (*firm*)
staunch•ly
staunch•ness

staunch (*var. of stanch*)

stave
past and *past part.* stove
or staved

Stav•ro•pol

stay
stay•er

stead

stead•fast
stead•fast•ly
stead•fast•ness

stead•y
stead•i•er, stead•i•est
stead•ies, stead•ied
pl. stead•ies
stead•i•ly
stead•i•ness

steak (*meat; see* STAKE)

steal (*take; see* STEEL)
past stole; *past part.*
sto•len
steal•er
steal•ing

stealth

stealth•y
stealth•i•er, stealth•i•
est
stealth•i•ly
stealth•i•ness

steam

steam·boat

steam·er

steam·roll·er

steam·ship

steam·y
steam·i·er, steam·i·est
steam·i·ly
steam·i·ness

steed

steel (*metal*; see STEAL)
steel·i·ness
steel·y
steel·i·er, steel·i·est

steel·works
steel·work·er

steel·yard

steep
steep·en
steep·ly
steep·ness

stee·ple
stee·pled

stee·ple·chase
stee·ple·chas·er
stee·ple·chas·ing

stee·ple·jack

steer
steer·a·ble
steer·er
steer·ing

steer·age

steg·o·sau·rus
also steg·o·saur

Stein (*proper name*)

stein (*mug*)

Stein·beck

ste·la
pl. ste·lae

stel·lar
stel·li·form

stem
stemmed, stem·ming
stem·less
stem·like

stench

sten·cil
sten·ciled, sten·cil·ing
or sten·cilled, sten·
cil·ling

Sten·dhal

ste·nog·ra·phy
ste·nog·ra·pher
sten·o·graph·ic

sten·to·ri·an

step (*movement*; see
STEPPE)
stepped, step·ping
step·ping-stone
step·like

step·broth·er

step·child

step·daugh·ter

step·fa·ther

step·lad·der

step·moth·er

step·par·ent

steppe (*grassy plain*; see
STEP)

step·sis·ter

step·son

ster·e·o
pl. ster·e·os

ster·e·o·phon·ic
ster·e·o·phon·i·cal·ly

ster·e·o·scope
ster·e·o·scop·ic

ster·e·o·scop·i·cal·ly
ster·e·os·co·py

ster·e·o·type
ster·e·o·typ·ic
ster·e·o·typ·i·cal
ster·e·o·typ·i·cal·ly

ster·ile
ster·ile·ly
ste·ril·i·ty

ster·i·lize
ster·i·li·za·tion
ster·i·liz·er

ster·ling

stern (*ship's rear part*)
sterned
stern·most
stern·ward
stern·wards

stern (*strict*)
stern·ly
stern·ness

ster·num
pl. ster·nums *or* ster·na

ster·oid
ster·oid·al

ste·rol

ster·to·rous

stet
stet·ted, stet·ting

steth·o·scope

Stet·son (*trademark*)

Steu·ben

ste·ve·dore

Ste·vens

Ste·ven·son

stew

stew·ard
stew·ard·ship

stew·ard·ess

stick (*branch*)
  stick•like

stick (*adhere*)
  past and *past part.* stuck
  stick-in-the-mud
  stick-up

stick•ball

stick•er

stick•ler

stick•y
  stick•i•er, stick•i•est
  stick•i•ly
  stick•i•ness

stiff
  stiff-necked
  stiff•ish
  stiff•ly
  stiff•ness

stiff•en
  stiff•en•er
  stiff•en•ing

sti•fle
  sti•fler
  sti•fling•ly

stig•ma
  pl. stig•mas *or* stig•
  ma•ta

stig•ma•tize
  stig•ma•ti•za•tion

stile (*gate*; see STYLE)

sti•let•to
  pl. sti•let•tos

still
  still•ness

still•birth

still•born

stilt

stilt•ed
  stilt•ed•ly
  stilt•ed•ness

stim•u•lant

stim•u•late
  stim•u•lat•ing
  stim•u•la•tion
  stim•u•la•tive
  stim•u•la•tor

stim•u•lus
  pl. stim•u•li

sting
  past and *past part.* stung
  sting•er
  sting•ing•ly
  sting•less
  sting•like

sting•ray

stin•gy
  stin•gi•er, stin•gi•est
  stin•gi•ly
  stin•gi•ness

stink
  past stank *or* stunk; *past
  part.* stunk

stink•er

stink•ing
  stink•ing•ly

stint
  stint•er
  stint•less

sti•pend

stip•ple
  stip•pler
  stip•pling

stip•u•late
  stip•u•la•tion
  stip•u•la•tor

stir
  stirred, stir•ring
  stir•rer

stir-fry
  stir-fries, stir-fried

stir•ring
  stir•ring•ly

stir•rup

stitch
  stitch•er
  stitch•er•y

stoat

stock
  stock-in-trade
  stock-still
  stock•er
  stock•less

stock•ade

stock•brok•er
  stock•brok•er•age
  stock•brok•ing

stock•hold•er
  stock•hold•ing

Stock•holm

stock•ing
  stock•inged
  stock•ing•less

stock•pile
  stock•pil•er

stock•room

stock•tak•ing

Stock•ton

stock•y
  stock•i•er, stock•i•est
  stock•i•ly
  stock•i•ness

stock•yard

stodg•y
  stodg•i•er, stodg•i•est
  stodg•i•ly
  stodg•i•ness

Sto•ic
  also sto•ic

sto•i•cal
  sto•i•cal•ly

Sto•i•cism
  also sto•i•cism

stoke

Stoke-on-Trent

stole

sto·len

stol·id
sto·lid·i·ty
stol·id·ly
stol·id·ness

stom·ach
stom·ach·ful
pl. stom·ach·fuls

stom·ach·ache

stomp
stomp·er

stone
stone·less
ston·er

stoned

stone·ma·son
stone·ma·son·ry

stone·wall
stone·wall·er
stone·wall·ing

stone·ware

stone·washed

stone·work
stone·work·er

ston·y
ston·i·er, ston·i·est
ston·i·ly
ston·i·ness

stood

stooge

stool

stoop

stop
stopped, stop·ping
stop·less
stop·pa·ble

stop·cock

stop·gap

stop·o·ver

stop·page

Stop·pard

stop·per

stop·watch

stor·age

store
stor·a·ble
stor·er

store·house

store·keep·er

store·room

sto·ried

stork

storm
storm·less
storm·proof

storm·y
storm·i·er, storm·i·est
storm·i·ly
storm·i·ness

sto·ry
pl. sto·ries

sto·ry·board

sto·ry·tell·er
sto·ry·tell·ing

stout
stout·ish
stout·ly
stout·ness

stout·heart·ed
stout·heart·ed·ly

stove

stove·pipe

stow (*pack*; see STOWE)

stow·a·way

Stowe (*proper name*; see STOW)

stra·bis·mus
stra·bis·mal
stra·bis·mic

strad·dle
strad·dler

Stra·di·va·ri

strafe

strag·gle
strag·gler
strag·gly
strag·gli·er, strag·gli·est

straight (*direct*; see STRAIT)
straight·ly
straight·ness

straight·a·way

straight·en
straight·en·er

straight·for·ward
straight·for·ward·ly
straight·for·ward·ness

strain
strain·a·ble

strained

strain·er

strait (*channel*; see STRAIGHT)
strait·ly
strait·ness

strait·ened

strait·jack·et

strait·laced

strand

strange
strange·ly
strange·ness

strang·er

stran·gle
stran·gler

stran·gle·hold

stran·gu·late

stran·gu·la·tion

strap
strapped, strap·ping

strap·ping

Stras·bourg

stra·ta

strat·a·gem

stra·te·gic
stra·te·gi·cal
stra·te·gi·cal·ly
stra·te·gics

strat·e·gy
pl. strat·e·gies
strat·e·gist

strat·i·fy
strat·i·fies, strat·i·fied
strat·i·fi·ca·tion

strat·o·sphere
strat·o·spher·ic

stra·tum
pl. stra·ta *or* stra·tums
stra·tal

Strauss

Stra·vin·sky

straw

straw·ber·ry
pl. straw·ber·ries

stray
stray·er

streak
streak·er
streak·ing

streak·y
streak·i·er, streak·i·est
streak·i·ly
streak·i·ness

stream

stream·er

stream·line

street

street·car

street·walk·er
street·walk·ing

street·wise

strength

strength·en
strength·en·er

stren·u·ous
stren·u·ous·ly
stren·u·ous·ness

strep·to·coc·cus
pl. strep·to·coc·ci
strep·to·coc·cal

strep·to·my·cin

stress
stress·less

stress·ful
stress·ful·ly
stress·ful·ness

stretch
stretch·a·ble
stretch·a·bil·i·ty
stretch·y
stretch·i·ness

stretch·er

strew
past part. strewn *or*
strewed
strew·er

stri·ate
also stri·at·ed
stri·a·tion

strick·en

strict
strict·ly
strict·ness

stric·ture

stride
past strode; *past part.*
strid·den
strid·er

stri·dent
stri·den·cy
stri·dent·ly

strife

strike
past struck; *past part.*
struck *or* strick·en
strik·a·ble
strik·er

strike·break·er
strike·break

strik·ing
strik·ing·ly

Strind·berg

string
past and *past part.*
strung
string·less
string·like

stringed

strin·gent
strin·gen·cy
strin·gent·ly

string·er

string·y
string·i·er, string·i·est
string·i·ly
string·i·ness

strip
stripped, strip·ping

stripe

striped

strip·ling

strip·per

strip·tease
strip·teas·er

strive
 past strove; *past part.*
 striv•en
 striv•er

strobe

stro•bo•scope
 stro•bo•scop•ic

strode

stroke

stroll

stroll•er

strong
 strong•er; strong•est
 strong-arm
 strong•ly

strong•box

strong•hold

strong•room

stron•ti•um

strop
 stropped, strop•ping

strove

struck

struc•ture
 struc•tur•al
 struc•tured
 struc•ture•less

stru•del

strug•gle
 strug•gler

strum
 strummed, strum•ming
 strum•mer

strum•pet

strung

strut
 strut•ted, strut•ting
 strut•ter
 strut•ting•ly

strych•nine
 strych•nic

Stu•art

stub
 stubbed, stub•bing

stub•ble
 stub•bled
 stub•bly

stub•born
 stub•born•ly
 stub•born•ness

stub•by
 stub•bi•er, stub•bi•est
 stub•bi•ly
 stub•bi•ness

stuc•co
 pl. stuc•coes *or* stuc•cos
 stuc•coes, stuc•coed

stuck

stuck-up

stud
 stud•ded, stud•ding

stu•dent

stu•di•o
 pl. stu•di•os

stu•di•ous
 stu•di•ous•ly
 stu•di•ous•ness

stud•y
 pl. stud•ies
 stud•ies, stud•ied

stuff
 stuff•er

stuff•ing

stuff•y
 stuff•i•er, stuff•i•est
 stuff•i•ly
 stuff•i•ness

stul•ti•fy
 stul•ti•fies, stul•ti•fied
 stul•ti•fi•ca•tion
 stul•ti•fi•er

stum•ble
 stum•bler
 stum•bling•ly

stump
 stump•y
 stump•i•er, stump•i•est

stun
 stunned, stun•ning

stung

stunk

stun•ning
 stun•ning•ly

stunt
 stunt•ed•ness

stu•pe•fy
 stu•pe•fies, stu•pe•fied
 stu•pe•fa•cient
 stu•pe•fac•tion
 stu•pe•fy•ing
 stu•pe•fy•ing•ly

stu•pen•dous
 stu•pen•dous•ly
 stu•pen•dous•ness

stu•pid
 stu•pid•er, stu•pid•est
 stu•pid•i•ty
 pl. stu•pid•i•ties
 stu•pid•ly

stu•por
 stu•por•ous

stur•dy
 stur•di•er, stur•di•est
 stur•di•ly
 stur•di•ness

stur•geon

stut•ter
 stut•ter•er
 stut•ter•ing•ly

Stutt•gart

Stuy•ve•sant

sty (*eye swelling*)
 also stye
 pl. sties *or* styes

sty (*pigpen*)
  pl. sties

style (*fashion*; see STILE)

styl·ish
  styl·ish·ly
  styl·ish·ness

styl·ist

sty·lis·tic
  sty·lis·ti·cal·ly

styl·ize
  styl·i·za·tion

sty·lus
  pl. sty·li *or* sty·luses

sty·mie
  also sty·my
  pl. sty·mies
  sty·mies, sty·mied, sty·
    my·ing *or* sty·mie·ing

styp·tic

sty·rene

Sty·ro·foam (*trademark*)

sua·sion
  sua·sive

suave
  suave·ly
  suave·ness
  suav·i·ty
  pl. suav·i·ties

sub
  subbed, sub·bing

sub·a·tom·ic

sub·base·ment

sub·branch

sub·cat·e·go·ri·za·tion

sub·cat·e·go·rize

sub·cat·e·go·ry

sub·class

sub·clause

sub·com·mit·tee

sub·com·pact

sub·con·scious
  sub·con·scious·ly
  sub·con·scious·ness

sub·con·ti·nent
  sub·con·ti·nent·al

sub·con·tract
  sub·con·trac·tor

sub·cra·ni·al

sub·cul·ture
  sub·cul·tur·al

sub·cu·ta·ne·ous
  sub·cu·ta·ne·ous·ly

sub·di·vide
  sub·di·vi·sion

sub·due
  sub·dues, sub·dued,
    sub·du·ing

sub·fam·i·ly

sub·form

sub·ge·nus

sub·group

sub·head
  also sub·head·ing

sub·hu·man

sub·ject
  sub·jec·tion
  sub·ject·less

sub·jec·tive
  sub·jec·tive·ly
  sub·jec·tive·ness
  sub·jec·tiv·i·ty

sub·join

sub·ju·gate
  sub·ju·ga·tion
  sub·ju·ga·tor

sub·junc·tive

sub·king·dom

sub·lease

sub·let
  sub·let·ting; *past* and
    past part. sub·let

sub·li·mate
  sub·li·ma·tion

sub·lime
  sub·lim·er, sub·lim·est
  sub·lime·ly
  sub·lim·i·ty

sub·lim·i·nal
  sub·lim·i·nal·ly

sub·ma·chine gun

sub·ma·rine
  sub·ma·rin·er

sub·merge
  sub·mer·gence
  sub·mer·sion

sub·mers·i·ble

sub·mis·sion

sub·mis·sive
  sub·mis·sive·ly
  sub·mis·sive·ness

sub·mit
  sub·mit·ted, sub·mit·
    ting
  sub·mit·ter

sub·nor·mal
  sub·nor·mal·i·ty

sub·or·der

sub·or·di·nate
  sub·or·di·nate·ly
  sub·or·di·na·tion

sub·orn
  sub·or·na·tion
  sub·orn·er

sub·phy·lum

sub·plot

sub·poe·na
  past and *past part.*
    sub·poe·naed

sub·ro·sa

sub·scribe
  sub·scrib·er

sub·script

sub·scrip·tion

sub·sec·tion

sub·se·quent
  sub·se·quent·ly

sub·ser·vi·ent
  sub·ser·vi·ence
  sub·ser·vi·ent·ly

sub·set

sub·side
  sub·sid·ence

sub·sid·i·ar·y
  pl. sub·sid·i·ar·ies

sub·si·dize
  sub·si·di·za·tion
  sub·si·diz·er

sub·si·dy
  pl. sub·si·dies

sub·sist
  sub·sist·ent

sub·sist·ence

sub·soil

sub·son·ic
  sub·son·i·cal·ly

sub·spe·cies

sub·stance

sub·stand·ard

sub·stan·tial
  sub·stan·tial·ly

sub·stan·ti·ate
  sub·stan·ti·a·tion

sub·stan·tive
  sub·stan·ti·val
  sub·stan·tive·ly

sub·sti·tute
  sub·sti·tut·a·ble
  sub·sti·tu·tion
  sub·sti·tu·tive

sub·strate

sub·stra·tum
  pl. sub·stra·ta *or* sub·stra·tums

sub·struc·ture
  sub·struc·tur·al

sub·sume
  sub·sum·a·ble

sub·ter·fuge

sub·ter·ra·ne·an

sub·text

sub·ti·tle

sub·tle
  sub·tler, sub·tlest
  sub·tle·ness
  sub·tle·ty
  sub·tly

sub·to·tal

sub·tract
  sub·tract·er
  sub·trac·tion
  sub·trac·tive

sub·trop·ics
  sub·trop·i·cal

sub·urb
  sub·ur·ban

sub·ur·bi·a

sub·ver·sive
  sub·ver·sion
  sub·ver·sive·ly
  sub·ver·sive·ness

sub·vert
  sub·vert·er

sub·way

sub·ze·ro

suc·ceed

suc·cess

suc·cess·ful
  suc·cess·ful·ly
  suc·cess·ful·ness

suc·ces·sion
  suc·ces·sion·al

suc·ces·sive
  suc·ces·sive·ly
  suc·ces·sive·ness

suc·ces·sor

suc·cinct
  suc·cinct·ly
  suc·cinct·ness

suc·cor (*help*; see SUCKER)

suc·co·tash

suc·cu·lent
  suc·cu·lence
  suc·cu·lent·ly

suc·cumb

such

such·like

suck

suck·er (*fool, candy*; see SUCCOR)

suck·le
  suck·ler

suck·ling

Su·cre

su·crose

suc·tion

Su·dan

sud·den
  sud·den·ly
  sud·den·ness

suds
  suds·y

sue (*take to court;* see
  SIOUX)
  sues, sued, su•ing
  su•er (*one who sues;* see
  SEWER)

suede

su•et
  su•et•y

Sue•to•ni•us

Su•ez

suf•fer
  suf•fer•a•ble
  suf•fer•er
  suf•fer•ing

suf•fer•ance

suf•fice

suf•fi•cien•cy
  pl. suf•fi•cien•cies

suf•fi•cient
  suf•fi•cient•ly

suf•fix

suf•fo•cate
  suf•fo•cat•ing
  suf•fo•cat•ing•ly
  suf•fo•ca•tion

suf•fra•gan

suf•frage
  suf•fra•gist

suf•fra•gette

suf•fuse
  suf•fu•sion

Su•fi
  pl. Su•fis
  Su•fic
  Su•fism

sug•ar
  sug•ar-coat•ed
  sug•ar•less

sug•ar•y
  sug•ar•i•ness

sug•gest
  sug•gest•er

sug•gest•i•ble

sug•ges•tion

sug•ges•tive
  sug•ges•tive•ly
  sug•ges•tive•ness

su•i•cid•al
  su•i•cid•al•ly

su•i•cide

su•i ge•ne•ris

suit

suit•a•ble
  suit•a•bil•i•ty
  suit•a•ble•ness
  suit•a•bly

suit•case
  suit•case•ful
  pl. suit•case•fuls

suite (*set;* see SWEET)

suit•or

Su•kar•no

Su•la•we•si

Su•lei•man I

sul•fa

sul•fate

sul•fide

sul•fite

sul•fon•a•mide

sul•fur
  also sul•phur
  sul•fur•ous
  sul•fur•y

sul•fu•ric ac•id

sulk
  sulk•er

sulk•y
  sulk•i•er, sulk•i•est
  sulk•i•ly
  sulk•i•ness

Sul•la

sul•len
  sul•len•ly
  sul•len•ness

sul•ly
  sul•lies, sul•lied

sul•phur
  var. of sul•fur

sul•tan
  sul•tan•ate

sul•ta•na

sul•try
  sul•tri•er, sul•tri•est
  sul•tri•ly
  sul•tri•ness

sum (*total;* see SOME)
  summed, sum•ming

su•mac
  also su•mach

Su•ma•tra

Sum•ga•it

sum•ma•rize
  sum•ma•ri•za•tion
  sum•ma•riz•er

sum•ma•ry (*synopsis;* see
  summery [SUMMER])
  pl. sum•ma•ries
  sum•mar•i•ly

sum•ma•tion
  sum•ma•tion•al

sum•mer
  sum•mer•less
  sum•mer•y (*warm;* see
  SUMMARY)

sum•mer•time

sum•mit
  sum•mit•less

sum•mon
  sum•mon•er

sum•mons
  pl. sum•mons•es

su•mo
  pl. su•mos

sump

sump•tu•ous
  sump•tu•ous•ly
  sump•tu•ous•ness

sun (*star*; see SON)
  sunned, sun•ning
  sun•less
  sun•proof

sun•bathe
  sun•bath•er

sun•beam

sun•burn

Sun•chon

sun•dae (*ice cream*; see SUNDAY)

Sun•da Is•lands

Sun•day (*day of the week*; see SUNDAE)

sun•der

sun•di•al

sun•down

sun•dry
  pl. sun•dries

sun•fish

sun•flow•er

sung

sun•glass•es

sunk

sunk•en

sun•light

sun•lit

Sun•ni
  pl. same or Sun•nis
  also Sun•nite

sun•ny (*bright*; see SONNY)
  sun•ni•er, sun•ni•est
  sun•ni•ly
  sun•ni•ness

Sun•ny•vale

sun•rise

sun•roof

sun•set

sun•shine

sun•spot

sun•stroke

sun•tan
  sun•tanned, sun•tan•ning

sun•up

Sun Yat-sen
  also Sun Yi-xian

sup
  supped, sup•ping

su•per

su•per•a•bun•dant
  su•per•a•bun•dance
  su•per•a•bun•dant•ly

su•per•an•nu•ate
  su•per•an•nu•a•tion

su•perb
  su•perb•ly
  su•perb•ness

su•per•charge

su•per•charg•er

su•per•cil•i•ous
  su•per•cil•i•ous•ly
  su•per•cil•i•ous•ness

su•per•con•duc•tiv•i•ty
  su•per•con•duct•ing
  su•per•con•duc•tive

su•per•con•duc•tor

su•per•e•go
  pl. su•per•e•gos

su•per•er•o•ga•tion
  su•per•e•rog•a•to•ry

su•per•fi•cial
  su•per•fi•ci•al•i•ty
  pl. su•per•fi•ci•al•i•ties
  su•per•fi•cial•ly

su•per•flu•i•ty
  pl. su•per•flu•i•ties

su•per•flu•ous
  su•per•flu•ous•ly
  su•per•flu•ous•ness

su•per•high•way

su•per•hu•man
  su•per•hu•man•ly

su•per•im•pose
  su•per•im•po•si•tion

su•per•in•tend
  su•per•in•tend•ence
  su•per•in•tend•en•cy

su•per•in•tend•ent

su•pe•ri•or
  fem. also su•pe•ri•or•ess

su•pe•ri•or•i•ty

su•per•la•tive
  su•per•la•tive•ly
  su•per•la•tive•ness

su•per•man
  pl. su•per•men

su•per•mar•ket

su•per•nat•u•ral
  su•per•nat•u•ral•ism
  su•per•nat•u•ral•ist
  su•per•nat•u•ral•ly

su•per•no•va
  pl. su•per•no•vae or su•per•no•vas

su•per•nu•mer•ar•y
  pl. su•per•nu•mer•ar•ies

su•per•pow•er

su•per•script

su·per·sede
  su·per·sed·ence

su·per·son·ic
  su·per·son·i·cal·ly

su·per·star
  su·per·star·dom

su·per·sti·tion
  su·per·sti·tious
  su·per·sti·tious·ly

su·per·struc·ture
  su·per·struc·tur·al

su·per·vene
  su·per·ven·ient
  su·per·ven·tion

su·per·vise
  su·per·vi·sion
  su·per·vi·sor
  su·per·vi·so·ry

su·pine
  su·pine·ly
  su·pine·ness

sup·per
  sup·per·less

sup·plant
  sup·plant·er

sup·ple
  sup·pler, sup·plest
  sup·ple·ness

sup·ple·ment
  sup·ple·men·tal
  sup·ple·men·tal·ly
  sup·ple·men·ta·tion

sup·ple·men·ta·ry

sup·pli·ant
  sup·pli·ant·ly

sup·pli·cate
  sup·pli·cant
  sup·pli·ca·tion

sup·ply
  sup·plies, sup·plied
  pl. sup·plies
  sup·pli·er

sup·port
  sup·port·a·ble
  sup·port·er

sup·port·ive
  sup·port·ive·ly
  sup·port·ive·ness

sup·pose
  sup·pos·a·ble

sup·pos·ed·ly

sup·po·si·tion
  sup·po·si·tion·al

sup·pos·i·to·ry
  pl. sup·pos·i·to·ries

sup·press
  sup·pres·sion
  sup·pres·sor

sup·pu·rate
  sup·pu·ra·tion
  sup·pu·ra·tive

su·pra·na·tion·al

su·prem·a·cy
  pl. su·prem·a·cies

su·preme
  su·preme·ly
  su·preme·ness

Su·ra·ba·ya

Su·rat

sur·cease

sur·charge

surd

sure
  sure-fire
  sure-foot·ed
  sure·ness

sure·ly

sur·e·ty
  pl. sur·e·ties

surf (*waves*; see SERF)
  surf·er

sur·face
  sur·faced
  sur·fac·er

surf·board

sur·feit

surge (*rush*; see SERGE)

sur·geon

sur·ger·y
  pl. sur·ger·ies

sur·gi·cal
  sur·gi·cal·ly

Su·ri·na·me
  Su·ri·na·mese

sur·ly
  sur·li·er, sur·li·est
  sur·li·ness

sur·mise

sur·mount
  sur·mount·a·ble

sur·name

sur·pass
  sur·pass·ing·ly

sur·plice (*robe*; see
  SURPLUS)
  sur·pliced

sur·plus (*extra*; see
  SURPLICE)

sur·prise
  sur·pris·ed·ly
  sur·pris·ing
  sur·pris·ing·ly

sur·re·al
  sur·re·al·ly

sur·re·al·ism
  sur·re·al·ist
  sur·re·al·is·tic
  sur·re·al·is·ti·cal·ly

sur·ren·der

sur·rep·ti·tious
  sur·rep·ti·tious·ly

sur•ro•gate
  sur•ro•ga•cy

sur•round
  sur•round•ing

sur•round•ings

sur•tax

sur•veil•lance

sur•vey

sur•vey•or

sur•viv•al

sur•vive
  sur•vi•vor

sus•cep•ti•bil•i•ty
  pl. sus•cep•ti•bil•i•ties

sus•cep•ti•ble
  sus•cep•ti•bly

su•shi

sus•pect

sus•pend
  sus•pens•i•ble

sus•pend•ers

sus•pense
  sus•pense•ful

sus•pen•sion

sus•pi•cion

sus•pi•cious
  sus•pi•cious•ly

sus•tain
  sus•tain•a•ble
  sus•tain•er
  sus•tain•ment

sus•te•nance

Suth•er•land

su•ture
  su•tured

Su•va

Su•won

svelte

Sverd•lovsk

swab
  swabbed, swab•bing

swad•dle
  swad•dling

swag

swag•ger
  swag•ger•er
  swag•ger•ing•ly

Swa•hi•li
  pl. same

swain

swal•low
  swal•low•er

swam

swa•mi
  pl. swa•mis

swamp
  swamp•y
  swamp•i•er, swamp•
  i•est

swan
  swan•like

swank

swank•y
  swank•i•er, swank•i•est
  swank•i•ly
  swank•i•ness

Swan•sea

swap
  also swop
  swapped, swap•ping
  swap•per

swarm

swarth•y
  swarth•i•er, swarth•
  i•est
  swarth•i•ness

swash

swash•buck•ler

swash•buck•ling

swas•ti•ka

swat
  swat•ted, swat•ting

swatch

swath

swathe

sway

Swa•zi•land

swear
  past swore; *past part.*
  sworn
  swear•er

sweat
  past and *past part.* sweat
  or sweat•ed

sweat•band

sweat•er

sweat•pants

sweat•shirt

sweat•y
  sweat•i•er, sweat•i•est
  sweat•i•ly
  sweat•i•ness

Swe•den
  Swede

Swed•ish

sweep
  past and *past part.* swept
  sweep•er

sweep•ing
  sweep•ing•ly

sweep•stake

sweet (*sugary*; see SUITE)
  sweet-talk
  sweet•ly

sweet•bread

sweet•bri•er

sweet•en
  sweet•en•ing

sweet•en•er

sweet•heart

sweet•meat

sweet•ness

swell
  past part. swol•len *or*
  swelled

swell•ing

swel•ter
  swel•ter•ing•ly

swept

swerve
  swerv•er

Swift (*proper name*)

swift (*fast*)
  swift•ly
  swift•ness

swig
  swigged, swig•ging
  swig•ger

swill
  swill•er

swim
  swim•ming; *past* swam;
  past part. swum
  swim•ma•ble
  swim•mer

swim•ming•ly

swim•suit

Swin•burne

swin•dle
  swin•dler

swine
  pl. swine *or* swines
  swin•ish
  swin•ish•ly

swing
  past and *past part.*
  swung
  swing•er

swipe
  swip•er

swirl
  swirl•y

swish

switch
  switch•er

switch•back

switch•board

Switz•er•land
  Swiss
  pl. same

swiv•el

swiz•zle

swol•len

swoon

swoop

swop
  var. of swap

sword
  sword•like

sword•fish

swords•man
  pl. swords•men
  swords•man•ship

swore

sworn

swum

swung

syb•a•rite

syc•a•more

syc•o•phant
  syc•o•phan•cy
  syc•o•phan•tic
  syc•o•phan•ti•cal•ly

Syd•ney

syl•lab•ic
  syl•lab•i•cal•ly

syl•lab•i•fi•ca•tion
  also syl•lab•i•ca•tion
  syl•lab•i•fy
  syl•lab•i•fies, syl•lab•
    i•fied

syl•la•ble
  syl•la•bled

syl•la•bus
  pl. syl•la•bus•es *or* syl•
    la•bi

syl•lo•gism
  syl•lo•gis•tic
  syl•lo•gis•ti•cal•ly

sylph
  sylph•like

syl•van
  also sil•van

sym•bi•o•sis
  pl. sym•bi•o•ses
  sym•bi•ot•ic
  sym•bi•ot•i•cal•ly

sym•bol (*sign;* see
  CYMBAL)
  sym•bol•ic
  sym•bol•i•cal•ly
  sym•bol•o•gy

sym•bol•ism
  sym•bol•ist
  sym•bol•is•tic

sym•bol•ize
  sym•bol•i•za•tion

sym•me•try
  pl. sym•me•tries
  sym•met•ric
  sym•met•ri•cal
  sym•met•ri•cal•ly

sym•pa•thet•ic
  sym•pa•thet•i•cal•ly

sym•pa•thize
  sym•pa•thiz•er

sym·pa·thy
  pl. sym·pa·thies

sym·pho·ny
  pl. sym·pho·nies
  sym·phon·ic
  sym·phon·i·cal·ly

sym·po·si·um
  pl. sym·po·si·ums *or*
  sym·po·si·a

symp·tom

symp·to·mat·ic
  symp·to·mat·i·cal·ly

syn·a·gogue
  also syn·a·gog
  syn·a·gog·al
  syn·a·gog·i·cal

syn·apse

sync (*harmony*; see SINK)
  also synch

syn·chron·ic
  syn·chron·i·cal·ly

syn·chro·nize
  syn·chro·ni·za·tion
  syn·chro·niz·er

syn·chro·nous
  syn·chro·nous·ly

syn·cline
  syn·cli·nal

syn·co·pate
  syn·co·pa·tion
  syn·co·pa·tor

syn·di·cate
  syn·di·ca·tion

syn·drome
  syn·drom·ic

syn·ec·do·che
  syn·ec·doch·ic

syn·er·gism
  also syn·er·gy
  syn·er·get·ic
  syn·er·gic
  syn·er·gist
  syn·er·gis·tic
  syn·er·gis·ti·cal·ly

Synge

syn·od

syn·o·nym
  syn·o·nym·ic
  syn·o·nym·i·ty

syn·on·y·mous
  syn·on·y·mous·ly
  syn·on·y·mous·ness

syn·op·sis
  pl. syn·op·ses
  syn·op·size
  syn·op·tic

syn·o·vi·a
  syn·o·vi·al

syn·tax
  syn·tac·tic
  syn·tac·ti·cal·ly

syn·the·sis
  pl. syn·the·ses

syn·the·size

syn·the·siz·er

syn·thet·ic
  syn·thet·i·cal·ly

syph·i·lis
  syph·i·lit·ic

Syr·a·cuse

Syr·i·a
  Syr·i·an

sy·ringe

syr·up
  syr·up·y

sys·tem

sys·tem·at·ic
  sys·tem·at·i·cal·ly

sys·tem·a·tize
  sys·tem·a·ti·za·tion
  sys·tem·a·tiz·er

sys·tem·ic
  sys·tem·i·cal·ly

sys·to·le
  sys·tol·ic

Szcze·cin

T

tab
  tabbed, tab•bing

Ta•bas•co

tab•by
  pl. tab•bies

tab•er•na•cle

ta•bla

tab•la•ture

ta•ble
  ta•ble•ful
  pl. ta•ble•fuls
  ta•bling

tab•leau
  pl. tab•leaux or tab•leaus

ta•ble•cloth

ta•ble•land

ta•ble•spoon
  ta•ble•spoon•ful
  pl. ta•ble•spoon•fuls

tab•let

tab•loid

ta•boo
  ta•boos, ta•booed

tab•o•ret
  also tab•ou•ret

Ta•briz

tab•u•lar

ta•bu•late
  tab•u•la•tion
  tab•u•la•tor

ta•chom•e•ter

tac•it
  tac•it•ly

tac•i•turn
  tac•i•tur•ni•ty
  tac•i•turn•ly

Tac•i•tus

tack
  tack•er

tack•le
  tack•ler
  tack•ling

tack•y
  tack•i•er, tack•i•est
  tack•i•ly
  tack•i•ness

ta•co
  pl. ta•cos

Ta•co•ma

tact
  tact•ful
  tact•ful•ly
  tact•ful•ness

tac•tic
  tac•ti•cal
  tac•ti•cal•ly

tac•tics
  tac•ti•cian

tac•tile
  tac•til•i•ty

tact•less
  tact•less•ly
  tact•less•ness

tad

tad•pole

Ta•dzhik•i•stan
  Ta•dzhik

Tae•gu

Tae•jon

tae kwon do

taf•fe•ta

taff•rail

taf•fy
  pl. taf•fies

Taft

tag
  tagged, tag•ging

Ta•ga•log

Ta•gore

Ta•gus Riv•er

ta•hi•ni

Ta•hi•ti
  Ta•hi•tian

Ta•hoe, Lake

t'ai chi ch'uan
  also t'ai chi

Tai•chung

Ta•if

tail (rear; see TALE)
  tailed
  tail•less

tail•back

tail•coat

tail•gate
  tail•gat•er

tail•light

tai•lor
  tai•lor-made
  tai•lor•ing

tai•lored

tail•pipe

tail•spin
  tail•spin•ning; past and past part. tail•spun

Tai•nan

taint

Tai·pei

Tai·wan
Tai·wan·ese

Tai·yuan

take
past took; *past part.*
tak·en
tak·a·ble
also take·a·ble
tak·er

take·off

take·o·ver

tak·ing

talc
talcked, talck·ing

tal·cum

tale (*story*; see TAIL.)

tal·ent
tal·ent·ed
tal·ent·less

tal·is·man
pl. tal·is·mans
tal·is·man·ic

talk
talk·er

talk·a·tive

talk·ie

tall
tall·ish

Tal·la·has·see

tall·boy

**Tal·ley·rand-Pé·ri·
gord**

Tal·linn

tal·low
tal·low·ish
tal·low·y

tal·ly
pl. tal·lies
tal·lies, tal·lied
tal·li·er

tal·ly·ho
pl. tal·ly·hos
tal·ly·hoes, tal·ly·hoed

Tal·mud
Tal·mud·ic
Tal·mud·i·cal
Tal·mud·ist

tal·on
tal·oned

ta·lus
pl. ta·li

tam

ta·ma·le

tam·a·rack

tam·a·rind

Ta·mau·li·pas

tam·bou·rine
tam·bou·rin·ist

tame
tam·a·ble
tame·ly
tame·ness
tam·er

Tam·er·lane

Tam·il
Tam·il·ian

tam·ing

tam-o'-shan·ter

tamp
tamp·er
tamp·ing

Tam·pa

tam·per
tam·per·er
tam·per·proof

Tam·pi·co

tam·pon

tan
tanned, tan·ning
tan·na·ble
tan·ning
tan·nish

tan·a·ger

tan·dem

tan·door·i

tang

Tan·gan·yi·ka, Lake

tan·ge·lo
pl. tan·ge·los

tan·gent
tan·gen·cy

tan·gen·tial
tan·gen·tial·ly

tan·ger·ine

tan·gi·ble
tan·gi·bil·i·ty
tan·gi·ble·ness
tan·gi·bly

Tan·gier
also Tan·giers

tan·gle

tan·go
pl. tan·gos
tan·goes, tan·goed

tan·gram

Tang·shan

tang·y
tang·i·er, tang·i·est
tang·i·ness

tank
tank·ful
pl. tank·fuls

tan·kard

tank·er

tan·ner

tan•ner•y
  pl. tan•ner•ies

tan•nic

tan•sy
  pl. tan•sies

tan•ta•lize
  tan•ta•li•za•tion
  tan•ta•liz•er
  tan•ta•liz•ing•ly

tan•ta•lum
  tan•tal•ic

tan•ta•mount

tan•tra

tan•trum

Tan•za•ni•a
  Tan•za•ni•an

Tao•ism
  Tao•ist
  Tao•is•tic

Taos

tap (*faucet*)
  tapped, tap•ping
  tap•pa•ble

tap (*strike lightly*)
  tapped, tap•ping
  tap-dance (*verb*)
  tap•per

tape
  tape-re•cord
  tape•a•ble

ta•per (*candle*; see TAPIR)

tap•es•try
  pl. tap•es•tries

tape•worm

tap•i•o•ca

ta•pir (*animal*; see
  TAPER)

tap•pet

tap•room

tar
  tarred, tar•ring

tar•an•tel•la

ta•ran•tu•la

tar•dy
  tar•di•er, tar•di•est
  tar•di•ly
  tar•di•ness

tare (*weight*; see TEAR)

tar•get
  tar•get•a•ble

tar•iff

Tar•king•ton

Tar•mac (*trademark*)
  also tar•mac
  tar•macked, tar•mack•
    ing

tar•mac•ad•am

tarn

tar•na•tion

tar•nish
  tar•nish•a•ble

ta•ro (*plant*; see TAROT)
  pl. ta•ros

ta•rot (*fortune-telling
  cards*; see TARO)

tar•pau•lin
  also tarp

tar•pon

tar•ra•gon

tar•ry
  tar•ries, tar•ried
  tar•ri•er

tar•sus
  pl. tar•si
  tar•sal

tart (*pastry*)
  tart•let

tart (*prostitute*)
  tart•y
  tart•i•er, tart•i•est

tart (*tangy*)
  tart•ly
  tart•ness

tar•tan

Tar•tar (*proper name*)
  also Ta•tar
  Tar•tar•i•an

tar•tar (*tooth deposit*)

Tash•kent

task

task•mas•ter
  fem. task•mis•tress

Tas•ma•ni•a
  Tas•ma•ni•an

tas•sel
  tas•seled

taste
  taste•a•ble
  tast•er

taste•ful
  taste•ful•ly
  taste•ful•ness

taste•less
  taste•less•ly
  taste•less•ness

tast•y
  tast•i•er, tast•i•est
  tast•i•ly
  tast•i•ness

tat
  tat•ted, tat•ting

Ta•tar
  var. of Tar•tar

ta•ter

tat•ter
  tat•tered

tat•ting

tat•tle

tat•tle•tale

tat•too
  tat•too•er
  tat•too•ist

tat•ty

tau

taught (*past of teach*; see TAUT)

taunt
  taunt•er
  taunt•ing•ly

taupe

Tau•rus
  Tau•re•an

taut (*tight*; see TAUGHT)
  taut•en
  taut•ly
  taut•ness

tau•tol•o•gy
  pl. tau•tol•o•gies
  tau•to•log•ic
  tau•to•log•i•cal
  tau•to•log•i•cal•ly
  tau•tol•o•gist
  tau•tol•o•gize
  tau•tol•o•gous

tav•ern

taw•dry
  taw•dri•er, taw•dri•est
  taw•dri•ly
  taw•dri•ness

taw•ny
  taw•ni•er, taw•ni•est
  taw•ni•ness

tax
  tax•a•ble
  tax•er

tax•a

tax•a•tion

tax-ex•empt

tax•i
  pl. tax•is
  tax•is, tax•ied, tax•i•
    ing *or* tax•y•ing

tax•i•cab

tax•i•der•my
  tax•i•der•mist

tax•i•me•ter

tax•on
  pl. tax•a

tax•on•o•my
  tax•o•nom•ic
  tax•o•nom•i•cal
  tax•o•nom•i•cal•ly
  tax•on•o•mist

tax•pay•er

Tay•lor

Tbi•li•si

T-bone

Tchai•kov•sky

te
  var. of ti

tea (*beverage*; see TEE, TI)

teach
  past and *past part.*
   taught
  teach•a•ble

teach•er

teach•ing

tea•cup
  tea•cup•ful
  pl. tea•cup•fuls

teak

tea•ket•tle

teal
  pl. same

team (*group*; see TEEM)

team•mate

team•ster

team•work

tea•pot

tear (*rip*; see TARE)
  past tore; *past part.* torn
  tear•a•ble
  tear•er

tear (*teardrop*; see TIER)
  tear•like

tear•ful
  tear•ful•ly
  tear•ful•ness

tear•jerk•er

tea•room

tease (*taunt*; see *tees*
  [TEE])
  teas•er
  teas•ing•ly

tea•sel
  also tea•zel, tea•zle
  tea•sel•er

tea•spoon
  tea•spoon•ful
  pl. tea•spoon•fuls

teat

tech

tech•ne•ti•um

tech•ni•cal
  tech•ni•cal•ly

tech•ni•cal•i•ty
  pl. tech•ni•cal•i•ties

tech•ni•cian

Tech•ni•col•or
  (*trademark*)

tech•nique

tech•noc•ra•cy
  pl. tech•noc•ra•cies
  tech•no•crat
  tech•no•crat•ic

tech•nol•o•gy
  pl. tech•nol•o•gies
  tech•no•log•i•cal
  tech•no•log•i•cal•ly
  tech•nol•o•gist

tec·ton·ic
 tec·ton·i·cal·ly

tec·ton·ics

Te·cum·seh

ted·dy
 pl. ted·dies

te·di·ous
 te·di·ous·ly
 te·di·ous·ness

te·di·um

tee (*golfing aid*; see TEA, TI)
 tees (see TEASE), teed

tee-hee
 also te-hee
 tee-hees, tee-heed

teem (*swarm*; see TEAM)

teen

teen·age
 teen·aged

teen·ag·er

teens

teen·sy
 teen·si·er, teen·si·est
 teen·sy-ween·sy

tee·ny
 tee·ni·er, tee·ni·est
 tee·ny-ween·y

tee·ny·bop·per

tee·pee
 var. of te·pee

tee-shirt
 var. of T-shirt

tee·ter

teeth

teethe
 teeth·ing

tee·to·tal
 tee·to·tal·er

also tee·to·tal·ler
 tee·to·tal·ism

Tef·lon (*trademark*)

Te·gu·ci·gal·pa

Teh·ran
 also Tehran

Teil·hard de Char·din

Te Ka·na·wa

Tel A·viv
 also Tel A·viv-Jaf·fa *or*
 Tel A·viv-Ya·fo

tel·e·cast
 tel·e·cast·er

tel·e·com·mu·ni·ca·tion

tel·e·com·mute
 tel·e·com·mut·ed,
 tel·e·com·mut·ing

tel·e·con·fer·ence
 tel·e·con·fer·enc·ing

tel·e·gram

tel·e·graph
 te·leg·ra·pher
 tel·e·graph·ic
 tel·e·graph·i·cal·ly
 te·leg·ra·phy

tel·e·ki·ne·sis
 tel·e·ki·net·ic

tel·e·mar·ket·ing
 tel·e·mar·ket·er

tel·e·ol·o·gy
 tel·e·o·log·i·cal
 tel·e·ol·o·gist

te·lep·a·thy
 tel·e·path·ic
 tel·e·path·i·cal·ly
 te·lep·a·thist

tel·e·phone
 tel·e·phon·ic
 tel·e·phon·i·cal·ly

te·leph·o·ny

tel·e·pho·to
 pl. tel·e·pho·tos

tel·e·pho·tog·ra·phy
 tel·e·pho·to·graph·ic

Tel·e·Promp·Ter
 (*trademark*)

tel·e·scope
 tel·e·scop·ic
 tel·e·scop·i·cal·ly

tel·e·thon

Tel·e·type (*trademark*)

tel·e·vise

tel·e·vi·sion

tel·ex
 also Tel·ex

tell
 past and past part. told
 tell·a·ble

Tel·ler (*proper name*)

tell·er (*bank worker*)

tell·ing
 tell·ing·ly

tell·tale

tel·lu·ri·um
 tel·lu·ride
 tel·lu·rite
 tel·lu·rous
 tel·lu·ric

te·mer·i·ty

temp

Tem·pe

tem·per
 tem·per·a·ble
 tem·pered

tem·per·a

tem·per·a·ment

tem·per·a·men·tal
 tem·per·a·men·tal·ly

tem·per·ance

tem·per·ate
  tem·per·ate·ly
  tem·per·ate·ness

tem·per·a·ture

tem·pest
  tem·pes·tu·ous
  tem·pes·tu·ous·ly
  tem·pes·tu·ous·ness

tem·plate

tem·ple

tem·po
  pl. tem·pos *or* tem·pi

tem·po·ral
  tem·po·ral·ly

tem·po·rar·y
  pl. tem·po·rar·ies
  tem·po·rar·i·ly

tem·po·rize
  tem·po·ri·za·tion
  tem·po·riz·er

tempt
  tempt·a·ble
  tempt·er
  tempt·ress

temp·ta·tion

tempt·ing
  tempt·ing·ly

tem·pu·ra

ten

ten·a·ble
  ten·a·bil·i·ty
  ten·a·ble·ness

te·na·cious
  te·na·cious·ly
  te·na·cious·ness
  te·nac·i·ty

ten·an·cy
  pl. ten·an·cies

ten·ant

tend

ten·den·cy
  pl. ten·den·cies

ten·den·tious
  ten·den·tious·ly
  ten·den·tious·ness

ten·der
  ten·der·er, ten·der·est
  ten·der-heart·ed
  ten·der·ly
  ten·der·ness

ten·der·foot

ten·der·ize
  ten·der·iz·er

ten·der·loin

ten·don

ten·dril

ten·e·ment

ten·et

ten·fold

Teng Hsiao-p'ing
  var. of Deng Xiao·ping

Ten·nes·see
  Ten·nes·see·an

ten·nis

Ten·ny·son

ten·on

ten·or

ten·pins

tense
  tense·ly
  tense·ness
  ten·si·ty

ten·sile
  ten·sil·i·ty

ten·sion

ten·sor

tent

ten·ta·cle
  ten·ta·cled

ten·ta·tive
  ten·ta·tive·ly
  ten·ta·tive·ness

ten·ter·hook

tenth
  tenth·ly

ten·u·ous
  ten·u·ous·ly
  ten·u·ous·ness

ten·ure
  ten·ured

te·pee
  also tee·pee

Te·pic

tep·id
  te·pid·i·ty
  tep·id·ly
  tep·id·ness

te·qui·la

ter·bi·um

ter·cen·te·nar·y
  pl. ter·cen·te·nar·ies

ter·cen·ten·ni·al

Te·re·sa

ter·gi·ver·sate
  ter·gi·ver·sa·tion

ter·i·ya·ki

term

ter·ma·gant

ter·mi·na·ble

ter·mi·nal
  ter·mi·nal·ly

ter·mi·nate
  ter·mi·na·tion
  ter·mi·na·tor

ter·mi·nol·o·gy
  pl. ter·mi·nol·o·gies
  ter·mi·nol·o·gist

ter•mi•nus
  pl. ter•mi•ni *or* ter•mi•
  nus•es

ter•mite

tern (*bird; see* TURN)

terp•si•cho•re•an

ter•race

ter•ra-cot•ta

ter•ra fir•ma

ter•rain

ter•ra•pin

ter•rar•i•um
  pl. ter•rar•i•ums *or*
  ter•ra•ri•a

Ter•re Haute

ter•res•tri•al

ter•ri•ble
  ter•ri•ble•ness

ter•ri•bly

ter•ri•er

ter•rif•ic
  ter•rif•i•cal•ly

ter•ri•fy
  ter•ri•fies, ter•ri•fied
  ter•ri•fi•er
  ter•ri•fy•ing
  ter•ri•fy•ing•ly

ter•ri•to•ri•al
  ter•ri•to•ri•al•ly

ter•ri•to•ry
  pl. ter•ri•to•ries

ter•ror
  ter•ror-strick•en
  ter•ror-struck

ter•ror•ist
  ter•ror•ism
  ter•ror•is•tic

ter•ror•ize
  ter•ror•i•za•tion
  ter•ror•iz•er

ter•ry
  pl. ter•ries

terse
  ters•er, ters•est
  terse•ly
  terse•ness

ter•ti•ar•y

Tes•la (*proper name*)

tes•la (*unit of magnetism*)

tes•sel•lat•ed
  tes•sel•la•tion

test
  test-tube
  test•a•ble
  test•a•bil•i•ty
  test•er

tes•ta•ment
  tes•ta•men•ta•ry

tes•tate
  tes•ta•cy
  pl. tes•ta•cies

tes•ta•tor
  fem. tes•ta•trix

tes•tes

tes•ti•cle
  tes•tic•u•lar

tes•ti•fy
  tes•ti•fies, tes•ti•fied
  tes•ti•fi•er

tes•ti•mo•ni•al

tes•ti•mo•ny
  pl. tes•ti•mo•nies

tes•tis
  pl. tes•tes

tes•tos•ter•one

tes•ty
  tes•ti•er, tes•ti•est
  tes•ti•ly
  tes•ti•ness

tet•a•nus

tête-à-tête

teth•er

Te•ton Range

tet•ra•cy•cline

Tet•ra•gram•ma•ton

tet•ra•he•dron
  pl. tet•ra•he•dra *or*
  tet•ra•he•drons
  tet•ra•he•dral

te•tral•o•gy
  pl. te•tral•o•gies

te•tram•e•ter

tet•ra•pod
  tet•ra•pod•ous

te•trarch
  te•trarch•ate
  te•trar•chi•cal
  te•trar•chy
  pl. te•trar•chies

Teu•ton

Teu•ton•ic

Tex•as
  Tex•an

Tex-Mex

text

text•book
  text•book•ish

tex•tile

tex•tu•al
  tex•tu•al•ly

tex•ture
  tex•tur•al
  tex•tur•al•ly

Thack•er•ay

Thai•land
  Thai (*of Thailand; see*
  TIE)
  pl. same *or* Thais

thal•a•mus
  pl. thal•a•mi
  tha•lam•ic

Tha·les

tha·lid·o·mide

thal·li·um
thal·lic
thal·lous

Thames

than

Tha·na

thane

thank

thank·ful
thank·ful·ness

thank·ful·ly

thank·less
thank·less·ly
thank·less·ness

thanks·giv·ing

Thant

that

thatch
thatch·er

Thatch·er

thaw

the

the·a·ter
also the·a·tre
the·a·ter-go·er
the·a·ter-in-the-round

the·at·ric

the·at·ri·cal
the·at·ri·cal·ism
the·at·ri·cal·i·ty
the·at·ri·cal·ly

thee

theft

their (*of them;* see THERE, THEY'RE)

theirs

the·ism
the·ist
the·is·tic

them

theme
the·mat·ic
the·mat·i·cal·ly

them·selves

then

thence

thence·forth

thence·for·ward

the·o·cen·tric

the·oc·ra·cy
pl. the·oc·ra·cies
the·o·crat
the·o·crat·ic
the·o·crat·i·cal·ly

the·od·o·lite
the·od·o·lit·ic

the·o·lo·gian

the·ol·o·gy
pl. the·ol·o·gies
the·o·log·i·cal
the·o·log·i·cal·ly
the·ol·o·gist

the·o·rem

the·o·ret·ic

the·o·ret·i·cal
the·o·ret·i·cal·ly

the·o·rist

the·o·rize
the·o·riz·er

the·o·ry
pl. the·o·ries

the·os·o·phy
pl. the·os·o·phies

the·o·soph·i·cal
the·o·soph·i·cal·ly
the·os·o·phist

ther·a·peu·tic
ther·a·peu·ti·cal·ly

ther·a·peu·tics

ther·a·py
pl. ther·a·pies
ther·a·pist

there (*that place;* see
THEIR, THEY'RE)

there·a·bouts
also there·a·bout

there·af·ter

there·by

there·fore

there·in

there·of

there·to

there·up·on

ther·mal
ther·mal·ly

ther·mo·dy·nam·ics
ther·mo·dy·nam·ic
ther·mo·dy·nam·i·cal·
ly

ther·mom·e·ter

ther·mo·nu·cle·ar

ther·mo·plas·tic

ther·mos

ther·mo·stat
ther·mo·stat·ic
ther·mo·stat·i·cal·ly

the·sau·rus
pl. the·sau·ri *or*
the·sau·rus·es

these

the·sis
  pl. the·ses

thes·pi·an

Thes·sa·lo·ni·ke
  also Sa·lo·ni·ka

the·ta

they

they'd

they'll

they're (*they are;* see
  THEIR, THERE)

they've

thi·a·mine
  also thi·a·min

Thi·bault

thick
  thick-skinned
  thick·ish
  thick·ly

thick·en
  thick·en·er

thick·et

thick·head·ed
  thick·head·ed·ness

thick·ness

thick·set

thief
  pl. thieves

thieve
  thiev·ish
  thiev·ish·ly
  thiev·ish·ness

thiev·er·y

thieves

thigh

thim·ble
  thim·ble·ful
  pl. thim·ble·fuls

Thim·phu

thin
  thin·ner, thin·nest
  thinned, thin·ning
  thin-skinned
  thin·ly
  thin·ness
  thin·nish

thine

thing

thing·a·ma·bob
  also thing·a·ma·jig

think
  past and past part.
    thought
  think·er

think·ing

thin·ner

third
  third-class
  third-de·gree
  third-rate
  third·ly

thirst
  thirst·y
  thirst·i·ly
  thirst·i·ness

thir·teen
  thir·teenth

thir·ty
  pl. thir·ties
  thir·ty-first, thir·ty-sec·
    ond, etc.,
  thir·ty-one, thir·ty-two,
    etc.,
  thir·ti·eth

this
  pl. these

this·tle

thith·er

tho'
  var. of though

Thom·as

Thom·as à Kem·pis

thong

tho·rax
  pl. tho·rax·es or tho·
    ra·ces
  tho·rac·ic

Tho·reau

tho·ri·um

thorn

thorn·y
  thorn·i·er, thorn·i·est
  thorn·i·ly
  thorn·i·ness

thor·ough
  thor·ough·ly
  thor·ough·ness

thor·ough·bred

thor·ough·fare

thor·ough·go·ing

those

thou

though

thought

thought·ful
  thought·ful·ly
  thought·ful·ness

thought·less
  thought·less·ly
  thought·less·ness

thou·sand
  pl. thou·sands or thou·
    sand
  thou·sand·fold
  thou·sandth

thrall
  thrall·dom
  also thral·dom

thrash
  thrash·ing

thrash·er

thread
thread·er
thread·like

thread·bare

threat

threat·en
threat·en·er
threat·en·ing
threat·en·ing·ly

three
three-di·men·sion·al
three-ring

three·fold

three·score

three·some

thren·o·dy
also thre·node
pl. thre·no·dies *or*
three·nodes

thresh
thresh·er

thresh·old

threw (*past of throw*; see
THROUGH)

thrice

thrift

thrift·y
thrift·i·er, thrift·i·est
thrift·i·ly
thrift·i·ness

thrill
thrill·ing
thrill·ing·ly

thrill·er

thrive
past throve *or* thrived;
past part. thriv·en *or*
thrived

throat

throat·y
throat·i·er, throat·i·est

throat·i·ly
throat·i·ness

throb
throbbed, throb·bing

throe (*anguish*; see
THROW)

throm·bo·sis
pl. throm·bo·ses
throm·bot·ic

throne (*chair*; see *thrown*
[THROW])

throng

throt·tle

through (*preposition*; see
THREW)
also thru

through·out

through·put

through·way
also thru·way

throve

throw (*toss*; see THROE)
past threw; *past part.*
thrown (see THRONE)
throw·a·ble
throw·er

throw·a·way

throw·back

thru
var. of through

thrum
thrummed, thrum·
ming

thrush

thrust
past and past part.
thrust

thru·way
var. of throughway

Thu·cyd·i·des

thud
thud·ded, thud·ding
thud·ding·ly

thug
thug·ger·y
thug·gish
thug·gish·ly
thug·gish·ness

thu·li·um

thumb
thumbed

thumb·nail

thumb·print

thumb·screw

thumb·tack

thump
thump·er

thun·der
thun·der·er

thun·der·bolt

thun·der·clap

thun·der·cloud

thun·der·head

thun·der·ous
thun·der·ous·ly
thun·der·ous·ness

thun·der·show·er

thun·der·storm

thun·der·struck

Thur·ber

Thurs·day

thus

thwart

thy
also thine

thyme (*herb*; see TIME)

thy·mi

thy•mus
  pl. thy•mus•es *or* thy•mi

thy•roid

thy•self

ti (*musical note;* see TEA,
   TEE)
   also te

Tian•jin

ti•ar•a

Ti•be•ri•us

Ti•bet
  Ti•bet•an

tib•i•a
  pl. tib•i•ae
  tib•i•al

tic (*spasm;* see TICK)

tick (*click;* see TIC)
  tick-tack-toe
  also tic-tac-toe

tick•er

tick•et
  tick•et•ed

tick•ing

tick•le
  tick•ler
  tick•ly

tick•lish
  tick•lish•ly
  tick•lish•ness

tid•al
  tid•al•ly

tid•bit

tid•dly-winks

tide

tide•ta•ble

tide•wa•ter

ti•dings

ti•dy
  ti•di•er, ti•di•est
  ti•dies, ti•died
  ti•di•ly
  ti•di•ness

tie (*fasten;* see *Thai*
   [THAILAND])
  ty•ing
  tie-dye
  tie-in

Tien•tsin

tie•pin

tier (*row;* see TEAR)
  tiered

Ti•er•ra del Fue•go

tiff

ti•ger
  ti•ger-eye
  also ti•ger's-eye

tight
  tight-fist•ed
  tight-lipped
  tight•ly
  tight•ness

tight•en

tight•rope

tights

tight•wad

ti•gress

Ti•gris

Ti•jua•na

tike
  var. of tyke

Til•burg

til•de

tile
  til•er

til•ing

till (*cultivate*)
  till•a•ble
  till•er

till (*up to the time of*)

till•age

till•er

Til•lich

tilt
  tilt•er

tim•ber
  tim•ber•ing

tim•ber•line

tim•bre

Tim•buk•tu

time (*progress of events;*
   see THYME)
  time-hon•ored
  time-share
  time-shar•ing

time•keep•er
  time•keep•ing

time•less
  time•less•ly
  time•less•ness

time•ly
  time•li•er, time•li•est
  time•li•ness

time•piece

tim•er

time•ta•ble

tim•id
  ti•mid•i•ty
  tim•id•ly
  tim•id•ness

tim•ing

Ti•mi•soa•ra

tim•o•rous
  tim•or•ous•ly
  tim•or•ous•ness

tim•pa•ni
  also tym•pa•ni
  tim•pa•nist

tin
  tinned, tin•ning
  tin-plate

tinc•ture

tin•der

tin•der•box

tine
  tined

tinge
  tinge•ing *or* ting•ing

tin•gle
  tin•gly

tin•ker
  tin•ker•er

tin•kle

tin•ni•tus

tin•ny
  tin•ni•er, tin•ni•est
  tin•ni•ly
  tin•ni•ness

tin•sel
  tin•seled

tint
  tint•er

tin•tin•nab•u•la•tion

Tin•to•ret•to

ti•ny
  ti•ni•er, ti•ni•est
  ti•ni•ness

tip
  tipped, tip•ping
  tip-off
  tip•per

tip•ple
  tip•pler

tip•sy
  tip•si•er, tip•si•est
  tip•si•ly
  tip•si•ness

tip•toe
  tip•toes, tip•toed, tip•
   toe•ing

tip-top

ti•rade

Ti•ra•në

tire

tired
  tired•ly
  tired•ness

tire•less
  tire•less•ly
  tire•less•ness

tire•some
  tire•some•ly
  tire•some•ness

'tis

tis•sue

tit

Ti•tan
  also ti•tan

ti•tan•ic
  ti•tan•i•cal•ly

ti•ta•ni•um

tithe
  tith•ing

Ti•tian

Ti•ti•ca•ca, Lake

tit•il•late
  tit•il•lat•ing•ly
  tit•il•la•tion

ti•tle

ti•tled

tit•mouse
  pl. tit•mice

Ti•to

tit•ter

tit•tle

tit•u•lar
  tit•u•lar•ly

tiz•zy
  pl. tiz•zies

Tlax•ca•la

Tlin•git

to (*toward*; see TOO, TWO)

toad (*animal*; see *toed*
  [TOE])
  toad•ish

toad•stool

toad•y
  pl. toad•ies
  toad•ies, toad•ied
  toad•y•ish
  toad•y•ism

toast

toast•er

toast•mas•ter
  fem. toast•mis•tress

toast•y

to•bac•co
  pl. to•bac•cos

to•bog•gan
  to•bog•gan•er
  to•bog•gan•ing
  to•bog•gan•ist

to•coph•er•ol

Tocque•ville

toc•sin (*bell*; see TOXIN)

to•day

tod•dle

tod•dler

tod•dy
  pl. tod•dies

to-do

toe (*part of foot*; see TOW)
  toes, toed (see TOAD),
   toe•ing
  toe•less

toe·nail

tof·fee

Tof·fler

to·fu

tog

to·ga
 to·gaed

to·geth·er

to·geth·er·ness

tog·gle

To·go

toil
 toil·er

toile

toi·let

toi·let·ry
 pl. toi·let·ries

toi·lette

toil·some

To·jo

to·ken

to·ken·ism

To·ky·o

told

tole (*metalware;* see TOLL)

To·le·do

tol·er·a·ble
 tol·er·a·bly

tol·er·ance

tol·er·ant
 tol·er·ant·ly

tol·er·ate
 tol·er·a·tion
 tol·er·a·tor

Tol·kien

toll (*payment;* see TOLE)

toll·booth

Tol·stoy

Tol·tec

To·lu·ca

tom

tom·a·hawk

to·ma·to
 pl. to·ma·toes
 to·ma·to·ey

tomb

tom·boy
 tom·boy·ish
 tom·boy·ish·ness

tomb·stone

tome

tom·fool·er·y
 pl. tom·fool·er·ies

tom·my gun
 also Tom·my gun

tom·my·rot

to·mog·ra·phy

to·mor·row

tom-tom

ton (*2,000 pounds;* see
 TONNE, TUN)

ton·al
 ton·al·ly

to·nal·i·ty
 pl. to·nal·i·ties

tone
 tone-deaf
 tone·less
 tone·less·ly

ton·er

Ton·ga
 Ton·gan

tongs

tongue
 tongues, tongued,
  tongu·ing
 tongue-and-groove
 tongue-in-cheek
 tongue-lash·ing
 tongue-tied
 tongued
 tongue·less

ton·ic
 ton·i·cal·ly

to·night

ton·nage

tonne (*metric ton;* see
 TON, TUN)

ton·sil

ton·sil·lec·to·my
 pl. ton·sil·lec·to·mies

ton·sil·li·tis

ton·so·ri·al

ton·sure

too (*also;* see TO, TWO)

took

tool (*implement;* see
 TULLE)
 tool·er

tool·box

tool·mak·er
 tool·mak·ing

toot
 toot·er

tooth
 pl. teeth
 toothed
 tooth·less
 tooth·like

tooth·ache

tooth·brush

tooth·paste

tooth·pick

tooth·some
tooth·some·ly
tooth·some·ness

tooth·y
tooth·i·er, tooth·i·est

too·tle
too·tler

top
topped, top·ping
top-draw·er
top-notch
top·most

to·paz

top·coat

To·pe·ka

top-heav·y
top·-heav·i·ness

to·pi·ar·y
pl. to·pi·ar·ies

top·ic

top·i·cal
top·i·cal·i·ty
top·i·cal·ly

top·knot

top·less
top·less·ness

top·mast

to·pog·ra·phy
to·pog·ra·pher
top·o·graph·ic
top·o·graph·i·cal
top·o·graph·i·cal·ly

to·pol·o·gy

top·ping

top·ple

top·sail

top·side

top·soil

top·spin

top·sy-tur·vy

toque

tor (hill; see TORE)

torch

tore (past of tear; see
TOR)

tor·e·a·dor

to·ri·i
pl. same

To·ri·no

tor·ment
tor·men·tor

torn

tor·na·do
pl. tor·na·does

To·ron·to

tor·pe·do
pl. tor·pe·does
tor·pe·does, tor·pe·
doed

tor·pid
tor·pid·i·ty
tor·pid·ly
tor·pid·ness

tor·por
tor·por·if·ic

torque

Tor·que·ma·da

Tor·rance

tor·rent
tor·ren·tial
tor·ren·tial·ly

Tor·re·ón

tor·rid
tor·rid·ly
tor·rid·ness

tor·sion

tor·so
pl. tor·sos or tor·si

tort

torte

tor·til·la

tor·toise
tor·toise·like

tor·toise·shell

tor·tu·ous
tor·tu·os·i·ty
pl. tor·tu·os·i·ties
tor·tu·ous·ly
tor·tu·ous·ness

tor·ture
tor·tur·er
tor·tur·ous
tor·tur·ous·ly

To·ry
pl. To·ries
To·ry·ism

Tos·ca·ni·ni

toss
toss-up
toss·er

tot

to·tal
to·taled, to·tal·ing or
to·talled, to·tal·ling
to·tal·ly

to·tal·i·tar·i·an
to·tal·i·tar·i·an·ism

to·tal·i·ty

tote
tot·er

to·tem
to·tem·ic
to·tem·ism

tot·ter
tot·ter·er
tot·ter·y

tou·can

touch
  touch-me-not
  touch-type
  touch-typ·ist
  touch·a·ble
  touch·er

touch·down

tou·ché

touch·ing
  touch·ing·ly

touch·stone

touch·y
  touch·i·er, touch·i·est
  touch·i·ly
  touch·i·ness

tough
  tough·en
  tough·en·er
  tough·ly
  tough·ness

Tou·lon

Tou·louse

Tou·louse-Lau·trec

tou·pee

tour

tour de force

tour·ism

tour·ist

tour·ma·line

tour·na·ment

tour·ney

tour·ni·quet

Tours

tou·sle

tout
  tout·er

tow (*pull*; see TOE)

to·ward
  also to·wards

tow·el
  tow·el·ing

tow·er

tow·head
  tow·head·ed

town

town house
  also town·house

town·ie

towns·folk

town·ship

towns·peo·ple

tox·e·mi·a

tox·ic
  tox·ic·i·ty

tox·i·col·o·gy
  tox·i·co·log·i·cal
  tox·i·col·o·gist

tox·in (*poison*; see
  TOCSIN)

toy

Toyn·bee

trace
  trace·a·ble
  trace·a·bil·i·ty

trac·er

trac·er·y
  pl. trac·er·ies

tra·che·a
  pl. tra·che·ae *or* tra·
  che·as
  tra·che·al

tra·che·ot·o·my
  pl. tra·che·ot·o·mies

trac·ing

track

tract

trac·ta·ble
  trac·ta·bil·i·ty

trac·tion

trac·tor
  trac·tor-trail·er

Tra·cy

trade
  trade-in
  trade-off
  trad·a·ble *or* trade·
    a·ble

trade·mark

trad·er

trades·man
  pl. trades·men; *fem.*
  trades·wom·an, *pl.*
  trades·wom·en

trad·ing

tra·di·tion
  tra·di·tion·al
  tra·di·tion·al·ly

tra·di·tion·al·ism
  tra·di·tion·al·ist

tra·duce
  tra·duce·ment
  tra·duc·er

traf·fic
  traf·ficked, traf·fick·ing
  traf·fick·er

tra·ge·di·an
  fem. tra·ge·di·enne

trag·e·dy
  pl. trag·e·dies

trag·ic
  trag·i·cal·ly

trag·i·com·e·dy
  pl. trag·i·com·e·dies
  trag·i·com·ic

trail

trail•blaz•er
  trail•blaz•ing

trail•er

train
  train•ee
  train•ing

train•er

traipse

trait

trai•tor
  fem. trai•tress
  trai•tor•ous
  trai•tor•ous•ly

tra•jec•to•ry
  pl. tra•jec•to•ries

tram•mel

tramp

tram•ple

tram•po•line
  tram•po•lin•ist

trance

tran•quil
  tran•quil•li•ty
  tran•quil•ly

tran•quil•ize

tran•quil•iz•er

trans•act
  trans•ac•tor

trans•ac•tion

trans•at•lan•tic

tran•scend
  tran•scend•ence
  tran•scend•en•cy
  tran•scend•ent
  tran•scend•ent•ly

tran•scen•den•tal
  tran•scen•den•tal•ism

tran•scen•den•tal•ist
tran•scen•den•tal•ly

trans•con•ti•nen•tal

tran•scribe
  tran•scrib•er
  tran•scrip•tion

tran•script

trans•duc•er

tran•sect
  tran•sec•tion

tran•sept

trans•fer
  trans•ferred, trans•fer•
  ring
  trans•fer•a•ble

trans•fer•al
  also trans•fer•ral

trans•fer•ence

trans•fig•ure
  trans•fig•u•ra•tion

trans•fix

trans•form
  trans•for•ma•tion

trans•form•er

trans•fuse
  trans•fu•sion

trans•gress
  trans•gres•sion
  trans•gres•sor

tran•sient
  tran•sience

tran•sis•tor

tran•sit

tran•si•tion

tran•si•tive

tran•si•to•ry
  tran•si•to•ri•ly
  tran•si•to•ri•ness

trans•late
  trans•lat•a•ble
  trans•la•tion
  trans•la•tor

trans•lit•er•ate
  trans•lit•er•a•tion

trans•lu•cent
  trans•lu•cence
  trans•lu•cen•cy
  trans•lu•cent•ly

trans•mi•grate
  trans•mi•gra•tion

trans•mis•sion

trans•mit
  trans•mit•ted, trans•
  mit•ting
  trans•mis•si•ble
  trans•mit•ta•ble
  trans•mit•tal

trans•mit•ter

trans•mog•ri•fy
  trans•mog•ri•fies,
  trans•mog•ri•fied
  trans•mog•ri•fi•ca•tion

trans•mute
  trans•mut•a•ble
  trans•mut•a•bil•i•ty
  trans•mu•ta•tion

trans•o•ce•an•ic

tran•som

trans•par•en•cy
  pl. trans•par•en•cies

trans•par•ent
  trans•par•ent•ly

tran•spire
  tran•spi•ra•tion

trans•plant
  trans•plan•ta•tion

trans•pon•der

trans•port
  trans•port•a•ble
  trans•port•er

trans·por·ta·tion

trans·pose
    trans·pos·er
    trans·po·si·tion

trans·sex·u·al
    trans·sex·u·al·ism

trans·ship
    trans·shipped, trans·
    ship·ping
    trans·ship·ment

tran·sub·stan·ti·a·tion

Trans·vaal

trans·verse
    trans·verse·ly

trans·ves·tite
    trans·ves·tism

Tran·syl·va·nia

trap
    trapped, trap·ping

trap·door

tra·peze

tra·pe·zi·um
    pl. tra·pe·zi·a *or* tra·
    pe·zi·ums

trap·e·zoid
    trap·e·zoi·dal

trap·per

trap·pings

Trap·pist

trash

trash·y
    trash·i·er, trash·i·est
    trash·i·ness

trau·ma
    pl. trau·ma·ta *or*
    trau·mas
    trau·ma·tize
    trau·ma·ti·za·tion

trau·mat·ic
    trau·mat·i·cal·ly

tra·vail

trav·el
    trav·el·er
    trav·el·ing

trav·eled

trav·e·logue
    also trav·e·log

tra·verse
    tra·vers·al
    tra·vers·er

trav·es·ty
    pl. trav·es·ties
    trav·es·ties, trav·es·tied

trawl

trawl·er

tray (*flat board*; see TREY)

treach·er·ous
    treach·er·ous·ly
    treach·er·ous·ness

treach·er·y
    pl. treach·er·ies

trea·cle
    trea·cly

tread
    past trod; *past part.*
    trod·den *or* trod

trea·dle

tread·mill

trea·son
    trea·son·a·ble
    trea·son·ous

treas·ure

treas·ur·er

treas·ur·y
    pl. treas·ur·ies

treat
    treat·a·ble
    treat·er
    treat·ing

trea·tise

treat·ment

trea·ty
    pl. trea·ties

tre·ble

tree
    tree·less

trek
    trekked, trek·king
    trek·ker

trel·lis

trem·a·tode

trem·ble
    trem·bly

tre·men·dous
    tre·men·dous·ly

trem·o·lo

trem·or

trem·u·lous
    trem·u·lous·ly
    trem·u·lous·ness

trench

trench·ant
    trench·an·cy
    trench·ant·ly

trench·er·man
    pl. trench·er·men

trend

trend·set·ter
    trend·set·ting

trend·y
    trend·i·er, trend·i·est
    trend·i·ly
    trend·i·ness

Tren·ton

trep·i·da·tion

tres·pass
  tres·pass·er

tress

tres·tle

Trev·i·thick

trey (*three*; see TRAY)

tri·ad

tri·age

tri·al

tri·an·gle
  tri·an·gu·lar

tri·an·gu·late
  tri·an·gu·la·tion

Tri·as·sic

tri·ath·lon
  tri·ath·lete

tribe
  trib·al
  trib·al·ism

tribes·man
  pl. tribes·men

trib·u·la·tion

tri·bu·nal

trib·une

trib·u·tar·y
  pl. trib·u·tar·ies

trib·ute

trice

tri·ceps

tri·cer·a·tops

trich·i·no·sis

trick

trick·er·y
  pl. trick·er·ies

trick·le

trick·ster

trick·y
  trick·i·er, trick·i·est
  trick·i·ly
  trick·i·ness

tri·col·or
  tri·col·ored

tri·corn
  also tri·corne

tri·cot

tri·cy·cle

tri·dent

tried

tri·en·ni·al
  tri·en·ni·al·ly

Tri·este

tri·fec·ta

tri·fle

tri·fling

tri·fo·cal

tri·fo·ri·um
  pl. tri·fo·ri·a

trig

trig·ger
  trig·ger-hap·py
  trig·gered

trig·o·nom·e·try
  trig·o·no·met·ric
  trig·o·no·met·ri·cal

tri·lat·er·al

trill

tril·lion
  pl. same *or* tril·lions
  tril·lionth

tri·lo·bite

tril·o·gy
  pl. tril·o·gies

trim
  trimmed, trim·ming
  trim·ly
  trim·ness

tri·ma·ran

tri·mes·ter

trim·e·ter

trim·ming

Trin·i·dad and To·ba·go

tri·ni·tro·tol·u·ene
  also tri·ni·tro·tol·u·ol

trin·i·ty
  also Trin·i·ty
  pl. trin·i·ties

trin·ket
  trin·ket·ry

tri·o
  pl. tri·os

trip
  tripped, trip·ping

tri·par·tite

tripe

tri·ple

trip·let

trip·li·cate
  trip·li·ca·tion

tri·pod

Trip·o·li

trip·tych

tri·sect
  tri·sec·tion
  tri·sec·tor

tris·mus

trite
  trite·ly
  trite·ness

tri·ti·um

tri·umph

tri·um·phal

tri·um·phant
  tri·um·phant·ly

tri·um·vi·rate

tri·va·lent
  tri·va·lence
  tri·va·len·cy

triv·et

triv·i·a

triv·i·al
  triv·i·al·i·ty
  pl. triv·i·al·i·ties
  triv·i·al·ly

triv·i·al·ize
  triv·i·al·i·za·tion

tro·che (*lozenge;* see
  TROCHEE)

tro·chee (*poetic foot;* see
  TROCHE)

trod

trod·den

trog·lo·dyte
  trog·lo·dyt·ic

troi·ka

Tro·jan

troll

trol·ley

trol·lop

trom·bone
  trom·bon·ist

trompe-l'œil

Trond·heim

troop (*soldiers;* see
  TROUPE)

troop·er

tro·phy
  pl. tro·phies

trop·ic
  trop·i·cal

tro·po·sphere
  tro·po·spher·ic

trot
  trot·ted, trot·ting

troth

trou·ba·dour

trou·ble

Trot·sky

trou·ble·mak·er
  trou·ble·mak·ing

trou·ble·shoot·er
  trou·ble·shoot·ing

trou·ble·some

trou·bling

trough

trounce
  trounc·er
  trounc·ing

troupe (*actors;* see
  TROOP)

troup·er

trou·sers

trous·seau
  pl. trous·seaus *or* trous·
  seaux

trout
  pl. same *or* trouts

trove

trow·el

Troy (*proper name*)
  Tro·jan

troy (*weight*)

tru·ant
  tru·an·cy

truce

truck
  truck·er

truck·le
  truck·ler

tru·cu·lent
  truc·u·lence
  truc·u·lent·ly

Tru·deau

trudge

true
  trues, trued, true·ing
  or tru·ing
  true-blue

truf·fle

tru·ism

Tru·ji·llo

tru·ly

Tru·man

trump

trum·per·y
  pl. trum·per·ies

trum·pet
  trum·pet·er

trun·cate
  trun·ca·tion

trun·cheon

trun·dle

trunk

truss

trust

trust·ee
  trust·ee·ship

trust·ful
  trust·ful·ly
  trust·ful·ness

trust·ing
  trust·ing·ly

trust·wor·thy
  trust·wor·thi·ness

trust·y
  trust·i·er, trust·i·est

truth
  pl. truths

truth·ful
  truth·ful·ly
  truth·ful·ness

try
  tries, tried
  pl. tries

try·ing

tryst

tsar
  var. of czar

tsa·ri·na
  var. of cza·ri·na

tset·se

T-shirt
  also tee shirt

Tsing·tao

Tsi·tsi·har

T square

tsu·na·mi
  pl. tsu·na·mis

Tswa·na
  also Set·swa·na

tub

tu·ba
  pl. tu·bas

tub·by
  tub·bi·er, tub·bi·est
  tub·bi·ness

tube
  tube·like

tu·ber
  tu·ber·ous

tu·ber·cle
  tu·ber·cu·lar
  tu·ber·cu·lous

tu·ber·cu·lo·sis

tub·ing

Tub·man

tu·bu·lar

tu·bule

Tuch·man

tuck

tuck·er

Tuc·son

Tu·dor

Tues·day

tuft
  tuft·ed
  tuft·y

tug
  tugged, tug·ging
  tug-of-war

tug·boat

tu·i·tion

tu·lip

tulle (*silk*; see TOOL)

Tul·sa

tum·ble

tum·ble·down

tum·bler

tum·ble·weed

tum·brel
  also tum·bril

tu·mes·cent
  tu·mes·cence

tu·mid
  tu·mid·i·ty
  tu·mid·ly

tum·my
  pl. tum·mies

tu·mor
  tu·mor·ous

tu·mult

tu·mul·tu·ous
  tu·mul·tu·ous·ly

tun (*cask*; see TON,
  TONNE)

tu·na
  pl. same *or* tu·nas

tun·dra

tune
  tun·a·ble
  also tune·a·ble

tune·ful
  tune·ful·ly
  tune·ful·ness

tune·less
  tune·less·ly
  tune·less·ness

tun·er

tung·sten

tu·nic

tun·ing

Tu·nis

Tu·ni·sia
  Tu·ni·sian

tun·nel
  tun·nel·er

tu·pe·lo
  pl. tu·pe·los

Tu·pi
  pl. same *or* Tu·pis

tur·ban
  tur·baned

tur·bid
  tur·bid·i·ty

tur·bine

tur·bo·charg·er

tur·bo·jet

tur·bo·prop

tur·bot

tur·bu·lent
  tur·bu·lence
  tur·bu·lent·ly

tu·reen

turf

Tur·ge·nev

tur·gid
  tur·gid·i·ty

Tu·rin

Tur·key (*country*)
  Turk
  Tur·kish

tur·key (*bird*)

Turk·me·ni·stan
  Turk·men

Turks and Cai·cos
  Is·lands

tur·mer·ic

tur·moil

turn (*movement; see* TERN)
  turn-on

turn·a·bout

turn·a·round

turn·buck·le

turn·coat

Tur·ner

turn·ing

tur·nip
  tur·nip·y

turn·key

turn·off

turn·out

turn·o·ver

turn·pike

turn·stile

turn·ta·ble

tur·pen·tine

tur·pi·tude

tur·quoise

tur·ret
  tur·ret·ed

tur·tle

tur·tle·dove

tur·tle·neck

Tus·ca·loo·sa

Tus·ca·ro·ra

tusk
  tusked

tus·sle

tus·sock
  tus·sock·y

Tut·ankh·a·men

tu·te·lage

tu·te·lar·y

tu·tor
  tu·tor·ship

tu·to·ri·al

tut·ti

tut·ti-frut·ti

Tu·tu (*proper name*)

tu·tu (*dancewear*)

Tu·va·lu

tux

tux·e·do
  pl. tux·e·dos *or* tux·e·does

Tux·tla Gu·tiér·rez

Tver

twad·dle

Twain (*proper name*)

twain (*two*)

twang
  twang·y

'twas

tweak

Tweed (*proper name*)

tweed (*cloth*)

tweet

tweet·er

tweeze

tweez·ers

twelfth

twelve

twelve·fold

twen·ty
  pl. twen·ties
  twen·ty-twen·ty *also* 20/20
  twen·ti·eth

'twere

twerp
  also twirp

twice

twid·dle
  twid·dler
  twid·dly

twig
  twig·gy

twi·light

twi·lit

twill (*fabric*)
  twilled

'twill (*it will*)

twin
  twinned, twin·ning

twine
  twin·er

twinge

twin·kle
  twin·kler
  twin·kling

twirl
  twirl·er
  twirl·y

twirp
  var. of twerp

twist
  twist·y
  twist·i·er, twist·i·est

twist·er

twit
  twit·ted, twit·ting

twitch

twit·ter
  twit·ter·y

two (*number*, see TO, TOO)
  two-bit
  two-di·men·sion·al
  two-faced
  two-ply
  two-step
  two-time
  two-tim·er
  two-tone
  two-way

two·fer

two·fold

two·some

'twould

ty·coon

ty·ing

tyke
  also tike

Ty·ler

tym·pa·ni
  var. of tim·pa·ni

tym·pa·num
  pl. tym·pa·nums *or* tym·pa·na
  tym·pan·ic

Tyn·dale

type

type·cast
  past and *past part.* type·cast

type·face

type·script

type·set·ter
  type·set·ting

type·writ·er

type·writ·ten

ty·phoid

ty·phoon

ty·phus
  ty·phous

typ·i·cal
  typ·i·cal·i·ty
  typ·i·cal·ly

typ·i·fy
  typ·i·fies, typ·i·fied
  typ·i·fi·ca·tion
  typ·i·fi·er

typ·ist

ty·po
  pl. ty·pos

ty·pog·ra·phy
  ty·pog·ra·pher
  ty·po·graph·i·cal
  ty·po·graph·i·cal·ly

ty·ran·ni·cal
  ty·ran·ni·cal·ly

tyr·an·nize

ty·ran·no·sau·rus
  also ty·ran·no·saur

tyr·an·ny
  pl. tyr·an·nies
  tyr·an·nous
  tyr·an·nous·ly

ty·rant

ty·ro
  pl. ty·ros

U

u·biq·ui·tous
 u·biq·ui·tous·ly
 u·biq·ui·tous·ness
 u·biq·ui·ty

U-boat

ud·der

U·fa

UFO
 also ufo
 pl. UFOs *or* ufos

u·fol·o·gy
 u·fol·o·gist

U·gan·da
 U·gan·dan

ugh

ug·ly
 ug·li·er, ug·li·est
 ug·li·ness

U·jung Pan·dang

u·kase

U·kraine
 U·krain·i·an

u·ku·le·le

U·lan Ba·tor
 also U·laan·baa·tar

ul·cer
 ul·cered
 ul·cer·ous

ul·cer·ate
 ul·cer·a·ble
 ul·cer·a·tion
 ul·cer·a·tive

Ulm

ul·na
 pl. ul·nae *or* ul·nas
 ul·nar

Ul·san

Ul·ster (*place*)

ul·ster (*coat*)

ul·te·ri·or
 ul·te·ri·or·ly

ul·ti·mate
 ul·ti·mate·ly
 ul·ti·mate·ness

ul·ti·ma·tum
 pl. ul·ti·ma·tums *or* ul·
 ti·ma·ta

ul·ti·mo

ul·tra

ul·tra·high

ul·tra·ma·rine

ul·tra·mon·tane

ul·tra·son·ic
 ul·tra·son·i·cal·ly

ul·tra·sound

ul·tra·vi·o·let

ul·u·late
 ul·u·lant
 ul·u·la·tion

um

um·bel
 um·bel·lar
 um·bel·lif·er·ous

um·ber

um·bil·i·cal

um·bil·i·cus
 pl. um·bil·i·ci *or* um·
 bil·i·cus·es

um·bra
 pl. um·bras *or* um·brae
 um·bral

um·brage

um·brel·la
 um·brel·laed
 um·brel·la·like

u·mi·ak

um·laut

ump

um·pire

ump·teen
 ump·teenth

un·a·bashed

un·a·bat·ed
 un·a·bat·ed·ly

un·a·ble

un·a·bridged

un·ac·a·dem·ic

un·ac·cept·a·ble
 un·ac·cept·a·bly

un·ac·com·pa·nied

un·ac·com·plished

un·ac·count·a·ble
 un·ac·count·a·bil·i·ty
 un·ac·count·a·ble·ness
 un·ac·count·a·bly

un·ac·count·ed

un·ac·cus·tomed
 un·ac·cus·tomed·ly

un·a·chiev·a·ble

un·ac·knowl·edged

un·ac·quaint·ed

un·a·dorned

un·a·dul·ter·at·ed

un·ad·ver·tised

un·ad·vis·a·ble

un·ad·vised
un·ad·vis·ed·ly
un·ad·vis·ed·ness

un·af·fect·ed
un·af·fect·ed·ly
un·af·fect·ed·ness

un·af·fil·i·at·ed

un·a·fraid

un·aid·ed

un·al·ien·a·ble

un·a·ligned

un·al·loyed

un·al·ter·a·ble
un·al·ter·a·bly

un·al·tered

un·am·bi·gu·i·ty

un·am·big·u·ous
un·am·big·u·ous·ly

un·am·bi·tious

un-A·mer·i·can
un-A·mer·i·can·ism

u·nan·i·mous
u·na·nim·i·ty
u·nan·i·mous·ly

un·an·nounced

un·an·swer·a·ble
un·an·swer·a·bly

un·an·swered

un·an·tic·i·pat·ed

un·ap·peal·ing
un·ap·peal·ing·ly

un·ap·pe·tiz·ing

un·ap·pre·ci·at·ed

un·ap·pre·cia·tive

un·ap·proach·a·ble
un·ap·proach·a·bil·i·ty
un·ap·proach·a·bly

un·ap·pro·pri·at·ed

un·ap·proved

un·apt
un·apt·ly
un·apt·ness

un·ar·gu·a·ble

un·armed

un·ar·tic·u·lat·ed

un·ar·tis·tic
un·ar·tis·ti·cal·ly

un·a·shamed
un·a·sham·ed·ly
un·a·sham·ed·ness

un·asked

un·as·sail·a·ble

un·as·sist·ed

un·as·sum·ing
un·as·sum·ing·ly

un·at·tached

un·at·tain·a·ble

un·at·tend·ed

un·at·trac·tive
un·at·trac·tive·ly

un·at·trib·ut·a·ble
un·at·trib·ut·a·bly

un·au·thor·ized

un·a·vail·a·bil·i·ty

un·a·vail·a·ble

un·a·vail·ing
un·avail·ing·ly

un·a·void·a·ble
un·a·void·a·bly

un·a·ware
un·a·ware·ness

un·a·wares

un·bal·ance

un·bear·a·ble
un·bear·a·bly

un·beat·a·ble

un·be·com·ing
un·be·com·ing·ly

un·be·known
also un·be·knownst

un·be·lief
un·be·liev·er
un·be·liev·ing

un·be·liev·a·ble
un·be·liev·a·bly

un·bend
past and past part. un·
bent

un·bend·ing

un·bi·ased

un·bleached

un·blem·ished

un·blink·ing
un·blink·ing·ly

un·bolt

un·born

un·bos·om

un·bound

un·bound·ed

un·break·a·ble

un·bri·dle

un·bro·ken

un·buck·le

un·budg·ing

un·bur·den

un·but·ton

un·called

un·can·ny
un·can·ni·er, un·can·
ni·est
un·can·ni·ly

un·cared-for

un·car·ing

un·ceas·ing
  un·ceas·ing·ly

un·cen·sored

un·cer·e·mo·ni·ous
  un·cer·e·mo·ni·ous·ly

un·cer·tain
  un·cer·tain·ly
  un·cer·tain·ty

un·chal·lenged

un·change·a·ble

un·changed

un·chang·ing

un·chap·er·oned

un·char·ac·ter·is·tic
  un·char·ac·ter·is·ti·
  cal·ly

un·char·i·ta·ble
  un·char·i·ta·bly

un·chart·ed

un·checked

un·chris·tian

un·ci·al

un·civ·il
  un·civ·il·ly

un·civ·i·lized

un·claimed

un·clas·si·fied

un·cle

un·clean

un·clear
  un·clear·ly

un·cloud·ed

un·clut·tered

un·coil

un·combed

un·com·fort·a·ble
  un·com·fort·a·bly

un·com·mit·ted

un·com·mon
  un·com·mon·ly
  un·com·mon·ness

un·com·mu·ni·ca·tive

un·com·plain·ing
  un·com·plain·ing·ly

un·com·plet·ed

un·com·pli·cat·ed

un·com·pli·men·ta·ry

un·com·pre·hend·ing

un·com·pro·mis·ing
  un·com·pro·mis·ing·ly

un·con·cealed

un·con·cern
  un·con·cerned
  un·con·cern·ed·ly

un·con·di·tion·al
  un·con·di·tion·al·ly

un·con·di·tioned

un·con·fined

un·con·firmed

un·con·nec·ted

un·con·quer·a·ble

un·con·quered

un·con·scion·a·ble
  un·con·scion·a·bly

un·con·scious
  un·con·scious·ly
  un·con·scious·ness

un·con·sti·tu·tion·al
  un·con·sti·tu·tion·al·ly

un·con·strained

un·con·tam·i·nat·ed

un·con·test·ed

un·con·trol·la·ble
  un·con·trol·la·bly

un·con·trolled

un·con·ven·tion·al
  un·con·ven·tion·al·i·ty
  un·con·ven·tion·al·ly

un·con·vinced

un·con·vinc·ing
  un·con·vinc·ing·ly

un·cooked

un·co·op·er·a·tive

un·co·or·di·nat·ed

un·cork

un·cor·rob·o·rat·ed

un·count·ed

un·cou·ple

un·couth

un·cov·er

un·crit·i·cal

un·cross

unc·tion

unc·tu·ous
  unc·tu·ous·ly

un·cul·ti·vat·ed

un·cured

un·cut

un·dam·aged

un·dat·ed

un·daunt·ed

un·de·bat·a·ble

un·de·cid·ed

un·de·clared

un·de·feat·ed

un·de·fend·ed

un·de·fined

un·de·mand·ing

un·dem·o·crat·ic

un·de·mon·stra·tive

un·de·ni·a·ble
un·de·ni·a·bly

un·de·pend·a·ble

un·der
un·der·most

un·der·a·chieve
un·der·a·chiev·er

un·der·act

un·der·age

un·der·arm

un·der·bel·ly
pl. un·der·bel·lies

un·der·bid
un·der·bid·ding; past and past part. un·der·bid
un·der·bid·der

un·der·brush

un·der·car·riage

un·der·charge

un·der·class

un·der·clothes

un·der·coat
un·der·coat·ing

un·der·cov·er

un·der·cur·rent

un·der·cut
un·der·cut·ting; past and past part. un·der·cut

un·der·de·vel·oped
un·der·de·vel·op·ment

un·der·dog

un·der·done

un·der·em·ployed
un·der·em·ploy·ment

un·der·es·ti·mate
un·der·es·ti·mation

un·der·ex·pose
un·der·ex·po·sure

un·der·foot

un·der·gar·ment

un·der·gird

un·der·go
un·der·goes; past un·der·went; past part. un·der·gone

un·der·grad·u·ate

un·der·ground

un·der·growth

un·der·hand

un·der·lie
un·der·ly·ing; past un·der·lay; past part. un·der·lain

un·der·line

un·der·ling

un·der·mine

un·der·neath

un·der·pants

un·der·pass

un·der·pay
past and past part. un·der·paid
un·der·pay·ment

un·der·pin
un·der·pinned, un·der·pin·ning

un·der·play

un·der·pop·u·lat·ed

un·der·priv·i·leged

un·der·rate

un·der·score

un·der·sea

un·der·sec·re·tar·y
pl. un·der·sec·re·tar·ies

un·der·sell
past and past part. un·der·sold

un·der·shirt

un·der·shoot
past and past part. un·der·shot

un·der·shorts

un·der·side

un·der·signed

un·der·skirt

un·der·staffed

un·der·stand
past and past part. un·der·stood
un·der·stand·a·ble
un·der·stand·a·bly

un·der·stand·ing
un·der·stand·ing·ly

un·der·state
un·der·state·ment

un·der·stood

un·der·stud·y
pl. un·der·stud·ies
un·der·stud·ies, un·der·stud·ied

un·der·take
past un·der·took; past part. un·der·tak·en

un·der·tak·er

un·der·tak·ing

un·der·things

un·der·tone

un·der·tow

un·der·val·ue
  un·der·val·ues, un·der·
  val·ued, un·der·val·
  u·ing
  un·der·val·u·a·tion

un·der·wa·ter

un·der·wear

un·der·weight

un·der·whelm

un·der·world

un·der·write
  past un·der·wrote; *past*
  part. un·der·writ·ten
  un·der·writ·er

un·de·served
  un·de·serv·ed·ly

un·de·serv·ing

un·de·signed

un·de·sir·a·ble
  un·de·sir·a·bil·i·ty

un·de·tect·a·ble
  un·de·tect·a·bly

un·de·tect·ed

un·de·ter·mined

un·de·terred

un·de·vel·oped

un·de·vi·at·ing

un·did

un·dies

un·dif·fer·en·ti·at·ed

un·di·gest·ed

un·dig·ni·fied

un·di·lut·ed

un·di·min·ished

un·dip·lo·mat·ic

un·dis·ci·plined

un·dis·closed

un·dis·cov·ered

un·dis·guised

un·dis·mayed

un·dis·put·ed

un·dis·tin·guished

un·dis·turbed

un·di·vid·ed

un·do (*reverse*; see
  UNDUE)
  un·does; *past* un·did;
  past part. un·done

un·doc·u·ment·ed

un·do·ing

un·doubt·ed
  un·doubt·ed·ly

un·dreamed
  also un·dreamt

un·dress

un·dressed

un·drink·a·ble

un·due (*excessive*; see
  UNDO)
  un·du·ly

un·du·late
  un·du·la·tion

un·dy·ing
  un·dy·ing·ly

un·earned

un·earth

un·earth·ly
  un·earth·li·ness

un·ease

un·eas·y
  un·eas·i·er, un·eas·i·
  est
  un·eas·i·ly
  un·eas·i·ness

un·eat·en

un·ec·o·nom·ic

un·ec·o·nom·i·cal
  un·ec·o·nom·i·cal·ly

un·ed·it·ed

un·ed·u·cat·ed

un·e·mo·tion·al

un·em·phat·ic

un·em·ploy·a·ble
  un·em·ploy·a·bil·i·ty

un·em·ployed
  un·em·ploy·ment

un·en·cum·bered

un·end·ing

un·en·dur·a·ble
  un·en·dur·a·bly

un·en·light·ened

un·en·thu·si·as·tic
  un·en·thu·si·as·ti·
  cal·ly

un·en·vi·a·ble

un·e·qual
  un·e·qual·ly

un·e·qualed

un·e·quiv·o·cal
  un·e·quiv·o·cal·ly

un·err·ing
  un·err·ing·ly
  un·err·ing·ness

un·eth·i·cal
  un·eth·i·cal·ly

un·e·ven
  un·e·ven·ly
  un·e·ven·ness

un·e·vent·ful
  un·e·vent·ful·ly

un·ex·am·pled

un·ex·cep·tion·a·ble
  un·ex·cep·tion·a·bly

un·ex·cep·tion·al
  un·ex·cep·tion·al·ly

un·ex·pect·ed
  un·ex·pect·ed·ly
  un·ex·pect·ed·ness

un·ex·plain·a·ble
  un·ex·plain·a·bly

un·ex·plained

un·ex·plored

un·ex·posed

un·ex·pressed

un·ex·pur·gat·ed

un·fad·ing

un·fail·ing
  un·fail·ing·ly

un·fair
  un·fair·ly
  un·fair·ness

un·faith·ful
  un·faith·ful·ly
  un·faith·ful·ness

un·fal·ter·ing

un·fa·mil·iar

un·fa·mil·i·ar·i·ty

un·fash·ion·a·ble
  un·fash·ion·a·bly

un·fas·ten
  un·fas·tened

un·fath·o·ma·ble

un·fa·vor·a·ble

un·fa·vor·a·bly

un·feel·ing
  un·feel·ing·ly

un·feigned

un·fin·ished

un·fit

un·fit·ting
  un·fit·ting·ly

un·fix

un·flag·ging
  un·flag·ging·ly

un·flap·pa·ble
  un·flap·pa·bil·i·ty
  un·flap·pa·bly

un·flat·ter·ing
  un·flat·ter·ing·ly

un·flinch·ing
  un·flinch·ing·ly

un·fold

un·forced

un·fore·see·a·ble

un·fore·seen

un·for·get·ta·ble
  un·for·get·ta·bly

un·for·giv·a·ble
  un·for·giv·a·bly

un·for·giv·en

un·for·giv·ing

un·for·got·ten

un·formed

un·for·tu·nate
  un·for·tu·nate·ly

un·found·ed

un·friend·ly
  un·friend·li·er, un·
    friend·li·est
  un·friend·li·ness

un·ful·filled

un·fun·ny
  un·fun·ni·er, un·fun·
    ni·est
  un·fun·ni·ly

un·furl

un·fur·nished

un·gain·ly
  un·gain·li·ness

un·gen·tle·man·ly

un·glued

un·god·ly
  un·god·li·ness

un·gov·ern·a·ble
  un·gov·ern·a·bil·i·ty
  un·gov·ern·a·bly

un·grace·ful
  un·grace·ful·ly

un·grac·ious
  un·gra·cious·ly
  un·gra·cious·ness

un·gram·mat·i·cal
  un·gram·mat·i·cal·ly

un·grate·ful
  un·grate·ful·ly

un·grudg·ing
  un·grudg·ing·ly

un·guard·ed
  un·guard·ed·ly
  un·guard·ed·ness

un·guent

un·gu·late

un·hal·lowed

un·ham·pered

un·hand

un·hap·py
  un·hap·pi·er, un·hap·
    pi·est
  un·hap·pi·ly
  un·hap·pi·ness

un·harmed

un·health·y
  un·health·i·er, un·
    health·i·est
  un·health·i·ly
  un·health·i·ness

un·heard

un·help·ful
  un·help·ful·ly

un·hes·i·tat·ing
  un·hes·i·tat·ing·ly

un·hin·dered

un·hinge

un·hitch

un·ho·ly
  un·ho·li·er, un·hol·i·est
  un·ho·li·ness

un·hook

un·hoped-for

un·hur·ried

un·hurt

u·ni·cam·er·al

u·ni·cel·lu·lar

u·ni·corn

u·ni·cy·cle
  u·ni·cy·clist

un·i·den·ti·fi·a·ble

un·i·den·ti·fied

u·ni·di·rec·tion·al

u·ni·fi·ca·tion

u·ni·form
  u·ni·formed
  u·ni·form·i·ty
  u·ni·form·ly

u·ni·fy
  u·ni·fies, u·ni·fied
  u·ni·fi·er

u·ni·lat·er·al
  u·ni·lat·er·al·ly

un·im·ag·i·na·ble

un·im·ag·i·na·tive
  un·im·ag·i·na·tive·ly

un·im·paired

un·im·peach·a·ble
  un·im·peach·a·bly

un·im·ped·ed

un·im·por·tant

un·im·pressed

un·im·pres·sive

un·im·proved

un·in·cor·po·rat·ed

un·in·formed

un·in·hab·it·a·ble

un·in·hab·it·ed

un·in·hib·it·ed

un·in·i·ti·at·ed

un·in·jured

un·in·spired

un·in·sured

un·in·tel·li·gi·ble

un·in·tend·ed

un·in·ten·tion·al
  un·in·ten·tion·al·ly

un·in·ter·est·ed
  un·in·ter·est·ed·ly

un·in·ter·rupt·ed

un·in·vit·ing
  un·in·vit·ing·ly

un·ion

un·ion·ize
  un·ion·i·za·tion

Un·ion of So·vi·et So·cial·ist Re·pub·lics

u·nique
  u·nique·ly
  u·nique·ness

u·ni·sex

u·ni·son

u·nit

un·i·tard

U·ni·tar·i·an
  U·ni·tar·i·an·ism

u·ni·tar·y

u·nite

U·nit·ed Ar·ab E·mir·ates

U·nit·ed King·dom

U·nit·ed States of A·mer·i·ca

u·ni·ty
  pl. u·ni·ties

u·ni·va·lent

u·ni·valve

u·ni·ver·sal
  u·ni·ver·sal·i·ty
  u·ni·ver·sal·ize
  u·ni·ver·sal·ly

u·ni·verse

u·ni·ver·si·ty
  pl. u·ni·ver·si·ties

un·just

un·jus·ti·fi·a·ble
  un·jus·ti·fi·a·bly

un·jus·ti·fied

un·just·ly

un·kempt
  un·kempt·ly
  un·kempt·ness

un·kind
  un·kind·ly
  un·kind·ness

un·know·a·ble

un·know·ing
  un·know·ing·ly

un·known

un·la·beled

un·lace

un•law•ful
un•law•ful•ly
un•law•ful•ness

un•lead•ed

un•learn
past and *past part.* un•learned *or* un•learnt

un•learn•ed

un•leash

un•leav•ened

un•less

un•let•tered

un•li•censed

un•like

un•like•ly
un•like•li•er, un•like•li•est
un•like•li•hood
un•like•li•ness

un•lim•it•ed
un•lim•it•ed•ness

un•lined

un•list•ed

un•lit

un•load
un•load•er

un•lock

un•looked-for

un•loose
also un•loos•en

un•luck•y
un•luck•i•er, un•luck•i•est
un•luck•i•ly
un•luck•i•ness

un•made

un•make
past and *past part.* un•made

un•man

un•manned, un•man•ning

un•man•age•a•ble
un•man•age•a•bly

un•man•ly

un•man•ner•ly

un•marked

un•mar•ried

un•mask
un•mask•er

un•matched

un•men•tion•a•ble
un•men•tion•a•bly

un•mer•ci•ful
un•mer•ci•ful•ly

un•mer•it•ed

un•mind•ful

un•mis•tak•a•ble
un•mis•tak•a•bly

un•mit•i•gat•ed
un•mit•i•gat•ed•ly

un•mor•al
un•mo•ral•i•ty
un•mor•al•ly

un•moved
un•mov•a•ble
also un•move•a•ble

un•named

un•nat•u•ral
un•nat•u•ral•ly

un•nec•es•sar•y
un•nec•es•sar•i•ly

un•need•ed

un•nerve
un•nerv•ing•ly

un•no•tice•a•ble
un•no•tice•a•bly

un•no•ticed

un•num•bered

un•ob•jec•tion•a•ble

un•o•blig•ing

un•ob•serv•ant

un•ob•served

un•ob•struct•ed

un•ob•tain•a•ble

un•ob•tru•sive
un•ob•tru•sive•ly
un•ob•tru•sive•ness

un•oc•cu•pied

un•of•fi•cial
un•of•fi•cial•ly

un•o•pened

un•op•posed

un•or•gan•ized

un•or•tho•dox

un•pack
un•pack•er

un•paid

un•paint•ed

un•pal•at•a•ble
un•pal•at•a•bil•i•ty

un•par•al•leled

un•par•don•a•ble
un•par•don•a•bly

un•pa•tri•ot•ic

un•paved

un•per•turbed

un•planned

un•pleas•ant
un•pleas•ant•ly
un•pleas•ant•ness

un•plug
un•plugged, un•plug•ging

un•plumbed
un•plumb•a•ble

un·pol·ished

un·pol·lut·ed

un·pop·u·lar
un·pop·u·lar·i·ty
un·pop·u·lar·ly

un·prac·ticed

un·prec·e·dent·ed
un·prec·e·dent·ed·ly

un·pre·dict·a·bil·i·ty

un·pre·dict·a·ble
un·pre·dict·a·bly

un·pre·dict·ed

un·prej·u·diced

un·pre·med·i·tat·ed

un·pre·pared

un·pre·pos·sess·ing

un·pre·ten·tious
un·pre·ten·tious·ly
un·pre·ten·tious·ness

un·prin·ci·pled

un·print·a·ble
un·print·a·bly

un·pro·duc·tive

un·pro·fes·sion·al
un·pro·fes·sion·al·ly

un·prof·it·a·ble

un·prompt·ed

un·pro·nounce·a·ble

un·pro·pi·tious

un·pro·tect·ed

un·pro·voked

un·pub·lished

un·pun·ished

un·qual·i·fied

un·quench·a·ble

un·ques·tion·a·ble
un·ques·tion·a·bly

un·ques·tioned

un·ques·tion·ing
un·ques·tion·ing·ly

un·qui·et
un·qui·et·ly
un·qui·et·ness

un·quote

un·rav·el

un·read

un·read·a·ble
un·read·a·bil·i·ty
un·read·a·bly

un·re·al
un·re·al·i·ty
un·re·al·ly

un·re·al·is·tic
un·re·al·is·ti·cal·ly

un·re·al·iz·a·ble

un·re·al·ized

un·rea·son

un·rea·son·a·ble
un·rea·son·a·ble·ness
un·rea·son·a·bly

un·rec·og·niz·a·ble

un·rec·on·ciled

un·re·cord·ed

un·re·fined

un·re·gen·er·ate
un·re·gen·er·a·cy
un·re·gen·er·ate·ly

un·reg·is·tered

un·re·hearsed

un·re·lat·ed

un·re·lent·ing
un·re·lent·ing·ly

un·re·li·a·ble

un·re·li·a·bil·i·ty
un·re·li·a·bly

un·re·lieved

un·re·mit·ting
un·re·mit·ting·ly
un·re·mit·ting·ness

un·re·pent·ant·ly

un·re·quit·ed
un·re·quit·ed·ly

un·re·served
un·re·serv·ed·ly

un·re·solved

un·re·spon·sive

un·rest

un·re·strained

un·re·strict·ed

un·right·eous
un·right·eous·ly
un·right·eous·ness

un·ri·valed

un·roll

un·ruf·fled

un·ru·ly
un·ru·li·er, un·ru·li·est
un·ru·li·ness

un·sad·dle

un·safe

un·said

un·salt·ed

un·san·i·tar·y

un·sat·is·fac·to·ry
un·sat·is·fac·to·ri·ly

un·sat·u·rat·ed
un·sat·u·ra·tion

un·saved

un·sa·vor·y
un·sa·vor·i·ness

un·scarred

un·scathed

un·sched·uled

un·schooled

un·sci·en·tif·ic
un·sci·en·tif·i·cal·ly

un·scram·ble
un·scram·bler

un·screw

un·script·ed

un·scru·pu·lous
un·scru·pu·lous·ly
un·scru·pu·lous·ness

un·seal

un·sea·son·a·ble
un·sea·son·a·bly

un·sea·soned

un·seat

un·see·ing

un·seem·ly
un·seem·li·er, un·seem·li·
est
un·seem·li·ness

un·seen

un·self·con·scious
un·self·con·scious·ly

un·self·con·scious·ness

un·self·ish
un·self·ish·ly
un·self·ish·ness

un·sen·ti·men·tal

un·set·tle
un·set·tling
un·set·tled

un·shak·a·ble
also un·shake·able
un·shak·a·bil·i·ty
un·shak·a·bly

un·shrink·ing
un·shrink·ing·ly

un·sight·ly
un·sight·li·ness

un·signed

un·sink·a·ble

un·skilled

un·skill·ful

un·sliced

un·snap

un·so·cia·ble

un·sold

un·so·lic·it·ed

un·solved

un·so·phis·ti·cat·ed
un·so·phis·ti·cat·ed·ly

un·sought

un·sound
un·sound·ly
un·sound·ness

un·spar·ing
un·spar·ing·ly

un·speak·a·ble
un·speak·a·ble·ness
un·speak·a·bly

un·spe·cif·ic

un·spec·i·fied

un·spec·tac·u·lar
un·spec·tac·u·lar·ly

un·spoiled

un·sports·man·like

un·sta·ble
un·sta·bler, un·sta·
blest
un·sta·ble·ness
un·sta·bly

un·stat·ed

un·stead·y
un·stead·i·er, un·
stead·i·est

un·stead·i·ly
un·stead·i·ness

un·stint·ing
un·stint·ing·ly

un·stop
un·stopped, un·stop·
ping

un·stop·pa·ble

un·stressed

un·string
past and *past part.* un·
strung

un·struc·tured

un·stud·ied

un·sub·stan·tial
un·sub·stan·ti·al·i·ty
un·sub·stan·tial·ly

un·sub·stan·ti·at·ed

un·suc·cess·ful
un·suc·cess·ful·ly

un·suit·a·ble
un·suit·a·bly

un·suit·a·bil·i·ty

un·suit·ed

un·sul·lied

un·sung

un·su·per·vised

un·sup·port·ed

un·sure

un·sur·passed

un·sus·pect·ed

un·sus·pect·ing

un·sweet·ened

un·swerv·ing
un·swerv·ing·ly

un·tan·gle

un·tapped

un·taught

un·ten·a·ble
un·ten·a·bil·i·ty
un·ten·a·bly

un·test·ed

un·think·a·ble
un·think·a·bly

un·think·ing
un·think·ing·ly

un·ti·dy
un·ti·di·er, un·ti·di·est
un·ti·di·ly
un·ti·di·ness

un·tie
pres. part. un·ty·ing

un·til

un·time·ly
un·time·li·ness

un·tir·ing

un·ti·tled

un·to

un·told

un·touch·a·ble
un·touch·a·bil·i·ty
un·touch·a·ble·ness

un·touched

un·to·ward
un·to·ward·ly
un·to·ward·ness

un·trained

un·tram·meled

un·treat·ed

un·tried

un·trou·bled

un·true
un·tru·ly

un·trust·wor·thi·ness

un·trust·wor·thy

un·truth
pl. un·truths
un·truth·ful
un·truth·ful·ly
un·truth·ful·ness

un·tu·tored

un·twist

un·us·a·ble

un·used

un·u·su·al
un·u·su·al·ly

un·ut·ter·a·ble
un·ut·ter·a·bly

un·var·nished

un·var·y·ing

un·veil

un·voiced

un·want·ed

un·war·rant·ed

un·war·y
un·war·i·ly
un·war·i·ness

un·washed

un·wa·ver·ing
un·wa·ver·ing·ly

un·wea·ry·ing
un·wea·ry·ing·ly

un·wel·come

un·well

un·whole·some
un·whole·some·ly
un·whole·some·ness

un·wield·y
un·wield·i·er, un·wield·i·est
un·wield·i·ness

un·will·ing
un·will·ing·ly
un·will·ing·ness

un·wind

past and *past part.* un·wound

un·wise
un·wise·ly

un·wit·ting
un·wit·ting·ly
un·wit·ting·ness

un·wont·ed
un·wont·ed·ly
un·wont·ed·ness

un·work·a·ble
un·work·a·bly

un·world·ly
un·world·li·ness

un·wor·thy
un·wor·thi·er, un·wor·thi·est
un·wor·thi·ly
un·wor·thi·ness

un·wound

un·wrap
un·wrapped, un·wrap·ping

un·writ·ten

un·yield·ing
un·yield·ing·ly
un·yield·ing·ness

un·zip

up
upped, up·ping
up-and-com·ing
up-front

up·beat

up·braid
up·braid·ing

up·bring·ing

up·chuck

up·com·ing

up·date
up·dat·er

Up·dike

up•end

up•grade
  up•grad•er

up•heav•al

up•hill

up•hold
  past and *past part.*
  up•held
  up•hold•er

up•hol•ster
  up•hol•ster•er

up•hol•ster•y

up•keep

up•land

up•lift
  up•lift•er
  up•lift•ing

up•mar•ket

up•on

up•per

up•per•case

up•per•cut

up•per•most
  also up•most

up•pi•ty

Upp•sa•la

up•right
  up•right•ly
  up•right•ness

up•ris•ing

up•roar

up•roar•i•ous
  up•roar•i•ous•ly

up•root
  up•root•er

up•scale

up•set
  up•set•ting; *past* and
  past part. up•set
  up•set•ter
  up•set•ting•ly

up•shot

up•side down
  also up•side-down

up•si•lon

up•stage

up•stairs
  also up•stair

up•stand•ing

up•start

up•state
  up•stat•er

up•stream

up•surge

up•swept

up•swing

up•take

up•thrust

up•tight

up•town
  up•town•er

up•turn

up•ward
  also up•wards

up•ward•ly

up•wind

U•ral Moun•tains

u•ra•ni•um
  u•ran•ic

U•ra•nus

ur•ban

ur•bane
  ur•bane•ly
  ur•ban•i•ty

ur•ban•ite

ur•ban•ize
  ur•ban•i•za•tion

ur•chin

Ur•du

u•re•a
  u•re•al

u•re•mi•a

u•re•ter

u•re•thane

u•re•thra
  pl. u•re•thras *or* u•re•
  thrae

Ur•fa

urge

ur•gent
  ur•gen•cy
  ur•gent•ly

urg•ing

u•ric

u•ri•nal

u•ri•nal•y•sis
  pl. u•ri•nal•y•ses

u•ri•nar•y

u•ri•nate
  u•ri•na•tion

u•rine

urn (*vase*; see EARN)
  urn•ful
  pl. urn•fuls

u•ro•gen•i•tal

u•rol•o•gy
  u•ro•log•ic
  u•rol•o•gist

ur•sine

U•ru•guay
  U•ru•guay•an

Ü·rüm·qi

us

us·a·ble
  also use·a·ble
  us·a·bil·i·ty
  us·a·ble·ness

us·age

use
  us·er

use·ful
  use·ful·ly
  use·ful·ness

use·less
  use·less·ly
  use·less·ness

us·er-friend·ly

ush·er

u·su·al
  u·su·al·ly

u·surp
  u·sur·pa·tion
  u·surp·er

u·su·ry
  u·su·rer
  u·su·ri·ous

U·tah
  U·tah·an

Ute
  pl. same *or* Utes

u·ten·sil

u·ter·us
  pl. u·ter·i *or* u·ter·us·es
  u·ter·ine

u·til·i·tar·i·an
  u·til·i·tar·i·an·ism

u·til·i·ty
  pl. u·til·i·ties

u·ti·lize
  u·ti·liz·a·ble
  u·ti·li·za·tion
  u·ti·liz·er

ut·most

U·to·pi·a
  U·to·pi·an

U·trecht

ut·ter (*complete*)
  ut·ter·ly

ut·ter (*say*)
  ut·ter·a·ble
  ut·ter·er

ut·ter·ance

ut·ter·most

U-turn

u·vu·la
  pl. u·vu·las *or* u·vu·lae
  u·vu·lar

ux·o·ri·al

ux·o·ri·ous
  ux·o·ri·ous·ly
  ux·o·ri·ous·ness

Uz·bek·i·stan
  Uz·bek *or* Uz·beg

V

va·can·cy
  pl. va·can·cies

va·cant
  va·cant·ly

va·cate

va·ca·tion
  va·ca·tion·er

vac·ci·nate
  vac·ci·na·tion

vac·cine

vac·il·late
  vac·il·la·tion
  vac·il·la·tor

va·cu·i·ty

vac·u·ole
  vac·u·o·lar
  vac·u·o·la·tion

vac·u·ous
  va·cu·i·ty
  vac·u·ous·ly

vac·u·um
  pl. vac·u·ums *or* vac·u·a
  vac·u·um-packed

va·de me·cum

Va·duz

vag·a·bond
  vag·a·bond·age

va·ga·ry
  pl. va·ga·ries
  va·gar·i·ous

va·gi·na
  pl. va·gi·nas *or* va·gi·nae
  vag·i·nal
  vag·i·ni·tis

va·grant
  va·gran·cy
  va·grant·ly

vague
  vague·ly
  vague·ness

vain (*proud; see* VANE, VEIN)
  vain·ly
  vain·ness

vain·glo·ry
  vain·glo·ri·ous
  vain·glo·ri·ous·ly

val·ance (*curtain; see* VALENCE)
  val·anced

vale (*valley; see* VEIL)

val·e·dic·tion

val·e·dic·to·ri·an

val·e·dic·to·ry
  pl. val·e·dic·to·ries

va·lence (*atomic property; see* VALANCE)

Va·len·ci·a

val·en·tine

va·le·ri·an

Va·lé·ry

val·et

val·e·tu·di·nar·i·an
  val·e·tu·di·nar·i·an·ism

Val·hal·la

val·iant
  val·iant·ly

val·id
  va·lid·i·ty
  val·id·ly

val·i·date
  val·i·da·tion

va·lise

Val·i·um (*trademark*)

Val·kyr·ie

Va·lla·do·lid

Val·le·jo

Val·let·ta

val·ley
  pl. val·leys

val·or
  val·or·ous

Val·pa·rai·so (*Indiana*)

Val·pa·ra·í·so (*Chile*)

val·u·a·ble
  val·u·a·bly

val·u·a·tion
  val·u·ate

val·ue
  val·ues, val·ued, val·u·ing
  value-add·ed
  val·ue·less

valve
  val·vate
  valved
  valve·less
  val·vu·lar

va·moose

vamp

vam·pire

van

va·na·di·um

Van Bu·ren

Van·cou·ver

van·dal
  van·dal·ism
  van·dal·ize

Van·der·bilt

Van Dyck

Van Dyke

Van·dyke beard

vane (*pointer*; see VAIN, VEIN)
  vaned
  vane·less

Van Eyck

Van Gogh

van·guard

va·nil·la

van·ish

van·i·ty
  pl. van·i·ties

van·quish
  van·quish·a·ble
  van·quish·er

van·tage

Va·nu·a·tu

vap·id
  va·pid·i·ty
  vap·id·ly
  vap·id·ness

va·por
  va·por·ous
  va·por·ous·ly
  va·por·y

va·por·ize
  va·por·iz·a·ble
  also va·por·a·ble
  va·por·i·za·tion
  va·por·iz·er

Va·ra·na·si

var·i·a·ble
  var·i·a·bil·i·ty
  var·i·a·bly

var·i·ance

var·i·ant

var·i·a·tion
  var·i·a·tion·al

var·i·col·ored

var·i·cose
  var·i·cos·i·ty

var·ied
  var·ied·ly

var·i·e·gat·ed
  var·i·e·ga·tion

va·ri·e·tal
  va·ri·e·tal·ly

va·ri·e·ty
  pl. va·ri·e·ties

var·i·ous
  var·i·ous·ly

var·let
  var·let·ry

var·mint

Var·na

var·nish
  var·nish·er

var·si·ty
  pl. var·si·ties

var·y (*change*; see VERY)
  var·ies, var·ied

vas·cu·lar
  vas·cu·lar·ly

vas de·fe·rens
  pl. va·sa de·fe·ren·ti·a

vase
  vase·ful
  pl. vase·fuls

vas·ec·to·my
  pl. vas·ec·to·mies

Vas·e·line (*trademark*)

vas·o·mo·tor

vas·sal
  vas·sal·age

vast
  vast·ly
  vast·ness

vat
  vat·ful
  pl. vat·fuls

Vat·i·can

vaude·ville
  vaude·vil·lian

Vaughan

Vaughan Wil·liams

vault
  vault·er

vault·ing

vaunt
  vaunt·er
  vaunt·ing·ly

veal

vec·tor
  vec·to·ri·al

Ve·da
  Ve·dic

vee·jay

veer

veg

veg·an

veg·e·ta·ble

veg·e·tar·i·an
  veg·e·tar·i·an·ism

veg·e·tate
  veg·e·ta·tive

veg·e·ta·tion
  veg·e·ta·tion·al

veg·gie

ve·he·ment
  ve·he·mence
  ve·he·ment·ly

ve·hi·cle
ve·hic·u·lar

veil (*covering*; see VALE)
veil·less

veiled

vein (*blood vessel*; see
VAIN, VANE)
vein·less
vein·like
vein·y
vein·i·er, vein·i·est
veined

ve·lar

Ve·láz·quez

Vel·cro (*trademark*)
Vel·croed

veld
also veldt

vel·lum (*parchment*; see
VELUM)

ve·loc·i·pede

ve·loc·i·ty
pl. ve·loc·i·ties

ve·lo·drome

ve·lour
also ve·lours

ve·lum (*membrane*; see
VELLUM)
pl. ve·la

vel·vet
vel·vet·ed
vel·vet·y

vel·vet·een

ve·nal
ve·nal·i·ty
ve·nal·ly

vend
ven·dor

ven·det·ta

ve·neer

ven·er·a·ble
ven·er·a·bil·i·ty
ven·er·a·ble·ness
ven·er·a·bly

ven·er·ate
ven·er·a·tion
ven·er·a·tor

ve·ne·re·al
ve·ne·re·al·ly

ve·ne·tian blind

Ve·ne·zia

Ven·e·zue·la
Ven·e·zue·lan

ven·geance

venge·ful
venge·ful·ly
venge·ful·ness

ve·ni·al
ve·ni·al·i·ty
ve·ni·al·ly

Ven·ice
Ve·ne·tian

ven·i·son

Venn di·a·gram

ven·om
ven·om·ous
ven·om·ous·ly

ve·nous (*of veins*; see
VENUS)
ve·nos·i·ty
ve·nous·ly

vent
vent·less

ven·ti·late
ven·ti·la·tion

ven·ti·la·tor

ven·tral
ven·tral·ly

ven·tri·cle
ven·tric·u·lar

ven·tril·o·quism
ven·tril·o·quist
ven·tril·o·quize

Ven·tu·ra

ven·ture

ven·ture·some
ven·ture·some·ly
ven·ture·some·ness

ven·ue

Ve·nus (*planet*; see
VENOUS)
pl. Ve·nus·es
Ve·nu·si·an

ve·ra·cious (*true*; see
VORACIOUS)
ve·ra·cious·ly
ve·rac·i·ty

Ve·ra·cruz

ve·ran·da
also ve·ran·dah

verb
ver·bal
ver·bal·ly

ver·bal·ize
ver·bal·i·za·tion
ver·bal·iz·er

ver·ba·tim

ver·be·na

ver·bi·age

ver·bose
ver·bose·ly
ver·bos·i·ty

ver·dant
ver·dan·cy
ver·dant·ly

Ver·di

ver·dict

ver·di·gris

ver·dure
ver·dured

verge

verg·ing

ve·rid·i·cal

ver·i·fy
ver·i·fies, ver·i·fied
ver·i·fi·a·ble
ver·i·fi·a·bly
ver·i·fi·ca·tion
ver·i·fi·er

ver·i·ly

ver·i·si·mil·i·tude

ver·i·ta·ble
ver·i·ta·bly

ver·i·ty
pl. ver·i·ties

Ver·meer

ver·mi·cel·li

ver·mi·cide

ver·mic·u·lite

ver·mi·form

ver·mil·ion

ver·min
ver·min·ous

Ver·mont
Ver·mont·er

ver·mouth

ver·nac·u·lar
ver·nac·u·lar·ism
ver·nac·u·lar·ly

ver·nal
ver·nal·ly

Verne

ver·ni·er

Ve·ro·na

ver·sa·tile
ver·sa·til·i·ty

verse

versed

ver·si·cle

ver·si·fy
ver·si·fies, ver·si·fied
ver·si·fi·ca·tion
ver·si·fi·er

ver·sion
ver·sion·al

ver·so
pl. ver·sos

ver·sus

ver·te·bra
pl. ver·te·brae
ver·te·bral

ver·te·brate

ver·tex
pl. ver·ti·ces *or* ver·tex·es

ver·ti·cal
ver·ti·cal·i·ty
ver·ti·cal·ly

ver·tig·i·nous
ver·tig·i·nous·ly

ver·ti·go

verve

ver·y (*extremely*; see VARY)

ves·i·cle
ve·sic·u·lar
ve·sic·u·late
ve·sic·u·la·tion

ves·pers

Ves·puc·ci

ves·sel

vest
vest-pock·et

ves·tal

ves·tib·u·lar

ves·ti·bule

ves·tige
ves·tig·i·al

vest·ment

ves·try
pl. ves·tries
ves·tral

Ve·su·vi·us

vet
vet·ted, vet·ting

vetch

vet·er·an

vet·er·i·nar·i·an

vet·er·i·nar·y

ve·to
pl. ve·toes
ve·toes, ve·toed
ve·to·er

vex
vex·er
vex·ing
vex·ing·ly

vex·a·tion
vex·a·tious

vexed
vex·ed·ly

vi·a

vi·a·ble
vi·a·bil·i·ty
vi·a·bly

vi·a·duct

vi·al (*container*; see VILE, VIOL)
vi·al·ful
pl. vi·al·fuls

vi·and

vi·at·i·cum
pl. vi·at·i·ca *or* vi·at·i·cums

vibes

vi·brant
vi·bran·cy
vi·brant·ly

vi·bra·phone
vi·bra·phon·ist

vi·brate
vi·bra·tor
vi·bra·to·ry

vi·bra·tion
vi·bra·tion·al

vi·bra·to

vi·bur·num

vic·ar

vic·ar·age

vi·car·i·ous
vi·car·i·ous·ly
vi·car·i·ous·ness

vice (*immorality*; see VISE)
vice·less

vice pres·i·dent
also vice-pres·i·dent
vice pres·i·den·cy
pl. vice pres·i·den·cies
vice-pres·i·den·tial

vice·roy

vi·ce ver·sa

vi·chys·soise

vi·cin·i·ty
pl. vi·cin·i·ties

vi·cious
vi·cious·ly
vi·cious·ness

vi·cis·si·tude

vic·tim

vic·tim·ize
vic·tim·i·za·tion
vic·tim·iz·er

vic·tor

Vic·to·ri·a

Vic·to·ri·an
Vic·to·ri·an·ism

vic·to·ri·ous
vic·to·ri·ous·ly

vic·to·ry
pl. vic·to·ries

vict·ual
vict·ual·less

vict·ual·er

vi·cu·ña
also vi·cu·na

Vi·dal

vi·de·li·cet

vid·e·o
pl. vid·e·os
vid·e·oes, vid·e·oed

vid·e·o·cas·sette

vid·e·o·tape

vie
vy·ing

Vi·en·na
Vi·en·nese
pl. same

Vien·tiane

Vi·et·nam
Vi·et·nam·ese
pl. same

view
view·a·ble

view·er

view·er·ship

view·find·er

view·ing

view·point

vig·il

vig·i·lance
vig·i·lant

vig·i·lan·te

vi·gnette
vi·gnet·tist

Vi·go

vig·or
vig·or·ous
vig·or·ous·ly

Vi·king

Vi·la

vile (*disgusting*; see VIAL, VIOL)
vile·ly
vile·ness

vil·i·fy
vil·i·fies, vil·i·fied
vil·i·fi·ca·tion
vil·i·fi·er

Vil·la (*proper name*)

vil·la (*house*)

vil·lage
vil·lag·er

Vi·lla·her·mo·sa

vil·lain
vil·lain·ous
vil·lain·y

vil·lein
vil·lein·age

Vil·lon

vil·lus (*tiny hair*)
pl. vil·li
vil·lous (*covered with villi*)

Vil·ni·us

vim

vin·ai·grette

vin·di·cate
vin·di·ca·tion
vin·di·ca·tor

vin·dic·tive
vin·dic·tive·ly
vin·dic·tive·ness

vine
vin·y

vin·e·gar

vin·e·gar·ish
vin·e·gar·y

vine·yard

vi·no

vin·tage

vint ner

vi·nyl

vi·ol (*musical instrument*; see VIAL, VILE)

vi·o·la

vi·o·late
vi·o·la·ble
vi·o·la·tion
vi·o·la·tor

vi·o·lence

vi·o·lent
vi·o·lent·ly

vi·o·let

vi·o·lin
vi·o·lin·ist

vi·o·lon·cel·lo
pl. vi·o·lon·cel·los
vi·o·lon·cel·list

vi·per
vi·per·ous

vi·ra·go
pl. vi·ra·gos

vi·ral
vi·ral·ly

vir·e·o
pl. vir·e·os

Vir·gil
also Ver·gil

vir·gin
vir·gin·al
vir·gin·i·ty

Vir·gin·ia
Vir·gin·ian

Vir·gin Is·lands

Vir·go
pl. Vir·gos

vir·gule

vir·ile
vi·ril·i·ty

vi·rol·o·gy
vi·ro·log·i·cal
vi·ro·log·i·cal·ly
vi·rol·o·gist

vir·tu·al
vir·tu·al·i·ty
vir·tu·al·ly

vir·tue
vir·tue·less

vir·tu·o·so
pl. vir·tu·o·si *or* vir·tu·o·sos
vir·tu·os·i·ty

vir·tu·ous
vir·tu·ous·ly
vir·tu·ous·ness

vir·u·lent
vir·u·lence
vir·u·lent·ly

vi·rus

vi·sa

vis·age
vis·aged

Vi·sa·kha·pat·nam

vis-à-vis

vis·cer·a

vis·cer·al
vis·cer·al·ly

vis·cid
vis·cid·i·ty

vis·cose

vis·cos·i·ty

vis·count

vis·count·ess

vis·cous
vis·cous·ly

vise (*clamp*; see VICE)
vise·like

Vish·nu
Vish·nu·ism

vis·i·bil·i·ty

vis·i·ble
vis·i·ble·ness
vis·i·bly

vi·sion
vi·sion·less

vi·sion·ar·y
pl. vi·sion·ar·ies

vis·it
vis·i·tor

vis·i·tant

vis·i·ta·tion

vi·sor
vi·sored
vi·sor·less

vis·ta
vis·taed

vis·u·al
vis·u·al·ly

vis·u·al·ize
vis·u·al·i·za·tion

vi·tal
vi·tal·ly

vi·tal·i·ty

vi·tal·ize
vi·tal·i·za·tion

vi·ta·min

vi·ti·ate
vi·ti·a·tion
vi·ti·a·tor

vit·i·cul·ture
vit·i·cul·tur·al
vit·i·cul·tur·ist

vit·re·ous
vit·re·ous·ness

vit·ri·fy
vit·ri·fies, vit·ri·fied
vit·ri·fac·tion
vit·ri·fi·a·ble
vit·ri·fi·ca·tion

vit·ri·ol
vit·ri·ol·ic

vi·tu·per·ate
vi·tu·per·a·tion
vi·tu·per·a·tive

vi·va

vi·va·ce

vi·va·cious
vi·va·cious·ly
vi·va·cious·ness
vi·vac·i·ty

Vi·val·di

viv·id
viv·id·ly
viv·id·ness

viv·i·fy
viv·i·fies, viv·i·fied
viv·i·fi·ca·tion

vi·vip·a·rous
vi·vip·a·rous·ly

viv·i·sec·tion
viv·i·sect
viv·i·sec·tion·al
viv·i·sec·tion·ist
viv·i·sec·tor

vix·en
vix·en·ish
vix·en·ly

vi·zier
vi·zier·i·al
vi·zier·ship

Vla·di·kav·kaz

Vla·di·vos·tok

vo·cab·u·lar·y
pl. vo·cab·u·lar·ies

vo·cal
vo·cal·i·ty
vo·cal·ly

vo·cal·ist

vo·cal·ize
vo·cal·i·za·tion
vo·cal·iz·er

vo·ca·tion
vo·ca·tion·al

voc·a·tive

vo·cif·er·ate
vo·cif·er·a·tion

vo·cif·er·ous
vo·cif·er·ous·ly
vo·cif·er·ous·ness

vod·ka

vogue
vogu·ish

voice
voice-o·ver

void
void·a·ble

voile

vol·a·tile
vol·a·til·i·ty

vol·can·ic
vol·can·i·cal·ly

vol·ca·no
pl. vol·ca·noes

vole

Vol·ga

Vol·go·grad

vo·li·tion
vo·li·tion·al
vo·li·tion·al·ly
vol·i·tive

vol·ley
pl. vol·leys
vol·leys, vol·leyed
vol·ley·er

vol·ley·ball

volt

Vol·ta

volt·age

vol·ta·ic

Vol·taire

volt·me·ter

vol·u·ble
vol·u·bil·i·ty
vol·u·ble·ness
vol·u·bly

vol·ume
vol·umed

vo·lu·mi·nous
vo·lu·mi·nous·ly
vo·lu·mi·nous·ness

vol·un·ta·rism

vol·un·tar·y
pl. vol·un·tar·ies
vol·un·tar·i·ly

vol·un·teer

vo·lup·tu·ar·y
pl. vo·lup·tu·ar·ies

vo·lup·tu·ous
vo·lup·tu·ous·ly
vo·lup·tu·ous·ness

vo·lute
vo·lut·ed

vom·it
vom·it·er

Von·ne·gut

voo·doo
voo·doo·ism
voo·doo·ist

vo·ra·cious (*greedy;* see
VERACIOUS)
vo·ra·cious·ly
vo·ra·cious·ness
vo·rac·i·ty

Vo·ro·shi·lov·grad

vor·tex
  pl. vor·ti·ces *or* vor·
    tex·es
  vor·ti·cal
  vor·ti·cal·ly
  vor·tic·i·ty
  vor·ti·cose

vo·ta·ry
  pl. vo·ta·ries; *fem.* vo·
    ta·ress
  vo·ta·rist

vote
  vot·a·ble
  vote·less
  vot·er

vo·tive

vouch

vouch·er

vouch·safe

vow

vow·el
  vow·eled
  vow·el·less

vox po·pu·li

voy·age
  voy·ag·er

vo·ya·geur

vo·yeur
  vo·yeur·ism
  voy·eur·is·tic
  voy·eur·is·ti·cal·ly

vul·can·ize
  vul·can·i·za·tion
  vul·can·iz·er

vul·gar
  vul·gar·i·ty
  vul·gar·ly

vul·gar·i·an

vul·gar·ism

vul·gar·ize
  vul·gar·i·za·tion

Vul·gate

vul·ner·a·ble
  vul·ner·a·bil·i·ty
  vul·ner·a·ble·ness
  vul·ner·a·bly

vul·pine

vul·ture
  vul·tur·ine
  vul·tur·ous

vul·va
  pl. vul·vas

vy·ing

W

Wa·bash Riv·er

wack·o
 also whack·o
 pl. wack·os *or* wack·oes

wack·y
 also whack·y
 wack·i·er, wack·i·est
 pl. wack·ies
 wack·i·ly
 wack·i·ness

Wa·co

wad
 wad·ded, wad·ding

wad·ding

wad·dle
 wad·dler

wade
 wad·a·ble
 also wade·a·ble

wad·er

wa·di
 also wa·dy
 pl. wa·dis *or* wa·dies

wad·ing

wa·fer
 wa·fer-thin
 wa·fer·y

waf·fle
 waf·fler
 waf·fly

waft

wag (*joker*)

wag (*shake*)
 wagged, wag·ging

wage

wa·ger

wag·gish
 wag·gish·ly
 wag·gish·ness

wag·gle

wag·gly

wag·ing

Wag·ner

wag·on

waif
 waif·ish

wail (*cry*; see WALE, WHALE)
 wail·er (*one who wails*; see WHALER)
 wail·ing·ly

wain (*wagon*; see WANE)

wain·scot

wain·scot·ing

wain·wright

waist (*part of body*; see WASTE)
 waist·ed
 waist·less

waist·band

waist·line

wait (*delay*; see WEIGHT)

wait·er

wait·ing

wait·per·son

wait·ress

waive (*give up*; see WAVE)

waiv·er (*a giving up*; see WAVER)

wake
 past woke *or* waked;
 past part. wok·en *or* waked
 wak·er

wake·ful
 wake·ful·ly
 wake·ful·ness

wak·en

Wald·heim

wale (*ridge*; see WAIL, WHALE)

Wales

Wa·le·sa

walk (*go*; see WOK)

walk·er

walk·ie-talk·ie

Walk·man (*trademark*)
 pl. Walk·mans

walk·out

walk·way

wall
 wall·ing
 wall-less

wal·la·by
 pl. wal·la·bies

Wal·lace

wall·board

wal·let

wall·eye
 wall·eyed

wall·flow·er

Wal·loon

wal·lop
 wal·lop·er
 wal·lop·ing

wal·low
  wal·low·er

wall·pa·per

wal·nut

Wal·pole

wal·rus

Wal·ton

waltz
  waltz·er

wam·pum

wan
  wan·ly
  wan·ness

wand

wan·der
  wan·der·er
  wan·der·ing

wan·der·lust

wane (*decrease*; see WAIN)
  waning

wan·gle
  wan·gler

Wan·kel

wan·na·be

want
  want·er

want·ing

wan·ton
  wan·ton·ly
  wan·ton·ness

wap·i·ti

war (*fight*; see WORE)
  warred (*past of war*; see
  WARD), war·ring

war·ble

war·bler

ward (*hospital area*; see
  warred [WAR])

war·den

ward·er

ward·robe

ward·room

ware (*merchandise*; see
  WEAR, WHERE)

ware·house

war·fare

war·head

War·hol

war·horse

war·i·ly

war·like

war·lock

war·lord

warm
  warm-blood·ed
  warmed-up
  warmed-o·ver
  warm-up
  warm·er
  warm·ish
  warm·ly
  warm·ness

warm·heart·ed
  warm·heart·ed·ly
  warm·heart·ed·ness

war·mon·ger
  war·mon·ger·ing

warmth

warn (*advise*; see WORN)
  warn·er

warn·ing
  warn·ing·ly

warp
  warp·age

war·path

war·rant
  war·rant·or *or* war·
  ran·ter

war·ran·tee (*person*; see
  WARRANTY)

war·ran·ty (*guarantee*;
  see WARRANTEE)
  pl. war·ran·ties

War·ren (*proper name,
  city*)

war·ren (*rabbit home*)

war·ring

war·ri·or

War·saw

war·ship

wart
  wart·y

wart·hog

war·y (*cautious*; see
  WHERRY)
  war·i·er, war·i·est
  war·i·ly
  war·i·ness

was

wash
  wash-out
  wash·a·bil·i·ty
  wash·a·ble

wash·board

wash·cloth

wash·er

wash·er·wom·an
  pl. wash·er·wom·en
  also wash·wom·an

wash·ing

Wash·ing·ton
  Wash·ing·to·ni·an

Wash·ing·ton, D.C.

wash·room

wash·stand

was·n't

WASP (*white Anglo-
Saxon Protestant*)
also Wasp
Wasp•y

wasp (*insect*)
wasp•like

wasp•ish
wasp•ish•ly
wasp•ish•ness

was•sail
was•sail•er

wast•age

waste (*squander; see*
WAIST)
waste•less

waste•bas•ket

waste•ful
waste•ful•ly
waste•ful•ness

waste•land

waste•pa•per

wast•rel

watch
watch•a•ble
watch•er

watch•band

watch•dog
watch•dogged, watch•
dog•ging

watch•ful
watch•ful•ly
watch•ful•ness

watch•man
pl. watch•men

watch•tow•er

watch•word

wa•ter
wa•ter-re•pel•lent
wa•ter•er
wa•ter•less

Wa•ter•bur•y

wa•ter•col•or
wa•ter•col•or•ist

wa•ter•course

wa•ter•cress

wa•ter•fall

wa•ter•fowl

wa•ter•front

wa•ter•line

wa•ter•logged

Wa•ter•loo

wa•ter•man
pl. wa•ter•men

wa•ter•mark

wa•ter•mel•on

wa•ter•pow•er

wa•ter•proof

wa•ter•shed

wa•ter•spout

wa•ter•tight

wa•ter•way

wa•ter•works

wa•ter•y
wa•ter•i•ness

Wat•son

watt

watt•age

Wat•teau

wat•tle
wat•tled

Waugh

wave (*gesture; see* WAIVE)
wave•less
wave•like

wave•form

wave•length

wave•let

wa•ver (*hesitate; see*
WAIVER)
wa•ver•er
wa•ver•ing•ly

wav•y
wav•i•er, wav•i•est
wav•i•ly
wav•i•ness

wax
wax•er
wax•i•ly
wax•i•ness
wax•y
wax•i•er, wax•i•est

wax•en

wax•wing

wax•work

way (*road; see* WEIGH,
WHEY)
way-out

way•far•er
way•far•ing

way•lay
past and past part. way•
laid
way•lay•er

Wayne

way•side

way•ward
way•ward•ly
way•ward•ness

we (*1st person pl.; see*
WEE)

weak (*not strong; see*
WEEK)
weak-kneed
weak-mind•ed

weak•en
weak•en•er

weak•ling

weak·ly
weak·li·er, weak·li·est
weak·li·ness

weak·ness

weal (*prosperity*; see
WE'LL, WHEEL)

wealth

wealth·y
wealth·i·er, wealth·
i·est
wealth·i·ly
wealth·i·ness

wean

weap·on
weap·oned
weap·on·less

weap·on·ry

wear (*be dressed in*; see
WARE, WHERE)
past wore; *past part.*
worn
wear·a·ble
wear·a·bil·i·ty
wear·er
wear·ing
wear·ing·ly

wea·ri·some
wea·ri·some·ly
wea·ri·some·ness

wea·ry
wea·ri·er, wea·ri·est
wea·ries, wea·ried
wea·ri·less
wea·ri·ly
wea·ri·ness
wea·ry·ing·ly

wea·sel
wea·sel·ly

weath·er (*climate*; see
WETHER, WHETHER)
weath·er-beaten
weath·er-strip

weath·er·cock

weath·er·man
pl. weath·er·men

weath·er·proof
weath·er·proofed

weave (*make fabric*; see
WE'VE)
past wove; *past part.*
wo·ven *or* wove
weav·er

web
web-foot·ed
webbed

web·bing

We·ber

web·er

Web·ster

we'd (*we would*; see
WEED)

wed
wed·ding; *past and
past part.* wed·ded
or wed

Wed·dell Sea

wed·ding

wedge
wedge·like
wedge·wise

Wedg·wood

wed·lock

Wednes·day

wee (*small*; see WE)
we·er; we·est

weed (*plant*; see WE'D)
weed·er
weed·less

weeds

weed·y
weed·i·er, weed·i·est
weed·i·ness

week (*seven days*; see
WEAK)

week·day

week·end

week·ly
pl. week·lies

weep
past and past part. wept
weep·er
weep·ing·ly
weep·y
weep·i·er, weep·i·est

wee·vil
wee·vil·y

weft

weigh (*measure heaviness*;
see WAY, WHEY)
weigh·a·ble
weigh·er

weight (*heaviness*; see
WAIT)

weight·less
weight·less·ly
weight·less·ness

weight·lift·ing
weight·lift·er

weight·y
weight·i·er, weight·i·
est
weight·i·ly
weight·i·ness

Weill

weir (*dam*; see WE'RE)

weird
weird·ly
weird·ness

weird·o
pl. weird·os

Weiz·mann

welch
var. of welsh

wel·come
wel·come·ly
wel·come·ness
wel·com·er
wel·com·ing·ly

weld
  weld•a•ble
  weld•a•bil•i•ty
  weld•er

wel•fare

wel•kin

well
  well-ad•vised
  well-ap•point•ed
  well-bal•anced
  well-be•ing
  well-bred
  well-dis•posed
  well-done
  well-found•ed
  well-groomed
  well-ground•ed
  well-heeled
  well-in•formed
  well-in•ten•tioned
  well-known
  well-mean•ing
  well-off
  well-pre•served
  well-read
  well-round•ed
  well-spok•en
  well-to-do
  well-worn

we'll (*we will*; see WEAL, WHEEL)

well•born

well•head

Wel•ling•ton

well•ness

well-nigh

Wells

welsh (*go back on*)
  also welch
  welsh•er

Welsh (*of Wales*)
  Welsh•man
  pl. Welsh•men

Welsh•wom•an
  pl. Welsh•wom•en

welt

wel•ter

wel•ter•weight

Wel•ty

wen

wench
  wench•er

wend

went

wept

were (*past of be*; see WHIR)

we're (*we are*; see WEIR)

were•n't

were•wolf
  also wer•wolf
  pl. were•wolves

Wes•ley

west

west•er•ly
  pl. west•er•lies

west•ern
  west•ern•most

west•ern•er

west•ern•ize
  also West•ern•ize
  west•ern•i•za•tion

West In•dies

West Vir•gin•ia
  West Vir•gin•ian

west•ward
  also west•wards

wet (*not dry*; see WHET)
  wet•ter, wet•test
  wet•ting; *past and past part.* wet *or* wet•ted
  wet-nurse
  wet•ly
  wet•ness
  wet•ta•ble
  wet•ting
  wet•tish

wet•back

weth•er (*sheep*; see WEATHER, WHETHER)

wet•lands

we've (*we have*; see WEAVE)

whack
  whack•er
  whack•ing

whale (*animal*; see WAIL, WALE)
  pl. same *or* whales

whale•bone

whal•er (*whale hunter*; see *wailer* [WAIL])

wham
  whammed, wham•ming

wham•my
  pl. wham•mies

wharf
  pl. wharves *or* wharfs

Whar•ton

what

what•ev•er

what•not

what•so•ev•er

wheat
  wheat•en

Wheat•ley

Wheat•stone

whee•dle
  whee•dler
  whee•dling
  whee•dling•ly

wheel (*round object*; see WEAL, WE'LL)
  wheel•er-deal•er
  wheeled
  wheel•less

wheel·bar·row

wheel·base

wheel·chair

wheel·house

wheel·ie

Whee·ling

wheel·wright

wheeze
  wheez·er
  wheez·ing·ly
  wheez·y
  wheez·i·er, wheez·i·est
  wheez·i·ly
  wheez·i·ness

whelk

whelm

whelp

when

whence

when·ev·er

when·so·ev·er

where (*what place*; see
  WARE, WEAR)

where·a·bouts

where·as

where·by

where·fore

where·in

where·of

where·up·on

wher·ev·er

where·with·al

wher·ry (*boat*; see WARY)
  pl. wher·ries

whet (*arouse*; see WET)
  whet·ted, whet·ting
  whet·ter

wheth·er (*if*; see
  WEATHER, WETHER)

whet·stone

whew

whey (*milk product*; see
  WAY, WEIGH)

which (*what one*; see
  WITCH)

which·ev·er

whiff

Whig (*political party*; see
  WIG)
  Whig·ger·y
  Whig·gish
  Whig·gism

while (*during which*; see
  WILE)

whim

whim·per
  whim·per·er
  whim·per·ing·ly

whim·si·cal
  whim·si·cal·i·ty
  whim·si·cal·ly
  whim·si·cal·ness

whim·sy
  also whim·sey
  pl. whim·sies *or* whim·
  seys

whine
  whin·er
  whin·ing·ly
  whin·y
  whin·i·er, whin·i·est

whin·ny
  pl. whin·nies
  whin·nies, whin·nied

whip
  whipped, whip·ping
  whip·less
  whip·like
  whip·per
  whip·ping

whip·cord

whip·lash

whip·per·snap·per

whip·pet

whip·ping

whip·poor·will

whir (*buzz*; see WERE)
  also whirr
  whirred (*past of whir*;
  see WORD), whir·ring

whirl
  whirl·er
  whirl·ing·ly

whirl·i·gig

whirl·pool

whirl·wind

whisk

whisk·er
  whisk·er·ed
  whisk·er·y

whis·key
  also whis·ky
  pl. whis·keys *or* whis·
  kies

whis·per
  whis·per·er
  whis·per·ing

whist

whis·tle
  whis·tle-stop

whis·tle·blow·er

Whis·tler

whit (*little bit*; see WIT)

white
  white-col·lar
  white-out
  white·ly
  white·ness
  whit·ish

white·cap

White·head

white·head

White·horse

whit·en
  whit·en·er
  whit·en·ing

white·wall

white·wash
  white·wash·er

whith·er (*where*; see
  WITHER)

whit·ing

Whit·man

Whit·ney

Whit·sun·day

Whit·ti·er

whit·tle

whiz
  also whizz, wiz
  pl. whiz·zes
  whizzed, whiz·zing

who

whoa (*command to horse*;
  see WOE)

who'd

who·dun·it

who·ev·er

whole (*complete*; see
  HOLE)
  whole-wheat
  whole·ness

whole·heart·ed
  whole·heart·ed·ly
  whole·heart·ed·ness

whole·sale
  whole·sal·er

whole·some
  whole·some·ly
  whole·some·ness

whol·ly (*completely*; see
  holey [HOLE], HOLY)

whom

whom·ev·er

whom·so·ev·er

whoop

whop·per

whop·ping

whore (*prostitute*; see
  HOAR)
  whor·er

whorl
  whorled

who's (*who is*; see WHOSE)

whose (*belonging to which*;
  see WHO'S)

whos·ev·er

who·so·ev·er

why
  pl. whys (see WISE)

Wich·i·ta

wick

wick·ed
  wick·ed·er, wick·ed·est
  wick·ed·ly
  wick·ed·ness

wick·er

wick·er·work

wick·et

wide
  wide-eyed
  wide·ness
  wid·ish

wide-a·wake

wide·ly

wid·en
  wid·en·er

wide·spread

widg·eon
  also wig·eon

widg·et

wid·ow
  wid·ow·hood

wid·ow·er

width
  width·ways
  width·wise

wield
  wield·er

wie·ner

Wies·ba·den

wife
  pl. wives
  wife·hood
  wife·less
  wife·like
  wife·ly
  wife·li·ness

wig (*hairpiece*; see WHIG)
  wigged
  wig·less

wig·eon
  var. of widg·eon

wig·gle
  wig·gler

Wight, Isle of

wig·wag
  wig·wagged, wig·wag·
  ging

wig·wam

wild
  wild·ish
  wild·ly
  wild·ness

wild·cat

Wilde

wil·de·beest

Wil·der

wil·der·ness

wild·fire

wild·fowl
  pl. same

wild·life

wile (*trick*; see WHILE)

will (*document*)
  willed
  will·less

will (*shall*)

Wil·lard

will·ful
  will·ful·ly
  will·ful·ness

Wil·liam

Wil·liams

wil·lies

will·ing
  will·ing·ly
  will·ing·ness

will-o'-the-wisp

wil·low

wil·low·y

will·pow·er

wil·ly-nil·ly

Wil·ming·ton

Wil·son

wilt

wil·y
  wil·i·er, wil·i·est
  wil·i·ness

wimp
  wimp·ish
  wimp·ish·ly
  wimp·ish·ness
  wimp·y

wim·ple

win
  win·ning; *past* and *past part.* won
  win·na·ble

wince
  winc·er
  winc·ing·ly

winch
  winch·er

wind (*breeze*)
  wind·less

wind (*turn*)
  past and *past part.* wound

wind·bag

wind·break

wind·break·er

wind·burn

wind·chill

wind·fall

Wind·hoek

wind·ing

wind·jam·mer

wind·lass

wind·mill

win·dow
  win·dow-shop
  win·dow·shopped,
    win·dow·shop·ping
  win·dow-shop·per
  win·dowed
  win·dow·less

win·dow·pane

win·dow·sill

wind·pipe

wind·shield

Wind·sor

wind·surf·ing
  wind·surf
  wind·surf·er

wind-swept

wind·up

wind·ward

wind·y
  wind·i·er, wind·i·est
  wind·i·ly
  wind·i·ness

wine
  wine·less
  win·y
  win·i·er, win·i·est

win·er·y
  pl. win·er·ies

wing
  winged
  wing·less
  wing·let
  wing·like

wing·span

wink
  wink·er

Win·ne·ba·go
  (*trademark*)

win·ner

win·ning
  win·ning·ly
  win·ning·ness

Win·ni·peg

win·now
  win·now·er

wi·no
  pl. wi·nos

win·some
  win·some·ly
  win·some·ness

Win·ston-Sa·lem

win·ter
  win·ter·er
  win·ter·less

win·ter·green

win·ter·ize
win·ter·i·za·tion

win·ter·time

win·try
also win·ter·y
win·tri·er, win·tri·est
win·tri·ly
win·tri·ness

wipe
wipe·a·ble
wip·er

wire
wir·er

wire·haired

wire·less

wire·tap
wire·tapped, wire·tap·
ping
wire·tap·per
wire·tap·ping

wir·ing

wir·y
wir·i·er, wir·i·est
wir·i·ly
wir·i·ness

Wis·con·sin
Wis·con·sin·ite

wis·dom

wise (*experienced*; see
whys [WHY])
wise·ly

wise·a·cre

wise·crack
wise·crack·er

wish
wish·er

wish·bone

wish·ful
wish·ful·ly
wish·ful·ness

wish·y-wash·y

wisp
wisp·y
wisp·i·er, wisp·i·est
wisp·i·ly
wisp·i·ness

wis·te·ri·a
also wis·tar·i·a

wist·ful
wist·ful·ly
wist·ful·ness

wit (*intelligence*; see WHIT)
wit·ted

witch (*sorceress*; see
WHICH)
witch-hunt
witch·ing
witch·like

witch·craft

witch·er·y

with (*preposition*; see
WITHE)
with-it

with·al

with·draw
past with·drew; *past
part.* with·drawn
with·draw·er

with·draw·al

withe (*twig*; see WITH)

with·er (*droop*; see
WHITHER)
with·er·ing·ly

with·ers

with·hold
past and *past part.* with·
held
with·hold·er

with·in

with·out

with·stand
past and *past part.* with·
stood
with·stand·er

wit·less
wit·less·ly
wit·less·ness

wit·ness

Witt·gen·stein

wit·ti·cism

wit·ty
wit·ti·er, wit·ti·est
wit·ti·ly
wit·ti·ness

wives

wiz·ard
wiz·ard·ly
wiz·ard·ry

wiz·ened
also wiz·en

wob·ble
wob·bler
wob·bli·ness
wob·bly
wob·bli·er, wob·bli·est

Wode·house

woe (*misfortune*; see
WHOA)

woe·be·gone

woe·ful
woe·ful·ly
woe·ful·ness

wok (*cooking pan*; see
WALK)

woke

wok·en

wolf
pl. wolves
wolf·ish
wolf·ish·ly
wolf·like

Wolfe

wolf•hound

wolf•ram

Wol•las•ton

Wol•sey

Wol•ver•hamp•ton

wol•ver•ine

wom•an
　pl. wom•en
　wom•an•less
　wom•an•like

wom•an•hood

wom•an•ish
　wom•an•ish•ly
　wom•an•ish•ness

wom•an•ize
　wom•an•iz•er

wom•an•kind
　also wom•en•kind

wom•an•ly
　wom•an•li•ness

womb
　womb•like

wom•bat

wom•en

wom•en•folk

wom•en•kind

won

Won•der

won•der
　won•der•er

won•der•ful
　won•der•ful•ly
　won•der•ful•ness

won•der•land

won•der•ment

won•drous
　won•drous•ly
　won•drous•ness

wont

won't (will not)

wont•ed

woo
　woos, wooed
　woo•a•ble
　woo•er

Wood

wood (tree product; see
　WOULD)
　wood•ed
　wood•less

wood•bine

wood•chuck

wood•cock
　pl. same

wood•craft

wood•cut

wood•cut•ter

wood•en
　wood•en•ly
　wood•en•ness

wood•land
　wood•land•er

wood•peck•er

wood•pile

wood•shed

woods•man
　pl. woods•men

woods•y

wood•wind

wood•work
　wood•work•er
　wood•work•ing

wood•y
　wood•i•er, wood•i•est
　wood•i•ness

woof

woof•er

wool
　wool•like

wool•en
　also wool•len

Woolf

wool•ly
　also wool•y
　wool•li•er, wool•li•est
　wool•li•ness

woo•zy
　woo•zi•er, woo•zi•est
　woo•zi•ly
　woo•zi•ness

Worces•ter

Worces•ter•shire sauce

word (language element;
　see whirred [WHIR])
　word-of-mouth
　word•age
　word•less
　word•less•ly
　word•less•ness

word•ing

word•play

Words•worth

word•y
　word•i•er, word•i•est
　word•i•ly
　word•i•ness

wore (dressed in; see WAR)

work
　past and past part.
　worked or wrought
　work•less

work•a•ble
　work•a•bil•i•ty
　work•a•ble•ness
　work•a•bly

work•a•day

work•a•hol•ic

work·bench

work·day

work·er

work·force

work·horse

work·ing
  work·ing-class

work·load

work·man
  pl. work·men

work·man·like

work·man·ship

work·out

work·place

work·shop

work·sta·tion

world
  world-class
  world-wea·ry

world·ly
  world·li·er, world·li·
    est
  world·ly-wise
  world·li·ness

world·wide

worm
  worm·er
  worm·i·ness
  worm·like
  worm·y

worm·wood

worn (*past part. of wear*;
  see WARN)

wor·ri·some
  wor·ri·some·ly

wor·ry
  wor·ries, wor·ried
  pl. wor·ries
  wor·ried·ly
  wor·ri·er
  wor·ry·ing·ly

wor·ry·wart

worse

wors·en

wor·ship
  wor·shiped, wor·ship·
    ing *or* wor·shipped,
    wor·ship·ping
  wor·ship·er *or* wor·
    ship·per

wor·ship·ful

worst

wor·sted

wort

worth

worth·less
  worth·less·ly
  worth·less·ness

worth·while
  worth·while·ness

wor·thy
  wor·thi·er, wor·thi·est
  pl. wor·thies
  wor·thi·ly
  wor·thi·ness

Wouk

would (*past of will*; see
  WOOD)
  would-be

would·n't

wound (*injury*)
  wound·ing·ly
  wound·less

wound (*past of wind*)

wove

wo·ven

wow

wrack (*torment*; see
  RACK)

wraith
  wraith·like

wran·gle

wran·gler

wrap (*cover*; see RAP)
  wrapped (*past of wrap*;
    see *rapped* [RAP],
    RAPT), wrap·ping

wrap·a·round

wrap·per

wrap·ping

wrasse

wrath
  wrath·ful
  wrath·ful·ly
  wrath·ful·ness

wreak (*produce*; see
  REEK)
  wreak·er

wreath
  pl. wreaths

wreathe

wreck

wreck·age

wreck·er

Wren

wren

wrench

wrest (*take away*; see
  REST)

wres·tle
  wres·tler
  wres·tling

wretch (*unfortunate
  person*; see RETCH)

wretch·ed
  wretch·ed·er, wretch·
    ed·est
  wretch·ed·ly
  wretch·ed·ness

wrig·gle
  wrig·gler
  wrig·gly
  wrig·gli·er, wrig·gli·est

Wright (*proper name*)

wright (*builder*; see
  RIGHT, RITE, WRITE)

wring (*squeeze; see* RING)
  past and *past part.*
  wrung

wring•er (*one that wrings;*
  see *ringer* [RING])

wrin•kle
  wrin•kly
  wrin•kli•er, wrin•kli•
  est

wrist

wrist•watch

writ

write (*record; see* RIGHT,
  RITE, WRIGHT)
  past wrote; *past part.*
  writ•ten
  write-in
  write-off
  write-up

writ•er

writhe

writ•ing

writ•ten

Wroc•law

wrong
  wrong•ly

wrong•do•er
  wrong•do•ing

wronged

wrong•ful
  wrong•ful•ly
  wrong•ful•ness

wrong•head•ed
  wrong•head•ed•ly
  wrong•head•ed•ness

wrote (*past of write; see*
  ROTE)

wrought

wrung (*past of wring; see*
  RUNG)

wry (*ironic; see* RYE)
  wry•er, wry•est *or* wri•
  er, wri•est
  wry•ly
  wry•ness

Wu•han

Wup•per•tal

wurst

wuss
  wuss•y

Wy•eth

Wy•o•ming
  Wy•o•ming•ite

WYSIWYG
  also wysiwyg

XYZ

x-ax•is

X chro•mo•some

Xa•vi•er

xe•non

xe•no•pho•bi•a
  xe•no•phobe
  xe•no•pho•bic

Xen•o•phon

xe•rog•ra•phy
  xe•ro•graph•ic
  xe•ro•graph•i•cal•ly

Xe•rox (*trademark*)

Xerx•es I

xi

Xi•an
  also Si•an

X•mas

X ray
  also x-ray

xy•lem

xy•lo•phone
  xy•lo•phon•ic
  xy•lo•phon•ist

Y chro•mo•some

yacht
  yacht•ing

yachts•man
  pl. yachts•men; *fem.*
  yachts•wom•an,
  *pl.*yachts•wom•en

ya•hoo

Yah•weh
  also Yah•veh

yak

yak•king

yam

yam•mer
  yam•mer•er

Ya•mous•sou•kro

yang

Yan•gon

Yang•tze River

Yank (*Yankee*)

yank (*pull*)

Yan•kee

Ya•oun•dé

yap
  yapped, yap•ping
  yap•per

yard

yard•age

yard•arm

yard•stick

Ya•ren

yar•mul•ke
  also yar•mul•ka, yar•
  mel•ke

yarn

yar•row

yaw

yawl

yawn
  yawn•er
  yawn•ing•ly

yawp
  also yaup

yaws

y-ax•is

ye

yea

yeah

year

year•book

year•ling

year•ly

yearn
  yearn•er
  yearn•ing
  yearn•ing•ly

yeast
  yeast•less
  yeast•like

yeast•y
  yeast•i•er, yeast•i•est
  yeast•i•ly
  yeast•i•ness

Yeats

yegg

Ye•ka•te•rin•burg

yell

yel•low
  yel•low•ish
  yel•low•ly
  yel•low•ness
  yel•low•y

Yel•low•knife

Yel•low•stone

yelp
  yelp•er

Yelt•sin

Yem•en
  Yem•en•ite *or* Yem•en•i

yen

yeo·man
  pl. yeo·men

yeo·man·ry
  pl. yeo·man·ries

yep
  also yup

Ye·re·van

yes
  yes-man
  pl. yes-men

ye·shi·va
  also ye·shi·vah

yes·ter·day

yes·ter·year

yet

yew (*tree*; see EWE, YOU)

Ye·zo

yield
  yield·er
  yield·ing
  yield·ing·ly

yin

yip
  yipped, yip·ping

yip·pee

yo·del
  yo·del·er

yo·ga
  yo·gic

yo·gi
  yo·gism

yo·gurt
  also yo·ghurt

yoke (*frame*; see YOLK)
  pl. same *or* yokes

yo·kel

Yo·ko·ha·ma

Yo·ko·su·ka

yolk (*center of egg*; see
    YOKE)
  yolked
  yolk·less
  yolk·y

Yom Kip·pur

yon

yon·der

Yon·kers

yoo-hoo

yore (*old days*; see YOUR,
    YOU'RE)

York

York·town

Yo·sem·i·te

you (*2nd person*; see EWE,
    YEW)

you'd

you'll (*you will*; see YULE)

Young

young
  young·er; young·est
  young·ish
  young·ling

young·ster

Youngs·town

your (*belonging to you*;
    see YORE, YOU'RE)

you're (*you are*; see YORE,
    YOUR)

yours

your·self
  pl. your·selves

youth
  pl. youths

youth·ful
  youth·ful·ly
  youth·ful·ness

you've

yowl

yo-yo
  pl. yo-yos
  yo-yoes, yo-yoed, yo-
    yoing

yt·ter·bi·um

yt·tri·um

yuan
  pl. same

Yu·ca·tán

yuc·ca

yuck
  yuck·y
  yuck·i·er, yuck·i·est

Yu·go·sla·vi·a
  Yu·go·sla·vi·an *or* Yu·
    go·slav
  also Ju·go·slav

Yu·kon

yule (*Christmas*; see
    YOU'LL)
  also yule·tide

Yu·ma

yum·my
  yum·mi·er, yum·mi·est

yum-yum

yup

yup·pie
  also yup·py
  pl. yup·pies

yurt

za·ba·glio·ne

Za·ca·te·cas

zag
  zagged, zag·ging

Za·greb

Za·ire

Zam·be·zi

Zam·bi·a
Zam·bi·an

za·ny
za·ni·er, za·ni·est
za·ni·ly
za·ni·ness

Zan·zi·bar

zap
zapped, zap·ping

Za·pa·ta

zap·per

Za·ra·go·za

Zar·a·thus·tra

Zar·a·thus·tri·an
var. of Zo·ro·as·tri·an

zeal
zeal·ous
zeal·ous·ly
zeal·ous·ness

zeal·ot
zeal·ot·ry

ze·bra
pl. same or ze·bras
ze·brine

ze·bu

zed

Zeit·geist
also zeit·geist

Zen
Zen·ist
also Zen·nist

ze·nith

zeph·yr

Zep·pe·lin

zep·pe·lin

ze·ro
pl. ze·ros
ze·roes, ze·roed
ze·ro-sum

zest
zest·ful

zest·ful·ly
zest·i·ncss
zest·y
zest·i·er, zest·i·est

ze·ta

Zhdan·ov

zig
zigged, zigging

Zhou En·lai
also Chou En-lai

Zhu·kov

Zieg·feld

zig·gu·rat

zig·zag
zig·zagged, zig·zag·
ging
zig·zag·ged·ly

zilch

zil·lion
zil·lionth

Zim·bab·we

zinc
zinced
also zincked

zing
zing·er
zing·y
zing·i·er, zing·i·est

zin·ni·a

Zi·on
also Si·on

Zi·on·ism
Zi·on·ist

zip
zipped, zip·ping

zip code
also ZIP code

zip·per
zip·pered

zip·py
zip·pi·er, zip·pi·est
zip·pi·ly
zip·pi·ness

zir·con

zir·co·ni·um

zit

zith·er
zith·er·ist

zo·di·ac
zo·di·a·cal

Zo·la

Zom·ba

zom·bie

zone
zon·al
zon·ing

zonked

zoo

zo·ol·o·gy
zo·o·log·i·cal
zo·ol·o·gist

zoom

zo·o·phyte
zo·o·phyt·ic

Zo·ro·as·ter
also Zar·a·thus·tra

Zo·ro·as·tri·an
also Zar·a·thus·tri·an
Zo·ro·as·tri·an·ism

zuc·chi·ni
pl. same or zuc·chi·nis

Zu·lu

Zu·ni
also Zu·ñi

Zu·rich

zwie·back

zy·gote
zy·got·ic
zy·got·i·cal·ly

zy·mur·gy

Good Speller's Toolkit

Modern English has its origins in languages from around the world. It has evolved over several centuries and continues to evolve along with the ever-changing and ever-broadening society of English speakers and writers. Largely because of this diversity, English is noted for its inconsistencies, especially where spelling is concerned.

Nevertheless, there are many helpful guidelines to English spelling, the most useful of which are discussed here:

> "Timeless Tips"
> Capitalization
> Plurals
> Suffixes and Other Word Endings
> Prefixes

"Timeless Tips"

Perhaps the best known spelling tips for English regard the proper usage of *ie* and *ei*. Two familiar rhymes that teach these tips are as follows:

> *I* before *e*
> Except after *c*,
> But only if you
> Can hear a long *e*.

> *I* before *e*
> Except after *c*,
> Or when sounded like *a*
> As in *neighbor* and *weigh*.

These are helpful rules to remember because most of the time they are in agreement with correct spelling (*relieve, conceive*). However, it is important to know that these are rules with a number of notable exceptions (*caffeine, protein, seizure, weird*).

Capitalization

Correct capitalization is an important element of good spelling. In brief, English capitalization rules are as follows:

1. The first letter of the first word in a sentence is capitalized.
   My house is just around the corner.

2. The first letter of the first word of a direct quotation is capitalized.
   As he ran out the door, he shouted, "Don't forget to feed the dog!"
   "It was a wonderful parade," she said, "and the band played better than ever."

3. The first word, the last word, and all the principal words in the titles of books, magazines, plays, songs, movies, television shows, works of art, etc., are capitalized. A general rule of thumb is "do not cap the CAP" (where "CAP" stands for "conjunctions," "articles," and "prepositions"). Sometimes this rule is modified to allow the capitalization of prepositions that are at least five or six letters long.
   This month's best seller is The Life and Times of a Space Traveler *by E. P. Drake.*
   He read his poem "Somewhere under My Yellow Sky" to us.
   This week's episode of City Hospital *is titled "An Apple a Day Keeps the Doctor Away."*

4. Proper nouns are capitalized. Among the many designations of proper nouns are those enumerated below. Pay close attention to the examples, noting when *not* to capitalize (in general, do not capitalize an indefinite, nonspecific name or a title that follows a modifier):

   personal names
   I introduced Sasha to the Douglases.

   titles with names
   Where is the book about King George that Aunt Claire gave to me?
   My aunt Claire gave me a book about the king.

   titles that replace names
   Dear Sir or Madam

   definite place-names
   My cousin from North Dakota left his snapshots of Yellowstone National Park at the bus stop on South Union Street.
   It was on this street that my cousin from North Dakota lost his snapshots of a national park.

ildings and institutions

> *The students from West Central Elementary School took a field*
> *trip to Springfield Public Library.*
>
> *The students from the elementary school took a field trip to the*
> *main branch of the public library.*

organizations

> *Several agents of the Federal Bureau of Investigation were once*
> *members of the Girl Scouts of America.*
>
> *She belonged to a scouting organization years before landing*
> *a job with a federal agency.*

definite events and observances

> *If it were not for the American Revolution, we would not be*
> *celebrating the Fourth of July.*
>
> *On the eighth of March, he finally finished his book on the*
> *aftermath of the political revolution.*

languages, nationalities, and religions

> *Very few Latvians in the group converted to Buddhism.*

trademarks and brand names

> *She insists on using only Fireburst Charcoal in her new Cook-*
> *master Grill.*
>
> *The only charcoal she will use in her new grill, which is a*
> *Cookmaster, is the kind made by Fireburst.*

Plurals

Most nouns are made into plural nouns by simply adding an *s*. For many nouns, this is not so, as shown in the following guidelines:

1. Add *es* to pluralize a noun that ends in *s, ss, sh, x, z*, or soft *ch* (*plus, pluses; boss, bosses; wish, wishes; fox, foxes; waltz, waltzes; couch, couches*).

2. Add just an *s* to pluralize a noun that ends in *y* if the *y* is preceded by a vowel (*donkey, donkeys*), but if the *y* is preceded by a consonant or *qu*, change the *y* to *i* and add *es* (*cooky, cookies; soliloquy, soliloquies*).

3. Add *es* to pluralize most nouns that end in long *o* (*potato, potatoes*). Be aware that there are some exceptions, as in the case of several musical terms that were borrowed from Italian (*alto, altos; piano, pianos; soprano, sopranos*).

4. For many nouns that end in a single *f* or *ife*, the way to pluralize is to change the *f* or *fe* to *v* and add *es* (*leaf, leaves; knife, knives*). Most of the exceptions to this include certain nouns that end in *ief*, *oof*, and *rf* (*beliefs, roofs, serfs*).

Suffixes and Other Word Endings

Suffixes can be tricky because adding a suffix to a word often, but not always, involves a respelling of the root word. Also, certain suffixes may cause confusion owing to their similar meanings yet different spellings.

Adding a suffix

1. When a one-syllable word ends in single consonant that is preceded by a short vowel sound (*sad*), do not double the final consonant if the suffix begins with a consonant (*sadly*).

2. When a one-syllable word ends in single consonant that is preceded by a short vowel sound (*sad*), double the final consonant if the suffix begins with a vowel (e.g., *sadder*, adding the *-er* suffix for comparative degree).

3. When adding a suffix to a word that ends with an *r*, double the *r* if the word has only one syllable or if the stress is on the syllable with the *r* (*blur/blurred, deter/deterring*). But if the *r* is preceded by two vowels, do not double the *r* (*near/neared, engineer/engineering*).

4. When a two-syllable word ends in a single consonant (*carpet*), do not double the final consonant if the stress is on the first syllable (*carpeted*). If the stress is on the second syllable (*forget*), double the final consonant if the suffix begins with a vowel (*forgetting*), but do not double it if the suffix begins with a consonant (*forgetful*).

5. When adding the suffix *-ous* to a word that ends with a *y*, replace the *y* with an *e* (*bounty, bounteous*).

6. When adding the suffix *-ous* to a word that ends with *ce*, replace the *e* with an *i* (*grace, gracious*).

Choosing the right suffix

In most cases, the word endings **-ance** and **-ant** sound very similar to **-ence** and **-ent**. When a *c* or *g* precedes the ending, two general rules help in choosing the correct spelling:

1. The endings *-ance* and *-ant* follow a hard *c* or *g* (*insignificant, elegance*).

2. The endings *-ence* and *-ent* follow a soft *c* or *g* (*indulgent, magnificence*).

Another easily confused pair of word endings is **-able** an.
Where these similar-sounding, same-meaning suffixes are conc
a number of guidelines are useful:

1. When a noun ending in *-ation* has a related adjective ending
-ble, the suffix used is *-able* (*consideration, considerable*).

2. When a noun ending in *-ion* (but not ending in *-ation*) has a
related adjective ending in *-ble*, the suffix used is most often *-ible*
(*division, divisible*).

3. The suffix *-ible* is very often preceded by a double *s* (*permissible*).

4. If the root word ends in a silent *e*, drop the *e* when adding *-ible*
(*forcible, reversible*).

5. The preceding rule also applies when adding *-able* (*unbeliev-
able*), EXCEPT when the silent *e* follows a soft *c* or *g*, in which case
do not drop the *e* (*embraceable, changeable*).

6. It may be helpful to remember that there are far fewer words
that end in *-ible* than end in *-able*. Most of the commonly encountered
-ible words are listed below:

accessible	discernible	irascible
admissible	divisible	irresistible
audible	edible	legible
collapsible	eligible	negligible
collectible	fallible	perceptible
combustible	feasible	permissible
compatible	flexible	plausible
comprehensible	forcible	possible
contemptible	fusible	reprehensible
convertible	gullible	responsible
credible	horrible	reversible
deductible	incorrigible	sensible
defensible	indelible	susceptible
destructible	intelligible	terrible
digestible	invincible	visible

Other confusing word endings

Knowing which to choose of the same-sounding word endings
-cede, *-ceed*, and *-sede* may seem confusing, but the rule actually is
quite simple. The correct choice is *-cede* (*antecede, precede*) in all but
four instances:

1. There are only three common words that end in *-ceed*: *exceed,
proceed, succeed.*

2. There is only one common word that ends in *-sede*: *supersede.*

s that end with the sound "cul," are spelled with the ending
or -*cal*. Nearly always, two rules are true:

he endings -*cle* and -*kle* are used for nouns (*tentacle*, *wrinkle*).

The ending -*cal* is used for adjectives (*cynical*, *spherical*).

Prefixes

Unlike suffixes, prefixes never change the spelling of the root word. Some of the most commonly used prefixes are listed below:

Prefix	Meaning	Usage Examples
a-	in, on	aflame, atop
a-	not, without	atypical, asymmetry
ab-	away from	abnormal
ante-	before	antedate
anti-	against	antiwar
auto-	self	autobiography
bi-	twice, two, both	biannual, bicolor, bicoastal
circum-	around	circumnavigate
co-, com-, con-	with, together	copilot, commingle, confluent
contra-, counter-	against, opposite	contradistinction, counterclockwise
de-	reverse, reduce, remove	desegregation, degrade, dehumidify
dis-	apart	disassociate
hyper-	above, beyond	hypersensitive
hypo-	beneath	hypothermic
il-, im-, in-	not	illicit, immoral, insensitive
inter-	among, between	international
intra-	within	intramuscular
ir-	not	irreversible
macro-	large (or very large)	macromolecule
micro-	small (or very small)	microorganism
mid-	at or near the middle	midafternoon
mini-	small, limited	minibike, minirecession
mis-	wrongly, badly	misguided
multi-	many, much, more than one	multifaceted, multistory
non-	not, without	noncompliant, nonfat
over-	excessive	overjoy
per-	through	perforce
post-	after	postwar
pre-	before	pregame
pro-	in favor of	prodemocracy
pseudo-	false, pretended	pseudocharitable
re-	again, back	retrace
semi-	half, somewhat	semicircle, semiliterate
sub-	under	subfloor
super-	above, excessive	superimpose, supergrowth
trans-	across	transatlantic
ultra-	beyond, extremely	ultrareligious
un-	not	unfeeling
under-	beneath, insufficiently	undercarriage, undernourished